C000137182

ADVANCED LEVEL ACCOUNTING

HAROLD RANDALL
FCA, FCCA, ACMA, ATII, MICM

DP PUBLICATIONS LTD
Aldine Place
142/144 Uxbridge Road
Shepherds Bush Green
London W12 8AW
1990

ACKNOWLEDGEMENTS

EXAMINATION QUESTIONS

The author would like to express thanks to the following for giving permission to reproduce past examination questions.

The Associated Examining Board (AEB)

University of Cambridge Local Examinations Syndicate (Cambridge)

University of London School Examinations Board (London)

University of Oxford Delegacy of Local Examinations (Oxford)

Joint Matriculation Board (JMB)

Welsh Joint Education Committee (WJEC)

Northern Ireland General Certificate of Education Examinations (Northern Ireland)

Each question used is cross referenced to the appropriate examination board and the title of the paper.

ISBN 1 870941 36 5

© Harold Randall

First Edition 1990
Reprinted with corrections 1991

All rights reserved.
No part of this publication may be reproduced, stored
in a retrieval system, or transmitted in any form or
by any means, electronic, mechanical, photocopying,
recording, or otherwise, without the prior permission
of the copyright owner.

Printed in Great Britain by
   The Guernsey Press Co. Ltd.,
   Guernsey, Channel Islands.

Pageset by
   Kai, 21 Sycamore Rise,
   Cinderhill, Nottingham.

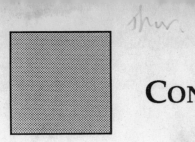

CONTENTS

PREFACE

AIM

Advanced Level Accounting aims to provide all the support needed for the successful pursuit of studies leading to Advanced Level Accounting examinations. In one volume it encompasses the financial, management and social accounting aspects of the subject that are included in the syllabuses for single subject accounting at Advanced Level.

The book assumes that the principles of the subject have been taught and contains a resume of those principles in the explanatory text which is, however, sufficient also to be used as a course text book.

NEED

Teachers, lecturers, and students studying Advanced Level accounting have long been aware of the dearth of texts prepared specifically for their requirements. All Advanced Level syllabuses embrace financial, cost and management accounting. An awareness of social accounting is also expected by some of the examining Boards. Accounting text books abound but none has been prepared with all these requirements adequately met within the covers of a single volume; all of which invariably means that two text books must be selected from those that have been written with other syllabuses and needs in mind.

The principles of double entry bookkeeping and accounting remain the same regardless of the differences of approach by examiners; but it is those differences of approach that often put a particular gloss, some would even say a peculiar gloss on occasions, on Advanced Level accounting questions.

Hence the need for a text prepared specifically for these examinations.

Advanced Level Accounting embraces some parts of the topics which are not treated adequately, or at all, in most of the other standard texts. Indeed, in the author's experience as an examiner, it is evident that many students taking Advanced Levels are ill prepared both in the substance of topics and in the techniques required for attempting them in examinations.

The author hopes and believes that Advanced Level Accounting will meet the perceived needs for a specially written text for Advanced Levels.

APPROACH

Each chapter begins with an introduction to the topic or topics to be considered. Aspects of each topic are then explained in sections of manageable length.

The text leads the student step by step through the stages of each topic from what would be the known to the unknown had the subject not already been taught. It serves the dual purpose of reminding students of what they should already have been taught and, hopefully, helping to clarify areas of study in which they have not already a good understanding.

Each principle is clearly demonstrated by an example and followed by one of the many self-test exercises to which answers are given at the back of the book. The text is rounded off on a positive note with 'Key Points to Remember' including examination hints and a brief mention of errors commonly committed in examination scripts.

Finally, each chapter concludes with additional exercises drawn from all the Advanced Level examining bodies in the U.K.

Answers to the Advanced Level examining body questions/exercises are provided free of charge to lecturers using the book as a course text (applications by lecturers should be on departmental headed notepaper).

STUDY AND EXAMINATION HINTS

STUDY

1. Accounting at Advanced Level is by no means easy; some would say it can be difficult at times. It certainly makes demands upon those who would study it. You will achieve success only if you are diligent in your studies throughout the duration of your course. Given the right determination to succeed, you will find Advanced Level Accounting fully supportive of your efforts.

2. Set aside regular periods of study. Allow nothing and nobody to interfere with these periods.

3. Plan a programme of work which will include regular revision sessions and ensure that you complete the syllabus in ample time before the examination.

4. When concentration begins to wane during your study period, take a short break and then return to your study refreshed. Time spent when concentration has gone is wasted time.

5. Master each part of a topic before moving on to the next part. Work through all examples; make sure you understand them. Tick each figure to show you have understood where it has come from, how it is calculated and how it is being used.

6. Use the examination questions at the ends of chapters for additional practice and for revision. It is always helpful to try questions set by other Boards as well as those of the Board for which you are studying. Reworking the same question more than once at intervals can be helpful. The results will show you whether or not you have mastered the solution to that question and other similar ones; it will also help you to become more familiar with the examiner's style.

7. Attempt some questions under simulated examination conditions and time yourself. In the examination you will be able to spend $1^3/_4$ minutes on each question for each mark allocated to it. In a three hour paper, for instance, where you are required to complete four 25 mark questions, you should allocate 45 minutes to each question. It takes discipline to adhere to this time constraint and that discipline must be developed as part of the exercises you do in your studies.

IN THE EXAMINATION

1. Make sure you have all your equipment, pens, calculator etc. ready and in good order on the day before your examination.

    - Do not use coloured inks; continually changing pens for headings, underlinings etc. wastes time which is very precious in the examination room. You are sitting an examination in accounting, not in art! The examiner marks the papers in red and may be irritated by the confusion caused by your use of the same colour.

    - Do not use correcting fluids; not only do they also waste time but they should not be permissible in accounting work anyway. Correct an error by deleting it with a single horizontal stroke and rewriting the correct amount in full above the deletion.

    - Do not write your answers in pencil. It may be difficult to read and examiners are not expected to mark scripts which are too difficult to read.

2. Arrive at the centre in good time. Arriving late and flustered is no way to sit an examination.

3. Familiarise yourself with the rubrics (instructions) on the front of the examination paper.

4. Read all questions through before starting to write. Begin with the question you can do best and do the others in the order of your preference. You do not have to do the questions in numerical order, but you should assemble them in that order if you have answered the questions on loose sheets as opposed to an answer booklet.

5. Read the questions carefully and make sure you understand them and know what you are required to do. There is no point in wasting time giving the examiner something he has not asked for; it will not gain any marks.

6.   Calculate the amount of time you should allocate to each question. It is a good idea to write on the question paper the time you should quit a question even if it is unfinished - and keep to it.

7.   Submit all workings. You should not waste any valuable time in jotting down your workings but they should be Legible (the examiner should be able to read them) Logical (the steps should follow in order; do not omit any.) Labelled (indicate briefly what each figure is.) Lucid (the examiner should be able to follow them easily.)

1 REVISION OF BASIC PRINCIPLES, CONCEPTS AND TECHNIQUES

1.1 Students at this level should already have a good grasp of the basic principles, concepts and techniques of accounting. This chapter is intended as a brief summary of these as they are important for a proper understanding of the chapters that follow; they are:

- concepts of entity, duality and money measurement, realisation, matching, prudence and 'going concern'
- classification of ledger accounts; understanding the significance of debit and credit entries and balances
- trial balances; their uses and limitations
- trading and profit and loss accounts
- balance sheets
- provision accounts
- books of prime entry

1.2 Since a sound grasp of these topics is essential to the successful study of advanced level accounting this chapter is intended as a brief revision of them. Students requiring a fuller treatment of any of the topics dealt with in this chapter should refer to *Intermediate Accounting* by J.R.Dyson or *Foundation Accounting* by A.H.Millichamp (D.P.Publications).

1.3 NINE CONCEPTS

(i) **CONCEPT OF ENTITY.** For accounting purposes, every business is deemed to have a separate existence from that of its owner(s).

   (a) Money or money's worth introduced into the business by a proprietor is deemed to be owed to him/her by the business. (Capital.) A person does not owe money to himself.

   (b) A proprietor's private financial affairs outside the business are not recorded in the business books.

(ii) **CONCEPT OF DUALITY.** The twofold aspect of every transaction (i.e. 'giving' and 'receiving') is recognised in accounting records.

A trader starts his business by providing it with capital; that is, he gives the business money which the business, in turn, owes to him.

The ownership of assets by a business (what it receives) is correspondingly represented by what it owes to other people (owner's capital and liabilities to other people).

Form the habit of thinking of both aspects of every transaction in your exercises, and how each aspect will be recorded in the books and its effect on the final accounts of the business.

(iii) **THE ACCOUNTING EQUATION.** Assets = Capital + Liabilities

or, Capital = Assets – Liabilities

This is an essential aid for solving very many accounting problems.

(iv) **CONCEPT OF REALISATION.** Revenue is not recorded in the accounts until it has been realised.

A sale is deemed to take place when the goods which are the subject of the sale are replaced by cash or a debtor or some other asset received in exchange.

Revenue must not be overstated by sales which have not been realised; e.g. although a promise or statement of intention to purchase goods in the future may be received, the sales may not materialise.

(v) **CONCEPT OF MATCHING** (or accruals concept). Revenue and income should be brought into the period to which it relates, whether it has been received in that period or not.

Expenses should be accounted for in the period to which they relate. They may be related to revenue, e.g salesmen's commission, which should be brought into the same period as the sales revenue. Other expenses are related to time and should be charged in the profit and loss account covering that period.

(vi) **CONCEPT OF PRUDENCE.** Profits are not anticipated before they are realised. All known losses should be provided for as soon as recognised.

Profits should not be knowingly overstated; unwitting depletion of capital by excessive drawings or dividends must be avoided.

(vii) **CONCEPT OF CONSISTENCY.** All items of a similar nature should be treated in the same way within each accounting period and from one period to the next.

    (a)   All fixed assets of a similar nature should be depreciated on the same basis in the same accounting period; the same basis should be applied consistently from one period to the next.

    (b)   The same basis used for valuing stock in trade at the end of one period should be used for valuing stock at the end of the next period.

(viii) **GOING CONCERN CONCEPT.** Financial statements are prepared on the assumption that the business will continue on the same scale and that there is no intention to curtail significantly any of its operations in the foreseeable future.

Fixed assets will be shown at cost or valuation, less any amounts provided for depreciation to date. Stock will be valued at the lower of cost, net realisable value or replacement cost. Otherwise these assets would have to be shown at 'break-up' values, i.e. what they would be likely to fetch in an enforced sale.

(ix) **CONCEPT OF MONEY MEASUREMENT.** The only events which can be recorded in accounts are those which can be measured in money or money's worth.

Matters which cannot be measured in terms of money or money's worth cannot be recorded in accounts; e.g. quality of management, morale of staff, the standing of a business in public esteem, ecological matters. You need to bear constantly in mind that financial accounts cannot tell us all we would like to know about a business.

1.4   THE DOUBLE ENTRY MODEL

A ledger account is the history of a particular type of transaction or of the dealings of a business with a particular person.

The 'giving' of a benefit is credited to the account of the 'giver'; the corresponding 'receipt' appears as a debit in the account 'receiving' the benefit.

Entries in ledger accounts represent:

ACCOUNT

Debit side	*Credit side*
Cash, goods or services received	Cash, goods or services given
Assets	Liabilities
Expenses	Revenue, income
Losses	Profits

Classification of ledger accounts.

See the diagram on the opposite page and memorise it to help you remember

1.   Which accounts normally have credit balances and which debit.

2.   In which financial statement balances on these accounts are expected to appear.

1.5   TRIAL BALANCE

A trial balance is a list of all balances existing on ledger accounts at a given date. Always describe it as a 'trial balance at (date)'.

The trial balance distinguishes between those accounts with debit balances and those with credit balances. If the total of the debit balances equals the total of the credit balances, the ledger accounts are, on the face of it, arithmetically correct.

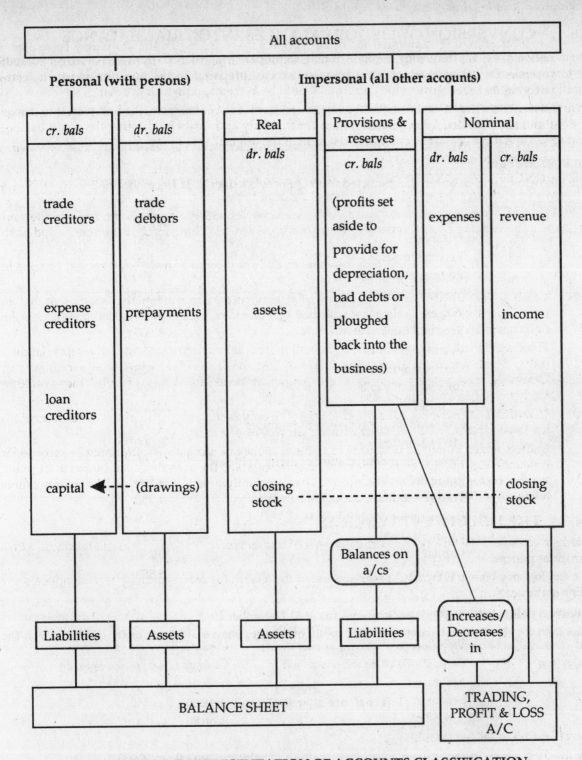

DIAGRAMMATIC REPRESENTATION OF ACCOUNTS CLASSIFICATION

Six types of error do not affect the trial balance:

1. Errors of omission: transactions completely omitted from the books.
2. Errors of commission: transactions posted to wrong account but to one of correct type.
3. Errors of principle: postings not only to wrong account, but also to wrong type of account.
4. Errors of original entry: wrong amount used to record transaction entirely.
5. Complete reversal of entries: account which should be credited is debited, and account which should be debited is credited.
6. Compensating errors: two or more errors completely cancel each other out arithmetically.

1.6   CONVERSION OF LIST OF BALANCES INTO TRIAL BALANCE

Examination questions frequently require students to prepare trial balances from lists of ledger balances or to correct trial balances which have been incorrectly prepared in the question paper. It tests a candidate's ability to recognise which accounts should be in credit and which in debit.

In any case, where final accounts have to be prepared from a list of balances, the best plan is to convert the list into a trial balance at once. This can be done quickly and easily by deleting the credit balances and re-writing them in another column to the right of the original.

1.6.1   EXAMPLE

The following list of balances was extracted from Quincey's ledger at 31 December 19-2

	£
Sales	36,000
Purchases	25,000
Returns inwards	820
Returns outwards	400
Stock at 1.1.-9	2,500
Wages	4,000
Rent and rates	1,600
Carriage inwards	750
Carriage outwards	925
Interest receivable	600
Premises	20,000
Provision for depreciation of premises	2,000
Motor vehicles	8,000
Provision for depreciation of motor vehicles	4,000
Trade debtors	4,500
Trade creditors	1,250
Provision for doubtful debts	200
Balance at bank	1,225
Capital	30,750
Drawings	5,880

REQUIRED:

Prepare a trial balance for Quincey's business as at 31 December 19-2.

(*Note to student:* Draft the answer by converting the list of balances into a trial balance on the question paper. The answer may then be quickly 'fair-copied' onto the answer sheet.)

ANSWER

Quincey
Trial balance as at 31 December 19-2

	Dr.	Cr.
	£	£
Sales	~~36,000~~	36,000
Purchases	25,000	
Returns inwards	820	
Returns outwards	~~400~~	400
Stock at 1.1.-9	2,500	
Wages	4,000	
Rent and rates	1,600	
Carriage inwards	750	
Carried forward	34,670	36,400

4

	Dr.	Cr.
	£	£
Brought forward	34,670	36,400
Carriage outwards	925	
Interest receivable	~~600~~	600
Premises	20,000	
Provision for depreciation of premises	~~2,000~~	2,000
Motor vehicles	8,000	
Provision for depreciation of motor vehicles	~~4,000~~	4,000
Trade Debtors	4,500	
Trade Creditors	~~1,250~~	1,250
Provision for doubtful debts	~~200~~	200
Balance at bank	1,225	
Drawings	5,880	
Capital	~~30,750~~	30,750
	75,200	75,200

1.6.2   EXERCISE 1 (For practice in correcting trial balances)

Colombo is an inexperienced accounts assistant and has prepared the following trial balance at 31.12.19-9:

	Dr.	Cr.
	£	£
Premises	80,000	
Plant and machinery	65,000	
Office furniture	15,000	
Provision for depreciation: plant and machinery	35,000	
Provision for depreciation: office furniture	10,000	
Stock at 1.1.-9	6,000	
Stock at 31.12.-9		7,200
Debtors	5,500	
Creditors		2,700
Purchases	47,000	
Carriage inwards	1,200	
Carriage outwards		2,100
Sales		90,000
Returns inwards		2,600
Returns outwards	1,400	
Provision for doubtful debts	500	
Selling and distribution expenses	20,800	
Administration expenses	15,400	
Discounts receivable	2,000	
Discounts allowed	1,800	
Drawings		12,600
Capital		133,400
	306,600	250,600

You are required to prepare a corrected trial balance for Colombo as at 31 December 19-9.

1.7   DEPRECIATION

Depreciation is the difference between the cost of an asset and its sale or scrap proceeds on disposal.

Depreciation is spread over the useful life of an asset by one of the following methods in order to match the cost of the use of that asset to the revenue earned by it.

Main methods of calculating annual depreciation charges:

1. **Straight line.** The depreciation is a fixed charge every year calculated as a percentage of the original cost, as follows:

$$\frac{\text{Cost of asset less estimated residual value at end of useful life}}{\text{estimated useful life (in years)}}$$

2. **Reducing balance.** Depreciation is calculated as a fixed percentage of the written down value of the asset at the beginning of the year. The percentage is calculated as follows:

$$1 - \sqrt[n]{\frac{R}{C}}$$

        where n = number of years of estimated useful life

                    R = estimated residual value of asset

                    C = cost of asset.

3. **Depletion unit.** Used for mines, quarries, oil wells etc. The annual charge is calculated as follows:

$$\text{Cost of asset} \times \frac{\text{quantity of material extracted}}{\text{estimated total resources of asset}}$$

4. **Machine hour.** For machinery, aircraft, ships etc. It is calculated as follows:

$$\text{Cost of machine} \times \frac{\text{no. of hours used in year}}{\text{estimated total hours of use during useful life}}$$

5. **Revaluation.** Used for assets for which detailed records cannot conveniently be maintained e.g. loose tools and other small items of equipment. It is calculated as follows:

Value of asset at beginning of year plus additions during the year less value of asset at end of year.

6. **Sum of the digits.** For various assets. Calculated as in the following example:

       Cost of asset: £30,000.

       Estimated useful life 5 years

	Cost	Depreciation
	£30,000	£
Year 1	$\times \, ^5/_{15}$	10,000
2	$\times \, ^4/_{15}$	8,000
3	$\times \, ^3/_{15}$	6,000
4	$\times \, ^2/_{15}$	4,000
5	$\times \, ^1/_{15}$	2,000
	$^{15}/_{15}$	£30,000

Accounting entries to record provision for depreciation:

Annual charge for depreciation	Debit Profit & loss a/c	Credit Provision for depreciation of (asset) a/c.

The annual charge for depreciation is an attempt to match a proportion of the cost of an asset to revenue earned by it in a year. It is a bookkeeping entry. It does not involve any payment of money; it is a non-monetary item in the profit and loss account.

In the balance sheet, deduct the balances on the Provisions for depreciation accounts from the relevant assets in order to show the net book (or written down) values of the fixed assets. See 1.10 for a preferred layout of fixed assets in a balance sheet.

The net book value of an asset, as shown in a balance sheet, is the balance of the original cost not yet written off against revenue; it is the amount being carried forward at the date of the balance sheet to be written off against future revenue from that asset. It is not intended to represent what the asset is worth; still less is it a statement of what the asset will fetch if sold.

Profits and losses on disposal of fixed assets. These frequently have to be calculated in examination questions.

Calculation: Proceeds of disposal less (original cost - aggregate depreciation to date of disposal) = profit/(loss)

i.e. Proceeds of disposal - written down value at date of sale.

1.8 PROVISIONS FOR DOUBTFUL DEBTS AND DISCOUNTS

Provisions for doubtful debts

The provisions may be:

specific – against identified debts
or general – based on a percentage of debtors
or a combination of both methods.

Accounting entries:

| Increase in existing provision | Debit Profit & loss a/c | Credit Provision for doubtful debts |
| Decrease in existing provision | Debit Provision for doubtful debts | Credit Profit & loss a/c |

Provisions for discounts allowed. Calculate as percentage of those debts which have not become overdue, after deducting any part of the provision for doubtful debts based on those debtors.

In the balance sheet, deduct the provisions for doubtful debts and discounts allowed from the trade debtors.

Discounts receivable on outstanding creditors should be ignored in order not to anticipate profits. (Prudence.)

1.9 TRADING AND PROFIT AND LOSS ACCOUNTS

Give every financial statement you prepare a proper heading; without it the statement will be meaningless. Trading and profit and loss account headings should be as follows:

Name
Trading and profit and loss account
Period covered by the account

For example:

John Brown
Trading and profit and loss account for the year ended 31 December 19-9

Within the trading account, the form in which 'cost of sales' is presented should recognise the correct calculation of the amount of purchases for the period. This figure should include the cost of the goods, less goods returned, plus the cost of getting the goods to their present location (carriage inwards).

Recommended presentation of a trading account where all the above elements are present:

	£	£	£
Sales			25,000
less cost of sales:			
Opening stock		5,000	
Purchases	12,000		
less returns outwards	900		
	11,100		
add carriage inwards	400	11,500	
		16,500	
less closing stock		4,000	12,500
Gross profit			12,500

1.10   BALANCE SHEETS

A balance sheet heading should recognise that it is the 'position' statement of a business at a particular point in time.

For example:

John Brown

Balance sheet as at 31 December 19-9

Within a balance sheet, the order in which fixed assets are shown is important. Start with the most permanent assets, progressing to the less permanent ones:

e.g.   Freehold property

Leasehold property

Plant and machinery

Motor vehicles

Office furniture, machinery, etc.

Fixed assets should be displayed where possible to show the total 'cost' and total 'depreciation' as well as the total of 'net book values' where the information is available.

Recommended lay-out of the 'fixed asset' section of a balance sheet:

Fixed assets	Cost £	Depn £	Net £
Premises	50,000	20,000	30,000
Plant and machinery	35,000	25,000	10,000
Office furniture	4,000	3,000	1,000
	89,000	48,000	41,000

Current assets should be shown in inverse order of liquidity. The most liquid form of current asset is cash; the least liquid form is stock. The usual order items is:

Stock

Debtors

Prepayments

Bank balance

Cash in hand

(The published accounts of limited companies must be considered separately; see Chapter 10.)

1.11   PROVISIONS AND RESERVES

Provisions are amounts set aside out of profits to provide for:

(i)   depreciation of fixed assets;

(ii)   possible losses caused by bad debts;

(iii)   liabilities, the amounts of which cannot be estimated with substantial accuracy when a balance sheet is being prepared.

All other amounts set aside out of profits are reserves.

Provisions and reserves are always represented by credit balances.

In a balance sheet, provisions for depreciation should always be deducted from the fixed assets to which they refer,and provision for bad debts should be deducted from debtors.

1.12   BOOKS OF PRIME ENTRY

You must have a thorough understanding of the purposes of the books of prime entry, and the manner in which the items in them are posted to the books of double entry.

The books of prime entry with which you should be familiar are:

Cash book (and petty cash book where one is kept)

Purchases day book (Purchases journal)

Purchases returns book (Goods outwards book)

Sales day book (Sales journal)

Sales returns book (Goods inwards book)

Journal

The cash book is the only book of prime entry which is also a ledger account, and therefore part of the double entry system. The other books are memoranda books only and both aspects of every transaction in them must be posted to the appropriate ledger accounts.

Never prepare a journal entry showing a posting to be made to a book of prime entry; such books are not ledger accounts or, indeed, part of the double entry system at all.

The functions of the books of prime entry are to:

(i)   collect together all transactions of a similar nature in order.

(ii) facilitate reference back to original documents (invoices, etc.)

(iii) control the completeness of all information posted to the accounts.

(iv) reduce volume of entries made in nominal ledger accounts as only daily (weekly, or monthly) totals need be posted to the sales, purchases etc. accounts.

The purposes of, and the postings made from, the books of prime entry, other than the cash book and journal are:

Book of prime entry	Individual items posted to:	Period totals posted to:
Purchases day book (purchases on credit)	Credit of suppliers' accounts	Debit of Purchases account
Purchases returns book (goods returned to suppliers)	Debit of suppliers' accounts	Credit of Purchases Returns/Goods outwards
Sales day book (Sales on credit)	Debit of customers' accounts	Credit of Sales account
Sales returns (goods returned by customers)	Credit of customers' accounts	Debit of Sales returns/Goods inwards

The journal is used as a book of prime entry for:

–   correction of errors

–   transfers between ledger accounts

–   purchases and sales of fixed assets

–   opening entries in new set of ledgers

–   any other transaction for which there is no other book of prime entry

1.13   KEY POINTS TO REMEMBER

1.   A good understanding of your first-year studies in book-keeping and accounting is essential as you approach advanced level accounting. If you find difficulty with any of the topics in this chapter, revise your first-year studies thoroughly before you proceed any further.

2.   Many advanced level accounting questions are concerned to test your understanding of basic concepts: entity, duality, money measurement, realisation, matching, prudence, consistency and going concern.

3.   The application of the accounting equation is an essential technique in solving many questions, especially those concerned with incomplete records.

4.   Make sure you fully understand the principles of double entry book-keeping, in particular, which account should be debited and which credited to record any transaction. Learn to think in terms of 'double-entry'.

5.   You should be able to distinguish readily between those accounts which normally have debit balances and those which have credit balances.

6. Many examination marking schemes reserve marks for the following points, which you should learn and practice in all your exercises.

(i) When required to write up ledger accounts, take trouble to write them up properly. Each account should be appropriately headed, each transaction dated and the name of the other account in which the corresponding debit or credit entry will be found should be entered as part of each posted amount. Keep to the normal 'T' account format.

(ii) If an account has a balance to be carried down, show the balance also as brought down on the following day to complete the double entry.

(iii) Trading and profit and loss accounts and balance sheets should be headed correctly as in 1.9 and 1.10 above.

(iv) Whenever appropriate, set Trading accounts out as shown in 1.9 above.

(v) Whenever appropriate, set fixed assets out in balance sheets as shown in 1.10 above. Marks may be awarded for total cost and total depreciation figures.

7. Present all your answers neatly and tidily; give them suitable headings which accurately describe them. If you make a mistake, cross the whole amount in question out and re-write the correct amount above it. You will not lose marks for crossings out.

1.14 EXAMINATION QUESTIONS

QUESTION 1 (Cambridge June 1987)

The following draft balance sheet as at 31 March 19-7 of David Sparks, retail trader, was prepared quickly after the year end.

	£	£
Fixed assets:		
Freehold property – at cost	24,000	
provision for depreciation	4,800	19,200
Motor vehicles – at cost	18,000	
provision for depreciation	9,000	9,000
		28,200
Current assets:		
Stock	13,000	
Debtors	9,000	
Balance at bank	1,600	
	23,600	
Less: Current liabilities - Creditors and accruals	3,800	19,800
		48,000
Represented by:		
Capital – At 1 April 19-6		50,000
Add net profit for the year ended 31 March 19-7		10,000
		60,000
Less drawings		12,000
		48,000

After the draft balance sheet had been prepared, the following discoveries were made:

(a) A quantity of goods sent to T.Beal on a sale or return basis remained unsold on 31 March 19-7. These goods had cost David Sparks £600 and were expected to sell for £1,000. In preparing the draft accounts for the year ended 31 March 19-7, it was assumed that all the goods had been sold, on credit, by T.Beal as planned. T.Beal is to be paid a commission of 2% on the gross proceeds of all sales made for David Sparks.

(b) Debtors include £200 due from K.Peacock who has now been declared bankrupt. It is unlikely that any money will be received for this debt.

(c) A provision for doubtful debts at 31 March 19-7 of 2% of debtors at that date is to be created.

(d) Provision is to be made for electricity charges of £700 accrued due at 31 March 19-7.

(e) On 1 October 18-6, David Sparks hired (leased) a motor van for one year from Hire Vehicles Limited; the hire charge of £3,000 was paid in advance. However, in preparing the above draft accounts, it was assumed that the motor van had been purchased for £3,000.

Additional information:

The depreciation policy applied in the accounts of David Sparks is as follows:

Freehold property	10% per annum on cost;
Motor vehicles	25% per annum on cost.

REQUIRED

A corrected balance sheet as at 31 March 19-7   *(25 marks)*

QUESTION 2 (WJEC June 1988)

The following trial balance has been extracted from the books of Idyia Evans.

	£	£
Stocks at 1 May, 19-7	25,187	
Personal drawings	18,500	
Trade debtors and creditors	22,776	10,238
Rent and rates	12,800	
Advertising and promotion	1,750	
Insurance premiums	1,900	
Purchases and sales	99,817	182,208
Bad debts written off	218	
Development agency loan		50,000
Repairs and modifications to plant	1,581	
Vehicle operating expenditure	2,575	
Wages and salaries	45,012	
Loan interest at 15%	3,750	
Provision for doubtful debts		500
Heating and lighting	7,500	
Plant and machinery – cost	63,260	
– provision for depreciation		18,925
Office expenses	5,817	
Owner's capital account at 1 May, 19-7		53,000
Motor vehicles – cost	21,557	
– provision for depreciation		11,317
Bank overdraft		7,812
	334,000	334,000

11

Additional information is to be taken account of as follows:

(i)   Stock at 30 April, 19-8 was valued at £27,515.

(ii)   Loan interest for the six months ended 30 April, 19-8 is outstanding. Reconciliation of the bank account with statements received from the bank indicate that interest of £851 and charges of £1,025 have been entered by the bank. These amounts had not been included in the cash book at 30 April, 19-8.

(iii) Rent paid in advance at 30 April, 19-8 amounts to £870. Rates assessed as due but not yet paid are to be included at £1,200.

(iv)   Of the repairs and modifications to plant, £1,000 was expended on safety equipment as required by government health and safety regulations.

(v)   Depreciation of plant is to be provided for at 10% of cost and of motor vehicles at 20% of their written-down values.

(vi)   Advertising costs of £250 and wages and salaries due of £415 are to be allowed for.

REQUIRED

Trading and profit and loss accounts for the year ended 30 April, 19-8 and the balance sheet as at that date.
(28 marks)

QUESTION 3 (JMB June 1986)

You are required to explain to a friend with no accounting knowledge why revenues and expenses recorded in a profit and loss account do not necessarily represent receipts and payments made during the period which the profit and loss account covers. Use **three** examples to illustrate your explanation, and finally respond to your friend's query as to why the complications involved in your explanation are felt to be necessary.
(16 marks)

QUESTION 4 (JMB June 1987)

Ms. Price set up a business on 1 January 19-6 with a loan of £10,000 from a friend and £10,000 of her own. With this cash she purchased a machine for manufacturing a new board game called 'Chairmanship'. She submits the following account for her first year's trading.

		£
Cash Received from Sale of Games(2,000 @ £20 each)		40,000
Less: Cash Paid:	Wages	14,000
	Rent	4,000
	Raw Materials	6,800
	General Expenses	2,400
	Part Repayment of Loan	3,000
Net Income		£9,800

Ms. Price is somewhat doubtful whether the above statement is very reliable and asks you to prepare a Trading and Profit and Loss Account and Balance Sheet. In addition to the above information you discover:

(i)   Ms. Price has sold a further 300 units at £20 each for which she has not yet been paid;

(ii)   she owes £1,800 for materials already received;

(iii)   the machine has a ten year life and no anticipated scrap value;

(iv)   Ms. Price owes her secretary £400 for working overtime;

(v)   there are raw materials at cost £800 left in stock but no work in progress or finished goods;

(vi)   the rent payment covers the period from 1 January 19-6 to 31 March 19-7;

(vii)   the wages include £8,000 withdrawn by Ms. Price for her own use;

(viii) she has incurred further general expenses of £200 which she has not yet paid.

You are required to:

(a) prepare a revised Trading and Profit and Loss Account for the year ended 31 December 19-6 and a Balance Sheet as at that date; *(18 marks)*

(b) explain to Ms. Price the accounting conventions you have adopted which are primarily responsible for the difference between the original account and your revised Trading and Profit and Loss Account and why such conventions are considered necessary. *(7 marks)*

(25 Marks)

QUESTION 5 (JMB June 1988)

A company has recently acquired a new machine at a cost of £30,000. The machine has an estimated useful life of three years and an anticipated disposal value of £3,000. Details of units produced by the machine and repair and maintenance costs are as follows.

	Units	Repair and maintenance
		£
Year to 31 December 19-7 (actual)	14,000	600
Year to 31 December 19-8 (estimate)	16,000	1,400
Year to 31 December 19-9 (estimate)	10,000	2,000

(a) You are required to calculate the annual depreciation charge for each of the three years using the following methods:

(i) straight line;

(ii) reducing balance using the rate of 54%;

(iii) units produced. *(6 marks)*

(b) Draft a report to the directors on the merits and problems associated with each of the above methods. *(11 marks)*

(Total 17 marks)

EXERCISE 6 (London June 1988)

The following report appeared in a newspaper:

'Small computers are replaced typically in a period between nine months and two years after their purchase date. Users are becoming increasingly worried about the speed of obsolescence, which is seen as a major problem.

Many companies, however, still depreciate small computers over a much longer period than their useful life.'

You are required to:

(a) Explain the nature and purpose of depreciation. *(6 marks)*

(b) Advise a company regarding the way in which a depreciation policy should be formulated in respect not only of assets such as small computers, but also longer term assets such as land and buildings. *(14 marks)*

(Total 20 marks)

2 CONTROL (OR TOTAL) ACCOUNTS

For this topic you should be able to:-

- state the uses of control accounts
- recognise the sources of the entries in control accounts
- prepare control accounts from given information
- correct errors in control accounts and purchases and sales ledgers when the control account balances disagree with the ledgers they are controlling

2.1   CONTROL ACCOUNTS

Purposes of control accounts

1. To act as independent checks on the arithmetical accuracy of the aggregates of the balances in the sales and purchases ledgers.
2. To provide totals of debtors and creditors quickly when a trial balance is being prepared.
3. To identify the ledger or ledgers in which errors have been made when there is a difference on a trial balance.
4. To act as an independent internal check on the work of the sales and purchase ledger clerks, to detect errors and deter fraud. Duties should be so divided between staff that the sales and purchases ledger clerks have no access to the control accounts, and the person who maintains the total accounts has no access to the sales and purchases ledger accounts. For this purpose, it is important that the control accounts should be kept in the nominal ledger and not in the Purchases and Sales ledgers.

Form of control accounts

They contain in total form all transactions which have been posted as individual items to the sales and purchases ledgers. They are often known as Total accounts.

The periodic totals of each type of transaction are obtained from the books of prime entry.

The usual contents of the sales ledger control account are as follows with the sources of the entries shown in brackets.

SALES LEDGER CONTROL ACCOUNT

(Debit side)	(Credit side)
Total of sales ledger debit balances brought forward from previous period	Total of sales ledger credit balances brought forward from previous period
Credit sales for period (total of sales day book)	Sales Returns for period (total of sales returns book)
Refunds to customers (cash book)	Cash received from debtors (cash book)
Dishonoured cheques (cash book)	Cash discounts allowed (discount column of cash book)
Interest charged to customers on overdue accounts (journal)	Bad debts written off (journal)
Bad debts previously written off now recovered (journal)	Cash received in respect of bad debts previously written off (cash book)
	Sales ledger balances offset against balances in purchases ledger (journal)
Total of any sales ledger credit balances at end of period carried forward	Total of sales ledger debit balances at end of period carried forward

Notes:

1. Cash sales are not recorded in the sales ledger control account.
2. Provisions for doubtful debts do not feature in sales ledger control accounts because the provision accounts are not kept in the sales ledger.

PURCHASE LEDGER CONTROL ACCOUNT

(Debit side)	(Credit side)
Total of purchase ledger debit balances (if any) brought forward from previous period	Total of purchase ledger credit balances brought forward from previous period
Total of goods returned to suppliers (purchases returns book)	Total credit purchases (purchases day book)
Total of cash paid to suppliers (cash book)	Refunds from suppliers (cash book)
Cash discounts received (discount column of cash book)	
Purchases ledger balances offset against balances in sales ledger (journal)	Interest charged by suppliers on overdue invoices (purchases day book or journal)
Total of credit balances at end of period carried forward	Total of debit balances, if any, at end of period carried forward

Note: Purchases made for cash do not feature in the purchases ledger control account.

Double entry book-keeping requires that either the sales and purchases ledger accounts are treated as part of the double-entry system and the control accounts are regarded as memoranda accounts only; or the control accounts are treated as part of the double entry and the sales and purchases ledger accounts are regarded as memoranda accounts.

2.1.1 EXAMPLE

The following data has been extracted from the books of Universal Controls plc for the month of May 19-9:

			£
May 1	Purchases ledger balances brought forward	– dr	405
		cr	6,210
	Sales ledger balances brought forward	– dr	21,566
		cr	975
May 31	Monthly totals of: Purchases day book		44,220
	Purchases returns book		2,630
	Sales day book		86,920
	Sales returns book		4,220
	Cash book		
	– cash paid to suppliers		38,900
	– cash received from debtors		77,840
	– discounts received column		1,400
	– discounts allowed column		3,120
	Dishonoured cheques		784
	Analysis of journal: Bad debts written off		1,260
	Sales ledger balances offset against purchases ledger balances		2,640
	Debit balances on purchases ledger accounts at 31 May 19-9		600
	Credit balances on sales ledger accounts at 31 May 19-9		800

REQUIRED

From the information given above prepare a sales ledger control account and a purchases ledger control account for Universal Controls plc for the month of May 19-9.

ANSWER

Universal Controls plc
Purchase ledger control account for the month of May 19-9

19-9			£	19-9			£
May 1	Balance b/d		405	May 1	Balance b/d		6,210
31	Purchases returns		2,630	31	Purchases		44,220
	Cash book	– payments	38,900		Balance c/d		600
		– discounts	1,400				
	Contra	– Sales ledger	2,640				
	Balance c/d		5,055				
			51,030				51,030
June 1	Balance b/d		600	June 1	Balance b/d		5,055

Sales ledger control account for the month of May 19-9

19-9		£	19-9		£
May 1	Balance b/d	21,566	May 1	Balance b/d	975
31	Sales	86,920	31	Sales returns	4,220
	Dishonoured cheques	784		Cash book	
				– receipts	77,840
	Balance c/d	800		– discounts	3,120
				Bad debts written off	1,260
				Contra – Purchase ledger	2,640
				Balance c/d	20,015
		110,070			110,070
June 1	Balance b/d	20,015	June 1	Balance b/d	800

2.1.2 EXERCISE (for practice in preparing control accounts)

The following information has been extracted from the books of Total Controls Ltd. for the month of September 19-0.

			£
Sales ledger balances at 1 September 19-0		– Dr	5,000
		– Cr	76
Purchases ledger balances at 1 September 19-0		– Dr	124
		– Cr	3,600
Sales for September	– cash		2,400
	– credit		21,790
Purchases for September	– cash		1,020
	– credit		14,500
Goods returned by credit customers			1,760
Goods returned to suppliers (originally bought on credit)			440
Cash received from debtors			20,450
Cash paid to creditors			11,120
Discounts allowed			580
Discounts received			276
Bad debts written off			424
Cash received in respect of a bad debt previously written off			70
Debtors' cheques returned by bank unpaid			826
Interest debited to accounts of overdue debtors			36
Balances in sales ledger offset against purchases ledger accounts			1,200
Balance on Provision for Doubtful Debts account at 1 September 19-0			200
Sales ledger credit balances at 30 September 19-0			150
Purchases ledger debit balances at 30 September 19-0			80

The directors of Total Controls Ltd. have decided that the Provision for Doubtful Debts should be adjusted to 5% of debtors at 30 September 19-0.

REQUIRED

The Sales Ledger Control account and the Purchases Ledger Control account for the month of September 19-0 for Total Controls Ltd.

Tutorial note: Not all of the information in this question is required for your answer.

2.2 CONTROL ACCOUNTS AND TRADE DISCOUNTS

Trade discount is not recorded in double entry book-keeping. Examiners may introduce trade discount into control account questions: the entries in the control accounts should be net of trade discount. Do not credit the Purchases ledger control account with the full list price of purchases, with a 'contra' entry for the trade discount on the debit side; this will not be acceptable to the examiner.

Cash discount, which is a discount for prompt payment, is, of course, recorded in the ledger accounts, including the control accounts.

2.2.1 EXAMPLE

P.Witte is a retailer of goods and he obtains his supplies from various sources, all of which allow him 10% discount off list prices.
Witte's records show the following information for the month of October, 19-4

		£
Purchases ledger balances at 1. 10.-4	Cr	16,420
	Dr	1,724
Purchases at list prices		210,000
Purchases returns at list prices		4,640
Cheques sent to suppliers		189,500
Cash discounts received		4,700
Purchases ledger balances at 31.10.-4	Dr	1,360
	Cr	?

REQUIRED

P. Witte's Purchases ledger control account for the month of October 19-4.

ANSWER

P.Witte
Purchases ledger control account for the month of October 19-4

19-4		£	19-4		£
Oct 1	Balance b/d	1,724	Oct 1	Balance b/d	16,420
31	Purchases returns	4,176	31	Purchases	189,000
	Cheques	189,500		Balance c/d	1,360
	Discounts	4,700			
	Balance c/d	6,680			
		206,780			206,780
Nov 1	Balance b/d	1,360	Nov 1	Balance b/d	6,680

Workings

	List price £	less 10% £	Net £
Purchases	210,000	21,000	189,000
Purchases returns	4,640	464	4,176

2.2.2 EXERCISE (for practice in treatment of trade discount in control accounts)

Dodgson deals in specialised electronic equipment. The following information is extracted from his records for the three months ended 30 June 19-3.

		April	May	June
		£	£	£
Balances on purchases ledger				
at 1 April	dr	625		
	cr	32,000		
Purchases at retail prices		150,000	200,000	180,000
Purchases returns at retail prices		4,000	6,000	5,000
Cheques sent to creditors		100,200	148,000	130,000
Discounts received		2,500	3,800	2,700
Debit balances at month end		410	570	220

Dodgson buys his goods at 20% less than the retail price.

REQUIRED

Dodgson's Purchases ledger control account for each of the three months for the period in question.

2.3 CORRECTION OF ERRORS

These questions are favourites with examiners. It is not possible to frame a concise set of rules to deal with this sort of problem. The best approach is to ask the following questions:

About the book-keeping errors

1. What entries, if any, have been made in the accounting records?

2. What entries should have been made?

3. What entries are required to correct the errors?

About the records affected

4. Has the error affected the sales/purchases ledger accounts?

5. Has the error affected the control account?

2.3.1 EXAMPLE

Tortelier has extracted the balances from his sales ledger as at 31 July 19-1 and they total £17,200, which total Tortelier has inserted as trade debtors in his trial balance. The trial balance does not agree, neither does the schedule of debtors, with the balance on the sales ledger control account.

An examination of the records reveals the following errors:

1. The discount allowed column in the cash book has been overcast by £200.

2. An invoice for a sale to Jones has been completely omitted from the books. The invoice is for £84.

3. Goods returned by Smithson, which had been invoiced to him in the sum of £160, had been correctly entered in the Sales Returns book, but debited to his account as £106.

4. Goods with a selling price of £1,000 had been sent on 'Sale or Return' to Gregson. Although Gregson has not yet indicated his intention to purchase the goods, the transaction has been entered in the Sales Day Book.

5. A bad debt of £50 has been written off in the Sales ledger but this item was not entered in the journal.

REQUIRED

(a) The Sales Ledger Control account, showing clearly the original balance on the account at 31 July 19-1, and the entries required to adjust the account for the above items.

(b) A calculation of Tortelier's corrected trade debtors figure at 31 July 19-1.

ANSWER

Tutorial notes:

Error 1   Sales ledger accounts not affected but the total of discounts allowed in the total account is £200 too much. Correct control account by debiting it with £200.

Error 2   Invoice £84 omitted entirely from books. Correct by debiting Jones' account in sales ledger, and the total account, with £84. (Credit sales account: £84).

Error 3   Returns from Smithson: his account in the sales ledger only affected. Credit his account with £106 to cancel erroneous debit plus £160 to record the return of goods.

Error 4   Goods on sale or return should not be treated as sales until the consignee has indicated his intention to purchase the goods. The sale should be eliminated from both Gregson's account in the sales ledger and the total account by credit entries in both. Sales account should be debited with the amount.

Error 5   The sales ledger account is correct, only the total account is affected. Credit the £50 written off to control account.

(a)

Tortelier

Sales Ledger Control Account

19-1		£	19-1		£
July 31	Balance b/d (balancing figure)	16,784	July 31	Adjustment of goods on sale or return	1,000
	Adjustment of discounts	200		Bad debt w/o	50
	Adjustment of omission of Jones invoice	84		Balance c/d [see part (b)]	16,018
		17,068			17,068
Aug 1	Balance b/d	16,018			

(b)   **Calculation of revised trade debtors balance at 31 July 19-1**

	£	£
Total of schedule of trade debtors before adjustment		17,200
Add: further debit - Jones		84
		17,284
Deduct: credit – to cancel wrong debit to Smithson	106	
– to record goods returned by Smithson	160	
	266	
– to cancel goods wrongly debited to Gregson	1,000	1,266
		16,018

2.3.2 EXERCISE (for practice in correcting errors in the Purchases ledger and its total account)

Datchett extracted the balances from his Purchases ledger on 31 January 19-9 and the totals of the lists were: credit balances £15,240; debit balances £540 (made up of W. Lynne £300; P. Francis £240).

When these balances were inserted in the trial balance, there was a difference on the trial balance. Furthermore, the Purchases ledger balances did not agree with the position shown by the Purchases ledger total account.

Subsequently, Datchett discovered the following errors which had been made in January 19-9.

1. One page of the Purchases Day Book had not been included in the monthly total of that book; the total of the missing page was £1,250.

2. Goods returned to Sawyer, supplier, amounting to £300 had been entered in the Purchases Returns Book, but had been credited to Sawyer's account in error.

3. A credit note for £400 received from L. Wynne, supplier, had been debited to W. Lynne's account in error. (There is at present a credit balance of £800 on L. Wynne's account.)

4. A contra entry between James' account in the Purchases ledger and his account in the Sales ledger had been entered in the journal and posted to the Sales ledger account correctly but the corresponding entry had not been made in the Purchases ledger. The amount concerned was £380. The transfer had been recorded in the relevant control accounts.

5. The total of cheques sent to trade creditors in the month was £13,575. This had been posted to the Purchases ledger control account as £15,375.

6. The total of the discounts allowed column in the cash book, £1,321, had been credited to the Sales Ledger Control account, but had also been posted to the debit of the Purchases Ledger Control account as discounts received. The total of the discounts received column in cash book was £1,026.

REQUIRED

(a) The Purchases Ledger Control Account for the month of January 19-9 showing clearly the balances brought forward and carried forward, and the correcting entries.

(b) A calculation of the correct totals of the debit and credit balances in the purchases ledger.

2.4   KEY POINTS TO REMEMBER

1. Control accounts enable trial balances to be prepared sooner than if the purchases and sales ledger balances had to be extracted first.
2. Control accounts help to identify the ledgers in which there are errors contributing to a trial balance difference.
3. Entries in Control accounts consist of periodic totals of the books of prime entry.
4. When an examination question gives a list of 'list' prices of purchases and the amount of trade discount, show the purchases 'net' in the control account.

COMMON ERRORS

–   Items posted to wrong sides of control accounts.
–   Purchases/sales not posted to control accounts net of trade discount.
–   Contra entries between the Sales and Purchases ledgers entered in one control account only.
–   Failure to identify the Purchases and Sales Ledgers or the control accounts as memoranda records only when correcting errors.
–   Bad debts recovered not posted to both sides of the sales ledger control account.

2.5   EXAMINATION QUESTIONS

QUESTION 1   (Oxford June 86)

(a) List the advantages of using an account to control the debtors' ledger.   *(6 marks)*

(b) Prepare such an account from the following:

	£
Total debtors' balances at 1 May 19-6	22,000
Cash sales for the month of May	142,000
Credit sales for May	86,000
Credit sales returned during May	420
Cash received from debtors	87,210
Discounts allowed to debtors	1,415
Bad debts written off	250
Doubtful debts provision created	220
Customer's cheque returned by bank marked 'return to drawer'. The customer assures us that the cheque will be settled in June. The customer was allowed a cash discount of £16.	144
A customer has an account in the creditors ledger and it is decided to settle the two by a transfer.	85

(6 marks)

(c) State where the information for each entry in your account would be recorded before being entered in the ledger.

(6 marks)

(Total 18 marks)

QUESTION 2 (WJEC June 87)

The following figures appeared in the purchases ledger control account of Hudson and Co. Ltd. on 31 March 19-7.

	£
Creditor balances 1 April 19-6	36,846
Debtor balances 1 April 19-6	328
Discount received	1,957
Purchases	276,220
Payments to creditors	258,972
Purchase returns	3,116
Cash refunded from creditors	262
Bills payable	1,118
Debtor balances 31 March 19-7	419
Contras: sales ledger	784

The control account creditor balance at 31 March 19-7 failed to agree with the total of the list of balances of creditors extracted from the purchase ledger. Subsequent examination revealed the following errors.

(i)   A credit balance of £176 on the account of a creditor had been omitted from the list of creditors balances.

(ii) Discount received of £28 had been entered in the cash book and discount received account but not in the creditors account in the ledger.

(iii) The purchase day book had been undercast by £200.

(iv) An item of £186 in the purchase day book had been posted to the creditors account as £168.

(v)   Discount received for the month of £137 had been posted to the debit instead of the credit side of the discount received account.

(vi) Goods returned to a supplier valued at £82 had been correctly entered in the creditors account but entered in the purchases returns account as £182.

REQUIRED

(i)   Show how the control account would appear in the ledger before making any corrections.

(ii) Prepare a statement showing the adjustment of the balance in the control account in (i) above to the correct balance, giving details of the errors.

(iii) Prepare a statement reconciling the corrected balance with the totals as shown by the list of balances before the errors were found, giving details of the relevant errors.   *(18 marks)*

QUESTION 3 (WJEC June 1986)

(a) Explain the principle on which control accounts are based and give a simple illustration of their operation.   *(6 marks)*

(b) Explain how control accounts are used for **either** a debtors **or** creditors ledger.   *(6 marks)*

(c) Explain the difference between the operation of control accounts in a manually operated accounting system and a mechanised or computerised system using batch posting, and explain the main advantage of the method used for operation of control accounts in a mechanised or computerised system as compared with a manual system.   *(6 marks)*

(Total 18 marks)

Tutorial notes:

Many students think that this type of question is an easy alternative to computational type questions. In fact, the experience of examiners is that candidates generally score very badly on 'essay' type answers.

Each part of the question requires you to explain something. An explanation is not the same as a description or a discussion. You must explain each point in the question clearly and in as much depth as you can in the time allowed. Do not be vague or wander on to some irrelevant point.

An examiner will give minimum marks for a vague or bare recognition of a point. To score good marks, you must demonstrate good understanding of the topic. Where appropriate it is often best to tabulate the points in your answer.

QUESTION 4 (London June 1987)

The sales ledger control account of Jack Hill for the year ended 31 December 19-5 had a closing balance of £15,380, made up as follows:

	£
W. Hopper Limited	12,340
Other debtors	3,610
	15,950
Credit balances	570
	15,380

A summarised list of entries in W. Hopper Limited's sales ledger account in the books of Hill, for the year ended 31 December 19-6, is shown in the following table:

	£
Opening balance	12,340
Invoices	6,930
Cheque returned due to insufficient funds being available	150
Journal entry (1)	260
Cheques paid to Jack Hill	5,100
Goods returned	75
Journal entry (2)	1,405

Notes:

Journal entry (1) related to the correction of an error, whereby a cheque received from a creditor in repayment of a duplicated payment made by Hill had been posted incorrectly to Hopper's account.

Journal entry (2) was made to record the transfer of a balance on Hill's purchases ledger for goods purchased from Hopper.

Other information relevant to the personal ledgers of Hill for the year ended 31 December 19-6 is:

	£
Opening creditors	16,330
Purchases	128,400
Sales (other than to W. Hopper Limited)	214,960
Cheques to creditors	97,450
Cheques from debtors (including those from W. Hopper Limited)	179,910

Jack Hill decided that half of the balance on W. Hopper Limited's sales ledger account should be provided for as a doubtful debt on 31 December 19-6. There were no other doubtful debts.

You are required to prepare,

(a) the Sales Ledger Control Account in Hill's books for the year to 31 December 19-6   *(13 marks)*

(b) Purchase Ledger Control account in Hill's books for the year to 31 December 19-6   *(8 marks)*

(c) the entry relating to debtors appearing in Hill's balance sheet as at 31 December 19-6.   *(4 marks)*

(Total 25 marks)

QUESTION 5 (AEB November 1986)

At the end of the financial year of Extra Ltd. the debit balance of £8,792 on the sales ledger control account did not agree with the total of balances extracted from the sales ledger; the latter being included in the trial balance. The following errors have subsequently been discovered.

(1) The total of the discount allowed account in the cash book had been overcast by £190.

(2) No entry had been made in the accounts relating to the writing off as irrecoverable a balance of £650 owed by James.

(3) The return of goods value £210 from Jackson, a customer, had been debited to the returns inward account but had not been posted to Jackson's account.

(4) Goods value £460 sent to a customer on a sale or return basis have been included in the sales day book. The customer has not indicated whether or not he will purchase the items.

(5) The receipt of £1,450 cash from S. Austin had been treated as a payment from S.J. Austin, a customer. The amount received related to the cash sale of a delivery van which was surplus to requirements.

REQUIRED

(a) A sales ledger control account showing clearly all the amendments to the original balance.

(8 marks)

(b) The journal entries to correct items (1), (3) and (5) above. Narratives are required. *(4 marks)*

(Total 12 marks)

QUESTION 6 (AEB June 1987)

Sellabrick, a firm trading as builders' merchants, purchases stock on credit from a large number of suppliers. The company maintains a purchase ledger control account as an integral part of its double entry book-keeping system and in addition maintains supplier accounts on a memoranda basis in a purchase ledger. At the end of the financial year ended 31 May 19-7 the balance of £25,450 on the purchase ledger control account failed to agree with the total of balances from the purchase ledger. The following errors have subsequently been discovered.

(1) Goods which cost £350 and which were purchased on credit from Green, a supplier, had been entered in the purchase day book at their retail price of £600.

(2) An amount of £1,500 paid to Hunt, a supplier, had been correctly entered in the cash book but had been entered in Jackson's Account as £1,550.

(3) The return of goods purchased on credit and costing £800 had been completely omitted from the books.

(4) The purchase day book had been undercast by £2,220.

REQUIRED

(a) A purchase ledger control account showing clearly all of the amendments to the original balance.

(7 marks)

(b) A calculation showing the total of the balances in the purchase ledger before the corrections were made. *(6 marks)*

(Total 13 marks)

SUSPENSE ACCOUNTS

For this topic you should be able to:-

● distinguish between errors which affect the trial balance and those which do not
● draft suitable journal entries to correct errors
● write up suspense accounts, from journal entries
● revise the net profit or loss per draft accounts to take account of the correction of errors

3.1 SUSPENSE ACCOUNTS

When a difference exists on a trial balance and immediate checks do not disclose the cause of the difference, a suspense account may be opened in the nominal ledger. It is debited or credited with the trial balance difference. The suspense account balance is then inserted into the trial balance to make it agree, and work on production of final accounts may then proceed.

The causes of the trial balance difference must be investigated at the earliest opportunity and correcting entries made, through the suspense account where appropriate, until the difference has been eliminated.

3.2 CORRECTION OF ERRORS

The best approach is to ask the following questions:

– about the nature of the error:

(i) Is it one of the six types of error which do not affect the trial balance? (Refer to 1.5) If it is, do not adjust it through the suspense account. (In the rest of this chapter we shall refer to such errors as the 'six types of error').

– about the correcting entries required:

(ii) What entries, if any, have already been made in the accounts?

(iii) What entries should have been made?

(iv) What entries are required to correct the error?

3.2.1 EXAMPLE

Kay Singh extracted a trial balance from the books of her business as at 31 December 19-2. The trial balance totals were: £11,942 (debit) and £12,428 (credit).

Kay debited the difference of £486 to a suspense account so that she could prepare draft accounts, and the draft profit and loss account showed a provisional net profit of £4,200.

Subsequently, Kay found the following errors:

1. The debit side of the wages account had been overcast by £100.
2. Discounts received, £45, had been posted to the suppliers' accounts but not to the Discounts Received account.
3. A sale of goods on credit to Paul Song for £120 had not been entered in the books at all.
4. A cheque received from a debtor, Ken Toon, £62, had been posted to the debit of his account.
5. The refund of an insurance premium, £30, had been debited in the cash book but no other entry had been made.
6. The purchase of some office equipment for £590 had been debited to office expenses.
7. Rent paid, £400, had been credited to Rent Receivable account.

8. Goods returned to Fast Sales Ltd., a supplier, had been credited to Fast Sales Ltd.'s account and debited to Purchases Returns account. The goods had originally cost £200.

9. A credit balance in the Purchases Ledger, £15, had been omitted from the list of balances extracted from that ledger. The total of the list had been included in the trial balance as trade creditors.

10. A purchase of office stationery, £110, had been debited to Telephones and Postages account in error.

REQUIRED

(a) The journal entries to correct the foregoing errors. (Narratives are not required.)

(b) The suspense account showing the correcting entries.

(c) A revised profit figure for the year ended 31 December 19-2.

ANSWER

(a) **Error 1** *Tutorial note:* the debit balance on wages a/c is overstated by £100. Reduce this by a credit to the account of the same amount. Not one of the 'six errors'; adjust through suspense a/c.

Journal	Dr.	Cr.
	£	£
Suspense	100	
Wages		100

Error 2 *Tutorial note:* Discounts Received a/c is short by £45 (credit). Credit that amount to the a/c. Not one of the 'six errors'; adjust through suspense a/c.

Journal	Dr.	Cr.
	£	£
Suspense	45	
Discounts Received		45

Error 3 *Tutorial note:* Paul Song £120. This is error of omission, one of the 'six types'; do not adjust through suspense a/c.

Journal	Dr.	Cr.
	£	£
Paul Song	120	
Sales		120

Error 4 *Tutorial note:* £62 posted to wrong side of Toon's a/c; item posted to wrong side of a/c produces error twice its own size. Not one of 'six types'; adjust through suspense a/c.

Journal	Dr.	Cr.
	£	£
Suspense	124	
Ken Toon		124

Error 5 *Tutorial note:* omission of credit to Insurance a/c has resulted in debit balance on this a/c being overstated by £30. Credit £30 to insurance a/c. Not one of 'six types'; adjust through suspense a/c.

Journal	Dr.	Cr.
	£	£
Suspense	30	
Insurance		30

25

Error 6 *Tutorial note:* purchase of office equipment treated as revenue expense instead of as capital expenditure; error of principle, one of 'six types'. Do not adjust through suspense a/c.

Journal	Dr.	Cr.
	£	£
Office equipment	590	
Office expenses		590

Error 7 *Tutorial note:* rent paid posted not only to wrong a/c, but to wrong side of wrong account. Error is £800 (2x£400). Not one of 'six types'; adjust through suspense a/c.

Journal	Dr.	Cr.
	£	£
Rent Receivable	400	
Rent Payable	400	
Suspense		800

Error 8 *Tutorial note:* Fast Sales Ltd. This is an example of complete reversal of entries and one of the 'six types'; do not adjust through suspense a/c. Reverse the original entries, using twice the cost of the goods.

Journal	Dr.	Cr.
	£	£
Fast Sales Ltd.	400	
Purchases Returns		400

Error 9 *Tutorial note:* Balance omitted from list extracted from ledger not an error in the double entry. Correct by adding balance to list and amending item of trade creditors in trial balance. Adjust through suspense a/c by 'one sided' journal entry.

Journal	Dr.	Cr.
	£	£
Suspense	15	

Error 10 *Tutorial note:* Purchase of office stationery debited to wrong expense a/c.; error of commission, one of the 'six errors'. Do not adjust through suspense a/c.

Journal	Dr.	Cr.
	£	£
Office stationery	110	
Telephone and postages		110

(b) *Tutorial note:* In this part of the question, open the Suspense account with the trial balance difference and post from your journal entries from part (a).

Kay Singh

Suspense account

19-2		£	19-2		£
Dec 31	Difference on trial		Dec 31	Rent payable	400
	balance	486		Rent receivable	400
	Wages	100			
	Discounts received	45			
	K. Toon	124			
	Insurance	30			
	Increase in trade				
	creditors	15			
		800			800

(c) *Tutorial note:* You must now select those journal entries which affect the profit and loss account i.e. adjustments to nominal accounts. Ignore corrections which affect personal accounts or real accounts only.

Kay Singh
Calculation of corrected net profit for the year to 31 December 19-2

		Decrease	Increase	
		£	£	£
Net profit per draft accounts				4,200
(1)	Reduction in wages		100	
(2)	Increase in discounts received		45	
(3)	Increase in sales		120	
(5)	Reduction in insurance premiums		30	
(6)	Reduction in office expenses		590	
(7)	Reduction in rent receivable	400		
	Increase in rent payable	400		
(8)	Increase in purchases returns		400	
		800	1,285	
		800		485
Revised net profit				£4,685

Items (4) and (9) do not affect profit.

Tutorial note: Adopt the above lay-out for 'revision of net profit' type questions. Untidy, 'straggly' answers without a logical lay-out do not commend themselves to examiners.

3.2.2   EXERCISE (To test your ability to correct accounting errors and to calculate a revised profit figure.)

G. Sobers extracted the balances from his ledgers on 30 June 19-3 and prepared a trial balance as at that date. The trial balance failed to agree and Sobers opened a suspense account to enable him to proceed with the preparation of draft final accounts.

Subsequently, Sobers discovered the following errors:

(1)   A cheque received from C.Lloyd, a debtor, had been correctly entered in the cash book as £105, but had been credited to Lloyd's account as £150.

(2)   An improvement to a machine at a cost of £750 had been debited to Machinery Repairs instead of to the Machinery (asset) account. (Assets are depreciated on the straight line basis at 10% of cost; a full year's depreciation is calculated in the year of purchase.)

(3)   The total of the Sales Day Book for February,19-3, was £10,860; this had been posted to the Sales account as £10,680.

(4)   An invoice for the purchase of goods from F.Engineer on 1 June 19-3 had been entirely omitted from the books. The invoice amounted to £300.

(5)   A debt of £100 in the sales ledger had proved to be bad and had been written off in the sales ledger, but the appropriate entry had not been made in the Bad Debts account.

REQUIRED

(a)   Prepare the suspense account in Sober's ledger showing clearly the difference on the trial balance at 30 June 19-3 and the entries made to adjust the above mentioned errors.

(b)   Journal entries for errors 2 and 4 above (narratives not required.)

(c)   A calculation of the corrected net profit for the year to 30 June 19-3. Sober's first draft of the profit and loss account had disclosed a net profit of £7,550.

Tutorial note: The trial balance difference in the Suspense account will be the figure required to make that account balance after the adjustments have been posted to it.

3.2.3   EXERCISE (A more difficult one)

P.Hendrie's trial balance at 31 March 19-2 had a difference of £4,510, the total of the debit side being larger by that amount.

Hendrie opened a suspense account until such time as the error(s) could be found. Meanwhile, he prepared final accounts for the business which showed a net loss of £2,300 for the year.

Subsequently, Hendrie found the following errors:

(1) Major repair work to a damaged motor car, in the sum of £2,780, had been debited in error to the motor cars (asset) account as £2,870.

(2) An invoice for the sale on credit to Boon of goods with a selling price of £500 had been debited to Boon's account but had not been entered in the Sales Day Book.

(3) The figure of stock at 1 April 19-1 had been entered into the trial balance as £14,000 instead of £10,400 as shown in the Stock account.

(4) A stock sheet totalling £1,300 had been inadvertently omitted from the closing stock summary at 31 March 19-2.

(5) A credit balance of £160 in the Sales ledger had been extracted as a debit balance.

REQUIRED

(a) The journal entries required to correct the above mentioned errors in Hendrie's books.

(b) The suspense account showing the entries for the original difference and the correction of errors.

(c) A calculation of the revised profit or loss of P.Hendrie's business for year ended 31 March 19-2.

3.3 KEY POINTS TO REMEMBER

1. Journal entries should always be prepared in proper form with the accounts to be debited shown before those to be credited. Include concise narratives unless the question states that narratives are not required.

2. Identify those errors which do not affect the trial balance and will not therefore be adjusted through the suspense account; the remaining errors must be adjusted through the suspense account.

3. When calculating revised profit identify those errors which have affected the profit and loss account. Present your calculation in the form used in this chapter.

COMMON ERRORS
- failure to differentiate between errors which must be adjusted through the suspense account and other errors.
- failure to identify the proper entries required to correct errors.
- making journal entries to other books of prime entry.
- failure to identify errors that affect the profit and loss account and those that do not.
- increasing profit when it should be reduced and vice versa.

3.4 EXAMINATION QUESTIONS

QUESTION 1 (AEB June 1986)

At the completion of the financial year ended 30 April 19-4 the trial balance of Rock Ltd. failed to agree and the difference was recorded in a suspense account.

The company does not maintain control accounts.

The following information has been subsequently discovered prior to the preparation of the final accounts.

(1) The purchase of a secondhand delivery van costing £1,500 has been debited to the motor vehicle expenses account.

(2) No entry has been made in the accounts to record the theft of £250 cash from the business by a dishonest former employee. The cash will not be recovered.

(3) The total of the discount allowed column in the cash book has been overcast by £187.

(4) The receipt of £289 from Hand, a customer, has been correctly entered in the cash book but has been debited to Hand's account in the sales ledger as £298.

(5) Although the return of goods, sold for £45, from Brown, a customer, has been correctly entered in the returns inwards account no entry has been made in Brown's account in the sales ledger.

REQUIRED

(a) Journal entries correcting each of the five errors given above. Narratives are not required. *(5 marks)*

(b) A suspense account showing clearly the original discrepancy on the trial balance. *(5 marks)*

(Total 10 marks)

QUESTION 2   (Oxford June 1987)

Mrs. Beatrice Morgan has prepared the following trial balance at 31 December 19-6 for the business of her husband:

	£	£
Capital 1 January 19-6		53,780
Purchases and sales	9,000	18,400
Returns Inward	100	
Returns Outward		250
Depreciation for year written off	890	
Wages	4,300	
Discounts allowed		450
Discounts received	270	
Debtors and Creditors	1,250	2,750
Premises	45,000	
Fixtures and fittings	8,900	
Bank Overdraft	1,200	
Cash	150	
Carriage Inwards	370	
Stock 1 January 19-6	2,500	
Carriage Outwards		140
Sundry Expenses	1,420	
Provision for Doubtful Debts	420	—
	£75,770	£75,770

Although the trial balance balances, Mrs. Morgan is sure that something is on the wrong side, but before she can check it she is rushed into hospital for an operation. Mr. Morgan asks you to check it for him.

(a) **You are required** to rewrite the trial balance correctly entering the difference (if any) as a suspense account balance.

(b) Mr. Morgan asks you to check the books to see if there are any errors and you find the following:

   (i)   A page of the purchases day book has been undercast by £3,000.

   (ii) A total in the sales book has been carried forward as £1,000, instead of £1,600.

   (iii) The sale of some old fixtures for cash for £300 has been credited to the sales account.

   (iv) Returns inward of £100 have been posted to the returns outward account.

Prepare Journal entries to correct the above errors. (Narrations are not required.)

(c) Write up the suspense account, starting with the balance from your trial balance. *(Total 18 marks)*

4 INCOMPLETE RECORDS

You should be able to:-

- calculate net profit or loss for a period using statements of affairs
- prepare receipts and payments accounts
- prepare trading and profit and loss accounts using total accounts, and ratios of gross profit to turnover or cost of sales
- prepare balance sheets
- calculate value of stock lost in fire or by theft

'Incomplete records' is a term which is used to describe situations where only single entry bookkeeping is employed (e.g. only a cash book or only personal accounts for debtors and creditors), or where no records are kept at all. As a result, transactions are not recorded in their two-fold aspects, the concept of duality is ignored and final accounts of the business cannot be prepared in the usual way.

Where sufficient information is available from such records as have been kept, including bank statements, bank paying-in book counterfoils, cheque counterfoils, copies of invoices, etc., trading and profit and loss accounts may be prepared. In the absence of such sources of information, the profit or loss may be ascertained by preparing statements of affairs.

4.1 STATEMENTS OF AFFAIRS

A statement of affairs lists the assets and liabilities of a business at a given date. The difference between the assets and liabilities represents capital. (Accounting equation: assets less liabilities = capital.)

Comparison of capital at different dates to ascertain profit or loss: profit increases capital; a loss decreases capital. Therefore: capital at end of period less capital at start of period = profit or loss for the period. Capital introduced during the period and capital withdrawn during the period (drawings) must be taken into account.

4.1.1 EXAMPLE

Ms. Perfect, hair stylist, has been in business for some years but has never kept records of her takings or expenditure. She has now received an estimated assessment for income tax from H.M.Inspector of Taxes and wishes to check the business profit shown in her assessment. Ms. Perfect provides the following information as at the 6 April 19-1 and 5 April 19-2.

	6 April 19-1	5 April 19-2
	£	£
Equipment	1,000	1,200
Stocks of hair styling sundries	70	45
Amounts owing from clients	60	72
Rent paid in advance	100	80
Balance at bank	265	180
Creditors for supplies	40	22
Electricity owing	20	35

Ms. Perfect has drawn £100 per week from the business.

ANSWER

Ms. Perfect
Calculation of profit for the year to 5 April 19-2
Statements of affairs as at

	6 April 19-1		5 April 19-2	
	£	£	£	£
Equipment		1,000		1,200
Stocks of hair styling sundries		70		45
Amounts owing from clients		60		72
Rent paid in advance		100		80
Balance at bank		265		180
		1,495		1,577
less creditors for supplies	40		22	
electricity owing	20	60	35	57
Net assets (= capital)		1,435		1,520
deduct capital at 6 April 19-1				1,435
				85
add drawings for year (52 × £100)				5,200
Profit for year				5,285

4.1.2 EXERCISE (calculation of profit using Statements of Affairs.)

Mr. Blower has carried on business as a plumber for some years. He has arranged a visit to his bank manager to arrange overdraft facilities, but he has never kept any proper records and wishes to provide his bank manager with the results of his business for the past year. The only information he has been able to produce is a schedule of his assets and liabilities as at 1 July 19-2 and 30 June 19-3. They are as follows:

	as at 1 July 19-2	as at 30 June 19-3
	£	£
Premises at cost	5,000	5,000
Motor van at cost	4,000	4,000
Motor car at valuation	–	5,500
Plant and equipment	900	1,000
Stock of materials	100	175
Debtors for work done	1,250	640
Balance at bank	2,400	120
Owing to suppliers	975	1,800
Rates owing	–	400
Telephone owing	15	40
Loan from father	–	2,000

The premises were purchased some years ago and were valued at £8,000 on 1 July 19-2; the valuation has not changed since then. The value of the motor van at 30 June 19-3 was £3,200. During the year, Mr.Blower brought his private car into the business at the valuation shown above.

Mr.Blower has drawn £80 per week from the business.

REQUIRED

A calculation of Mr. Blower's profit or loss for the year to 30 June 19-3.

Tutorial note: The valuation of assets rather than their cost should be used to calculate capital as the valuation represents the true worth of the owner's investment in the business.

4.2 TRADING AND PROFIT AND LOSS ACCOUNTS

If sufficient information is available, trading and profit and loss accounts may be prepared from incomplete records. Two techniques are useful for this purpose: total accounts and the use of the mark-up, margin and the relationship between these last two.

4.2.1 EXAMPLE

Total accounts may be used to calculate purchases and sales for a period.
The following information is available from Taylor's business records:

	At 1 Jan 19-4	At 31 Dec 19-4
	£	£
Trade debtors	2,220	2,600
Trade creditors	1,760	2,240

		£
For the year to 31 December 19-4		
Cash sales		5,600
Cash received from trade debtors		25,800
Cash paid to trade creditors		12,220

REQUIRED

Calculate Taylor's purchases and sales for the year to 31 December 19-4

Taylor
Purchases total account

19-4		£	19-4		£
Dec 1	Cash paid to creditors	12,220	Jan 1	Creditors b/d	1,760
31	Creditors c/d	2,240	Dec 31	Purchases- trading a/c	
				(balancing figure)	12,700
		14,460			14,460

Purchases to be debited in trading account: £12,700

Sales total account

19-4		£	19-4		£
Jan 1	Debtors b/d	2,220	Dec 31	Cash received from debtors	25,800
Dec 31	Sales (balancing figure)	26,180		Debtors c/d	2,600
		28,400			28,400

	£
Credit sales	26,180
Cash sales	5,600
Sales for the year	31,780

Tutorial note: Do not include cash sales in the total account.

4.2.2 EXERCISE (for practice in using total accounts to calculate purchases and sales)

The following information is extracted from the records of A. Smith:

	At 1 April 19-3	At 31 March 19-4
	£	£
Trade creditors	14,640	16,100
Trade debtors	19,730	21,150

Other information for the year to 31 March 19-4

	£
Cheques sent to suppliers	168,000
Discounts received	6,400
Cash received from debtors	199,700
Discounts allowed	4,820

REQUIRED

A calculation of Smith's purchases and sales for the year ended 31 March 19-4.

4.3 MARK-UP AND MARGIN

Mark-up is gross profit expressed as a percentage or fraction of cost of sales.

Example:

	£
Cost price of goods	100
Selling price	125
Gross profit	25

$$\frac{\text{Gross profit}}{\text{Cost price}} \times 100 = \frac{25}{100} \times 100 = 25\% \text{ or } \frac{1}{4}$$

Margin is gross profit expressed as a percentage or fraction of selling price.
Example (as above)

$$\frac{\text{Gross profit}}{\text{Selling price}} \times 100 = \frac{25}{125} \times 100 = 20\% \text{ or } \frac{1}{5}$$

(relationship between mark-up and margin – example as above)

$$\text{Mark-up} = \frac{1}{4} \text{ or } \frac{1}{5-1}$$

$$\text{Margin} = \frac{1}{5} \text{ or } \frac{1}{4+1}$$

Therefore, in general terms:

when mark-up is $\frac{a}{b}$, margin is $\frac{a}{b+a}$

and when margin is $\frac{a}{b}$, mark-up is $\frac{a}{b-a}$

thus: mark-up $\frac{1}{3}$,   margin $\frac{1}{3+1}$ or $\frac{1}{4}$

$\frac{2}{5}$ $\frac{2}{5+2}$ or $\frac{2}{7}$

margin $\frac{1}{6}$ mark-up $\frac{1}{6-1}$ or $\frac{1}{5}$

$\frac{2}{5}$ $\frac{2}{5-2}$ or $\frac{2}{3}$

4.3.1 EXAMPLES

(i)   Mr. Wedge's books showed the following information for the year to 31 December 19-2:

	£
Stock at 1 Jan 19-2	5,000
Purchases for year	25,000
Stock at 31 December 19-2	8,000

Mr. Wedge adds 25% to his cost of sales to arrive at the selling price. What were his sales for the year to 31 December 19-2?

ANSWER

	£
Stock at 1.1.-2	5,000
Purchases	25,000
	30,000
less stock at 31.12.-2	8,000
Cost of sales	22,000
add gross profit (25% of £22,000)	5,500 (20% of £27,500)
Sales for the year	27,500

(ii)   Miss Hodges' records showed the following:

	£
Stock at 1 July 19-3	12,000
Stock at 30 June 19-4	15,000
Sales for year to 30 June 19-4	180,000

Miss Hodges sells her goods so as to produce a gross margin of 33¹/₃%

Prepare Miss Hodges trading account for the year to 30 June 19-4, showing the amount of goods purchased.

ANSWER

Miss Hodges
Trading account for the year to 30 June 19-4

	£	£
Sales		180,000
Stock at 1 July -3	12,000	
Purchases (balancing figure 3)	123,000	
(balancing figure 2)	135,000	
less stock at 30 June -4	15,000	
Cost of sales (balancing figure 1)		120,000
Gross profit (33¹/₃% of £180,000)		60,000

Tutorial note: The 'missing' figures in this answer are 'balancing' figures found by working back from cost of sales to purchases.

4.3.2 EXERCISE (for practice in using the relationship between mark-up and margin.)

Mr. Peters' business records show the following information for the year to 30 September 19-5:

	£
Sales for the year	260,000
Stock at 1 October 19-4	11,000
Stock at 30 September 19-5	14,000

Mr. Peters adds 25% to his cost of sales to arrive at his selling prices.

REQUIRED

Prepare Mr. Peters' trading account for the year to 30 September 19-5, showing the amount of purchases for the year.

4.4   RECEIPTS AND PAYMENTS ACCOUNTS

Receipts and payments accounts are, in effect, cash books in summarised form
- they show the opening and closing bank or cash balances.
- they record all receipts and payments irrespective of whether they are capital or revenue in nature.
- they record all amounts received or paid in the period irrespective of the periods of time to which they relate.

It will be necessary to prepare a receipts and payments account when one is not already included in an incomplete records question. Prepare separate accounts for bank and cash. Make sure that the cash paid into the bank is the same figure in both accounts.

Treat any expenditure which is not accounted for in the question as drawings in a receipts and payments account.

4.5   PREPARATION OF FINAL ACCOUNTS FROM INCOMPLETE RECORDS.

Seven steps in preparing trading and profit and loss accounts and balance sheets from incomplete records;

1.   Prepare statement of affairs at beginning of period to calculate opening capital.
2.   Prepare receipts and payments account.
3.   Calculate sales and purchases using total accounts, mark-up and margin as appropriate.
4.   Open 'T' accounts from opening statement of affairs and complete double entry from receipts and payments accounts.
5.   Adjust 'T' accounts for accruals and prepayments at end of period.
6.   Make provisions for depreciation and bad debts as required by question.
7.   Copy out trading and profit and loss account and balance sheet.

4.5.1 EXAMPLE

T. Harman, a general dealer, has been in business for some years and has never kept proper records. He now wishes you to prepare accounts for his business for the year to 31 December 19-2. Harman supplies you with the following information:

	1 Jan 19-2	31 Dec 19-2
	£	£
Premises	20,000	20,000
Motor van	7,000	7,000
Equipment	4,000	4,600
Stock	3,000	5,000
Cash at bank	2,700	3,400
Cash in hand	100	80
Trade debtors	1,900	2,480
Trade creditors	1,100	700
Rates in advance	350	425
Insurance in advance	60	75
Garage rent owing	100	125
Electricity owing	230	480
Loan from brother		1,000

In addition the following information for the year is available:

		£
Receipts:	Takings from cash sales	11,450
	Receipts from debtors	15,225
	Loan from brother	1,000
	Interest received on personal holding of savings bonds	700
	Refund of insurance premium	100
Payments:	Trade creditors	11,000
	Purchase of equipment	1,200
	Rates	2,100
	Insurance	500
	Garage rent	475
	Electricity	1,300
	Drawings	5,000

Harman informs you that with the exception of takings from cash sales, all the above receipts and payments passed directly through the bank account. The cash sales money was used to pay wages of £100 per week and to purchase sundry small items totalling £700; the balance of the cash takings were then banked. The loan from Harman's brother was received on 1 July 19-2 and interest is payable on it at the rate of 10% per annum.

You are to provide for depreciation on the motor van at the rate of 20%, and make a provision for bad debts of 5% of debtors at 31 December 19-2.

REQUIRED

A trading and profit and loss account for T.Harman's business for the year to 31 December 19-2 and a balance sheet as at that date.

ANSWER

Step 1

Statement of affairs at 1 January 19-2

	£	£
Premises		20,000
Motor van		7,000
Equipment		4,000
Stock		3,000
Cash at bank		2,700
Cash in hand		100
Trade debtors		1,900
Prepayments – rates		350
– insurance		60
		39,110
less Trade creditors	1,100	
garage rent owing	100	
electricity owing	230	1,430
Capital at 1 January 19-2		37,680

Step 2

Receipts and payments account (bank)

19-2		£	19-2		£
Jan 1	Balance b/f	2,700	Dec 31	Trade creditors	11,000
Jun 1	Loan from brother	1,000		Purchase of equipment	1,200
Dec 31	Takings – cash sales			Rates	2,100
	(balancing figure)	5,250		Insurance	500
	Receipts from debtors	15,225		Garage rent	475
	Interest on savings bonds	700		Electricity	1,300
				Drawings	5,000
	Refund of insurance	100		Balance c/f	3,400
		24,975			24,975

Receipts and payments account (cash)

19-2		£	19-2		£
Jan 1	Balance b/f	100	Dec 31	Wages	5,200
Dec 31	Cash sales	11,450		Sundries	700
				Banked	5,250
				Drawings (bal.fig.)	320
				Balance c/f	80
		11,550			11,550

Step 3

Purchases total account

19-2		£	19-2		£
Dec 31	Cheques to suppliers	11,000	Jan 1	Creditors b/f	1,100
	Creditors c/f	700	Dec 31	Purchases (bal.fig.)	10,600
		11,700			11,700

Sales total account

19-2		£	19-2		£
Jan 1	Debtors b/f	1,900	Dec 31	Receipts from debtors	15,225
Dec 31	Credit sales (bal.fig.)	15,805		Debtors c/f	2,480
		17,705			17,705

			£
Total Sales:	credit		15,805
	cash		11,450
			27,255

Steps 4 and 5

Loan from brother

			19-2		£
			Jul 1	Bank	1,000

Capital

			19-2		£
			Jan 1	Balance b/f	37,680

Equipment

19-2		£	19-2		£
Jan 1	Balance b/d	4,000	Dec 31	P&L - depreciation	600
Dec 31	Purchases	1,200		Balance c/d	4,600
		5,200			5,200

Rates

19-2		£	19-2		£
Jan 1	Balance b/f	350	Dec 31	P&L	2,025
Dec 31	Cheques	2,100		Balance c/f	425
		2,450			2,450

Insurance

19-2		£	19-2		£
Jan 1	Prepayment b/d	60	Dec 31	Refund	100
Dec 31	Cheques	500		P&L	385
				Prepayment c/f	75
		560			560

Garage rent

19-2		£	19-2		£
Dec 31	Cheques	475	Jan 1	Accrual b/f	100
	Accrual c/f	125	Dec 31	P&L	500
		600			600

Electricity

19-2		£	19-2		£
Dec 31	Cheques	1,300	Jan 1	Accrual b/f	230
	Accrual c/f	480	Dec 31	P&L	1,550
		1,780			1,780

Wages

19-2		£	19-2		£
Dec 31	Cash	5,200	Dec 31	P&L	5,200

Sundries

19-2		£	19-2		£
Dec 31	Cash	700	Dec 31	P&L	700

Drawings

19-2		£	19-2		£
Dec 31	Cheques	5,000	Dec 31	Interest on savings bonds	
					700
	Cash	320	Dec 31	Balance	4,620
		5,320			5,320

Step 6

Provision for depreciation of motor van

			19-2		£
			Dec 31	P&L (20% of £7,000)	1,400

Provision for bad debts

			19-2		£
			Dec 31	P&L (5% of £2,480)	124

Interest on loan from brother

19-2		£	19-2		£
Dec 31	Accrual c/f (10% of £1,000 × $^6/_{12}$)	50	Dec 31	P&L	50

Step 7

T. HARMAN
Trading and profit and loss account for the year ended 31 December 19-2

		£	£
Sales			27,255
less	Stock at Jan 1	3,000	
	Purchases	10,600	
		13,600	
	deduct stock at Dec 31	5,000	8,600
Gross profit			18,655
less	Wages	5,200	
	Rates	2,025	
	Insurance	385	
	Garage rent	500	
Carried forward		8,110	18,655

	£	£
Brought forward	8,110	18,655
Electricity	1,550	
Sundries	700	
Interest on loan	50	
Provision for depreciation – motor van	1,400	
– equipment	600	
Provision for bad debts	124	12,534
Net profit		6,121

Balance sheet as at 31 December 19-2

			£
Fixed assets			
Premises			20,000
Motor van (7,000 - 1,400)			5,600
Equipment (4,000 + 1,200 - 600)			4,600
			30,200
Current assets			
Stock		5,000	
Debtors (2,480 - 124)		2,356	
Prepayments – rates	425		
– insurance	75	500	
Cash – at bank		3,400	
– in hand		80	
		11,336	
less Current liabilities			
Creditors	700		
Accrued expenses – garage rent	125		
electricity	480		
loan interest	50	1,355	9,981
			40,181
Deduct loan from brother			1,000
			39,181

	£
Represented by	
Capital at 1 January 19-2	37,680
Add profit for year	6,121
	43,801
Deduct drawings	4,620
	39,181

Tutorial notes:

1. Interest on brother's loan must be provided for the six months to 31 December 19-2.

2. Interest on savings bonds is not business income. Reduce Harman's drawings by this amount.

3. Cash takings banked will be amount required to make the bank balance; be sure to credit the same figure in the cash account.

4. Drawings shown in cash receipts and payments account is the amount required to make the account balance.
5. Depreciation of equipment. This is the difference between the opening balance of equipment at the beginning of the year, plus the additions, less the valuation of the equipment at the end of the year. (Revaluation method: see 1.7).

4.5.2 EXERCISE (for practice in preparing final accounts from incomplete records)

J.T.Forster has a small building and decorating business but has not kept proper records.

The following information is available for Forster's business:

	1.1.-3	31.12 -3
	£	£
Premises	45,000	45,000
Motor lorry CWT100R	8,000	-
Motor lorry HHH999X	–	10,000
Plant and equipment	10,000	11,000
Stock of materials	2,600	3,500
Debtors	3,000	6,000
Creditors for supplies	2,700	4,250
Prepayments – rates	400	500
– advertising	120	340
Cash at bank	1,276	3,540
Cash in hand	300	450
Motor expenses owing	900	–
Electricity owing	200	280

Bank paying-in slip and cheque counterfoils showed that the following amounts had been paid into or paid out of the bank during the year.

		£
Receipts:	takings banked	36,764
	proceeds of sale of motor lorry CWT100R	5,000
	wife's premium bond prize money	2,500
Payments:	creditors for supplies	9,000
	purchase of motor lorry HHH999X	10,000
	purchase of plant and equipment	2,400
	rates	1,000
	advertising	700
	motor lorry running expenses	2,100
	electricity	800
	drawings	10,000
	wages	6,000

In addition, the following amounts were passed through the cash account:

	£
receipts from clients	40,764
purchase of materials	2,000
wages	1,800

Motor lorry CWT100R was sold on 30 June 19-3; motor lorry HHH999X was purchased on 1 July 19-3. Motor lorries are to be depreciated at 20%p.a.

REQUIRED

A profit and loss account for the year ended 31 December 19-3 and a balance sheet as at that date.

Tutorial note: A trading account is not appropriate in this case as J.T.Forster is not buying and selling any commodity, i.e. he is not a trader. Credit his revenue for the period to the profit and loss account and show the cost of materials either as a deduction from receipts for work done, or as a debit in the profit and loss account.

4.6 STOCK LOST IN FIRE OR BY THEFT

When goods have been lost in a fire or by theft, the value of such loss must be calculated for:

(a) the loss to be reflected in the trading account at the year- end as a reduction of the cost of sales,

(b) a claim for compensation to be prepared for insurance compensation

(c) tax purposes.

If detailed stock records have not been kept or not survived the incident, the value of stock lost must be calculated using the incomplete records technique of finding a missing closing stock figure in a trading account. Any difference between the quantity of stock so calculated and actual stock remaining after the incident is the value of stock lost.

4.6.1 EXAMPLE

Mr. Georgiou's warehouse was burgled on 10th April 19-4. The thieves stole most of the stock, but left goods worth £1,250. Mr. Georgiou has to submit an insurance claim and provides the following information:

Extracted from his balance sheet at 31st December 19-3:

	£
Stock	15,000
Debtors	20,000
Creditors	10,000

Cash book summary 1st January to 10 April 19-4:

	£
Receipts from debtors	88,000
Payments to creditors	60,000

Other information:

	£
Sales invoices outstanding at 10 April 19-4	12,000
Suppliers' invoices unpaid at 10 April 19-4	13,000

Mr. Georgiou sells his goods at a mark-up of 25%

REQUIRED

A calculation of the cost of the goods stolen.

Mr. Georgiou
Proforma trading account for the period 1 January - 10 April 19-4

		£	£
Sales (W1)			80,000
Cost of sales:	Stock at 1.1.19-4	15,000	
	Purchases (W2)	63,000	
		78,000	
	Stock at 4.4.19-4		
	(missing figure)	14,000	64,000
Gross profit (£80,000 × 20%)			16,000

Tutorial note: Since mark-up is 25%, Margin is 20%.

	£
Calculated stock at 10 April 19-4	14,000
Stock not stolen	1,250
Stock stolen (at cost)	12,750

Workings: 1. Sales:

	£
Receipts from debtors	88,000
less debtors at 1.1.-4	20,000
	68,000
add debtors at 10.4.-4	12,000
	80,000

2. Purchases

	£
Payments to creditors	60,000
less creditors at 1.1.-4	10,000
	50,000
add creditors at 10.4.-4	13,000
	63,000

4.6.2 EXERCISE (practice in calculation of cost of goods lost in fire)

On the night of 5 November 19-1, the warehouse of Conn, Flagge, Raye & Son was burned down and most of the stock destroyed. The stock salvaged was valued at cost in the sum of £6,000. The firm claimed for compensation from its insurance company.

REQUIRED

Using the following information, calculate the amount of the claim.

Balance sheet as at 30 June 19-1 (extracts):

	£
Stock	23,750
Debtors	16,000
Creditors	11,520

Further information for period 1.7.-1 to 5.11.-1:

	£
Receipts from debtors	61,000
Cash sales	17,220
Payments to creditors	59,630

At 5 November 19-1:	Debtors	18,780
	Creditors	14,210

The firm achieves a margin of 33⅓% on all sales.

4.7   KEY POINTS TO REMEMBER

1. When required to calculate profit or loss for a period, and insufficient information is available to prepare a trading and profit and loss account, use statements of affairs to calculate the increase or decrease in capital during the period after allowing for any new capital introduced and drawings during the period.

2. If sufficient information is available, prepare a trading and profit and loss account.

3. Mark-up and margin are useful for calculating sales or cost of sales when it is not possible to prepare a sales or purchases total account.

4. Follow the 7 steps in preparing a trading and profit and loss account from incomplete records; if the question also requires a balance sheet, this will be prepared as part of step 7.

5. Steps 1-6 will generally be workings in support of the answer. If a question requires the preparation of an opening statement of affairs and/or a receipts and payments account, steps 1/2 will become part of the answer.

6. If steps 1-6 appear to be a formidable amount of work to do before you actually begin to write your answer, remember that examination regulations require all workings to be shown anyway.

7. Do not waste time on making your workings as neat as your answer to the question provided they are legible and clearly headed. 'T' accounts may be ruled free-hand, or not ruled at all provided the two sides are made distinct and all amounts shown in them are briefly described.

   An examiner is not bound to accept figures without descriptions as these may be meaningless.

8. One approach to step 7 is to prepare drafts of the trading and profit and loss account and balance sheet at an early stage so that figures may be inserted as they are calculated. In this way, you will start to accumulate marks at an early stage. Leave room to insert additional items which you may have overlooked.

9. Alternatively, step 7 may be left until all workings have been completed. Trading and profit and loss accounts and balance sheets can be fair-copied quite quickly, especially if you have had plenty of practice before the examination.

COMMON ERRORS

- no adjustments to cash receipts and payments for opening and closing debtors and creditors when calculating sales and purchases.
- failure to give effect to all the instructions in the question for the preparation of a profit and loss account and balance sheet.
- no statement of affairs prepared as at beginning of period. It is unwise to insert a balancing figure in the balance sheet for the opening capital; even if it happens to be the correct figure, the method of arriving at it may not be acceptable to the examiner.

4.8 EXAMINATION QUESTIONS

QUESTION 1 (Oxford June 1987)

Tim Jones runs his own business but has no idea of the way to keep his accounts; although he has been trading for twelve months he is not sure how much profit his business has made. He assumes that, since he put £200 into a bank account on 1 May 19-6 and at 30 April 19-7 he has twice as much in his account, he must have made a profit of £200 for the year.

You have a long talk with him during which you jot down a few figures. The following are your notes from which to work out what you estimate his profit for the year to be.

'Started with tools he already had valued at £2,500, working in his own bungalow and taking up half of it for his business. Market value of similar bungalow has risen during year from £32,000 to £38,000. Now uses the whole bungalow for his business and has bought a small house for himself which cost £40,000. Had to use bungalow as mortgage for this. He had some materials in stock when he started which he valued at £1,450.

Today stock is valued at £2,800, he is owed £450 by his customers and he owes £210 to a supplier. During year he borrowed £2,000 from a friend, who charges no interest and has paid £500 back to him. Has steadily built up his collection of tools and he guesses they are now worth at least £3,200. He has a small work bench he built himself during the year at a cost of £150. Had to have structural repair work done on the bungalow which cost £12,000, none of which has been paid.

Tim doesn't have much spare time but he has taken £100 from the business bank account towards a weekend break that he took in January, when business was slack.

You are required to show your calculations of Tim's profit for the year, giving any explanations that you think necessary to justify your use of any of the figures, remembering that Tim has no accounting knowledge.

(18 marks)

QUESTION 2 (Cambridge November 1988)

Ingar Hanson commenced trading on 1 August 19-8 with a balance at bank of £100,000 as his only asset; there were no liabilities at that date. At the end of his first three months' trading, Ingar Hanson reviewed his progress.

The following information has been extracted from the accounting records:

19-8	Sales		Credit sales
	Cash	Credit	returns
	£	£	£
August	24,000	98,000	3,070
September	37,000	150,072	7,900
October	34,896	168,000	5,398

19-8	Cash received for cash and credit sales	Discounts allowed on credit sales
	£	£
August	32,000	600
September	117,000	1,100
October	183,200	980

19-8	Debtors overdue at month end	Credit balances on customers' accounts at month end.
	£	£
August	–	190
September	11,300	320
October	3,190	570

The following additional information is given:

(a) A gross profit of 40% is obtained on the cost of all sales.

(b) A stock turnover rate of 10 has been achieved using the average of opening and closing stocks.

(c) Overhead expenses have amounted to £36,000 per month.

(d) It has been decided to create a provision for doubtful debts at 31 October 19-8 of 10% of overdue debtors and 2% of other debtors at that date.

REQUIRED

(a) The sales ledger control account for the three months ended 31 October 19-8 *(13 marks)*

(b) The trading and profit and loss account for the three months ended 31 October 19-8 of Ingar Hanson in as much detail as possible. *(12 marks)*

QUESTION 3 (Cambridge June 1989)

Harold Minter, a general dealer, has traded for several years but has never kept a full set of accounting records. However, the recent expansion of the business has put some strain on cash resources and Harold Minter is now obliged to prepare some 'accounts' in readiness for a forthcoming meeting with his bank manager.

The following information has now been produced by Harold Minter:

(a) Assets and liabilities at 28 February 19-9:

	£
Fixtures and fittings at cost 1 March 19-6	8,000
Motor van at cost 1 March 19-8	10,000
Stock	7,100
Trade debtors	6,300
Balance at bank	1,100
Trade creditors	8,200

(b) Depreciation is to be provided at the following rates per annum on a straight line basis:

Fixtures and fittings	12½%
Motor van	20%

(c) Bank receipts and payments during the three months ended 31 May 19-9 were as follows:

	March	April	May
	£	£	£
Receipts			
Sales - cash	4,000	5,000	3,000
credit	5,100	9,000	14,000
Loan from father,T.Minter (interest at 6% p.a.)	10,000	–	
	19,100	14,000	17,000
Payments			
Fixtures and fittings purchased	–	5,760	–
Purchases	7,800	17,000	9,000
Wages	2,100	2,340	2,300
Drawings	1,200	1,500	1,600
Overhead expenses	2,900	2,600	2,300
Rent of business premises year ending 28 February 19-0	15,000		
	29,000	29,200	15,200

Note: Assume all transactions take place on the last day of the month stated.

(d) Sales during the three months ended 31 May 19-9 amounted to £52,500 and purchases to £32,300. A gross profit of 30% is achieved on all sales.

(e) In view of current market conditions, it is prudent to create a provision for doubtful debts at 31 May 19-9 of 5% of debtors at that date.

REQUIRED

(a) A trading and profit and loss account for the three months ended 31 May 19-9 and a balance sheet as at that date. *(18 marks)*

(b) Identify from the 'final accounts' prepared three areas of concern and give reasons for your selection. *(7 marks)*

(Total 25 marks)

QUESTION 4 (London January 1987)

Dorothy has been trading as the 'Smash Hit' music shop for several years but has never kept full accounting records. A summary of the business bank account for the year ended 31 October 19-6 is given below.

	£		£
Opening balance	700	Paid to suppliers	23,600
Cash banked (see note 1)	42,900	Rent and rates	1,500
Closing balance	1,400	Light and heat	2,200
		Advertising	950
		Wages of assistants	5,530
		Drawings	10,300
		Sundry expenses	920
	45,000		45,000

Details of assets and liabilities (other than the bank balance) at the start and end of financial year are as follows:

	1 November 19-5	31 October 19-6
	£	£
Debtors	218	(see note 2)
Creditors	3,750	4,950
Advertising prepaid	–	600
Advertising accrued	250	–
Stocks at cost	6,120	(see note 3)
Shop fixtures	10,620	(see note 4)

Notes:

1. All takings were banked, with the exception of £830 which had been used to purchase new furniture for Dorothy's house.

2. Closing debtors were equivalent to one week's sales. A quarter of this total is considered 'doubtful' and should be provided for. Assume that the shop was open for fifty weeks in the year.

3. Closing stock valued at selling price was £10,395. Average mark-up on cost price was 75%.

4. Shop fixtures are to be depreciated by the 'straight line' method over a five-year period. By 31 October 19-6, the fixtures had been owned for exactly two years.

Prepare appropriate financial statements for Dorothy's business for the year ended 31 October 19-6.

(25 marks)

QUESTION 5 (AEB June 1988)

Jim Hastings commenced in business on 1 May 19-7 trading as 'Orbit Records', a retail outlet dealing in records, cassettes and hi-fi accessories. When he commenced business he brought in £6,500 cash, which was banked immediately. He also brought in his car at the start of the business which was valued at £4,100. On 1 August 19-7, the business borrowed £5,300 from a finance institution at an interest rate of 16% per annum. This loan was lodged in the business bank account 1 August 19-7 and is not repayable until 19-5. Jim maintains the minimum of accounting records, but does keep details of all cash and bank transactions. Summary details of cash and bank transactions for the year ended 30 April 19-8 are listed below.

Transaction	Cash	Bank
	£	£
Lease payments for premises		4,800
Wages to staff	3,200	7,050
Redecoration of premises		1,235
General operating expenses	320	1,375
Purchases of goods for resale		105,950
Lighting and heating	95	965
Fixtures and fittings		4,895
Interest payments on loan		424
Accountancy fees		355
Car expenses	155	1,050

Additional information.

(1) The lease agreement, which was entered into at the start of the business, detailed the cost as £960 per quarter payable in advance.

(2) Asset and liability balances at 30 April 19-8:

	£
Cash	125
Cash at bank	8,150
Car	3,150
Fixtures and fittings	4,200
Stocks	14,500
Creditors for purchases	10,950

(There have been no sales of fixed assets during the year to 30 April 19-8)

(3) All sales were made on a cash basis and after meeting cash payments the net amount was banked daily.

(4) Jim Hastings took £100 per week from the cash till for personal purposes and withdrew goods for personal use during the year valued at £335 in cost terms.

(5) Included within general operating expenses was the payment of a personal life assurance premium which amounted to £215.

(6) It has been estimated that one-fifth of the costs relating to the car are for private purposes.

REQUIRED

(a) Prepare a cash account and a bank account for the year to 30 April 19-8.   *(6 marks)*

(b) Prepare a trading and profit and loss account for the year ended 30 April 19-8 and a balance sheet as at that date.   *(16 marks)*

(Total 22 marks)

Tutorial note: You should preferably prepare your answer to Part (a) in the form of a two-column cash book.

5 ACCOUNTS OF NON-PROFIT MAKING ORGANISATIONS

> You should be able to prepare:-
> - Receipts and Payments accounts
> - Income and Expenditure Accounts
> - Trading accounts
> - Balance sheets
>   (for clubs, societies etc.)

Most clubs, societies etc. do not employ trained bookkeepers as their Honorary Treasurers, their accounting records are invariably incomplete and the techniques already learned in Chapter 4 are required for the preparation of their annual accounts.

5.1 MAIN FEATURES OF NON-PROFIT MAKING ORGANISATIONS

(a) An Income and Expenditure account replaces the Profit and Loss account.

(b) A trading account is only prepared for a subsidiary activity which is in the nature of trading and carried on to supplement the income of the club or to provide a service to members, e.g. bar sales.

(c) In the Income and Expenditure account, 'Surplus of income over expenditure' replaces the 'net profit' of a profit and loss account, and 'Excess of expenditure over income' replaces 'net loss'.

(d) In the balance sheet, 'Accumulated fund' replaces the 'capital' account found in the accounts of a sole trader.

Members' subscriptions

The total of subscriptions credited to the Income and expenditure account should equal the annual subscription per member multiplied by the number of members. If this information is not given, prepare a total subscriptions account.

Subscriptions in arrears.

Clubs can hardly take legal action against members to recover subscriptions in arrears. The policy of the club committee will determine how arrears of subscriptions will be dealt with in the accounts. Unfortunately, examiners do not always disclose the policy of the committee, which may be one of the following:

(i) To omit unpaid subscriptions from the Income and Expenditure account and the balance sheet. If the subscriptions are paid at a later date, they will be credited to the Income and Expenditure account in the year in which received.

(ii) To credit all subscriptions due for the year to the Income and Expenditure account whether received or not, and to show subscriptions in arrears in the balance sheet as current assets. Insofar as the arrears are not received in the following year, to write them off in that following year.

Course (i) above is the more prudent of the two as it tends to understate income and assets rather than overstate them. On the other hand, the second course has the merits of matching income to the period concerned and of highlighting the amounts of subscriptions in arrears and those that are subsequently written off. The normal method is to treat subscriptions as in (ii) above unless the question indicates that it is the club's policy to adopt a different treatment.

Life subscriptions and entry fees.

These are lump sums paid by members and should be dealt with in accordance with the matching concept; they should be credited when received to suspense accounts and credited to Income and expenditure account in equal annual instalments over such period as determined by the committee.

Gifts, legacies etc. made to the club.

These should not be credited to the Income and Expenditure account as if they were normal regular income of the club. They should be credited directly either to a special fund or to the general fund of the club.

5.2 ANCILLARY ACTIVITIES

Clubs often engage in activities which are ancillary to their main object in order to supplement their subscription income; these may include sales to members of equipment, publications, or bar facilities, which are in the form of trading. Other non-trading activities include the provision of refreshments and raffles. For any activity which constitutes trading, a separate trading account should be prepared and the balance on that account transferred to the Income and expenditure account. For non-trading activities, the income and expenditure should be 'netted' in that account; e.g.

	£	£
Sale of raffle tickets	90	
less cost of prizes and tickets	55	35

5.2.1 EXAMPLE

The Penny Black Philatelic Society offers its members the opportunity to attend weekly meetings, to hear talks on postage stamps, attend exhibitions and auctions of stamps and to buy and sell stamps and equipment through the society. Its financial year ends on 30 April.

The secretary of the society has supplied the following information:

	Balances at	
	1 May 19-1	30 April 19-2
	£	£
Fixed assets: Display cases	1,000	1,000
Equipment	1,600	1,840
Stock of stamps at cost	2,200	3,120
Debtors for stamp sales	200	110
Subscriptions in arrears	100	80
Subscriptions in advance	40	55
Cash at bank	416	to be found
Rent of hall in advance	100	70
Electricity owing	60	80
Printing expenses outstanding	15	40

Receipts in the year to 30 April 19-2: Subscriptions £1,100; sales of stamps £5,140; sales of raffle tickets £300; refreshments £440.

Payments in the year to 30 April 19-2: Purchase of stamps £3,000; purchase of equipment for use by the society £400; rent £900; electricity £230; printing £60; raffle prizes £100; secretary's expenses £35; refreshments £240.

Display cases are to be depreciated by 10% on book value.

REQUIRED:

The Income and expenditure account of the Penny Black Philatelic Society for the year to 30 April 19-2, and a balance sheet as at that date.

(The profit or loss on sale of stamps should be calculated separately, and the net income from other activities should be shown in the Income and expenditure account.)

Workings:

1. Accumulated fund at 1 May 19-1	£	£
Fixed assets: display cases		1,000
equipment		1,600
Stock of stamps		2,200
Debtors for stamps		200
Subscriptions in arrears		100
Cash at bank		416
Rent in advance		100
Carried forward		5,616

		£	£
Brought forward			5,616
less Subscriptions in advance		40	
Electricity		60	
Printing		15	115
Accumulated fund at 1.5.19-1			5,501

2. Receipts and payments account for year to 30 April 19-2:

	£		£
Balance at 1.1.19-1	416	Purchase of stamps	3,000
Subscriptions	1,100	Equipment	400
Sales of stamps	5,140	Rent	900
Sale of raffle tickets	300	Electricity	230
Refreshments	440	Printing	60
		Raffle prizes	100
		Secretary's expenses	35
		Refreshments	240
		Balance c/d	2,431
	7,396		7,396

3.

Sale of stamps

	£		£
Debtors at 1.1.19-1	200	Cash received	5,140
Stamp trading account	5,050	Debtors at 30.4.19-2	110
	5,250		5,250

Subscriptions

	£		£
Arrears b/f	100	In advance b/f	40
In advance c/f	55	Bank	1,100
I & E a/c	1,065	Arrears c/f	80
	1,220		1,220

Rent of hall

	£		£
Prepayment b/f	100	I & E a/c	930
Bank	900	Prepayment c/f	70
	1,000		1,000

Electricity

	£		£
Bank	230	Accrual b/f	60
Accrual c/f	80	I & E a/c	250
	310		310

Printing

	£		£
Bank	60	Accrual b/f	15
Accrual c/f	40	I & E a/c	85
	100		100

Equipment

	£		£
Bal b/f	1,600	I & E a/c	160
Additions	400	Balance c/f	1,840
	2,000		2,000

ANSWER

The Penny Black Philatelic Society
Stamp trading account for the year to 30 April 19-2

	£	£
Sales of stamps		5,050
less cost of stamps sold: Stock at 1.5.-1	2,200	
Purchases	3,000	
	5,200	
Stock at 30.4.-2	3,120	2,080
Profit on sale of stamps		2,970

Income and expenditure account for the year to 30 April 19-2

	£	£
Income: Subscriptions		1,065
Profit on sale of stamps		2,970
Raffles – sale of tickets	300	
less cost of prizes	100	200
Refreshments	440	
less cost of food	240	200
		4,435
Expenditure: Rent	930	
Electricity	250	
Printing	85	
Secretary's expenses	35	
Depreciation - display cases	100	
equipment	160	1,560
Surplus of income over expenditure		2,875

Balance sheet as at 30 April 19-2

	£	£	£
Fixed assets: Display cases (1,000 - 100)			900
Equipment (1,600 + 400 - 160)			1,840
			2,740
Current assets: Stock of stamps		3,120	
Debtors for stamps		110	
Subscriptions in arrears		80	
Rent in advance		70	
Balance at bank		2,431	
		5,811	
less Current liabilities:			
Subscriptions in advance	55		
Electricity	80		
Carried forward	135	5,811	2,740

	£	£	£
Brought forward	135	5,811	2,740
Printing	40	175	5,636
			8,376
Represented by: Accumulated fund at 1 May 19-1			5,501
Surplus of income over expenditure			2,875
			8,376

5.2.2 EXERCISE (practice in preparing club accounts)

The Diplock, Pibworth and Parkland Sports and Social Club's financial year ends on 31 December. The assets and liabilities of the club at the dates stated were as follows:

	At 31 Dec 19-0	At 31 Dec 19-1
	£	£
Equipment	2,500	2,800
Subscriptions in arrears	200	180
Subscriptions in advance	130	110
Creditors for bar stocks	350	430
Bar stocks	800	600
Rent owing	150	100
Electricity owing	105	140
Bank balance (favourable)	723	1,300

In the year to 31 December 19-1, the cash receipts were:

	£
Subscriptions (including £60 of arrears from previous year)	2,100
Bar takings	4,100
Annual dinner/dance, sale of tickets	2,400
Sale of raffle tickets	180

In the same period the following payments have been made:

	£
Affiliation fees	100
Purchase of equipment	800
Bar stocks	2,050
Barman's wages	750
Catering (dinner/dance)	1,440
Hire of band (dinner/dance)	300
Raffle prizes	60
Rent of hall	1,500
Printing and postage	200
Electricity	581
Hon. secretary's expenses	122
Repairs to equipment	300

REQUIRED

Diplock, Pibworth and Parkland Sports and Social Club's Income and expenditure account for the year to 31 December 19-1 and the balance sheet as at that date.

5.3 KEY POINTS TO REMEMBER

1. Follow the seven steps demonstrated in Chapter 4 (incomplete records) to prepare accounts of non-profit making organisations.

2. Non-profit making organisations have: Income and expenditure accounts (instead of profit and loss accounts); Surplus of income over expenditure (instead of profits); Excess of expenditure over income (instead of losses); Accumulated funds (instead of capital accounts).

3. Prepare a trading account for any trading activity used to raise funds, e.g. a bar, and carry the profit or loss only to the Income and expenditure account.

4. 'Net' expenditure against income in the Income and expenditure account for fund raising activities which do not constitute trading e.g. dinner/dances, raffles.

COMMON ERRORS

- Failure to prepare trading accounts, or to show 'net' results in the Income and Expenditure account for activities for which trading accounts are not appropriate.
- Preparation of Profit and loss account instead of an Income and expenditure account and the use of incorrect terminology (see 5.1 above).
- Entrance fees, life membership subscriptions, gifts and legacies credited to Income and expenditure account when received.
- Subscriptions in arrears treated incorrectly.
- Accruals and prepayments of expenses, depreciation, ignored or treated incorrectly.

5.4 EXAMINATION QUESTIONS

QUESTION 1 (Cambridge November 1989)

The following information was available from the books of The Triangle Flower Club as at 1 July 19-8.

	£
Balance at Bank	12,200
Club Premises	120,000
Members' Subscriptions due	1,250
Creditors – bar supplies	1,100
– flower and bulb supplies	3,700
Stock of flowers and bulbs	10,100
Greenhouses	27,000
Vehicles	21,500
Stock - bar	5,400

Receipts and Payments for the year ended 30 June 19-9

Members' Subscriptions	12,900	Staff Wages – General		21,300
Event receipts	21,600	– Bar		9,100
Bar Sales	55,450	Heating Costs		15,200
Sale of old greenhouse	1,000	Purchase of new greenhouse		17,500
Sales of flowers and bulbs	17,100	Vehicle repairs and maintenance		2,200
		Rates		2,100
		Sundry Expenses		750
		Flowers and Bulbs		14,200
		Bar Supplies		32,300

Additional information

1. Stocks at 30 June 19-9 were:

	Bar	£2,900
	Flowers and bulbs	£9,200

2. Members' subscriptions received during the year ended 30 June 19-9 included £1,000 in respect of 19-7 to 19-8 and £1,100 in respect of 19-9 to 19-0.

3. Creditors at 30 June 19-9 were: Bar supplies   £1,700

                                     Flowers and Bulbs   £2,050

4. The greenhouse sold during the year had been written down to £1,500 prior to sale. Depreciation on the remaining greenhouses plus any addition should be written down by 20% of the net book value.

   Motor Vehicles should be written down by 25% of the present net book value.

5. Sundry expenses include an insurance account which was prepaid by £50 as at 30 June 19-9.

REQUIRED

(a) A bar account for the year ended 30 June 19-9.   *(5 marks)*

(b) An Income and Expenditure account for the year ended 30 June 19-9 (clearly showing profit on sale of flowers and bulbs.)   *(12 marks)*

(c) A Balance Sheet as at 30 June 19-9.   *(8 marks)*

                                                             (Total 25 marks)

QUESTION 2 (AEB June 1987)

Although the Golden Valley Sports and Social Club has enjoyed a thriving existence over several years a record of financial transactions has never been properly maintained. The treasurer of the club is able to provide only the following information for the financial year ended 31 May 19-7.

	31 May 19-6	31 May 19-7
	£	£
Bar stocks at cost	1,800	3,600
Bar suppliers	3,400	4,800
Subscriptions received in advance	400	500
Equipment at cost less depreciation	5,000	7,200
Stationery stock at cost	300	150
Balance at bank	2,400	700
10% Loan to Club		3,000

The following information is also available.

(1) Included in the closing bar stock figure were some items which cost £350 but which in fact were unsaleable and have a scrap value of £60.

(2) An exceptional item, a gift of £1,500, was received during the year from a former member of the club.

(3) Equipment was purchased on 1 June 19-6 at a cost of £3,000 and was financed by a loan for that amount raised on that date. Interest at the rate of 10% per annum is payable on the loan although no payment has yet been made.

REQUIRED

(a) A statement of affairs of the Golden Valley Sports and Social Club as at 31 May 19-7 showing clearly, as part of the accumulated fund, the surplus or deficit for the year ended 31 May 19-7.

                                                             (13 marks)

(b) Draft a memorandum to the committee of the club stating why it is necessary to introduce a method of financial record keeping and suggest a suitable approach to adopt.   *(12 marks)*

                                                             (Total 25 marks)

QUESTION 3 (AEB November 1987)

The Micro Friendly Club is an association which provides members with the following facilities:

(i)   periodic social functions.

(ii)   a selling service for members' old micro terminals. The club charges 10% of the gross proceeds as a commission.

(iii) arranging the interfacing of members' home computers with the club Primate Mini-computer.

In addition the club organises 'Micro Learn' computer courses for non-members.

(1) The following financial information was available as at 1 June 19-6:

Freehold premises at book value £50,000, Primate Mini-computer at book value £25,000, various terminals and printers £25,000, computer software £15,000, members' subscriptions due £400, social functions expenses owing £150, balance at bank £8,700.

Two of the terminals included above at cost of £900 belong to a member, and are held by the Club pending being sold.

(2) Receipts and Payments during the year ended 31 May,19-7.

	£		£	£
Members' subscriptions	3,500	Purchases of stocks for		
Receipts from micro		social functions		9,000
learn courses	2,750	Maintenance charges		
Sales of members'		- computers		1,150
terminals	4,000	Payments for micro-		
Social functions		learn courses		
takings	16,900	Visiting staff	1,500	
Interface connection		Expenses	360	1,860
charges received from		Social functions		
members	2,400	expenses		3,500
		Establishment expenses		7,800
		Purchase of micro		
		terminal 31 May 19-7		3,000
		Payments to members for		
		sales of terminals		2,800

Additional information.

(3) At 31 May 19-7 members' subscriptions in arrears were £900.

(4) All the terminals sold belonged to members. The Club accepted no responsibility for loss or damage to the terminals whilst on club premises.

(5) Social functions stocks as at 31 May 19-7 were £2,000.

(6) A visiting lecturer was owed £300 for his tuition services on a course given in April 19-7

(7) Ten members had interface connections to the mini-computer installed during the year. The installation charge was £480 per member, of which the club agreed to pay half.

The club had not yet paid the interface contractor for the work done.

(8) The club's telephone bill was outstanding £750, covering the period 1 March 19-7 to 31 May 19-7

(9) It was club policy to depreciate its computer equipment as follows:

Mini-computer, terminals and printers	20% on the balances as at 1 June 19-6
Software	25% on the balances as at 1 June 19-6

REQUIRED

(a) An income and expenditure account for the year ended 31 May 19-7. *(10 marks)*

(b) A balance sheet as at 31 May 19-7. *(7 marks)*

(c) As club treasurer you are required to prepare a report on the club's financial position for the Annual General Meeting. Your report should include any appropriate recommendations you think necessary. *(8 marks)*

(Total 25 marks)

QUESTION 4 (Oxford June 1987)

The Baldac Engineering Co has a social club which provides social and leisure activities for all employees. The club is assisted by the company, but is run as a separate entity with its own officers and committee. Any employee and his immediate family may join by paying an annual fee of

(i) £5 for the employee

(ii) £8 for the employee's husband/wife

(iii) £3 for each child up to the age of 18 years.

Members joining after 31 December in any year are charged half a year's subscription.

Every year the company donates to the club a sum equal to 50% of the total membership fees due from employees, this sum to be calculated on the membership at 31 May each year, and paid in the following July.

The club is able to purchase certain goods through the company's Central Purchasing department at a discount. Some of these are sold to members at cost to the club plus 25%.

The company's monthly magazine 'Baldac Review' is distributed to employees through the social club; the company makes a contribution of two pence for each magazine distributed and the club pays members five pence for every magazine that they are able to distribute to employees who are not members of the social club.

The club's accounting year ends on 31 May each year, and for the year ended 31 May 19-7 the following information concerning the club activities is available.

RECEIPTS		£
Subscriptions received from members:	Employees	3,180
	Husband/wife	2,800
	Under 18	1,800
Receipts from social functions:	Horticultural Show	8,750
	Christmas Dinner and Dance	13,450
	Old time Music Halls	4,700
	Prize draws held at social functions	5,420
	Gala and Sports Day	4,750
	Other social functions	5,350
Receipts from refreshments at social functions		1,400
Receipts from the Company:	Distribution costs 'Baldac Review'	480
	Donations based on membership	1,500
Receipts from sales of goods to members (note 6)		45,375
Receipts from sales in the bar		84,100

PAYMENTS		
Lighting and Heating of Club premises		8,830
Telephone and postage		1,625
Insurance		1,415
Repairs and Maintenance of premises and equipment		3,630
Costs of functions held:	Horticultural Show	450
	Dinner/Dance	7,640
	Old Time Music Halls	1,140
	Gala and Sports Day	1,285
	Other Functions	2,100
Prizes: Horticultural Show		2,480
Gala and Sports Day		1,760
Prize Draws		820
Purchases through the company's Central Purchasing		42,800
Purchases of Bar stocks		71,750
Purchase of Refreshments		14,800
Payments for distributing 'Baldac Review'		216
Purchase of equipment for club house		12,000
Club Stewards' wages		12,460

Notes

1. The club owns its own premises which at 1 June 19-6 were valued at £242,000.

2. Equipment owned by the club at 1 June 19-6 had a book value of £41,000 (cost £74,000). It is club policy to depreciate equipment at 15% per annum on cost on 31 May. The club also has trophies valued at £54,000 at 1 June 19-6.

3. At 1 June 19-6 £60 was owing by members for subscriptions for the year to 31 May 19-6.

4. The club has the following membership:

	31 December 19-6	31 May 19-7
Employees	500	800
Husbands/wives	300	400
Under 18	400	800

No members had left during the year, and at 31 December 19-6 all membership fees had been paid.

5. Cost of refreshments is to be apportioned between the Horticultural show, Christmas Dinner/Dance, Old Time Music Hall, Gala and Sports Day and other social functions in proportion to receipts from these functions, (excluding receipts from refreshments at social functions).

6. Of the goods purchased through the company's Central Purchasing department

    £6,450 were used in the bar

    £1,400 were used in the prize draw

    £450 were used at other social functions. The remainder apart from the closing stock, was sold to members on a strictly cash basis. The stock of goods unsold at cost at 31 May 19-6 was £3,800.

At 31 May 19-6 the club had £4,750 in the bank, and at 31 May 19-7 bar stocks had increased by £100 to £4,750. One quarter of the stewards' wages is paid to the barman.

You are required to prepare:

(a) A Revenue account (Income and Expenditure) for the year ended 31 May 19-7, showing the profits made by the various club activities as far as can be ascertained.   *(21 marks)*

(b) A Balance Sheet at 31 May 19-7.   *(19 marks)*

(Total 40 marks)

QUESTION 5 (Northern Ireland 1986)

The Glenbeg Adventure Club was formed in January 19-5 as an association of individuals who had participated in outdoor activity courses at the Glenbeg Outdoor Pursuits Centre which is administered by the Mid-Ulster Education and Library Board. The Club levied an annual subscription of £3 and organised monthly meetings to which guest speakers were invited.

In order to give the new club fresh impetus it organised an overland expedition from Fair Head, the northern extremity of County Antrim, to Mizzen Head, the south-western extremity of County Cork. The expedition took place during the 19-5 Summer holidays and was successfully completed by a combination of three self propelled means of transport: canoe, cycle and foot. The expedition was accompanied by a minibus which carried equipment and personal belongings between overnight stops. Eight participants each paid £100 and an additional four unemployed participants each paid £25.

The following is a summary of the bank statements of the Club for the year ended 31 December 19-5.

RECEIPTS	£
Subscriptions from 45 members and contributions from 12 expedition participants	1,035
Expedition fund raising and sponsorship	1,250
Mountaineering and Canoeing federations -	
priming grant for new clubs	50
expedition grant	300
Grant from Mid-Ulster Education and Library Board	2,500
Receipts from monthly club meetings	15
Revenue from advertisements in Expedition report	125
Sales of Expedition report (50@£1)	50
Royalties, takings etc from showings of Expedition film	200
	5,525

PAYMENTS	£
Secretarial expenses including telephone	28
Rent of room for Club meetings	8
Expedition food	214
CIE for travel home from Cork for expedition participants	125
New Canoes and camping equipment	3,200
Rent of minibus	176
Carried forward	3,751

	£
Brought forward	3,751
Levies to Mountaineering and Canoeing federations	23
Contributions to cost of training courses for unemployed members	60
Liability insurance for the year ended 31 October 19-6	36
Cost of producing expedition film	480
Cost of producing expedition report (500 copies @ 65p)	325
Petty cash imprest to expedition leader	340
	5,015
BANK BALANCE ON 31 December 19-5	510

You are furnished with the following additional information.

(i) A receipt for £25 for advertising in the expedition report was credited in the bank statement in February 19-6; other advertisers had been invoiced for a total of £40 but no amounts had so far been received.

(ii) Creditors of £45 for expedition food and of £80 for film developing have not yet been paid.

(iii) The expedition leader accounted for his petty cash imprest as follows:-

	£
Petrol for minibus	65
Food	91
Pocket money advanced to participants	150
Unaccounted for	34
	340

(iv) The grant received from the Mid-Ulster Education and Library Board was advanced towards the cost of expedition equipment on the condition that all equipment purchased with its assistance was placed at the disposal of the Glenbeg Outdoor Pursuits Centre on the completion of the expedition.

(v) The Club committee have expressed a wish·for separate expedition funding and it is their intention to open a second bank account for the funding of future expeditions.

REQUIRED

(a) You are required to prepare statement(s) of account of the Glenbeg Adventure Club for the year ended 31 December 19-5 in a format suitable for presentation to the members of the Club and to grant awarding authorities. Such statements should allocate receipts, payments and net assets between two capital funds of the Club: a general fund and an expedition fund.   *(17 marks)*

(b) You are required to explain the advantages and disadvantages to the treasurer of a club of segregating receipts and payments made by or on behalf of different purposes or functions of the club into separate bank accounts.   *(3 marks)*

(c) A Club may present an income and expenditure account and balance sheet to its members, or alternatively a statement based on cash flow principles. What are the advantages of this latter type of statement over the traditional type of accounting statements from the point of view of a club?   *(5 marks)*

(Total 25 marks)

6 PARTNERSHIP ACCOUNTING

Questions on this topic test a wide range of knowledge and abilities:-
- appreciation of the differences between sole traders and partnerships
- knowledge of partnership law and accounting
- application of accounting concepts
- preparation of trading and profit and loss accounts and balance sheets, including the ability to prepare these as forecast statements
- correction of errors
- preparation of partnership accounts from incomplete records

6.1   PARTNERSHIP

The relationship which subsists between persons carrying on business in common with a view of profit (Partnership Act 1890)

Advantages of partnerships:

(a)   May enable more capital to be raised for firm than would otherwise be possible for a sole trader.

(b)   May result in more diversity of knowledge, experience and expertise in the management of the business.

(c)   Partners can 'cover' for each other during holidays and sickness.

Disadvantages:

(a)   Partners not able to act as independently as sole traders.

(b)   A partner's plans for the direction and development of the firm may be frustrated by the other partners.

(c)   Number of partners is limited to 20 except for certain professional partnerships such as firms of accountants or solicitors.

A partnership agreement should include reference to the following:

(1)   Amount of capital to be subscribed by each partner.

(2)   Rate of interest, if any, on partners' loans to firm.

(3)   Rate of interest, if any, to be allowed on partners' capitals.

(4)   Rate of interest, if any, to be charged on partners' drawings.

(5)   Amounts of partners' salaries, if any.

(6)   Ratio in which profits and losses are to be shared between the partners.

Partnership Act 1890. The following provisions apply only insofar as they are not covered in the partnership agreement:

(1)   All partners may contribute equally to the capital of the partnership.

(2)   Partners not entitled to:

> (a) interest on capital:

> (b) salaries.

(3)   Partners not to be charged interest on drawings.

(4)   Partners to share balance of profits and losses equally.

(5)   Partners entitled to interest at 5% p.a. on loans made to firm in excess of their agreed capitals.

Tutorial notes:

1.   Questions include, as part of the data, such of the above items as are contained in the partnership agreement. If the question is silent on any point, it implies that the point is not covered in the agreement and that the Partnership Act 1890 applies.

2.   You are expected to know the provisions of the Act and to apply them when appropriate.

3.   Read every partnership question carefully and avoid making invalid assumptions about partners' rights.

Partners' salaries and interest on capitals are methods of regulating the division of profits amongst partners to reward them for extra responsibilities or their relative contributions of capital to the firm.

6.2   SPECIAL FEATURES OF PARTNERSHIP ACCOUNTS

The following are required:

For each partner: Capital account

Drawings account

Current account

A Profit and Loss Appropriation account.

Treat the balances on partners' capital accounts as fixed. Unless a question specifically requires it, do not post interest, salaries or profit shares to the capital accounts.

Debit interest on partners' loans to Profit and loss account; it is not an appropriation of profit and should not be debited in the Appropriation account. When a question gives the net profit before charging such interest, the interest must be deducted to arrive at the profit brought down to the Appropriation account.

Accounting Entries:	Debit	Credit
Interest on partners' loans to firm	Profit & Loss a/c	Partners' Current a/cs
Interest on drawings	Partners' Current a/cs	Appropriation a/c
Interest on capitals } Partners' salaries } Shares of profit }	Appropriation a/c	Partners' Current a/cs
Shares of loss	Partners' Current a/cs	Appropriation a/c
Partners' drawings	Partners' Current a/cs	Partners' Drawings a/cs

6.2.1 Example 1 (Partnership agreement provides for sharing of profits and losses.)

Abel and Baker make up their accounts annually to 31 December and have been in partnership for some years. Interest is charged on drawings at the rate of 10% p.a. and is allowed on capitals also at 10% p.a. Baker receives a salary of £4,000 p.a. The balance of profits or losses is to be shared: Abel $^2/_3$ Baker $^1/_3$.

At 1 January 19-1, the following balances appeared in the firm's books:

		£	
Capital accounts:	Abel	10,000	
	Baker	6,000	
Current accounts:	Abel	5,000	(Cr)
	Baker	3,000	(Cr)

The net profit for the year to 31 December 19-1 amounted to £15,000 and at that date the balances on the partners' Drawings accounts were: Abel £6,000; Baker £5,000.

REQUIRED

(a)   The profit and loss appropriation account of the partnership for the year to 31 December 19-1

(b)   The partners' current accounts as at 31 December 19-1

(c)   A balance sheet extract as at 31 December 19-1 showing the partners capital and current account balances.

ANSWER

Abel and Baker

(a)   Profit and loss appropriation account for the year ended 31 December 19-1

	£	£		£
Current accounts:			Net profit b/d	15,000
Interest on			Current accounts:	
capitals - Abel	1,000		Interest on drawings – Abel	600
Carried forward	1,000			15,600

	£	£			£
Brought forward	1,000				15,600
Baker	600	1,600		Baker	500
Salary – Baker		4,000			
		5,600			
Share of profit					
Abel (2/3)	7,000				
Baker (1/3)	3,500	10,500			
		16,100			16,100

(b)

Partners' Current accounts as at 31 December 19-1

		Abel	Baker			Abel	Baker
19-1		£	£	19-1		£	£
Dec 31	Interest on			Jan 1	Bal b/d	5,000	3,000
	drawings	600	500	Dec 31	Interest on		
	Drawings	6,000	5,000		capitals	1,000	600
	Balances c/d	6,400	5,600		Salary		4,000
					Share of profit	7,000	3,500
		13,000	11,100			13,000	11,100
				19-2			
				Jan 1	Bal. b/d	6,400	5,600

(c) Balance sheet (extract) as at 31 December 19-1

	£	£	£
	Abel	Baker	
Capital accounts	10,000	6,000	16,000
Current accounts	6,400	5,600	12,000
	16,400	11,600	28,000

Tutorial note: When a question requires the Current accounts to be shown as in (b) above, it is only necessary to show the closing balances on the current accounts in the balance sheet as in (c) above. If the question does not require the Current accounts to be shown separately, you should show the details in the balance sheet as in the next example.

EXAMPLE 2 (Partnership agreement does not state how profits are to be shared. The provisions of the Partnership Act 1890 are applied.)

The facts are as stated as in Example 1 except that the agreement makes no mention of interest on drawings or capital or of partners' salaries or profit sharing ratio.

REQUIRED

(a) Profit and loss appropriation account for the year to 31 December 19-1, and

(b) balance sheet extract as at 31 December 19-1 showing the partners' capital and current accounts.

ANSWER:

(a)

Abel and Baker
Profit and Loss Appropriation Account
for the year to 31 December 19-1

	£	£
Net profit brought down		15,000
Current accounts – share of profits		
Abel (1/2)	7,500	
Baker (1/2)	7,500	15,000

(The account has been shown this time in vertical format – the form of final accounts preferred by examiners.)

(b) Balance sheet (extract) as at 31 December 19-1

		£	£
Capital accounts:	Abel	10,000	
	Baker	6,000	16,000

Current accounts	Abel £	Baker £	
Balances at 1.1.-1	5,000	3,000	
Profit for year	7,500	7,500	
	12,500	10,500	
less drawings	6,000	5,000	
	6,500	5,500	12,000
			28,000

EXAMPLE 3 (This example requires the preparation of a forecast trading and profit and loss account, and a recognition of differences between sole trader and partnership entities.)

Addison carries on business as a sole trader selling office equipment, and his trading and profit and loss account for the year to 31 December 19-1 was as follows:

	£	£
Sales		100,000
less cost of sales		58,000
Gross profit		42,000
Salaries and wages	20,000	
Rent, rates and insurance	3,800	
Heating and lighting	2,320	
Advertising	4,000	
Delivery expenses	2,000	
Sundry expenses	2,200	34,320
Net profit		7,680

Addison's net profits for the previous two years were:

19-9	£12,000
19-0	£ 9,600

The forecast for the foreseeable future is not good and profits seem set to decline at the same rate as for the past three years.

Addison has not followed the latest trends in information technology and has confined his trading to older, conventional types of equipment which has steadily become more obsolete every year.

Addison has employed Steele as manager since January 19-9 at a salary of £8,000 per annum. Steele previously worked for a high technology firm and has acquired considerable knowledge and experience in selling micro-computers and word processors.

In order to arrest the decline in his profits, Addison is now considering taking Steele into partnership and making Steele responsible for marketing micro-computers and word processors as a new line of business.

Steele would introduce £20,000 into the business as capital and would continue to receive his present salary in addition to $1/3$ share of the balance of profits. Both partners would be entitled to interest on capital at the rate of 10% p.a. Addison's capital account balance at 31 December 19-1 was £50,000.

If Steele is admitted as a partner, to manage the new line of business whilst Addison continues to manage the existing business, the following results are forecast.

	Existing business	New business
	£	£
Sales	80,000	100,000
Gross profit	46,400	20,420

In addition, it will be necessary to engage a new sales assistant at an annual salary of £6,000. Insurance premium will increase by £500 p.a. Advertising and delivery expenses will each increase by 50%.

REQUIRED

(a) A forecast trading and profit and loss account for the year to 31 December 19-2 assuming Addison takes Steele into partnership.

(b) State whether, in your opinion, Addison should admit Steele as a partner, with reasons.

(c) Give your views on the proposed profit sharing arrangements and, in particular, whether or not you think Steele would be justified in accepting only one third share of the balance of profits.

ANSWER

(a)

Addison and Steele
Forecast trading and profit and loss account
for the year to 31 December 19-2

	£	£
Sales (80,000 + 100,000)		180,000
less: Cost of sales (balancing figure)		113,180
Gross profit (46,400 + 20,420)		66,820
Salaries and wages (20,000 - 8,000 + 6,000)	18,000	
Rent, rate and insurance (3,800 + 500)	4,300	
Heating and lighting	2,320	
Advertising (4,000 + 2,000)	6,000	
Delivery expenses (2,000 + 1,000)	3,000	
Sundry expenses	2,200	35,820
Net profit		31,000
Steele – salary	8,000	
Interest on capitals: Addison	5,000	
Steele	2,000	15,000
		16,000
Share of profit: Addison ($^2/_3$)	10,667	
Steele ($^1/_3$)	5,333	16,000

(b) (Outline answer)

1. Addison should take Steele into partnership. As a sole trader he could expect his net profit in 19-2 to be about £6,144. (His profits have been falling by 20% year on year.) As a partner, he can expect to receive £15,667.

2. Steele's expertise can be used more fully, increasing his motivation at the same time as the business benefits.

3. A new lease of life is injected into the business by the introduction of a new line in technology.

4. The introduction of new capital by Steele will increase the liquidity of the firm; but the new line of business will result in an increase in stock, debtors and creditors.

(c) 1. Interest on capital rewards partners proportionately to their unequal capitals.

2. Addison's $^2/_3$ share of profits maintains his position of seniority.

3. Steele's salary guarantees him a minimum share of profits; he will receive it even if no profits are available. (It could actually increase a loss.)

EXAMPLE 4 (Guaranteed shares of profit.)

Donald, Peter and Paul are in partnership sharing profits in the ratio of 3:2:1. Paul is guaranteed a minimum share of profits of £8,000.

		£
Profit for the year to:	31 December 19-0	60,000
	31 December 19-1	40,000

REQUIRED

Show the share of profit due to each partner for each of the years 19-0 and 19-1.

Appropriation account for the year to 31 December 19-0

		£	£
Net profit b/d			60,000
Shares of profit:	Donald $3/6$	30,000	
	Peter $2/6$	20,000	
	Paul $1/6$	10,000	60,000

Appropriation account for the year to 31 December 19-1

		£	£
Net profit b/d			40,000
Shares of profit:	Donald ($3/5$ of £32,000)	19,200	
	Peter ($2/5$ of £32,000)	12,800	
	Paul (guaranteed)	8,000	40,000

Tutorial notes:

1.   As Paul is entitled to a minimum share of £8,000, Donald and Peter share the balance of £32,000.

2.   The profit sharing ratio between Donald and Peter is 3:2, or $3/5$ and $2/5$; not $3/6$ and $2/6$

6.2.2 EXERCISE 1 (for practice in preparing a partnership appropriation account applying the provisions of the Partnership Act 1890)

Gray and Green have been carrying on business in partnership for a few years but have never prepared a partnership agreement. At 1 April 19-9, the following balances appeared in their books:

		£	
Capital accounts:	Gray	20,000	
	Green	14,000	
Current accounts:	Gray	7,000	(Cr.)
Green		2,000	(Cr.)
Loan account:	Gray	10,000	

In the year ended 31 March 19-0, the partnership made a profit of £8,000 before interest on Gray's loan. At 31 March 19-0 the balances on the partners' Drawing accounts were: Gray £4,000; Green £3,000.

REQUIRED

Prepare the partnership appropriation account for the year ended 31 March 19-0 and a balance sheet extract as at that date showing the partners' capital accounts, and their current accounts in detail.

EXERCISE 2 (practice in (i) the application of terms of partnership agreement and (ii) adjustments for accruals and prepayments.)

Palmer and Green have been in partnership for some years. The terms of their agreement provide for interest at 10 per cent per annum on partners' loans to the firm. It also allows for interest at 10 per cent per annum on capitals and drawings. Green receives a salary of £8,000 per annum and the balance of profits are to be shared: Palmer $3/5$, Green $2/5$.

The following balances had been extracted from the books at 31 December 19-0 after the trading account for the year had been prepared:

		£			£
Capitals:	Palmer	35,000	Premises at cost		100,000
	Green	20,000	Provision for		
Loan by Palmer		8,000	depreciation of		
Current accounts:	Palmer	4,000 (Cr)	premises		25,000
	Green	3,000 (Dr)	Motor cars		16,000
Drawings:	Palmer	7,000	Provision for		
	Green	8,000	depreciation of		
Gross profit for year		80,000	motor cars		8,000
Selling and distribution			Stock at 31,12.-0		12,000
expenses		23,500	Debtors		36,000
Administration expenses		16,400	Creditors		8,300
Bank overdraft		3,600	Bank loan (repayable 1.1.-2)		30,000

The following adjustments are to be made in the preparation of the profit and loss account:

1. Selling and distribution expenses accrued at 31 December 19-0: £1,500
2. Administration expenses prepaid at 31 December 19-0 £800
3. Depreciation is to be provided for the year as follows: Premises: 4% on cost Motor cars: 20% on cost

REQUIRED

(a) The partnership profit and loss and appropriation accounts for the year to 31 December 19-0

(b) The current accounts of the partners as at 31 December 19-0

(c) The balance sheet as at 31 December 19-0

EXERCISE 3 (in which a partner has a guaranteed share of profit.)

Doyle, Lee and Carter are in partnership sharing profits and losses in the ratio of 5:3:2. Carter, however, is guaranteed a minimum share of £5,000. At 31 December, 19-2, the partners' capital account balances were as follows: Doyle £25,000, Lee £17,000, Carter £6,000. By the partnership agreement, they are entitled to interest on capital at 10% per annum.

In the year to 31 December, 19-3, the net profit of the firm was £7,000.

REQUIRED

The appropriation account of the partnership for the year ended 31 December, 19-3.

EXERCISE 4 (forecast trading and profit and loss account and balance sheet of partnership; choice between alternatives of (a) continuing to trade as a sole trader, and (b) forming a partnership.)

Bath has been in business as a sole trader for some years and at 31 December 19-0 the final accounts of his business were as follows:

Trading and profit and loss account for the year to 31 December 19-0

	£	£
Sales		70,000
Cost of sales		42,000
Gross profit		28,000
less Salaries and wages	10,000	
Rent and rates	3,600	
Insurance	800	
Entertainment expenses	500	
Car expenses	2,600	
Bank overdraft interest	240	
Advertising	1,500	
Sundry expenses	660	
Depreciation: Motor car	1,000	
Fixtures and fittings	750	21,650
Net profit		6,350

Balance sheet as at 31 December 19-0

		£	£	£
Fixed assets:	Motor car		4,000	
	less depreciation		1,000	3,000
	Fixtures and fittings		3,750	
	less depreciation		750	3,000
				6,000
Current assets:	Stock		2,200	
	Debtors		3,000	
			5,200	
less Current liabilities;				
	Bank overdraft	2,500		
	Creditors	1,900	4,400	800
				6,800
Capital account				6,800

Profit has remained static in recent years and the liquidity of the business is beginning to cause Bath some concern.

Wells is a friend of Bath, and has engaged in his spare time in a business which could successfully be combined with Bath's. Wells, however, lacks suitable business premises and there would be room in Bath's premises for both businesses. Bath sees that his own liquidity position could be improved by the additional capital which Wells would introduce if they went into partnership.

Wells would enter into partnership on 1 January 19-1 on the following terms: Wells to pay into the firm £5,000 in addition to bringing in his car at a valuation of £5,000; Bath's capital to remain unchanged; both capital accounts to be regarded as fixed; interest to be allowed on capitals at 10% per annum., and Wells to be entitled to a salary of £8,000 per annum.

Bath estimates that the partnership would result in the following:

Bath's business: Sales would increase by £10,000 and the gross profit percentage would remain unchanged.Well's business: Sales would be £120,000 on which the margin would be 30%

Salaries and wages would increase by £4,000 Entertainment expenses and car expenses would double.Advertising costs would increase by £1,800 Sundry expenses would be £1,000.

Motor cars would be depreciated at the rate of 25% on the reducing balance. Fixtures and fittings would be depreciated at the rate of 20%, also on the reducing balance.

Bath's stock would remain constant and Well's stock at 31 December 19-1 would be £8,000.

Debtors would increase by 200% whilst creditors would increase by 100%

REQUIRED

(a) A forecast trading and profit and loss account for the year to 31 December 19-1 and a forecast balance sheet as at that date on the assumption that Bath admits Wells as a partner on the terms shown above.

(b) Whether in your opinion Bath should go into partnership with Wells, giving your reasons.

Tutorial note: The item 'Bank' in your balance sheet will be the figure required to make your balance sheet balance.

6.3   KEY POINTS TO REMEMBER

1. Advantages of partnership:
   a.   Provision of capital.
   b.   Diversity of knowledge, experience and expertise.
   c.   'Cover' for partners during sickness and holidays.
   Disadvantages:
   All partners must agree on policy etc. Sole trader is free agent to run his own business.

2. Partnership Act 1890:
   a. All partners entitled to contribute equally to capital of firm.
   b. NO interest on capitals or drawings.
   c. NO partners' salaries.
   d. Interest on partners' loans to firm 5% p.a.

   These provisions only apply where not covered by partnership agreement.

3. Partnership accounts:

   Appropriation account for division of profits including interest on capital and drawings (but not on loans).

   For each partner: Capital account

      Current account

      Drawings account.

4. Always debit interest on partners' loan to firm in profit and loss account, not in appropriation account.

5. Unless question requires otherwise, treat partners' capitals as fixed and complete double entry from appropriation account to their current accounts.

   Interest on loans will also be credited to the current accounts.

   For accounting entries see 6.2.

6. Always transfer balances on partners' Drawings accounts to their current accounts at the year end.

7. Partnership questions are not difficult for examinees who think about what they are doing and apply all the information in the questions. Avoid omitting to give effect to all the data and requirements by ticking each item on the question paper as you give effect to it.

   Check that everything has been ticked before you complete your answer.

COMMON ERRORS

– Interest on partners' loans shown in Appropriation account;
– Interest on capitals, loans, drawings, omitted although stated by question to be included in the partnership agreement;
– Appropriations of profit posted to capital accounts when capitals are fixed;
– Failure to transfer balances on Drawings accounts to Current accounts at year end.

6.4 EXAMINATION QUESTIONS

QUESTION 1 (AEB June 1987)

The following draft balance sheet as at 31 May 19-7 of the partnership of X and Y has been produced following the completion of the revenue accounts for the year ended 31 May 19-7. X and Y share profits and losses equally.

	Cost	Aggregate depreciation	
	£	£	£
Fixed Assets			
Plant and machinery	50,000	24,000	26,000
Motor vehicles	40,000	13,000	27,000
	90,000	37,000	53,000
Current Assets			
Stock at cost	28,000		
Debtors	14,000		
Balance at bank	10,000	52,000	
Carried forward		52,000	53,000

67

	£	£	£
Brought forward		52,000	53,000
less Current Liabilities			
Creditors		12,000	40,000
			93,000
Capital Accounts			
X		30,000	
Y		50,000	80,000
Current Accounts			
X		18,000	
Y		(5,000)	13,000
			93,000

After the preparation of the draft final accounts the following information became available.

(1) Included in the stock figure of £28,000 was an item valued at cost of £4,000. The item is now in short supply and would cost £9,000 to replace. The recommended selling price of the item is £15,000.

(2) No entry has been made in the accounts to record the sale on credit to J. Smith of an item of plant and machinery for £5,000 on 25 April 19-7. The machinery was purchased on June 1 19-3 for £15,000. It is company policy to depreciate plant and machinery by 10% per annum based on the cost of assets shown in the books at the end of the financial year.

(3) Included in the figure for debtors is a debt of £3,000 which was owed by Green, a long established customer. Green, in partial payment of the debt, had given X some materials for his house extension which had a value of £2,000. No entry has been made in the accounts to record that transaction nor the fact that Green is unable to pay the balance of his debt.

(4) On 29 May 19-7 the firm formally agreed to purchase on credit items of stock at a cost of £8,000 and accepted the invoice dated that day. The stock has not been received by 31 May but it has been despatched by the supplier. No entry has been made in the accounts to record the transaction.

REQUIRED

(a) The journal entries to record transaction (2) above.
    Narratives are not required. *(6 marks)*

(b) A statement showing the effect, if any, of each of the four items above on the Current Account balances of X and Y. *(8 marks)*

(c) A redrafted balance sheet as at 31 May 19-7 of X and Y after the items above had been taken into consideration. *(5 marks)*

(Total 19 marks)

QUESTION 2 (AEB November 1988)

Franklin, Michael and Longman are trading in partnership. The following information has been extracted from the partnership agreement and books of account for the year ended 31 October 19-8:

(1) Partners are to be credited with interest on capital account balances at the rate of 9% per annum. Interest is to be charged on cash drawings only, at the rate of 10% per annum.

(2) The partnership net trading profit for the year per the draft accounts amounted to £72,190 and the profit is to be appropriated in the following ratios:
    Franklin 1: Michael 2: Longman 2.

(3) Cash drawings during the year amounted to:

	£
Franklin	5,500
Michael	6,200
Longman	4,900

It should be assumed that all cash drawings took place on 30 April 19-8

(4) The balances on the partners' capital and current accounts at 1 November 19-7 were:

	Capital account	Current account
	£	£
Franklin	18,000	Cr. 9,310
Michael	40,000	Cr. 4,650
Longman	33,000	Cr. 2,170

(5) Each partner had taken goods for his own use during the year at cost as follows:

Franklin £3,200, Michael £1,900 and Longman £2,500. No entries had been made in the books of account to record these transactions.

(6) The partnership disposed of a motor vehicle on 25 October 19-8 for £4,200 and the proceeds of sale were recorded as income in arriving at the profit for the year. The vehicle had a book value of £6,100 at the time of sale and this amount had been transferred to a suspense account at 31 October 19-8.

(7) An insurance premium of £230 relating to Michael's home was paid by the partnership and charged to the profit and loss account.

REQUIRED

(a) A statement of the corrected net trading profit for the partnership for the year ended 31 October 19-8
(6 marks)

(b) The profit and loss appropriation account for the year ended 31 October 19-8 *(6 marks)*

(c) The capital and current accounts of Franklin, Michael and Longman as they would appear in the balance sheet at 31 October 19-8.
(6 marks)

(Total 18 marks)

QUESTION 3 (Cambridge June 1988)

The following draft balance sheet as at 31 March 19-8 has been prepared for Leaf and Branch who are trading in partnership:

	£	£
Fixed assets		
Fixtures and fittings		
At cost	30,000	
Less: Aggregate depreciation	23,000	7,000
Current assets		
Stock	19,000	
Debtors	16,000	
Balance at bank	6,000	
	41,000	
Less: Current liabilities		
Creditors	8,000	33,000
		40,000
Less: Long term loan - Leaf		
At 1 April 18-7		10,000
		£30,000
Represented by:		
Capital accounts		
At 1 April 19-7 - Leaf		15,000
Branch		9,000
Carried forward		24,000

	£	£
Brought forward		24,000
Current accounts - Leaf	5,000	
Branch	1,000	6,000
		£30,000

After preparing the above draft balance sheet, the following discoveries have been made:

(a) A quantity of fixtures and fittings was sold for £2,000 in July 19-7: the cost of the items sold was £10,000 and their net book value at 31 March 19-7 was £3,000. The proceeds of the sale have been credited to the fixtures and fittings at cost account; no further accounting entries have been made for this sale.

Note: The policy of the partnership is for depreciation on the straight line basis at the rate of 10% to be provided on the balance of the fixtures and fittings at cost account at the end of each financial year.

(b) Interest at the rate of 12$\frac{1}{2}$% per annum is to be provided on the long-term loan for the year ended 31 March 19-8.

(c) The valuation of stock-in-trade at 31 March 19-7 should have been included in the accounts for the year ended on that date at £24,000, instead of the amount incorrectly shown in the accounts of £16,000.

The partners agree that the correct stock valuation at 31 March 19-7 should be incorporated in the partnership accounts.

(d) A provision for doubtful debts of 2$\frac{1}{2}$% of debtors outstanding at 31 March 19-8 should be made in the draft accounts.

(e) An adjustment is to be made for rent prepaid at 31 March 19-8 of £500.

(f) No entries have been made in the accounts for goods costing £600 withdrawn from the business during the year by Branch for his own use.

Additional information:

In addition to the interest on partners' loans, the partnership agreement provides for interest at the rate os 5% per annum on partners' capital account balances. It also provides for the balance of profits and losses to be divided between Leaf and Branch in the ratio 3:2 respectively up to 31 March 19-7, and subsequently to be divided equally.

REQUIRED

A corrected balance sheet for the partnership as at 31 March 19-8. *(25 marks)*

QUESTION 4 (Cambridge November 1988)

Joey and Jasmine operate a boutique in partnership. Their agreement states that after allowing interest at 12% per annum on their fixed capitals, the remaining profits are shared equally, except that Jasmine is to receive a minimum share of profit (after allowing for interest on capital) of £15,000.

The partnership balance sheet at 30 April 19-7 was as follows:

	£	£		£	£
Fixed Assets		44,000	Fixed Capital Accounts		
Current Assets			Joey		40,000
Stock	72,500		Jasmine		20,000
Debtors	14,600		Current Accounts		
Bank	1,200		Joey	9,500	
		88,300	Jasmine	5,500	15,000
			Current Liabilities		
			Bank Loan	32,000	
			Trade Creditors	22,000	
			Accruals	3,300	57,300
		132,300			132,300

The partnership does not keep full accounting records but you are able to ascertain the following information:

i) Joey takes out of the business £600 a month and Jasmine £800 a month to meet personal expenses

ii) During the year Fixed Assets with a written down value of £2,000 were sold for £1,500 and new Fixed Assets were purchased for £16,000. Depreciation is calculated at $12^1/_2$% on the book value of Fixed Assets at the end of the year.

iii) The Bank Loan carries interest at a rate of 15% per annum and is repayable in annual instalments of £8,000.

iv) At 30 April 19-8 the following year end balances were ascertained:

Stock cost £90,000 but its net realisable value is £86,000.

Debtors total £18,000 but it is decided to make a general provision for doubtful debts of £1,200.

Trade creditors total £23,600.

There is a contingent liability of £3,000 (maximum) under a guarantee given by the partnership.

Accruals total £4,150.

Bank statements show an overdraft of £7,700 and there are unpresented cheques still to be paid amounting to £1,600.

REQUIRED

(a) A statement showing the assets and liabilities of the partnership at 30 April 19-8.   *(8 marks)*

(b) A calculation of the profit for the year and its division between the partners.   *(7 marks)*

(c) Partners' Current Accounts for the year ended 30 April19-8.   *(5 marks)*

(d) Briefly explain to the partners why it is necessary to put a value on Goodwill if they decide to admit a new partner.   *(5 marks)*

(Total 25 marks)

QUESTION 5   (Oxford June 1986)

Misfit and Wartz are in partnership. At 31 December 19-4 they agree that their assets are worth:

	£
Premises	200,000
Fixtures	80,000
Motor Vehicles	60,000
Stock	20,000
Debtors	8,200
Bank	1,200
Cash	300

At the same date they have creditors of   5,700

During the year ended 31 December 19-5 the following transactions took place:

1. On 1 July 19-5 Misfit loaned the partnership £20,000 for ten years.
2. At the same date, Wartz increased his capital by £36,000 to make it equal to Misfit's.
3. Cash sales for the year were £300,000.
4. £490,200 was paid into the bank during the year.
5. Expenses paid in cash during the year were £2,400.
6. Expenses paid by cheque during the year were:
    (i) Wages £56,000
    (ii) Lighting and heating and rates £9,700
    (iii) Motor vehicle expenses £18,300
    (iv) Carriage on purchases £3,400
    (v) Other expenses £18,800
7. Some small items of goods for resale were purchased and paid for out of the cash £10,000.
8. Goods which cost £1,200 had been returned to credit suppliers.

9. £288,720 was paid to creditors during the year. 10% cash discount had been deducted from all payments.

10. No discounts were allowed to debtors, but £200 had been written off as bad.

11. One of the vehicles is used occasionally by Misfit's wife. The cost of this usage (included in the Motor vehicle expenses) is estimated to be £3,400; this is to be charged to Misfit.

12. Both partners had taken goods from the business during the year valued at cost. These were estimated at:

               Misfit   £2,800   Wartz   £1,900

13. At 31 December 19-5, Fixtures and Motor vehicles were valued at £72,000 and £60,341 respectively, stocks were valued at £22,500. Debtors owed £5,500 and creditors were owed £6,400.

14. A small amount of cash is kept in the business from cash sales for paying expenses and at 31 December19-5 there is £500 not paid into the bank.

15. On 1 June 19-5 a small van with a book value of £750 was sold for £900 and replaced by a new one at a cost of £7,800. The difference was paid by cheque.

16. During the year the partners had withdrawn from the bank for their own use: Misfit £3,840: Wartz £18,200.

17. Watkinson is the general manager for the partnership and apart from his wages he is entitled to a bonus of 10% of the net profit of the business calculated after charging this bonus. The bonus will be paid on 1 February 19-6.

18. Interest is allowed on partnership capitals of 5% per annum and Wartz is allowed a salary of £15,000 per annum. Interest is charged on drawings, but apart from these no other agreements have been made.

19. The interest on drawings for the year has been calculated at Misfit £300 and Wartz £550.

You are required to prepare:

(a) the Trading and Profit and Loss account of the partnership for the year ended 31 December 19-5,

(b) the partners' current accounts and

(c) the Balance Sheet at 31 December 19-5.

(Total 40 marks)

7 PARTNERSHIP CHANGES

> *This aspect of partnership accounting entails:-*
> ● preparation of separate profit and loss accounts for the periods before, and after, the change.
> ● revaluation of partnership assets on partnership change
> ● goodwill

The admission of a new partner, or the retirement or death of an existing partner, constitute the termination of one partnership and the commencement of a new one.

7.1 ACCOUNTING FOR CHANGES

Separate accounts should be prepared for the old partnership and the new one.

Examination questions on this topic invariably pose situations where no new entries are made in the partnership books to reflect changes as they occur, and require the separate accounts for the two firms to be produced at the end of the financial year.

Prepare the profit and loss accounts for the two firms in columnar form, one for the period to the date of change, the other for the period following the change.

Split the expenses in the profit and loss accounts in the manner indicated in the question. Expenses which vary with turnover should be split in proportion to turnover, e.g salesmen's commission on sales; those which are related to time, e.g. rent, rates, should be split on a time basis. Other items may be split on some other basis stated in the question, e.g. provisions for doubtful debts which will depend upon the debtors outstanding at the date of change in the partnership, and those outstanding at the year end.

Any expenses applicable only to the old partnership, or to the new one only, will not be split but entered in the appropriate period. In this connection, take care to calculate partners' salaries and interest on their loans, capitals and drawings on a time basis when these are expressed in the question on an annual basis.

7.1.1 EXAMPLE.

East and New are in partnership as general traders, sharing profits and losses equally after allowing East a salary of £4,000 p.a. At 1 January 19-1, their capital accounts were: East £10,000, New £8,000. Their current account balances were East £3,000 (Cr.), New £2,000 (Cr.)

On 1 July 19-1, they admitted Barnet as a partner. From that date profits were to be shared between East, New and Barnet in the ratio 2:2:1. Barnet is to receive a salary of £3,000 p.a.

It was agreed that from 1 July 19-1 East would transfer £2,000 from his capital account to a loan account on which interest would be paid at 10% p.a.

Barnet brought his private car into the firm at a valuation of £5,000.

No entries to reflect the foregoing matters were made in the books before the end of the financial year on 31 December 19-1.

The following information is available for the year to 31 December 19-1:

	£
Sales (spread evenly throughout the year)	80,000
Cost of sales	35,000
Rent and rates	10,000
Wages	14,000
General expenses	6,000

The car is to be depreciated over 4 years on the straight line basis; it is assumed it will have a nil residual value.

Of the General expenses, £2,000 was incurred in the six months to 30 June 19-1.

All sales produce a uniform rate of gross profit.

REQUIRED

(1) The trading and profit and loss and appropriation accounts of the partnership for the year to 31 December 19-1.

(2) The partners' current accounts as at 31 December 19-1.

ANSWER

(a)

East, New and Barnet
Trading and profit and loss account
for the year to 31 December 19-1

		£
Sales		80,000
less cost of sales		35,000
Gross profit		45,000

	6 months to 30 Jun		6 months to 31 Dec		Total	
	£	£	£	£	£	£
Gross profit b/d		22,500		22,500		45,000
Rent and rates	5,000		5,000		10,000	
Wages	7,000		7,000		14,000	
General expenses	2,000		4,000		6,000	
Interest on loan	–		100		100	
Depreciation						
- car	–	14,000	625	16,725	625	30,725
Net profit		8,500		5,775		14,275
Salary - East		2,000				2,000
Salary - Barnet				1,500		1,500
		6,500				
Share of profit						
East ($^1/_2$)	3,250		($^2/_5$) 1,710			4,960
New ($^1/_2$)	3,250		($^2/_5$) 1,710			4,960
Barnet	–		($^1/_5$) 855			855
		6,500		5,775		14,275

Tutorial note: When a partnership change involves only a change in the profit sharing ratios of existing partners without affecting profit and loss account items, it is necessary to split the appropriation account only.

7.1.2 EXERCISE 1 (involving a change in the profit sharing ratios only)

Toll, Puddle and Martyn have been in partnership for some years sharing profits in the ratio 3:2:1.

The following data for the year ended 31 December 19-2 has been extracted from the partnership books:

	£
Sales for the year	74,000
Cost of sales	38,000
Wages	8,000
General expenses	3,000
Depreciation of fixed assets	1,000

The partners have agreed that from 1 July 19-2, Toll shall be entitled to a salary of £3,000 p.a. and the balance of the profits shall be shared equally. Sales have taken place evenly throughout the year and all sales earned a uniform rate of gross profit. No entries to reflect the change in profit sharing ratio have been made in the books before the year end.

REQUIRED

The trading and profit and loss and appropriation accounts of the firm for the year to 31 December 19-2.

EXERCISE 2 (Introduction of a new partner during financial year)

Crook and Shank were in partnership in a firm of general dealers, sharing profits in the ratio of 3:2. They made up their accounts annually to 31 March. On 1 October 19-1, they admitted Spindle as a partner; Spindle paid £20,000 into the firm's bank account on that date as capital.

The new partnership agreement allowed interest on capital at 10% p.a. Spindle would receive a salary of £4,000 p.a. and the balance of profit would be divided as follows: Crook $^2/_5$, Shank $^2/_5$, Spindle $^1/_5$.

Information extracted from the books of the firm for the year to 31 March 19-2 was as follows:

	£
Sales	190,000
Cost of sales	100,000
Salaries and wages	21,000
Rent and rates	8,500
Lighting and heating	3,200
General expenses	2,400
Loan made to firm by Crook on 1 October 19-1 with interest at 12% p.a.	10,000
Motor cars at cost 1 April 19-1	20,000
Motor car brought into partnership on 1 October 19-1 by Spindle at valuation	8,000
Provision for doubtful debts at 1 April 19-1	500
Debtors at 30 September 19-1	12,000
Debtors at 31 March 19-2	14,000
Capital accounts at 1 April 19-1: Crook	40,000
Shank	30,000

The following further information is also available:

1. Rent and rates prepaid at 31 March 19-2: £2,500.

2. Heating and lighting owing at 31 March 19-2: £800.

3. General expenses incurred to 30 September 19-1: £1,100.

4. Motor cars are to be depreciated at the rate of 20% on cost or valuation as appropriate.

5. The provision for doubtful debts to be maintained at the rate of 4% of debtors.

6. Owing to the seasonal nature of the business, one third of the sales occurred in the first six months of the financial year.

7. All sales produced a uniform rate of gross profit.

REQUIRED

The trading and profit and loss and appropriation accounts of the partnership for the year to 31 March 19-2.

7.2 REVALUATION OF ASSETS

On a change in the profit sharing arrangements in a partnership, which obviously includes the admission or retirement of a partner, the partners' capital accounts should show their true interests in the firm.

Partners' capitals equal the net worth of their business. The real net worth of a business depends upon the realistic valuation of the assets and liabilities. Therefore it is usual to review the values of these items on a partnership change.

Accounting entries:

A Revaluation account must be opened in the general ledger.

	Account to be debited	Account to be credited
Increases in values of assets	Asset	Revaluation
Decreases in values of assets	Revaluation	Asset
Provisions for depreciation on revalued assets	Provision for depreciation	Revaluation
Profit on revaluation	Revaluation	Capitals*
Loss on revaluation	Capitals*	Revaluation

* In the proportion in which partners shared profits and losses before the change.

Tutorial note: Profits and losses on revaluation of assets affect the partners' investment in the firm: the profits or losses are unrealised profits or losses of a capital nature unlike trading profits and losses. Therefore they must be adjusted through the capital accounts. If they were entered in the partners' current accounts, that would imply that any profits were realised profits which could be drawn out by the partners, and that would deplete the long term capital of the firm, perhaps with serious results.

7.2.1 EXAMPLE.

Daisy and Pansy are in partnership sharing profits and losses in the ratio 3:2. They decide to admit Poppy as a partner on 1 May 19-2 when the profit sharing ratio will become: Daisy $1/2$, Pansy $1/3$ and Poppy $1/6$.

The balance sheet of Daisy and Pansy on 30 April 19-2 was:

		£	£
Fixed assets:	Motor car		6,000
	Office furniture		4,000
			10,000
Current assets:	Stock	2,000	
	Debtors	1,200	
	Bank	2,500	
		5,700	
less Current liabilities			
	Creditors	300	5,400
			15,400
Capital accounts:	Daisy	9,000	
	Pansy	6,000	15,000
Current accounts	Daisy	800	
	Pansy	(400)	400
			15,400

It is agreed that the assets shall be revalued as follows:

Motor car £4,000; office furniture (some of which has been found to be genuinely antique) £7,000; stock which originally cost £200 is damaged and is considered to be of no value. No provision has been made for doubtful debts and it is agreed that a provision of 10% of debtors should be created.

The adjustments are made in the books at 30 April 19-2 and Poppy is admitted as a partner on the following day, paying £2,500 into the firm's bank account as capital.

REQUIRED

(a) Journal entries to show the entries in the books of the firm on 30 April 19-2 to give effect to the above adjustments. (Narratives are not required.)

(b) The Revaluation account.

(c) The capital accounts of Daisy and Pansy at 30 April 19-2.

(d) The opening balance sheet of the firm of Daisy, Pansy and Poppy as at 1 May 19-2.

ANSWER

(a)

Daisy and Pansy
Journal

	Dr	Cr
	£	£
Revaluation	2,000	
Motor car		2,000
Office furniture	3,000	
Revaluation		3,000
Revaluation	200	
Stock		200
Revaluation	120	
Provision for doubtful debts		120

(b)

Revaluation account

19-2		£	19-2		£
April 30	Motor car	2,000	April 30	Office furniture	3,000
	Stock	200			
	Provision for doubtful debts	120			
Capitals:	Daisy	408			
	Pansy	272			
		3,000			3,000

(c)

Partners' capital accounts (old firm)

		Daisy	Pansy			Daisy	Pansy
		£	£			£	£
19-2				19-2			
April 30	Balance c/d	9,408	6,272	April 30	Balance b/d	9,000	6,000
					Revaluation	408	272
		9,408	6,272			9,408	6,272
				May 1	Balance b/d	9,408	6,272

(d)

Daisy, Pansy and Poppy
Opening Balance sheet as at 1 May 19-2

		£	£	£
Fixed assets:	Motor car			4,000
	Office furniture			7,000
				11,000
Current assets:	Stock		1,800	
	Debtors		1,200	
	less provision		120	1,080
	Bank			5,000
				7,880
less Current liabilities:	Creditors			300	7,580
				18,580

		£	£	£
Capitals:	Daisy	9,408		
	Pansy	6,272		
	Poppy	2,500		18,180
Current accounts:	Daisy	800		
	Pansy	(400)		400
				18,580

Tutorial note: Had the profit on realisation been credited to the current accounts of Daisy and Pansy, that would have implied that they could withdraw the profits. However, the profits have not been realised and must go to their capital accounts with the clear implication that if the partners withdraw those profits they will reduce their permanent capitals in the business, which would be imprudent.

7.2.2 EXERCISE (revaluation of assets on admission of new partner.)

Legge and Spinner were in partnership sharing profits equally. At 31 December 19-2, their balance sheet was as follows:

	£	£
Fixed assets:		
Freehold premises		40,000
Plant and machinery		15,000
Motor vans		16,000
		71,000
Current assets:		
Stock	14,000	
Debtors	12,000	
Balance at bank	7,500	
	33,500	
less Current liabilities: Creditors:	7,500	26,000
		97,000
Capital accounts: Legge	40,000	
Spinner	40,000	80,000
Current accounts: Legge	9,000	
Spinner	8,000	17,000
		97,000

Legge and Spinner agreed to admit Bowler as a partner on 1 January 19-3 when the assets were revalued as follows:

	£
Freehold premises	70,000
Plant and machinery	10,000
Motor vans	8,000

It was also agreed that stock which had cost £7,000 was now worth £3,000, and further stock which had cost £2,000 now had nil value.

Debtors at 31 December 19-2 included bad debts of £2,000; no provision for doubtful debts had been made in the past but a provision equal to 4% of debtors as at 31 December 19-2 should be created.

The adjustments for the foregoing matters were made in the books as at 31 December 19-2 and Bowler was duly admitted as a partner on 1 January 19-3 and subscribed £25,000 as capital.

REQUIRED

(a) Journal entries to adjust for the revaluation of assets referred to above. (Narratives are not required.)

(b) The revaluation account at 31 December 19-2.

(c) The capital accounts of Legge and Spinner as at 31 December 19-2.

(d) The opening balance sheet of the partnership of Legge, Spinner and Bowler as at 1 January 19-3.

7.3 REVALUATION OF FIXED ASSETS WHICH HAVE BEEN SUBJECT TO PROVISIONS FOR DEPRECIATION

In addition to adjusting the 'fixed asset at cost' accounts for increases or decreases in values on revaluation, transfer any provisions for depreciation on those assets at the date of revaluation to the Revaluation account. If this is not done, the assets will be recorded in the books at the new valuation less the amount of a depreciation provision which is now redundant.

7.3.1 EXAMPLE.

The following is an extract from the balance sheet of Dandy and Pixie at 28 February 19-1; they share profits and losses equally.

Fixed assets	Cost	Depn	Net
	£	£	£
Freehold property	80,000	30,000	50,000
Plant and machinery	45,000	25,000	20,000
Motor vehicles	38,000	23,000	15,000
	163,000	78,000	85,000
Current assets			
Debtors	24,000		
less provision for doubtful debts	1,200	22,800	

Dandy and Pixie agreed to admit Puck as a partner on 1 March 19-1, on which date the assets were valued as follows:

	£
Freehold property	100,000
Plant and machinery	15,000
Motor vehicles	12,000

It was also agreed that the provision for doubtful debts should be adjusted to $2^1/_2\%$ of debtors.

REQUIRED

Journal entries to give effect to the revaluation of the partnership assets at 28 February 19-1. (The answer should include the transfers to the partners' capital accounts from the Revaluation account.)

ANSWER

	Dr	Cr
	£	£
Freehold property	20,000	
Provision for depreciation of freehold property	30,000	
Revaluation account		50,000
Revaluation account	5,000	
Provision for depreciation of plant and machinery	25,000	
Plant and Machinery		30,000
Revaluation account	3,000	
Provision for depreciation of motor vehicles	23,000	
Motor vehicles		26,000

	Dr £	Cr £
Provision for doubtful debts	600	
Revaluation account		600
Revaluation account	42,600	
Capital accounts:		
Dandy		21,300
Pixie		21,300

(Transfer of profit on revaluation of assets to partners' capital accounts)

Note 1. Provision for doubtful debts:	£
Balance at 28.2.19-1	1,200
Provision required (2$^{1}/_{2}$% of £24,000)	600
Balance transferred to Revaluation account	600

Note 2. Profit on revaluation: £(50,000 + 600 - 5,000 - 3,000) = £42,600

7.3.2 EXERCISE (preparation of Revaluation account involving provisions for depreciation of fixed assets.)

Carey and Street are in partnership sharing profits in the ratio 3:2. They propose to admit Court as a partner on 1 July 19-2. The following is an extract of Carey and Street's balance sheet at 30 June 19-2.

Fixed assets	£	£
Plant and equipment at cost	14,000	
less provision for depreciation	9,000	5,000
Motor vans	11,000	
less provision for depreciation	8,300	2,700
Office machinery	5,000	
less provision for depreciation	2,800	2,200
		9,900
Current assets		
Debtors	6,000	
less provision for doubtful debts	120	5,880

It is agreed that the partnership assets should be revalued as follows:

	£
Plant and equipment	4,000
Motor vans	2,000
Office machinery	4,000

On 1 July, the partners learned that a debtor owing £800 had become bankrupt. They also decided to increase the provision for doubtful debts to 5% of debtors.

REQUIRED

(a)   Journal entries to give effect to the above mentioned adjustments. Narratives should be included.

(b)   Show all the relevant ledger accounts concerned after the necessary postings have been made.

7.4   GOODWILL

'The goodwill of a business is the advantage ... which a person gets by continuing to carry on ... a business which has been carried on for some time previously'.

Goodwill may be regarded as that which enables a business to earn greater profits than the return normally expected on the net tangible assets of a business because of the reputation or special advantages which the business enjoys with the rest of the world.

In accounting, goodwill is an intangible asset and is only recorded as an asset in the accounts if it has a monetary value, i.e. the price at which it may be sold. Sole traders and partnerships do not usually record goodwill in their books unless they have actually paid for it on purchasing a ready-made business because of the difficulty of placing a value on it, or even of proving that goodwill actually exists. Even if it is recorded in the books, prudence requires that it should be written off to the profit and loss account within a reasonable period as 'purchased goodwill' will progressively be replaced by the goodwill created by the new owner of the business.

Statement of Standard Accounting Practice (SSAP) 22 defines goodwill as the difference between the value of a business as a whole and the aggregate of the fair value of its separable net assets.

For the purpose of this topic, therefore, goodwill will be regarded as the difference between the price paid for a business and the net asset value acquired by the purchaser. (If the price paid is less than the net asset value, the difference is 'negative goodwill', not 'badwill'.)

Since a change in the constitution of a partnership amounts to the dissolution of one partnership and the commencement of another, the new partnership acquires the business of the old. The old partners are entitled to and should agree a figure of goodwill with the new partners, who will benefit from this. It makes no difference that the partners in the old firm may well continue as partners in the new firm.

7.4.1 EXAMPLE:

Sweeney and Todd's balance sheet at 31 December 19-3 was as follows:

		£	£
Fixed assets:	Plant and equipment		3,000
	Motor van		4,000
	Office equipment		1,500
			8,500
Current assets:	Stock	800	
	Debtors	300	
	Bank	1,000	
		2,100	
less: Current liabilities: Creditors		450	1,650
			10,150
Capital accounts: Sweeney		5,100	
	Todd	5,050	10,150

On 1 January 19-4 Sweeney and Todd sold their business to Barber and Leech who took over the fixed assets, stock and debtors at the following valuations: plant and equipment £2,500; motor van £3,000; office equipment £1,200 and stock £1,000. Barber and Leech paid £10,000 for the fixed assets, stock and debtors, and agreed to pay the creditors.

REQUIRED

A calculation of the price paid for goodwill by Barber and Leech.

ANSWER

	£
Net value of assets taken over:	
Plant and equipment	2,500
Motor van	3,000
Office equipment	1,200
Stock	1,000
Debtors	300
	8,000
less creditors	450
Net asset value	7,550
Price paid for business	10,000
Goodwill	2,450

Tutorial note: Assets may not be taken over at their balance sheet values; the values to be taken in calculating goodwill are those which the purchaser is prepared to pay for the assets.

7.5   TREATMENT OF GOODWILL ON A CHANGE IN A PARTNERSHIP

Goodwill should be valued and the following accounting entries made in the partnership books before the change:

	Account to be debited	Account to be credited
A. If goodwill is to be retained in the books	Goodwill	Capital accounts of partners in old firm(in old profit sharing ratios.)
B. If goodwill is not to be retained in the books	(i) Goodwill	Capital accounts of partners in old firm(in old profit sharing ratios.)
	(ii) Capital accounts of partners in new firm (in new profit sharing ratio.)	Goodwill (to close goodwill account again.)

An alternative method to B above, and the one to be preferred, when goodwill is not to be recorded in the books is to credit or debit each partner's capital account in the old and new partnerships with the net amount of any change in his share of goodwill after the change.

7.5.1 EXAMPLE

Datchett and Petworth are partners in a firm and share profits equally. Their capitals are: Datchett £50,000, Petworth £30,000. On 1 January 19-2 they admit Polbrook as a partner when the profit sharing ratio will be Datchett $^2/_5$, Petworth $^2/_5$, Polbrook $^1/_5$. Goodwill is valued at £12,000 but is not to be recorded in the firm's books.

Polbrook pays £30,000 into the firm's bank account as capital.

REQUIRED

Show the entries in the partners' capital accounts to adjust for goodwill.

ANSWER:

Working:

	(a) Old firm (in old profit sharing ratios		(b) New firm (in new profit sharing ratios		Entries in capital accounts [col(a)-col(b)] + = credit; − = debit
		£		£	£
Datchett	($^1/_2$)	6,000	($^2/_5$)	4,800	+ 1,200 (Cr.)
Petworth	($^1/_2$)	6,000	($^2/_5$)	4,800	+ 1,200 (Cr.)
Polbrook	–	–	($^1/_5$)	2,400	− 2,400 (Dr.)
		12,000		12,000	−

Partners' capital accounts

		Dat chett £	Pet worth £	Pol brook £			Dat chett £	Pet worth £	Pol brook £
19-1					19-1				
Jan1	Goodwill			2,400	Jan 1				
	Balance c/d	51,200	31,200	27,600		Balance b/d	50,000	30,000	
						Bank			30,000
						Goodwill	1,200	1,200	
		51,200	31,200	30,000			51,200	31,200	30,000
						Balance b/d	51,200	31,200	27,600

7.5.2 EXERCISE (adjustment of capital accounts on admission of new partner.)

Parchment and Deedes, partners in a firm of solicitors, share profits and losses equally. At 31 December 19-3 their balance sheet was as follows:

			£	£
Fixed assets:				
	Freehold premises			100,000
	Motor cars			40,000
	Office furniture and equipment			6,000
				146,000
Current assets:	Estimated undelivered costs	20,000		
	Unpaid delivered costs	48,000		
	Balance at bank	12,000		
		80,000		
less:				
Current liabilities: Creditors		8,000	72,000	
				218,000
Capital accounts:	Parchment		100,000	
	Deedes		100,000	200,000
Current accounts:	Parchment		12,000	
	Deedes		6,000	18,000
				218,000

Parchment and Deedes admitted Tape, their senior clerk, as a partner on 1 January 19-4 and he introduced £50,000 as capital plus his private car which was valued at £12,000 on the same day. It was agreed that the freehold premises should be revalued at £130,000, the motor cars of the old firm at £35,000, and the office furniture and equipment at £1,000. The partners agreed that a provision of 5% of unpaid delivered costs should be created.

The new profit-sharing ratio was to be Parchment $2/5$ Deedes $2/5$, Tape $1/5$.

Goodwill was valued at £50,000 but was not to be recorded in the books.

REQUIRED

(a) Journal entries to record the entries in the accounts of the partnership on the admission of Tape as a partner.

(b) The partners' capital accounts as at 1 January 19-4.

(c) The opening balance sheet of the firm of Parchment, Deedes and Tape, Solicitors, as at 1 January 19-4.

Tutorial note: Estimated undelivered costs are solicitors' equivalent of work in progress; unpaid delivered costs are debtors for work done.

7.6.1 EXAMPLE (a comprehensive example to illustrate all the aspects of partnership changes covered in this chapter.)

Dragge and Pullen have been in partnership for some years and their partnership agreement provided as follows:

1. Accounts to be prepared annually to 31 December.

2. Interest on capital to be allowed at 10% p.a.

3. Pullen to be entitled to a salary of £12,000 p.a.

4. Profits and losses to be shared in the ratio 2:1.

At 31 December 19-0 the balance sheet of Dragge and Pullen was as follows:

Fixed assets	Cost	Depn.	Net
	£	£	£
Freehold premises	87,000	17,000	70,000
Plant and machinery	45,000	31,000	14,000
Motor cars	36,000	27,000	9,000
Office equipment	12,000	8,000	4,000
	180,000	83,000	97,000

Current assets			
Stock		13,000	
Debtors	11,800		
less provision for bad debts	600	11,200	
		24,200	
Current liabilities			
Trade creditors	7,400		
Bank overdraft	4,800	12,200	12,000
			109,000

less: Long term liability: Loan from Shover (Carrying interest at 15% p.a.)			25,000
			84,000

Represented by:	Capitals	Current Accounts	
	£	£	£
Dragge	50,000	2,600	52,600
Pullen	30,000	1,400	31,400
	80,000	4,000	84,000

Note to accounts: Depreciation has been calculated on the fixed assets at cost as follows: freehold premises 4%; plant and machinery 20%; motor cars 25%; office equipment 10%.

On 1 September 19-1, Dragge and Pullen admitted their manager, Pushkin, as a partner. Pushkin had been receiving a salary of £15,000 p.a. as manager.

Under the revised partnership agreement Pullen's salary would be increased to £18,000 p.a.; interest would continue to be allowed at the rate of 10% p.a. on capital; profits and losses would be divided equally.

The partners agreed that the assets should be revalued at 31 August 19-1 as follows:

	£
Freehold premises	120,000
Plant and machinery	12,000
Motor cars	6,000
Office equipment	3,000

Stock costing £2,000 was to be written off.

Goodwill was valued at £30,000, but no goodwill account was to be opened in the firm's books.

Fixed assets would be depreciated at the same rates as hitherto, but calculated on their revalued amounts.

No additions to, or sales of, fixed assets had taken place between 31 December 19-0 and 31 August 19-1.

On the 1 September, 19-1, Pushkin paid £30,000 into the firm's bank account as capital and also brought his private car, valued at £10,000, into the business.

On the same day, the loan to Shover was repaid together with the accrued interest, and Dragge transferred £20,000 from his capital account to a loan account on which interest would be paid at 10% p.a.

The following data was available from the partnership books for the year to 31 December 19-1:

	£
Receipts from debtors	299,800
Payments to suppliers	159,400
Wages and salaries	52,000
Rent rates and insurance	20,000
Heating and lighting	2,500
Sundry expenses	4,000
Shover: repayment of loan with accrued interest	27,500

Notes:
1. Sales were spread evenly throughout the year and a uniform rate of gross profit was earned on all sales.
2. Stock at 31 December 19-1 was valued at cost, £15,000
3. Accrued expenses at 31 December 19-1: Rent £5,000 Heating and lighting £200
4. Prepaid expenses at 31 December 19-1: Rates £3,000, Insurance £1,000
5. Trade debtors at 31 August 19-1 £9,000; at 31 December 19-1 £12,000
6. Trade creditors at 31 December 19-1 £8,000
7. The provision for doubtful debts is to be adjusted to 6 % of trade debtors
8. Drawings in year to 31 December 19-1: Dragge £15,000; Pullen £20,000; Pushkin £3,000
9. Sundry expenses: £3,000 of these related to the eight months to 31 August 19-1

REQUIRED

(a) The trading and profit and loss and appropriation accounts of the firm of Dragge and Pullen for the eight months to 31 August 19-1.

(b) The trading and profit and loss and appropriation accounts of the firm of Dragge, Pullen and Pushkin for the four months ended 31 December 19-1.

(c) The balance sheets of the firm of Dragge, Pullen and Pushkin as at 31 December 19-1.

(d) The capital accounts and current accounts of Dragge, Pullen and Pushkin for the year to 31 December 19-1.

ANSWER

(a) and (b)

DRAGGE, PULLEN AND PUSHKIN
Trading and profit and loss account
for the year to 31 December 19-1

	£
Sales	300,000
less cost of sales	156,000
Gross profit carried down	144,000

	8 mths. to 31 Aug £	4 mths. to 31 Dec £	Total £
Gross profit b/d	96,000	48,000	144,000
less:			
Wages and salaries	38,000	14,000	52,000
Rent, rates & insurance	14,000	7,000	21,000
Heating and lighting	1,800	900	2,700
Sundry expenses	3,000	1,000	4,000
Carried forward	56,800	22,900	79,700

	8 mths. to 31 Aug	4 mths. to 31 Dec	Total
	£	£	£
Brought forward	56,800	22,900	79,700
Interest on loans – Shover	2,500		2,500
– Dragge		667	667
Provision for doubtful debts	(60)	180	120
Provision for depreciation:			
Freehold premises	2,320	1,600	3,920
Plant & machinery	6,000	800	6,800
Motor cars	6,000	1,333	7,333
Office equipment	800	100	900
	74,360	27,580	101,940
Net profit	21,640	20,420	42,060
less:			
Salary – Pullen	8,000	6,000	14,000
Interest on capital – Dragge	3,333	2,602	5,935
Pullen	2,000	1,634	3,634
Pushkin		1,000	1,000
	13,333	11,236	24,569
	8,307	9,184	17,491
Shares of profit – Dragge	5,538	3,061	8,599
Pullen	2,769	3,061	5,830
Pushkin		3,062	3,062
	8,307	9,184	17,491

(c)

Balance sheet as at 31 December 19-1

Fixed assets	At valuation	Depn.	Net
	£	£	£
Freehold premises	120,000	1,600	118,400
Plant and machinery	12,000	800	11,200
Motor cars	16,000	1,333	14,667
Office equipment	3,000	100	2,900
	151,000	3,833	147,167
Current assets			
Stock		15,000	
Trade debtors	12,000		
less provision	720	11,280	
Prepayments		4,000	
Bank		21,600	
		51,880	
less Current liabilities			
Trade creditors	8,000		
Carried forward	8,000	51,880	147,167

	£	£	£
Brought forward	8,000	51,880	147,167
Expense creditors	5,200	13,200	38,680
			185,847
Long term liability: Loan from Dragge			20,000
			165,847

	Capitals	Current A/cs	
	£	£	£
Dragge	78,080	2,801	80,881
Pullen	49,040	4,864	53,904
Pushkin	30,000	1,062	31,062
	157,120	8,727	165,847

(d)

Capital accounts for the year to 31 December 19-1

		Dragge	Pullen	Pushkin
		£	£	£
19-1				
Jan 1	Balances b/f	50,000	30,000	
Aug 31	Revaluation account	38,080	19,040	
	Goodwill	10,000		
Sep 1	Bank			30,000
	Motor cars			10,000
		98,080	49,040	40,000
	Goodwill			(10,000)
	Transfer to loan a/c	(20,000)		
		78,080	49,040	30,000

Current accounts for the year to 31 December 19-1

		Dragge	Pullen	Pushkin
		£	£	£
19-1				
Jan 1	Balances b/f	2,600	1,400	
Dec 31	Salary		14,000	
	Interest on loan	667		
	Interest on capital	5,935	3,634	1,000
	Share of profit	8,599	5,830	3,062
		17,801	24,864	4,062
	Drawings	(15,000)	(20,000)	(3,000)
		2,801	4,864	1,062

Workings

1. Revaluation account

	£		£
Plant and machinery	33,000	Freehold premises	33,000
Motor cars	30,000	Provision for depn:	
Office equipment	9,000	*Freehold premises	19,320
Stock	2,000	* Plant & machinery	37,000
		* Motor cars	33,000
Carried forward	74,000		122,320

Brought forward	74,000		122,320
Capital accounts:		* Office equipment	8,800
Dragge ($^2/_3$)	38,080		
Pullen ($^1/_3$)	19,040		
	131,120		131,120

* Depreciation is made up of the balances on the provisions for depreciation as at 31 December 19-0 (per the balance sheet) plus the additional depreciation for the eight months to 31 August 19-1 (per the profit and loss account).

2. Goodwill

		Old firm		New firm	Adjustment	
		£		£	£	
Dragge	($^2/_3$)	20,000	($^1/_3$)	10,000	10,000	(Cr)
Pullen	($^1/_3$)	10,000	($^1/_3$)	10,000	–	
Pushkin			($^1/_3$)	10,000	10,000	(Dr)
		30,000		30,000		

3. Bank account

	£		£
Sales	299,800	Balance b/f	4,800
Pushkin – capital	30,000	Purchases	159,400
		Wages and salaries	52,000
		Rent, rates and insurance	20,000
		Heating & lighting	2,500
		Sundry expenses	4,000
		Shover – interest	2,500
		repayment	25,000
		Drawings Dragge	15,000
		Pullen	20,000
		Pushkin	3,000
		Balance c/d	21,600
	329,800		329,800

7.6.2 EXERCISE (a comprehensive exercise to test overall grasp of topic)

Johanne, Sebastian and Bach were in partnership, making up their accounts annually to 30 June. At 30 June 19-2 their balance sheet was as follows:

	Cost	Depn.	Net	
	£	£	£	
Fixed assets				
Freehold premises	40,000	10,000	30,000	
Motor cars	20,000	12,000	8,000	
Office machinery	18,000	8,000	10,000	
	78,000	30,000	48,000	
Current assets				
Stock		8,000		
Debtors		3,000		
Bank		9,000		
		20,000		
less Current liabilities				
Creditors		6,000	14,000	
			62,000	

Capitals		Current a/cs	
	£	£	£
Johanne	30,000	5,000	35,000
Sebastian	15,000	3,000	18,000
Bach	15,000	(6,000)	9,000
	60,000	2,000	62,000

The partners' policy was to provide for depreciation on fixed assets on cost as follows: freehold premises $2^{1}/_{2}$%; motor cars 20%; office machinery 25%.

Johanne received a salary of £10,000 p.a. and the partners were allowed interest on capitals at 10% p.a. and were charged with interest at the same rate on drawings. Profits and losses were shared: Johanne $^{1}/_{2}$, Sebastian $^{1}/_{4}$ Bach $^{1}/_{4}$.

Johanne retired on 31 December 19-2 and the partners agreed the following:

1. Johanne should take over one of the firm's cars at a valuation of £4,000. The car had been purchased for £8,000 on 1 July 19-1. Of the amount due to Johanne on his retirement, £30,000 should be transferred from his capital account to a loan account carrying interest at 10% p.a. The balance of his capital account was paid to him on 31 December 19-2.

2. The fixed assets should be revalued as follows at 31 December 19-2: Freehold premises £60,000; motor cars (other than the one taken by Johanne) £6,000; office machinery £4,000.

3. Goodwill to be valued at £20,000, but not to be recorded in the books.

4. Sebastian and Bach would continue as partners after Johanne's retirement on the following terms:

    (i) The balances on their current accounts at 31 December 19-2 should be transferred to their capital accounts as at that date. They would adjust the balances on their capital accounts as at 31 December 19-2 (after the transfers from their current accounts) to £25,000 by payments into or withdrawals from the firm's bank account.

    (ii) Sebastian and Bach would share Johannes' duties between them, for which Sebastian would receive a salary of £7,000 p.a. and Bach a salary of £3,000 p.a.

    (iii) The balance of profits and losses would be shared equally.

    (iv) Depreciation of fixed assets would be charged at the same rates as before, but calculated on the new valuations.

The following details were extracted from the books of the partnership for the year to 30 June 19-3:

		£
Receipts:	Cash sales	60,000
	Cash received from debtors	34,000
Payments:	Purchases	28,000
	Selling expenses	6,000
	Distribution expenses	4,000
	Wages and salaries	20,000
	General expenses	3,000
	Drawings: (to 31.12. 19-2)	
	Johanne	4,000
	Sebastian	6,000
	Bach	5,000
	(1 Jan - 30 June 19-3):	
	Sebastian	4,000
	Bach	5,000
Trade debtors at 30 June 19-3		5,000
Trade creditors at 30 June 19-3		7,000

The following were owing at 30 June 19-3:

Selling expenses £1,200; distribution expenses £800; general expenses £200.

Stock at 30 June was £4,000.

Sales occurred evenly throughout the year and a uniform profit margin was earned on all sales.

REQUIRED

(a) The trading and profit and loss and appropriation accounts of the firm of Johanne, Sebastian and Bach for the six months to 31 December 19-2.

(b) The trading and profit and loss and appropriation accounts of the firm of Sebastian and Bach for the six months to 30 June 19-3.

(c) The balance sheet of Sebastian and Bach as at 30 June 19-3.

(d) The partners' capital and current accounts for the year to 30 June 19-3.

7.7 KEY POINTS TO REMEMBER

1. A partnership change constitutes the termination of one partnership and the commencement of a new one.

2. Separate accounts should be prepared for the old and new partnerships. Do this by preparing the profit and loss and appropriation accounts for the two firms in columnar form.

3. Apportion revenue and expenses as directed by the question and perform the arithmetical calculations very carefully.

4. Accruals and prepayments of expenses must be treated with care; adjust for these before apportioning the revenue and expenses in the profit and loss accounts.

5. Remember that partners' salaries, interest on capitals and drawings, although stated in questions on an annual basis, must be calculated on a time basis before and after the partnership change.

6. Revaluation of fixed assets. Adjust the fixed asset accounts for revaluation using a Revaluation account to complete the double entry. Credit increases in values to the Revaluation account and debit that account with decreases in values. Transfer all provisions for depreciation on those assets up to the date of the revaluation to the credit of the Revaluation account.

7. Profits or losses on revaluation of fixed assets. Transfer the balance on the Revaluation account to the old partners' capital accounts in their old profit sharing ratios.

8. Goodwill. Note carefully whether or not goodwill is to be recorded in the ledger for inclusion in future balance sheets. Do not leave the goodwill in the books if the question states that a goodwill account is not to be opened or that goodwill account is not to be shown in the balance sheet in future. Make the goodwill adjustments in the partners' capital accounts. The old partners' accounts must be credited with their shares of goodwill in their old profit sharing ratios; the capital accounts of the partners in the new firm must be debited with goodwill in their new profit sharing ratios. Follow the method shown in 7.5.1 above.

9. Outgoing partners. Transfer the balance on an outgoing partner's Drawings account to his Current account and, after the Current account has been adjusted for the partner's share of profit to the date of retirement, close the Current account off to his Capital account. Note carefully how the question requires the final balance on the outgoing partner's Capital account to be treated, i.e. repaid to him, or transferred to a loan account.

10. Read the question very carefully two or three times before commencing your answer. Tick every figure and instruction in the question as you deal with it in your answer to make sure you do not miss anything.

COMMON ERRORS

- failure to apportion the gross profit correctly between the periods before and after a change.
- failure to prepare separate profit and loss accounts for the periods before and after a partnership change.
- arithmetic errors in calculating the apportionment of revenue and expenses.

- failure to apportion annual salaries to partners or annual rates of interest on capitals and drawings on a time basis.
- failure to transfer the depreciation provisions on revalued assets up to the date of revaluation to the Revaluation account.
- failure to deal with the revaluation of fixed assets altogether.
- showing revalued assets in subsequent balance sheets as 'at cost' instead of 'as at valuation'.
- failure to deal correctly, or at all, with goodwill.

7.8   EXAMINATION QUESTIONS

QUESTION 1   (Author's question, after JMB)

Holley and Iveagh are in partnership sharing profits equally after allowing for interest on capitals of 10 per cent per annum. They admit Sprigge as a partner on 1 January 19-3, on which date Sprigge pays £25,000 into the partnership bank account as his capital and payment for goodwill. Goodwill is calculated as 3 year's purchase of the average profits for the past two years, which were as follows: year to 31 December 19-1: £24,000; year to 31 December 19-2: £28,000. No goodwill account is to be opened in the books.

It is agreed that Sprigge will receive interest on his capital account and a salary of £8,000 per annum. Profits are to be shared by Holley, Iveagh and Sprigge in the proportion 3:2:1 respectively.

The following information is available at 31 December 19-3:

	Capitals at 1 Jan 19-3	Current accounts at 1 Jan 19-3	Drawings in 19-3
	£	£	£
Holley	25,000	8,000 (Cr)	18,000
Iveagh	30,000	1,600 (Dr)	11,000
Sprigge			10,000

The net profit on trading for the year to 31 December 19-3 is £39,400.

You are required to prepare the partnership profit and loss appropriation account and the partners' capital and current accounts for the year to 31 December 19-3.   *(20 marks)*

QUESTION 2   (Cambridge November 1987)

The following trial balance as at 30 June 19-7 has been extracted from the books of Graham Pool, a car repairer:

	£	£
Sales		240,000
Cost of sales	144,000	
Establishment and administrative expenses	25,000	
Sales and distribution expenses	37,000	
Graham Pool – capital account at 1 July 19–6		92,000
Graham Pool – drawings	15,000	
Freehold property: at cost	50,000	
provision for depreciation at 1 July 19-6		6,000
Fixtures and fittings: at cost	21,000	
provision for depreciation at 1 July 19-6		4,200
Stock	32,000	
Debtors	7,000	
Creditors		4,000
Balance at bank	15,200	
	£346,200	£346,200

It has now been discovered that effect has not yet been given, in the accounting records of Graham Pool, to the admission of Thomas Stream into partnership with Graham Pool as from 1 April 19-7.

On becoming a partner, Thomas Stream brought in as his capital motor vehicles valued at £20,000 and stock valued at £10,000; neither of these items has been included in the above trial balance. However, all the stock brought into the business by Thomas Stream was sold before 30 June 19-7 and the proceeds have been included in the sales of £240,000 shown in the above trial balance.

Goodwill was valued at £32,000 at 1 April 19-7, but it has been decided that a goodwill account will not be opened.

The partnership agreement provides for interest of 10% per annum on the balance of partners' capital accounts and the balance of the profit or loss to be shared between Graham Pool and Thomas Stream in the ratio 3:1 respectively.

A current account is to be opened for each partner for transfers from the profit and loss appropriation account and drawings.

The partners have agreed to continue the depreciation policy introduced by Graham Pool as follows:

**Percentage per annum on cost of assets
held at each accounting year end**

Freehold property	2
Fixtures and fittings	10
Motor vehicles	25

It can be assumed that gross profit, establishment and administrative expenses, and sales and distribution expenses have accrued uniformly during the year ended 30 June 19-7.

REQUIRED

Prepare in good style the trading and profit and loss account for the year ended 30 June 19-7 and a balance sheet as at that date. *(25 marks)*

QUESTION 3 (Associated Examining Board June 1988)

Page, Dickson and Saville are in partnership and own a sports business which manufactures sports clothing and retails sports goods and equipment. The latest available partnership balance sheet as at 29 February 19-8 revealed the following:

	£	£
Fixed assets, at net book value		116,325
Current assets		
Stocks	73,500	
Debtors	51,900	
	125,400	
Creditors, less than one year		
Bank overdraft	11,900	
Creditors	63,000 (74,900)	50,500
		£166,825
Capital accounts		
Page	40,000	
Dickson	35,000	
Saville	50,000	
		125,000
Current accounts		
Page	16,325	
Dickson	12,100	
Saville	13,400	
		41,825
		166,825

Additional information.

(1) Page and Dickson wish to expand the retail base of the business and to raise the necessary capital they have agreed to transfer the manufacturing activities to Saville.

(2) After settlement of his capital and current account balances Saville has agreed to pay cash for the net assets of the manufacturing business transferred to him.

(3) The net assets to be transferred to Saville were as follows:

	Values in the balance sheet of Page, Dickson and Saville	Agreed transfer value to Saville
	£	£
Fixed assets	64,950	76,500
Stocks	41,500	39,200
Debtors	43,200	41,450
Creditors	39,000	39,000

(4) Any profit or loss on transfer of net assets to Saville is to be shared equally by the remaining two partners and debited/credited to their capital accounts.

(5) Page and Dickson have agreed the following terms and details for their new partnership:

(i) Each partner would bring in additional capital of £15,000 on 1 March 19-8.

(ii) Each partner would be entitled to interest on capital at 8% per annum for the year ending 28 February 19-9 and the balance of profits and losses would be shared equally.

(iii) Partnership salaries have been agreed at: Page £9,000 and Dickson £7,000 p.a.

(iv) The new partnership estimate that profits from the retail business before interest on capital and partners' salaries will be £65,000 for the year to 28 February 19-9.

REQUIRED

(a) Prepare a balance sheet for the partnership of Page and Dickson on 1 March 19-8, assuming that Saville takes over the manufacturing business on the terms agreed.   *(12 marks)*

(b) Prepare a forecast profit and loss appropriation account for the new partnership of Page and Dickson on the basis of the above information for the year ending 28 February 19-9.   *(7 marks)*

(c) Briefly discuss the advantages and disadvantages to Page and Dickson of selling the sports clothing manufacturing business to Saville.   *(4 marks)*

(Total 23 marks)

QUESTION 4   (Cambridge November 1989)

Short and Tall have been trading in partnership for several years. The partnership agreement provides for

- annual accounts to be drawn up for each financial year to 31 December.

- partnership salaries of £10,000 per annum for each partner.

- the balance of profits or losses to be shared in the ratio Short 2 parts to Tall 1 part.

The partners have employed a Manager, Long, for the last two years and paid him a salary of £15,000 per annum.

As from 1 September 19-8 Short and Tall have admitted Long to the partnership. The new partnership agreement has retained the same financial year but amended the salaries to £12,000 per annum for each of the three partners and also provides for profits or losses to be shared by Short, Tall and Long in the ratio 3:2:1 respectively.

You are to take the following details into account for the financial year ended 31 December 19-8.

	£
Sales	600,000
Purchases	420,000
Rent & Rates	6,000
Light & Heat	12,600
Staff Salaries	
(including Long when employee)	40,000
Selling expenses	21,000
Distribution expenses	9,300
Interest on Bank Loan and Overdraft	7,500
Bad debts	8,700
The stock valuation at 1/1/-8 was	60,000
and at 31/12/-8 was	90,000

The new partnership got off to a good start and sales in the period 1 September to 31 December 19-8 amounted to £280,000.

REQUIRED

(a) Prepare trading profit and loss and appropriation accounts for the year ended 31 December 19-8 showing clearly the results attributable to each of the TWO partnerships. *(19 marks)*

(b) Give three reasons why a manager might be offered a partner's role in a business. *(6 marks)*

QUESTION 5 (London June 1988)

Winston, Nancy and Maurice are in partnership, sharing profits and losses in the ratio 2:2:1. Interest is charged on drawings at 5% per annum, and interest is credited on capital at 6% per annum. On 31 May 19-8, the balance sheet of the partnership was as follows:

	£	£	£
Fixed Assets:			
Freehold Land and Buildings			180,000
Machinery			60,000
Office Equipment			15,000
Motor Vehicles			35,000
			290,000
Current Assets:			
Stock		34,000	
Debtors		41,000	
		75,000	
Current Liabilities:			
Creditors	45,000		
Bank	10,000	55,000	20,000
			310,000
Capital Accounts:			
Winston		140,000	
Nancy		100,000	
Maurice		70,000	310,000

The partners have now realised that their capital account balances do not reflect the following matters:

(i) Interest had not been charged on the following drawings:

Date	Winston	Nancy	Maurice
19-7	£	£	£
1 June	6,000	15,000	10,000
1 December	9,000	–	5,000

94

(ii) Interest on partners' capital at 6% per annum has not been credited.

Partners' capital, *for the purpose of interest* calculations, is taken as:

	£
Winston	70,000
Nancy	50,000
Maurice	30,000

These amounts were unchanged throughout the year.

Maurice decided to retire on 1 June 19-8, on the following terms:

(1) He will receive £8,000 payable by cheque immediately.

(2) The freehold land and buildings are to be revalued at £250,000.

(3) Goodwill is to be valued at £100,000.

(4) Maurice will take ownership of a partnership vehicle at its balance sheet value of £9,000.

(5) The balance of Maurice's capital will be left on loan with the partnership.

It was decided to open a goodwill account in the partnership books.

You are required:

(a) To prepare the capital accounts of the three partners, showing in detail all the adjustments necessary, and the revised balances both at (i) 31 May 19-8 and (ii) after Maurice's retirement on 1 June 19-8. *(14 marks)*

(b) To prepare the balance sheet of the partnership of Winston and Nancy as at 1 June 19-8. *(6 marks)*

(c) To give two reasons why the partnership should charge interest at only 5% per annum on partners' drawings when it is having to pay 14% per annum to the partnership's bank in respect of its overdraft. *(5 marks)*

(Total 25 marks)

8 PARTNERSHIP AMALGAMATIONS, DISSOLUTION; SALE OF PARTNERSHIPS TO LIMITED COMPANIES

> Questions on these topics
> - require application of principles already learned in Chapter 7
> - test understanding of entries required to close partnership books

8.1 PARTNERSHIP AMALGAMATIONS

Sometimes two or more partnerships amalgamate. Be prepared to suggest reasons for such amalgamations:

(a) the firms have worked together well in the past.

(b) the businesses are similar and amalgamation will enable them to achieve economies of scale e.g. they may be able to purchase goods more cheaply by taking advantage of bulk discount; or they may be able to share the same premises.

(c) the businesses are complementary e.g. car sales and car servicing.

(d) a variety of skills, expertise and experience may be concentrated in one firm.

(e) the enlarged firm may be in a position to fulfil larger, more profitable contracts or act for more prestigious clients. e.g. firms of accountants amalgamate to enable them to act for larger, more profitable clients.

(f) the geographical area of operations may be enlarged where the firms are situated in different parts of the country or of the world.

Accounting procedure

Basically, the procedure for answering questions of this type is to add the balance sheets of the firms together after making any adjustments necessary to the separate balance sheets to ensure that the partners' capital accounts realistically reflect their true interests in their respective firms.

The procedure involved in adjusting the balance sheets are those already covered in Chapter 7:

For each firm

1. Adjust the partners' capital accounts for goodwill and profits or losses on revalued assets.

2. Deal with any assets not being transferred to the new firm. Assets taken over by partners should be debited to their capital accounts at the agreed value. Assets sold should be dealt with as normal disposals and profit or loss on disposal transferred to the capital accounts in the partners' old profit sharing ratios.

3. Give effect to any other requirements of the question such as transfers of current account balances to capital accounts, or adjustment of capital account balances to be included in the new firm by the introduction or withdrawal of cash.

4. The adjusted balance sheets may now be combined.

8.1.1 EXAMPLE.   Joyner & Co.

John and George are partners in the firm of John & Co., sharing profits and losses equally. Nerissa and Sally are partners in the firm of Nerissa & Co. and share profits and losses in the ratio of $3/5$ and $2/5$ respectively.

The partners in each of the firms agree to amalgamate under the name of Joyner & Co. as from 1 October 19-9. The profits and losses in the new firm will be shared as follows:

John	25%	
George	30%	
Nerissa	25%	
Sally	20%	

The balance sheets of the separate partnerships at 30 September 19-9 are:

	John & Co.	Nerissa & Co.
	£	£
Fixed assets	12,000	16,000
Stocks	8,400	24,000
Cash	9,600	4,000
	30,000	44,000
Capital accounts: John	10,000	
George	20,000	
Nerissa		20,000
Sally		24,000
	30,000	44,000

For the purpose of the amalgamation the assets are to be valued at the following amounts:

	John & Co.	Nerissa & Co.
	£	£
Fixed assets	18,000	20,000
Stocks	11,200	17,600
Goodwill	8,000	32,000

The new partnership does not intend to show goodwill in its balance sheet.

The capitals of the partners in the new firm are to be:

	£
John	10,000
George	15,000
Nerissa	30,000
Sally	25,000

REQUIRED

(a)   The capital accounts of the partners showing the entries required as a result of the amalgamation.

(b)   The opening balance sheet of Joyner & Co. as at 1 October 19-9.

ANSWER

(a)

Capital accounts

	John	George	Nerissa	Sally
	£	£	£	£
Balances b/f	10,000	20,000	20,000	24,000
Revaluation account	4,400	4,400	(1,440)	(960)
Goodwill	(6,000)	(8,000)	9,200	4,800
	8,400	16,400	27,760	27,840
Bank	1,600	(1,400)	2,240	(2,840)
Balance c/f	10,000	15,000	30,000	25,000

(b)
Joyner & Co.
Balance sheet as at 1 October 19-9

			£	£
Fixed assets (18,000 + 20,000)				38,000
Stocks (11,200 + 17,600)			28,800	
Cash (13,600 +1,600 + 2,240 - 1,400 - 2,840)			13,200	42,000
				80,000
Capital accounts:	John		10,000	
	George		15,000	
	Nerissa		30,000	
	Sally		25,000	80,000

Working: Revaluation accounts

		John & Co. £	Nerissa & Co. £
Fixed assets		6,000	4,000
Stocks		2,800	(6,400)
		8,800	(2,400)
Capital accounts	John ($^1/_2$)	(4,400)	
	George ($^1/_2$)	(4,400)	
	Nerissa ($^3/_5$)		1,440
	Sally ($^2/_5$)		960

Goodwill		Old firms £	New firm £	Adjustment £
John & Co £8,000				
	John ($^1/_2$)	4,000	(25%) 10,000	6,000 (dr.)
	George ($^1/_2$)	4,000	(30%) 12,000	8,000 (dr.)
Nerissa & Co £32,000				
	Nerissa $^3/_5$	19,200	(25%) 10,000	9,200 (cr.)
	Sally $^2/_5$	12,800	(20%) 8,000	4,800 (cr.)
		40,000	40,000	

8.1.2 EXERCISE (for practice in partnership amalgamation.)
Fortnum, Marks & Co.

Chas. Fortnum and Tony Mason are carrying on business in partnership; Stan Marks and Mike Spencer are also in partnership and carrying on a similar type of business to that of Fortnum and Mason. The two firms agree to amalgamate as from 1 September 19-1 as Fortnum, Marks & Co.

Fortnum and Mason have shared profits and losses in the ratio of 8:7; Marks and Spencer have shared profits and losses in the ratio 3:2. The balance sheets of the two firms on 31 August 19-1 are as follows:

	Fortnum & Mason £	Marks & Spencer £
Freehold property	15,000	10,000
Fixtures	3,600	2,800
Vehicles	5,000	3,400
Stock	11,800	13,400
Debtors	14,200	13,000
Carried forward	49,600	42,600

	£	£
Brought forward	49,600	42,600
Investments	3,000	
Balance at bank	8,400	6,200
	61,000	48,800
Capital accounts: Fortnum	24,000	
Mason	21,000	
Marks		22,000
Spencer		15,600
Current accounts: Fortnum	2,000	
Mason	1,200	
Creditors	12,800	11,200
	61,000	48,800

The partners agree that the following provisions should be made effective on the amalgamation:

1. The freehold property and fixtures of Marks and Spencer are to be sold and this is done on 1 September 19-1. The proceeds of sale amount to £20,000.

2. Fortnum, Marks & Co. are to take over the assets of the old partnerships at the following values:

	Fortnum & Mason £	Marks & Spencer £
Stock	11,400	12,400
Vehicles	4,600	3,000
Fixtures	4,000	
Freehold property	19,000	

3. Provision is to be made for doubtful debts in the sums of £800 by Fortnum and Mason, and £1,000 by Marks and Spencer; both firms are to allow for discounts of $2^1/2\%$ to be received from their creditors.

4. Fortnum is to take over his firm's investments at £2,400.

5. Fortnum and Mason's goodwill is valued at £15,000 and that of Marks and Spencer at £10,000. Fortnum, Marks and Co. will not show goodwill in its balance sheet.

6. As from 1 September 19-1 the profit sharing ratios are to be:

Fortnum	30%
Mason	25%
Marks	25%
Spencer	20%

7. Fortnum, Marks & Co. will have a capital of £100,000 which will be provided by the partners in the same ratios as they share profits and losses; any adjustments necessary for this purpose will be made by the partners paying cash to or withdrawing cash from the firm's bank account.

REQUIRED

For the old firms:
(a) the revaluation accounts
(b) the partners' capital accounts;

For Fortnum, Marks & Co.
(c) the partners' capital accounts
(d) the cash account
(e) the opening balance sheet as at the start of business on 1 September 19-1.

99

8.2 DISSOLUTION OF PARTNERSHIPS

Partnership assets are sold; profits or losses on realisation are apportioned to the partners' capital accounts in their profit sharing ratio; the balance of cash is used to pay creditors and expenses of dissolution and, finally, to repay the balances on their capital accounts to the partners.

Note: Unrecorded goodwill and asset revaluation are not relevant in this topic.

Accounting:

Open a Realisation account to record the sale of assets and proceed to make the accounting entries in the following order:

		Debit	Credit
1	Assets at net book value	Realisation a/c	Asset a/cs
2	Proceeds of sale of assets	Bank (cash)	Realisation a/c
3	Assets taken over by partners (at valuation)	Capital a/c of partner concerned	Realisation a/c
4	Costs of dissolution	Realisation a/c	Bank (cash)
5	Payment of creditors	Creditors' a/cs	Bank (cash)
6	Discounts received from creditors	Creditors' a/cs	Realisation a/c
7	Cash received from debtors	Bank (cash)	Debtors' a/cs
8	Bad debts and discounts allowed	Realisation a/c	Debtors' a/cs
9	Credit balance on Realisation a/c (profit on realisation)	Realisation a/c	Partners' capital a/cs
or	Debit balance on Realisation a/c (loss on realisation)	Partners' capital a/cs	Realisation a/c
	(in profit/loss sharing ratio)		
10	Repayment of partner's loan to firm	Partner's loan a/c	Bank
11	Repayment of partners' capitals	Partners' capital a/cs	Bank
	Debit balance on partner's capital account	Bank	Partner's capital a/c

All accounts should now be closed.

8.2.1 EXAMPLE

Lilley, Dilley and Willey have been carrying on business in partnership for some years sharing profits in the ratio 3:2:1. On 31 December 19-3 they decided to dissolve the partnership. On that date the firm's balance sheet was as follows:

		Cost	Depn	Net
		£	£	£
Fixed assets:	Plant and equipment	25,000	13,000	12,000
	Motor vehicles	18,000	15,000	3,000
	Office machinery	3,000	2,400	600
		46,000	30,400	15,600
Current assets:				
Stock			21,000	
Debtors			6,400	
Bank			3,800	
			31,200	
less Current liabilities: Creditors			2,700	28,500
Carried forward				44,100

		£	£
Brought forward			44,100
less Loan from Lilley			5,000
			39,100
Capitals:	Lilley	20,000	
	Dilley	10,000	
	Willey	2,000	32,000
Current accounts:	Lilley	4,000	
	Dilley	5,000	
	Willey	(1,900)	7,100
			39,100

Willey was allowed to retain his car which was valued at £4,000. The remaining assets realised the following amounts on the 1 January 19-4.

	£
Plant and equipment	10,000
Motor cars	5,000
Office machinery	400
Stock	24,000
Debtors	6,200

All creditors were paid and discount received amounted to £74.
The expenses of dissolution amounted to £800.

REQUIRED

Show the following accounts with the entries in them to record the dissolution of the partnership:
(i) Realisation account
(ii) the partners' capital accounts in columnar form
(iii) the firm's bank account.

ANSWER

Workings   **Journal entries to close asset accounts:**

	Dr.	Cr.
	£	£
Realisation account	12,000	
Provision for depreciation of plant and equipment	13,000	
Plant and equipment at cost		25,000
Realisation account	3,000	
Provision for depreciation of motor vehicles	15,000	
Motor vehicles at cost		18,000
Realisation account	600	
Provision for depreciation of office machinery	2,400	
Office machinery at cost		3,000
Realisation account	21,000	
Stock		21,000
Capital account – Willey	4,000	
Realisation account		4,000
Realisation account	200	
Sundry debtors		200
Sundry creditors	74	
Realisation account		74

(i)

Realisation account

	£		£
Plant and equipment	12,000	Capital - Willey	4,000
Motor vehicles	3,000	Bank	39,400
Office machinery	600	Sundry creditors	74
Stock	21,000		
Sundry debtors	200		
Bank – dissolution expenses	800		
Capitals – Lillee ($^3/_6$) 2937			
Dilley ($^2/_6$) 1958			
Willey ($^1/_6$) 979	5,874		
	43,474		43,474

(ii)

Capital accounts

	Lillee	Dilley	Willey
	£	£	£
Balances b/f	20,000	10,000	2,000
Current accounts	4,000	5,000	(1,900)
Realisation account	2,937	1,958	979
Bank			2,921
	26,937	16,958	4,000
Realisation account – car			(4,000)
Bank	(26,937)	(16,958)	
	–	–	–

(iii)

Bank

	£		£
Balance b/f	3,800	Sundry creditors	2,626
Realisation a/c	39,400	Realisation a/c costs	800
Sundry debtors	6,200	Lillee - loan account	5,000
Capital – Willey	2,921	Capitals – Lillee	26,937
		– Dilley	16,958
	52,321		52,321

8.2.2 EXERCISE (for practice in closing partnership books on dissolution of firm.)

Penn, Punch and Staple, partners in an office supplies business, made up their accounts to 30 June 19-0. The following was their balance sheet at that date:

Fixed assets	Cost	Depn.	Net
	£	£	£
Leasehold premises	21,000	16,000	5,000
Delivery vans	7,000	5,000	2,000
Fixtures and fittings	3,000	1,000	2,000
	31,000	22,000	9,000
Current assets: Stocks		12,000	
Debtors		3,400	
Carried forward		15,400	9,000

		£	£	£
Brought forward			15,400	9,000
less Current liabilities:				
Trade creditors		3,900		
Bank overdraft		900	4,800	10,600
				19,600
Less: Loan from Quire				3,000
				16,600
Capitals:	Penn	5,000		
	Punch	2,000		
	Staple	2,000		9,000
Current accounts	Penn	3,400		
	Punch	2,500		
	Staple	1,700		7,600
				16,600

Penn, Punch and Staple have always shared profits and losses in the ratio 2:2:1.

On 30 June 19-0, the partners agreed to terminate the partnership; Penn took over one of the delivery vans, which had a net book value of £1,000, at a valuation of £2,500. Staple took over, at a valuation of £6,000, stock which had cost £6,500.

A ready buyer was found for the leasehold premises, the remaining delivery vans, fixtures and fittings, and the balance of the stock, at an agreed price of £11,500. Debtors realised the sum of £3,225.

After the creditors had been paid in full, the partners received the monies due to them on capital account or paid what was due to the firm from them.

REQUIRED

The entries to record the above events in

(i) the Realisation account

(ii) the firm's bank account, and

(iii) the partners' capital accounts.

8.3 INSOLVENT PARTNERS (Garner v. Murray)

It may happen that a partner is insolvent and unable to clear a debit balance on his capital account on the dissolution of the firm. The debit balance on his capital account must be shared by the other partners in the ratio of the last agreed balances on their capital accounts; in practice, this means the balances shown on their latest balance sheet. This follows the decision in a case known as Garner v. Murray. It must only be applied when the partner concerned is insolvent, and this is clearly stated or implied in an examination question.

8.3.1 EXAMPLE:

Hall, Cotton, and Loss were in partnership sharing profits and losses equally. On 1 April 19-2, the partners decided to dissolve the partnership. After realising all the assets, the balance sheet appeared as follows:

		£
Cash at bank		27,000
Capital accounts:	Hall	18,000
	Cotton	12,000
	Loss	(3,000)
		27,000

Loss was unable to pay the amount of the balance due from him to the firm.

REQUIRED

The partners' capital accounts showing the entries required to close the books.

ANSWER

Partners' capital accounts

19-2		£ H	£ C	£ L	19-2		£ H	£ C	£ L
Apr 1	Bal b/f L-Cap.			3,000	Apr 1	Bal b/f Cap.a/cs	18,000	12,000	
	(18:12)	1,800	1,200			L & C			3,000
	Bank	16,200	10,800						
		18,000	12,000	3,000			18,000	12,000	3,000

Note: The debit balance on Loss's capital account is NOT shared by Hall and Cotton in their profit/loss sharing ratios.

8.3.2 EXERCISE (on the application of Garner v. Murray.)

Bent, Bold and Broke have been in partnership for some years sharing profits and losses in ratio 3:2:1.

At 31 December 19-1, their summarised balance sheet was as follows:

		£	£
Fixed assets			22,000
Current assets	Stock	18,000	
	Debtors	5,000	
	Bank	3,000	
		26,000	
less Current liabilities			
	Trade creditors	6,000	20,000
			42,000

	Capitals	Current accounts
	£	£
Bent	20,000	2,000
Bold	20,000	(2,000)
Broke	5,000	(3,000)
	45,000	(3,000) 42,000

On 1 January 19-2 the firm was dissolved and only £20,000 was obtained from the sale of the fixed assets and stock. Debtors realised £4,000. The creditors were paid in full.

Broke proved to be insolvent and therefore unable to contribute cash to meet the debit balance on his capital account.

REQUIRED

The Realisation account, the bank account and the partners' capital accounts, showing the entries required to close the books of the partnership.

8.4   SALE OF PARTNERSHIP TO LIMITED COMPANY

A partnership may be sold to an existing limited company, or the partners may form a limited company and sell the partnership business to it in order to obtain the benefits of limited liability. In either case, it makes no difference to the entries required in the partnership books.

The limited company may pay for the partnership business in cash, or by issuing shares and possibly debentures to the partners; or by a combination of cash, shares and debentures.

Accounting entries. Steps 1-9 for the dissolution of a partnership still apply (see 8.2) but the procedure which follows step 9 is modified as follows:

	Dr.	**Cr.**
Purchase consideration	Account opened for --- Ltd.	Realisation a/c
Payment in cash	Bank	--- Ltd.
Payment in preference shares	Preference shares in ---Ltd,	--- Ltd.
Payment in ordinary shares	Ordinary shares in ---Ltd.	--- Ltd.
Payment in debentures	Debentures in ---Ltd.	--- Ltd.
Closure of partners' capital accounts	Partners' capital accounts	Bank, preference, ordinary shares, debentures, in--Ltd. co. a/cs.

Follow the distribution of shares, debentures and cash to the partners as directed in the question.

In the absence of any directions in the question, where the partners are to continue as directors of the limited company, receiving salaries and shares of profits as hitherto, use the following procedure:

Partners' salaries:

Award the partners directors' salaries equal to their partnership salaries.

Partners' loans to the partnership.

Allocate debentures to any partner who has made to the partnership a loan which will be transferred to the limited company. Where the rate of interest on the debentures is different from that paid on the loan, the amount of the debentures allocated to the partner must be such as will give him the same amount of interest each year as he received from the partnership.

Partnership shares of profit.

Preserve the partners' profit sharing ratio by allocating ordinary shares in their respective capital/profit sharing ratio, so that the balance on the capital account of the partner with the lowest capital/profit sharing ratio is satisfied in full by his allocation of ordinary shares.

Satisfy any balances remaining on partners' capital accounts with preference shares (or cash).

8.4.1 EXAMPLE (sale of a partnership to a limited company.)

Arthur, Bill and Charles had been in partnership for some years sharing profits in the ratio 2:2:1. At 30 June 19-4 their summarised balance sheet was as follows:

		£	£
Fixed assets (at net book value)			140,000
Current assets:	Stock	40,000	
	Debtors	28,000	
	Bank	9,000	
		77,000	
less Current liabilities		17,000	60,000
			200,000
less Loan from Arthur (carrying interest at 10% p.a.)			20,000
			180,000
Capitals	Arthur		80,000
	Bill		60,000
	Charles		40,000
			180,000

On 1 July 19-4, the partners decided to form a limited company, ABC Ltd. to take over the business of Arthur, Bill and Charles.The purchase consideration was satisfied by the issue to the partners of 180,000 ordinary shares of £1 each, 25,000 12% Preference shares of £1 each and sufficient 8% debenture stock to give Arthur the same return on his loan as he had received from the partnership.

REQUIRED

The entries to close the partnership books in:

(a) Realisation account

(b) ABC Ltd. account

(c) Accounts for the purchase consideration

(d) Partners' capital accounts.

ANSWER

Working: Allocation of 8% debenture stock:

In partnership, Arthur received annual interest on his loan of £20,000 × 10% = £2,000. Amount of 8% debenture stock which will give Arthur £2,000 p.a. on loan of £20,000 = £20,000 × $^{10}/_8$ = £25,000

Total purchase consideration will be:	£
180,000 ordinary shares of £1 each	180,000
25,000 preference share of £1 each	25,000
£25,000 8 % debenture stock	25,000
	230,000

(a) **Realisation account**

		£		£
Fixed assets		140,000	Creditors	17,000
Stock		40,000	ABC Ltd.	230,000
Debtors		28,000		
Bank		9,000		
Capitals: Arthur	12,000			
Bill	12,000			
Charles	6,000	30,000		
		247,000		247,000

(b) **ABC Ltd.**

	£		£
Realisation account	230,000	10% debenture stock	25,000
		12% Preference shares	25,000
		Ordinary shares	180,000
	230,000		230,000

10 % Debenture stock in ABC Ltd.

	£		£
ABC Ltd.	25,000	Arthur capital account	25,000

12% Preference shares in ABC Ltd.

	£		£
ABC Ltd.	25,000	Capital accounts:	
		Arthur	15,000
		Charles	10,000
	25,000		25,000

Ordinary shares of £1 in ABC Ltd.

	£		£
ABC Ltd.	180,000	Capital accounts	
		Arthur	72,000
		Bill	72,000
		Charles	36,000
	180,000		180,000

Arthur – Loan account

	£		£
Capital account	20,000	Balance b/f	20,000

Capital accounts

	A	B	C		A	B	C
	£	£	£		£	£	£
Ordinary shares	72,000	72,000	36,000	Bal b/f	80,000	60,000	40,000
12% Pref. shares	15,000		10,000	Realisation	12,000	12,000	6,000
8% debenture							
stock	25,000			Loan	20,000		
	112,000	72,000	46,000		112,000	72,000	46,000

Note: Allocation of ordinary shares:

	Arthur	Bill	Charles
Capitals	80,000	60,000	40,000
Profit shares	2	2	1
=	40,000	30,000	40,000

Bill has the least Capital/profit sharing ratio, so will receive whole balance on his capital account in ordinary shares; the allocation of ordinary shares will therefore be:

	Profit sharing ratio	Ordinary share allocation
Arthur	2	72,000
Bill	2	72,000
Charles	1	36,000
		180,000

8.4.2 EXERCISE (for practice in closing partnership books when firm is sold to a limited company)

Dee, Emma and Fay are in partnership sharing profits equally. At 31 March 19-5, the following was the summarised balance sheet of the firm:

		£
Fixed and current assets		75,000
less loan from Dee (carrying interest at 8% p.a.)		5,000
		70,000
Capitals:	Dee	30,000
	Emma	25,000
	Fay	15,000
		70,000

On the same date, Dee, Emma and Fay decided to accept an offer of £90,000 from Enterprise Ltd., an old established company, for their business. The offer consisted of sufficient 10% debenture stock in Enterprise Ltd. to guarantee Dee the same interest annually as she had received on her loan to the partnership, 60,000 ordinary shares of £1 each and the balance in cash.

REQUIRED

(a) The realisation account of the partnership.

(b) The accounts necessary to record the purchase consideration paid by Enterprise Ltd.

(c) The partners' capital accounts.

8.5   KEY POINTS TO REMEMBER

Amalgamation of partnerships.

1. Before amalgamating the businesses, adjust the balance sheets of the individual firms to reflect revised values of assets, asset disposals, or assets taken over by partners, using Revaluation accounts. The resulting balances on the partners' capital accounts will more truly reflect their real investments in the firms being merged.

2. Add the revised balance sheets together. Give effect to any further capital adjustments to be made by the partners in cash.

Dissolution of partnerships.

3. Open a Realisation account. Debit the Realisation account with the net book values of assets being disposed of and the costs of dissolution. Credit the Realisation account with the proceeds of the sale of assets. Transfer any balance on the Realisation account, profit or loss, to the Partners' capital accounts.

4. Repay creditors, then loans by partners and, last of all, settle the balances on the partners' capital accounts.

Debit balance on partner's capital account.

5. Normally settle this by showing a payment by the partner, of the amount required to clear the balance, into the firm's bank account.

6. If, and only if, the question indicates that the partner in question is insolvent, apply the rule in Garner v. Murray. Transfer the debit balance on the insolvent partners' capital account to the other partners in proportion to their last agreed capitals (i.e. capitals shown on their latest balance sheet.)

Sale of partnership to limited company.

7. Open a Realisation account, and accounts for the limited company and for each constituent item of the purchase consideration.

8. Debentures may be allocated to partners who have made loans to the partnership.

9. Where the partners' former profit sharing ratios are to be preserved, allocate the ordinary shares to all partners in profit sharing ratio so that the balance on the capital account of the partner with the lowest capital/profit sharing ratio will be satisfied in full.

10. Close the remaining partners' capital accounts by allocations of preference shares, cash.

COMMON ERRORS

- failure to adjust partners' capital accounts correctly before amalgamation of balance sheets.

- failure to transfer net book values of assets being sold to Realisation account. (Confusion with Revaluation account to which only increases/decreases in asset values are transferred.)

- application of Garner v. Murray when question does not state that partner is insolvent.

- apportioning debit balance on insolvent partner's capital account to other partners' capital accounts in profit/loss sharing ratios.

- inability to choose appropriate method of allocating shares to partners when partnership is sold to a limited company.

8.6 EXAMINATION QUESTIONS

QUESTION 1 (London June 1987)

Beryl and Gordon, who shared profits and losses in the ratio 5:3 respectively, decided to dissolve their partnership on 1 January 19-7. The partnership's balance sheet at that date was as follows:

Fixed Assets:			£	£
Tangible	Premises			45,000
	Vehicle			15,000
Intangible	Goodwill			5,000
				65,000
Current Assets:				
	Stock	7,500		
	Debtors	14,000		
	Bank	12,000		
		33,500		
Current liabilities				
	Creditors	12,500		
			21,000	
				86,000
Capital accounts				
	Beryl	50,000		
	Gordon	36,000		
			86,000	

The premises were sold for £48,000 and Gordon took over the car at an agreed valuation of £8,000. The stock was sold for £6,000, the debtors realised £13,500, and the creditors were paid in full. Expenses of realisation amounted to £600.

(a) Prepare the realisation account, the bank account and the partners' capital accounts to record the above information. *(11 marks)*

(b) Part of the 'expenses of realisation' was a fee of £150 from the accountant who 'closed' off the business books. The partners sent a letter to the accountant asking him to explain why it was considered necessary to make closing entries. They argue that 'no-one is interested in a business which is no longer in existence'. State, with reasons one of the justifications for making the closing entries. *(4 marks)*

(Total 15 marks)

QUESTION 2 (Oxford June 1988)

The partnership of Allegro, Lento and Largo, sharing profits/losses in the ratio 4:3:2, has been in business for many years. Recently, the firm's market share has been declining, and thus, when Largo decides to retire on 31 May19-8, the partnership is dissolved. The final balance sheet of the partnership is:

	£	£	£
Fixed assets (net)			
Premises			103,500
Motor vehicles			20,360
Office equipment			26,000
Carried forward			149,860

	£	£	£
Brought forward			149,860
Current assets			
Stock		12,628	
Debtors		14,734	
Bank		5,282	
		32,644	
Current liabilities			
Creditors	13,260		
Accruals - loan interest	2,250		
	15,510		
		17,134	
		166,994	
Long term liability			
15% Bank loan			50,000
			116,994
Capital:	Allegro	50,000	
	Lento	20,000	
	Largo	40,000	
		110,000	
Current a/cs:	Allegro	10,358	
	Lento	(12,341)	
	Largo	8,977	
		6,994	
		116,994	

Allegro feels that he could run a similar business successfully on a smaller scale from his own home, and therefore elects to take some of the partnership's assets at agreed valuations as follows:

Motor vehicle	£5,200
Office equipment	£7,850

The premises realise £120,000, the remaining vehicles and office equipment £2,080 and £3,160 respectively, and the stock is sold for £2,810. Debtors settle for £11,455, and dissolution costs amount to £1,277. Creditors accept £12,750 in full settlement.

Lento is unable to meet his final obligation to the partnership.

You are required to provide

(i)   The realisation account, bank account and partners' capital accounts, showing the closing entries of the business.   (13 marks)

(ii)   A comment on the advantages and disadvantages faced by Allegro in running a similar business as a sole trader instead of being a member of a partnership.   (4 marks)

(iii)   An indication of the problems that would have faced Allegro and Lento if they had decided to form a new partnership on Largo's retirement.   (3 marks)

(Total 20 marks)

QUESTION 3   (JMB June 1987)

James and Dance were in partnership sharing profits and losses in the ratio 3:1. The Balance Sheet for the partnership at 31 March 19-7 was as follows:

Balance Sheet as at 31 March 19-7

	£	£		£	£
Capital accounts			Fixed Assets		
James	30,000		Plant		37,000
Dance	21,000	51,000	Cars		6,500
Current accounts			Current Assets		
James	4,500		Stock	18,600	
Dance	300		Debtors	9,300	
		4,800	Bank	2,400	
					30,300
Loan: James		6,000			
Creditors		12,000			
		73,800			73,800

The partners agreed to dissolve the partnership on 31 March 19-7. The loan was repaid, the creditors were paid £11,700 in full and final settlement. Dance took over one car for £1,000 and the remaining assets realised the following amounts:

	£
Plant	46,000
Cars	3,500
Stock	17,100
Debtors	8,700

You are required to prepare the following ledger accounts for the dissolution of the partnership:

(a) the Realisation account (9 marks)

(b) the Bank account (5 marks)

(c) the Partners' Capital accounts. (4 marks)

(Total 18 marks)

QUESTION 4 (AEB November 1986)

Mallard, Swan and Coote were trading as partners, but without a partnership agreement. On 30 June 19-6 they decided to form a limited company, Wildbirds Ltd. to take over the partnership's business activities. The company was incorporated with an authorised capital of 100,000 ordinary shares of £1 each.

The balance sheet of the partnership as at 30 June 19-6 was as follows:

	Mallard	Swan	Coote	Total
	£	£	£	£
Capital accounts	18,000	12,000	8,000	38,000
Current accounts				
Balances at 1 July 19-5	11,500	6,000	7,500	
Net profit share for year	9,000	9,000	9,000	
	20,500	15,000	16,500	
less drawings	11,000	8,500	6,500	
	9,500	6,500	10,000	26,000
				64,000
Long term loan from Mallard				24,000
				88,000

Represented by:

	At cost £	Aggregate Depreciation £	Net £
Fixed assets			
Freehold land and buildings	40,000	8,000	32,000
Plant and machinery	30,000	11,000	19,000
Motor vehicles	15,000	6,000	9,000
	85,000	25,000	60,000
Current assets			
Stock in trade		15,000	
Trade debtors		18,000	
Balance at bank		12,000	
		45,000	
less Current liabilities			
Trade creditors		17,000	28,000
			88,000

The following additional information is given.

(1) It was agreed that Swan and Coote would take over privately all the motor vehicles at a total valuation of £5,900. (Swan's share £4,000, Coote £1,900).

(2) It was agreed that the new company would require a commencing bank balance of £10,000.

(3) The assets below are to be transferred to Wildbirds Ltd. at the following valuations

	£
Freehold premises	50,000
Plant and machinery	10,000
Stock in trade	14,000
Trade debtors	17,300

As a result of the asset re-valuations in notes (1) and (3) a profit of £4,200 was made by the partnership.

(4) Wildbirds Ltd. are to take over the trade creditors at book value.

(5) No interest had been charged in the profit and loss account on Mallard's loan for the year ended 30 June 19-6.

Mallard agreed that the settlement of the total amount owing to him in respect of the loan, would be: £12,000 10% debenture stock at par for half the capital value of the loan and the remainder owing to him would be settled by the issue of ordinary shares at par.

(6) The purchase consideration for the partnership's assets and liabilities (other than the loan) is to be settled by Wildbirds Ltd issuing £1 ordinary shares at par.

The partners are to receive these shares in their profit sharing ratio.

(7) The balance of funds due to or from a partner is to be settled in cash.

REQUIRED

(a) The partners' capital accounts showing all the necessary entries to close the business. *(12 marks)*

(b) The balance sheet of Wildbirds Ltd. after the acquisition of the partnership. *(8 marks)*

(c) A statement of the principal advantages which may be gained by forming a limited company.

(5 marks)

(Total 25 marks)

QUESTION 5 (Cambridge November 1987)

Town, City and Hamlet have been trading in partnership for several years: their partnership agreement has provided for interest to be credited to the partners on their capital account balances at the rate of 5% per annum and the balance of the profits and losses to be divided between Town, City and Hamlet in the ratio 5:3:2 respectively. The partners have decided to sell their business to Shires Limited for the sum of £100,000; the sale will involve all the fixed assets and net current assets of the partnership, which will be the only assets of the company.

The partners have agreed that the partnership should be dissolved on 1 November 19-7, immediately upon receipt of the purchase consideration for the business, and that the investments received in Shires Limited should be distributed to the partners so that their future income from the business will be the same, proportionately, as they would have received if the partnership had continued.

Shires Limited have invited Town, City and Hamlet to select one of the following ways of satisfying the purchase consideration:

Either: 50,000 Ordinary shares of £1 each, fully paid, in Shires Limited.

Or: 30,000 Ordinary shares of £1 each, fully paid, in Shires Limited and £40,000 10% Loan stock, at par, in Shires Limited.

The summarised balance sheet as at 31 October 19-7 of the partnership is as follows:

	£		£	£
Fixed assets	30,000	Capital accounts:		
Current assets	68,000	Town	50,000	
	98,000	City	20,000	
		Hamlet	10,000	80,000
Less: Current liabilities	12,000			
		Current accounts:		
		Town	4,000	
		City	1,500	
		Hamlet	500	6,000
	86,000			86,000

The partners have agreed to pay cash into the partnership, or withdraw cash, so that the partnership accounts may be closed.

REQUIRED

(a) Advise the partners as to the best way for the purchase consideration to be satisfied. Answers should be supported briefly by reasons. *(5 marks)*

(b) Prepare the partners' capital accounts covering the sale of the business, the distribution of the investments in Shires Limited to the partners and the closure of the accounts. *(20 marks)*

Note: Assume the purchase consideration is satisfied in the way advised in (a).

(Total 25 marks)

QUESTION 6 (London January 1987)

Adams, Brown and Clements are in partnership, sharing profits and losses in the ratio 5:4:3 respectively. At 31 December 19-6 their balance sheet was as follows:

	£	£
Fixed Assets		71,096
Current Assets		
Stock	47,396	
Debtors	28,437	
Bank	16,590	
	92,423	
Less Trade creditors	23,519	
		68,904
		140,000

113

Capital accounts		
Adams	70,000	
Brown	35,000	
Clements	16,000	
		121,000
Current accounts		
Adams	16,000	
Brown	6,000	
	22,000	
Clements (debit)	(3,000)	
		19,000
		140,000

Clements retired from partnership on 1 January 19-7, and the following matters were agreed:

1. The current account balances would be transferred to and merged with the capital account balances within the general ledger.
2. Goodwill was valued at £12,000, and entered in the general ledger.
3. Fixed assets were revalued at £65,000.
4. The amount due to Clements would be satisfied by an immediate cash payment of £3,000 and the balance repaid over the following four years.

The remaining partners decided to form a limited company, Bradams Ltd., to take over the partnership as from 2 January 19-7. The company is to have an authorised share capital of 200,000 ordinary shares of £1 each, and shares are to be issued, at par value, to Adams and Brown in the ratio 3:1 respectively, with an appropriate cash transfer being made privately between the two partners. No further revaluations are to be made to the partnership's asset values in respect of this take-over, but the debt to Clements was assumed by the company.

REQUIRED

(a) the capital accounts of Adams, Brown and Clements showing the entries in respect of Clements' retirement and the take-over by Bradams Ltd. *(16 marks)*

(b) the opening balance sheet of Bradams Ltd. as at 2 January 19-7. *(6 marks)*

(c) a calculation of the amount of the cash transfer to be made privately between Adams and Brown in respect of the allocation of shares in the new company. State which partner has to make the payment. *(3 marks)*

(25 marks)

QUESTION 7 (Northern Ireland 1987)

Patrick and Carol have been in partnership for many years manufacturing shirts which they sell from a factory shop. Patrick has been production manager and Carol the sales manager.

The partnership profit sharing agreement provided for-

(i) salary to Carol of £3,500 per annum,

(ii) interest on fixed capital account balances of 6% per annum,

(iii) balance of profits or losses shared between Patrick and Carol in the ratio 3:2.

The trial balance extracted from the books of the firm at 31 December 19-6 after profit calculations for 19-6 had been made was as follows:

	£	£
Capital accounts at 31 December 19-5:		
Patrick		100,000
Carol		50,000
Current accounts at 31 December 19-5		
Patrick		7,500
Carol		5,000
Carried forward	–	162,500

	£	£
Brought forward	–	162,500
Fixed assets at net book value:		
Factory buildings	85,000	
Plant and machinery	37,500	
Shop fittings	14,000	
Stock in trade at 31 December 19-6	44,500	
Sundry debtors	28,000	
Cash at bank	13,500	
Sundry creditors		57,500
Net profit for 19-6		45,000
Drawings: Patrick	27,000	
Carol	15,500	
	265,000	265,000

On 1 January 19-7 the partnership was dissolved: a company, Patrick Textiles Ltd. was formed to take over the manufacturing activities previously carried on by the partnership; the retail business of the firm was transferred to Carol who continued in business as a sole trader boutique owner.

The following values of assets and liabilities were agreed for the purposes of the re-organisation

	Assets/liabilities taken over by	
	Patrick Textiles Ltd. (production assets)	Carol Boutique (retail assets)
	£	£
Factory buildings	100,000	
Plant and machinery	35,000	
Shop fittings		10,000
Goodwill	10,000	2,500
Stock	20,000	22,500
Debtors	27,500	
Cash at bank	13,500	
Creditors	(56,000)	
	150,000	35,000

The issued share capital of Patrick Textiles Ltd. was £150,000 in shares of £1 each of which 118,000 were issued to Patrick and 32,000 to Carol, credited as fully paid.

Also on 1 January 19-7 in order to increase working capital, Patrick Textiles Ltd. issued £25,000 10% debenture stock at a discount of 4%. The issue was fully taken up and the subscription monies received in cash.

REQUIREMENT

You are required to prepare

(a) current accounts of Patrick and Carol for 19-6 in columnar form   *(8 marks)*

(b) ledger accounts to record the dissolution of the partnership; and   *(9 marks)*

(c) the opening balance sheet of Patrick Textiles Ltd at 1 January 19-7.   *(8 marks)*

                   (Total 25 marks)

9 ACCOUNTS OF LIMITED COMPANIES

(In this chapter we are concerned only with accounts produced for internal use by the directors and management. The form of accounts for publication and distribution to shareholders and other interested parties is dealt with in Chapter 10.)

Examination questions on this topic cover the following:-
- differences between partnerships and limited companies
- distinction between public and private limited companies
- types of share capital
- distinction between shares and debentures
- accounting for issues of shares and debentures
- reserves and provisions
- dividend policy
- correction of errors and other accounting adjustments

9.1 LIMITED COMPANIES

A limited company is a separate legal entity; i.e. it is regarded in law for all purposes as having a separate existence from that of its members. This is not to be confused with the concept of entity, referred to in Chapter 1, which treats all businesses as having separate existences from their owners for accounting purposes only and has no legal consequences.

The members, or shareholders, of a limited company are not liable for the debts of the company beyond the amounts they have agreed to pay on their shares, except in certain unfortunate circumstances which are outside the scope of this study.

Much of the legislation concerning limited companies is concerned with the protection of creditors.

A limited company is formed by the registration of certain documents with the Registrar of Companies, compliance with certain legal requirements and the payment of stamp duties and fees.

The Memorandum and Articles of Association are two of the documents which have to be filed. The Memorandum defines the relationship of the company to the outside world; the Articles are the internal rules governing the rights of members and the running of the company.

9.2 LIMITED COMPANIES AND PARTNERSHIPS COMPARED

	Limited companies	Partnerships
(i)	Not less than two members	Not less than two partners
(ii)	Maximum number of members determined by number of shares.	Not more than 20 partners (except in certain professional firms.)
(iii)	Liability of members for debts of company is limited to amounts they have agreed to pay on their shares.	Liability of partners for debts of firm is not limited (except in limited partnerships); their private assets may be seized to pay the creditors.
(iv)	Amount of capital limited only by authorised capital stated in Memorandum of Association, but this may be increased.	Capital as determined in partnership agreement and limited by personal resources of partners.
(v)	Profits are distributed by way of dividend. Amount dependant upon shareholding Some profits may be retained in the company.	All profits are credited, losses debited, to the partners' current accounts in accordance with partnership agreement.

| (vi) | Companies are liable to pay Corporation Tax on their Profits. | Partnerships are not assessed to income tax on profits; income tax is assessed upon the partners on their shares of profit. |
| (vii) | Shareholders not entitled to take part in the management of the company. Directors are appointed for this purpose. | Normally, all partners entitled to take part in running of the firm. |

9.3 LIMITED COMPANIES – PUBLIC AND PRIVATE

Public Company

The company registers as a public company and describes itself as such in its Memorandum. The name of the company must end with 'Public limited company' or the abbreviation 'plc'. If it is a Welsh company, the name will end with the Welsh for public limited company (cwmni cyfyngedig cyhoeddus'). The issued capital must be at least £50,000.

A public company may offer its shares to the public and its shares will be traded on the Stock Exchange.

Private Company

 The company does not describe itself as a public company and its name will end with 'Limited' or 'Ltd.' The authorised capital may be less than £50,000.

A private company may not offer its shares to the public; they will not, therefore be traded on the Stock Exchange.

9.4 SHARE CAPITAL

Authorised Share Capital

The amount of share capital stated in the Memorandum of Association. This must not be exceeded; but the company may comply with certain formalities required by law to increase the amount of authorised capital.

Issued Share Capital

The share capital which has actually been issued to shareholders.

Called-Up Capital

That part of the share capital which has been called up. A company may not require all the money due on its shares to be paid by the shareholders immediately and may 'call up' only sufficient for its immediate requirements.

Uncalled Capital

That part of the share capital which has not yet been called up; if a company gets into financial difficulties, the liability of the shareholders for its debts is limited to the amount unpaid on their shares.

Paid-Up Capital

That part of the share capital for which the company has actually received cash from the shareholders.

Calls In Advance

Money received from shareholders in advance of calls made by the company.

Calls In Arrear

Calls on share capital made by a company for which money has not yet been received from shareholders.

Forfeited Shares

Shares which have been forfeited by the holders in accordance with the Articles of Association when they have not paid arrears of allotment money or calls.

TYPES OF SHARES

Preference Shares

Preference shareholders are entitled to a fixed rate of dividend in priority to any dividend payable to ordinary shareholders. Preference shareholders are also entitled to receive the return of their capital before the ordinary shareholders when a company is 'wound up' or liquidated (the terms used for terminating the existence of a company.)

Non-Cumulative Preference Shares

If the profits of a company are insufficient in any year to meet the dividend on preference shares, and the shares are non-cumulative preference shares, the holders of these shares will lose all or part of their dividend for that year.

Cumulative Preference Shares

The holders of cumulative preference shares are entitled to have any arrears of dividend made good in future years when sufficient profits are available.

Ordinary Shares (The 'Equity')

The holders of ordinary shares must wait until the preference shareholders have been allocated their dividend before they can receive any share of the profits. In the liquidation of a company, the ordinary shareholders must wait until the preference shareholders have had their capital repaid before they can receive the return of their own capital. However, in a company which is being run successfully, the ordinary shareholders' share of profits may be very good and, in a liquidation they may stand to receive repayment in excess of their original capital outlay.

Nominal Value

Shares are described as having a particular face value known as their nominal (or par) value. They may have a nominal value of £1, 50p, 25p, 10p or even 5p; on the other hand the nominal value could be more than £1, say £5.

Shares Issued at a Premium

The directors of a company may consider that shares to be issued are worth more than their nominal (or par) value. In that case, they may issue them at a premium. For instance, ordinary shares of £1 each may be issued at £1.20 i.e. at a premium of 20p.

9.4.1   EXAMPLE   To show the difference between non-cumulative and cumulative preference shares.

Ebbanflow Ltd. was formed with 10,000 ordinary shares of £1 each and 5,000 8% Non-cumulative Preference shares of £1 each.

The profits available for dividend were as follows:

19-1 £1,100; 19-2 £500; 19-3 £200; 19-4 £600; 19-5 £300; 19-6 £800.

Year	19-1	19-2	19-3	19-4	19-5	19-6
	£	£	£	£	£	£
Profit	1,100	500	200	600	300	800
Pref.div.	400	400	200 *	400	300 *	400
Ord.div.	700	100	–	200	–	400
do. %	7	1	–	2	–	4

* The preference shareholders lose the balance of their dividends in these years.

If the Preference shares had been 8% Cumulative Preference shares, the dividends would have been as follows:

Year	19-1	19-2	19-3	19-4	19-5	19-6
	£	£	£	£	£	£
Profit	1,100	500	200	600	300	800
Pref.div.	400	400	200	600 *	300	500 *
Ord.div.	700	100	–	–	–	300
do. %	7	1	–	–	–	3

* In these years the preference shareholders receive arrears of dividends.

9.4.2   EXERCISE (To test understanding of the effect on preference and ordinary dividends of fluctuating profits.)

Chance Ltd. had the following share capital: 80,000 10% Preference shares of £1 each, and 120,000 Ordinary shares of £1 each. Profits of the company were as follows:

19-1 £22,000; 19-2 £6,000; 19-3 £11,000; 19-4 £7,000 19-5 £10,000.

REQUIRED

Tables showing the dividends on the Preference and Ordinary shares if the Preference shares are (i) non-cumulative, and (ii) cumulative.

9.5   ISSUE OF SHARES

Like other contracts, the issue of shares involves offer, acceptance and consideration.

The *application* for shares constitutes an offer to subscribe for them.

The *allotment* of shares by the company to applicants constitutes acceptance of the offer.

The Consideration is the money paid by the members for their shares.

The sequence of events is as follows:

1.   The company issues an invitation (prospectus) for applications for shares in the company.
2.   Investors (the applicants) apply for shares; with their applications they send the cash due on application.
3.   The company allots shares to the applicants who are now known as the allottees. At the same time, application money is returned to unsuccessful applicants.
4.   The allottees send the money due on allotment to the company.
5.   Any further calls are made and the shareholders pay the calls as and when due.

Accounting Entries

Issue of prospectus:	No entries are made in the books.

Receipt of applications with money due on application	Debit Bank
	    Credit Application and Allotment account
	    with money received on application.

Allotment of shares	Debit Application and Allotment account
	    Credit Share capital account
	    with money due on application and allotment

Receipt of money due on allotment	Debit Bank
	    Credit Application and Allotment account
	    with money received on allotment.

Making of call	Debit Call account
	    Credit Share capital account
	    with money due on call

Receipt of call money	Debit Bank
	    Credit Call account
	    with money received on call.

Share Premium

The premium must not be credited to the share capital account. The accounting entries will be:

When premium becomes due (often with allotment money)	Debit Application and Allotment account (or call account) Credit Share Premium account

Rights Issues

A rights issue is one in which the shares are offered to existing shareholders, not to the general public. The right is one to apply for a specified number of shares at a stated price, and the number is based upon the shareholder's present holding. The offer price of the shares is usually an advantageous one to the shareholder and the company is saved the expense and inconvenience of preparing a full prospectus as for a public issue. If a shareholder does not wish to exercise his right, he may sell the right to another person.

Underwritten Issues

A company may have its issue of shares underwritten by one or more financial houses to ensure that the share issue is successful. The underwriters guarantee to subscribe for any shares which are not taken up by the public.

9.5.1   EXAMPLE

New Venture Plc was formed with an authorised share capital of 100,000 ordinary shares of £1 each at £1.20. These shares were offered to the public on the following terms:

On application: 25p per share.

On allotment: 45p per share (including 20p premium.)

First and final call: the balance of 50p per share.

Applications were received for 141,000 shares.

The directors rejected applications for 21,000 shares and allotted shares to the remaining applicants on the basis of 5 shares for every 6 applied for.

REQUIRED

The ledger accounts in the books of New Venture Plc to record the above transactions.

ANSWER

New Venture Plc

Ordinary share capital

	£		£
Balance c/d	100,000	Application & allotment	50,000
		First & final call	50,000
	100,000		100,000
		Balance b/d	100,000

Share Premium

	£		£
		Application & allotment	20,000

Bank

	£		£
Application & allotment	35,250	Application & allotment	5,250
		Balance c/d	120,000
Application & allotment	40,000		
Call	50,000		
	125,250		125,250
Balance b/d	120,000		

Application and allotment account

	£		£
Ordinary Share capital	50,000	Bank (application money)	35,250
		Bank (bal. on allotment)	40,000
Share premium	20,000		
Bank (refunds)	5,250		
	75,250		75,250

First and final call

	£		£
Share capital	50,000	Bank	50,000

9.5.2 EXERCISE (Practice in recording an issue of shares)

The Goodbuy Co. plc. has invited applications for its new issue of 300,000 Ordinary shares of £1 each at £1.25p per share. The terms of the issue are: Payable on application: 50p; on allotment: 50p. (including the premium); on call three months after allotment: 25p.

Applications for 373,500 shares were received and the directors decided not to allot shares to applicants for 23,500 shares and to allot shares to the other applicants on the basis of 6 shares for every 7 applied for. Application monies were returned to the unsuccessful applicants and all monies due on allotment and call were received on the due dates.

REQUIRED

The accounting entries to record the issue of the shares by The Goodbuy Co. plc.

9.6 FORFEITURE AND RE-ISSUE OF SHARES

When shares are forfeited for non-payment of allotment or call money and subsequently reissued, use a Forfeited Shares account and a Forfeited Shares Reissued account.

Accounting Entries

On forfeiture of shares:

> Debit Share Capital
>> Credit Forfeited Shares

with the total amount paid and due on the forfeited shares.

> Debit Forfeited Shares
>> Credit Allotment (or Call, as the case may be)

with the amount due and unpaid on the forfeited shares.

On reissue of shares as fully paid:

> Debit Forfeited Shares Reissued
>> Credit Share Capital

with the nominal value of the reissued shares

> Debit Bank
>> Credit Forfeited Shares Reissued

with the money received from the new holder

> Debit Forfeited Shares
>> Credit Forfeited Shares Reissued

with any discount on reissue of the shares to new holder

OR

> Debit Forfeited Shares Reissued
>> Credit Forfeited Shares

with any premium on reissue of the shares to the new holder

> Debit Forfeited Shares
>> Credit Share Premium

with balance on Forfeited Shares account (being the total, or net, premium on reissue).

9.6.1 EXAMPLE

Lost Horizons plc invited applications for 500,000 ordinary shares of £1 each at £1.30, payable as to 40p on application, 70p (including 30p premium) on allotment, and 20p on first and final call 4 months after allotment. Applications for all the shares were received and the shares duly allotted. All the allotment money was received but the holder of 1,000 shares failed to meet the call and forfeited his shares in accordance with the Articles of the company.

All the forfeited shares were subsequently reissued as fully paid shares at 80p each.

ANSWER

Ordinary share capital

	£		£
Forfeited shares	1,000	Application and Allotment	400,000
Balance c/d	500,000	Call	100,000
		Forfeited shares reissued	1,000
	501,000		501,000
		Balance b/d	500,000

Share Premium

	£		£
Balance c/d	150,600	Application and Allotment	150,000
		Forfeited shares reissued	600
	150,600		150,600
		Balance b/d	150,600

Bank

	£		£
Application &Allotment	200,000	Balance c/d	650,600
Application and Allotment	350,000		
Call	99,800		
Forfeited shares reissued	800		
	650,600		650,600
Balance b/d	650,600		

Application and Allotment

	£		£
Ordinary share capital	400,000	Bank	200,000
Share premium	150,000	Bank	350,000
	550,000		550,000

Call

	£		£
Ordinary share capital	100,000	Bank	99,800
		Forfeited shares	200
	100,000		100,000

Forfeited Shares

	£		£
Call	200	Ordinary share capital	1,000
Forfeited shares reissued	200		
Share Premium	600		
	1,000		1,000

Forfeited Shares Reissued.

	£		£
Ordinary share capital	1,000	Bank	800
		Forfeited shares	200
	1,000		1,000

Tutorial note: When shares are forfeited, the Forfeited Shares account shows them at the amount actually paid on them up to the time of forfeiture (£1,000 – £200 = £800) The Forfeited Shares Reissued account shows the discount given to the new holder. (£1,000 – £800 = £200). When the discount is transferred to the Forfeited Shares account, the balance remaining on that account represents additional premium on the shares and must be credited to the share premium account.

9.6.2   EXERCISE (Practice in accounting for forfeiture and reissue of shares.)

Jollysticks Ltd. issued 60,000 ordinary shares of 50p each at a premium of 7p. The terms of the issue were that 30p was payable on application and the balance, including the premium, was payable on allotment.

Applications were received for 71,000 shares. The directors allotted 60,000 shares to successful applicants and returned application money to the unsuccessful applicants.

The money due on allotment was received from allottees of 58,900 shares; the remaining shares were forfeited and later reissued to another applicant as fully paid on payment of 40p per share.

REQUIRED

Prepare the ledger accounts necessary to record the foregoing transactions.

9.7   DEBENTURES

A debenture is a document containing details of a loan made to a company. The loan may be secured on the assets of the company, when it is known as a *mortgage debenture*. If the security for the loan is on certain specified assets of the company, the debenture is said to be secured by a *fixed charge* on the assets. If the assets are not specified, but the security is on the assets as they may exist from time to time, it is known as a *floating charge* on the assets.

Debentures carry the right to a fixed rate of interest which must be paid whether or not the company makes a profit. The interest is debited in the Profit and Loss account of the company in order to arrive at the profit. This is one of the distinctions between debentures, and shares on which dividends may only be paid if profits are available. Dividends are debited in the company's Profit and Loss Appropriation account.

Debentures are usually *redeemable* on or before a specified date.

Debenture holders are not members of the company in the same way as shareholders are, and debentures must not be confused with the share capital and reserves in the balance sheet. Debentures should always be shown as long term liabilities (amounts falling due after more than one year) unless they are to be redeemed within one year of the date of the balance sheet.

9.8   RESERVES, PROVISIONS AND LIABILITIES

The distinctions between reserves, provisions and liabilities are of the utmost importance and must be learned.

Reserves are either *revenue* reserves or *capital* reserves.

Revenue reserves are profits which are ploughed back into the company by debiting Profit and Loss Appropriation account and crediting the appropriate reserve account.

Specific reserves are revenue reserves which have been set aside for some specific purpose such as replacement of fixed assets or in anticipation of an expansion of the business.

General reserves are other revenue reserves considered desirable or necessary to reinforce the financial position of the company.

Setting profits aside as revenue reserves reduces the amount available for dividends at least for the time being. If at some future date the revenue reserves are found to be unnecessary or excessive, they may be credited back to the profit and loss account and made available for dividends.

Capital reserves are reserves which cannot be transferred to Profit and Loss account and used to pay cash dividends. If they are distributed they will be distributed in the form of bonus shares. The Share Premium account is a capital reserve, and so are Revaluation Reserves and Capital Redemption Reserves.

Share premium account. The creation of this has already been dealt with in 9.5 above. The Share Premium account may be applied:

1.   In paying up unissued shares as fully paid bonus shares. (see below)

2.   To write off:

(i)   preliminary expenses (expenses incurred in forming the company)

(ii)   expenses of, or the commission paid or discount allowed on, any issue of shares or debentures

3.   To provide any premium payable on the redemption of shares or debentures.

Revaluation Reserve

A Revaluation Reserve is created when an asset is revalued to reflect an increase in value. The asset account is debited with the increase and the corresponding credit is entered in a Revaluation Reserve account.

Capital Redemption Reserve

If a company redeems or buys back any of its own shares otherwise than out of the proceeds of a new issue of shares, it must protect the creditors by replacing the shares so redeemed or purchased with profits that would otherwise be available for distribution as dividends. The Capital Redemption Reserve created in this way may be used to issue unissued shares as fully paid bonus shares.

All reserves, regardless of whatever kind, form part of the ordinary shareholders' interest in the company.

When a company uses reserves to issue fully paid up *bonus shares* to its shareholders, the reserves are credited to the share capital account. Revenue reserves capitalised in this way no longer become available for distribution as dividends. The shares are called 'bonus' shares because the shareholders do not have to pay for them; the reserves were theirs anyway. (This topic is dealt with more fully in Chapter 13.) Distinguish between a bonus issue, and a rights issue in which the shareholder buys the shares for cash.

Provisions are:

> amounts written off or retained by way of providing for depreciation, renewals or diminution in the value of assets,

or, retained by way of providing for any known liability of which the amount cannot be determined with substantial accuracy.

Increases and decreases in provisions are debited or credited in the Profit and Loss account and credited or debited to a Provision account as the case may be.

Liabilities are amounts owing which can be determined with substantial accuracy.

9.8.1 EXAMPLE (To show valuation of shares using balance sheet values)

The summarised balance sheet of Jack Ltd. is as follows:

	£	£
Fixed assets		8,000
Current assets	10,000	
less creditors	3,000	7,000
		15,000
Capital and reserves		
Share capital		
12,000 ordinary shares of £1 each		12,000
Revenue reserve		2,500
Retained profit		500
		15,000

REQUIRED

Assuming the fixed and current assets are shown in the balance sheet at realistic values, calculate the value of one ordinary share.

ANSWER

> Total net assets: £15,000
>
> No. of shares: 12,000
>
> Each share is therefore worth £15,000/12,000 = £1.25p (based on balance sheet values.)

Tutorial notes

1. The net assets of the company are equal to the share capital plus the reserves.
2. If the assets are not shown in the balance sheet at their realisable values, these must be substituted for their balance sheet values.
3. The creditors must be paid before any money that would be returnable to the shareholders; the money due to the creditors must therefore be deducted from the total assets to arrive at the value of the share capital.

9.8.2 EXERCISE (In the valuation of shares)

Jill Ltd.'s summarised balance sheet is as follows:

	£	£
Fixed assets		102,000
Current assets	54,000	
less creditors	9,000	45,000
		147,000
Share capital and reserves		
75,000 Ordinary shares of £1 each		75,000
25,000 8% Preference shares of £1 each		25,000
Share Premium		15,000
Asset Replacement Reserve		20,000
Retained profit		12,000
		147,000

A realistic valuation of the assets shows that the fixed assets would realise £86,000 and the current assets have a realisable value of £48,000.

REQUIRED

Calculation of the value of one ordinary share based on: (i) balance sheet values and (ii) the realisable values of the assets.

9.9 DIVIDEND POLICY

Distributable profits are accumulated realised profits less accumulated realised losses. Realised profits (in general) = the credit balance on Profit and Loss account + the revenue reserves.

In recommending a dividend the directors of a company will have regard to the following:

1. The availability of distributable profits.
2. The availability of liquid funds to pay the dividend.
   (A cash forecast statement is essential.)
3. Whether the revenue reserves are adequate or need to be increased by further profits ploughed back into the business.
4. A balance between dividend growth and capital growth.
5. The effect of the dividend policy on the market price of the shares.
6. The liability to advance corporation tax which arises from the payment of a dividend.

Directors may pay interim dividends providing they are satisfied that profits for the purpose have been realised and that the liquid resources and requirements of the company will permit the payment of the dividend.

Directors, however, may only recommend payment of Final Dividends. The necessary resolution to pay the dividend must be passed by the members at the Annual General Meeting. Therefore, proposed final dividends will appear in the balance sheet as current liabilities. (Creditors: amounts falling due within one year.)

9.9.1 EXAMPLE

The following is an extract from the balance sheet of Box and Cox plc.:

	£
Share capital and reserves	
100,000 Ordinary shares of £1 each	100,000
Share Premium	25,000
Property Revaluation Reserve	70,000
Asset Replacement Reserve	45,000
General Reserve	20,000
Retained profit	10,000
	270,000

A major shareholder has written to the chairman of the company expressing the view that since the reserves of the company total £170,000 and belong to the shareholders, they should be used to pay a good dividend to the shareholders, especially as the dividends paid for some years past have been low.

REQUIRED

Prepare a report to the chairman of Box and Cox plc. suggesting points that he should bear in mind in his reply to the shareholder.

ANSWER

To the Chairman,
Box and Cox plc

Profits available for dividend to ordinary shareholders.

You have received a request from a shareholder that the reserves of the company, totalling £170,000, should be used to increase the dividend payable to the shareholders to compensate for allegedly low dividends in past years.

1. The shareholder is quite correct in stating that all the reserves of the company belong to the ordinary shareholders. However, not all the reserves are available for distribution in cash as dividends.

2. The Share Premium and the Property Revaluation Reserve are capital reserves which, by the Companies Act 1985, may not be used to pay cash dividends to shareholders.

3. On the face of the balance sheet the only profits which are available for dividend are the Retained Profit £10,000 which could be used to pay a dividend of 10% (10p per share).

4. The Asset Replacement Reserve and the General Reserve are revenue reserves which could, in theory, be used to pay a dividend.

5. Unless the directors are of the opinion that the Asset Replacement Reserve is no longer needed because of a change in policy or that it is excessive, it should not be used to pay a dividend.

6. General reserves are normally created in order to conserve or increase working capital as a shield against inflation or to provide additional working capital for business expansion. The General Reserve may be used to pay dividends only to the extent that the directors consider the reserve to be excessive to requirements.

7. Any proposal to pay a dividend must be covered by available cash, and the directors will need to consider the cash budget of the company to see if the payment of any dividend now will cause liquidity problems later. They must take into their reckoning the liability to pay advance corporation tax.

8. The directors will also bear in mind the rates of dividends being paid by other companies of similar size and in the same line of business.

(Signed)
(Date)

Tutorial note: The question has asked for a report; the answer must be drafted in report form, addressed to the appropriate person, mentioning the subject of the report, signed and dated.

9.9.2 EXERCISE (A calculation of the maximum dividend payable on ordinary shares)

The following is the summarised draft balance sheet of Splendiferous plc as at 31 March 19-2 before any interest payable has been charged in the profit and loss account or any appropriations made for dividends.

	£
Net assets (other than cash at bank)	30,000
Cash at bank	8,000
	38,000
12% debentures	(5,000)
	33,000

	£
Share capital and reserves	
10,000 Ordinary shares of £1 each	10,000
2,000 8% Preference shares of £1 each	2,000
Share premium	1,000
General reserve	10,000
Retained profit	10,000
	33,000

REQUIRED

A calculation of the maximum amount that can be paid to the ordinary shareholders as dividend for the year to 31 March 19-2.

9.10   KEY POINTS TO REMEMBER

1. A company is a separate legal entity.
2. The liability of members is limited to the amount they have paid, or have agreed to pay, on their shares.
3. A company can raise more capital than a partnership.
4. Public companies may issue shares to the general public; private companies must include a restriction on the issue of shares in their Articles of Association.
5. The differences between limited companies and partnerships (9.2).
6. The differences between non-cumulative preference shares, cumulative preference shares, ordinary shares and debentures.
7. The accounting entries for the issue and forfeiture of shares.
8. The definitions of capital reserves, revenue reserves, provisions and liabilities.
9. All reserves form part of the ordinary shareholders' interest in the company.
10. Factors affecting dividend policy.

COMMON ERRORS:
- showing debentures as part of the company's share capital and reserves.
- failure to ensure that a full year's interest on debentures is debited in the Profit and Loss account.
- omission of outstanding debenture interest from the balance sheet as a liability.
- failing to include interim dividends paid during the year in the Profit and Loss Appropriation account.
- omission of the final dividend for the year from the balance sheet as a liability.

9.11   EXAMINATION QUESTIONS

QUESTION 1   (London June 1988)

The agenda for the Annual General Meeting of a public limited company contains the following resolution:

'The final dividend for the year ended 31 May 19-8 shall be 0.7p per share.'

An extract from the company's profit and loss account for the year ended 31 May 19-8 is given below:

	£'000
Net profit after taxation	2,370
Proposed dividend	280
Retained profit for the year	2,090
Retained profit brought forward	7,560
Retained profit carried forward	9,650

The company chairman has received a letter from a shareholder who is unhappy about the size of the proposed dividend. The shareholder wants to see the dividend significantly increased to 10p per share.

(a) Advise the chairman regarding the options which are available to directors when deciding upon the appropriation of profits.   *(12 marks)*

(b) Prepare a reasoned reply from the chairman to the shareholder in defence of the company's dividend policy.   *(8 marks)*

(Total 20 marks)

QUESTION 2   (Oxford June 1988)

(a) Sforzando plc made a public issue of 500,000 £2 ordinary shares at £2.50 each on 1 October 19-7, requiring £1.20 per share to be sent on application. The issue was overscribed, and the directors decided to reject applicants for 30,000 shares. The remaining applicants were allocated two-thirds of the shares applied for, the balance of the application money being retained against the £0.90 per share, including share premium, due on allotment on 15 October 19-7. The final call was made on 4 May 19-8, and all due money was received.

(b) Sforzando's shareholders' interest at 30 September 19-7 was:

	£
1,500,000 £2 ordinary shares	3,000,000
Revaluation reserve	750,000
General reserve	250,000
Profit and loss	60,000
	4,060,000

It has an authorised capital of	£
2,500,000 £2 ordinary shares	5,000,000
1,000,000 £1 8% Preference shares	1,000,000
	6,000,000

One of the directors had argued that the authorised preference shares should be issued instead of more ordinary shares. Other directors had supported a rights issue, while a director who has since resigned felt that a bonus issue would be more appropriate.

You are required to provide

(i)   Journal entries covering the transactions in (a) above, with suitable narratives.   *(14 marks)*

(ii) A comment on the views expressed by the directors in (b) before the public issue.   *(6 marks)*

(Total 20 marks)

QUESTION 3   (JMB June 1986)

A friend with no accounting knowledge has been studying the balance sheets of a partnership and a limited company. He has asked you to explain the differences and the similarities between the two financial statements.   *(16 marks)*

QUESTION 4   (JMB June 1988)

Bandana Ltd. has an authorised share capital of 75,000 £1 ordinary shares. On 31 March 19-8 the following balances were extracted from its books.

	£
Ordinary shares, fully paid	50,000
Other reserves	70,000
Leasehold Land & Buildings, at cost	65,500
Motor vehicles, at cost	10,650
Plant & machinery, at cost	54,400
Creditors	39,400
Cash and bank	98,410
Stock at 1 April 19-7	10,640
Sales	280,520

	£
Purchases	182,530
Wages	19,456
Selling expenses	16,428
Administrative expenses	22,392
Profit & Loss Account at 1 April 19-7	29,246
Debtors	56,750
Interim dividend, paid	2,500
Provision for depreciation	
Leasehold land & building	32,750
Motor vehicles	6,420
Plant & Machinery	30,290
Provision for bad debts	1,030

The following information is relevant.

(i) Stock on hand at 31 March 19-8 amounted to £11,450

(ii) Provision for bad debts is to be adjusted to 2% of the outstanding debtors as on 31 March 19-8

(iii) Provision is to be made for:

(a) Audit fee £1,000

(b) Depreciation on leasehold land and buildings at 5% on cost, plant and machinery at 10% on cost, and motor vehicles at 20% on cost.

(iv) The directors wish to transfer £10,000 to general reserve and recommend a final dividend of 10%

(v) Administrative expenses include insurance payments of £2,000 which cover a 15 month period to 30 June 19-8.

(vi) The company is being sued for £19,000 in respect of costs arising from the expiration of a lease on a property formerly occupied by the company. The company's legal advisers are of the opinion that the company will not be held liable for this amount.

You are required to:

(a) prepare, not necessarily in a form for publication, a Trading and Profit and Loss Account for the year ending 31 March 19-8 and a Balance Sheet as at that date; *(22 marks)*

(b) explain and justify your treatment of the claim against the company in respect to the expiration of the lease. *(3 marks)*

(Total 25 marks)

QUESTION 5 (London January 1989)

The following is an extract from a letter received by Jill Chan, the managing director of Quip Limited, from her bank manager:

'The bank is prepared to lend your company the amount requested, but we shall require a *floating charge* over its assets. These include several *wasting assets*, so the bank may require an additional *fixed charge* to be arranged in due course.

'We note from your consolidated accounts that your *associated company* has produced better results this year.'

Explain the meaning of the four terms shown in italics in the bank manager's letter. *(20 marks)*

QUESTION 6 (Oxford June 1986)

Compare Ordinary shares with Debenture stock, mentioning at least four differences between them.

(8 marks)

10 LIMITED COMPANIES: PUBLISHED ACCOUNTS

Questions on published accounts of limited companies test ability to:-
- prepare profit and loss accounts and balance sheets from given information in forms prescribed by the fourth schedule of the Companies Act 1985
- prepare notes to the balance sheet and profit and loss account to provide information required to be disclosed by the Companies Act 1985.
- discuss or explain the purpose of the requirements to disclose certain information in the accounts

---

The published accounts of limited companies are used by:
- shareholders
- prospective investors
- debenture holders
- creditors
- financial analysts
- the financial Press.

Statutory regulations governing the requirements of published accounts of limited companies have existed for a very long time. The Companies Act 1981 sought to bring the presentation of accounts of U.K. companies into line with those of the rest of the European Common Market.

The requirements are now embodied in the Companies Act 1985 which provides in Section 227 that

'In the case of every company, the directors shall in respect of every accounting reference period of the company prepare a profit and loss account for the financial year... ...and shall prepare a balance sheet as at the last day of the period.'

Section 228 of the Act provides that 'A company's accounts prepared under section 227 shall comply with the requirements of Schedule 4 (so far as applicable) with respect to the form and content of the balance sheet and profit and loss account and any additional information to be provided by way of notes to the accounts.

Schedule 4 of the Act gives two balance sheet formats and four profit and loss account formats together with a statement of accounting principles and rules and notes to be appended to the accounts.

Schedule 5 deals with miscellaneous matters to be disclosed in the notes to the accounts.

Section 239 states that a company's accounts for a financial year are to be taken as comprising:

(a) the company's profit and loss account and balance sheet

(b) the directors' report

(c) the auditors' report, and

(d) group accounts where applicable.

Section 240 requires every company to send a copy of the company's accounts, not less than 21 days before the Annual General Meeting, to the following persons:

(a) every shareholder

(b) every debenture holder

(c) all other persons entitled to receive copies (e.g. the auditors.)

The directors of a company may adopt any format they wish for accounts produced for internal use within the company, but will probably adopt a form close to that required for the published accounts as that will facilitate the production of the published accounts. The accounts for internal use will be much more detailed than the published ones as the directors will not wish to include any information in the latter which will be of use to competitors. Nevertheless, published accounts often include more information than is required by law, the additional matter being calculated to improve the information given to the public and to improve the image of the company.

When answering questions on published accounts, adhere strictly to the requirements of the Companies Act; any departure, giving more or less information than legally required, will be interpreted as a display of an inadequate knowledge of the topic.

10.1   PROFIT AND LOSS ACCOUNT FORMAT 1

1. Turnover
2. Cost of sales *
3. Gross profit or loss
4. Distribution costs *
5. Administrative expenses *
6. Other operating income
7. Income from shares in group companies
8. Income from shares in related companies
9. Income from other fixed asset investments **
10. Other interest receivable and similar income **
11. Amounts written off investments
12. Interest payable and similar charges ***
13. Tax on profit or loss on ordinary activities
14. Profit or loss on ordinary activities after taxation
15. Extraordinary income
16. Extraordinary charges
17. Extraordinary profit or loss
18. Tax on extraordinary profit or loss
19. Other taxes not shown under the above items
20. Profit or loss for the financial year.

* Items 2,4 and 5. These items shall be stated after taking into account any necessary provisions for depreciation or diminution in value of assets.

** Items 9 and 10. Income and interest derived from group companies shall be shown separately from income and interest derived from other sources.

*** Item 12. The amount payable to group companies shall be shown separately.

10.2   BALANCE SHEET FORMAT 1

A. Called up share capital not paid *

B. Fixed assets
    I   Intangible assets
         1. Development costs
         2. Concessions, patents, licenses, trade marks and similar rights and assets
         3. Goodwill #
         4. Payments on account
    II   Tangible assets
         1. Land and buildings
         2. Plant and machinery
         3. Fixtures, fittings, tools and equipment
         4. Payments on account and assets in course of construction
    III Investments
         1. Shares in group companies
         2. Loans to group companies
         3. Shares in related companies
         4. Loans to related companies
         5. Other investments other than loans
         6. Other loans
         7. Own shares

C. Current assets
  I   Stocks
    1. Raw materials and consumable stores.
    2. Work in progress
    3. Finished goods and goods for resale
    4. Payments on account
  II   Debtors
    1. Trade debtors
    2. Amounts owed by group companies
    3. Amounts owed by related companies
    4. Other debtors
    5. Called up share capital not paid *
    6. Prepayments and accrued income **
  III Investments
    1. Shares in group companies
    2. Own shares
    3. Other investments
  IV   Cash at bank and in hand

D. Prepayments and accrued income **

E. Creditors: amounts falling due within one year
    1. Debenture loans
    2. Bank loans and overdrafts
    3. Payments received on account ##
    4. Trade creditors
    5. Bills of exchange payable
    6. Amounts owed to group companies
    7. Amounts owed to related companies
    8. Other creditors including taxation and social security
    9. Accruals and deferred income ***

F. Net current assets (liabilities) ###

G. Total assets less current liabilities

H. Creditors: amounts falling due after more than one year
    1. Debenture loans
    2. Bank loans and overdrafts
    3. Payments received on account ##
    4. Trade creditors
    5. Bills of exchange payable
    6. Amounts owed to group companies
    7. Amounts owed to related companies
    8. Other creditors including taxation and social security
    9. Accruals and deferred income ***

I. Provisions for liabilities and charges
    1. Pensions and similar obligations
    2. Taxation including deferred taxation
    3. Other provisions

J. Accruals and deferred income ***

K. Capital and reserves
  I   Called up share capital
  II   Share premium account

   III Revaluation reserve
   IV Other reserves
     1. Capital redemption reserve
     2. Reserve for own shares
     3. Reserves provided for by the articles of association
     4. Other reserves
   V Profit and loss account.

*   Called up share capital not paid. This item may be shown in either of the two positions given.

**   Prepayments and accrued income. This item may be shown in either of the two positions given.

***   Accruals and deferred income. The two positions given for this item at E.9 and H.9 are an alternative to the position at J, but if the item is not shown in a position corresponding to that at J it may be shown in either or both of the other two positions (as the case may require).

\#   Goodwill. Amounts representing goodwill shall only be included to the extent that goodwill was acquired for valuable consideration.

\#\#   Payments received on account. Payments received on account of orders shall be shown for each of these items in so far as they are not shown as deductions from stocks.

\#\#\#   Net current assets(liabilities). In determining the amount to be shown for this item any amounts shown under 'Prepayments and accrued income' shall be taken into account wherever shown.

10.3   ACCOUNTING PRINCIPLES

The amounts to be included in respect of all items shown in a company's accounts shall be determined in accordance with the following principles:

1.   The company shall be presumed to be carrying on business as a going concern.

2.   Accounting policies shall be applied consistently from one financial year to the next.

3.   The amount of any item shall be determined on a prudent basis:

  (a) only profits realised at the balance sheet date shall be included in the profit and loss account; and

  (b) all liabilities and losses which have arisen or are likely to arise in respect of the financial year to which the accounts relate or a previous financial year shall be taken into account.

4.   All income and charges relating to the financial year to which the accounts relate shall be taken into account, without regard to the date of receipt or payment.

5   In determining the aggregate amount of any item the amount of each individual asset or liability that falls to be taken into account shall be determined separately.

Departure from the Accounting Principles

If it appears to the directors of a company that there are special reasons for departing from any of the principles stated above in preparing the company's accounts in respect of any financial year they may do so, but particulars of the departure, the reasons for it and its effect shall be given in a note to the accounts.

Tutorial note: The accounting principles stated above are the concepts of going concern, consistency, prudence and accruals with which the student should already be familiar. See Chapter 1.

10.4   NOTES TO THE ACCOUNTS

The following information, if not given in the company's accounts, must be shown by way of notes to the accounts:

Disclosure of Accounting Policies

The accounting policies adopted by the company in determining the amounts to be included in respect of items shown in the balance sheet and in determining the profit or loss of the company shall be stated. (This includes such policies as those relating to the depreciation and diminution in value of assets.)

NOTES RELATING TO THE PROFIT AND LOSS ACCOUNT.

Turnover

Turnover means the amounts derived from the provision of goods and services falling within the company's ordinary activities, after deduction of:

(a)   trade discounts

(b)   value added tax, and

(c)   any other taxes based on the amounts so derived

Where, during a financial year, the business of a company has consisted of two or more classes that differ substantially from each other, a note to the accounts shall state the amount of the turnover attributable to each class and the amount of profit or loss before taxation attributable to that class.

If a company has supplied substantially different geographical markets, the amount of turnover attributable to each market shall be shown by way of note.

EXAMPLE

Profit and loss account: Turnover £99m

Note to profit and loss account:

	Turnover	Profit before tax
	£m	£m
Food	36	2.1
Furniture	54	16.0
Travel & tourism	9	0.9
	99	19.0

	Turnover
	£m
United Kingdom	54
Europe	30
North and South America	15
	99

The following items shall be shown by way of note to supplement the information given in the profit and loss account:

Interest

The amount of interest on or any similar charges in respect of:

(a)   bank loans and overdrafts, loans made to the company (except bank loans and overdrafts) which:

　(i)   are repayable otherwise than by instalments and fall due for repayment within five years of the date to which the accounts are made up; or

　(ii)   are repayable by instalments the last of which falls due for payment before the end of that period; and

(b)   loans of any other kind made to the company.

Income

The amount of income from investments listed on a recognised stock exchange.

Rent from Land

The net amount to be shown if it forms a substantial part of the company's revenue for the year.

Hire of Plant and Machinery

The amount charged in the profit and loss account in respect of sums payable for the hire of plant and machinery.

Auditors' Remuneration

The amount shown must include the amount of auditors' expenses paid by the company.

Taxation

Details should be given of the charge in the accounts showing:

(a)   UK corporation tax and the basis upon which it has been computed.

(b)   UK income tax and the basis upon which it has been computed.

(c)   irrecoverable advance corporation tax.

(d)   tax attributable to dividends received from other UK companies (known as franked investment income.)

Particulars of Staff

(a) The average number of persons employed by the company in the financial year;

(b) The average number of persons so employed within each category of persons employed by the company. (e.g. manufacturing, clerical etc.)

(c) (i)   wages and salaries paid or payable in the year

(ii) social security costs incurred by the company on their behalf

(iii) other pension costs

(d) The number of employees earning over £30,000 within each band of £5,000 over that amount. e.g.

Emoluments	Number of employees
£30,000 – £35,000	6
£35,001 – £40,000	2
£40,001 – £45,000	1
	9

Particulars of Directors' Emoluments

(a) (i)   Total emoluments including pension contributions and benefits in kind (e.g.company car), distinguishing between fees as director and other emoluments.

(ii) Total of pensions paid to past directors

(iii) Total of compensation for loss of office.

(b) Where the total of the directors' emoluments exceeds £60,000, the following must be shown:

(i)   The emoluments of the chairman.

(ii) The emoluments of the highest paid director if he is not the chairman,

(iii) The number of directors whose emoluments fall within the range £0 – £5,000, and of each higher band of £5,000. e.g.

Directors emoluments:	£'000
Total emoluments paid to directors	185
Chairman's emoluments	40
Emoluments of highest paid director	52

Number of directors not included above receiving	
£5,000 – £10,000	2
£10,001 – £15,000	4
£15,001 – £20,000	1

Earnings per Share

Statement of Standard Accounting Practice 3 requires listed companies (i.e.those dealt with on a stock exchange) to show the earnings per share.

NOTES RELATING TO THE BALANCE SHEET

Share Capital and Debentures

Note should show:

(a) authorised share capital

(b) number and aggregate nominal value of each class of shares allotted.

(c) with regard to any redeemable shares:

(i)   the earliest and latest dates on which company has power to redeem the shares

(ii) whether shares are redeemable in any event, or at option of the company or of shareholder

(iii) amount of any premium payable on redemption

Fixed Assets

The various classes of fixed assets should be shown at cost, or revaluation where appropriate, at beginning of the year. Additions during the year at cost, and the original cost or revaluation amounts of assets disposed of during the year should be shown.

The provisions for depreciation of fixed assets at the beginning of the year, together with such provisions on assets disposed of during the year and the charges for depreciation for the year for each class of asset should be shown.

EXAMPLE

Note to balance sheet:

Fixed assets	Freehold property	Plant & Machinery	Motor Vehicles
	£'000	£'000	£'000
At cost at beginning of year (see note 1)	1,600	852	660
Additions during year	–	280	206
Disposals	–	(97)	(147)
	1,600	1,035	719
Depreciation			
At beginning of year	280	568	410
Charge for the year	28	207	180
On disposals	–	(83)	(122)
	308	692	468
Net book value at end of year	1,292	343	251

Note 1. Freehold property: freehold land £200,000; buildings £1,400,000

(Statement of Standard Accounting Practice 12 requires that the following should also be disclosed:
1. Method of depreciation used
2. Economic life or depreciation rate in use.)

Revaluation of Fixed Assets

Revaluation of fixed assets is accounted for in a revaluation reserve. The directors must reduce the reserve if in their opinion any part of it is no longer necessary; the adjustment may only be made through the profit and loss account if the amount in question was originally charged to the profit and loss account, or it represents a realised profit.

Losses on the revaluation of certain fixed assets, or classes of assets, are realised losses (unless they offset an unrealised surplus previously recorded for the same asset); individual surpluses should be treated as unrealised profits.

If all the fixed assets are revalued, individual deficits should be regarded as unrealised losses.

In the year of revaluation of a fixed asset, a note to the balance sheet must state the names of the valuers or their qualifications, and the method of valuation used.

The annual depreciation charge on a revalued asset should be based on the revalued amount and the estimated remaining useful life of the asset.

10.4.1   EXAMPLE (Disclosure requirements relating to fixed assets)

Snook, Erdwell, Potter, Black and Co. plc had the following fixed assets at 31 December 19-1:

	Cost	Provision for depreciation to date
	£'000	£'000
*Freehold land and buildings	1,200	400
Plant and machinery	640	210
Motor vehicles	275	135

* (Land cost £200,000; buildings cost £1,000,000)

The depreciation policy of the company is to provide for depreciation as follows:

Freehold buildings	2% p.a. straight line
Plant and machinery	15% p.a. straight line
Motor vehicles	20% p.a. straight line

During the year to 31 December 19-2, the following events occurred:

1. On 1 January 19-2, the freehold property was professionally revalued by Billyard and Billyard, chartered surveyors, at £1,800,000, of which £400,000 was attributable to the land. The buildings were estimated to have a further useful life of 25 years.
2. Plant and machinery which originally cost £140,000 was scrapped for £5,000. It had a written down value of £40,000.
3. New plant and machinery was acquired at a cost of £240,000 on 1 April 19-2.
4. Motor vehicles which had cost £35,000 were sold for £15,000, making a profit on disposal of £5,000.
5. New motor vehicles were purchased on 1 July 19-2 at a cost of £80,000.

At a meeting of the directors on 1 December, 19-2, the sales director suggested that as freehold property tended to appreciate in value, no depreciation need be provided in future years on that property. The personnel director suggested that it would be more prudent to continue with the depreciation policy followed hitherto for freehold property. After a lengthy discussion, the directors agreed that the freehold property should be depreciated on generally accepted accounting principles.

REQUIRED

(a) A note, prepared in suitable form, for inclusion in the published accounts of the company, showing the information required to be disclosed in relation to tangible fixed assets.

(b) Your comments on the discussion that took place at the directors' meeting on 1 December 19-2 regarding the depreciation policy as it affected freehold property.

ANSWER

(a) Note to balance sheet

Tangible fixed assets

	Freehold land & buildings £'000	Plant & machinery £'000	Motor vehicles £'000
Balance at 31 December 19-1	1,200	640	275
Increase on revaluation	600		
Additions at cost		240	80
Disposals at cost		(140)	(35)
	1,800	740	320
DEPRECIATION			
Provisions at 31 December 19-1	400	210	135
Transfer to Revaluation Reserve	(400)		
Provisions on disposals		(100)	(25)
Charge for the year	56	102	56
	56	212	166
Balance sheet	1,744	528	154

Note to be included under 'Principal accounting policies'

Tangible Fixed Assets

Depreciation is calculated so as to write off the cost of the fixed assets on a straight line basis over the expected useful economic lives of the assets concerned.

The annual rates used for this year are:

Freehold buildings	4%
Plant and machinery	15%
Motor vehicles	20%

The rates shown above for the plant and machinery and motor vehicles are consistent with those used in the previous year.

The rate used for freehold buildings, consequent upon revaluation, is 4%, based upon the revalued amount and the expected remaining useful economic life of 25 years. The additional annual charge for depreciation for freehold buildings resulting from the revaluation amounts to £36,000.

Freehold land is not depreciated.

(b)   The sales director overlooked the fact that although freehold property may appreciate in value, buildings do not have an infinite life and must be replaced at some time in the future.

The personnel director recognised that buildings have finite lives, but overlooked the fact that the previous depreciation policy, at 2% p.a, would write the buildings off over 50 years, whereas the estimated remaining useful economic life is 25 years.

The policy adopted by the Board is to write off the revalued amount of the buildings over 25 years; this conforms with the requirements of SSAP 12.

10.4.2 EXERCISE (Based on the disclosure requirements for tangible fixed assets)

The Wooden Box Co. Ltd. had the following balances in its books at 30 June 19-2:

	£
Freehold land and buildings which cost £250,000 in 1964, and had been revalued in 1971 at	400,000
Plant and machinery purchased on 1 July 19-0 at a cost of	240,000
Plant and machinery purchased on 1 July 19-1 at a cost of	156,000
Motor vehicles purchased on 1 January 19-1 at a cost of	80,000
Motor vehicles purchased on 1 July 19-1 at a cost of	50,000

The annual rates of depreciation, based on cost with estimated nil residual values, and which have always been consistently used are:

Freehold land and buildings	not depreciated
Plant and machinery	20% straight line
Motor vehicles	25% straight line

When the freehold land and buildings were purchased in 1964, the cost was allocated as follows: land £50,000; buildings £200,000. The revalued amount for this asset in 1971 was allocated as follows: land £100,000; buildings £300,000.

In the year to 30 June 19-3, the following events took place:

1.   Freehold land and buildings were again revalued by Coffyn, Paul, Bayer and Stone, chartered surveyors, on 1 July 19-2 at £1,000,000, of which £200,000 related to the land. The freehold buildings were estimated to have a residual life of 20 years.

2.   The following sales took place:

1 January 19-3 Plant and machinery which had been purchased on 1 July 19-0
    at a cost of £100,000

1 April 19-3 Plant and machinery which had been purchased on 1 July 19-1
    at a cost of £6,000

1 April 19-3 Motor vehicles which had been purchased on 1 January 19-1
    at a cost of £20,000

3.   The following purchases were made:

1 July 19-2 A lease on property for 20 years for £100,000

1 October 19-2 Motor vehicles for £32,000

1 January 19-3 Plant and machinery for £110,000

The directors decided to depreciate freehold property and to amortise the lease as from 1 July 19-2 in accordance with accepted accounting practice. The depreciation policy for the other fixed assets was continued consistently with previous years.

REQUIRED

Prepare a note or notes for inclusion in the published accounts of The Wooden Box Company Ltd. to show the information that should be disclosed concerning the tangible fixed assets in the balance sheet at 30 June 19-3.

10.5 THE DIRECTORS' REPORT is required by the Companies' Act 1985 to contain the following matters:

1. Review of the business during the year and of its position at the end of the year. Principal activities of company during year and significant changes in those activities

2. Particulars of significant changes in fixed assets during the financial year. Where the market value of land differs substantially from the value shown in the balance sheet, and that difference is significant, an indication of that difference as precisely as is practicable.

3. Particulars of important events affecting the company since the end of the financial year.

4. An indication of likely future developments in business of company.

5. An Indication of the company's activities in research and development.

6. Amounts of any recommended dividends and proposed transfers to reserves.

7. Names of persons who were directors of company at any time during the year. Their interests in shares or debentures of the company.

8. If money given for political or charitable purposes exceeds £200 in the financial year, a disclosure of the total given for each purpose. If the amount given to a political party exceeds £200, disclosure of the identity of the party and the amount given.

9. Information regarding the arrangements in force for securing the health, safety and welfare at work of the employees.

10. If the average number of employees exceeds 250, a statement of the company's policy regarding the employment of disabled persons.

10.6 MODIFIED ACCOUNTS FOR SMALL AND MEDIUM-SIZED COMPANIES

Small and medium-sized companies are permitted to file modified final accounts with the Registrar of Companies, although they are still required to distribute full accounts to their shareholders. To qualify for this concession they must satisfy at least two of the following criteria:

	Small Companies	Medium Companies
Turnover	Not more than £1,400,000	Not more than £5,750,000
Balance sheet total	Not more than £700,000	Not more than £2,800,000
Average number of employees	Not exceeding 50	Not exceeding 250

Small companies need not file a profit and loss account or directors' report. They may file a modified balance sheet showing only those items to which a letter or a Roman number is assigned in the format (see 10.2)

Medium sized companies must file a profit and loss account in which items 1,2,3 and 6 (turnover, cost of sales, other operating income) in Format 1 may be combined under the heading 'gross profit or loss', which will be the first item in that financial statement. Analyses of turnover and profit are not required. The balance sheet must be prepared in full and the directors' report filed with the accounts..

10.7 AUDITORS' REPORT

The auditors report to the shareholders, not to the directors.

They must satisfy themselves that the company has kept proper accounting records and that the balance sheet and profit and loss account are in agreement with those records. They must state whether in their opinion

(a) the balance sheet and the profit and loss account have been prepared in accordance with the requirements of the Companies Act; and

(b) the balance sheet gives a true and fair view of the company's affairs at the end of the financial year, and the profit and loss account gives a true and fair view of the company's profit or loss for the financial year.

10.8   KEY POINTS TO REMEMBER

1. Memorise the order of items within the formats of the Profit and Loss account and the balance sheet. As far as possible try to keep to the wording prescribed by the Companies' Act.

2. Make yourself familiar with the notes that should be appended to the profit and loss account and the balance sheet, including the forms in which such notes should be prepared as shown in this chapter.

3. Although information required for a note may not be given in a question, you should make reference in your answer to the requirement for the note and its content.

4. When required to prepare accounts in a form suitable for publication, you may be penalised just as severely for disclosing too much information as for disclosing too little; either way, you show that you are unfamiliar with the statutory requirements.

5. In most cases, it is best to treat discounts receivable as a reduction of administrative expenses in published accounts.

COMMON ERRORS

- failure to observe the order of headings within the prescribed format.
- inclusion of items within the wrong headings.
- notes to the accounts omitted as a result of ignorance, oversight; no reference to note because requisite information is not given in question.

10.9   EXAMINATION QUESTIONS

QUESTION 1   (AEB November 1986)

Sagunto Ltd. has an authorised capital of 1.5 million £1 ordinary shares, of which 1 million have been issued as fully paid.

The following information was extracted from the accounts for the year ended 30 September 19-6.

	£	£		£
Freehold premises at cost		250,000	Purchases	430,000
			Returns inward	18,000
Carriage inwards		13,500	Returns outward	25,000
Sales		750,000	Directors' remuneration	20,000
Stock 1 Oct 19-5		80,000		
Wages & salaries:			Auditors' fees	2,500
Administration	20,000		General administrative expenses	9,000
Distribution	40,000	60,000		
Motor vehicle running costs		11,000	Discounts allowed	2,500
			Retained earnings (Cr. Bal. 1 Oct 19-5)	260,000

Additional information

(1) The closing stock was valued at £90,000 cost.

(2) The ordinary share dividends for the year were:

Interim   3% Already paid.

Final   8% Proposed.

(3) The directors decided to transfer £100,000 to General Reserve

(4) Expenses in arrears at 30 September 19-6 were:

	£
Motor vehicle running costs	1,100
Salaries and wages: distribution staff	3,000

(5)   Expenses paid in advance at 30 September 19-6 were:

	£
General administrative expenses	1,500

(6)   The liability for corporation tax for the year ended 30 September 19-6 had been agreed at £95,000

(7)   The company depreciated freehold premises at 4% per annum on cost. Aggregate depreciation to 30 September 19-5 was £40,000.

(8)   On 1 October 19-5 the company's assets included:

	£
Motor vehicles at cost	40,000
Depreciation to date	16,000

Depreciation is provided at 20% per annum on a reducing balance basis.

The above figures include a motor vehicle which cost £8,000, and which had been in company ownership for exactly two years. It was sold for £2,500 on 1 October 19-5. There were no other purchases or sales of vehicles during the year.

(9)   The company's motor vehicles were used by staff as follows

Distribution staff	30,000 miles per annum
Administration staff	10,000 miles per annum

REQUIRED

(a)   The trading and profit and loss account for the year ended 30 September 19-6   *(13 marks)*

(b)   The appropriation account for the year ended 30 September 19-6   *(4 marks)*

(c)   From your answer to (a) above, list those items which the company would be required to include in its published accounts under the Companies' Acts 1948-81.   *(8 marks)*

(Total 25 marks)

Tutorial note: The requirements of the Companies' Acts 1948-81, in so far as they relate to this question, were consolidated in the Companies Act 1985.

QUESTION 2   (AEB November 1989)

Blairgowrie plc produces its annual report and accounts for publication by 31 October. The company has a year end of 31 August and below are details relating to the tangible fixed assets of the company.

(1)   The tangible fixed assets of the company at 31 August 19-8 were as follows:

	Cost	Aggregate depreciation	Net book value
	£'000	£'000	£'000
Land	500	–	500
Buildings	725	145	580
Plant and machinery	490	201	289
Fixtures and fittings	91	33	58

(2)   The company had the land revalued by Mitchie and Partners, chartered surveyors, on 1 September 19-8 at £750,000. The directors have decided to incorporate the revaluation in the accounts.

(3)   Plant and machinery with a cost of £35,000 and aggregate depreciation of £20,664 at 31 August 19-8 was disposed of during the year.

(4)   Plant and machinery costing £53,000 was acquired on 28 February 19-9 and fixtures and fittings costing £6,000 were acquired on 31 May 19-9.

(5)   The methods and rates of depreciation applied to tangible assets are as follows:

Asset	Method	Rate per annum
Land	not depreciated	–
Buildings	straight-line	$2^{1}/_{2}\%$
Plant and machinery	reducing balance	20%
Fixtures and fittings	reducing balance	15%

(6)   No depreciation is charged in the year of disposal of an asset and depreciation is presumed to accrue evenly in the year of acquisition

REQUIRED

(a) What information regarding fixed assets is a public limited company required to disclose to shareholders. *(3 marks)*

(b) Prepare a detailed working note showing the figures relating to tangible fixed assets to be included in the annual accounts of Blairgowrie plc for the year ended 31 August 19-9. *(12 marks)*

(c) Explain why Blairgowrie plc has provided for depreciation of buildings, but not of land. *(2 marks)*

(Total 17 marks)

QUESTION 3 (London June 1988)

Borsetshire Limited's trial balance at 31 May 19-8 was as follows:

	£	£
Advertising	10,500	
Bad debts	587	
Bank interest	2,030	
Bank overdraft		17,750
Cash in hand	370	
Creditors		31,272
Delivery expenses	15,103	
Debtors	107,810	
Debenture interest	1,300	
Directors' salaries	33,600	
Fixtures and fittings (cost £35,000)	17,900	
General reserve		70,000
Insurance	1,900	
Issued share capital:		
100,000 Ordinary shares of £1 each		100,000
43,750 8% Preference shares of £1 each		43,750
Leasehold premises (cost £280,000)	245,000	
Motor Vehicles (cost £56,200)	53,550	
Profit and Loss account		34,895
Provision for bad debts		2,400
Purchases	268,464	
Rent and rates	11,550	
Sales (exclusive of VAT)		468,570
Share premium account		35,250
Stock	20,280	
Sundry expenses	8,268	
Wages and salaries	31,675	
10% debenture 19-0/-5		26,000
	829,887	829,887

Notes:

(1) Stock at 31 May 19-8 was valued at £37,100.

(2) The delivery expenses were the only distribution costs during the year.

(3) Authorised share capital is as follows:
200,000 Ordinary shares of £1 each.
50,000 8% Preference shares of £1 each.

(4) The remainder of the debenture interest is to be accrued.

(5) Depreciation is to be provided as follows:
Leasehold premises at 4% p.a. on cost
Motor vehicles at 20% p.a. on cost
Fixtures and fittings at 40% on reducing balance

142

(6) A dividend of 5% is proposed on the ordinary shares, and the full year's preference dividend is to be provided for

(7) £4,200 is owing for wages and salaries, and £200 has been prepaid for rent at 31 May 19-8

(8) Corporation Tax for the year is to be provided for in the sum of £19,000

(9) The provision for bad debts is to be increased to £2,900

(10) No fixed assets were bought or sold in the year

You are required to prepare:

Borsetshire Limited's profit and loss account for the year ended 31 May 19-8 and a balance sheet as at that date, in a form suitable for publication and complying, in so far as the information permits, with the disclosure requirements of the Companies Act 1985.

(25 marks)

QUESTION 4   (JMB June 1986)

(a) You are required to arrange the following balances in a format that would be acceptable for publication in the audited accounts of Sigma Signs plc. The balances relate to the year ended 31 December 19-5

	£'000s	
	Dr.	**Cr.**
Interest receivable		1,200
Cost of Sales	12,362	
Distributive Costs	893	
Administrative Expenses	1,121	
Interest payable	960	
Turnover		18,326
Taxation on Profit on Ordinary Activities	870	
Extraordinary Loss (net of Taxation)	738	
Proposed Ordinary Dividend	1,200	

(12 marks)

(b) Explain the logic of the presentation that you have used in presenting the accounts of Sigma Signs plc.

(6 marks)

(Total 18 marks)

QUESTION 5   (Cambridge June 1988)

The following balances are taken from the books of Robinson PLC at 30 April 19-8:

	£'000s
Turnover	2,290
Interest payable on short term loans	22
Equipment, at cost	1,420
Provision for depreciation on equipment at 1 May 19-7	570
Quoted investments, at cost	110
Marketing and administration expenses	320
Distribution costs	51
Cost of sales	760
Ordinary share capital, 8 million shares of 25p each	2,000
Investment income, on quoted investments	6
Retained profits at 1 May 19-7	645
Freehold properties, at cost	900

Notes:

1. The above is not a complete list of balances in the Company's books.

2. Marketing and administration expenses (£320,000 above) includes:

	£
Directors' remuneration	115,000
Hire charges under operating leases	47,000
Bad and doubtful debts	15,000
Salesmen's expenses and commissions	29,000

No adjustment has been made to the above figures to take account of the following matters:

3. Depreciation is to be provided on equipment at the rate of 25% on cost.

4. No account has yet been taken of a loss of £450,000 arising following the closure of the Company's business interests in the USA.

5. The basis of the valuation of stock is to be changed in the accounts so that stock values include a proportion of production overhead expenses. The effect of this change of policy is to increase stock valuation figures by 20%.

The relevant stock values are:

	Former basis	New basis
	£	£
1 May 19-7	150,000	180,000
30 April 19-8	200,000	240,000

Note that the 'former basis' was used in calculating the cost of sales given above.

6. Following a professional revaluation it is agreed that the Freehold properties should be revalued at £1,500,000. No depreciation has yet been provided in the Accounts on freehold properties and it is agreed that they have a further useful life of 25 years and should be depreciated over this period.

7. An interim dividend of 2p per share was paid on 1 January 19-8 and provision is to be made for a proposed dividend of 4p a share payable on 1 August 19-8.

REQUIRED

(a) Prepare a Profit and Loss Account for Robinson PLC for the year ended 30 April 19-8 in good style and suitable for publication in the Annual Report and Accounts. *(14 marks)*

(b) A calculation of Earnings per Share for the year. *(3 marks)*

(c) Prepare a note to appear in the Accounts explaining to shareholders the change in the basis of stock valuation. *(5 marks)*

(d) Explain the term 'Extraordinary Item' giving an example of such an item. *(3 marks)*

(Total 25 marks)

QUESTION 6 (Oxford June 1986)

The White Valley Trading plc has the following balances in its books at 31 May 19-6:

	£		£
Premises at cost	3,000,000	Preference dividend paid	70,000
Furniture and Fittings at cost	726,000	Debenture interest paid	80,000
Motor vehicles at cost	450,000	ACT owing	154,900
Equipment at cost	82,400	ACT recoverable	308,571
Stocks at 1 June 19-5	65,700	Goodwill	262,000
Trade Creditors	42,000	Share Premium	83,000
Investments in Green Vale plc	54,000	Capital Reserve	56,000
Administration expenses	152,600	Bank balance (debit)	358,000
Selling and Distribution Expenses	254,529	Prepayments	5,400
Purchases of goods resale	1,720,000	Profit and Loss A/C for 1 June 19-5	120,400
Sales	3,430,000	Share Capital	2,200,000
Trade Debtors	152,300		

	£	Provision for depreciation:	£
Returns Inwards	20,000	Furniture & Fittings	280,000
Returns Outwards	30,000	Motor Vehicles	210,000
Discounts Allowed	14,000	Equipment	22,200
Discounts Received	22,000	Other reserves	70,000
8% Debentures	1,000,000	Debenture RedemptionReserve	150,000
Patents and Trade Marks	95,000		

Notes

1. Included in the administration expenses are:

Depreciation –	Furniture & Fittings	£72,600
	Equipment	3,090

2. Included in Selling & Distribution expenses are:

Depreciation –	Motor Vehicles	£45,000
	Equipment	1,030

3. Stocks at 31 May 19-6   £74,100

4. Amounts owing at 31 May 19-6 are:

Directors' Fees	£8,000
Auditors' Fees	4,200

5. The Directors propose to transfer:

   £50,000 to Debenture Redemption Reserve

   £30,000 to other reserves

   and to pay a dividend to the ordinary shareholders of 15p per share.

6. The Authorised Share Capital of the company is £3,000,000, of this all the preference shares of 10% have been issued and £1,500,000 of the ordinary shares.

   All the shares have a nominal value of £1.

7. The Corporation tax on the year's profits is estimated to be £580,200.

8. Green Vale plc is a subsidiary of White Valley Trading.

9. £400,000 of the debentures are redeemable in January 19-7.

You are required to:

(a) Calculate the Profit and Loss Account balance that would be included in the Balance Sheet at 31 May 19-6,

(b) List in good order and total the items which you would include under the following headings in the published Balance Sheet:

    (i) Intangible Fixed Assets

    (ii) Tangible Fixed Assets

    (iii) Current Assets

    (iv) Creditors' amounts falling due within one year

    (v) Total Assets less Current Liabilities

    (vi) Capital and Reserves

(c) Show what information would be shown in the fixed assets schedule attached to the accounts,

(d) Show the note concerning the called up share capital,

(e) Calculate the total of the published Balance Sheet.

Ignore ACT on Proposed Dividends

(40 marks)

QUESTION 7 (WJEC June 1987)

The following trial balance was extracted from the books of Bardon Trading PLC on 31 March 19-7:

	£	£
Called-up capital:		
1,760,000 Ordinary shares of 25p each		440,000
200,000 10% Preference shares of £1 each,75p called		150,000
Delivery vehicles, at cost	51,000	
Provision for depreciation of delivery vehicles		21,000
Bank loan		60,000
Sales		1,321,000
Cost of sales	1,025,005	
Fixtures and fittings at cost	43,100	
Provision for depreciation of fixtures and fittings		19,040
Stock at 31 March 19-7	278,122	
Freehold premises, at cost	390,000	
13% Loan stock 1997, unsecured		200,000
Profit and loss account balance	62,550	
Trade debtors	322,160	
Trade creditors		181,200
General reserve		50,000
Management expenses	62,600	
Calls on Preference shares unpaid	500	
Interest on loan stock	13,000	
Insurances	3,000	
Directors' fees	33,300	
Interest on bank loan	4,100	
Cash at bank and in hand	52,703	
Wages and salaries	101,100	
	2,442,240	2,442,240

The following matters have to be taken into consideration in preparing the final accounts:

(i) A half year's interest is due on the 13% loan stock

(ii) Depreciation is to be provided as follows:

Fixtures and fittings at the rate of 10 % per annum on cost.

Delivery vehicles at the rate of 20% per annum on cost. They include a new delivery vehicle which was purchased at a cost of £8,000 on 1 October 19-6.

(iii) Authorised capital is as follows:

Ordinary shares of 25p each	£500,000
Preference shares of £1 each	£200,000

(iv) The following apportionments are made between administration expenses and selling and distribution expenses:

	Administration	Selling & distribution
Wages and salaries	75%	25%
Directors' Fees	100%	
Insurance	two-thirds	one-third
Management	80%	20%

(v) Wages and salaries owing amount to £900 and insurance prepaid amounts to £300.

(vi) One year's dividend is to be provided for on the nominal value of the preference shares.

(vii) One quarter of the bank loan is repayable during the year ended 31 March, 19-8 and the remainder after that date.

REQUIRED

Prepare a Profit and Loss Account for the year ended 31 March 19-7 and a Balance Sheet as at that date, drawn up in vertical form incorporating all the information provided, for internal use and for publication, in so far as possible from the information provided. *(28 marks)*

QUESTION 8 (Northern Ireland June 1988)

The fixed asset accounts of the Orb Manufacturing Co Ltd showed the following information at 31 December 19-6:

	£
Freehold properties which cost £300,000 in 19-6, but their book value was a 19-5 valuation of	450,000
Machinery purchased in 19-4, cost	156,000
Machinery purchased in 19-6, cost	72,000
Motor cars purchased in 19-5, cost	30,000

The company maintains separate accounts for properties, machinery and motor cars.

The company has always depreciated machinery over an estimated life of eight years ($12^{1}/_{2}$% on cost straight-line) and motor cars at the rate of 20% by the reducing balance method. A full year's depreciation is provided for in the year of purchase. The company does not provide for depreciation on its freehold property.

The following transactions and other events occurred in the company's accounting year ended 31 December 19-7:

(i) Freehold property which cost £100,000 in 19-6 (19-5 valuation £150,000) was sold for £185,000. The remaining properties were professionally valued in the sum of £360,000 and this valuation is to be incorporated in the books.

(ii) A motor car which cost £6,000 in 19-5 was sold for £2,750.

(iii) A new motor car was leased for an indefinite period (finance lease); under the terms of the lease agreement the company was to pay an annual rental of £3,000 in each of the years 19-7 to 19-0 inclusive and after 19-0 had an option to continue leasing the car for a nominal sum. The cost of the car if it had been purchased outright would have been £10,500 (fair value). The company decided to write off one-half of the finance charge against profits in 19-7, one third in 19-8 and one-sixth in 19-9.

(iv) A review of the expected life of the machinery was carried out which determined the remaining life (irrespective of date of purchase) at just under seven years including 19-7. Accordingly the unamortised cost at 1 January 19-7 is to be written off at 15% straight-line.

REQUIRED

(a) *Reproduced below is a partially completed fixed asset schedule which, when fully completed, will enable the Orb Manufacturing Co Ltd to comply with the disclosure requirements of the Companies Act in relation to fixed assets for the year ended 31 December 19-7.*

	Freehold property	Machinery	Motor Cars	Leased Motor Car
	£	£	£	£
COST OR VALUATION				
Book value at 31 December 19-6 in relation to 19-5 valuation	450,000	–	–	–
Cost at 31 December 19-6	–	228,000	30,000	–
Additions	–	–	–	–
Disposals	–	–	–	–
Amount added on revaluation	–	–	–	–
Book value at 31 December 19-7 in relation to 19-7 valuation	–	–	–	–
Cost at 31 December 19-7	–			

	Freehold property	Machinery	Motor Cars	Leased Motor Cars
	£	£	£	£
DEPRECIATION				
At 31 December 19-6	–			
Charge for 19-7	–		–	
Eliminated on disposals	–	–	(2,160)	–
At 31.December 19-7				
Net Book Value at 31 December 19-7				

You are required to reproduce the above proforma schedule and complete it in accordance with the information supplied

(12 marks)

(b) You are required to prepare for the year ended 31 December 19-7:

   (i) profit and loss account and balance sheet extracts (not including the fixed asset schedule) relating to the costs and financing of fixed assets; *(5 marks)*

and (ii) movements on reserves (both unrealised and realised capital reserves). *(4 marks)*

(c) You are required to indicate the extent to which the accounting policies of the Orb Manufacturing Co Ltd are *not* in agreement with SSAP No. 12 (Accounting for Depreciation). *(4 marks)*

(Total 25 marks)

_11_ STATEMENTS OF STANDARD ACCOUNTING PRACTICE

Statements of Standard Accounting Practice (SSAPs) are a very important topic at Advanced Level and are specifically included in the syllabi; they may be examined either

- directly in questions requiring explanations or discussion of the principles involved in one or more specified Standards
- directly in questions requiring an explanation of the correct accounting treatment of certain transactions or situations according to Standards not specified in the question
- indirectly in accounting questions where the correct treatment of transactions or situations will only result from an application of an appropriate Standard

---

ABOUT SSAPs.

1. An unsatisfactory situation existed in company reporting up to the end of the 1960's.

2. Treatment by companies of certain kinds of transactions and the way they reported certain situations was not necessarily incorrect, but relied upon opinions of directors and accountants.

3. As result of 2. above, the objectivity upon which company reporting should be based suffered, and so did public confidence in the accounting profession.

4. To remedy the situation, the major professional accountancy bodies established the Consultative Committee of Accountancy Bodies (CCAB) to coordinate future policies and pronouncements regarding recommended practices.

5. The Accounting Standards Committee (ASC) is a sub-committee of the CCAB and its purpose is to set standards, the objects of which are:

   1. To narrow the areas of difference and variety in accounting;
   2. To recommend disclosure of accounting bases;
   3. To require disclosure of departure from standards;
   4. To introduce a system for wide consultation on standard setting;
   5. To seek improvements in existing disclosure requirements of company law and the Stock Exchange.

6. All members of the professional accountancy bodies comprising the CCAB are expected to comply with SSAPs currently in use. All auditors of limited companies belong to one of four of the bodies as do many company directors and company accountants.

7. Any significant departure from any of the standards must be disclosed in the accounts unless it would be impracticable or misleading to do so in the context of giving a true and fair view.

8. Deliberate failure to comply with the standards can result in the appropriate professional body taking disciplinary action against the offending member or members.

11.1 SUMMARIES OF THE STATEMENTS OF STANDARD ACCOUNTING PRACTICE

SSAP 1 ACCOUNTING FOR ASSOCIATED COMPANIES

Tutorial note: We have already met the term 'Related company' in the balance sheet format in Chapter 10. The Companies Act 1985 defines 'Related company' slightly differently from the definition given to 'Associated company' in this SSAP. Advanced level students may take the two terms as being synonymous.

Associated company: A company in which:

(a) the interest of the investing company (or group) is effectively that of a partner in a joint venture or consortium and the investing company (or group) is in a position to exercise significant influence over the company in which the investment is made; or

(b) The interest of the investing company (or group) is for the long term and is substantial and having regard to the disposition of the other shareholdings, the investing company (or group) is in a position to exercise a significant influence over the company in which the investment is made.

Accounting requirements:

Profit and loss account:	Dividends received and receivable must be shown
Balance sheet:	Interest in associated company must be shown at valuation, or at cost less amounts written off.

The names of the principal associated companies should be disclosed in the financial statements of the investing company with details, for each of the companies, of the proportion of the number of the issued shares of each class held and an indication of the nature of its business.

Tutorial note: The requirements of the SSAP regarding consolidated accounts are outside the scope of this work.

SSAP 2 DISCLOSURE OF ACCOUNTING POLICIES

Tutorial note: This SSAP is an important examination topic and students should be familiar with its contents.
The SSAP defines three terms:

Fundamental Accounting Concepts

Broad basic assumptions which underlie the periodic financial accounts of business enterprises.
The SSAP mentions four concepts in particular: going concern; accruals; consistency; prudence.

Accounting Bases

The methods which have been developed for expressing or applying fundamental accounting concepts to financial transactions and items.

The SSAP mentions a number of matters for which different accounting bases are recognised: depreciation of fixed assets; (e.g straight line, reducing balance, etc.) treatment and amortisation of intangibles (such as research and development expenditure, patents and trade marks); stocks and work in progress (e.g. FIFO, LIFO AVCO, etc.); long term contracts etc.

Accounting Policies

The specific accounting bases judged by business enterprises to be most appropriate to their circumstances, and adopted by them for the purpose of preparing their financial accounts.
The SSAP defines the four concepts mentioned above.

(a) *The Going Concern Concept:* the enterprise will continue in operational existence for the foreseeable future. This means in particular that the profit and loss account and the balance sheet assume no intention or necessity to liquidate or curtail significantly the scale of operation.

(b) *The Accruals Concept:* revenue and costs are accrued (that is, recognised as they are earned or incurred, not as money is received or paid), matched with one another so far as their relationship can be established or justifiably assumed, and dealt with in the profit and loss account of the period to which they relate; but if the accruals concept conflicts with the concept of prudence in any particular circumstance, the latter prevails.

(c) *The Consistency Concept:* there is consistency of accounting treatment of like items within each accounting period and from one period to the next.

(d) *The Prudence Concept:* revenue and profits are not anticipated, but are recognised by inclusion in the profit and loss account only when realised in the form either of cash or of other assets the ultimate cash realisation of which can be assessed with reasonable certainty: provision is made for all known liabilities (expenses and losses) whether the amount of these is known with certainty or is a best estimate in the light of the information available.

Requirements of SSAP

If accounts are prepared using different concepts from the four mentioned above, that fact must be disclosed. In the absence of a clear statement to the contrary, there is a presumption that the four fundamental concepts have been observed.

The accounting policies followed for dealing with items which are judged to be material or critical in determining profit or loss for the year and in stating the financial position should be disclosed by way of a note to the accounts.

Tutorial note: The Companies Act 1985 includes all four of the above concepts as the accounting principles stated in schedule 4 of the Act.

SSAP 3 EARNINGS PER SHARE

This SSAP applies only to companies listed on a recognised stock exchange; such companies are required by this SSAP to show the earnings per share on the face of the profit and loss account.

Earnings = profit after tax and any preference share dividends.

Earnings per share is found by dividing the earnings by the number of ordinary shares.

The SSAP deals with complications in calculating the EPS as a result of taxation, changes in share capital and dilution of earnings and a further consideration of these matters is beyond the scope of this work.

SSAP 4 ACCOUNTING FOR GOVERNMENT GRANTS

Under certain circumstances, businesses may obtain government grants towards expenditure incurred. The grants may be towards revenue expenditure (for example, wages in an area having high unemployment), or capital expenditure.

Revenue-based grants should be credited to revenue in the same period in which the revenue expenditure to which they relate is charged.

Grants relating to fixed assets should be credited to revenue over the expected useful life of the asset by:

(a) crediting the amount of the grant to the fixed asset account; or

(b) crediting the amount to a special account, and transferring a portion of the amount to revenue annually.

Tutorial note: both methods achieve the result of spreading the grant over the useful life of the asset: the grant either reduces the annual charge for depreciation (method (a)), or results in a credit annually to the profit and loss account (method (b)).

SSAP 5 ACCOUNTING FOR VALUE ADDED TAX.

In the case of businesses registered for VAT purposes, sales should be credited to the Sales account net of VAT and the VAT credited to 'H.M.Customs and Excise' account. Similarly, purchases should be debited net of VAT to Purchases account, and the VAT debited to 'H.M.Customs and Excise' account. Any credit balance on 'H.M.Customs and Excise' account is an amount due to them; a debit balance represents the amount of refund due from H.M.Customs and Excise.

In the following cases, VAT is not recoverable on purchases:

(a) businesses not registered for VAT

(b) businesses carrying on exempted activities, such as banks and insurance companies

(c) 'non-deductible inputs', VAT on private motor cars and entertainment of UK customers. In these cases, the gross amount of expenditure (including VAT) will be debited to the accounts concerned.

In all other cases, sales, purchases and expenses will be shown 'net' in the accounts.

SSAP 6 EXTRAORDINARY ITEMS AND PRIOR YEAR ADJUSTMENTS.

Tutorial note: Questions requiring a knowledge of the contents of this SSAP are set to test students' recognition of 'Extraordinary items' which are required to be shown separately in the balance sheet as distinct from 'exceptional items which should be separately disclosed by way of note. It is also important to distinguish between prior year adjustments which require a restatement of the retained profits brought forward from the previous year, and those items to be adjusted through the current profit and loss account.

Extraordinary items are material items which derive from events or transactions that fall outside the ordinary activities of the company and which are therefore expected not to recur frequently or regularly. Amongst the examples mentioned in the SSAP are:

- discontinuance of part of a business (involving, for example, redundancy payments)
- sale of an investment not originally acquired for the purpose of resale, such as investments in subsidiary and associated companies
- material profit or loss on sale of fixed asset
- provision for permanent diminution in value of fixed asset because of extraordinary events during the period.

Extraordinary items must be shown in the profit and loss account in one of the positions shown in the format for published accounts.(See Chapter 10) Particulars of such items must be disclosed either on the face of the profit and loss account or by way of note.

Exceptional items are material items which derive from events or transactions that fall within the ordinary activities of the company, but which need to be disclosed separately by virtue of their size or incidence if the financial statements are to give a true and fair view. Amongst the examples mentioned in the SSAP are:
- redundancy costs relating to a continuing part of the business
- material profit or loss on sale of fixed asset
- abnormal charges for bad debts and write-offs of stock and work in progress
- abnormal provisions for losses on long-term contracts

Exceptional items require separate disclosure for the financial statements to give a true and fair view; it is normally sufficient for this to be by way of a note to the financial statements provided they are clearly identified as exceptional items.

Prior Year Adjustments are those material adjustments applicable to prior years arising from changes in accounting policies or from the correction of fundamental errors.

They do not include normal recurring corrections or adjustments of accounting estimates made in prior years.

Prior year adjustments should be made by adjusting the balance of retained profit brought forward from the previous year; full disclosure of such adjustments should be made in the accounts.

Normal corrections or adjustments of accounting estimates made in prior years must be corrected through the profit and loss account of the current year.

SSAP 8 THE TREATMENT OF TAXATION UNDER THE IMPUTATION SYSTEM IN THE ACCOUNTS OF COMPANIES

Tutorial note: Companies are subject to Corporation tax on their profits, the tax being payable 9 months after the end of the financial year. When a company pays a dividend, it must make an advance payment of part of the corporation tax due on the profit of the year on which the dividend is paid. This payment of Advance Corporation Tax (ACT) is 'imputed' to the recipients of the dividend, who receive the dividend and a tax credit (a 'certificate') equal to their 'share' of the ACT. 'Franked Investment Income' is a dividend received by one company from another UK company.

The SSAP requires the following:

Companies must show:

Franked Investment Income in their profit and loss account gross; ie the amount of cash received plus the tax credit.

Dividends paid or proposed in their profit and loss account net ie only the amount of cash paid or payable.

Corporation tax must be shown in the appropriate place in the profit and loss account format.

In the balance sheet, proposed dividends net, and the ACT relating to those dividends as a current liability

SSAP 9 STOCKS AND WORK IN PROGRESS

Tutorial note: This is probably the SSAP which forms the basis of examination questions more than any other. It is one with which the student must be properly acquainted because of the considerable impact which the valuation of stocks and work in progress can have on profit and the working capital of a business. The topic is dealt with further in Chapter 16.

Definitions:

Stocks and work in progress include:

(a) goods or other assets purchased for resale

(b) consumable stores

(c) raw materials and components purchased for incorporation into products for sale

(d) products and services in intermediate stages of completion

(e) finished goods

Cost: expenditure which has been incurred in the normal course of business in bringing the product or service to its present location and condition.

Cost of conversion comprises:

(a) costs which are specifically attributable to units of production, i.e. direct labour, direct expenses and sub-contracted work;

(b) production overheads (see below);

(c) other overheads, if applicable.

Production overheads: overheads incurred in respect of materials, labour or services for production, based on the normal level of activity, taking one year with another.

Net realisable value: the actual or estimated selling price

less:

(a)   all further costs to completion; and

(b)   all costs to be incurred in marketing, selling and distributing.

FIFO (first in, first out): the calculation of the cost of stocks and work in progress on the basis that the quantities in hand represent the latest purchases or production.

LIFO (last in, first out): the calculation of the cost of stocks and work in progress on the basis that the quantities in hand represent the earliest purchases or production.

Long term contract: a contract entered into for manufacture or building of a single substantial entity or the provision of a service where the time taken to manufacture, build or provide is such that a substantial proportion of all such contract work will extend for a period exceeding one year.

Requirements of SSAP

Stocks and Work in Progress (other than long term contract work in progress) should be stated at the total of the lower of cost and net realisable value of the separate items of stock and work in progress or of groups of similar items.

Valuation at replacement cost, where this is less than net realisable value, is not acceptable if the effect would be to take account of a loss greater than that which is expected to be incurred.

To compare the total realisable value of stocks with the total cost could result in an unacceptable setting off of foreseeable losses against unrealised profit.

Manufactured Goods and Work in Progress should be valued at total cost and not marginal cost even though some of the production overheads may accrue on a time basis.

Tutorial note: This will result in some overheads being carried forward to a future period in the closing stock instead of being borne in the period in which they were incurred. This seems to conflict with the concepts of matching and prudence; but the SSAP takes the view that the recommended practice results in truer figures for profit and closing stock.

SSAP 9 does not recommend the use of LIFO for valuing stock and work in progress as it does not usually bear a reasonable relationship to actual costs obtaining during a period. (In contrast, the Companies Act 1985 appears to regard LIFO as acceptable.)

Long Term Contracts These should be valued at cost plus any attributable profit, less any foreseeable losses and progress payments received and receivable. If anticipated losses on individual contracts exceed cost incurred to date less progress payments received and receivable, such excesses should be shown separately as provisions. (Attributable profit is that part of the total profit currently estimated to arise over the duration of the contract which fairly reflects the profit attributable to that part of the work performed at the accounting date.)

SSAP 10 STATEMENTS OF SOURCE AND APPLICATION OF FUNDS

The SSAP requires a statement of source and application of funds to be included in the audited financial accounts of companies with a turnover or gross income of £25,000 or more per annum.

The statement should show the profit or loss for the period together with the adjustments required for items which did not use (or provide) funds in the period. The following items, being sources and applications of funds, should, where material, be shown:

(a)   dividends paid

(b)   acquisitions and disposals of fixed and other non-current assets

(c)   funds raised by increasing, or expended in repaying or redeeming, medium or long-term loans or the issued capital of the company

(d)   increase or decrease in working capital sub-divided into its components, and movements in net liquid funds.

Net Liquid Funds = cash at bank and in hand and investments etc. held as current assets less bank overdrafts and other borrowings repayable within one year of the accounting date.

The funds statement will provide a link between the balance sheet at the beginning of the period, the profit and loss account for the period and the balance sheet at the end of the period.

A minimum of 'netting off' should take place as this may tend to mask the significance of individually important figures.

The figures from which a funds statement is constructed should be identifiable in the profit and loss account, balance sheet and related notes.

Tutorial note: Statements of source and application of funds are dealt with in detail in Chapter 12.

SSAP 12 ACCOUNTING FOR DEPRECIATION

Tutorial note: This is another important examination topic; students should familiarise themselves thoroughly with the requirements of this SSAP.

Depreciation is the measure of the wearing out, consumption or other loss of value of a fixed asset whether arising from use, effluxion of time or obsolescence through technology and market changes. (as defined by SSAP 12).

Accounting treatment:

Provision for depreciation of fixed assets having a finite useful life should be made by allocating the cost (or revalued amount) less estimated residual values of the assets as fairly as possible to the periods expected to benefit from their use.

Where there is a revision of the estimated useful life of an asset, the unamortised cost should be charged over the revised remaining useful life.

If at any time the unamortised cost of an asset is seen to be irrecoverable in full, it should be written down immediately to the estimated recoverable amount which should be charged over the remaining useful life.

A change from one method of providing depreciation to another is permissible only on the grounds that the new method will give a fairer presentation of the results and of the financial position.

Where there is a change from one method of depreciation to another, the unamortised cost of the asset should be written off over the remaining useful life on the new basis commencing with the period in which the change is made. The effect should be disclosed in the year of change, if material.

Where assets are revalued in the financial statements, the provision for depreciation should be based upon the revalued amount and current estimate of remaining useful life, with disclosure in the year of change, of the effect of the revaluation, if material.

It is not appropriate to omit charging depreciation of a fixed asset on the grounds that its market value is greater than its net book value.

Freehold land, unless subject to depletion by, for example, the extraction of minerals or to reduction in value due to other circumstances, will not normally require a provision for depreciation. However, the value of freehold land may be adversely affected by considerations such as the desirability of its location either socially or in relation to available sources of materials, labour or sales and in these circumstances it should be written down.

Buildings have a limited life which may be materially affected by technological and environmental changes and they should be depreciated having regard to the same criteria as in the case of other fixed assets.

An increase in the value of land and buildings does not remove the necessity for charging depreciation on the buildings.

This SSAP does not apply to investment properties, see SSAP19.

The following should be disclosed in the financial statements for each major class of depreciable asset:

(a) the depreciation methods used;

(b) the useful lives or the depreciation rates used;

(c) total depreciation allocated for the period;

(d) the gross amount of depreciable assets and the related accumulated depreciation.

SSAP 13 ACCOUNTING FOR RESEARCH AND DEVELOPMENT

Definitions:

Pure research

Original investigation undertaken in order to gain new scientific or technical knowledge and understanding; not primarily directed towards any specific practical aim or objective.

Applied research

Original investigation undertaken in order to gain new scientific or technical knowledge and directed towards a specific practical aim or objective.

Development

The use of scientific or technical knowledge in order to produce new or substantially improved materials, devices, products, processes, systems or services prior to the commencement of commercial production.

Accounting treatment

The cost of **fixed assets** acquired or constructed to provide facilities for research and development activities over a number of accounting periods should be capitalised and written off over their useful life.

Tutorial note: In other words, treated like any other fixed asset.

Other expenditure on **pure and applied research** should be written off in the year of expenditure

Development expenditure should be written off in the year of expenditure except in the following circumstances when it may be deferred to future periods:

(a) there is a **clearly defined project**

(b) the related expenditure is **separately identifiable**

(c) The outcome of such a project has been assessed with reasonable certainty as to

    (i) its **technical feasibility**

    (ii) its ultimate **commercial viability**

(d) If further development costs are to be incurred on the same project the **aggregate of such costs** are reasonably expected to be **more than covered** by related future revenues.

(e) **Adequate resources** exist, or are reasonably expected to be available, to enable the project to be completed and to provide any consequential increases in working capital.

SSAP 14 GROUP ACCOUNTS

If Company A owns more than 50 per cent of the ordinary shares of Company B or, being a shareholder in Company B controls the composition of B's board of directors, Company A is the holding company of Company B, and Company B is a subsidiary company of Company A.

The SSAP requires a holding company to prepare group accounts for itself and its subsidiary companies in the form of a consolidated profit and loss account and consolidated balance sheet as if they were the financial statements of a single entity.

If a holding company owns less than 100 per cent of the equity share capital in a subsidiary, some of the profits and net assets of the subsidiary will belong to other shareholders, known as the 'minority interests'.

Group accounts are outside the scope of this text. Suffice it to say that the topic is a rather complex one, and SSAP 14 sets out the standard accounting practice to be adopted in the preparation of group accounts.

SSAP 15 ACCOUNTING FOR DEFERRED TAX

This SSAP is outside the scope of this book but since 'deferred tax' has of necessity been alluded to in Chapter 10 in the balance sheet format (item I 2), a very brief account of it is included now.

The liability to tax is calculated on a different profit figure from that appearing in the profit and loss account of a company. That is because some items of expense not deductible for tax purposes have been deducted in the profit and loss account, whilst other items, not subject to corporation tax have been credited in the profit and loss account.

There are other items which are taxable, or allowable as deductions for tax purposes, but not in the same period as they appear in the profit and loss account; they are recognised for tax purposes in a later period. Income accrued but not received will be credited in the profit and loss account in the year in which it is receivable, but will not be taxed until it is actually received in a later period. A general provision for bad debts will not be allowed for tax purposes, but the debts will be allowed if they actually become bad in a later period. These are examples of timing differences. Depreciation is another such item.

The SSAP states that provision should be made for tax on items which are the subject of timing differences and sets out the accounting treatment for the provision for 'deferred tax'.

SSAP 17 ACCOUNTING FOR POST BALANCE SHEET EVENTS

Events arising after the balance sheet date need to be reflected in the financial statements of a company if they provide additional evidence of conditions that existed at the balance sheet date and materially affect the amounts to be included.

Definitions:

Adjusting events are post balance sheet events which provide additional evidence of conditions existing at the balance sheet date. e.g. fixed assets may have been purchased or sold before the balance sheet date, but the purchase or selling price, as the case may be, was not determined until after the balance sheet date. The valuation of property after the balance sheet date may provide evidence of the value of that property at the balance sheet date.

Non-adjusting events are post balance sheet events which concern conditions which did not exist at the balance sheet date; e.g. losses of fixed assets or stocks after the balance sheet date as a result of a catastrophe such as fire or flood; closing a significant part of the trading activities after the balance sheet date if this was not anticipated at the year end.

A material post balance sheet event requires **changes** in the amounts to be included in the financial statements where:

(a) it is an adjusting event; or

(b) it indicates that application of the going concern concept to the whole or a material part of the company is not appropriate.

A material post balance sheet event should be **disclosed** where:

(a) it is a non-adjusting event of such materiality that its non-disclosure would affect the ability of the users of the financial statements to reach a proper understanding of the financial position; or

(b) it is the reversal or maturity after the end of the year end of a transaction entered into before the year end, the substance of which was primarily to alter the appearance of the company's balance sheet.

In this case, the following information should be stated by way of notes in the financial statements:

(a) the nature of the event; and

(b) an estimate of the financial effect, or a statement that it is not practicable to make such an estimate.

SSAP 18 ACCOUNTING FOR CONTINGENCIES

Definition: A contingency is a condition which exists at the balance sheet date, where the outcome will be confirmed only on the occurrence or non-occurrence of one or more uncertain future events.

Accounting practice: A material contingent material loss should be accrued in the financial statements where it is **probable** that a future event will confirm a loss which can be estimated with reasonable accuracy at the date on which the financial statements are approved by the board of directors.

A material contingent loss not accrued should be disclosed except where the possibility of loss is **remote**.

Contingent gains should not be accrued in the financial statements. A material contingent gain should be disclosed in financial statements only if it is probable that the gain will be realised.

The following information should be stated by way of notes in respect of each contingency which is required to be disclosed:

(a) the nature of the contingency

(b) the uncertainties which are expected to affect the ultimate outcome; and

(c) a prudent estimate of the financial effect, or a statement that it is not practicable to make such an estimate.

SSAP 19 ACCOUNTING FOR INVESTMENT PROPERTIES

Investment properties should not be subject to periodic charges for depreciation on the basis set out in SSAP 12, except for properties held on lease which should be depreciated on the basis set out in SSAP 12 at least over the period when the unexpired term is 20 years or less.

Investment properties should be included in the balance sheet at their open market value.

Changes in the value of investment properties should not be taken to the profit and loss account but should be disclosed as a movement on an investment revaluation reserve. There should never be a debit balance on the investment revaluation reserve; any deficit should be charged in the profit and loss account in the period in which it arises.

SSAP 22 ACCOUNTING FOR GOODWILL

Definitions

Goodwill is the difference between the value of a business as a whole and the aggregate of the fair values of its separable net assets.

Purchased goodwill is goodwill which is established as a result of the purchase of a business accounted for as an acquisition.

Non-purchased goodwill is any goodwill other than purchased goodwill.

Accounting practice

Non-purchased goodwill should not be shown in the balance sheet.

The amount to be attributed to goodwill should be the difference between the fair value of the consideration given and the aggregate of the fair values of the separable net assets acquired.

The amount attributed to purchased goodwill should not include any value for separable intangibles. The amount of these, if material, should be included under the appropriate heading within intangible fixed assets in the balance sheet.

Purchased goodwill should not be carried in the balance sheet of a company as a permanent item

Purchased goodwill (other than negative goodwill) should normally be eliminated from the accounts immediately on acquisition against reserves, or may be amortised through the profit and loss account in arriving at profit or loss on ordinary activities on a systematic basis over its useful life.

Negative goodwill should be credited directly to reserve.

The accounting policy followed in respect of goodwill should be explained in the notes to the accounts.

SSAP 23 ACCOUNTING FOR ACQUISITIONS AND MERGERS

This SSAP is outside the scope of this work.

SSAP 24 ACCOUNTING FOR PENSION COSTS

Tutorial note: This is a long Statement and a detailed examination is outside the scope of this work; but the student should be aware of the purpose this SSAP as stated in the introduction to the Explanatory note.

Importance of pension costs.

The provision of a pension is part of the remuneration package of many employees. Pension costs form a significant proportion of total payroll costs and they give rise to special problems of estimation and of allocation between accounting periods. Accordingly, it is important that standard accounting practice exists concerning the recognition of such costs in the employers' financial statements. This statement deals with the accounting for, and the disclosure of, pension costs and commitments in the financial statements of enterprises that have pension arrangements for the provision of retirement benefits for their employees.

11.2   KEY POINTS TO REMEMBER

1. Try to understand the concepts that underlie each SSAP. This will help you to remember the requirements of each one more easily and accurately than if you try to learn them parrot-fashion.

2. You should be able to explain and discuss the requirements of SSAPs clearly and concisely in your own words to show that you understand them. Illustrate your answers with simple but apt examples where appropriate.

3. Look for occasions in the production of financial statements where you will be expected to demonstrate your knowledge of SSAPs.

COMMON ERRORS

- insufficient attention paid in the preparation for examinations to the contents and requirements of SSAPs.

- failure to recognise the application of SSAPs in the preparation of financial statements, especially those requiring the statements to be prepared in a form suitable for publication.

11.3 EXAMINATION QUESTIONS

QUESTION 1 (AEB June 1988)

A member of the board of Shoprite Enterprises plc has suggested two accounting policies for consideration by the financial director in preparing the latest set of accounts. These have been summarised as follows:

(i) The incorporation of goodwill in the accounts as a permanent fixed asset in recognition of the favourable trading situations of several of the business's outlets and also to reflect the quality of management experience in the business.

(ii) No depreciation to be provided in future on the buildings owned by the company because their market value is constantly appreciating and, in addition, this will result in an increase of the profit of the company.

REQUIRED

(a) Briefly explain your understanding of each of the following:

    (i)   goodwill

    (ii)   depreciation. *(3 marks)*

(b) Discuss the acceptability of each of the above suggested accounting policies, highlighting any conflict with accounting concepts. *(8 marks)*

(Total 11 marks)

QUESTION 2 (AEB November 1988)

There are a number of accounting conventions (sometimes called concepts), of which the following are examples:

(1) The materiality convention.

(2) The going concern convention.

(3) The consistency convention.

(4) The accruals convention.

REQUIRED

(a) A concise explanation of the meaning of the above conventions. *(12 marks)*

(b) Give examples to illustrate each of your answers to (a) using figures where appropriate.

(13 marks)

(Total 25 marks)

QUESTION 3 (London January 1987)

The auditors' report to the shareholders of a public limited company included the following two paragraphs:

'The accounts have been prepared on a going concern basis and the validity of this depends on the company's bankers continuing their support by providing adequate overdraft facilities'.

'Because of the materiality of the matters referred to in a previous paragraph we are unable to form an opinion as to whether the accounts give a true and fair view of the state of affairs of the company.'

You are required to explain the following terms:

(a) Going concern basis

(b) Materiality. *(10 marks)*

QUESTION 4 (London June 1987)

The auditor's report on the accounts of a public limited company included the following two paragraphs:

'As explained in the note on accounting policies, it is the Company's policy to capitalise costs incurred on the research and development of the Company's inventions. The costs capitalised during the year have been quantified by the Directors and represent their allocation and apportionment of expenditure incurred for these purposes. We have been unable to determine whether the amounts capitalised of £3,600,000 have been properly quantified or whether it is appropriate to carry forward these amounts in the balance sheet.'

'The Accounts have been prepared on a going concern basis, and the validity of this depends on the Company's bankers continuing their support by providing adequate overdraft facilities.'

(a) In relation to the first paragraph, discuss the circumstances where it *might* be appropriate for a company to carry forward these amounts in the balance sheet. *(9 marks)*

(b) In relation to the second paragraph, explain the meaning 'going concern basis' and discuss the possible changes to a balance sheet which had *not* been prepared on such a basis. *(6 marks)*

(Total 15 marks)

QUESTION 5   (Author's question, after JMB)

The turnover of Laburnam PLC is £250 million per annum and the pre-tax profit is £32 million. Its financial year ends on 31 December and the following matters have arisen in the year to 31 December 19-1:

(i)   A loss of £40m. on a major long-term contract, which is due for completion in 19-2, is now a certainty. Provision for the loss must be made in the accounts for the year to 31 December 19-1.

(ii) The company's freehold properties have been professionally revalued during the year revealing an unrealised surplus of £18.4 million. Accordingly, the properties are to be shown in the balance sheet as at 31 December 19-1 at the amount of the revaluation.

(iii) One of the company's factories was closed down during the year; the cost of the closure amounted to £3 million.

(iv) Goodwill was shown in the balance sheet at 31 December 19-0 at £400,000. The directors are now of the opinion that it is valueless and should be written off.

(v)   During the year, expenditure of £5.6 million was incurred on research and development. The directors have now concluded that the project is no longer viable and must be abandoned.

You are required to classify each of the above items into one of the following categories and explain the reason for the classification in each case:

(a) Extraordinary item

(b) Exceptional (abnormal) item

(c) Transfer to reserves. *(20 marks)*

QUESTION 6   (JMB June 1986)

The ledgers of Gamma plc have been closed for the year ending 31 March 19-6, and the following items have been referred to the directors by the company accountant and all are considered to be of material significance.

(i)   A Government grant of £265,000 for a new factory has been approved and, although the funds have not been received, the project was completed during the financial year. The new factory is to be depreciated over 15 years.

(ii) Theta Limited, which owes Gamma plc £138,000 at 31 March 19-6, has gone into receivership and it is forecast that the unsecured creditors of Theta Limited are likely, in due course, to receive approximately 25 pence in the pound.

(iii) During the stocktaking it was found that, of the total stock of £835,000, approximately £93,000 of stock was missing and had been misappropriated. A further £50,000 of stock was estimated to be obsolete, with very little likelihood of resale.

(iv) The directors have received a professional valuation of the company's properties valuing them at £2,850,000 as against the cost of £1,935,000 which is recorded in the accounts.

(v)   Due to unusual market conditions, Gamma plc has managed to negotiate the sale of an existing contract with Sigma Limited to Alpha plc for £385,000, with no costs to be borne by Gamma plc.

You are required:

(a) to advise the directors how each item should be treated in the company's audited accounts; *(13 marks)*

(b) to explain any alternative treatments and refer to Statements of Standard Accounting Practice where appropriate. *(12 marks)*

(Total 25 marks)

QUESTION 7   (JMB June 1986)

(a) The Accounting Standards Committee has produced its Statement of Standard Accounting Practice Number 18, Accounting for Contingencies.

(i)   What is a contingency?   *(2 marks)*

(ii) What are the alternative accounting treatments for contingencies?   *(3 marks)*

(iii) Explain how the alternative accounting treatments are determined.   *(3 marks)*

(b) The Delta Company manufactures and sells a fluorescent thermostat. The financial year end was 31 March 19-6. How should the following items be dealt with in the accounts for the year ended 31 March 19-6?

(i)   A competitor has started producing a similar product which, it is believed, is in breach of a patent owned by Delta. On 25 February 1 19-6 the company commenced legal proceedings. These are progressing slowly, but the company's lawyers believe that there is a 70 per cent chance that within twelve months the company could receive damages in the region of £250,000.   *(5 marks)*

(ii) A customer has also commenced legal proceedings against Delta for damages based on a claim that the thermostat has caused ill health due to radiation. The company's lawyers believe that the £500,000 claim for damages has only a 30 per cent chance of success. At 31 March 19-6 correspondence between the two parties was at a preliminary stage. *(5 marks)*

(Total 18 marks)

QUESTION 8   (JMB June 1987)

Snak-pak Limited manufactures packaging for the retail food market. The following information relates to the year ending 30 April 19-7.

(i)   On 1 April 19-7 the directors decided to close down a subsidiary engaged in the manufacture of freezer packaging materials. The estimated cost of termination of this activity is £417,000.

(ii) During the year, the company spent £300,000 on research and development. £200,000 of this expenditure related to the development of a new packaging material for hot foods. A major hamburger chain has been conducting trials of the new product and it is anticipated full scale production of this product will commence in August 19-7. The remaining research expenditure has been spent in trying, without success, to improve the durability of their microwave packaging material.

(iii) The moulding equipment currently being used to produce hot foods packaging has a net book value of £320,000 and is being depreciated at 20% per annum on the reducing balance. This equipment is not suitable for processing the new material referred to above, and the directors estimate the realisable value of this equipment to be £40,000.

(iv) After the company's year end on 24 May 19-7, the company moved its distribution organisation from Macclesfield to Telford. It is estimated that the capital expenditure in connection with this move will be in the region of £400,000.

(v)   A decision was taken during the year to change the depreciation policy on certain major items of plant from the reducing balance method to the straight line method.

You are required to advise the directors on the treatment of the above matters in the Profit and Loss Account and Balance Sheet. Make reference, where appropriate, to any relevant Statement of Standard Accounting Practice.

(25 marks)

QUESTION 9   (JMB June 1987)

(a) Define goodwill and explain how it arises in a company's accounts.   *(5 marks)*

(b) Outline the alternative treatments of goodwill that are permitted by Statement of Standard Accounting Practice Number 22, Accounting for Goodwill.   *(4 marks)*

(c) Explain the principles underlying the treatments permitted by the Standard.   *(8 marks)*

(Total 17 marks)

QUESTION 10 (JMB June 1988)

The following is a list of unrelated transactions of different companies and shows the proposed treatment of these transactions in the accounts of the company concerned.

(i) Buildings which originally cost £240,000 have been professionally revalued at £450,000. It is proposed to state these buildings at their current market value in the balance sheet and credit the surplus to the profit and loss account. In addition, it is proposed to continue to depreciate the buildings on their historic cost.

(ii) £420,000 was spent during the year on research into the creation of a vaccine to prevent the spread of a newly discovered virus. In previous years similar expenditure has been charged to the profit and loss account. It is proposed to treat this expenditure as an asset in the balance sheet at the year end.

(iii) A specialised piece of equipment with an estimated useful life of six years was purchased during the year. It is proposed that the total cost of this equipment be charged against the current year's revenue on the grounds that if the company were to go into liquidation it would have no resale value.

(iv) Stocks which cost £20,000 can now be replaced for £14,000. The estimated net realisable value of this stock is £17,000. It is proposed that the stock should be written down to £17,000.

(v) As a result of a declining order book the directors have decided to cut back production. They estimate that this will result in the loss of two hundred production employees and thirty administrative employees early in the firm's next financial year. It is estimated that redundancy costs will be £900,000. It is proposed to create a provision for these costs in the current year by charging them as an extraordinary item in the profit and loss account.

You are required to state, giving your reasons, which accounting principles or conventions are followed or violated in each of the above proposals and how you think each transaction should be treated in the accounts. Make reference where appropriate to any relevant Statement of Standard Accounting Practice.

(25 marks)

12 STATEMENT OF SOURCE AND APPLICATION OF FUNDS

The preparation of statements of source and application of funds tests ability to:-

● prepare statements in accordance with the requirements of SSAP 10 in the format prescribed by that statement

● recognise various sources and applications of funds

● recognise 'non-cash' events and transactions

● explain the purpose of statements of source and application of funds

● distinguish between profitability and liquidity

This chapter should be studied in conjunction with the section on SSAP 10 (Statements of Source and Application of Funds) in Chapter 11.

12.1 THE PURPOSE OF STATEMENTS OF SOURCE AND APPLICATION OF FUNDS

The statements are intended to ask the important question of any business: 'Where have our funds come from and how have we used them?' SSAP 10 goes one step further and asks: 'What difference has it made to the working capital and, in particular, to the net liquid funds of the business?' The importance of this lies in the fact that the working capital of a business is its life-blood and a proper degree of liquidity is essential to the health of any business.

Examination questions are often based upon businesses that are profitable and yet short of cash. The student has to explain the difference between profitability and liquidity and why an increase in the former does not necessarily result in a corresponding increase in the latter.

Profit and loss accounts show the results of carrying on business over a period of time but they do not relate liquidity to profit because

(a) they are prepared on an accruals basis and not a cash basis

(b) they exclude items of a capital nature, and

(c) they contain non-cash items (i.e. items not involving the movement of cash into or out of the business)

Balance sheets show the position of businesses at particular moments in time and show the working capital at the balance sheet dates. A comparison of two balance sheets will show the changes in the component parts of working capital between the dates of the two balance sheets, but not why the changes have taken place.

Statements of source and application of funds explain the changes in working capital and net liquid funds by forming a link between the balance sheet at the beginning of a period, the profit and loss account for that period, and the balance sheet at the end of the period.

12.2 FORMAT OF STATEMENT OF SOURCE AND APPLICATION OF FUNDS

SSAP 10 gives an example of a statement of source and application of funds. The example is an illustration only and the SSAP concedes that 'other methods of presentation may equally comply with the accounting standard. The format used should be selected with a view to demonstrating clearly the manner in which the operations of the company have been financed and in which its financial resources have been utilised'. The format is reproduced below; the headings in bold print are part of the format in SSAP 10; the author has added items of detail (not in bold print) to show typical entries that may appear under each heading, together with figures to introduce a semblance of realism.

Given take Ltd.
Statement of source and application of funds
for the year ended 31 December 19--

	£'000	£'000	£'000
SOURCES OF FUNDS			
Profit before tax			700
Adjustments for items not involving the movement of funds:			
Depreciation		205	
Loss/(profit) on sale of fixed assets		94	
Amount written off goodwill		100	399
Total generated from operations			1099
Funds from other sources			
Issue of shares for cash		200	
Issue of debentures		–	
Proceeds of sale of fixed assets		184	384
			1483
Application of funds			
Redemption of shares		–	
Redemption of debentures		(100)	
Purchase of fixed assets		(685)	
Tax paid		(280)	
Dividends paid		(300)	(1365)
	118		
Increase/(decrease) in working capital			
Increase in stocks	151		
Increase in debtors	72		
Increase in creditors (excluding taxation and proposed dividends)	(111)	112	
Movement in net liquid funds:			
Increase (decrease) in:			
Cash balances	2		
Bank balances	92		
Short-term investments	(88)	6	118

Note that although tax and dividends proposed appear in the working capital section of balance sheets, those two items are not included in the working capital section of a statement of source and application of funds.

Students should adhere to the above format and learn the kinds of entries that may be expected to occur under each heading.

It is worth pausing at this stage to see what information we can gain from the statement of Given take Ltd. which would not be available from a study of its profit and loss account and balance sheet:

The total funds available to the company during the year amounted to £1,483k, of which £1,283k were generated internally (£1,099k from operations and £184k from sale of fixed assets), and £200k came from external sources.

The proceeds of the share issue replaced the funds that had previously been provided by the debentures, and the other applications apart from the redemption of the debentures were met out of internally produced funds.

There was a net increase of £118k in funds which financed an increase in working capital; an increase in stocks (£151k) was accompanied, as might be expected, by an increase in creditors (£111). The proceeds of the sale of short term investments increased the bank balance correspondingly.

12.3 PREPARATION OF SIMPLE STATEMENT OF SOURCE AND APPLICATION OF FUNDS (SSAF) OF SOLE TRADER.

Since the SSAF is a link between two balance sheets, the very simplest SSAF can be produced by deducting one balance sheet from another.

12.3.1 EXAMPLE

Georgina's balance sheets for her business at 31 December 19-1 and 19-2 were as follows:

	19-1		19-2	
Fixed assets:	£	£	£	£
Equipment at cost	6,000		8,000	
less depreciation	2,400	3,600	3,200	4,800
Motor car at cost	4,000		4,000	
less depreciation	3,000	1,000	3,500	500
Office machinery at cost	2,000		–	
less depreciation	1,800	200	–	–
		4,800		5,300
Current assets:				
Stock	2,000		3,500	
Debtors	3,800		3,000	
Bank	2,100		3,250	
	7,900		9,750	
less Current liabilities				
Creditors	1,700	6,200	2,300	7,450
		11,000		12,750
Capital at 1 January		8,000		11,000
Profit for year		10,000		9,000
		18,000		20,000
less Drawings		7,000		9,250
		11,000		10,750
Loan from father				2,000
				12,750

There was neither profit nor loss on the sale of the office machinery.

REQUIRED

A statement of the source and application of funds for the year ended 31 December 19-2.

ANSWER

GEORGINA
Statement of source and application of funds
for the year ended 31 December 19-2

	£	£
Net profit		9,000
Add Depreciation for year [(3,200 - 2,400) + (3,500 - 3,000)]		1,300
Funds generated by operations (carried forward)		10,300

	£	£
Brought forward		10,300
Funds from other sources		
Loan from father	2,000	
Sale of office machinery (sold at net book value)	200	2,200
		12,500
Application of funds		
Purchase of equipment (8,000-6,000)	2,000	
Drawings	9,250	11,250
		1,250
Increase/(decrease) in working capital		
Increase in stock (3,500-2,000)	1,500	
Decrease in debtors (3,000-3,800)	(800)	
Increase in creditors (2,300-1,700)	(600)	
	100	
Movement in net liquid funds:		
Increase in bank balance (3,250-2,100)	1,150	1,250

Tutorial notes:

1. Always deduct the earlier balance sheet from the later one.

2. Depreciation is debited in the profit and loss account, but it is only a book entry; it involves no movement of cash. It must therefore be added back to net profit to reflect the funds generated by operations. (Profits or losses on sales of fixed assets must be treated similarly for the same reason.)

3. Working capital is increased when there is an increase in a current asset or a decrease in a current liability; conversely, working capital is decreased when there is a decrease in a current asset or an increase in a current liability.

12.3.2 EXERCISE (for practice in the preparation of a simple SSAF)

Mary owns a successful boutique and makes up her accounts to 31 March in each year. She informs you that she made a good profit in the year to 31 March 19-4, but was surprised to find that the bank balance had reduced in spite of the profit and the fact that her drawings from the business were less than usual. She seeks your advice, and shows you the following balance sheets of the business:

	Balance sheets as at			
	31 March 19-3		31 March 19-4	
	£	£	£	£
Fixed assets				
Leasehold property		20,000		18,000
Equipment at cost	8,000		17,000	
less depreciation	3,000	5,000	4,400	12,600
Motor van at cost	6,400		6,400	
less depreciation	3,200	3,200	4,800	1,600
Office equipment at cost	4,000		3,000	
less depreciation	2,800	1,200	2,400	600
		29,400		32,800
Current assets				
Stock	5,000		8,000	
Debtors	1,800		2,800	
Bank	2,060		1,740	
Cash	100		100	
	8,960		12,640	
less: creditors	1,980	6,980	4,560	8,080
		36,380		40,880

	£	£	£
Capital at 1 April	31,416		36,380
Profit for the year	20,584		18,940
	52,000		55,320
less Drawings	15,620		14,440
	36,380		40,880

Mary informs you that she is amortising the leasehold property over the remainder of the lease which expires in 9 years.

She has not sold any equipment during the year to 31 March 19-4 but she has sold a word processor which cost £1,000 to a friend at its net book value, £200.

REQUIRED

(a) Prepare for Mary a statement of source and application of funds which will show clearly the funds available for the business, and their sources and applications during the year to 31 March 19-4.

(b) Using the information contained in your answer to part (a), draft a letter to Mary explaining to her why the balance at the bank is less than a year ago in spite of the profit made during the year.

12.4 ASCERTAINMENT OF PROFIT OF COMPANY

When an extract of a company's profit and loss account is available the profit to be included in a SSAF is the net profit before tax, not the retained profit:

Extract of profit and loss account:

	£'000	£'000
Profit before tax		400
Tax		(118)
Profit after tax		282
Transfer to reserve	(100)	
Proposed dividend	(80)	(180)
Retained profit for the year		102
Retained profit b/f		74
Retained profit c/f		176

In the SSAF show 'Profit before tax £400k.'

When the profit and loss account is not given in a question the profit before tax must be found from the balance sheet.

12.4.1 EXAMPLE

The following are extracts from the balance sheets of Mario plc as at 31 December 19-1 and 19-2:

	19-1 £'000	19-2 £'000
Creditors: amounts due within one year		
Taxation	125	232
Dividends proposed	220	280
Capital and reserves		
Share capital	1,200	1,200
Reserve for replacement of fixed assets	600	800
Retained profit	950	1,132

Calculation of profit before tax for the year to 31 December 19-2:	£'000
Retained profit at 31 December 19-2	1,132
less Retained profit at 31 December 19-1	950
Carried forward	182

	£'000	£'000
Brought forward		182
add taxation provision for the year 19-2		232
proposed dividend as at 31 December 19-2		280
transfer to asset replacement reserve (800–600)		200
Profit for the year to 31 December 19-2 before tax		894

Proof:

Profit and loss account for the year to 31 December 19-2

	£'000	£'000
Profit before tax		894
Tax		(232)
Profit after tax		662
Transfer to reserve for replacement of fixed assets	(200)	
Proposed dividend	(280)	(480)
Retained profit for the year		182
Retained profit brought forward		950
Retained profit carried forward		1,132

12.4.2 EXERCISE (Calculation of a company's profit before tax from its balance sheets)

The following are extracts from the balance sheets of Andrew and Demetriou plc as at 31 March 19-3 and 19-4:

	at 31 March 19-3	at 31 March 19-4
	£'000	£'000
Creditors: amounts due within one year:		
Taxation	700	540
Proposed dividends	340	600
Debenture interest	100	100
Share capital and reserves		
Share capital	500	600
Share premium account	50	70
Asset revaluation reserve	–	150
Asset replacement reserve	160	185
General reserve	200	230
Retained profit	110	85

REQUIRED

A statement of source and application of funds is being prepared for Andrew and Demetriou plc and you are to calculate the item 'net profit before tax' to be included in that statement.

12.5 TANGIBLE FIXED ASSETS – PURCHASE, SALE, DEPRECIATION, AND PROFIT OR LOSS ON DISPOSAL

When preparing SSAFs, take care to account properly for:
(a) funds applied in the purchase of fixed assets
(b) proceeds of sales of fixed assets
(c) depreciation provided in the year
(d) profits/losses on disposals of fixed assets.

Examination questions often do not give all the information about these items and they have to be found by the 'missing figure' technique.

12.5.1 EXAMPLE.

The following are extracts from the balance sheets of Malani, Priya and Co. Ltd. as at 30 June 19-2 and 19-3:

	at 30 June 19-2		at 30 June 19-3	
	£'000	£'000	£'000	£'000
Freehold premises		750		1,000
Plant and machinery at cost	400		430	
less provision for depreciation	220	180	230	200
Motor vehicles at cost	250		281	
less provision for depreciation	175	75	205	76
		1,005		1,276
Capital and reserves				
Asset revaluation reserve		–		250

In the year to 30 June 19-3, plant and machinery which had cost £80,000 and had been written down to £10,000 was sold for £7,000. In addition, motor vehicles which had cost £33,000 were sold for £8,000 at a profit of £2,000.

REQUIRED

Calculate the figures to be included in a statement of source and application of funds for the year to 30 June 19-3 to account for the movements in tangible fixed assets.

ANSWER

Tutorial note: reconstruct the ledger accounts to find the 'missing figures'.

Plant and machinery at cost

	£'000		£'000
Balance b/f	400	Plant & machinery sold	80
* Plant purchased		Balance c/f (per question)	430
(balancing figure)	110		
	510		510

Provision for depreciation of plant and machinery

	£'000		£'000
Disposal	70	Balance b/f	220
Balance c/f * (per question)	230	Profit and loss (balancing figure)	80
	300		300

Plant & machinery disposal account

	£'000		£'000
Plant and machinery at cost	80	Provision for depreciation	70
		Sale proceeds	7
		* Loss on sale (P&L a/c)	3
	80		80

Motor vehicles at cost

	£'000		£'000
Balance b/f	250	Motor vehicles sold	33
* Motor vehicles purchased		Balance c/f (per question)	281
(balancing figure)	64		
	314		314

Provision for depreciation of motor vehicles

	£'000		£'000
* Disposal(per Disposal account)	27	Balance b/f	175
Balance c/f (per question)	205	* Profit & loss (balancing figure)	57
	232		232

Motor vehicles disposal account

	£'000		£'000
Motor vehicles (at cost)	33	* Provision for depreciation	
Profit on sale (P&L a/c)	2	(balancing figure)	27
		Sale proceeds	8
	35		35

Tutorial note: The items marked * are balancing figures.

Information for SSAF

Funds generated by operations:

	£'000	£'000
Depreciation for year to be added to profit before tax:		
on plant and machinery	80	
on motor vehicles	57	137
Loss on disposal of plant and machinery to be added to net profit		3
Profit on disposal of motor vehicles to be deducted from net profit		(2)
Net loss on disposals		1
Other sources of funds:		
Proceeds of sales of fixed assets (£7,000+£8,000)		£15,000
Application of funds		
Purchases of fixed assets (£110,000+£64,000)		£174,000

Tutorial note: Look out for asset revaluation reserves; these will be created when fixed assets, notably freehold property, are revalued upwards. In the above example, the freehold premises have increased in value by £250,000 between the dates of the two balance sheets. During the same period, a revaluation reserve of the same amount has been created indicating that the increase in freehold property arises from revaluation and not because of further expenditure.

12.5.2 EXERCISE (to calculate details regarding tangible fixed assets for SSAF)

Pondayne plc's balance sheets for the years to 31 December 19-3 and 19-4 contained the following extracts:

	at 31 Dec 19-3		at 31 Dec 19-4	
	£'000	£'000	£'000	£'000
Freehold premises at valuation		900		1,200
Plant and machinery at cost	450		690	
less provision for depreciation	376	74	520	170
Fixtures and fittings at cost	60		40	
less provision for depreciation	54	6	30	10
		980		1,380
Capital and reserves				
Property revaluation reserve		150		450

During the year to 31 December 19-4 plant and machinery which had cost £80,000 and which, at the time of sale, had a written down value value of £16,000 was sold for £8,000. Also fixtures and fittings were sold for £5,000; they had originally cost £40,000, and £38,000 had been provided for depreciation on these fixtures and fittings.

REQUIRED

Calculate

(a) the non-cash items relating to the tangible fixed asset information given above,

(b) the utilisation of funds during the year for the purchase of tangible fixed assets and

(c) the amount of funds spent on acquiring additional tangible fixed assets during the year.

12.6   INTANGIBLE FIXED ASSETS

Intangible fixed assets, such as goodwill, written off in the profit and loss account are non-cash items and should be added back to profit before tax in the same way as depreciation.

12.7   SHARE CAPITAL AND DEBENTURES

Increases in share capital and debentures for cash are sources of funds; shares or debentures issued for other consideration will be non-cash items. *Bonus shares* are non-cash items and must be ignored for SSAF purposes but do not confuse these with *rights issues* which are made for cash and must be included in the statement if made in the period.

Premium on shares issued in the period will be a source of funds, and should be identified separately from the increase in share capital in order to comply with the requirement of SSAP 10 that the figures in the statement should be identifiable in the profit and loss account, balance sheet and notes thereto.

Redemption or purchase by a company of its own shares or debentures is an application of funds; the remarks regarding share premium on issues of shares also apply to redemption.

12.8   TAXATION

Taxation shown as a current liability (creditor, payment due within one year) in a balance sheet will be paid in the year before the next annual balance sheet. Taxation shown in the earlier of two balance sheets will therefore be an application of funds in an SSAF produced at the date of the second balance sheet.

Taxation shown in a balance sheet, however, is not necessarily the amount which will eventually be agreed as the liability by the Inland Revenue. The amount actually paid in respect of the liability may be different and it could therefore be misleading to show the balance sheet amount as the actual payment in an SSAF.

To be sure of the tax payment to be shown in an SSAF it is often advisable to reconstruct the taxation account on the following lines:

Taxation
£   £

Tax liability carried forward (per later balance sheet)	Tax liability brought forward (per earlier balance sheet)
<u>Tax payment</u> during year (balancing figure)	Tax debited in profit and loss account.

12.8.1 EXAMPLE

The taxation liability shown in Albrind plc's balance sheet at 31 December 19-1 was £345,000. The liability for taxation shown in the balance sheet at 31 December 19-2 was £410,000. In the company's profit and loss account for the year ended 31 December 19-2, the following item appeared:

	£'000
Taxation	398

REQUIRED

A calculation of the taxation paid in the year to 31 December 19-2.

ANSWER

Taxation account

	£		£
Taxation c/f	410,000	Taxation b/f	345,000
Tax paid during the year (balancing figure)	333,000	Profit and Loss a/c	398,000
	743,000		743,000

Tutorial note: The taxation liability provided for in 19-1 was £12,000 too much; this excess of £12,000 reduces the amount that needs to be debited in the profit and loss account in 19-2 (410,000 - 12,000 = 398,000)

12.8.2 EXERCISE (calculation of taxation paid for the inclusion in an SSAF)

The following extracts are taken from the balance sheets of The Vortex Puzzle Co. Ltd:

	As at 30 June 19-5 £'000	As at 30 June 19-6 £'000
Creditors: amounts falling due within one year		
Taxation	157	201

The following is an extract from the company's profit and loss account for the year to 30 June 19-6:

	£'000
Profit before taxation	974
Taxation	(210)
Profit after taxation	764

REQUIRED

Calculate the amount of taxation paid by The Vortex Puzzle Company Ltd. in the year to 30 June 19-6.

12.9   DIVIDENDS

Proposed dividends are shown in company balance sheets. Interim dividends paid during the year are debited in the profit and loss account together with the proposed final dividend for the year.

If, in examination questions, interim dividends have been paid they must be included in the dividend payments shown in SSAFs.

The payment of dividends in an SSAF will therefore represent the payment of the final dividend for the previous year plus interim dividends paid in respect of the year covered by the SSAF.

Unless a question states that an interim dividend has been paid during the year and the amount of the dividend, then, where such a dividend has been paid, the question must provide an extract from the profit and loss account for the year.

As with taxation above, it will probably be as well to reconstruct the dividends account:

Dividends paid and proposed account

	£		£
Proposed dividend for current year c/f (per later balance sheet)		Proposed dividend for previous year b/f (per earlier balance sheet)	
Dividends paid during current year (balancing figure)		Dividends debited in profit and loss account	

12.9.1 EXAMPLE

The following extracts are taken from the balance sheets of Imitation Bunting Ltd.

	at 30 April 19-0 £'000	at 30 April 19-1 £'000
Creditors: amounts falling due within one year		
Proposed dividends	75	120

The profit and loss account for the year to 30 April 19-1 contained the following: 'Dividends paid and proposed £170,000'.

REQUIRED

Calculate the amount paid as dividends by Imitation Bunting Ltd. in the year to 30 April 19-1.

ANSWER

Dividends

	£'000		£'000
Proposed dividend c/f	120	Proposed dividend b/f	75
Paid during the year	125	Profit and loss account	170
	245		245

Dividends paid during the year to 30 April 19-1: £125 (i.e final dividend for 19-1 £75,000 plus interim dividend for 19-2 £50,000).

12.9.2 EXERCISE (calculation of dividends paid)

The following extracts are taken from the balance sheets of Portable Grummitts plc.:

	as at 31 May 19-3	as at 31 May 19-4
	£'000	£'000
Dividends proposed	300	250

The company's profit and loss account for the year to 31 May 19-4 contained the following item:

	£'000
Dividends paid and proposed	280

REQUIRED

An extract from Portable Grummitts plc's Statement of Source and Application of Funds for the year to 31 May 19-4 showing the information regarding the application of funds for dividend payments in that year.

12.10   WORKED EXAMPLE AND EXERCISE

12.10.1 EXAMPLE

The Homer Double Glazing Company plc's balance sheets as at 31 December 19-1 and 19-2, and the profit and loss account for the year to 31 December 19-2 are as follows:

Balance Sheet

	as at 31 December 19-2		as at 31 December 19-1	
	£'000	£'000	£'000	£'000
Fixed assets:				
Freehold property at valuation		1,000		850
Plant and machinery at cost	780		695	
less provision for depreciation	320	460	280	415
Motor vehicles at cost	400		332	
less provision for depreciation	185	215	170	162
Office computer equipment at cost	60		55	
less provision for depreciation	30	30	28	27
		1,705		1,454
Current assets:				
Stocks	250		222	
Debtors	102		107	
Short term investments	300		–	
Cash at bank	54		75	
Carried forward	706	1,705	404	1,454

	£'000	£'000	£'000	£'000
Carried forward	706	1,705	404	1,454
Creditors: amounts due within one year				
Trade creditors	(45)		(68)	
Taxation	(140)		(86)	
Proposed dividends	(120)		(100)	
Net current assets		401		150
Total assets less current liabilities		2,106		1,604
Creditors: amounts falling due after more than one year				
10% Debenture stock		100		150
		2,006		1,454
Capital and reserves				
Issued share capital		1,000		600
Share premium		30		210
Freehold property revaluation reserve		150		–
Asset replacement reserve		250		200
General reserve		400		300
Retained profit		176		144
		2,006		1,454

Profit and loss account (extract) for the year to 31 December 19-2

	£'000	£'000
Profit before tax		494
Taxation		(132)
Profit after tax		362
Transfer to asset replacement reserve	(50)	
Transfer to general reserve	(100)	
Dividends paid and proposed	(180)	(330)
Retained profit for the year		32
Retained profit brought forward from 31 December 19-1		144
Retained profit carried forward at 31 December 19-2		176

Notes

1. During the year to 31 December 19-2 the following transactions took place:
   (i) Plant and machinery which cost £120,000 and on which depreciation of £95,000 had been provided, was sold for £22,000.
   (ii) Motor vehicles which had cost £85,000 and which had a written down value of £15,000 at the date of sale were sold for £28,000.
   (iii) Office computer equipment which had cost £10,000 and on which depreciation of £5,000 had been provided was sold at a loss of £2,000.
2. During the year to 31 December 19-2 a bonus issue of shares was made on the basis of one bonus share for every three shares already held. This was done by using part of the share premium account. The company then made a rights issue on the basis of one share for each four held, the new shares being offered at a premium of 10p on each share.
3. There had been no additions to freehold property during the year to 31 December 19-2.
4. The 10% debenture stock is redeemable at par.

REQUIRED

A statement of source and application of funds for the year to 31 December 19-2 for The Homer Double Glazing Company plc.

ANSWER

The Homer Double Glazing Company plc
Statement of source and application of funds for the year to 31 December 19-2

	£'000	£'000
Source of funds		
Profit before tax		494
Adjustments of items not involving the movement of funds:		
Depreciation		227
Profit on disposal of fixed assets		(8)
Total generated from operations		713
Funds from other sources		
Issue of shares for cash		200
Premium on issue of shares		20
Proceeds of sales of fixed assets		53
		986
Application of funds		
Redemption of debenture stock	(50)	
Purchase of fixed assets	(373)	
Taxation paid	(78)	
Dividends paid	(160)	(661)
		325
Increase/(decrease) in working capital		
Increase in stocks	28	
Decrease in debtors	(5)	
Decrease in creditors	23	
	46	
Movement in net liquid funds		
Increase/(decrease) in:		
Bank balance	(21)	
Short term investments	300	279	325

Workings
Fixed assets

Plant & machinery

b/f	695	Disp.	120
*Pchse	205	c/f	780
	900		900

Provn for depn.

Disp	95	b/f	280
c/f	320	*P&L	135
	415		415

Disposals

P&M	120	Depn	95
		Cash	22
		*Loss	3
	120		120

Motor Vehicles

b/f	332	Disp.	85
*Pchse	153	c/f	400
	485		485

Provn for depn.

*Disp	70	b/f	170
c/f	185	* P&L	85
	255		255

Disposals

M.V	85	Depn	70
*Prft	13	Cash	28
	98		98

Office Computer

b/f	55	Disp	10
*Pchse	15	c/f	60
	70		70

Provn for depn.

*Disp	5	b/f	28
c/f	30	* P&L	7
	35		35

Disposals

Comp	10	Depn	5
		*Cash	3
		Loss	2
	10		10

Purchases (205+153+15) Depn for year = Proceeds =
= 373 (135+85+7) = 227 (22+28+3) = 53
Profit less losses on disposals =
(13-3-2) = 8

	Taxation				**Dividends**		
*Paid	78	b/f	86	*Paid	160	b/f	100
c/f	140	P&L	132	c/f	120	P&L	180
	218		218		280		280

Tutorial notes:

1. Items marked * in workings are balancing figures.

2. Revaluation of freehold property is a non-cash item; see increase in freehold property revaluation reserve.

3. Bonus shares issued: 600,000/3 = 200,000 (non cash item; £200,000 transferred from share premium account to share capital account.)

4. Rights issue: 800,000/4 = 200,000 shares issued for cash.

   Addition to share premium account = 10% of £200,000 = £20,000.

12.10.2 EXERCISE (Preparation of Statement of Source and Application of Funds.)

The Ovid Egg Products Ltd.'s balance sheets at 31 December 19-0 and 19-1 were as follows:

	At 31 December 19-1		**At 31 December 19-0**	
	£'000	£'000	£'000	£'000
Tangible fixed assets (note 1)		435		434
Current assets				
Stock	110		70	
Debtors	61		35	
Bank	37		24	
	208		129	
Creditors: amounts due within one year				
Creditors	(25)		(38)	
Taxation	(51)		(45)	
Dividends proposed	(30)	(106)	(35)	(118)
Net current assets		102		11
Total assets less current liabilities		537		445
Creditors: amounts due after one year				
12% Debentures		(80)		(50)
		457		395
Capital and reserves				
Share capital (Ordinary shares of £1 fully paid)		250		200
Share premium		25		15
General reserve		130		80
Retained profits		52		100
		457		395

Notes
1.

Tangible fixed assets	Freehold property	Plant & machinery	Motor vehicles	Office equipment	Total
At cost	£'000	£'000	£'000	£'000	£'000
Balance at 31.12 -0	375	72	111	20	578
Additions		58	50	10	118
Disposals at cost	(49)	(20)	(23)		(92)
At cost at 31.12 -1	326	110	138	30	604
Provisions for depreciation					
Balance at 31.12 -0	-	(60)	(72)	(12)	(144)
Depreciation on disposals		18	20		38
Depreciation for year		(28)	(32)	(3)	(63)
	-	(70)	(84)	(15)	(169)
Net book value at 31 December 19-1	326	40	54	15	435

2. During the year to 31 December 19-1, freehold premises which were surplus to requirements were sold for £37,000; plant was sold for £3,000 and motor vehicles were sold for £5,000.

3. 50,000 shares of £1 each were issued at a premium of 20p each on 1 July 19-1.

4. An interim dividend of 5p per share was paid on 30 June 19-1.

5. Taxation in the sum of £55,000 had been debited in the profit and loss account.

REQUIRED

(a) A statement of source and application of funds for the year ended 31 December 19-1 for Ovid Egg Products Ltd.

(b) A concise report to the shareholders of Ovid Egg Products Ltd. on the reasons for the large increase in the working capital of Ovid Egg Products Ltd. so far as the information is available from your answer to part (a).

(c) State briefly the uses of statements of source and application of funds.

12.11   KEY POINTS TO REMEMBER

1. Memorise the format of statements of source and application of funds prescribed by SSAP 10 and the usual items to be found under each heading.

2. Recognise the usual non-cash items for which 'profit before tax' must be adjusted: depreciation; profits/losses on disposals of fixed assets; goodwill written off.

3. Recognise other non-cash items which are not sources or applications of funds: bonus shares; revaluation of properties.

4. An important examination technique is to start to earn marks as quickly as possible in an answer. A candidate who has adequately practised preparing SSAFs before the examination should be able to prepare a statement in outline without delay, leaving spaces for additional items which may have to be inserted as the answer proceeds. The figures may then be inserted in the outline as soon as they have been calculated. The easiest figures to insert are the ones for the components of working capital and these may be entered first; they may well each earn an easy mark at an early stage in your answer as well as providing the total for the sources and application section that precedes working capital.

5. Prepare 'T' accounts if necessary to calculate fixed asset, depreciation, taxation and dividend figures.
6. Answer questions about the causes of changes in working capital with references to the items appearing in the sources and applications sections that precede the working capital section in the SSAF. Do not refer to increases/ decreases in stocks, debtors, creditors etc; these are the changes, not the causes.

COMMON ERRORS:
- error in calculation of funds generated by operations.
- inability to calculate 'net profit before tax'.
- failure to adjust for non cash items when calculating 'net profit before tax'.
- confusing liabilities for tax and proposed dividends in current balance sheet with tax and dividends actually paid in the year.

12.12   EXAMINATION QUESTIONS

QUESTION 1   (Cambridge November 1989)

The following financial information was available from L. Square Limited

Balance sheet as at 30 April

	19-8 £'000	19-8 £'000	19-9 £'000	19-9 £'000
Fixed Assets				
Land and buildings(at cost)		250		350
Plant & Equipment				
Cost	170		240	
Less Depreciation	86	84	96	144
Goodwill		110		55
		444		549
Current Assets				
Stocks	175		250	
Trade Debtors	95		75	
Expenses Prepaid	22		22	
Bank	108		78	
Cash	10		15	
	410		440	
Current Liabilities				
Trade Creditors	55		85	
Interest Accrued	5		10	
Proposed Dividend	25		20	
	85		115	
		325		325
		£769		£874

Financed by:	£'000	£'000
Share Capital £1 ord. Shares fully paid	400	400
Share Premium	320	320
General Reserves	20	20
Profit and Loss	29	34
10% Debentures 1998/9	–	100
	£769	£874

Additional information

1. Plant and equipment which originally cost £135,000 was sold for £30,000. At the date of sale, 1 May 19-8, the book value was £75,000.
2. Depreciation of £70,000 was provided against plant and equipment held during the year.
3. The profit and loss appropriation account for the year ended 30 April 19-9 showed:

		£
Net Profit		40,000
Less Net Dividends		
Interim (Paid)	15,000	
Final (Proposed)	20,000	35,000
Retained		£5,000

REQUIRED

(a) A source and application of funds statement for the year ended 30 April 19-9 showing clearly the changes in working capital over the year. *(18 marks)*

(b) An explanation of the causes of the changes in the working capital position. *(5 marks)*

(c) Why are sources and applications of funds statements considered as an important part of business accounting information? *(2 marks)*

(Total 25 marks)

QUESTION 2 (London January 1989)

The balance sheets of Dowsing Ltd as at 31 December 19-8 and 19-7 are as follows:

31.12 -7		31.12.-8
£		£
32,000	Fixed Assets (net book value)	43,000
	Current Assets:	
18,000	Stock	19,000
7,500	Debtors	9,000
4,800	Bank	–
62,300		71,000
	Share Capital:	
16,000	Ordinary Shares of 25p each	19,000
17,000	Preference Shares of £1 each	5,000
–	Capital Redemption Reserve	12,000
200	Share Premium Account	300
13,200	Retained Earnings	17,900
	Current Liabilities:	
9,900	Creditors	6,100
4,000	Taxation	5,000
2,000	Proposed dividends	3,000
–	Bank	2,700
62,300		71,000

Notes:

1. A summary of the company's Fixed Assets Account in the general ledger for the year ended 31 December 19-8 is shown below:

		£			£
1 Jan 19-8	Cost b/f	76,000	31 Dec 19-8	Disposals A/c	8,000
31 Dec 19-8	Additions	22,000	31 Dec 19-8	Cost c/f	90,000
		98,000			98,000

The assets were sold for £1,800, which represented a loss of £3,200 compared with their book value.

2.   A bonus (scrip) issue of 1,000 shares was made during the year, the shares being paid up from the balance standing to the credit of the Share Premium Account.

3.   The preference shares were redeemed at par in November 19-8.

You are required to:

(a)   Prepare the profit and loss appropriation account for the year ended 31 December 19-8.   *(5 marks)*

(b)   Draw up a Source and Application of Funds Statement for the year ended 31 December 19-8.

(15 marks)

(c)   Explain the difference between a *bonus* issue and a *rights* issue.   *(5 marks)*

(Total 25 marks)

Tutorial note: Students unfamiliar with share redemption and bonus issues may come back to this question after reading Chapter 13.

QUESTION 3   (Oxford June 1988)

The balance sheets at the end of the last two years for Cantabile plc are shown below:

	31 May 19-7				**31 May 19-8**	
£	£	£	**Fixed Assets**	£	£	£
	32,650		Goodwill			23,500
	80,000		Premises	200,000	–	200,000
	158,200		Plant and Machinery	265,000	76,900	188,100
	82,100		Office Equipment	98,000	22,500	75,500
				563,000	99,400	
	125,260		Investments			152,750
		478,210				639,850
			Current Assets			
	67,815		Stock		88,890	
54,115			Debtors	60,265		
2,100			less provision for bad debts	2,375		
	52,015				57,890	
	–		Bank		9,210	
	119,830				155,990	
			Current Liabilities			
39,870			Creditors	49,820		
28,750			Corporation Tax	31,500		
18,160			Ordinary Share Dividend	26,000		
5,420			Accruals	2,320		
22,630			Bank overdraft	–		
	114,830				109,640	
		5,000				46,350
		483,210				686,200
			Long Term Liability			
		50,000	12% Bank Loan			62,900
		433,210				623,300
			Issued Share Capital			
		250,000	£1 ordinary shares			425,000
			£1 6% redeemable preference			
		160,000	shares 1987-9			75,000
		410,000	Carried forward			500,000

179

£	£	£		£	£
		410,000	Brought forward		500,000
			Reserves		
	–		Share Premium	33,000	
	–		Capital Redemption Reserve	30,000	
	12,000		General Reserve	38,000	
	11,210		Profit and Loss	22,300	
	23,210				123,300
		433,210			623,300

During the year ended 31 May 19-8, an interim ordinary dividend of £15,500 was paid. Some of the redeemable preference shares, which had been issued at par, were redeemed at a premium of 2%. Preference dividend was also paid but only on the preference shares still in issue.

Plant and machinery costing £42,000, book value £18,000, was sold for £20,500, and new plant and machinery was purchased for £69,615.

There was a revaluation of the premises and a subsequent bonus issue of £1 ordinary shares to the value of the revaluation reserve.

You are required to provide

(i)   A Statement of Sources and Applications of Funds for the year ended 31 May 19-8 for Cantabile plc.   *(30 marks)*

(ii) A comment on the performance and policies of the firm during the year ended 31 May 19-8 as revealed by your answer to (i)   *(10 marks)*

(Total 40 marks)

QUESTION 4   (JMB June 1987)

Happy Holidays Ltd. is in the business of providing package camping holidays in Europe. The following information is provided of its activities during the year to 31 March.

Transactions during the year ended 31 March 19-7

	£'000
Cash receipts from customers	2,000
Cash payments to ferry operators & camp site proprietors	710
Administration & advertising expense payments	245

Balances	At 31.3.-6	At 31.3.-7
	£'000	£'000
Deposits received from customers	200	230
Deposits paid to ferry operators & camp-site proprietors	110	160
Creditors (for camping equipment)	300	40
Camping equipment (at cost)	3,000	3,400
Advertising expenditure paid, but deferred to following period	60	60

Given that:

(i)   no camping equipment was lost or disposed of during the year;

(ii)   Camping equipment is to be depreciated at $33\frac{1}{3}\%$ of cost;

(iii) sales are regarded, for the purpose of calculating annual profit/loss, as the total value of holidays provided during the year.

You are required to:

(a) prepare a Profit and Loss Account for the year ended 31 March 19-7:   *(10 marks)*

(b) prepare a Sources and Uses of Cash Statement for the year ended 31 March 19-7.   *(10 marks)*

(Total 20 marks)

QUESTION 5 (JMB June 1988)

You have been asked to advise the board of directors of Omega Limited on the cashflow implications of the manufacture of a new product. The budgeted trading statement for the new product in its first year is as follows:

	£'000s	£'000s
Sales (all credit)		104.0
Raw materials	41.6	
Direct labour	31.2	
Direct overheads	15.0	
Depreciation	5.0	92.8
Budgeted profit		11.2

It is estimated that, on average, raw materials will be in stock for four weeks before they are issued to production, production will take three weeks and finished goods will be in stock for a further two weeks. Suppliers of raw materials will allow five weeks' credit and debtors are expected to take seven weeks' credit. The expenditures on direct labour and overheads will occur evenly throughout the year. To produce the new product a piece of equipment is required costing £40,000, and this will need to be paid for during the first year.

You are required to:

(a) draw up a funds flow statement for the new product for the first full year of production: *(15 marks)*

(b) note the assumptions you have made and indicate their significance.   *(5 marks)*

(Total 20 marks)

QUESTION 6 (AEB June 1989)

The summarised balance sheets as at 31 March 19-8 and 19-9 of Higher Limited are as follows:

	19-9		19-8		Additional information
	£'000	£'000	£'000	£'000	
Fixed assets; at net book value		175		150	1
Current assets	90		80		2
Creditors, less than one year	(70)	20	(50)	30	
		195		180	
Creditors, more than one year		(30)		(30)	
		165		150	
Capital and reserves					
Ordinary shares of £1 each		90		80	3
8% Redeemable preference shares of 50p each		–		30	3
Share premium account		25		20	3
Capital redemption reserve		15		–	
Profit and loss account		35		20	
		165		150	

Additional information	Cost	Depreciation	Net Book Value
	£'000	£'000	£'000
(1) Fixed assets			
Balance at 31 March 19-8	200	50	150
Additions	60	–	60
Disposals	(40)	(25)	(15)
Carried forward	220	25	195

	£'000	£'000	£'000
Brought forward	220	25	195
Depreciation for the year to 31 March 19–9	–	20	(20)
Balance at 31 March 19-9	220	45	175

Fixed assets disposed of during the year were sold for £22,000.

(2) Current assets at 31 March for each of the two years comprise the following:

	19-9	19-8
	£'000	£'000
Stocks	35	27
Debtors	22	28
Bank	24	22
Cash	9	3
	90	80

(3) The preference shares were redeemed during the year ended 31 March 19-9. This redemption was funded by a new issue of ordinary shares at a premium.

(4) A transfer of £15,000 from the profit and loss account was made to the capital redemption reserve.

REQUIRED

(a) Prepare a Source and Application of Funds Statement for Higher Limited for the year ended 31 March 19-9, showing clearly the change in the working capital. *(15 marks)*

(b) Explain the purpose and uses of the Source and Application of Funds Statement. *(7 marks)*

(Total 22 marks)

Tutorial note: Students who have not studied the redemption of shares at this stage should study Chapter 13 before attempting this question.

QUESTION 7 (AEB November 1989)

The following summarised balance sheets have been prepared for Bentwater plc as at 30 September 19-8 and 30 September 19-9

Balance sheet as at 30 September

19-8				19-9		
£'000	£'000			£'000	£'000	£'000
		Fixed assets				
190		Freehold land and buildings (net book value)				450
120		Plant and machinery (net book value)				195
	310					645
	190	Investments (at cost)				20
		Currents assets				
120		Stocks			70	
148		Trade debtors			61	
–		Balance at bank			133	
19		Cash			45	
287					309	
		Less current liabilities				
35		Trade creditors		66		
18		Proposed dividend		26		
33		Bank overdraft		–		
86	201			92		217
	701					882

	Financed by:	
	Share Capital	
100	£1 Ordinary shares fully paid	300
	Reserves	
245	Share premium	195
–	Land revaluation	100
265	Retained earnings	196
610		791
	Loan capital	
91	10% Debentures 1989 - 96	91
701		882

Additional information

(1) Profit and loss appropriation for the year ended 30 September 19-9

	£'000
Net profit	7
Less final dividend proposed	26
Transfer to retained earnings	(19)

(2) (i) The freehold land and buildings were revalued on 1 June 19-9 by £100,000

    (ii) On 1 July 19-9 further freehold land and buildings were purchased at a cost of £160,000

    (iii) There were no sales or provision for depreciation of freehold land and buildings.

(3) (i) On 1 July 19-9 a bonus issue was made of 3 shares for every 2 shares held. The issue was financed from the share premium account £100,000, and the balance from retained earnings.

    (ii) On 1 August 19-9 50,000 new £1 ordinary shares were issued at £2 a share.

(4) During the financial year 19-8/-9 investments which cost £170,000 were sold for £200,000.

(5) The depreciation on plant and machinery was £40,000 for the year, and there were no revaluations or sales of plant and machinery.

REQUIRED

(a) A source and application of funds statement for Bentwater plc for the year ended 30 September 19-9. Show the change in working capital over the year. *(15 marks)*

(b) Write a brief report on Bentwater plc explaining:

    (i) How the company is able to finance an expansion in its productive capacity when in the current year profits are extremely poor.

    (ii) Why the company has made an issue of bonus shares. *(8 marks)*

(c) For the financial year 19-9/-0 the company has a budget target for return on equity capital employed (as at 30 September 19-9) of 18%.

What net profit must the company earn in order to meet its target? *(2 marks)*

(Total 25 marks)

Tutorial note: Students may return to this question after studying issues of bonus shares in Chapter 13.

13 COMPANIES: CAPITAL RECONSTRUCTION AND REDEMPTION

> *This chapter is concerned with:-*
> - how companies are permitted by the Companies Act 1985 to alter their share capital
> - the issue of bonus shares
> - capital reduction schemes
> - redemption of shares

A company's memorandum of association contains details of its authorised share capital. The Companies Act 1985 section 121 provides that a company may –

(a) increase its share capital by new shares of such amount as it thinks expedient;

(b) consolidate and divide all or any of its shares into shares of larger amount than its existing shares;

Tutorial note: i.e. if it has a share capital of 1,000 ordinary shares £1 each it may consolidate them into 200 shares of £5 each, or shares of any other denomination.

(c) convert all or any of its paid-up shares into stock, and re-convert that stock into paid-up shares of any denomination;

Tutorial note: stock consists of 'bundles of shares'. Shares may only be bought and sold in discrete amounts, i.e. £1 shares may only change hands in multiples of £1, £5 shares in multiples of £5 and so on. Stock may be traded in fractional amounts.

(d) sub-divide its shares, or any of them, into shares of smaller amount than is fixed by the memorandum;

Tutorial note: share capital of, say, 1,000 ordinary shares of £1 may be converted into 4,000 shares of 25p, or 5,000 shares of 20p or 10,000 shares of 10p or 20,000 shares of 5p, etc. This may happen when, for instance, the market price of £1 shares has risen permanently to such an extent that dealings are hindered by the large sums of money required to purchase a reasonable number of £1 shares.

(e) cancel shares which, at date of the passing of the resolution to cancel them, have not been taken or agreed to be taken by any person, and diminish the amount of the company's share capital by the amount of the shares so cancelled.

13.1 INCREASE OF SHARE CAPITAL – BONUS SHARES

Share capital may be increased by the issue of new shares for cash; this increases the assets (cash) of the company. Shares may also be issued for a consideration other than cash e.g. in payment for an asset such as property, plant and machinery etc.

This again results in an increase in the assets of the company.

Bonus shares do not result in an increase in the assets of a company; they are issued free to existing shareholders in recognition of the fact that the company's reserves, which already belong to the shareholders, are providing permanent finance to the company. The following illustrates this:

Balance sheet (summarised)

	£	£
Fixed assets		80,000
Current assets	7,000	
less Current liabilities	3,000	
		4,000
		84,000

	£	£
Share capital and reserves		
20,000 ordinary shares of £1		20,000
Share premium account		4,000
Profit and loss account		60,000
		84,000

In a typical examination question a shareholder complains that the directors are withholding profits from the shareholders and wants the profits distributed as a cash dividend. The objections to such a distribution, as exemplified above, are:

1. Obviously, the cash resources of the company will not allow such a distribution to be made.
2. Only £20,000 of the fixed assets are financed by share capital; the balance of £60,000 is financed by the reserves. The reserves could only be distributed by selling the fixed assets.
3. A distribution of £60,000 would amount to a dividend of 300% on the shares, which would be unpopular with the workers who never have pay rises of such proportions, and with the company's customers, who would infer that they are being grossly overcharged for the company's products.

All reserves belong to the ordinary shareholders, a point of which the shareholder in the question was aware, but one that is not usually recognised by workers or customers.

The solution is to distribute the reserves as bonus shares. This is one of the purposes for which the share premium account may be used; otherwise, as a capital reserve, its uses are rather restricted.

The directors could decide to issue to the shareholders 3 bonus shares for every share presently held by them, using the share premium account and as much of the profit and loss account balance as is required to make up the difference. The balance sheet would therefore appear as follows after this had been done.

	£	£
Fixed assets		80,000
Current assets	7,000	
less current liabilities	3,000	4,000
		84,000
Capital and reserves		
80,000 ordinary shares of £1		80,000
Profit and loss account		4,000
		84,000

The journal entries to show the accounting entries involved are:

	Dr	Cr
	£	£
Share premium	4,000	
Profit and loss	56,000	
Bonus account		60,000
Bonus account	60,000	
Ordinary share capital		60,000

13.1.1 EXAMPLE

Birchwood plc's balance sheet at 15 May 19-2 was as follows:

	£	£
Fixed assets		300,000
Current assets	65,000	
less Current liabilities	42,000	23,000
		323,000

185

	£	£
Share capital and reserves		
100,000 shares of £1 each		100,000
Share premium account		25,000
Asset revaluation reserve		80,000
Retained profits		118,000
		323,000

The directors proposed to issue bonus shares on the basis of two bonus shares for every share already held, using reserves for the purpose in such a way as to leave the remaining reserves in the most flexible form after the issue of the shares. The directors further proposed that following the bonus share issue there would be a rights issue on a one for three basis. These proposals were approved by the company and the shares duly issued.

REQUIRED

The balance sheet of the company after the rights issue has been made.

ANSWER

Balance sheet

	£	£
Fixed assets		300,000
Current assets	165,000	
Less Current liabilities	42,000	123,000
		423,000
Share capital and reserves		
400,000 ordinary shares of £1		400,000
Retained profits		23,000
		423,000

Tutorial note: The current assets are increased by the cash received from the rights issue. The bonus issue has been made out of the share premium, £25,000, asset revaluation reserve, £80,000 and retained profits, £95,000.

13.1.2   EXERCISE (involving a bonus issue followed by a consolidation of the share capital and a rights issue)

Pinewood plc's balance sheet at 31 January 19-3 was as follows:

	£	£
Fixed assets		852,000
Current assets	377,000	
less Current liabilities	191,000	186,000
		1,038,000
Share capital and reserves		
1,000,000 ordinary shares of 20p		200,000
Share premium account		53,000
General reserve		600,000
Profit and loss account		185,000
		1,038,000

On 1 February 19-3 the following following events took place in the order shown:

(i)   A bonus issue of 3,500,000 ordinary shares was made so as to leave the remaining reserves in the most flexible form.

(ii)   The ordinary shares were then consolidated into shares of £1.

(iii)   A rights issue, at a premium of 10p per share, was offered and fully taken up on the basis of one share for every three already held.

REQUIRED

The balance sheet of Pinewood plc after the above events had taken place.

13.2   CAPITAL REDUCTION

Debit balances on profit and loss accounts may lead to an erosion of capital and it may be necessary to recognise the fact by a capital reduction scheme. A Capital Reduction account is used for the purpose.

13.2.1 EXAMPLE

The following is the balance sheet of Oakwood Ltd. at 31 December 19-0:

	£	£
Fixed assets		50,000
Current assets	36,000	
less Current liabilities	24,000	12,000
		62,000
Capital and reserves		
100,000 ordinary shares of £1		100,000
Profit and loss account		(38,000)
		62,000

No provision has been made for depreciation of the fixed assets which, at the date of the balance sheet, were estimated to be worth £42,000, and it has been discovered that a major customer, owing £4,000 has become bankrupt.

However, the directors are of the opinion that the company will begin to make a profit of £5,000 per annum from now on.

REQUIRED

A scheme of capital reduction and the balance sheet as it will appear after the scheme has been put into effect.

ANSWER

The shares are worth 62p (£62,000/100,000) on balance sheet values, but it is necessary to substitute the estimated realisable values of the assets to find the real value of the shares. They are really worth £(42,000 + 8,000)/100,000 = 50p. Furthermore the shareholders will have to wait 8 years before the future profits will have eliminated the debit balance on the profit and loss account and they can look forward to a dividend.

This situation may be resolved in a number of ways, one of which would be to reduce the nominal value of the shares to 50p. Each £1 share could be cancelled and replaced by one new share of 50p.

The accounting entries will require the use of a Capital Reduction account:

	Dr	Cr
	£	£
Ordinary share capital	50,000	
Capital reduction account		50,000
Capital reduction account	50,000	
Fixed assets		8,000
Debtor (personal account)		4,000
Profit and loss		38,000

The resulting balance sheet will then be as follows:

	£	£
Fixed assets		42,000
Current assets	32,000	
less Current liabilities	24,000	8,000
		50,000

	£	£
Capital and reserves		
100,000 ordinary shares of 50p		50,000

Tutorial notes

1. The shareholders have not lost anything as a result of the reconstruction of the capital of the company as their shares had already lost 50p of their value; the reconstruction merely recognises this fact.

2. The debit balance has been eliminated from the profit and loss account. If the profit of £5,000 is achieved, it will be equivalent to a dividend of 10% payable to the shareholders immediately; they will not have to wait 8 years for a dividend.

13.2.2 EXERCISE (to record a scheme of reconstruction to reduce share capital)

The balance sheet of Pinewood Ltd. is as follows:

	£	£	£
Fixed assets at cost			45,000
Current assets		28,000	
Less Current liabilities:			
Creditors	12,000		
Bank overdraft	5,000	17,000	11,000
			56,000
Share capital and reserves			
100,000 ordinary shares of £1			100,000
Less Profit and loss account			(44,000)
			56,000

The directors consider that the fixed assets should be depreciated by £5,000 and a provision of £1,000 should be created for bad debts. It is decided to reduce the nominal value of the ordinary shares to 50p, to eliminate the debit balance on profit and loss account and to create provisions for depreciation of the fixed assets and for bad debts.

REQUIRED

(a) Prepare the Capital Reduction account showing the entries to record the above scheme of reconstruction;

(b) Redraft the balance sheet as it will appear immediately after the reduction of the share capital.

13.3 REDEMPTION AND PURCHASE OF OWN SHARES BY A COMPANY

A company is permitted by the Companies Act 1985, to issue redeemable shares.

A company may issue redeemable shares because

(i) They may be redeemed when there is a surplus of capital and the surplus funds cannot be put to profitable use.

(ii) Capital may be needed in the medium term for a project, but the project may be expected to generate sufficient funds in due course to enable the capital to be repaid.

(iii) Private companies may have difficulty in raising share capital as their shares are not traded on the Stock Exchange. A potential investor who may be wary of putting money into shares which cannot be sold again easily may be encouraged to invest if the shares are redeemable by the company.

(iv) If a shareholder in a 'family' company dies, his personal representatives may require money as a matter of some urgency to pay taxes.

The Act is concerned to protect the creditors of any company which decides to redeem shares; otherwise cash which should be used to pay the creditors could be paid instead to shareholders.

Companies are permitted to redeem their own shares either:

1. Out of the proceeds of a new issue of shares.

2. By capitalising profits that would otherwise be distributable to the shareholders, or

3. By a combination of both methods.

Method 2. requires the creation of a Capital Redemption Reserve.

Shares may be redeemed at a premium; the premium on redemption may be charged to share premium account only if:

1.   The shares to be redeemed were originally issued at a premium, and
2.   The shares are to be redeemed out of the proceeds of a new issue of shares.

The amount of the premium which may be debited to share premium account is limited to

(i)   the premium on the shares when they were issued, and
(ii) the balance presently standing to the credit of the share premium account (i.e. the share premium account must not end up with a debit balance)

Note:

(i)   Private limited companies may use capital reserves to create the Capital Redemption Reserve, but only to the extent that their distributable reserves are insufficient for this purpose.

(ii) If a private limited company's revenue and capital reserves together are insufficient to fill the 'gap' created by the redemption of shares, the Companies Act allows for a shortfall in the Capital Redemption Reserve.

Neither of the provisions mentioned in this note applies to public limited companies.

13.3.1 EXAMPLE 1

The balance sheet of Pelican Foods plc is as follows:

	£'000	£'000
Fixed assets		540
Current assets	284	
Less Current liabilities	177	107
		647
Share capital and reserves		
300,000 ordinary shares of £1		300
100,000 10% redeemable preference shares of £1		100
Share premium		60
Retained profits		187
		647

It has been decided to redeem the 10% redeemable preference shares at a premium of 10p per share. There will be a further issue of 50,000 ordinary shares at a premium of £1 to provide funds for the redemption of the preference shares. The preference shares were originally issued at a premium of 15p per share.

REQUIRED

Show the balance sheet as it will appear immediately after the above events have been complete.

ANSWER

Pelican Foods plc

	£'000	£'000
Fixed Assets		540
Current assets (284+100-110)	274	
Less Current liabilities	177	97
		637
Capital and reserves		
350,000 ordinary shares of £1		350
Share premium (60+50-10)		100
Retained profits		187
		637

EXAMPLE 2

The balance sheet for Pelican Foods Ltd. as in Example 1.

The company decides to redeem the preference shares at a premium of 10p. No new shares are to be issued.

REQUIRED

Show the balance sheet as it will appear immediately after the redemption of the preference shares.

ANSWER

Pelican Foods plc

	£'000	£'000
Fixed assets		540
Current assets (284-110)	174	
Less current liabilities	(177)	(3)
		537
Capital and reserves		
300,000 ordinary shares of £1		300
Share premium		60
Capital Redemption Reserve		100
Retained profits (187-100-10)		77
		537

Tutorial note: £100,000 of the distributable profit has been used to create the Capital Redemption Reserve; a further £10,000 has been used to write off the premium on the redemption of the preference shares.

13.3.2 EXERCISE 1

The balance sheet of Penguin Beakers Ltd. is as follows:

	£'000
Net assets	101
Capital and reserves	
75,000 ordinary shares of £1	75
10,000 8% redeemable preference shares of £1	10
Share premium account	6
Retained profits	10
	101

The directors intend to redeem the preference shares at a premium of 20p; the preference shares were originally issued at a premium of 10p. The redemption is to be financed out of the proceeds of a new issue of 10,000 £1 ordinary shares at a premium of 25p.

REQUIRED

The balance sheet of Penguin Beakers Ltd. after the new ordinary shares have been issued and the preference shares have been redeemed.

EXERCISE 2

The following is the balance sheet of Flamingo plc:

	£'000
Net assets	1,250

Capital and reserves
750,000 ordinary shares of £1	750
100,000 10% preference shares of £1	100
Share premium account	40
Revenue reserves	360
	1,250

The preference shares are to be redeemed at a premium of 10p each; no new shares are to be issued.

REQUIRED

The balance sheet of Flamingo plc after the preference shares have been redeemed.

EXERCISE 3

At 30 September 19-2 the balance sheet of Ostrich Ltd. a private limited company was as follows:

	£
Net assets	13,000
Capital and reserves	
6,000 ordinary shares of £1	6,000
4,000 10% preference shares of £1	4,000
Share premium account	1,000
Retained profits	2,000
	13,000

It has been decided to redeem the preference shares at par (nominal value) without the issue of any new shares.

REQUIRED

The balance sheet of Ostrich Ltd. a private limited company, after the redemption of the preference shares has been completed.

13.4   THE PURCHASE BY A COMPANY OF ITS OWN SHARES

Shares which have not been issued as 'redeemable' shares may be purchased from the holders by a company; the accounting entries are similar to those required for the redemption of shares.

13.5   REDEMPTION OF DEBENTURES

The accounting treatment of the redemption of debentures is similar to that for the repayment of any other loan. There is no legal obligation to replace the debentures with the equivalent of the Capital Redemption Reserve, but it is often considered prudent to recognise the nature of debentures as a source of long term finance by capitalising an equivalent amount of revenue reserves.

13.6   KEY POINTS TO REMEMBER

1. Bonus shares are created by transferring reserves to share capital account. No cash is received by the company for the shares.
2. Reduction of share capital requires the use of a Capital Reduction account to which is credited the reduction of share capital. The debit balance on profit and loss account, and reductions in asset accounts are debited to the Capital Reduction account.
3. Shares may be redeemed out of the proceeds of a new issue of shares; otherwise a Capital Redemption Reserve must be created. A premium payable on redemption of shares may only be debited to share premium if certain conditions are fulfilled. (See 13.3)

COMMON ERRORS

- confusion of bonus shares with rights issues.
- failure to adjust a balance sheet correctly after a capital reduction; make sure the double entry is completed properly for each adjustment.
- failure to observe the basic rules for the redemption of share capital; this often results from a failure to read the question carefully.

13.7   EXAMINATION QUESTIONS

QUESTION 1   (London January 1989)

Chesterton plc produced a set of draft accounts for the year ended 31 December 19-8. The trial balance at that date included the following balances:

	Dr	Cr
	£	£
Ordinary shares of 25p each, fully paid		260,000
8% Redeemable Preference Shares, of £1 each, fully paid		80,000
Share Premium Account		40,000
Interim Ordinary dividend	13,000	
Preference dividend	3,200	
Net Profit for the year		195,700
Retained Profit 1 January 19-8		156,078
Cash at Bank	24,000	
Debtors and Creditors	45,000	36,000
Stock at 31 December 19-8	129,000	

Note: Authorised share capital is 1.2 million ordinary shares of 25p each, and 80,000 8% Redeemable Preference Shares of £1 each.

The following decisions have been taken which will affect the draft accounts:

1. The preference shares are to be redeemed at par at the year end. No new shares will be issued in replacement.

2. Taxation of £30,000 is to be provided on the year's profit.

3. £10,000 is to be transferred to an Asset Replacement Reserve.

4. The remaining preference dividend is to be paid, together with a final ordinary dividend of 2 pence per share. Both dividends will be paid in February 19-9.

5. An adjustment is necessary in respect of directors' salaries due but unpaid at the year end, amounting to £8,000.

(a) You are required to prepare:

   (i)   The profit and loss appropriation account for the year ended 31 December 19-8.   *(8 marks)*

   (ii) Extracts from the balance sheet at 31 December 19-8 showing current assets, current liabilities, share capital and reserves.   *(10 marks)*

(b) After the redemption of shares it is usual for a company to maintain the total of its share capital and capital reserves at their pre-redemption level. Explain the reasons for this.   *(7 marks)*

(Total 25 marks)

QUESTION 2   (Oxford June 1986)

A company has an authorised capital of 2,000,000 £1 shares of which 1,500,000 have been issued. At 31 May 19-5 the balance sheet of the company shows the following items:

	£
Premium account	82,000
Profit and Loss account	515,000
£1 Ordinary shares	1,000,000
8% Preference shares (issued at a premium)	500,000
6% Convertible stock	200,000

The following transactions took place during the year ending 31 May 19-6:

June 19-5   A rights issue was made of 200,000 Ordinary shares at £1.50 each. These rights were all taken up and the proceeds received by the end of the month.

July 19-5   The 8% redeemable preference shares were redeemed at a premium of 5%.

Half of the stock holders opted to convert their stock to Ordinary shares at a rate of three shares for each £4 of stock held.

Aug 19-5   The company made a bonus issue of one ordinary share for every five shares held at that date.

You are required to show:

The journal entries, with narrations, to record the above transactions.   *(18 marks)*

QUESTION 3 (JMB June 1987)

The accounts of Coldstream plc showed the following balances on 31 December 19-6.

	£	£
Issued Share Capital:		
1,000,000 Ordinary Shares of £0.50 each, fully paid		500,000
400,000 10% Redeemable Preference Shares of £1.00 each, fully paid		400,000
		900,000
Share Premium	9,000	
General Reserve	340,000	
Profit and Loss	27,800	376,800
		1,276,800

The redeemable preference shares were issued in October 19-4.

In January 19-7, the following transactions were undertaken:

(i)   an issue of 200,000 ordinary shares of £0.50 each as a bonus issue utilising the general reserve;

(ii)   the redemption of 140,000 10% redeemable preference shares at a 20% premium.

You are required to:

(a)   prepare the appropriate ledger accounts, excluding bank, to record the above transactions:

(12 marks)

(b)   prepare the shareholders' funds section of the Balance Sheet immediately after the issue and redemption.   *(6 marks)*

(Total 18 marks)

QUESTION 4   (Cambridge November 1987)

The summarised balance sheet as at 31 October 19-7 of Teamer Limited is as follows:

	£'000
Net assets (current break up value £1.8m)	2,000
Represented by:	
Ordinary shares of £1.00 each, fully paid	4,000
7% Cumulative Preference shares of £1.00 each, fully paid	500
Reserves	(3,500)
10% Loan stock	1,000
	2,000

Consideration is now being given to the following scheme of re-construction:

(a)   the existing ordinary shares to be cancelled and the ordinary shareholders to be issued with 4,000,000 ordinary shares of 10p each, fully paid;

(b)   the 7% Cumulative Preference shareholders to receive 1,000,000 ordinary shares of 10p each, fully paid in settlement of the three years' arrears of the preference dividend;

(c)   the existing 10% Loan stock to be cancelled and the loan stock holders to be issued with £800,000 12% Loan stock and 2,000,000 ordinary shares of 10p each, fully paid.

It is anticipated that the company's annual earnings available for distribution in the next few years will be in the region of £400,000.

It is known that a number of ordinary shareholders are unhappy about the apparently great sacrifices to be made by the ordinary shareholders if the reconstruction scheme is approved.

REQUIRED

(a) The summarised balance sheet as at 1 November 19-7, assuming the implementation of the reconstruction scheme. *(10 marks)*

(b) A reply to the ordinary shareholders who are unhappy about the reconstruction scheme. Answers should be supported by appropriate computations showing how the reconstruction scheme will affect the various classes of investors in the company. *(15 marks)*

(Total 25 marks)

14 AMALGAMATIONS AND TAKE-OVERS; CONSOLIDATED ACCOUNTS

This chapter is concerned with:-
- one company acquiring the net assets of another or other companies i.e. an amalgamation of companies
- one company acquiring all or part of the share capital of another or other companies i.e a take-over
- simple consolidations of the profit and loss accounts and balance sheets of a group of companies

One company may acquire an interest in another company either by:
1. Purchasing the net assets of that other company or
2. Purchasing shares in that other company

or

3. A third company may be formed to acquire the share capitals of the other two.

14.1 AMALGAMATIONS

When two companies amalgamate, one of the companies purchases the net assets of the other company; in other words, the former company purchases the assets of the other company and assumes responsibility for paying its creditors.

The amalgamation is then recorded by combining the assets and liabilities of the companies concerned.

Three points to remember when amalgamating balance sheets:

1. The assets of the 'acquired' company may not be taken over at their balance sheet values. The values at which they are taken over must be substituted for their balance sheet values.
2. Any excess of the purchase price over the value of the net assets being acquired represents a payment for goodwill.
3. Adjust the 'acquiring' company's balance sheet for the cash it pays and/or the shares it issues as the purchase consideration.

14.1.1 EXAMPLE 1 (Simple acquisition in exchange for shares and cash)

The balance sheets of Laurel Ltd. and Hardy Ltd. at 31 March 19-0 were as follows:

	Laurel Ltd.		Hardy Ltd.	
	£	£	£	£
Fixed assets				
Freehold premises		20,000		–
Plant and equipment		19,000		12,000
Motor vehicles		11,000		8,000
Office computer		–		3,000
		50,000		23,000
Current assets				
Stock	4,000		1,200	
Debtors	5,400		900	
Bank	31,700		1,000	
	41,100		3,100	
less Creditors	3,600	37,500	475	2,625
		87,500		25,625

195

	£	£	£	£
Capital and reserves				
Ordinary shares of £1		75,000		25,000
Profit and loss account		12,500		625
		87,500		25,625

Laurel Ltd. acquires at their book values all the assets of Hardy Ltd except the bank account and assumes responsibility for paying the creditors. The purchase consideration will consist of 20,000 ordinary shares in Laurel Ltd at par, and the balance in cash.

REQUIRED

The balance sheet of Laurel Ltd. immediately after the acquisition of the net assets of Hardy Ltd.

ANSWER

(Working: The value of the net assets acquired is £25,625 – £1,000 (bank account) = £24,625. Purchase consideration will consist of £20,000 in shares and £4,625 in cash);

Laurel Ltd.
Balance sheet at 1 April 19 -0

	£	£
Fixed assets		
Freehold premises		20,000
Plant and equipment (19,000 + 12,000)		31,000
Motor vehicles (11,000 + 8,000)		19,000
Office computer		3,000
		73,000
Current assets		
Stock (4,000 + 1,200)	5,200	
Debtors (5,400 + 900)	6,300	
Bank (31,700 - 4,625)	27,075	
	38,575	
less Creditors (3,600 + 475)	4,075	34,500
		107,500
Share Capital and reserves		
Ordinary shares of £1 (75,000 + 20,000)		95,000
Profit and loss account		12,500
		107,500

EXAMPLE 2. (Acquisition of net assets at fair valuation and payment for goodwill)
The balance sheets of Pig Ltd. and Whistle Ltd. at 31 May 19-3 were as follows:

	Pig Ltd.		Whistle Ltd	
	£	£	£	£
Fixed assets				
Freehold property		–		25,000
Plant and machinery		40,000		19,000
Motor vehicles		31,000		27,000
Office equipment		5,000		8,000
		76,000		79,000
Current assets				
Stock	14,000		11,000	
Debtors	9,000		7,600	
Bank	27,000		9,400	
Carried forward	50,000	76,000	28,000	79,000

	£	£	£	£
Brought forward	50,000	76,000	28,000	79,000
less Creditors	17,000	33,000	14,000	14,000
		109,000		93,000
Share capital and reserves				
Ordinary shares of £1 each		100,000		100,000
Profit and loss account		9,000		(7,000)
		109,000		93,000

Pig Ltd. agreed to take over the assets of Whistle Ltd, except for the bank account, at the following valuations:

	£
Freehold property	30,000
Plant and machinery	16,000
Motor vehicles	24,000
Office equipment	3,000
Stock	10,000
Debtors	7,000

Pig Ltd. also agreed to settle Whistle Ltd.'s creditors.

The purchase price was fixed at £80,000 which was to be settled by the issue to Whistle Ltd's shareholders of 50,000 ordinary shares of £1 each in Pig Ltd. at a premium of 50p each, and the balance in cash.

REQUIRED

(a) The balance sheet of Pig Ltd. immediately after the completion of the acquisition of the business of Whistle Ltd.

(b) The balance sheet of Whistle Ltd. immediately following the sale of the business to Pig Ltd.

ANSWER

(a) Working: Value of net assets acquired:

	£
Total of assets per question	90,000
Less creditors	14,000
	76,000
Consideration:	80,000
Goodwill	4,000
Consideration: Shares: 50,000 × £1.50	75,000
Cash	5,000

Pig Ltd.
Balance sheet at 1 June 19-3

	£	£	£
Fixed assets			
Intangible assets			
Goodwill			4,000
Tangible assets			
Freehold property		30,000	
Plant and machinery (40,000 + 16,000)		56,000	
Motor vehicles (31,000 + 24,000)		55,000	
Office equipment (5,000 + 3,000)		8,000	149,000
Carried forward			153,000

	£	£	£
Brought forward			153,000
Current assets			
Stock (14,000 + 10,000)		24,000	
Debtors (9,000 + 7,000)		16,000	
Bank (27,000 - 5,000)		22,000	
		62,000	
less Creditors (17,000 + 14,000)		31,000	31,000
			184,000
Share capital and reserves			
150,000 shares of £1			150,000
Share premium			25,000
Profit and loss account			9,000
			184,000

(b)

Whistle Ltd.
Balance sheet as at 1 June 19-3

	£	£
Shares in Pig Ltd. at cost		75,000
Bank (9,400 + 5,000)		14,400
		89,400
Share capital and reserves		
Ordinary shares of £1		100,000
Profit and loss account	(7,000)	
add loss on sale of assets		
(*83,600 - 80,000)	(3,600)	(10,600)
		89,400

* Total net assets £93,000 less bank account not taken over £9,400

14.1.2 EXERCISE (Preparation of the balance sheet of a company after it has acquired two other businesses.)

Gerald Mercer for some years owned two businesses in Uptown: Gerald (Menswear) and Mercer Fashions. Both businesses required additional capital. Gerald's two brothers agreed to supply additional capital provided the two businesses were converted into a limited liability company.

Accordingly, a new company, Merger (19-1) Ltd. was formed on 1 July 19-1 to acquire the net assets of Gerald (Menswear) and Mercer Fashions. Mercer and his two brothers subscribed for a total of 100,000 ordinary shares of £1 each in Merger (19-1) Ltd. and paid the cash for the shares into the company's bank account.

At 1 July, 19-1 the balance sheets of Merger (19-1) Ltd., Gerald Menswear and Mercer Fashions were as follows:

	Merger (19-1) Ltd		Gerald (Menswear)		Mercer Fashions
	£'000	£'000	£'000	£'000	£'000
Fixed assets					
Freehold premises	–		40		15
Delivery vans			8		6
Fixtures and fittings			7		11
Office equipment			3		1
Carried forward			58		33

	Merger (19-1) Ltd	Gerald (Menswear)		Mercer Fashions	
	£'000	£'000	£'000	£'000	£'000
Brought forward			58		33
Current assets					
Stock		40		66	
Debtors		5		17	
Bank	100	–		–	
	100	45		83	
less Current liabilities					
Trade creditors		(32)		(76)	
Bank overdraft		(16)	(3)	(22)	(15)
	100		55		18
Capital					
100,000 ordinary shares of £1	100				
Gerald Mercer- Capital			55		18

It was agreed by the brothers that Merger (19-1) Ltd. should take over the assets of the two businesses at their net book values except for the following assets which would be taken over at the values shown.

	Gerald(Menswear)	Mercer Fashions
	£'000	£'000
Freehold premises	75	25
Delivery vans	net book value	5
Fixtures and fittings	4	net book value
Stock	38	55
Debtors	4	60

It was further agreed between the brothers that Merger(19-1) Ltd. would pay:

£100,000   for Gerald (menswear), to be settled by the allotment of 60,000 ordinary shares of £1 each in Merger(19-1) Ltd. and £28,000 in cash;

and   £60,000   for Mercer Fashions, to be settled by the allotment of 40,000 ordinary shares of £1 each in Merger(19-1) Ltd., and £12,000 in cash.

REQUIRED

Prepare the balance sheet of Merger (19-1) Ltd. as it would have appeared immediately after the above agreed matters had been implemented.

14.2 PURCHASE BY ONE COMPANY OF SHARES IN ANOTHER COMPANY

A company may gain control of another company by purchasing more than 50 percent of the shares that carry voting rights in that other company; that normally means the ordinary share capital.

The company acquiring the shares is known as the *holding company*; the company whose shares have been acquired is a *subsidiary company* of the holding company. A holding company and its subsidiary company or companies is known as a *group*.

In the balance sheet of the holding company the shareholding(s) will be shown under fixed assets as 'Investment' at cost, subject to the following:

Whilst dividends paid out of post-acquisition profits by the subsidiary company to the holding company may be credited to the holding company's profit and loss account, a dividend paid out of pre-acquistion profits to the holding company should be credited to the Investment account, thus reducing the cost of the asset in the balance sheet. (Pre-acquisition profits = profits made before the holding company acquired the shares; post-acquisition profits = those made after.)

This is the 'Acquisition method' of accounting, and the reason for treating dividends paid out of pre-acquisition profits in this way is because the cash used to pay the dividend formed part of the assets of the business when it was purchased. The payment of the dividend is really a return of purchase money for the shares.

An alternative known as the 'merger method' allows all dividends received by a holding company to be credited to its profit and loss account, whether paid out of pre- or post-acquisition profits.

14.3   CONSOLIDATED BALANCE SHEETS

A company having one or more subsidiary companies must prepare group accounts in addition to its own profit and loss account and balance sheet.

The Purposes of Consolidated Accounts

(a)   The holding company's own balance sheet gives no indication of the totality of assets and liabilities of the group in which it holds investments. A consolidated balance sheet discloses the details of the total assets and liabilities of the group.

(b)   Consolidated accounts enable shareholders in the holding company to assess their company's ability to invest wisely in other companies.

(c)   A consolidated balance sheet discloses the gearing of the group as a whole.

N.B. A consolidated balance sheet does not help creditors; they wish to know that the company which is indebted to them has sufficient assets readily available to pay its debts. Creditors cannot look to other companies, even in the same group, to pay the debts. Consolidated balance sheets do not identify assets with particular companies.

Preparation of Consolidated Balance Sheets

A consolidated balance sheet is prepared by adding together the balance sheets of the holding company and its subsidiaries, subject to the following:

(It is assumed for the present that the holding company has acquired the whole of the shares in its subsidiary and that the consideration for those shares is equal to the value of the net assets of the subsidiary company.)

1.   Cancel the item 'Investment in subsidiary' appearing in the holding company's balance sheet against the share capital and reserves in the subsidiary company's balance sheet.

2.   Cancel inter-company indebtedness from the creditors of one company and the debtors of the other company.

3.   Eliminate unrealised profit from the closing stock of a company which has bought that stock from another company in the same group; deduct the unrealised profit from the retained profit of the company which sold the stock within the group.

When the consideration paid for the shares is greater than the net asset value of subsidiary.

Treat the difference between the cost of the investment and the net assets as goodwill in the consolidated balance sheet.

When the consideration paid for the shares is less than the net asset value of the subsidiary.

Treat the difference between the cost of the investment and the net assets as a capital reserve in the consolidated balance sheet.

When the holding company acquires less than 100 percent of the shares in the subsidiary (i.e. there are minority interests.)

Show the minority interest in the consolidated balance sheet at the amount of its shares plus its proportion of the reserves at the date of the balance sheet.

14.3.1 EXAMPLE 1 (Holding company owning whole of share capital in subsidiary.)

Hotdogs Ltd. acquired the whole of the share capital of Chips Ltd. on 31 December 19-1 when the reserves of the latter amounted to £10,000.

The balance sheets of Hotdogs plc and Chips Ltd. at 31 December 19-2 were as follows:

	Hotdogs Ltd.		Chips Ltd.	
	£'000		£'000	
Tangible fixed assets		300		80
Investment in Chips Ltd. at cost		110		–
Current assets				
Stock	80		25	
Debtors	55		30	
Bank	30		4	
	165		59	
Less creditors	(35)	130	(14)	45
		540		125
Capital and reserves				
Ordinary shares of £1		400		100
Reserves		140		25
		540		125

Further information:

1. At 31 December 19-2, Chips Ltd. owed Hotdogs Ltd. £8,000.
2. Included in the stock of Hotdogs Ltd. are goods which Hotdogs Ltd. has purchased from Chips Ltd. for £10,000. Chips sells goods to Hotdogs Ltd at cost plus 25%.

REQUIRED

Prepare the consolidated balance sheet for the group as at 31 December 19-2.

ANSWER

Workings:

1. Calculation of unrealised profit:

    If mark-up is 25% ($^1/_4$), margin is 20% ($^1/_5$)

    Goods in stock cost Hotdogs £10,000; therefore unrealised profit = 20% of £10,000 = £2,000.

    Stock

Reduce stock of Hotdogs by £2,000: £(80,000 - 2,000) =	£78,000
Add stock in Chips balance sheet	£25,000
Stock to be included in consolidated balance sheet	£103,000

2. Inter-company indebtedness:

    In the balance sheet of Chips Ltd.:

reduce creditors by £8,000: £(14,000 - 8,000) =	£6,000
On consolidation creditors will be Hotdogs £35,000 + Chips £6,000 =	£41,000

    In balance sheet of Hotdogs Ltd:

reduce debtors by £8,000: £(55,000-8,000) =	£47,000
On consolidation debtors will be Hotdogs £47,000+ Chips £30,000 =	£77,000

3. Capital and reserves

Chips Ltd.	Share capital	Reserves
	£	£
Per balance sheet at 31.12. 19-2	100,000	25,000
Cancel against Investment in Hotdogs Ltd. balance sheet	(100,000)	(10,000)
Deduct unrealised profit on goods sold to Hotdogs Ltd.		(2,000)
Carried forward	–	13,000

	Share capital £	Reserves £
Brought forward	–	13,000
Add Hotdogs Ltd. capital and reserves	400,000	140,000
Per consolidated balance sheet	400,000	153,000

Hotdogs Ltd. and subsidiary company
Consolidated balance sheet
as at 31 December 19-2

	£'000	£'000
Tangible fixed assets (300,000 + 80,000)		380
Current assets		
Stock (see working 1)	103	
Debtors (see working 2)	77	
Bank (30,000 + 4,000)	34	
	214	
Creditors (see working 2)	41	173
		553
Share capital and reserves		
400,000 ordinary shares of £1 each		400
Reserves (see working 3)		153
		553

EXAMPLE 2 (Goodwill on consolidation)

Facts as in Example 1 above, except that investment is shown in Hotdogs Ltd.'s balance sheet at £125,000, and Hotdogs Ltd.'s reserves at 31 December 19-2 are £155,000.
Calculation of goodwill:

Cost of acquisition	£125,000
Share capital and reserves of Chips Ltd.	
31 December 19-1	£110,000
Goodwill per consolidated balance sheet	£15,000

Hotdogs Ltd. and subsidiary company
Consolidated balance sheet as at 31 December 19-2

	£'000
Intangible fixed asset:	
Goodwill	15
Tangible fixed assets	380
	395
Net working capital (as in example 1 above)	173
	568
Share capital and reserves	
400,000 ordinary shares of £1 each	400
Reserves (155,000 +13,000)	168
	568

EXAMPLE 3 (negative goodwill on consolidation)

Facts as in Example 1 above, except that investment is shown in Hotdogs Ltd. balance sheet at £96,000, and Hotdogs Ltd.'s reserves at 31 December 19-2 are £126,000.

Working:

Cost of acquisition	£96,000
Share capital and reserves of Chips Ltd.at	
31 December 19-1	£110,000
Negative goodwill – capital reserve	£14,000

Hotdogs Ltd. and subsidiary company
Consolidated balance sheet as at 31 December 19-2

	£'000
Tangible fixed assets	380
Net working capital (as in example 1)	173
	553
Share capital and reserves	
400,000 ordinary shares of £1	400
Capital reserve	14
Other reserves (126,000 + 13,000)	139
	553

EXAMPLE 4 (involving minority interests)

Facts as in Example 1, except that Hotdogs Ltd. acquired 80,000 ordinary shares of £1 each in Chips Ltd. for £110,000.

Working

1 Share capital of Chips Ltd. held as follows:

Hotdogs Ltd.	80%	
Minority interest	20%	

Proportion of net assets at 31 December 19-1 attributable to Hotdogs Ltd.'s holding = 80% of Chips Ltd.'s share capital and reserves at

31 December 19-1 = 80% of £110,000 =		£88,000
	Cost of acquisition =	£110,000
	Goodwill per consolidated balance sheet =	£22,000

2. Reserves:

Reserves per Hotdogs Ltd balance sheet at 31 December 19-2	£140,000
80% of Chips Ltd. increase in reserves at 31 December 19-2 (80% of £15,000)	£ 12,000
	£152,000
Less unrealised profit (see example 1)	£2,000
Per consolidated balance sheet	£150,000

3. Minority Interest:

20% of share capital of Chips Ltd.	£20,000
20% of reserves at 31 December 19-2 (20% of £25,000)	£ 5,000
	£25,000

Hotdogs Ltd. and subsidiary company
Consolidated balance sheet as at 31 December 19-2

	£'000
Intangible fixed asset	
Goodwill (working 1)	22
Tangible fixed assets	380
Net working capital	173
	575
Capital and reserves	
400,000 shares of £1 each	400
Reserves (working 2)	150
	550
Minority interest (working 3)	25
	575

14.3.2 EXERCISE 1 (Consolidated balance sheet for holding company and two subsidiaries)

The balance sheets at 31 December 19-1 of Doulla Ltd. and its two subsidiary companies, Rosalia Ltd. and Tracey Ltd. were as follows:

	Doulla Ltd		Rosalia Ltd		Tracey Ltd	
	£'000	£'000	£'000	£'000	£'000	£'000
Fixed assets						
Freehold property		100		–		–
Plant and equipment		80		65		40
Motor vehicles		42		35		28
Office machinery		30		15		20
		252		115		88
Investments						
150,000 ordinary shares in Rosalia Ltd.		200				
150,000 ordinary shares in Tracey Ltd.		150				
Current assets						
Stock	74		51		39	
Debtors	52		39		22	
Bank	60		27		30	
	186		117		91	
Less: Creditors	48	138	50	67	22	69
		740		182		157
Capital and reserves						
Ordinary shares of £1		600		150		150
Reserves		140		32		7
		740		182		157

REQUIRED

The consolidated balance sheet of Doulla Ltd. and its subsidiary companies as at 31 December 19-1.

EXERCISE 2 (consolidated balance sheet for holding company and two wholly owned subsidiaries where there are inter-company indebtedness and unrealised profit.)

Mei Yiu Ltd. and Sing Yiu Ltd. became wholly owned subsidiaries of Hon Wai Ltd. on 30 April 19-4. Their balance sheets immediately afterwards were as follows:

	Hon Wai Ltd		Mei Yiu Ltd		Sing Yiu Ltd	
	£'000	£'000	£'000	£'000	£'000	£'000
Fixed assets						
Freehold property		180		–		–
Plant and machinery		75		64		80
Motor vehicles		30		45		28
		285		109		108
Investments						
150,000 ordinary shares in Mei–Yiu Ltd.		195				
120,000 ordinary shares in Sing-Yiu Ltd.		150				
Current assets						
Stock	60		48		45	
Debtors	54		26		19	
Bank	31		13		4	
	145		87		68	
Creditors	36	109	19	68	21	47
		739		177		155
Capital and reserves						
Ordinary shares of £1		700		150		120
Reserves		39		27		35
		739		177		155

Further information:
1. At 30 April 19-4, Mei Yiu Ltd.'s stock included goods which had been purchased from Hon Wai Ltd. for £28,000. The goods had cost Hon Wai Ltd £20,000.
2. At 30 April 19-4 Sing Yiu Ltd. owed £5,000 to Mei Yiu Ltd.

REQUIRED

A consolidated balance sheet for Hon Wai Ltd. and its subsidiaries as at 30 April 19-4.

EXERCISE 3. (Preparation of a consolidated balance sheet with minority interests)

On 1 January 19-0, Buckle Ltd. acquired shares in Lace Ltd. and Pin Ltd. Their respective balance sheets were then as follows:

	Buckle Ltd		Lace Ltd.		Pin Ltd	
	£'000	£'000	£'000	£'000	£'000	£'000
Fixed assets						
Freehold premises		–		40		–
Motor vehicles		70		15		50
Equipment		25		20		30
		95		75		80
Investments						
80,000 ordinary shares in Lace Ltd.	100					
75,000 ordinary shares in Pin Ltd.	70					
		170				
Current assets						
Stock	42		50		14	
Debtors	54		28		10	
Bank	12		7		5	
	108		85		29	
Creditors	27	81	20	65	13	16
Carried forward		346		140		96

	Buckle Ltd		Lace Ltd.		Pin Ltd	
	£'000	£'000	£'000	£'000	£'000	£'000
Brought forward		346		140		96
		——		——		——
Share capital and reserves						
Ordinary shares of £1		300		100		100
8% Preference shares of £1		–		30		–
Retained profits		46		10		(4)
		——		——		——
		346		140		96
		——		——		——

REQUIRED

Prepare a consolidated balance sheet for Buckle Ltd. and its subsidiary companies as at 1 January 19-0.

EXERCISE 4 (Preparation of consolidated balance sheet with minority interests, inter-company indebtedness and unrealised profit)

Wader Ltd. acquired shares and debentures in Swan Ltd. and Heron Ltd. on 1 May 19-5, when the respective balance sheets of those companies were as follows:

	Wader Ltd.		Swan Ltd.		Heron Ltd.	
	£'000	£'000	£'000	£'000	£'000	£'000
Fixed assets						
Freehold property	300		–		84	
Plant and machinery	140		86		51	
Motor vehicles	45	485	28	114	15	150
	——		——		——	
Investments						
120,000 ordinary shares in Swan Ltd.	180					
20,000 preference shares in Swan Ltd.	20					
100,000 ordinary shares in Heron Ltd.	75					
£20,000 debentures in Heron Ltd.	20	295				
	——					
Current assets						
Stock	75		36		29	
Debtors	64		47		23	
Bank	33		35		17	
	——		——		——	
	172		118		69	
Creditors	45	127	27	91	39	30
	——		——		——	
		907		205		180
Less Debentures		–		–		60
		——		——		——
		907		205		120
		——		——		——
Capital and reserves						
Ordinary shares of £1		800		150		150
Preference shares of £1				25		
Retained profits		107		30		(30)
		——		——		——
		907		205		120
		——		——		——

The following information is relevant:

1. At 1 May 19-5 Heron Ltd. owed Swan Ltd. £7,000.

2. Included in the stock of Heron Ltd. is stock which it had bought from Wader Ltd. for £18,000. The goods had cost Wader Ltd. £12,000.

REQUIRED

A consolidated balance sheet for Wader Ltd. and its subsidiaries as at 1 May 19-5.

14.4 CONSOLIDATED PROFIT AND LOSS ACCOUNTS

Method of consolidating profit and loss accounts of a group:

1. *When there are no inter-company sales, dividends, unrealised profits in stock, or minority interests:*

   Add profit and loss accounts together.

2. *When there are inter-company sales:*

   Add profit and loss accounts together after deleting inter-company sales at selling price from sales of vending company and from cost of sales (purchases) of purchasing company.

3. *When closing stock includes unrealised profits on stock purchased within the group:*

   Deduct unrealised profit from closing stock (cost of sales) of company concerned. (This adjustment corresponds to the adjustment made to stock in the balance sheet, as demonstrated above.)

4. *Minority interests:*

   Deduct minority interest from 'profit on ordinary activities after taxation.'

5. *Calculation of minority interests:*

   Minority's share of preference dividends (if any) plus Minority's share of balance of profits (after preference dividends, if any).

6. *Extraordinary profit:*

   Aggregate holding company's extraordinary profits/losses with groups' share of subsidiaries' extraordinary profits/losses.

7. *Retained profits from previous year:*

   Add holding company's retained profit to group's share of post-acquisition profits of subsidiaries.

8. *Proposed dividends:*

   Show holding company's dividends only.

9. *Transfers to reserves:*

   Aggregate holding company's transfers to reserves and group's share of subsidiaries' transfers to reserves.

14.4.1 EXAMPLE

The issued share capital of Circle Ltd. consists of 100,000 £1 ordinary shares and 30,000 10% preference shares of £1 each.

Cone Ltd. holds 80,000 of the ordinary shares and 20,000 preference shares of Circle Ltd. During the year to 31 December 19-2 Cone Ltd. sold goods to Circle Ltd. for £25,000; these goods had cost Cone Ltd. £15,000. One half of these goods were still in Circle Ltd.'s stock at 31 December 19-2.

The profit and loss accounts of the two companies for the year to 31 December 19-2, and the consolidated profit and loss account for that year are as follows:

	Cone Ltd		Circle Ltd.		Group	
	£'000	£'000	£'000	£'000	£'000	£'000
Turnover		850		298		(A)1,123
Cost of sales		526		145		(B)(C) 651
Gross profit		324		153		472
Distribution costs	53		20		73	
Administration expenses	67	120	32	52	99	172
Profit on ordinary activities before taxation		204		101		300
Tax on profit on ordinary activities		42		27		69
Profit on ordinary activities after taxation		162		74		231
Minority interest						(D) 47
Carried forward		162		74		184

	£'000	£'000	£'000	£'000	£'000	£'000
Brought forward		162		74		184
Extraordinary profits net of tax		44		15	(E)	56
Profit for the financial year		206		89		240
Retained profits from last year		109		75	(F)	169
		315		164		409
Proposed dividends:						
Preference			3			
Ordinary	100		60		100	(G)
Transfer to reserves	80	180	30	93	104	(H) 204
Retained profits carried to next year		135		71		205

Workings

A   less £25,000 goods sold to Circle Ltd. (see 2. above)

B   less £25,000 goods bought from Cone Ltd. (see 2. above)

C   add £5,000: $1/2 \times £(25,000 - 15,000)$ (see 3. above)

D   minority interest = $1/3$ of preference dividend   £1,000
plus $1/5$ of: profit (after tax and after preference dividend):
$1/5 \times £(231,000 - 1,000)$ £46,000

(see 4 and 5 above)   £47,000

E   £44,000 + $4/5$ of £15,000 (see 6 above)

F   £109,000 + $4/5$ of £75,000 (see 7 above)

G   (see 8 above)

H   £80,000 + $4/5$ of £30,000 (see 9 above)

14.4.2 EXERCISE 1 (Consolidated profit and loss account of holding company with one wholly owned subsidiary company)

Cox Ltd. is the wholly owned subsidiary of Box Ltd. The profit and loss accounts of Box Ltd. and Cox Ltd. for the year to 31 March 19-1 were as follows:

	Box Ltd.		Cox Ltd.	
	£'000	£'000	£'000	£'000
Turnover		100		80
Cost of sales		60		50
Gross profit		40		30
Distribution costs	8		5	
Administration expenses	22	30	13	18
Profit on ordinary activities before taxation		10		12
Taxation on profit on ordinary activities		4		3
Profit on ordinary activities after taxation		6		9
Extraordinary profits net of tax		5		2
Profit for the financial year		11		11
Retained profits from the previous year		13		7
		24		18
Proposed dividend	8		5	
Transfer to reserve	10	18	8	13
Retained profit carried to next year		6		5

Further information:

Cox Ltd. has sold goods to Box Ltd. during the year for £18,000; the goods cost Cox Ltd. £15,000. All these goods were still in stock at Box Ltd. at 31 March 19-1.

REQUIRED

A consolidated profit and loss account for Box Ltd. and Cox Ltd. for the year ended 31 March 19-1.

EXERCISE 2 (Consolidated profit and loss account for a holding company and its subsidiary in which there are minority interests)

Bat plc owns 75 percent of the ordinary shares of Ball Ltd. and $^2/_3$rd of its preference shares. At the 30 September 19-3 the profit and loss accounts of the two companies were as follows:

	Bat plc		Ball Ltd.	
	£'000	£'000	£'000	£'000
Turnover		1,000		750
Cost of sales		684		525
Gross profit		316		225
Distribution costs	36		18	
Administrative expenses	84	120	36	54
Profit on ordinary activities before taxation		196		171
Taxation on profit on ordinary activities		67		50
Profit on ordinary activities after taxation		129		121
Extraordinary profit net of taxation		24		20
Profit for the financial year		153		141
Retained profit from previous year		116		80
		269		221
Proposed dividends				
Preference		–	42	
Ordinary	120		120	
Transfer to reserve	80	200	32	194
Retained profit carried to next year		69		27

Bat Ltd. sold goods for £24,000 to Ball Ltd. on 26 September 19-3; at 30 September 19-3 Bat Ltd. had not paid for these goods, all of which were still in stock. Ball Ltd. sells to Bat Ltd. at a mark-up of 50%.

REQUIRED

A consolidated profit and loss account for Bat Ltd. and its subsidiary for the year to 30 September 19-3.

14.5 KEY POINTS TO REMEMBER

1. Accounting for an amalgamation (or merger) requires the net assets acquired to be added to those of the purchasing company. The aggregation should take into account the fair values of the assets acquired if these are different from their net book values.
2. An excess of the purchase price over the aggregate of the fair values of net assets acquired represents the price paid for goodwill. If the price paid for the net assets is less than the aggregate of their fair values, the difference must be recorded as a capital reserve.
3. When one company acquires shares in another company, the investment should be shown in the balance sheet of the acquiring company at cost. Dividends received out of pre-acquisition profits from a subsidiary should be credited to the investment account to reduce the cost of the asset in the balance sheet. A note to the balance sheet should state the current market value of the investments, if quoted. A permanent reduction in value should be written off in the profit and loss account.

4. A take-over involving the acquisition of shares in another company does not give rise to goodwill in the balance sheet of the acquiring company.
5. When consolidating group company balance sheets proceed in the following order:
   (i) Calculate goodwill
   (ii) Calculate the group's share of reserves
   (iii) Calculate minority interests
   (iv) Cancel inter-company indebtedness
   (v) Deduct unrealised profit from stock
6. When consolidating profit and loss accounts,
   (i) Delete inter-company sales from turnover and cost of sales
   (ii) Delete unrealised profit from closing stock (i.e. add to cost of sales)
   (iii) Deduct minority interests from 'net profit after tax on ordinary activities'
   (iv) Items which occur after the deduction of minority interests represent the **group's share only** of those items; *except* that **only the holding company's dividends** will be shown.
6. Practice making adjustments in consolidation of profit and loss accounts and balance sheets by attempting as many questions as possible. Students should make up some examples of their own; much can be learned in this way.
7. As with all financial statements, you should head your consolidated accounts with appropriate headings.

COMMON ERRORS
- failure to recognise goodwill or negative goodwill when accounting for amalgamations.
- failure to calculate and adjust for goodwill, inter-company indebtedness, unrealised profit, group reserves, minority interests, in consolidated accounts.

14.6 EXAMINATION QUESTIONS

QUESTION 1 (Cambridge November 1986)

On 1 November 19-6, X Limited agreed to purchase the fixed assets, stock and debtors of Y Limited for £60,000 and also all the share capital of Z Limited for £105,000.

The balance sheets as at 31 October 19-6 of X Limited, Y Limited and Z Limited are as follows:

	X Limited	Y Limited	Z Limited
	£	£	£
Fixed assets	90,000	44,000	50,000
Current assets:			
Stock	30,000	6,000	36,000
Debtors	20,000	2,000	14,000
Balance at bank	70,000	3,000	16,000
	£210,000	£55,000	£116,000
Ordinary shares of £1 each			
fully paid	160,000	40,000	70,000
Retained earnings	45,000	10,000	30,000
Creditors	5,000	5,000	16,000
	£210,000	£55,000	£116,000

All the assets of the three companies have been recorded in the respective balance sheets at 31 October 19-6 at fair values.

The purchase price of £60,000 for the assets of Y Limited acquired by X Limited was settled by cash on 1 November 19-6. On the same day, X Limited issued 35,000 ordinary shares of £1 credited as fully paid in settlement for the share capital of Z Limited.

REQUIRED

(a) The balance sheets as at 1 November 19-6, immediately after the completion of the above transactions, of (i) X Limited and (ii) Y Limited. *(17 marks)*

(b) An outline of the possible reasons for the different forms of the transactions entered into by X Limited with regard to (i) Y Limited and (ii) Z Limited. *(8 marks)*

(Total 25 marks)

QUESTION 2 (Oxford June 1986)

On 30 April 19-6 a new company, Rainbow plc, was formed to take over three existing companies. The authorised capital of Rainbow plc was to consist of 1,000,000 Ordinary Shares of 50p each.

The terms of the takeover were as follows:

Blue plc The creditors and all the assets with the exception of the bank to be taken over at book values, settlement to be: nine ordinary shares in Rainbow for every fifty ordinary shares in Blue. Four ordinary shares in Rainbow for every two preference shares in Blue and a cash payment of £99,000. Blue plc is to redeem its own debentures at par.

Orange plc All the assets and liabilities except the bank overdraft to be taken over at a price of £98,000, half of the purchase price to be in ordinary shares in Rainbow.

Green plc Rainbow will not take over the creditors but will take over all the assets, including bank, and will settle with one ordinary share in Rainbow for each ordinary share in Green. The debenture holders are to receive 200 ordinary shares in Rainbow for every £100 debentures. £25,000 is to be paid to Green in cash.

All the necessary formalities are completed by 31 May 19-6 by which time Rainbow plc have issued all the remaining shares at a premium of 5p per share. Legal expenses of the takeover, £20,000, have been paid and land and buildings have been revalued at £100,000. Apart from this there are no other transactions for Rainbow for the month.

The following are the summarised balance sheets of the three companies at 30 April 19-6:

	Blue plc £'000s	Orange plc £'000s	Green plc £'000s
Goodwill	–	36	8
Land and Buildings	40	12	–
Plant and Machinery	44	20	12
Other fixed assets	25	10	5
Stocks	66	30	20
Debtors	120	90	18
Bank	50	(25) credit	4
Creditors	(80)	(70)	(6)
	265	103	61
Ordinary Shares of £1 each	110	108	50
8% Preference Shares of £1 each	60	–	–
6% debentures	70	–	8
Reserves	12	–	1
Retained Profits	13	(5) debit	2
	265	103	61

You are required to:

(a) Show the liquidation accounts, sundry shareholders' accounts and bank accounts in the books of the three selling companies.

(b) Show the Journal entry to record the take over of the three companies in the books of Rainbow plc.

(c) Draw up the Balance Sheet of Rainbow plc at 31 May 19-6.

IGNORE TAXATION

(40 marks)

QUESTION 3 (JMB June 1986)

On 31 December 19-5 Alpha Limited agreed to acquire all the assets and liabilities of Beta Limited for £880,000 in cash and the issue of £50,000 £1 Ordinary Shares. Prior to the acquisition Beta's stock is to be written down by £65,000. The balance sheets for the two companies at 31 December 19-5 were:

	Alpha		Beta	
	£'000s	£'000s	£'000s	£'000s
Net Fixed Assets		130		180
Investments		63		–
Current assets				
Stock	632		385	
Debtors	426		227	
Bank	581		326	
	1,639		938	
Current liabilities				
Creditors	563		210	
Taxation due	52	615	40	
Net current assets		1,024	250	688
Net Assets		1,217		868
Represented by Share Capital		275		130
Reserves		942		738
		1,217		868

(a) You are required to produce the balance sheet for Alpha Limited immediately after the acquisition of Beta Limited. *(10 marks)*

(b) Explain what goodwill is and how it can be treated in published accounts. What type of asset is it considered to be. *(6 marks)*

(Total 16 marks)

QUESTION 4 (Author's own question, after JMB)

Oak Limited and Ash Limited both have the same year end at 31 March. Oak Limited acquired the whole of the share capital of Ash Limited on 31 March 19-0 when their respective balance sheets were as follows:

Balance sheets as at 31 March 19-0

	Oak Limited	Ash Limited
	£	£
Assets		
Fixed assets	60,000	20,000
Current assets		
Stock	12,000	9,000
Debtors	14,000	8,000
Cash	30,000	3,000
	116,000	40,000
Represented by:		
Share capital (ordinary shares of £1)	75,000	25,000
Reserves	25,000	5,000
Current liabilities	16,000	10,000
	116,000	40,000

The consideration paid by Oak Limited to the shareholders of Ash Limited was £34,000, made up of 25,000 ordinary shares of £1 in Oak Limited and £4,000 in cash.

You are required to:

(i)   Prepare the balance sheet of Oak Limited immediately after the acquisition of the share capital of Ash Limited has been completed. (Assume that no other transactions have taken place in either company) *(14 marks)*

(ii) Explain why pre-acquisition profits are treated differently from post-acquisition profits in the accounts of a holding company. *(6 marks)*

(Total 20 marks)

QUESTION 5   (London January 1987)

A public limited company comprises a holding company and several subsidiaries. As a shareholder, you receive an annual report containing *consolidated* accounts.

(a)   Explain the purpose of consolidated accounts. *(5 marks)*

(b)   Suggest how the strengths or weaknesses of individual companies within the group may be revealed or concealed by the consolidation process. *(15 marks)*

(Total 20 marks)

QUESTION 6   (JMB June 1988)

The Balance Sheets of Sledge Ltd. and Hammer Ltd. as at 31 December 19-7 were as follows.

	SLEDGE LTD.		HAMMER LTD.
	£		£
Fixed Assets			
Land & Buildings		76,500	40,000
Plant & Equipment		40,000	28,500
		116,500	68,500
Investments			
Shares in Hammer Ltd.			
40,000 ordinary		60,000	–
10,000 preference		10,000	–
Current Assets			
Stock	27,000		25,100
Debtors	24,000		11,000
Cash	17,000		1,500
	68,000		37,600
Less			
Current Liabilities			
Creditors	45,500		7,100
Net Current Assets		22,500	30,500
Total Net Assets		209,000	99,000
Share Capital			
Ordinary Shares of £1		125,000	60,000
11% Preference Shares of £1		–	15,000
General Reserve		44,000	6,000
Profit & Loss Account		40,000	18,000
		209,000	99,000

Sledge Ltd. acquired its shares in Hammer Ltd. on 31 December 19-7.

(a)   You are required to produce a consolidated balance sheet for Sledge Ltd. as at 31 December 19-7 which incorporates the net assets of its subsidiary. *(15 marks)*

(b)   Explain what is meant by the term 'negative goodwill' and how it should be treated in company accounts. *(3 marks)*

(Total 18 marks)

QUESTION 7 (Northern Ireland 1986)

Robinson plc is the parent company of a group of companies which comprises itself and three subsidiary companies. Two of the subsidiaries are wholly owned by Robinson plc which owns 75% of the equity shares in the third subsidiary.

The following are the published consolidated profit and loss account of Robinson plc (the group) and the profit and loss account of Robinson plc as a separate legal entity (the company) for the year ended 31 December 19-5.

Profit and Loss Accounts for year ended 31 December 19-5		Robinson plc Group £'000		Company £'000
Turnover	(i)		3,250	–
Cost of sales			2,392	–
Gross profit			858	–
Dividends received and receivable from subsidiaries	(ii)		–	156
Operating expenses		(306)		(–)
Administrative expenses		(187)	(493)	(37) (37)
Profit before interest			365	119
Interest payable	(iii)		50	50
Profit on ordinary activities before taxation			315	69
Tax on profit on ordinary activities			123	5
Profit on ordinary activities after taxation			192	64
Minority interests	(iv)		17	–
Profit for financial year attributable to shareholders			175	64
Dividends – preference shares		(4)		(4)
ordinary shares, 4p per share	(v)	(40)	44	(40) 44
Retained profit for the year			131	20
Earnings per share			17.5p	6.4p

REQUIREMENT

You are required to

(a) compare the amounts which appear opposite each narrative which is marked by a roman numeral (i) to (v) in the two sets of accounts set out above and explain why the amounts differ between the two sets of accounts, or, if they do not differ, explain why the amounts are the same;   *(15 marks)*

and

(b) explain the method of calculation and purpose of the following items in a consolidated balance sheet:

   (i)   goodwill arising on consolidation, and

   (ii) minority interests.   *(10 marks)*

(Total 25 marks)

QUESTION 8   (Northern Ireland Pilot paper 1990)

The following is the balance sheet of Siblings Ltd on 31 December 19-6

	£'000		£'000	£'000
Capital and Reserves		Fixed Assets		
Share capital –		Plant and fixtures		
25 pence shares	100	at net book value		75
Profit and loss account	32			
	132			
Current Liabilities		Current Assets		
Sundry creditors	43	Stock	50	
		Sundry debtors	35	
		Cash at bank	15	100
	175			175

On 1 January 19-7 a management company, Holdings Ltd. was formed to acquire a 75% controlling interest in the share capital of Siblings Ltd. In exchange for 300,000 shares of 25p each in Siblings Ltd., Holdings Ltd. issued 80,000 shares of £1 issued at a premium of 50 pence.

As a result of the share exchange the opening balance sheet of Holdings Ltd. was

	£'000		£'000
Capital and Reserves		Shares in Subsidiary	
Share capital – £1 shares	80	300,000 shares of 25 pence	
Share premium account	40	each in Siblings Ltd.	120
	120		120

You are required to:

(i)   prepare the consolidated balance sheet of Holdings Ltd. as on 1 January 19-7;   *(12 marks)*

(ii) explain how the method of accounting used to prepare the consolidated accounts of a holding company differs from the method of accounting used to prepare the company's own accounts as a separate legal entity. Make special reference to TWO items which either do not appear in both sets of accounts or the amounts of the items differ as between the two sets of accounts.   *(8 marks)*

(Total 20 marks)

15 MANUFACTURING ACCOUNTS

This topic tests your ability to:-

- prepare the manufacturing, trading and profit and loss accounts of a manufacturing enterprise in good form
- recognise 'Prime Cost'
- distinguish between factory overheads and other overheads
- treat work in progress correctly
- account for manufacturing profit correctly
- provide for unrealised profit included in the valuation of closing stocks of finished goods
- disclose stocks of raw materials, work in progress and finished goods correctly in the balance sheet

---

15.1 Manufacturing, Trading and Profit and Loss Accounts

Businesses which manufacture all or some of the goods they sell preface their trading Account with a manufacturing account which shows the cost of goods produced. This 'cost of production' is transferred to the trading account to calculate the cost of goods sold.

The manufacturing account comprises two main sections:

1. Prime cost section:
   a. Direct materials (those contained in the goods made).
   b. Direct labour (wages of the operatives who actually make the goods).
   c. Other direct expenses (royalties, licence fees paid on each unit produced; electricity only if question indicates this is separately ascertainable for powering machinery).

2. Overheads section:

   Debit this with factory overheads:
   a. Indirect material (lubricating oil and cotton waste for cleaning machines and other materials not contained in the goods made).
   b. Indirect labour (wages of supervisors, storemen, cleaners, factory canteen staff etc.).
   c. Other indirect expenses (factory rent, rates, heating, lighting etc., depreciation of factory buildings, machinery, etc.).

All other overheads of the business which do not relate to the factory must be debited in the profit and loss account.

Stocks of raw materials and work in progress:

Purchases of raw materials must be adjusted by the difference in opening and closing stocks of raw materials to find cost of materials used in period.

Factory costs for the period must be adjusted by the difference in opening and closing stocks of work in progress to find cost of goods produced in period.

When apportioning overheads between the manufacturing and profit and loss accounts, and the overheads are subject to accruals and prepayments, adjust for the accruals and pre-payments before making the apportionment.

Outline form of Manufacturing, Trading and Profit and Loss Account

	£
Direct materials	X
Direct Labour	X
Other direct expenses	X
Prime Cost	X

		£
Factory overheads		X
		X
Add: Opening work in progress		X
		X
Deduct: Closing work in progress		X
Cost of goods produced transferred to Trading Account		X
Sales		X
Less Cost of sales		X
Gross Profit		X
Add other income		X
Less: Selling and distribution costs	X	
Administration costs	X	
Finance costs	X	X
Net profit		X

15.1.1. EXAMPLE

Ross, Wye Limited: extract from trial balance at 31st December 19-8

	Dr.	Cr.
	£	£
Stocks at 1.1.19-8		
Raw material	12,000	
Work in progress	14,200	
Finished goods	22,000	
Purchases:- raw materials	144,000	
indirect materials	1,000	
Factory wages – direct	210,000	
– indirect	32,500	
Rent and rates – factory	20,000	
– offices	12,600	
Heating and lighting		
– factory	7,100	
– offices	3,400	
Carriage inwards	1,360	
Carriage outwards	4,725	
Office salaries – salesmen	12,000	
– other	8,800	
Debenture interest	500	
Sales		556,135
Rent receivable		2,000

Other information:

Stocks at 31st December 19-8	£
Raw materials	10,100
Work in progress	15,900
Finished goods	16,000
Rent and rates paid in advance : factory	3,000
offices	800

217

Wages and salaries accrued: factory		£
	- direct	12,000
	- indirect	1,800
	salesmen	2,000
	other	700
Depreciation for the year:	- Machinery	15,000
	- Office equipment	1,000
	- Delivery vans	4,000

REQUIRED

(a) A manufacturing, trading and profit and loss account for Ross, Wye Ltd., for the year to 31st December 19-8.

(b) A balance sheet extract as at 31 December 19-8 showing stocks on hand at that date.

ROSS, WYE LIMITED
Manufacturing, Trading and Profit and Loss Account
for the year ended 31st December 19-8

	£	£	£
Raw materials: Stock at 1.1.-8		12,000	
Purchases	144,000		
Carriage inwards	1,360		
	145,360		
less Stock at 31.12.-8	10,100	135,260	147,260
Direct wages (W1)			222,000
PRIME COST			369,260
Add factory overheads:			
Indirect materials		1,000	
Indirect wages (W2)		34,300	
Rent and Rates (W3)		17,000	
Heating and lighting		7,100	
Depreciation – machinery		15,000	74,400
			443,660
Add: Work in progress at 1.1.-8		14,200	
less Work in progress at 31.12.-8		(15,900)	(1,700)
Cost of goods produced transferred to Trading Account			441,960
Sales			556,135
Less: Cost of sales			
Stock of finished goods at 1.1.-8		22,000	
Cost of goods produced		441,960	
		463,960	
less stock at 31.12.-8		16,000	447,960
Gross profit			108,175
Add: Rent receivable			2,000
			110,175
Less: Selling and distribution (W4)		22,725	
Administration (W5)		25,700	
Finance costs (Debenture Interest)		500	48,925
Net Profit			61,250

Balance sheet extract as at 31st December 19-8:

		£
Current assets		
Stocks: Raw materials		10,100
Work in progress		15,900
Finished goods		16,000
		42,000

Workings:

		T.B.	Accrued (Prepaid)	Total
		£	£	£
1.	Direct wages	210,000	12,000	222,000
2.	Indirect wages	32,500	1,800	34,300
3.	Factory rent and rates	20,000	(3,000)	17,000
4.	Selling and distribution			
	Salesmens' salaries	12,000	2,000	14,000
	Carriage outwards			4,725
	Depreciation – vans			4,000
				22,725
	Administration			
	Rent and rates – offices	12,600	(800)	11,800
	Heating and lighting			3,400
	Salaries	8,800	700	9,500
	Depreciation – office machinery			1,000
				25,700

15.1.2 EXERCISES

EXERCISE 1 THE JOBBITT CO. LTD. (To provide practice in the preparation of manufacturing, trading and profit and loss accounts in good form).

The Jobbitt Co. Ltd. commenced as manufacturers of window frames on 1st October 19-7. The following balances were extracted from the company's books at 30th September 19-8:

		Dr.	Cr.
		£	£
Sales			700,000
Raw materials		115,000	
Direct labour		200,000	
Indirect materials		10,000	
Indirect labour		25,000	
Rent and rates	– factory	35,000	
	– offices	15,000	
Electricity	– factory	8,000	
	– offices	2,000	
Salaries	– factory	20,000	
	– offices	40,000	
Sundry expenses	– administration	2,000	

Other information:

Stocks at 30th September 19-8	£
Raw materials	13,000
Work in progress	9,500
Finished goods	2,800

Provide for depreciation for the year as follows: £
Factory machinery   12,000
Office equipment   1,000

REQUIRED

Manufacturing, trading and profit and loss account for The Jobbitt Co. Ltd. for the year to 30th September 19-8 and an extract from the balance sheet as at that date showing the relevant entries for current assets.

EXERCISE 2 COLLETTE FABRICATIONS LTD. (To provide practice in the apportionment of overheads when accruals and prepayments are involved).

Prepare a manufacturing, trading and profit and loss account for the year to 30th April 19-9 from the following which has been extracted from the books of Collette Fabrications Ltd. at that date.

		£
Sales		800,000
Purchase of raw materials		176,000
Direct Wages		195,000
Indirect Wages		26,000
Rent and rates		60,000
Heating and lighting		56,400
Insurance		4,200
Office Salaries		68,600
Carriage inwards		15,340
Carriage outwards		3,360
Motor van expenses		8,000
Loose tools		9,000
Discounts receivable		4,125
Stocks at 1.5.19-8:	Raw materials	15,000
	Work in progress	24,000
	Finished goods	36,000
	Loose tools	5,000

Other information

Stocks at 30.4.19-9:	Raw materials	17,500
	Work in progress	21,000
	Finished goods	32,000
	Loose tools	4,000

The following expenses must be accrued at 30th April 19-9:

	£
Rent	5,000
Heating and Lighting	3,600

The following expenses were prepaid at 30th April 19-9:

	£
Rates	14,000
Insurance	1,200

Expenses are to be apportioned as follows:
Rent and rates: Factory 75%; Offices 25%
Heating and lighting: Factory $2/3$, Offices $1/3$
Insurance: Factory $9/10$, Offices $1/10$
Motor van costs: Factory 50%

Provide for depreciation as follows: £
Factory building   4,000
Machinery   14,000
Office machinery and equipment   5,000
Motor vans   10,000

15.2 PROFITS/LOSSES ON MANUFACTURE

Firms producing their own goods usually do so because they can make them more cheaply than they can buy them from outside ('bought-in' goods). The difference between costs of manufacture and cost of 'bought-in' goods is a factory profit, or profit on manufacturing, and increases the profits of the firm. The difference between the 'manufacturing profit' and 'gross profit on trading' is important and the two must be kept separate until they are aggregated in the profit and loss account.

(If the cost of production exceeds the cost of similar 'bought-in' goods, a factory loss results.)

Treatment of profits/losses on manufacture

In manufacturing account:

> Add factory profit to cost of production
> Deduct factory loss from cost of production

In profit and loss account:

> Add factory profit to net profit on trading
> Deduct factory loss from net profit on trading.

	Model:	£
	Prime cost	X
	Factory overheads	X
		X
	Work in progress adjustment	X
		X
	Add factory profit	A
or	Deduct factory loss	(B)
	Transfer to Trading account	X
	Sales	X
	Less cost of sales	(X)
	Gross profit	X
	Less administration etc. overheads	(X)
	Net profit on trading	X
	Add factory profit	A
or	Deduct factory loss	(B)
		X

15.2.1 EXAMPLE

The following data has been extracted from the books of Betta Widgetts Ltd. at 31st December 19-9:

		Dr.	Cr.
		£'000	£'000
Stocks at 1.1.-9:	Raw materials	16	
	Work in progress	24	
	Finished goods	40	
Purchase of raw materials		120	
Sales			650
Direct labour		260	
Rent and rates		80	
Electricity		40	
Office salaries		65	
Stocks at 31.12.-9	Raw materials	20	
	Work in progress	30	
	Finished goods	38	
Depreciation for the year:	Factory	40	
	Office	8	

Rent, rates and electricity are to be apportioned: Factory 75%, Offices 25%

Finished goods are to be transferred to the trading account at a profit of 15% on factory cost.

BETTA WIDGETTS LTD.
Manufacturing, Trading and Profit and loss account for the year ended 31st December 19-9.

		£'000	£'000
Raw materials:	Stock at 1.1.-9	16	
	Purchases	120	
		136	
	less stock at 31.12.-9	20	116
Direct labour			260
Prime cost			376
Add Factory Overheads:			
	Rent and rates	60	
	Electricity	30	
	Depreciation	40	130
			506
	Work in progress at 1.1.-9	24	
	Work in progress at 31.12.-9	(30)	(6)
			500
Add factory profit (15% of £500)			75
Transferred to Trading account			575
Sales			650
	less Cost of sales:		
	Stock of finished goods at 1.1.-9	40	
	Cost of goods produced	575	
		615	
	less stock at 31.12.-9	38	577
Gross profit			73
less:	Salaries	65	
	Rent and rates	20	
	Electricity	10	
	Depreciation	8	103
Net loss on trading			(30)
Add factory profit			75
	Net profit		45

15.2.2 EXERCISES

EXERCISE 1 BONNIE AND CLYDE (an exercise involving factory profit).

Bonnie and Clyde are in partnership, manufacturing kitchenware. The following details are extracted from their trial balance as at 31st March 19-7:

		Dr.	Cr.
		£'000	£'000
Sales			400
Stocks at 1.4..-6:	Raw materials	7	
	Work in progress	8	
	Finished goods	14	
Raw materials		96	
Direct labour		124	
Factory overheads		85	
Rent receivable			20
Office overheads		64	
Stocks at 31st March 19-7 were:		£'000	
	Raw materials	13	
	Work in progress	15	
	Finished goods	24	
Depreciation charges for the year:			
	Factory	8	
	Offices	2	

Completed production is to be transferred to the warehouse in the sum of £350,000.

REQUIRED

A Manufacturing, Trading and Profit and Loss account for Bonnie and Clyde for the year to 31st March 19-7.

EXERCISE 2 KONTAKKI LTD. (An exercise involving a factory loss.)

Kontakki Ltd., manufactures products for the leisure industry. The following information is extracted from the company's books at 30th June 19-8:

		£'000
Stocks at 1.7.-7:	Raw materials	40
	Work in progress	16
	Finished goods	32
Purchases:	Raw materials	110
	Finished goods	60
Direct wages		85
Office salaries		28
Rent and rates		40
Heating and lighting		16
Repairs to property - factory		20
Redecoration of offices		15
Depreciation charges for the year:		
	Machinery	30
	Salesmen's cars	15
Sales		300
Stocks at 30.6.-8:	Raw materials	55
	Work in progress	14
	Finished goods	30

Rent, rates heating and lighting are to be apportioned on the following basis: Factory 75% Office 25%
Finished goods are to be transferred to the trading account at £250,000.

REQUIRED

A Manufacturing, Trading and Profit and Loss Account for Kontakki Ltd., for the year to 30th Jun 19-8.

15.3 ELIMINATION OF UNREALISED MANUFACTURING PROFIT FROM UNSOLD STOCKS OF FINISHED GOODS

The Prudence Concept requires that profit shall not be anticipated before it is realised.

If the valuation of closing stocks of finished goods includes an element of factory profit, this unrealised profit must be eliminated in the profit and loss account and balance sheet by making an appropriate provision.

The entries to be made for the annual adjustment to the provision are as follows:

Increase in provision:

        debit profit and loss account;

        credit provision account with the amount of the increase

Decrease in provision:

        debit provision account;

        credit profit and loss account with the amount of the decrease

In balance sheet: deduct provision from stock of finished goods

EXAMPLE

Current assets		£	£
Stocks:	Raw materials		12,000
	Work in progress		20,000
	Finished goods	50,000	
less	provision for unrealised profit	8,000	42,000
			74,000

NOTE: Adjustment for unrealised profit on stock should only be made if required or implied by the question.

15.3.1 EXAMPLE

The following information is available after the preparation of the manufacturing and trading accounts of Dickery Dock Ltd.,for the year ended 31st December 19-6.

		Dr.	Cr.
		£	£
Gross profit on trading			38,000
Manufacturing profit			12,000
Selling, distribution and administration		24,000	
Provision for unrealised profit on stock at 1.1.19-6			2,000
Stocks at 31.12.19-6:	Raw materials	4,000	
	Work in progress	5,000	
	Finished goods	8,000	

The stock of finished goods at 31.12.-6 included unrealised profit on manufacture of £2,100.

DICKERY DOCK LTD
Profit and loss account for the year ended 31st December 19-6.

	£	£
Gross profit on trading		38,000
Selling, distribution and administration	24,000	
Increase in provision for unrealised profit	100	24,100
Net profit on trading		13,900
Manufacturing profit		12,000
		25,900

Balance sheet extract as at 31st December 19-6:

	£	£
Current Assets		
Stocks: Raw materials		4,000
Work in progress		5,000
Finished goods	8,000	
less provision for unrealised profit	2,100	5,900
		14,900

15.3.2 EXERCISES

EXERCISE 1 DORRITT AND DOMBIE LTD. (An exercise involving the treatment of provision for unrealised profit on stock of finished goods.)

Dorritt and Dombie Ltd. manufactures an electronic unit under licence. At 31st March 19-2, the following balances appeared in the trial balance:

		Dr.	Cr.
		£'000	£'000
Sales (4,500) units			1,800
Purchase	– Raw materials	300	
	– Finished goods (232 units)	58	
Stocks at 1.4.–1	– Raw materials	28	
	– Work in progress	58	
	– Finished goods (132 units)	33	
Wages	– direct	360	
	– indirect	88	
Licence fees		104	
Property expenses		82	
Canteen expenses		36	
Other administration		40	
Selling and distribution		37	
Office salaries		50	
Provision for unrealised profit at 1.4.–8			3

Further information:

Stocks at 31.3.–2	– Raw materials	32
	– Work in progress	54
	– Finished goods (264 units)	66

		£
Depreciation for year:	machinery	36
	canteen equipment	10
	Office machinery	5

The following expenses were owing at 31.3.-2:

	£'000
Property expenses	8
Canteen expenses	4
Other administration	5
Selling and distribution	3

Property and canteen expenses are to be apportioned as follows: Factory 80% Offices 20%.

Production is transferred to the warehouse at a mark-up of 10%.

The provision for unrealised profit on closing stock of finished goods at 31.3.-2 must be increased to £6,000.

REQUIRED:

(a) A manufacturing, trading and profit and loss account for Dorritt and Dombie Ltd. for the year ended 31st March 19-2.

(b) a balance sheet extract as at 31st March 19-2 showing the item of stocks.

(c) a calculation of the total (absorption) cost of each unit of production completed in the year.

EXERCISE 2 THE PREMIER MANUFACTURING CO LTD. (An exercise involving the calculation of unrealised profit in closing stock of finished goods.)

The following trial balance has been extracted from the books of The Premier Manufacturing Co. Ltd. at 31st December 19-8:

			Dr.	Cr.
			£	£
Stocks at 1.1.-8:	Raw materials		18,000	
	Work in progress		27,800	
	Finished goods		42,500	
	Loose tools		15,000	
Purchases:	Raw materials		245,500	
Direct wages			345,000	
Indirect wages			21,000	
Rent and rates	– factory		54,000	
	– offices		28,000	
Electricity	– factory		27,000	
	– offices		13,500	
Repairs and maintenance		– factory	10,000	
		– offices	8,200	
Insurance:		– factory	12,000	
		– offices	4,000	
Purchase of loose tools			13,650	
Sales				1,200,000
Motor vehicle expenses			17,600	
Carriage inwards			1,350	
Selling and distribution			52,190	
Administration			74,000	
Discounts			2,140	1,760
Debenture interest			800	
Freehold property (at cost)			240,000	
Provision for depreciation of freehold property				96,000
Plant and machinery (at cost)			215,000	
Provision for depreciation of plant and machinery				125,000
Motor vehicles (at cost)			84,000	
Provision for depreciation of motor vehicles				42,000
Office machinery and equipment (at cost)			26,000	
Provision for depreciation of office equipment				18,000
Debtors and creditors			114,640	23,540
Bank			54,260	
Provision for unrealised profit				4,000
Share capital (150,000 ordinary shares of £1 each)				150,000
8% debentures				20,000
Retained profits				86,830
			1,767,130	1,767,130

Notes

1. Stock at 31.12.-8:

	£
Raw materials	22,000
Work in progress	24,500
Finished goods	67,500
Loose tools	13,400

2. Accrued expenditure at 31.12.-8:

		£
Rent	– factory	5,000
	– offices	2,800
Direct wages		6,000
Indirect wages		1,900
Selling and distribution		3,000

3. Prepayments

		£
Rates	– factory	1,000
	– offices	800
Insurance	– factory	1,800
	– offices	600

4. Depreciation to be provided for the year on straight line basis:

Freehold premises – 4% on cost (75% factory)

Plant and machinery – 20% on cost

Motor vehicles – 25% on cost

Office machinery – 20% on cost

5. 50% of motor vehicles costs are to be apportioned to the factory.

6. Finished goods were transferred from the factory to the warehouse at £900,000.

7. Provide for unrealised profit on stock of finished goods at 31st December 19-8.

REQUIRED:

(a) The manufacturing, trading and profit and loss account of The Premier Manufacturing Co. Ltd. for the year to 31st December 19-8 and a balance sheet as at that date.

(b) State how the following concepts are relevant to the financial statements you have prepared for (a) above:

(i) accruals or matching concept

(ii) cost concept

(iii) going concern concept

15.4   KEY POINTS TO REMEMBER

1. Head your answers correctly with the name of the business, followed by 'Manufacturing, Trading and Profit and Loss Account for the (period) ended ---- 19--.' (This heading may need to be adapted to the requirement of the question.) It is best to avoid inserting headings between the manufacturing, trading and profit and loss accounts.

2. Recognize 'Prime Cost', 'Gross profit' and 'Net profit' by writing those descriptions against them.

3. Make sure you add factory overheads to prime cost; some candidates lose marks because they deduct the overheads instead.

4. Distinguish clearly between factory overheads, which appear in the manufacturing account, and the others which appear in the profit and loss account.

5. Make any adjustments to overheads for accruals and prepayments before apportioning them to the manufacturing and profit and loss accounts.

6. Check that you have calculated and treated factory profit and unrealised profit on stocks of finished goods correctly.

7. Distinguish between the manufacturing account and the trading accounts clearly; do not place the item 'Sales' in the manufacturing account.

8. Remember to make appropriate adjustments in the manufacturing account for opening and closing stocks of raw materials and work in progress.

COMMON ERRORS

- sales shown in the manufacturing account.
- prime cost not calculated correctly; not recognised as such in the manufacturing account.
- factory overheads, especially depreciation of machinery, shown in the profit and loss account instead of in the manufacturing account.
- opening and closing stocks of raw materials and work in progress not adjusted in manufacturing account.
- factory overheads deducted from prime cost instead of being added to prime cost.
- inability to deal with factory profit correctly.
- cost of finished goods in trading account does not correspond with amount for that item in the manufacturing account.
- incorrect treatment of the provision for unrealised profit.
- accruals and prepayments not treated correctly.

15.5 EXAMINATION QUESTIONS

QUESTION 1 (AEB November 1987)

Carter, a sole trader, commenced business on 1 September 19-6 as a manufacturer of three types of products.

The following balances were extracted from his trial balance at 31 August 19-7.

	Dr. £	Cr. £
Purchases of raw materials	280,000	
Returns	1,000	4,000
Carriage in	2,000	
Selling and distribution costs	20,000	
Rent	15,000	
Royalties	12,000	
Indirect factory labour	24,000	
Direct labour	125,000	
Administrative costs	35,000	
Sales		540,000
General factory expenses	15,000	
Plant and machinery at cost	140,000	
Delivery vans at cost	10,000	

The following information is also available.

(1) Rent was paid until the end of November 19-7 and was to be apportioned between the factory and general administration on the basis of 2:1.

(2) Selling and distribution costs of £8,000 were accrued on 31 August 19-7.

(3) Plant and machinery are depreciated by 20% per annum on cost and delivery vans are to be depreciated by 30% per annum on cost.

(4) The stock of raw materials at 31 August 19-7 was valued at £40,000.

(5) Although there was no work in progress at the end of the year there was a stock of finished goods of 3,000 units. Carter is uncertain as to how to value the goods which at present are selling for an average price of £30 per unit. During the year 25,000 units have been produced.

REQUIRED

(a) The manufacturing account for the year ended 31 August 19-7. (7 marks)

(b) Using **two** accepted methods of valuing the closing stock of finished goods complete the trading and profit and loss accounts for the year ended 31 August 19-7. (12 marks)

(c) Explain to Carter the difficulties involved in calculating a separate cost of sales figure for each of the three products produced. (6 marks)

(Total 25 marks)

QUESTION 2 (AEB June 1989)

Zacotex Ltd., a manufacturer, produced the following financial information for the year ended 31 March 19-9.

	£		£
Raw material purchases	250,000	Stocks at 1 April 19-8	
Direct labour	100,000	Raw materials	65,000
Direct expenses	80,900	Finished goods	48,000
Indirect factory labour	16,000	Work in progress	52,500
Factory maintenance costs	9,700	Other factory overhead	14,500
Machine repairs	11,500	Factory heating and lighting	19,000
Sales of finished goods during		Factory rates	11,500
the year	788,100	Administration expenses	22,000
		Selling and distribution expenses	36,800

Additional information.

(1) The stocks held at 31 March 19-9 were:

Raw materials	£51,400
Finished goods	£53,800
Work in progress	£41,000

N.B. Raw materials are valued at cost: finished goods at factory cost; work in progress at factory cost.

Of the raw materials held in stock at 31 March 19-9, £15,000 had suffered flood damage and it was estimated that they could only be sold for £2,500.

The remaining raw material stock could only be sold on the open market at cost less 10%.

(2) One quarter of the administration expenses are to be allocated to the factory.

(3) The raw materials purchases figure for the year includes a charge for carriage inwards. On 31 March 19-9 a credit note for £1,550 was received in respect of a carriage inwards overcharge. No adjustment had been made for this amount.

(4) Expenses in arrears at 31 March 19-9 were:

	£
Direct labour	6,600
Machine repairs	1,700
Selling and distribution expenses	4,900

(5) Plant and machinery at 1 April 19-8:

	£
at cost	250,000
aggregate depreciation	75,000

During the year an obsolete machine (cost £30,000, depreciation to date £8,000) was sold as scrap for £5,000.

On 1 October 19-8 new machinery was purchased for £70,000 with an installation charge of £8,000.

The company depreciates its plant and machinery at 10% per annum on cost, on all items in company ownership at the end of the accounting year. Items purchased during the year are allocated a full year's depreciation charge.

(6) An analysis of the sales of finished goods revealed the following:

	£
Goods sold for cash	105,000
Goods sold on credit	623,100
Goods sold on sale or return: returned	25,000
Goods sold on sale or return: retained and invoice confirmed	35,000
	788,100

(7) On 1 April 19-8 the company arranged a long term loan of £250,000 at a fixed rate of interest of 11% per annum. No provision had been made for the payment of the interest.

(8) The factory works manager felt that the preparation each year of a manufacturing account on an historical basis was inadequate for the control of costs. Thus he decided to seek the advice of an independent accountant on how to control his most important costs – direct labour and direct materials.

REQUIRED

(a) For the year ended 31 March 19-9:

(i) a manufacturing account showing prime cost and factory cost of goods produced.

(12 marks)

(ii) a trading and profit and loss account

(6 marks)

(b) As the independent accountant prepare a brief report advising the factory works manager what financial techniques are available to control direct labour and material costs. Give suitable numerical examples.

(7 marks)

(Total 25 marks)

QUESTION 3 (London June 1987)

The following balances refer to the workshops of the Cantalupe Engineering Company for the half year ended 31 December 19-6.

	£
Stocks at 1 July, 19-6:	
Raw materials	7,566
Work-in-progress	11,884
Finished goods	12,716
Direct factory wages	39,212
Indirect factory wages	26,076
Licence fees paid to patent holder	15,440
Heating and lighting	4,506
General factory expenses	12,710
Insurance of plant	5,274
Rates on factory premises	3,244
Purchases of raw materials	135,556
Raw materials returned to suppliers	1,652
Plant at cost	65,280
Depreciation provision: plant	26,112
Stocks at 31 December, 19-6	
Raw materials	6,354
Finished goods	10,034
Market value of goods completed	350,162

Notes:

1. Licence fees are to be treated as a direct expense.
2. Expenses owing at 31 December, 19-6 were: Direct wages £580; indirect wages £666; general expenses £223.
3. Expenses prepaid at 31 December, 19-6 were: Insurance £422; rates £274; heating and lighting £156.
4. Plant is to be depreciated at the rate of 5 per cent on cost for the period.

(a) Show the manufacturing account for the six months ended 31 December 19-6, assuming that the closing work-in-progress is valued at 5 per cent of full factory cost inclusive of work-in-progress.

(15 marks)

(b) State the manufacturing profit if closing work-in-progress is calculated at 5 per cent of prime cost.

(4 marks)

(c) Explain the meaning of the term 'equivalent production' and show how equivalence is used in the valuation of work-in-progress.

(6 marks)

(Total 25 marks)

QUESTION 4 (Cambridge June 1987)

The following list of balances as at 31 March 19-7 has been extracted from the books of Osogood Manufacturers Ltd:

	£
Ordinary share capital, ordinary shares of £1 fully paid	120,000
Share premium account	10,000
Retained earnings (at 1 April 19-6)	20,000
Freehold buildings, at cost (at 1 April 19-6)	68,000
Plant and machinery, at cost (at 1 April 19-6)	50,000
– provision for depreciation (at 1 April 19–6)	18,250
Sales	150,000
Office machinery, at cost (at 1 April 198-6)	18,000
– provision for depreciation (at 1 April 19–6)	1,600
Raw materials	25,000
Manufacturing wages	32,000
Factory overheads – variable	11,000
– fixed	9,000
Administrative expenses	17,250
Marketing expenses	9,800
Trade debtors	21,800
Trade creditors	7,400
Stocks, 1 April 19-6 - Raw materials	14,100
Finished goods	12,300
Work in progress, 1 April 19-6	36,000
Balance at bank	3,000

Additional information:

(a) Freehold buildings were revalued in April 19-6 at £80,000; the revalued figure is to be introduced into the accounts and the freehold buildings are to be depreciated for the year ended 31 March 19-7.

(b) Depreciation is to be provided on fixed assets as follows:

Straight line basis, assuming nil residual values and at the following annual rates on cost or revalued figures –

Freehold buildings	2%
Plant and machinery	12 1/2%
Office machinery	5%

The freehold buildings depreciation is to be apportioned 3/4 to the factory and 1/4 to sales and administration. The office machinery is used exclusively for sales and administration.

(c) Administrative expenses accrued due at 31 March 19-7 amounted to £500 and marketing expenses prepaid at 31 March 19-7 totalled £300.

(d) Stocks and work in progress valuations at 31 March 19-7 were as follows:

Raw materials	£16,000	
Work in progress	£40,000	
Finished goods	£20,000	(This represents 20% of the goods manufactured during the year ended 31 March 19-7)

231

All valuations are at cost price except that the finished goods have been valued at wholesale market prices; work in progress includes a proportion of variable and fixed overheads. The valuations of raw materials and work in progress are on the same basis as in previous years; however finished goods were valued in previous years at cost price.

(e) The wholesale market value of goods manufactured during the year ended 31 March 19-7 was £100,000.

(f) For the first time, the company requires its accounts to show prime cost and the profit on manufacturing.

(g) A dividend on the ordinary shares of 15p per share is proposed for the year under review.

REQUIRED

A manufacturing, trading and profit and loss account for the year ended 31 March 19-7.

(25 marks)

QUESTION 5 (Cambridge November 1988)

The following account balances have been extracted from the books of Circus and Green who for many years have operated a business manufacturing bathroom cabinets.

Balances as at 1 June 19-7

		£	
Land and Buildings (cost £152,000)		88,000	
Plant & Machinery (cost £93,000)		62,000	
Motor Vehicles (cost £17,500)		12,500	
Stocks	– Raw materials	21,600	
	– Work in Progress	25,800	
	– Finished Goods	24,000	
Capital A/C	– Circus	160,000	
	– Green	80,000	
Current A/C	– Circus	12,000	CR
	– Green	2,500	DR

Balances at 31 May 19-8 include:

	£
Creditors	51,700
Debtors	74,900
Factory Wages	141,000
Factory Expenses	10,200
Bank overdraft	11,300
Administrative Expenses	31,300
Selling Expenses	22,300
Discounts Allowed	1,700
Bad debts written off	4,500
Sales	521,000
Purchases of raw materials	197,000
Partners' Drawings – Circus	45,500
– Green	24,400

You are also informed that:

(a) Stocks were valued at cost as at 31 May 19-8 as follows:

	£
Raw Materials	18,200
Work in Progress	23,100
Finished Goods	31,404

It is business policy to transfer the value of fully completed bathroom cabinets to the Trading Account at factory cost plus 20% mark up.

(b) Depreciation is to be provided on

Land & Buildings	– 5% p.a. on cost
Plant & Machinery	– 20% p.a. on written down value
Motor Vehicles	– 20% p.a. on original cost.

These depreciation charges are then to be allocated thus:

Land & Buildings	– Factory	– 50%
	– Administration	– 50%
Plant & Machinery	– Factory	– 80%
	– Administration	– 20%
Motor Vehicles	– Factory	– 90%
	– Administration	– 10%

(c) The partnership agreement provides for interest on partners' capital at 10% per annum, for the award of a partnership salary of £12,500 per annum to Green and for the balance of profit or loss to be shared between the partners in the proportion Circus 3: Green 1.

REQUIRED

(a) Prepare Manufacturing Account for the year ended 31 May 19-8 showing clearly prime cost and the cost of goods manufactured.   *(8 marks)*

(b) Prepare Trading and Profit and Loss Account and a Profit & Loss Appropriation Account for the year ended 31 May 19-8.   *(12 marks)*

(c) Prepare an EXTRACT from the Balance Sheet as at 31 May 19-8 showing the partners' Capital and Current Accounts in full detail.   *(5 marks)*

(Total 25 marks)

16 REMUNERATION OF LABOUR; VALUATION OF STOCK

> Questions on these topics cover:-
> - the objectives to be met in setting a wages system
> - the employee relationship aspects to be considered in setting a wages system
> - methods of calculating remuneration; time rates, piece rates, incentive bonus schemes
> - accounting for labour
> - the financial considerations involved in stock valuation
> - different methods of valuing stock; their advantages and disadvantages

16.1 REMUNERATION OF LABOUR

Objectives:

1. Main objective of business is usually to obtain best return on capital employed; this involves maximising profits.

2. Subsidiary objectives usually aimed at helping to achieve main objective; e.g. maintaining good relations with the public, showing consideration for social and environmental factors etc.; but, very importantly, maintaining good staff relationships and motivating the staff. (Good conditions of employment including satisfactory level of remuneration.)

   Low staff morale leads to low productivity, spoilt work, industrial disputes, strike action etc.

3. Main objective will require 'cost of sales' to be minimised. This implies giving production staff incentive to improve productivity i.e. to produce more goods of an acceptable quality in less time.

Various methods of remuneration are aimed at achieving this.

METHODS OF REMUNERATION

Time Rates

Workers are paid an hourly or weekly rate.

Advantages:

1. Workers are guaranteed a fixed wage each week provided they work the agreed hours.
2. The method is uncomplicated and easy for the workers to understand.
3. The wages are easy to calculate.
4. The method can be applied to all workers.
5. Quality of work is not sacrificed as a consequence of attempts to increase earnings.

Disadvantages:

1. All workers are paid the same regardless of whether they work well or not.
2. There is no incentive for them to make any extra effort.
3. Workers may slack during normal hours in order to work overtime at enhanced rates of pay.
4. It may be necessary to instal rigid systems of control to ensure adequate productivity.

Straight Piece Rates

Workers are paid an agreed amount for every completed unit of production, e.g. If they complete one unit, they are paid £1; if they complete 5 units, they are paid £5 and so on.

Advantages:

1. Wages paid are proportionate to production.
2. Wages are easy to calculate.
3. The system encourages greater efficiency.
4. The work is completed more quickly and time wasting is discouraged.

Disadvantages:
1. May not be suitable for all workers; only suitable when a standard item is being produced or the work is of a repetitive nature.
2. Workers are unfairly penalised when production is halted because of shortage of materials, machinery breakdown, etc.
3. Unless careful control is exercised, workers will be tempted to rush the work in order to increase wages; this will lead to substandard work, spoilt production and unacceptable wastage of materials.
4. More rigid quality control may be needed.
5. Increased cost of supervision occasioned by need to check amount of each worker's output.
6. Unions may be contentious over fixing of piece rates.

High Day Rates

A higher than normal wage rate is offered for a continuously higher than normal performance.

Advantages:
1. Wage calculations are simple.
2. The firm benefits from high performance through lower unit costs.
3. Employment with such a firm is usually well sought after.
4. The firm is in a position to choose a better class of worker.

Disadvantage:
Standards must be continuously and closely monitored.

Time/Piece Rates

Workers are paid on a piece rate basis, but guaranteed a minimum weekly wage.

Advantage:
Some degree of uncertainty about the wage to be received at the end of the week is removed for the workers.

Disadvantages:
Most of those already mentioned above.

Premium Bonus Schemes

These are based on a guaranteed basic time rate with a bonus based on a proportion of the time saved.

Advantages:
1. Although the wage paid is less per unit of completed work than under the time rate basis, the hourly rate is higher and a worker can increase his wages very considerably.
2. Wages earned are related to output, but there is a guaranteed minimum weekly wage.
3. The firm gains from lower unit labour costs *and* lower unit fixed overhead allocation costs.

Disadvantage:
1. Difficulty of fixing a fair standard allowable time. Large amounts of bonus paid consistently may indicate poor fixing of the standard.
2. Bonus will not be paid if production is slowed or stopped by circumstances outside the workers' control e.g. shortage of material or machine breakdown.
3. Quality of products may suffer as a result of hasty work.
4. It may be necessary to instal a costly system of quality control.
5. Pay calculations may be complex.
6. Trade unions may be contentious in the agreeing of bonus rates with them.

Halsey system: guaranteed time rate + bonus based on a **fixed** proportion (usually 50% but may vary between 30% and 70%) of the standard time saved:

    e.g.   Standard time allowed for job: 10 hours.

            Time taken: 8 hours

            Hourly rate of pay £8

Amount paid: 8 hours × £8	=	£64
50% of (10-8) hours × £8	=	£ 8 £72

N.B. If the job had taken 10 hours payment would have been $10 \times £8 = £80$.

However the actual hourly rate of pay has increased from £8 to $£(^{72}/_8) = £9$

Rowan system: Guaranteed time rate + bonus based on such a proportion of the time taken as the time saved bears to the standard time allowed.

e.g. Standard time allowed for job: 10 hours.

Time taken: 8 hours

Hourly rate of pay £8

Amount paid: 8 hours $\times$ £8	= £64

(10-8) hours = 2 hours.

Time saved/Time allowed

$= ^2/_{10}$ or 20%

20% of Time taken = $^8/_5$

= 1hour 36 mins.

1hour 36 mins at £8 per hour	= £12.80
Total	£76.80

This is equivalent to an hourly rate of £9.60

(Compare this with the calculation for the Halsey system above.)

Note: A worker may earn more under the Rowan system than under the Halsey system up to the point where the time saved is 50% of the time allowed. (Thereafter the hourly rate of pay becomes less than under the Halsey system. Under the Rowan system, a worker is unable to double his wages.

Barth system: Earnings are calculated as follows:

Rate per hour $\times \sqrt{\text{Time allowed} \times \text{Time taken}}$

e.g. Time allowed 10 hours

Time taken 8 hours

Hourly rate of pay £8

amount paid $= £8 \times \sqrt{10 \times 8}$ $= £8 \times \sqrt{80}$

$= £8 \times 8.944$ $= £71.55$

Note: hourly rate = £8.94 (compare with Halsey and Rowan systems)

Note: The Barth system is suitable for trainee workers whose performance levels are not yet up to those of trained workers.

Installation of Bonus Systems

Management should consult trade unions and/or staff. The scheme must be explained clearly to the workforce and satisfactory terms need to be agreed. A scheme imposed upon the workforce may be counter productive and lead to a withdrawal of labour.

ACCOUNTING FOR LABOUR

Basic records

- clock cards for time rate workers. Clocking-in and out should be controlled to prevent 'clocking on' for late or absent workers.

- job cards or piece work cards for piece workers. These should be initialled by a foreman or manager as verification that the entries for work satisfactorily completed are correct.

Summaries

- details from the basic records should be copied onto summary sheets and the gross wages calculated and independently checked.

Pay roll sheets

- the gross wages should be copied onto the payroll sheets and the deductions for tax etc. and net pay calculated. The calculations should be independently checked.

Computerised payrolls

- The information will be input to the computer from the summary sheets. A print out of that information will then be obtained and checked by an independent, responsible official.

Cheque signatories for the pay roll should see that the payroll has been signed by the compiler and the checker, authorised by a senior manager, and that all appears to be in order.

Payment of wages should be witnessed by an independent person, or some other system of check should be installed to ensure that the wage packets are paid to bona fide employees.

16.1.1 EXAMPLE (calculation of wages at premium bonus rates)

Archer, Bowman and Chieftain all work for the same company. They work a 40 hour week and each has a standard output fixed at 120 units of production; but they are remunerated on different bases:

Archer: Basic wage of £80 per week plus a bonus equal to 50% of the time saved

Bowman: Basic wage of £80 per week plus a bonus calculated in the ratio that the time saved bears to the standard time for the job.

Chieftain: Earnings are based on an hourly rate of £2 which is multiplied by the following factor: $\sqrt{\text{standard time allowed} \times \text{time taken}}$

In one week Archer, Bowman and Chieftain each completed 150 units of production.

REQUIRED

A calculation of the wage paid to each of the three workers in the week and the hourly rate for each of them.

ANSWER

Standard time for 120 items = 40 hours; i.e. 20 minutes per item

Number of items completed = 150, equivalent to 50 standard hours.

Therefore time saved = 10 hours.

Archer:	Basic wage		£80
	Bonus: hourly rate = £2		
	£2 × 50% of 10 hours		£10
			£90 (£2.25 per hour)
Bowman:	Basic wage		£80
	Bonus: hourly rate = £2		
	£80 × ¹⁰/₄₀		£20
			£100 (£2.50 per hour)
Chieftain:	£2 × $\sqrt{50 \times 40}$ = £2 × 44.72		£89.44 (£2.236 per hour)

16.1.2 EXERCISE (Calculation of wages using the Halsey, Rowan and Barth schemes)

Following negotiations between their employer and the trade union, the working week of Archer, Bowman and Chieftain was reduced to one of 35 hours for which the basic wage was increased to £84. but the standard output was fixed at 115 units of production per working week. The bases for calculating the wages of Archer, Bowman and Chieftain respectively were retained as in the example 16.1.1 above.

REQUIRED

The wages paid to Archer, Bowman and Chieftain, and their respective hourly rates if they each achieve an output of

(a)   138 units and

(b)   184 units in their normal working week.

16.2   THE VALUATION OF STOCK

This section should be read in conjunction with SSAP 9 (Chapter 12)

Importance of stock valuation

Value of closing stock determines cost of sales and, therefore, gross profit. It also affects net working capital, of which it is a constituent item, in the balance sheet.

Stock should be valued at the lower of cost and net realisable value.

Net Realisable Value

Proceeds of sale less any further costs to be incurred in putting goods into saleable condition and conveying them to the place of sale.e.g. Goods cost £1,000; if sold, they will fetch £1,300. Before they can be sold, some work is required to put them into a saleable condition at a cost of £275. The cost of transporting the goods to the place of sale will be £65. Net realisable value is: £[1,300 -(275+65)] = £960. As this is less than cost, the goods should be valued at £960.

Cost

Where it is not possible or practicable to identify the cost of individual items of stock, cost is ascertained by making an assumption about the items in stock.

It may be assumed

- that stock has been used or sold in the order in which it has been received (First In, First Out – FIFO)
- that the most recently received stock has been used or sold before older stock (Last In, First Out – LIFO)

OR

- stock may be valued at a weighted average cost (AVCO)

    The use of a particular method of valuing stock does not mean that stock is actually used in that particular order; e.g. stock may be *valued* using the FIFO method, but actually *sold* in LIFO order or in random order.

FIFO

Advantages:

1. It is realistic because it is based on the assumption that goods are used or sold in that order.
2. The value of closing stock is easy to calculate.
3. The valuation is based on prices actually paid for stock.
4. Closing stock is valued at the most recent prices.
5. The FIFO method is acceptable under SSAP 9 (see Chapter 12).

Disadvantages:

1. In a manufacturing business, the prices at which raw materials are issued to production are probably not the most recent prices.
2. If prices are rising, FIFO contravenes the principle of prudence insofar as it produces higher profits than other methods of stock valuation. (But remember - it is preferred to LIFO by SSAP 9 because of its advantages as against the disadvantages of LIFO).

LIFO

Advantages:

1. The value of closing stock is easy to calculate.
2. Raw materials are used for manufacturing at the latest prices.

Disadvantages:

1. It is usually unrealistic because it is based on the assumption that the most recently acquired stock is used or sold before older stock.
2. Closing stock is not valued at the most recent prices.
3. LIFO is not recommended by SSAP 9.
4. LIFO is not acceptable by the Inland Revenue for the calculation of taxation liabilities.

AVCO

Advantages:

1. As prices paid for identical items purchased at different times are averaged, AVCO recognises that all such items have equal value.
2. Averaging has the effect of 'smoothing out' cost of production and cost of sales so that distortion of profits between one period and another is minimised.
3. The valuation of closing stock will usually be fairly close to current prices.
4. AVCO is acceptable for SSAP 9.

Perpetual and Periodic Inventories

A perpetual inventory is one in which a running balance is maintained of stock remaining after every receipt and issue of stock.

A periodic inventory is one in which only the totals of receipts and issues are recorded at the end of each accounting period and a new balance calculated at the period end only.

16.2.1 EXAMPLE (showing the effect of valuing stock on various bases.)

During the month of March the following were the purchases and sales of Igoxi:

		Receipts		Sales	
		Quantity kilos	Price per kilo	Quantity kilos	Price per kilo
			£		£
March	1	100	2		
	5			60	5
	8	80	2.50		
	12	40	3		
	14			80	5
	21	50	3.50		
	25			100	6
	28	100	4		
	31			100	6

REQUIRED

Trading accounts for the month of March showing the gross profit if closing stock is valued on each of the following bases:

(a) FIFO

(b) LIFO

(c) AVCO

ANSWER

Workings

FIFO	March		1	8	12	21	28
		Price	£2	£2.50	£3	£3.50	£4
		Received	100	80	40	50	100
Issues	5		(60)				
			40				
	14		(40)	(40)			
			–	40			
	25			(40)	(40)	(20)	
				–	–	30	
	31					(30)	(70)
						–	30

Closing stock: 30 kilos × £4 = £120

LIFO	March		1	8	12	21	28
		Price	£2	£2.50	£3	£3.50	£4
		Received	100	80	40	50	100
Issues	5		(60)				
Carried forward			40	80	40	50	100

March	1	8	12	21	28
Brought forward	40	80	40	50	100
14		(40)	(40)		
		40	–		
25	(10)	(40)		(50)	
	30	–		–	
31					(100)
					–

Closing stock: 30 kilos × £2 = £60

AVCO	Received (kilos)	£	Sales (kilos)	Balance (kilos)	Average £	Balance £
March 1	100	2		100	2	200
5			60	(60)		120
				40	2	80
8	80	2.50		80		200
				120	2.3333	280
12	40	3		40		120
				160	2.50	400
14			80	(80)		200
				80	2.50	200
21	50	3.50		50		175
				130	2.8846	375
25			100	(100)		288
				30		87
28	100	4		100		400
				130	3.7462	487
31			100	(100)		(374)
				30	3.7462	113

Closing stock: 30 kilos: £113

Trading account for the month of March

	FIFO		LIFO		AVCO	
	£	£	£	£	£	£
Sales (140 × £5 + 200 × £6)		1,900		1,900		1,900
Purchases	1,095		1,095		1,095	
less Closing stock	(120)	975	(60)	1,035	(113)	982
Gross profit		925		865		918

16.2.2 EXERCISE (Preparation of manufacturing accounts using different methods of valuing stock)
On 1 March 19-2 The Beta Manufacturing Co. Ltd. commenced to manufacture Betabits and took delivery of Stibateb, a material used in the manufacture of Betabits, as follows:

		Kilos	Price per kilo (£)
March	1	300	4
	17	200	4.50
April	5	400	5
	22	300	5.50
May	8	300	6
	24	400	6.50

Issues of Stibateb to production took place as follows:

		Kilos
March	8	240
	20	240
April	10	360
	28	300
May	12	240
	28	180

The other costs of production for the three months to 31 May 19-2 were as follows:

	£
Direct wages	16,500
Variable overheads	4,000
Depreciation	3,180
Other fixed overheads	11,200

There was no work in progress at 31 May 19-2

REQUIRED

Manufacturing accounts for the Beta Manufacturing Co. Ltd for the three months to 31 May 19-2 showing factory cost if closing stock is valued on the following bases:

(a) FIFO

(b) LIFO

(c) AVCO

16.3 KEY POINTS TO REMEMBER

1. Questions on remuneration of labour and valuation of stock generally require arithmetical calculations which should be done accurately.

2. It is very important to get adequate practice at calculating premium bonuses.

3. Apart from being able to calculate stock values on FIFO, LIFO and AVCO bases, be prepared to discuss the advantages and disadvantages of each method.

4. Learn the requirements of SSAP 9 and be ready to state and discuss them if required to do so.

5. Read questions carefully to ascertain whether they refer to the prices of stock issues or the value of stock on hand. It is most important to answer questions exactly as set.

COMMON ERROR

- to confuse the assumptions on which FIFO and LIFO are based with the actual way in which stock is issued.

16.4 EXAMINATION QUESTIONS

QUESTION 1 (London January 1987)

(i) With reference to wages systems, what is meant by:

(a) piece rates

(b) time rates

(c) standard hours? *(4 marks)*

(ii) Bath Ltd. has a payments scheme specifically designed for trainees. Under the scheme earnings are calculated as follows:

$$\text{Earnings} = \text{Rate per hour} \times \sqrt{(\text{Standard hours} \times \text{Clock hours})}$$

If the rate per hour is £3.60 and five standard hours are allowed for a job, show

(a) the earnings accruing if clock hours are seven;

(b) how standard rates are earned when clock hours equal standard hours. *(2 marks)*

(iii)   A firm's bonus scheme pays employees a bonus of 50 per cent of the time saved in completing a job. Harry Jones, a new employee, is confused because the basic pay for a job when no time is saved is greater than when four hours are saved.

Use the figures in the following table to resolve Harry's confusion:

Time allowed (Hours)	Time taken (Hours)	Rate per hour	Basic Pay	Bonus Pay	Total Pay
		£	£	£	£
8	8	4.50	36	–	36
8	4	4.50	18	9	27

(4 marks)

(iv)   What are the advantages and disadvantages to a firm of introducing a bonus system?   *(5 marks)*

(Total 15 marks)

QUESTION 2   (London June 1988)

The following information relates to three employees; Arnold, Brown and Carter.

	Workers		
	Arnold	Brown	Carter
Actual hours worked	37	41	35
Hourly pay rate (£)	3.20	2.75	4.10
Output (units); product S	50	–	174
product T	93	70	–
product U	99	75	225

The standard time for each item is product S 5 minutes; product T 10 minutes; product U 12 minutes. For piece rate purposes, each minute is valued at £0.05.

You are required to calculate the weekly pay for each of the three workers using:

(a)   guaranteed hourly rates only (basic pay);   *(3 marks)*

(b)   piece work, with earnings guaranteed at 80 per cent of basic pay;   *(6 marks)*

(c)   premium bonus, where the employee receives half of the time saved in additional pay.   *(6 marks)*

QUESTION 3   (Oxford June 1987)

Explain with a simple example the difference between a labour wage rate and labour hour rate, when calculating the cost of a particular job in a factory.   *(8 marks)*

QUESTION 4   (Oxford June 1986)

What is the difference between a labour rate and a labour hour rate? How would you use them both in a costing system?   *(8 marks)*

QUESTION 5   (Cambridge June 1987)

Jane North commenced trading as a distributor of 'Bigdeal' farm tractors on 1 January 19-6 with a capital of £50,000. During 19-6, Jane North made the following purchases and sales of 'Bigdeal' farm tractors:

January	Bought 3 tractors @ £10,000 each
February	Sold 1 tractor @ £15,000
April	Bought 2 tractors @ £12,000 each
June	Sold 3 tractors @ £15,000 each
August	Bought 4 tractors @ £13,000 each
November	Sold 3 tractors @ £15,000 each

All transactions during 19-6 involved the Mark A1 'Bigdeal' farm tractor.

Overhead expenses of £6,000 were incurred during 19-6.

Jane North had been employed previously as a sales representative by the manufacturers of 'Bigdeal' farm tractors at a salary of £17,000 per annum.

The retail price index of 100 at 1 January 19-6 increased to 110 by the end of the year.

REQUIRED

(a) Computations of Jane North's net profit or net loss for the year ended 31 December 19-6, using (i) the first in first out basis of stock valuation, and (ii) the last in first out basis of stock valuation.

Note: In both cases, the perpetual inventory method of valuation is to be used.

(12 marks)

(b) On the basis of her results for 19-6, advise Jane North whether on financial grounds she should continue as a distributor of 'Bigdeal' farm tractors.

Note: Make and state any necessary assumptions.

(7 marks)

(c) Outline the arguments in favour of
   (i)   the first in first out basis of stock valuation:
   (ii) the last in first out basis of stock valuation.

(6 marks)

QUESTION 6 (Cambridge November 1989)

Whilst on holiday in Germany three friends Albert, Bertie and Clive obtained the distribution rights for the UK market of a wine Kit.

On 1 January 19-9 the friends put £3,000 each from their savings into a bank account under the name of *Wineparts* – a partnership. They agreed to take nothing from the firm until six months had passed when they were to share any profits equally.

Their supplier said that because the main item in the Kit - wine concentrate - would fluctuate in price he could not guarantee a price to the partnership. The partners agreed that they would set a price – £1.50 per Kit - and maintain this for the first six months.

During the six months to 30 June 19-9 the following transactions took place.

	Purchases	Sales (all at £1.50 each)
January	10,000 kits @ £1.00 each	5,000 kits
February	5,000 kits @ £1.20 each	5,000 kits
March	10,000 kits @ £1.00 each	–
April	–	10,000 kits
May	5,000 kits @ £1.10 each	5,000 kits
June	5,000 kits @ £1.25 each	5,000 kits

On the 30 June 19-9 the partners met to consider the results of the first six months trading. However they disagreed over the business profits made, because they have different views re the pricing of stock. Albert uses the FIFO method, Bertie the LIFO method and Clive the average cost method (AVCO).

They ask you to

(a) Set out calculations of the different profits arrived at *for each partner* and closing stock valuations if
   1. LIFO method of pricing stock is used
   2. FIFO method of pricing stock is used
   3. AVCO method of pricing stock is used.

(18 marks)

(b) Explain why each method might have advantages using your calculations in (a) where appropriate.

(4 marks)

(c) Advance reasons why a business might use different bases of valuation for different purposes.

(3 marks)

(Total 25 marks)

QUESTION 7 (WJEC June 1986)

In relation to the valuation of stock in a trading business, explain how the terms *cost, net realisable value* and *replacement cost* may be interpreted.

(18 marks)

QUESTION 8 (N.I.June 1988)

Stuffit Ltd. manufactures rucksacks and other bags for the leisure industry from a basic canvas material which is priced per metre.

The following information relates to its purchases and issues to production of canvas for a 2-month budget period.

	Purchases		Issues	
January 4	50 metres @ £3.00 per metre		January 10	30 metres
January 21	150 metres @ £3.20 per metre		January 30	100 metres
February 15	100 metres @ £3.25 per metre		February 20	120 metres

The cost office uses LIFO (last in, first out) method of pricing issues to production.

You are *required* to write up the stores account in the records of the cost office for the 2-month budget period.

(Assume that there was no opening stock of canvas on 1 January.)   *(8 marks)*

QUESTION 9 (AEB November 1987)

In December 19-6, Terry Marshall, an established builders' merchant, introduced a new product, Barbrick, to the range of materials sold by the business. The product cost £200 per unit when introduced but increased in cost to £250 per unit with effect from 1 March 19-7. The selling price of the product increased from £300 to £350 per unit with effect from 1 April 19-7.

The following were the purchases and sales, in units, of Barbrick during the financial year ended 31 October 19-7.

Purchases on the first day of the month:

December 19-6	50
February 19-7	70
May	60
September	30

Sales during the month of

January 19-7	30
February	20
April	40
June	20
August	40
September	20

Because of the erratic demand for the product and difficulties in obtaining an adequate supply, Marshall decided at the end of September 19-7 to cease to hold stocks of Barbrick. In October Marshall anticipates that, during November 19-7, 10 Units of Barbrick were to be sold at the normal price but that any remaining units can only be sold at a price of £230 per unit up to the end of April 19-8. However Marshall operates a firm policy that stock must never be sold at below cost price in the belief that to do so must reduce profit.

REQUIRED

(a) Calculate the gross profits arising from the sale of Barbrick for the year ended 31 October 19-7 using both last in first out (LIFO) and first in first out (FIFO) methods of stock valuation.

(11 marks)

(b) Prepare draft trading accounts for the eighteen months up to 30 April 19-8 for the sale of Barbrick using (i) the LIFO and (ii) FIFO methods of stock valuation assuming that Marshall maintains his policy outlined above.

(9 marks)

(c) Advise Marshall as to the decision that should be made with regard to the sale of the stock of Barbrick remaining at 31 October 1987.

(5 marks)

(Total 25 marks)

17 ABSORPTION COSTING AND MARGINAL COSTING

Questions on these topics require:-
- an understanding and ability to define and explain costing terms
- ability to compare the two costing techniques, either descriptively or by using quantified data to produce comparative statements
- a knowledge of the uses and limitations of the respective techniques
- an understanding of how absorption and marginal costing can be used by management for decision-making
- ability to calculate and use contribution/sales (or profit/volume) ratio
- an ability to calculate profits/losses using absorption and marginal costing
- calculation of break-even points and margins of safety and the construction and interpretation of break-even charts, contribution charts and profit charts

17.1 SOME COSTING TERMS DEFINED

Direct Costs. Those costs which are directly attributable to a product or service i.e direct materials, direct labour and other direct expenses.

Direct Labour. The cost of employing those workers who are actually engaged in the production of goods or providing services i.e the wages etc. of the 'operatives' as distinct from non-productive workers such as supervisors, foremen etc.

Direct Materials. The cost of materials which actually form part of the goods being produced e.g. wood used in the construction of a desk, brass used for the desk drawer handles, but not, hopefully, the lubricating oil for the machinery! (This last would be an example of an indirect expense)

Direct Expenses. Other expenses directly connected with the goods produced or services provided e.g. royalties payable to an inventor or patentee for the right to produce certain goods.

Prime cost = direct labour + direct materials + direct expenses

Indirect Expenses. Any expenses other than direct expenses: indirect labour (foremen, storekeepers, factory canteen staff etc.); indirect materials (lubricating oil for machines, cotton waste for cleaning machines etc.); indirect expenses (rent of factory, depreciation of machinery etc.).

Overhead Cost. The total of all the indirect expenses.

Variable Cost. A cost which varies with the level of activity (production, sales etc.).

Fixed Cost. A cost which is time-based and is not dependent upon the level of activity e.g. rent of premises, depreciation of machinery.

NOTE: even fixed costs are usually only 'fixed' within certain limits; for instance, if manufacturing output needs to be increased beyond a certain point, it may be necessary to have additional machinery – increased depreciation; or even additional factory space – increased rent.

17.2 ABSORPTION COSTING (ALSO KNOWN AS TOTAL COSTING)

Absorption costing bases the cost of production on total costs i.e. direct cost plus overhead cost. All overheads are 'absorbed' into the cost of production (or total factory cost).

Example of absorption cost statement for the month of May 19-5

Production for the month of May 19-5: 1,000 units

	£
Direct labour	55,000
Direct materials	27,000
Direct expenses (royalties)	2,000
PRIME COST (carried forward)	84,000

245

	£
Brought forward	84,000
Indirect labour	8,500
Indirect materials	12,500
Depreciation	4,000
Other indirect expenses (including rent of factory, heat and light etc.)	9,000
Total cost of production	118,000
Selling expenses (all fixed)	22,000
Administration expenses (all fixed)	35,000
Total cost	175,000

overheads. (handwritten annotation bracketing indirect items)

On an absorption cost basis each unit has cost £$\frac{175,000}{1,000}$ = £175.

If 1,001 items had been produced, the total cost for the month would have been increased by $1/1,000$th of the variable costs, i.e. by direct labour, £55; by direct materials, £27; by direct expenses, £2 i.e. by a total of £84. Fixed costs would not have been affected.

On an absorption cost basis, then, each unit would have cost £175,084/1,001 = £174.909

If 1,010 units had been produced the cost of each unit on this basis of calculation would have been £175,840/1,010 = £174.099

The reason for the different answers to the question 'What has each unit cost' lies in the fact that the fixed costs are being spread over ('absorbed' by) different quantities of items produced in the month.

Limitations of Absorption Costs

They are an inadequate basis on which to make many management decisions.

Uses of Absorption Costs

Calculation of profit/loss when selling price is fixed, or calculation of selling price to achieve a predetermined level of profit.

17.2.1 EXAMPLE

Given the data in 17.2 for the production of 1,000 items calculate:

(a) the profit if the unit selling price is £220

(b) the selling price if a net profit of 20% on sales is required.

ANSWER

(a)
Sales = 1,000 × £220	£220,000
Total cost	£175,000 *80%*
Net profit	45,000 *20%*

(b) Net profit on sales of 20% = 25% of cost of sales; 25% of £175,000 = £43,750; therefore selling price to achieve 20% on sales must be £218,750/1,000 = £218.75 per unit

17.2.2 EXERCISE (To prepare an absorption cost statement.)

Bigthings Ltd. owns a freehold factory which it bought for £900,000, plant and machinery which cost £1,200,000 and a fleet of delivery vans which cost £60,000.

The annual budget for 19-2 includes the following:

	£
Factory overheads (not including depreciation)	510,000
Salaries of sales staff	50,000
Wages of delivery van drivers	34,000
Motor van running costs (excluding depreciation)	48,000
Office rent	33,000
Other administration costs	252,000

It is Bigthings Ltd.'s policy to provide for depreciation on a straight line basis as follows:

Freehold factory	2% on cost
Plant and machinery	20% on cost
Delivery vans	25% on cost

Bigthings Ltd. manufactures Whoppers, its only product, and it has a budgeted output for 19-2 of 24,000 Whoppers. Production is spread evenly over the months of the year.

The raw materials for each Whopper cost £15. Direct labour costs are £26 per Whopper.

REQUIRED

An absorption cost statement for Bigthings Ltd. for the month of March 19-2 showing:

(a) the total profit or loss for the month if the selling price of each Whoppers is £100.

(b) the selling price per Whopper if a profit of 40% of total cost is to be achieved in March 19-2.

17.3   MARGINAL COSTING

MARGINAL COST is the total of the variable costs incurred in producing one unit of a good or in the provision of a service.

All fixed costs i.e. those related to time and not to volume, are ignored for the purpose of ascertaining marginal cost. Marginal cost is often defined as the cost of producing one additional item.

Illustration:

Marginal Products Ltd. produces variable grommets under licence and its budget for the month of September 19-3 is as follows:

Production: 1,000 variable grommets.	£	£
Direct materials		56,000
Direct labour		84,000
Royalties		10,000
Prime cost		150,000
Other production costs:		
Variable	12,000	
Fixed	30,000	42,000
Selling and distribution costs:		
Variable	10,000	
Fixed	25,000	35,000
Administration expenses (all fixed)		55,000
Total cost		282,000
Budgeted net profit		148,000
Budgeted sales		430,000

The above could be redrafted as a marginal cost statement as follows:

	Total cost/1000 units	Marginal cost/unit
Variable costs:	£	£
Direct materials	56,000	56
Direct labour	84,000	84
Direct expenses – royalties	10,000	10
Production costs – variable	12,000	12
Selling and distribution costs – variable	10,000	10
MARGINAL COST	172,000	172
⚹CONTRIBUTION⚹	258,000	258
Sales (selling price)	430,000	430

Fixed costs have been omitted.

CONTRIBUTION is the difference between the marginal cost and the selling price; it represents the contribution each unit of production makes towards:

(i)   covering the fixed expenses

(ii)   the profit

in that order.

CONTRIBUTION/SALES RATIO – C/S Ratio (often misnamed the profit/volume ratio or p/v ratio): contribution is expressed as a percentage of sales. In the above illustration the c/s ratio is:

$$\frac{258}{430} \times 100 = 60\%$$

The c/s ratio is very useful for calculating profit at various levels of activity:

To find profit if sales of variable grommets reached (a) £300,000 (b) £600,000

(a)

		£'000
Contribution = 60% of £300,000		180
less fixed overheads: (30,000 + 25,000 + 55,000)		110
Net profit		70

(b)

		£'000
Contribution = 60% of £600:		360
less fixed overheads		110
Net profit		250

BREAK-EVEN POINT: The level of activity at which the business makes neither profit nor loss i.e. total contribution = total fixed costs.

Calculation of break-even point: divide total fixed costs by the contribution per unit.

Break-even point for variable grommets (above) is: $\frac{£110,000}{£258}$ = 426.36 grommets

As Marginal Products Ltd. can hardly sell 0.36 of a grommet, it will not have completely covered its fixed costs until it has sold the 427th. grommet.

When the break-even point is to be calculated in terms of sales revenue multiply the number of units by the unit price: 426.36 × £430 = £183,334.80

alternatively:

Divide the total fixed costs by the contribution per £ of revenue:

C/s ratio of variable grommets = 60%, or 60p per £1 of revenue.

$\frac{£110,000}{0.60}$ = £183,333 (the difference is in roundings)

BREAK-EVEN CHARTS show sales revenue plotted against total cost and provide, within limits, useful information about various aspects of a product or service (exhibit 1).

1.   Break-even occurs where the sales line intersects the total cost line; the sales at that point is denoted by the vertical scale and the number of units by the horizontal scale.

2.   **Profit** at any particular level of activity to the **right of break-even point** is represented by the **vertical distance** between the sales revenue line and the total cost line at that point.

3.   **Loss** at any particular level of activity **to the left of the break-even point** is represented by the vertical distance between the total cost line and the sales revenue line.

4.   **Margin of safety** is the distance between break-even point and expected level of activity. It depicts the amount by which actual activity can fall short of expected activity before a loss is incurred. It is a measure of risk.

Calculate margin of safety as follows:

$$\frac{\text{Profit}}{\text{C/S ratio}} \times 100$$

e.g. if budgeted sales of variable grommets is £430,000

margin of safety $= \dfrac{£148,000}{60} \times 100 = £246,666$ (or sales - b/e = £430,000 - £183,334) i.e. 57% of budgeted sales.

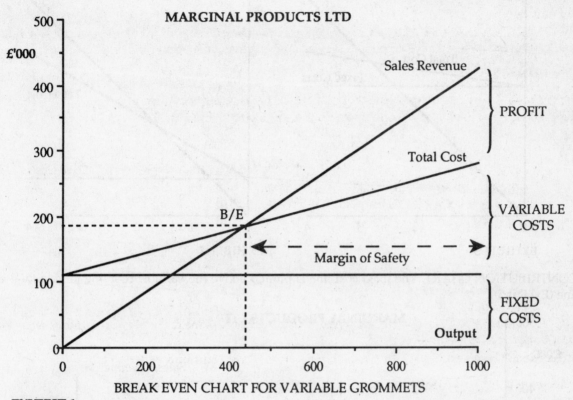

BREAK EVEN CHART FOR VARIABLE GROMMETS

EXHIBIT 1

5. The closer the break-even point is to the left of the chart, the earlier break-even is reached and the greater the margin of safety is likely to be. (The lower the risk for the product) Conversely, a break even-point nearer to the right of the chart indicates greater risk.

6. The position of the break-even point is decided by the slope of the sales line compared with that of the total cost line; the greater the angle between the two lines, the sooner break even point is reached. (Exhibit 2)

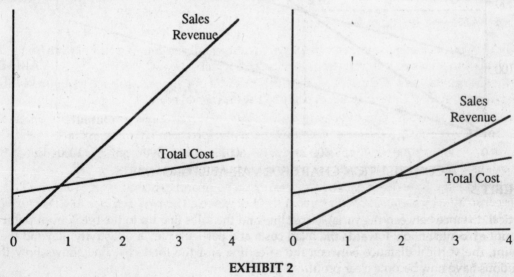

EXHIBIT 2

8. High fixed costs relatively to total cost will result in a high break even point (exhibit 3); low fixed costs relatively to total cost will result in a low break even point (exhibit 4):

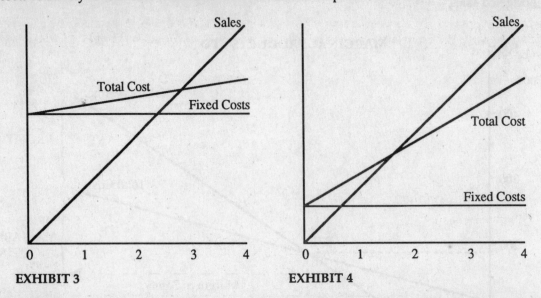

EXHIBIT 3   **EXHIBIT 4**

CONTRIBUTION CHART. The fixed cost line is plotted above the variable cost line to give total cost line (Exhibit 5).

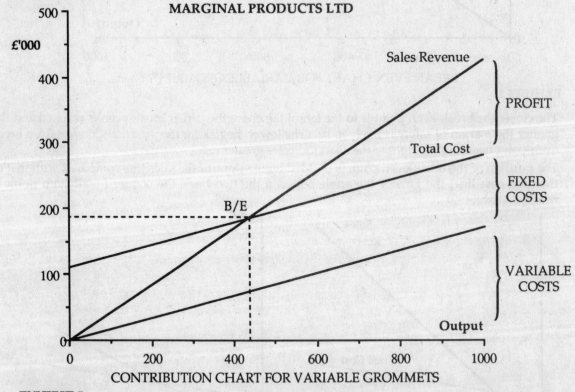

EXHIBIT 5

The vertical distance between the variable cost line and the sales line up to the break even point shows the amount of 'contribution' towards the fixed costs at a particular level of activity. Beyond the break even point, the vertical distance between the sales line and the total cost line shows how the unit contributions have now become clear profit.

PROFIT CHART (Contribution/sales chart): Sales revenue is plotted along the horizontal axis and profit/loss are plotted on the vertical axis (exhibit 6). The maximum loss occurs at zero sales and is equal to the total of fixed costs.

The budgeted profit at a particular level of sales is plotted and the two plots joined by a straight line which represents the cumulative contributions. The profit or loss for any intervening level of sales may then be read from the chart.

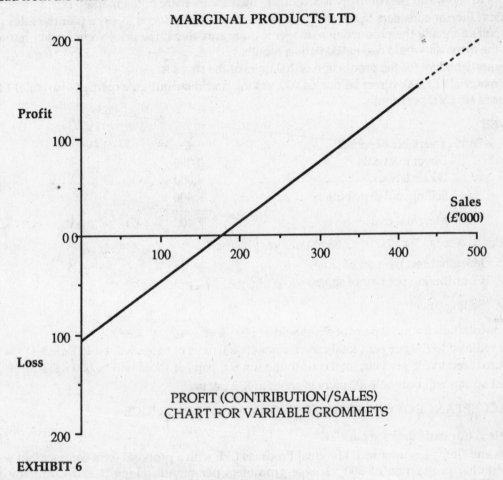

MARGINAL PRODUCTS LTD

PROFIT (CONTRIBUTION/SALES)
CHART FOR VARIABLE GROMMETS

EXHIBIT 6

LIMITATIONS OF BREAK EVEN CHARTS

1. Not all costs can be easily categorised as fixed or variable.

2. Fixed costs are generally only fixed within given parameters. The fixed cost line may need to rise in steps at certain levels of activity.

3. Sales revenue and costs can rarely be represented by straight lines; e.g. increased discounts given in order to achieve higher levels of turnover will tend to 'flatten out' the sales curve.

17.4 APPLICATIONS OF MARGINAL COSTING IN MANAGEMENT DECISIONS

(a) Pricing: circumstances may require a reduction in the selling price of a product e.g. the emergence of competition.

The product price may be reduced provided it is not set below the marginal cost. Any price above marginal cost will produce a contribution towards fixed costs. (However, there may be other factors to be taken into account to arrive at a decision.)

(b) Acceptance of order below normal selling price.

(c) 'Make or buy' decision as to whether to make own product or buy it in from an outside source.

(d) Optimum use of scarce resources.

17.4.1

(a) PRICING DECISION

EXAMPLE (Proposed reduction in selling price)

Peters Ltd. manufactures a special kind of shoe for buskers which sells at £40. The monthly turnover is 200 pairs of shoes and the company is anxious to increase its share of the market.

The Sales Director considers that if the price of the shoes was reduced to £39 a pair the sales would rise to 400 pairs a month; the production manager is quite sure that if the price were further reduced to £38 a pair, the turnover would rise to 600 pairs a month.

The monthly budget for the production of 200 pairs of the shoes is:

Direct materials £3,000; direct labour £4,000; selling and distribution expenses (variable) £400. Fixed overheads are £500 per month.

ANSWER

	£
Total of variable expenses:	
Direct materials	3,000
Direct labour	4,000
Selling and distribution	400
Marginal cost	7,400

÷ No of items 200

	£
Marginal cost per pair of shoes	37
Contribution per pair of shoes	3
Selling price	40

Total contribution from 200 pairs of shoes sold at £40 (40 - 37 × 200) = £600
If price reduced to £39 per pair, total contribution on 400 pairs of shoes will be 400 × £(3-1) = £800
If price reduced to £38 per pair, total contribution on 600 pairs of shoes will be 600 × £(3-2) = £600

ANS → The best option will be to sell 400 pairs of shoes at £39 per pair.

(b) ACCEPTANCE OF ORDER BELOW NORMAL SELLING PRICE

Example 2. (for basic data see page 247)

Floggitt and Company approach Marginal Products Ltd. with a proposal for a contract that will require an additional production of 300 variable grommets per month. Floggitt and Company would be prepared to pay £390 for each of the additional variable grommets produced.

At the same time, Baggett & Sons Ltd. require Marginal Products to produce an additional 200 variable grommets per month for which they will be prepared to pay £160 per grommet.

REQUIRED

A statement showing the effect on profit of each of the potential orders from Floggitt and Company and Baggett & Sons Ltd., and your opinion as to whether or not Marginal Products should accept either or both of the orders.

ANSWER

	Floggitt	Baggett
	£	£
Marginal cost of grommets	172	172
Price offered	390	160
Contribution	222	(12)
Additional profit on 300 grommets	£66,600	
Reduction of profit on 200 grommets		£2,400

Marginal Products Ltd. should accept the order from Floggitt and Company provided the supply to that company on terms far more favourable than those offered to their other customers will not have an adverse effect upon trading relationships with those other customers.

The order from Baggett & Sons Ltd. should be refused.

(c) 'MAKE OR BUY' DECISION →

Treat the cost of the ready-made goods bought from an outside supplier as their marginal cost.

EXAMPLE 3. Jayesh Ltd. manufactures Uggle Boxes.

The budget for March 19-4 is as follows:

			£
Direct materials			10,000
Direct labour			15,000
Factory overheads:	variable		5,000
	fixed		7,000
Selling and distribution expenses:			
	variable		4,000
	fixed		9,000
Administration expenses – fixed			32,000

Planned output for March: 2,000 Uggle Boxes

Each uggle box is sold for £45.

Jayesh Ltd. can buy uggle boxes from Devram's Super Box Manufacturing Co. Ltd. at a cost of £14 per box.

REQUIRED

(a) A financial statement for March 19-4 to show whether Jayesh Ltd. should continue to manufacture uggle boxes or should cease production of the boxes and retail those made by Devram's Super Box Manufacturing Co. Ltd.

(b) A calculation of the profit for March 19-4

    (i)   if Jayesh Ltd. continues to make and sell uggle boxes

    (ii)   if Jayesh Ltd. discontinues production and retails those made by Devram's Super Box Manufacturing Company Ltd.

ANSWER

		£
(a)	Marginal cost of own boxes:	
Per box:	Direct materials	5
	Direct labour	7.50
	Factory overheads – variable	2.50
	Marginal cost of production	15

As this is more than the boxes can be bought from outside, Jayesh Ltd. should discontinue production and 'buy-in' boxes from Devram's Super Box Manufacturing Co. Ltd. at £14 per box.(Variable selling and distribution expenses are ignored as these will presumably still be incurred anyway.)

(b)

Contribution if own boxes are made and sold:

£(selling price per unit - marginal cost per unit) × no. sold

= £(45 - 15) × 2,000 = £60,000.

Net profit = total contribution less fixed overheads

	£
Total contribution	60,000
less Fixed overheads £(7,000 + 9,000 + 32,000)	48,000
Net profit	12,000

Increase in total contribution if boxes bought from Devram's Super Box Manufacturing Co. Ltd £(15 - 14) × 2,000 = £2,000; therefore net profit would be £14,000

(d) OPTIMUM USE OF SCARCE RESOURCES

LIMITING FACTOR or KEY FACTOR: Any factor which places a limit on the level of activity; e.g. a shortage of raw materials, or of suitable labour.

Application: Where two or more products use the same raw material which is in short supply; or the number of man hours or machine hours available for the manufacture of two or more products is insufficient to meet the total demand.

Rank each product in the order of the contribution yielded per unit of the scarce resource.

EXAMPLE 4

Kelly Ltd. manufactures three products: Aonyx, Bionyx and Cronyx. Planned production for the three months to 31 March 19-1 is: Aonyx 10,000 units, Bionyx 7,000 units, Cronyx 4,000 units.

The following information about production costs for each of the products is available:

Per unit	Aonyx	Bionyx	Cronyx
Raw materials: Onyxium	5 kilos	6 kilos	4 kilos
Man hours (at £8 per hour)	10	8	12
Other variable expenses	£115	£144	£78
Selling price	£800	£880	£670

Onyxium costs £100 per kilo. and it has now been ascertained that while 108,000 kilos are needed to produce budgeted output, only 96,000 kilos will be available in the three months to 31 March 19-1.

Fixed overheads amount to £300,000 per month.

REQUIRED

A revised production budget which will produce the maximum net profit for the three months to 31 March 19-1.

ANSWER

Cost of producing each unit:	Aonyx	Bionyx	Cronyx
	£	£	£
Direct materials	500	600	400
Direct labour	80	64	96
Other variable expenses	115	144	78
Marginal cost	695	808	574
Selling price	800	880	670
Contribution	105	72	96

Contribution per kilo of onyxium:

	Aonyx	Bionyx	Cronyx
	$\frac{105}{5}$	$\frac{72}{6}$	$\frac{96}{4}$
	= £21	= £12	= £24
Ranking order	(2)	(3)	(1)

Revised production budget:

	kilos of Onyxium		Total contribution £
Available	96,000		
4,000 units Cronyx	(16,000)	4,000 × £96	384,000
	80,000		
10,000 units Aonyx	(50,000)	10,000 × £105	1,050,000
Carried forward	30,000		1,434,000

254

			£
Brought forward	30,000		1,434,000
5,000 units Bionyx	(30,000)	5,000 × £72	360,000
			1,794,000
Less fixed overheads (3 × £300,000)			900,000
Net profit			£894,000

EXAMPLE 5

Data as in exercise 4, but although adequate supplies of onyxium will be available to meet budgeted production, there is a shortage of skilled labour and it is estimated that the maximum number of man hours worked will be 180,000.

	Aonyx	Bionyx	Cronyx
Contribution per unit (as above)	£105	£72	£96
Contribution per man hour	$\frac{£105}{10}$	$\frac{£72}{8}$	$\frac{£96}{12}$
	= £10.50	= £9	= £8
Ranking order	(1)	(2)	(3)

Revised production budget:

	Man Hours		Total contribution £
Available	180,000		
10,000 units of Aonyx	(100,000)	10,000 × £105	1,050,000
	80,000		
7,000 units of Bionyx	(56,000)	7,000 × £72	504,000
	24,000		
2,000 units of Cronyx	24,000	2,000 × £96	192,000
			1,746,000
Less fixed overheads			900,000
Net profit			£846,000

17.4.2   EXERCISE 1 (Calculation of break even point and margin of safety)

D Brown Ltd. manufactures bicycles under licence; it sells the bicycles for £260. Planned production for the six months to 30 June 19-6 is for 5,000 bicycles and the budget for that period is as follows:

		£
Direct materials		300,000
Direct labour		400,000
Royalties under licence		50,000
Selling and distribution expenses:		
	variable	20,000
	fixed	200,000
Administration costs:	variable	10,000
	fixed	220,960

REQUIRED

Calculate (i) the break even point and (ii) the margin of safety from the data given above.

EXERCISE 2 (Calculation of 'best price')

Mei Ling Ltd. manufactures decorative lanterns. Each lantern requires materials costing £8 and requires 2 hours of labour at £6 an hour.

The lanterns are sold at £25 each and current output is 400 lanterns a week.

Fixed expenses amount to £700 a week.

If the price of the lanterns were reduced to £23 each, sales would rise to 600 lanterns a week.

A further reduction in price to £22 would increase sales to 1,100 a week. An increase in production above 1,000 lanterns, however, would require additional resources which would add 15% to fixed expenses.

REQUIRED

Calculations to show which price Mei Ling Ltd. should charge for the lanterns in order to make the most profit.

EXERCISE 3 (Acceptance of order below normal selling price)

T.Lambrou Ltd. manufactures an electronic accessory for the motor trade. Each accessory requires components costing £25 and requires 4 hours of labour at £9 an hour.

Other variable costs, per accessory, include selling and distribution £4 and administration £2.

Monthly fixed overheads are: selling and distribution £15,000, administration £18,000.

The list price charged by T. Lambrou Ltd. for the accessory is £80.

Manjeet Motors, specialists in custom built cars, has approached T. Lambrou Ltd. with the following proposals:

1. That T. Lambrou Ltd. produce an additional 1,000 units per month as a special order for Manjeet Motors, the latter to be allowed a special trade discount of 10% on the catalogue price.

2. That the special order be increased to 2,000 units per month provided the trade discount is increased to 20%.

REQUIRED

Prepare a report to the directors of T. Lambrou Ltd. explaining why they should accept or reject the offers made by Manjeet Motors. Your report should quantify the effect on T. Lambrou Ltd.'s profit of each proposal.

EXERCISE 4 ('Make or buy')

Ninasim & Son Ltd. makes three products: Ninabits, Simlabits and Sonybits.

The monthly budgets for the three products are as follows:

		Ninabits	Simlabits	Sonybits
No. of units of production		1,000	1,000	500
		£	£	£
Direct materials		18,000	7,000	4,500
Direct labour		25,000	21,000	13,000
Selling and distribution:				
	variable	5,000	4,000	–
	fixed	21,000	10,000	10,000
Administration:	fixed	9,000	9,000	9,000

Ninasim & Son Ltd. have the opportunity to purchase each of the three products from Husseyin & Husseyin and Co. Ltd. at the following prices:

Ninabits	£50 each
Simlabits	£30 each
Sonybits	£33 each

REQUIRED

A recommendation as to which product or products, if any, Ninasim & Son Ltd. should continue to manufacture, and which should be 'bought in' from Husseyin & Husseyin and Co. Ltd.

EXERCISE 5 (Maximising profit when there are limiting factors)

C. Yiannakou manufactures three products: Boxydons, Doxydons and Moxydons. Planned production for 19-4 is as follows:

Boxydons	10,000 units
Doxydons	9,000 units
Moxydons	11,000 units

Production details per unit are as follows:

	Boxydons	Doxydons	Moxydons
3/8" Boxium alloy sheeting	3 sq.metres	6 sq.metres	4 sq.metres
Labour (man hours)	4	5	5
Selling price per unit	£50	£64	£60

3/8" Boxium alloy sheeting costs £2 per sq. metre. All labour is remunerated at the standard rate of £8 an hour. All other costs of C Yiannakou are fixed.

Only one Boxium mine is known to exist in the world, and that has recently been put out of action by a geological fault and production of the mineral is not expected to resume until 19-5. C Yiannakou has, however, stockpiled 3/8" Boxium sheeting and has presently got 92,000 sq. metres available for use.

REQUIRED

A revised production schedule for C. Yiannakou in order to produce the maximum profit for the year 19-4.

17.5 KEY POINTS TO REMEMBER

1. Absorption cost has limited uses; it is not suitable for most decision making as absorption of fixed overheads per unit depends upon the number of units produced.
2. Marginal cost includes only those costs which vary with the level of activity.
3. Contribution is the difference between selling price and marginal cost.
4. Break-even point is found by dividing total fixed costs by unit contribution.
5. Margin of safety is the amount by which expected or budgeted output exceeds break-even point.
6. Marginal costing may be used to aid management decision making, particularly: 'make or buy',
   acceptance of orders below normal selling price
   maximising profit when resources are scarce.
7. SSAP 9 recommends absorption cost to be used for valuation of closing stock in published financial accounts as it recognises costs in the same period as related revenue arises, thus complying with the 'matching' concept. Either marginal or absorption costs may be used by management for their own use.
8. Marginal costing questions may be recognised by references in them to fixed and variable costs, 'break-even', limiting factors etc.
9. Draw break-even charts carefully and neatly to enable readings to be taken from them with an acceptable degree of accuracy.
10. Give clear, concise headings to break-even charts and indicate the total cost and sales revenue lines and break even point clearly.

COMMON ERRORS
- failure to recognise marginal costing questions.
- failure to use the contribution/sales ratio as a quick method of calculation.
- poor presentation of marginal cost statements (omission of heading etc.)
- badly drawn, untidy and inaccurate break even charts often without appropriate headings or keys.

17.6 EXAMINATION QUESTIONS

QUESTION 1 (London January 1987)
(i) Explain the meaning of
   (a) absorption costing,
   (b) marginal costing,
   (c) contribution.

(6 marks)

(ii)   A firm which uses cost plus (full cost) pricing makes 100 each of a range of products each month. The unit costs of the whole range are:

	J	K	L	M	N
	£	£	£	£	£
Direct materials	10	12	13	16	19
Direct labour	8	9	10	13	13
Variable overhead	4	5	7	9	10
	22	26	30	38	42
Fixed overhead	3	4	5	7	8
	25	30	35	45	50
Profit (20%)	5	6	7	9	10
	30	36	42	54	60

Market conditions have moved against the firm and competitors are charging the following prices for the whole range, beginning with J: £21; £34; £38; £51; £40.

Show how the firm can still compete at the new prices, and earn itself an overall profit of £200 per month by producing K,L and M. Explain fully how this can be so.   *(6 marks)*

(iii)   Why is the marginal costing approach *not* suitable for analysing long-term decisions?

(3 marks)

(Total 15 marks)

QUESTION 2   (Oxford June 1986)

How is the element of 'fixed costs' dealt with in marginal and absorption costing?   *(8 marks)*

QUESTION 3   (Cambridge November 1987)

(A)   Pelican Limited manufactures one product. The selling price of the product remained the same in September and October 19-7. Over the same period, variable costs per unit remained constant and fixed costs were the same each month. Stocks are maintained at constant levels and the trading results were as follows:

	September	October
	£	£
Sales	165,000	210,000
Profit	4,000	13,000

REQUIRED

From the above information, calculate
 (a)   the monthly fixed costs
 (b)   the sales revenue required to break even,
 (c)   the sales revenue required to earn a profit of £18,000
 (d)   the profit or loss arising from sales of £136,000

(16 marks)

(B)   Consider in turn each of the graphs below. The cost of certain items of expenditure is measured on the vertical axis and activity levels are measured along the horizontal axis.

(i)   (ii)   (iii)

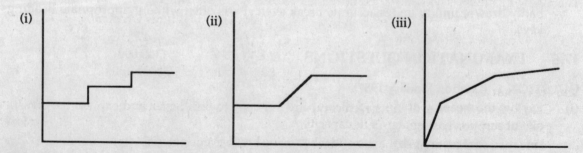

REQUIRED

In each case explain the pattern of cost behaviour shown and give an example of a cost which would behave in the way illustrated.
(9 marks)

QUESTION 4 (Cambridge June 1988)

Plonkers Limited manufactures a single product. During the year ended 30 April 19-8 the costs of manufacturing 100,000 units were as follows:

	Variable Costs £'000	Fixed Costs £'000	Total Costs £'000
Direct materials (3 lbs per unit)	150	–	150
Direct labour (15 mins per unit)	110	–	110
Direct manufacturing expenses (power)	45	–	45
Factory overhead	–	30	30
Selling expenses	35	60	95
	340	90	430

On 30 April 19-8, 33,000 lbs of raw material were in stock together with finished goods which were valued at £45,750. Finished goods in stock were valued at the marginal cost of manufacture, i.e. excluding any proportion of factory overheads. At 30 April 19-8 there was no work-in-progress and there were no opening stocks at 1 May 19-7.

Sales revenue for the year totalled £595,000.

All prices and costs remained stable throughout the year.

REQUIRED

(a) Calculate:

    (i)   the cost of raw material in stock at 30 April 19-8 *(2 marks)*

    (ii)   the labour cost per hour for the year ended 30 April 19-8 *(2 marks)*

    (iii) the number of unsold units of production in Finished Goods at 30 April 19-8 *(4 marks)*

    (iv) the selling price per unit *(2 marks)*

    (v)   the net profit of the Company for the year ended 30 April 19-8 *(6 marks)*

(b) (i)   Calculate the number of units required to be sold to break even using the selling price calculated above *(4 marks)*

    (ii)   Calculate the profit for the following year on the assumption that a TV advertising campaign costing £5,000 would increase sales to a total of 125,000 units at a selling price of £9 per unit. You may assume that production costs per unit will remain the same as in the previous year. *(5 marks)*

(Total 25 marks)

QUESTION 5 (Author's own question, after JMB)

Beech Limited and Willow Limited make identical products which they both sell at the same price of £9 each. Because the two companies use completely different methods of manufacture, their operating costs differ considerably.

The following data has been extracted from their records for the year 19-2:

	Beech Ltd.	Willow Limited
Variable costs per unit	£4	£7
Fixed costs for the year	£200,000	£140,000
Annual capacity	80,000 units	100,000 units

You are required to

(a) Calculate the number of units each company must sell to break-even and express the break even point of each as a percentage of its capacity, *(8 marks)*

(b) Name two assumptions that are made when using break-even analysis, *(12 marks)*

(c) Explain the risks of using break-even analysis in a business that produces several different products in the same factory, *(5 marks)*

(d) If the two companies simultaneously offered you a job as manager on equal terms, which of the two companies would you choose and why? (State clearly any assumptions you make and explain their significance)

(15 marks)

(Total 40 marks)

QUESTION 6 (Author's own question, after JMB)

Firtree PLC manufactures a variety of products and is currently operating at full capacity, represented in terms of 16,000 kilograms of materials each month. The sales director has suggested that the production of one product, Microgrummits, should be discontinued, and the available capacity used to manufacture Hypergrummits instead. The production manager has produced the following estimates of monthly revenues and costs for each product.

	Microgrummits	Hypergrummits
Selling price per product	£10	£16
Materials required	4,000 Kgs	4,000 Kgs
Revenues from sales	£60,000	£56,000
Production costs:		
Direct materials	£9,000	£9,750
Direct labour (variable)	£18,000	£13,000
Fixed overhead (50 per cent of direct labour)	£9,000	£6,500
Total production costs	£36,000	£29,250

Manufacture of Hypergrummits would require additional quality control inspection at a cost of £1,200 per month, otherwise the fixed factory overheads would remain unchanged. There will be no problem in obtaining adequate resources, either of direct labour or direct materials, and the overall labour force can be varied without penalty.

Selling and administrative expenses will not be affected whichever product is selected.

You are required to calculate

(a) The contribution per unit that each product will make, *(10 marks)*

(b) The net contribution per month if each product is sold at the given sales revenue *(10 marks)*

(c) How many Hypergrummits need to be produced to break even, *(8 marks)*

(d) Given limited capacity, which is the more profitable product? *(12 marks)*

(Total 40 marks)

QUESTION 7 (AEB June 1989)

Marlon Plc is a company operating a department store and the management are conducting an analysis of all departments. In department ZR products have been classified into three broad categories and the profit/volume graph on the opposite page has been compiled for the year ended 31 January 19-9.
Additional information.

The average selling prices of each product category in department ZR is as follows:

Product Category	Selling price each
	£
A	4.00
B	2.50
C	1.50

Department ZR – Profit/Volume Graph for the year ended 31 January 1989

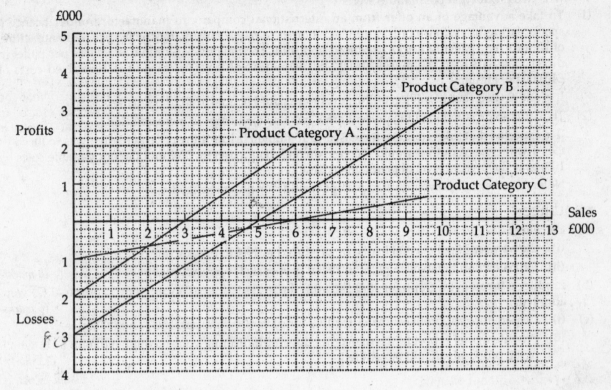

REQUIRED

(a) Using the profit/volume graph and the information given, prepare a total profit statement for department ZR for the year ended 31 January 19-9. *(5 marks)*

(b) Calculate the break-even point for each category of product and express your answer in sales units. *(3 marks)*

(c) Using the total figures in the statement you prepared in (a) above, prepare a break-even graph for the department. Reading from the graph you prepare, at what income did the department break even? *(5 marks)*

(d) By means of an accountancy equation utilising the total figures in your statement prepared in (a) above, calculate the *actual* income at which the department began to move into profit. *(3 marks)*

(Total 25 marks)

QUESTION 8 (AEB November 1989)

Skirb Ltd. manufacture bricks. In 19-8 they manufactured and sold 10 million bricks. All bricks were palletised for efficient handling and each pallet contained 1,000 bricks.

In the year ending 31 December 19-8 all bricks manufactured were sold at £100 per pallet. The unit costs of a pallet of bricks at the 19-8 level of output were:

	£
Direct materials	30
Direct labour	20
Factory costs: variable	11
fixed	5
Selling and distribution costs: variable	8
fixed	4
Other fixed costs	7
	85

The managing director was currently considering two different courses of action for the business in 19-9. The two production possibilities were:

(1) To take advantage of an offer from an international company to manufacture under licence a special facing brick. Skirb Ltd. would be required to pay a royalty, for the licence to manufacture, of £5 for every pallet of bricks produced and sold. The new brick would cost £3 less per pallet in direct materials than the present brick, but would involve an increase of factory fixed costs of £40,000 per annum.

It is anticipated that 12 million of the new bricks could be sold at £120 per pallet.

(2) To maintain production of the present brick but also to attempt to increase sales.

It is expected that sales could be increased to 15 million bricks if the price per pallet was reduced to £90. The increased output would increase direct labour costs by 20% and factory variable costs by 10% over the present level of pallet unit costs.

Note: All other cost/revenue relationships would remain unchanged.

REQUIRED

(a) Calculate:

    (i) the number of pallets that had to be produced in 19-8 to break-even

    (ii) the pallet unit break-even point in 19-9 if proposal (1) were adopted.   *(6 marks)*

(b) Produce a break-even graph for 19-9 showing the projected break-even point, if proposal (2) were adopted.   *(6 marks)*

(c) (i) Prepare forecast profit estimates for 19-9 for each of the proposals (1) and (2) above.

    (ii) Provide a brief report to the managing director indicating your recommendation as to which of the proposals should be selected.   *(13 marks)*

    (Total 25 marks)

18 BUDGETS AND BUDGETARY CONTROL

Questions on this topic require:-
● an ability to define and explain budgeting terms
● a knowledge of the uses and benefits of budgets
● an understanding of the control function of budgets
● ability to prepare operational and master budgets from given data

18.1 DEFINITIONS

Forecast

A prediction of the result of carrying on business over a future period of time, and of the position of the business at the end of that time if present and, as far as they are known, future conditions and trends are allowed to continue without management intervention.

Budget

A statement in money terms of management's plans for operating a business over a future period of time and their plans for the position of the business at the end of that time.

Operating Budgets (Functional Budgets)

Budgets prepared for each individual department, function etc. of a business showing the budget-responsibility of each manager.

Master Budget

A profit and loss account and balance sheet based upon the operating budgets. (Often referred to in examination questions as 'forecast' profit and loss accounts and balance sheets.)

Budget Periods

The period for which a budget is prepared, commonly for one year, but it will depend upon the particular business.

Budgetary Control

The use of budgets to monitor the performance of managers against their functional budgets. The system allows for the continuous comparison of actual with budgeted results at frequent intervals so that corrective action may be taken when necessary. Budget periods are broken down into control periods of, say, months or 4-weekly accounting periods

Illustration:

Budget for 4 weeks to 28 January 19-1

	Budget	Actual	Better/ (Worse)
	£'000	£'000	£'000
Staff costs	240	250	(10)
Property costs	105	98	7

Management By Exception (Exception reporting)

The focussing by management of its attention upon those items, processes etc. which are deviating from budget, on the principle that matters conforming to budget need no management intervention. Computers may be programmed to print out 'exception reports' of items deviating from budget.

Top Down Budgeting

Budgets are prepared for lower management by top management with, or without, discussion (The concept would usually imply little or no discussion.) Lower management tend to feel little commitment to this type of budget.

Bottom Up Budgeting

Lower management prepare their own functional budgets and submit them to higher management for approval and incorporation into the master budget. Lower management tends to set its targets low in order to reduce the risk of not meeting budget, or to appear to merit credit when actual performance is seen to be better than budget.

Budget Committee

A committee of senior management to co-ordinate the preparation of budgets.

Budget Manager (Or budget controller or officer)

Usually the accountant who gives assistance to managers in the compilation of their budgets, and to the Budget committee.

Budget Manual

Contents: Statement of objectives and procedures; the budget organisation structure (showing functional responsibilities); timetable for preparing budget; report format; frequency and distribution of reports.

Zero Base Budgeting

Budget preparation based on the principle that each item of expenditure and the amount thereof must be justified by the benefit which will accrue from it before it is included in the budget. This contrasts with the alternative method of starting with the previous year's budget and 'updating' it, including adding some percentage points for inflation. This latter method has the defect of perpetuating previous inaccuracies and inefficiencies.

Flexible Budget

A budget that recognises the different behaviours of fixed and variable costs at different levels of activity.

USES AND BENEFITS OF BUDGETS

(a) Budgets formalise management plans.

(b) Budget preparation ensures that all functions of a business are properly co-ordinated.

(c) Budgets may indicate possible future shortages of resources so that remedial action may be taken in good time, or other functional budgets modified (e.g. cash budget may give prior warning of shortage of liquidity and the need to re-phase expenditure, arrange bank overdraft, loan etc. in good time.)

(d) Budgets provide information for on-going control of business activities.

(e) Participation by management at all levels in budget preparation induces sense of commitment by all of them to the budget.

FACTORS TO BE CONSIDERED IN BUDGETING

(i) Long term objectives of business (Corporate, strategic planning)

(ii) Limiting factors

(iii) Internal factors (behavioural aspects of management when preparing budgets; number of each grade of employee; staff training and morale; available finance etc.)

(iv) External factors (International, political, economic, environmental etc.)

18.2   SALES BUDGET

Sales are frequently the key factor in a business and the sales budget will then largely determine the shape of the other budgets.

A simple sales budget will record quantities and prices and total revenue:

Sales budget for Product A for six months to 30 June 19-1

Month	Quantity	Price £	Revenue £
Jan	5,000	1.50	7,500
Feb	6,000	1.50	9,000
Mar	8,000	1.50	12,000
Carried forward	19,000		28,500

	£		£
Brought forward	19,000		28,500
Apr	7,000	1.60	11,200
May	7,500	1.60	12,000
Jun	8,000	1.60	12,800
	41,500		64,500

Additional columns will be used when more than one product is involved; a total column will then be necessary as well.

Further columns may be added to allow sales to be analysed over regions, departments. Alternatively, separate budgets may be prepared for each region or department and these combined into a summary statement.

18.2.1 EXAMPLE (Sales budget for a single product)

Naveed sells a single product, Deevan Beds, at a price of £160 each. During the three months to 31 December 19-1, he sold 1,500 beds; turnover was constant per month. He expects the volume of sales to remain unchanged for January 19-2, but to increase by 5% in February, and by a further 20% in April. The price of the beds will be increased by 10% in January and by a further 5% in June.

REQUIRED

Prepare a sales budget for Deevan Beds for the six months to 30 June 19-2.

ANSWER

Deevan Beds
Sales budget for the six months to 30 June 19-2

19-2	Quantity	Price £	Amount £
January	500	176	88,000
February	525	176	92,400
March	525	176	92,400
April	630	176	110,880
May	630	176	110,880
June	630	184.8	116,424
	3,440		610,984

18.2.2 EXERCISE (Preparation of a sales budget)

M. Cohen markets two products, A and B. The sales of Product A averaged 1,000 per month in 19-3 and in the same year an average of 500 of Product B were sold per month.

M. Cohen estimates that in 19-4, sales of Product A will increase by 5 per cent in March and by a further 8 per cent in August. Sales of Product B will increase by 6 per cent in February, by a further 10 per cent in June and then to increase to 600 a month by August with a further increase of 4 per cent by October.

Product A has been selling for £100 each and Product B for £120. The price of Product A will increase by 10 per cent in March 19-4 and by a further 5 per cent in the following September. The price of Product B will be increased by 5 per cent in May and again by a further $33^{1}/_{3}$ per cent in October.

REQUIRED

M.Cohen's sales budget for the year to 31 December 19-4.

18.3 PRODUCTION BUDGET

This is a budget for the production of finished goods

Even Production Budget

This type of budget is required by a firm employing skilled labour which cannot readily be hired, made redundant and then re-hired to meet seasonal fluctuations of business. Continuous employment of a stable, skilled workforce with an even flow of production, even if it results in seasonal stockpiling is preferable to a skilled labour shortage just when it is needed, or the costly training of new unskilled staff.

Uneven Production Budget

This could be required by a firm with a highly seasonal type of business in a product which it is not feasible to stockpile, e.g. icecream, and which can be produced by unskilled labour which can be hired and released as occasion demands, e.g. students seeking holiday jobs.

METHOD

(i) Read question through carefully to ascertain its requirements e.g. the exact period to be covered by the budget, whether even or uneven production is required, sales, opening stocks, minimum stocks, etc.

(ii) Prepare a column for each month, quarter or other period required.

(iii) Prepare rows for opening stocks of goods, units produced, sales and closing stocks.

(iv) Your template should now look like this:

Month	Jan	Feb	March	April
UNITS				
Opening stock b/f				
Production(sub total)				
Sales				
Closing stock c/f				

18.3.1 EXAMPLE 1 Even production

Sital Ltd. manufactures codgetts of which it produces 750 a month. Sales for the four months May to August are expected to be as follows: May 600; June 800; July 1,000; August 600.
At 30 April, Sital Ltd. will have 800 codgetts in stock.

REQUIRED

Sital Ltd.'s production budget for the four months May to August.

ANSWER

Sital Ltd.
Production Budget 4 months to 31 August

	May	June	July	August
Opening Stock	800	950	900	650
Production	750	750	750	750
	1550	1700	1650	1400
Sales	600	800	1000	600
Closing stock	950	900	650	800

EXAMPLE 2 Even production with minimum stock level

Hocus plc manufactures gas pokers with a regular monthly production of 1,000 pokers. Sales for the four months September to December are expected to be: September 900; October 1,000; November 1,300; December 900. Hocus Ltd. maintains a minimum stock of 600 pokers.

REQUIRED

Hocus plc's production budget for the four months to 31 December.

ANSWER

Tutorial note: No opening stock is given. Begin by preparing the budget, inserting monthly opening and closing stocks in pencil. (Insert 'negative' balances at this stage.) Find the month which has the biggest shortfall compared with minimum stock; the shortfall will be the required opening stock.

Hocus plc
Production Budget – 4 months to 31 December

	Sept	Oct	Nov	Dec
Opening stock b/f	?	*100	*100	*(200)
Production	1000	1000	1000	1000
Carried forward	1000	1100	1100	800

	Sept	Oct	Nov	Dec
Carried forward	1000	1100	1100	800
Sales	900	1000	1300	900
Closing stock c/f	*100	*100	*(200)	*(100)

* = balances 'pencilled in' at this stage

November has the greatest shortfall from minimum stock: 600 + 200= 800.

Enter 800 as the opening stock in September and substitute new balances for the ones pencilled in for opening and closing stocks for the other months:

	Sept	Oct	Nov	Dec
Opening stock b/f	800	900	900	600
Production	1000	1000	1000	1000
	1800	1900	1900	1600
Sales	900	1000	1300	900
Closing balance c/f	900	900	600	700

EXAMPLE 3 Uneven production

Okalas Ltd. produces Iyesan, a chemical product which they have patented. The stock of Iyesan at 1 January 19-1 was 1,200 kilos.

Sales for the four quarters of 19-1 are budgeted to be: Qtr. to 31 March 3,000 kilos; Qtr. to 30 June 5,000 kilos; Qtr. to 30 September 7,000 kilos; Qtr. to 31 December 4,000 kilos.

Closing stocks are required to be as follows: 31 March 1,500 kilos; 30 June 1,800 kilos; September 1600 kilos; December 1,300 kilos.

REQUIRED

Okalas Ltd.'s quarterly production budget for the year to 31 December 19-1.

Tutorial note: Production = sales + closing stock - opening stock. Therefore production for three months to 31 March = 3,000 + 1,500 - 1,200 = 3,300 kilos etc.

ANSWER

Okalas Ltd.
Production budget for the year to 31 December 19-1

Quarters ending	March 31	June 30	Sept 30	Dec 31
	kilos.	kilos.	kilos.	kilos
Opening stock	1,200	1,500	1,800	1,600
Production (balancing fig.)	3,300	5,300	6,800	3,700
	4,500	6,800	8,600	5,300
Sales	3,000	5,000	7,000	4,000
Closing stock	1,500	1,800	1,600	1,300

8.3.2 EXERCISE 1. (Budget for even production)

Murude plc manufactures beauty care packs and has a fixed production of 15,000 packs a month. The stock of beauty care packs at 1 January 19-2 was 16,000. Budgeted sales for 19-2 are as follows:

three months to		
	31 March	42,000 packs
	30 June	52,000 packs
	30 September	55,000 packs
	31 December	32,000 packs

REQUIRED

Murude plc's production budget for the four quarters of 19-2.

EXERCISE 2 (Even production and minimum stock level)

Shwish Ltd. produces cans of fizzy drink. 100,000 cans are produced each month and sales for 19-3 are budgeted to be as follows:

three months to		
	March 31	250,000 cans
	June 30	350,000 cans
	September 30	500,000 cans
	December 31	400,000 cans

The minimum stock at any time is to be 300,000 cans.

REQUIRED

Shwish Ltd's production budget for the four quarters of 19-3.

EXERCISE 3 (Uneven production)

The Aaisha Company produces fashion packs for home made garments. Budgeted sales and closing stocks are as follows:

	Sales (packs)	Closing stocks (packs)
December	7,000	1,000
January	6,000	2,000
February	8,000	4,000
March	7,000	5,000
April	8,000	4,000

REQUIRED

The Aaisha Company's production budget for the four months to 30 April 19-5.

18.4 STOCK PURCHASING BUDGETS

Budgets for the purchases of supplies of materials used for production will be compiled from production budgets. The procedure is similar to that followed for production budgets. Stock purchasing budgets may be produced either in units purchased or cost of purchases.

18.4.1 EXAMPLE (Stock purchasing budget based on month-end stocks being equivalent to the following month's production)

Maranah Med Ltd. manufactures a product each unit of which requires two kilos of a substance called 'prudice'. The closing stock at each month end has to be equivalent to the requirement for the following month's production.

Production for the months of September 19-1 to January 19-2 is budgeted as follows:

19-1	No. of units produced
September	1,000
October	3,000
November	4,000
December	2,000
19-2	
January	3,000

REQUIRED

The raw materials budget for Maranah Med Ltd. for the four months to 31 December 19-1.

ANSWER

Maranah Med Ltd. Raw Materials budget for the four months to December 19-1

Kilos	Sept	Oct	Nov	Dec
Opening stock	2,000	6,000	8,000	4,000
Purchases	6,000	8,000	4,000	6,000
Carried forward	8,000	14,000	12,000	10,000

	Sept	Oct	Nov	Dec
Brought forward	8,000	14,000	12,000	10,000
Issues	2,000	6,000	8,000	4,000
Closing stock	6,000	8,000	4,000	6,000

18.4.2 EXERCISE (Budget for purchase of raw materials at cost price.)

Pi Manufacturers Ltd. make product X. Each unit of product X requires 3 kilos of mucronium. Product X is made in the month prior to sale and the raw materials are purchased one month before production. Since 1 January 19-1, mucronium had cost £1.50 per kilo but the price was increased to £2 from 1 June 19-1. The FIFO basis is used for charging mucronium to production.

Budgeted sales of product X are as follows:

19-1	units
March	500
April	600
May	800
June	1,000
July	900
August	600

The stock of mucronium at 28 February 19-1 was equal to the production requirement for March.

REQUIRED

The budget for the purchase of mucronium by Pi Manufacturers Ltd. for the period March to June 19-1.

18.5   CASH BUDGET

METHOD

(i)   Examiners expect cash budgets to be prepared in a template similar to the following:

Periods	1	2	3	4	5	6 etc.
	£	£	£	£	£	£
Receipts (details)						
Payments (details)						
Net receipts/(payments)						
Balance b/f						
Balance c/f						

(ii)   Read the question very carefully at least twice before preparing the outline template, noting the nature of receipts and payments. Enter these in the template, leaving a few lines to allow for the insertion of additional items later which may have been overlooked.

(iii)   Once the outline template has been prepared, it is usually not too difficult to fill in the figures, but careful reading of the question, a little common sense and great care in performing calculations are essential.

(iv)   Sales and purchases on credit. Take care to enter receipts and payments in the period in which the money is expected to be received or paid. If some sales are for cash and others on credit, the receipts will be split between cash sales and the balance, received in a later period, as receipts from debtors.

Credit transactions require information for the period prior to the budget period to be given; do not be confused by this.

(v)   Other expenses may be paid currently or one period later than that in which they are incurred.

(vi)   Depreciation is a non-cash item and must be ignored.

(vii) Receipts and expenditure occurring before the period covered by the budget must be adjusted, if necessary, in the opening balance of cash brought forward and not shown as transactions in the first month, week etc.

(viii) Cash budgets are prepared on a cash and not an accruals basis. Any item, revenue or capital in nature, which should appear in the cash book in the period in question should be included in the budget; but all other items should be ignored.

18.5.1 EXAMPLE (Preparation of cash budget from supplied data.)

Niblick supplies golf equipment. Ten per cent of his sales are for cash; the remainder is on one month's credit. He receives one month's credit on all purchases. Sales and purchases are as follows:

	Sales £	Purchases £
December 19-1	30,000	16,000
January 19-2	25,000	14,000
February	18,000	20,000
March	22,000	25,000
April	28,000	30,000

Niblick pays wages of £2,000 per month. He pays rent of £10,000 per annum.; he paid one year's rent in advance on 1 January 19-2. Other expenses, £1,500 per month are paid currently.

On 6 February 19-2, Niblick sold a van for £2,300 but purchased a new one for £6,000 on 15 March 19-2. Niblick draws £1,000 a month for living expenses.

At 31 December 19-1, Niblick's bank balance was £7,000 (in hand). His father lent the business £4,000 on 1 April 19-2.

REQUIRED

Niblick's cash budget for the four months to 30 April 19-2.

ANSWER

Niblick.
Cash budget for 4 months to 30 April 19-2

	Jan £	Feb £	Mar £	Apr £
Receipts				
Cash sales	2,500	1,800	2,200	2,800
Receipts from debtors	27,000	22,500	16,200	19,800
Sale of van		2,300		
Loan from father				4,000
	29,500	26,600	18,400	26,600
Payments				
Creditors for supplies	16,000	14,000	20,000	25,000
Wages	2,000	2,000	2,000	2,000
Rent	10,000			
Other expenses	1,500	1,500	1,500	1,500
Purchase of van			6,000	
Drawings	1,000	1,000	1,000	1,000
	30,500	18,500	30,500	29,500
Net receipts/(payments)	(1,000)	8,100	(12,100)	(2,900)
Balance brought forward	7,000	6,000	14,100	2,000
Balance carried forward	6,000	14,100	2,000	(900)

18.5.2 EXERCISE (Preparation of a cash budget)

Kadriye commenced business on 1 January 19-2 trading as 'Kadriye's Kitchen Kabinets', selling 3-K kitchen furniture. She had opened a business bank account on 15 December 19-1, paying £25,000 into it as her opening capital. On 21 December 19-1, she rented premises, paying the first quarter's rent, due on 25 December 19-1, £1,200. Other expenditure in the same month was for the purchase of fixed assets for cash, £8,000, and stock £20,000 which was bought on one month's credit.

Kadriye estimates that her other purchases and the sales for the year to 31 December 19-2 will be as follows:

3 months to	Purchases	Sales
	£	£
March 31	12,000	15,000
June 30	18,000	24,000
September 30	21,000	30,000
December 31	15,000	36,000

All purchases and sales will be on one month's credit.

Other expenditure in 19-2 will be as follows:

January 5 Purchase of motor van for cash £5,000; the van is to be depreciated annually at the rate of 20% on cost.

Wages £2,000 per month paid currently.

Kadriye will draw £500 per month for living expenses. She plans to sell her private car in June for £3,500 and to pay the proceeds into the business as additional capital. A friend has also promised to lend the business £6,000 in September 19-2.

Kadriye's bank has agreed to allow overdraft facilities if they are required with interest at 10 per cent per annum. Interest will be debited in the bank statements on the last day of each half year and will be calculated on the average overdraft, if any, for the half year. For this purpose, the overdraft on the last day of the immediately preceding quarter is to be taken as the average for the half year.

REQUIRED

Kadriye's cash budget for the year to 31 December 19-2.

18.6 MASTER BUDGETS

The functional (or operational) budgets are summarised in the master budget which takes the form of a forecast profit and loss account and balance sheet.

In examinations, the preparation of a master budget is often required in conjunction with the preparation of a cash budget.

It is essential to remember the differences between a cash budget and a forecast profit and loss account:

- a cash budget is compiled on a 'cash' basis and includes all receipts and payments, capital as well as revenue. It does not include non-monetary items such as depreciation.
- a forecast profit and loss account is prepared on an accruals basis and includes revenue receipts and payments only. It includes non-monetary items such as depreciation, profits and losses on sales of fixed assets and provisions for bad debts.

18.6.1 EXAMPLE (Cash budget and master budget)

P. Blowers balance sheet at 30 June 19-3 was as follows:

Fixed assets	Cost	Depn	Net
	£	£	£
Equipment	5,000	3,000	2,000
Motor vehicles	8,000	5,000	3,000
	13,000	8,000	5,000
Current assets			
Stock		4,800	
Trade debtors		6,800	
Cash at bank		10,000	
Carried forward		21,600	5,000

	£	£
Brought forward	21,600	5,000
Less Current liabilities		
Trade creditors	3,100	
Net working capital		18,500
		23,500
Financed by Capital account: balance at 1 July 19-2		20,000
add profit for the year		8,500
		28,500
less Drawings		5,000
		23,500

P.Blowers estimates that his purchases and sales for the year to 30 June 19-4 will be as follows:

	Purchases £	Sales £
19-3		
July – September	18,000	33,000
October – December	24,000	51,000
19-4		
January – March	21,000	42,000
April – June	24,000	48,000

P.Blowers receives one month's credit on all purchases and allows one month's credit on all sales.

The following expenses will be incurred in the year to 30 June 19-4:

Rent £800 per quarter payable in advance on 1 January, 1 April, 1 July, 1 October.

Wages £1,800 per month payable currently

On 1 July 19-3 P.Blowers will pay an insurance premium in the sum of £1,500 up to 30 September 19-4. Other expenses will amount to £2,000 per month

P.Blowers will purchase additional equipment on 1 October 19-3 for £3,000.

A van which cost £4,000 and has a written down value at 30 June19-3 of £1,500 will be sold for £1,100 on 1 January 19-4.

A new van will be purchased on 1 October 19-3 for £8,000.

Motor vans are depreciated at $12\frac{1}{2}$% per annum on cost.

Equipment is depreciated by 10% per annum on cost.

P.Blowers will draw £1,000 per month for living expenses.

Stock of goods at 30 June 19-4 was £7,300.

REQUIRED

(a) P.Blowers cash budget for the year to 30 June 19-4 and

(b) A forecast trading and profit and loss account for the year to 30 June 19-4 and a balance sheet as at that date.

ANSWER

(a)

P.Blowers
Cash budget for the year to 30 June 19-4

	19-3		19-4	
	Jul-Sep £	Oct-Dec £	Jan-Mar £	Apr-Jun £
Receipts				
Sales	28,800	45,000	45,000	46,000
Proceeds of sale of van			1,100	
Carried forward	28,800	45,000	46,100	46,000

	£	£	£	£
Brought forward	28,800	45,000	46,100	46,000
Payments				
Purchases	15,100	22,000	22,000	23,000
Rent	800	800	800	800
Wages	5,400	5,400	5,400	5,400
Insurance	1,500			
Other expenses	6,000	6,000	6,000	6,000
Purchase of equipment		3,000		
Purchase of motor van		8,000		
Drawings	3,000	3,000	3,000	3,000
	31,800	48,200	37,200	38,200
Net receipts/(payments)	(3,000)	(3,200)	8,900	7,800
Balance b/f	10,000	7,000	3,800	12,700
Balance c/f	7,000	3,800	12,700	20,500

(b) **Forecast trading and profit and loss account for the year ending 30 June 19-4**

	£	£
Sales		174,000
Less Cost of sales: Stock at 1.7.-3	4,800	
Purchases	87,000	
	91,800	
less Stock at 30.6.-4	7,300	84,500
Gross profit		89,500
less		
Wages	21,600	
Rent	3,200	
Insurance	1,200	
Other expenses	24,000	
Loss on sale of motor van	150	
Depreciation: equipment	725	
motor vehicles	1,500	2,225	52,375
Net profit		37,125

Forecast Balance Sheet as at 30 June 19-4

Fixed assets	Cost £	Depn £	Net £
Equipment	8,000	3,725	4,275
Motor vehicles	12,000	3,750	8,250
	20,000	7,475	12,525
Current assets			
Stock		7,300	
Trade debtors		16,000	
Prepayment (insurance)		300	
Cash at bank		20,500	
		44,100	
Less Current liabilities			
Trade creditors		8,000	36,100
			48,625

Capital account: Balance at 1.7.-3		23,500
Profit for year		37,125
		60,625
less drawings		12,000
		48,625

Tutorial notes

1. Cash budget:

(a) Receipts in July 19-3 will include trade debtors shown in balance sheet at 30 June 19-3.

(b) One third of the sales in each quarter will be received in the following quarter. (Make a note of the receipts outstanding for the June sales for inclusion as trade debtors in the balance sheet.)

(c) Payments for purchases in July 19-3 will be to trade creditors shown in the balance sheet at 30 June 19-3.

(d) One third of purchases in each quarter will be paid for in the following quarter. (Make a note of the outstanding amount for June purchases for inclusion as trade creditors in the June balance sheet.)

(e) Make a note that £300 insurance paid in July 19-3 is to be shown as a prepayment in the balance sheet.

2. Profit and loss account:

(a) Loss on sale of motor van: Net book value at 30 June 19-3 = £1,500; further depreciation for 6 months = £250 making net book value £1,250 at date of sale.

(b) Depreciation of equipment includes depreciation on new equipment for 9 months.

(c) Depreciation of motor vehicles includes depreciation on motor van sold as above plus depreciation on new motor van for 9 months.

18.6.2 EXERCISE (Preparation of cash budget, forecast profit and loss account and balance sheet, and forecast statement of source and application of funds for a limited company)

Courante Ltd.'s balance sheet at 31 December 19-1 is as follows:

Fixed assets	Cost	Depn	Net
	£	£	£
Freehold premises	20,000	4,000	16,000
Plant and machinery	15,000	9,000	6,000
	35,000	13,000	22,000
Current assets			
Stock		12,000	
Trade debtors		17,000	
Cash at bank		9,500	
Administration expenses prepaid		2,400	
		40,900	
less Current liabilities			
Trade creditors	9,000		
Selling and distribution expenses accrued	1,200	10,200	30,700
			52,700
less Long term liabilities: 12 per cent debentures			10,000
			42,700
Share capital and reserves			
Ordinary shares of £1			25,000
General reserve			15,000
Retained profit			2,700
			42,700

Sales and purchases for the four months to 30 April 19-2 are as follows:

	Jan	Feb	Mar	Apr
	£	£	£	£
Sales	25,000	28,000	30,000	33,000
Purchases	10,000	8,000	12,000	15,000

40 per cent of sales are for cash; one month's credit is allowed on the remainder.

One month's credit is allowed on all purchases.

Additional information:

1. Selling and distribution expenses: 10 per cent of sales, payable in following month.
2. Administration expenses: £8,000 per month. Prepaid administration expenses at 30 April 19-2: £1,300.
3. Stock at 30 April 19-2: £9,000.
4. Additional machinery will be purchased on 1 March 19-2 at a cost of £24,000
5. Provision is made yearly for depreciation as follows: freehold premises: 3 per cent on cost; plant and machinery 20 per cent on cost. 50 per cent of all depreciation is charged to selling and distribution expenses and the balance to administration expenses.
6. Debenture interest is payable on 30 June and 31 December.
7. Payment of an interim dividend of 10p a share will be made in April 19-2.
8. It is planned to transfer a further £10,000 to general reserve at 30 April 19-2.

REQUIRED

(a) A cash budget for Courante Ltd. for the four months to 30 April 19-2.

(b) A forecast profit and loss account for the four months to 30 April 19-2 and a forecast balance sheet as at that date.

(c) A forecast statement of source and application of funds for the four months to 30 April 19-2.

18.7 KEY POINTS TO REMEMBER

1. Budgets need present little difficulty if
   (i) The question is read carefully
   (ii) All instructions are followed (tick them as you do them)
   (iii) All calculations are made accurately.

2. Learn the appropriate template to use for each type of budget. Prepare the outline as soon as you have read the question. Leave a few lines so that you can insert additional items at a later stage if you have overlooked any at the start.

3. SHOW ALL WORKINGS. This applies to all answers in examinations.

4. Give every budget a proper heading. This applies to all examination answers.

5. Cash budgets should be summaries of the entries which will be expected to appear in the cash book in the budget period. No other items (e.g.depreciation) should appear.

6. If asked how the liquidity of a business can be improved, make sensible suggestions based on the cash budget. e.g. capital expenditure may be deferred, or assets purchased on credit, or on hire purchase, or leased. Some suggestions may need qualification, e.g. getting debtors to pay more promptly may involve a cost (discounts allowed), or loss of custom. Delaying payment of creditors may result in loss of discounts receivable, stopping of supplies or a requirement to 'pay cash with order' in future. Do not make any suggestions that would be against the public interest or would result in penalties e.g. delaying payment of tax.

7. Forecast profit and loss accounts are compiled in the same way as such statements for past periods but remember the essential differences between a cash budget and a profit and loss account.

COMMON ERRORS
- inclusion of depreciation in cash budgets.
- failure to make any necessary adjustments to the opening bank balance for items occurring before the budget period. (Generally applicable to new business starting up.)
- failure to account for opening debtors, creditors, accruals and prepayments in cash budget.

18.8 EXAMINATION QUESTIONS

QUESTION 1 (JMB June 1987)

'The problem with budgetary control is that it is attempting to satisfy many purposes, some of which conflict. As I see it, a budget is required to co-ordinate future plans, to communicate these within the organization, and to provide information for decision-making and also, to provide a basis for personal motivation and subsequent evaluation of performance.'

You are required to:

(a) explain, with examples, the functions performed by a budget that are referred to in the above quotation;   *(20 marks)*

(b) provide an explanation of why the above functions may conflict in the production of budget information.   *(10 marks)*

(Total 30 marks)

QUESTION 2 (London January 1987)

A company's estimated pattern of costs and revenues for the first four months of 19-7 is as follows:

COSTS AND REVENUES: JANUARY - APRIL 19-7

(£'000)

Month	Sales	Materials	Wages	Overheads
JANUARY	410.4	81.6	16.2	273.6
FEBRUARY	423.6	84.8	16.8	282.4
MARCH	460.8	93.6	18.3	306.7
APRIL	456.3	91.2	18.6	304.5

1. One quarter of the materials are paid for in the month of production and the remainder two months later: deliveries received in November 19-6 were £78,600, and in December 19-6 £74,800.

2. Customers are expected to pay one-third of their debts a month after the sale and the remainder after two months: sales expected for November 19-6 are £398,400, and for December 19-6, £402,600.

3. Old factory equipment is to be sold in February 18-7 for £9,600. Receipt of the money is expected in April 19-7. New equipment will be installed at a cost of £38,000. One half of the amount is payable in March 19-7 and the remainder in August 19-7.

4. Two-thirds of the wages are payable in the month they fall due, and one-third a month later: wages for December 19-6 are estimated at £15,900.

5. £50,000 of total monthly overheads are payable in the month they occur, and the remainder one month later: total overheads for December 19-6 are expected to be £265,200.

6. The opening bank balance at 1 January 19-7 is expected to be an overdraft of £10,600

(a) Using the information above, prepare the firm's cash budget for the period January-April, 19-7.   *(16 marks)*

(b) Provide a statement to show those items in part (a) which would appear in a budgeted balance sheet as at 30 April 18-7.   *(9 marks)*

(Total 25 marks)

QUESTION 3 (Cambridge June 1988)

Peter Green is making plans for his business for the three months ending 30 September 19-8 and, as a result, has prepared the following estimated trading and profit and loss account for that period

	£	£
Sales		130,000
Less: Cost of sales		100,000
Gross profit (carried forward)		30,000

	£	£
Gross profit (brought forward)		30,000
Less: Wages	2,900	
Administrative expenses	3,600	
Depreciation – Motor vehicle	500	7,000
Net profit		23,000

The following additional information has been given:

(a) Sales are expected to arise as follows:

	£
July	26,000
August	39,000
September	65,000

(b) In each month, 50% in value of sales are for cash, the balance is on two months' credit.

(c) The stock in trade at 30 June 19-8 is valued at £10,000; however, it is proposed to increase the quantity of stock held to £20,000 in July 19-8.

(d) All goods purchased and administrative expenses are paid for on a monthly credit basis; wages are paid on a cash basis.

(e) The same rate of gross profit is obtained on all sales.

(f) The balance at bank at 30 June 19-8 is £12,000; there is no cash in hand. At 30 June 19-8, creditors amount to £29,200 (payable in July 19-8), and debtors are £39,000 (£23,000 due July 19-8 and the balance due August 19-8).

(g) Peter Green's cash drawings are expected to be:

	£
July	700
August	900
September	1,000

(h) It can be assumed that all receipts and payments occur at the end of the relevant month; wages are expected to increase by £100 per month in August and administrative expenses are at the same rate throughout the period.

(i) In August, Peter Green will take delivery of a motor van costing £8,000; payment is to be made in two equal instalments on 30 September and 31 October 19-8.

REQUIRED

(a) A cash budget for the three months ending 30 September 19-8, on a month by month basis.

(18 marks)

(b) Explain why it is important to distinguish between revenue expenditure and capital expenditure.

(7 marks)

(Total 25 marks)

QUESTION 4 (WJEC June 1987)

The summarised balance sheet of Newland Traders at 30 May 19-7 was as follows:

	£'000	£'000
Fixed assets at cost		610
Less depreciation		264
		346
Current assets		
Stocks	210	
Debtors	315	
Cash at bank and in hand	48	
	573	
Less Current liabilities		
Creditors	128	445
		791

	£'000
Capital and reserves	
Issued capital	600
General reserve	150
Profit and loss account	41
	791

Selling and materials prices at 30 May 19-7 provide for a gross profit at the rate of 25% of sales.

The creditors at 30 May 19-7 represent purchases for May 19-7, and the debtors the sales for April of £150,000 and May of £165,000.

Estimates of sales and expenditure for the six months to 30 November 19-7 are as follows.

(i) Sales for the period at current prices will be £800,000. Sales for the months of September and October will be twice those of the sales in each of the other months.

(ii) Stock at the end of each month will be the same as at 30 May 19-7 except that at 30 November 19-7 it will be increased to 20% above that level.

(iii) Creditors will be paid one month after the goods are supplied and debtors will pay two months after the goods are supplied.

(iv) Wages and expenses will be £20,000 a month and will be paid in the month in which they are incurred.

(v) Depreciation will be at the rate of £5,000 a month.

(vi) There will be capital expenditure of £80,000 on 1 September 19-7. Depreciation, in addition to that given in (v) above, will be at the rate of 10% per annum on cost.

(vii) There will be no changes in issued capital, general reserve or prices of sales or purchases.

REQUIRED

(i) Sales and purchases budgets and budgeted trading and profit and loss accounts for the six months ended 30 November 19-7.

(ii) A budgeted balance sheet as at 30 November 19-7.

(iii) A cash flow budget for the six months ended 30 November 19-7 indicating whether or not it will be necessary to make arrangements for extra finance and, if so, your recommendation as to what form it should take.

Show all your calculations.

(Total 28 marks)

QUESTION 5 (Oxford June 1988)

Andante Ltd has the following plans for the three months ending 31 August 19-8:

(1)

	June	July	August
Sales in units	2340	2460	2520
Production in units	2500	2400	2450
Selling price £ p.u.	21.50	21.50	22.00
Production Costs:			
Raw materials £ p.u.	9.50	9.50	9.50
Labour £ p.u.	4.60	4.80	4.80
Variable overhead £ p.u.	2.20	2.20	2.20
Purchases of raw materials	£25,000	£24,000	£24,500

(2) Fixed factory overhead will cost £2,375 per month, administrative overhead £1,850 per month and selling and distribution overheads 8% of sales value per month.

(3) At 30 April 19-8 Andante Ltd had a stock of £12,960 raw materials and 190 finished units, valued at factory variable cost of £16.30 p.u. using the FIFO method.

(4) £24,750 raw materials were purchased in May, 2,440 units were produced and 2,420 at £21.50 sold.

(5) Creditors for raw materials are paid in the month following purchase, as is fixed factory overhead, which has remained unchanged in 19-8. Labour, administrative overhead and selling and distribution costs are paid in the month they are incurred, as is 40% of variable factory overhead (the remaining 60% is paid in the following month). Variable costs per unit were unchanged in May 19-8.

278

(6) All sales are on credit. Customers pay in the month following sale and 20% obtain a cash discount of 5% for prompt payment.

(7) The firm has an overdrawn bank balance of £15,376 at 31 May 19-8 and a commitment to reduce this to £10,500 by 31 August 19-8.

You are required to provide

(i) A cash budget for the three months ending 31 August 19-8 *(9 marks)*

(ii) A calculation of the firm's gross profit for the three months ending 31 August 19-8 *(6 marks)*

(iii) A comment on the likelihood of the firm's overdraft reduction being adhered to. *(5 marks)*

(Total 20 marks)

QUESTION 6 (AEB June 1989)

Herbert Limited make a single product, whose unit budget details are as follows:

	£	£
Selling price		30
Less costs		
Direct material	9	
Direct labour	4	
Direct production expenses	6	
Variable selling expenses	4	23
Contribution		7

Additional information.

(1) Unit sales are expected to be :

June	July	August	September	October
1,000	800	400	600	900

(2) Credit sales will account for 60% of total sales. Debtors are expected to pay in the month following sale for which there will be a cash discount of 2%.

(3) Stock levels will be arranged so that production in one month will meet the next month's sales demand.

(4) The purchases of direct materials in one month will just meet the next month's production requirements.

(5) Suppliers of direct materials will be paid in the month following purchase.

(6) Labour costs will be paid in the month in which they are incurred. All other expenses will be paid in the month following that in which they are incurred.

(7) Fixed expenses are £2,000 per month and include £180 for depreciation.

(8) The bank balance at 1 July 19-9 is £3,900 favourable to the business.

REQUIRED

(a) A cash budget for Henry Limited for the three month period ending on 30 September 19-9 showing the balance of cash at the end of each month. *(16 marks)*

(b) List and explain **three** ways in which the preparation of a cash flow budget could be of advantage to the management of Herbert Limited. *(6 marks)*

(Total 22 marks)

QUESTION 7 (AEB June 1989)

Axon and Barrow, an old established partnership, produced the following summarised final accounts for the year ended 30 April 19-9.

Trading and profit and loss, and appropriation accounts

	£'000	£'000
Sales		350
Less cost of goods sold:		
Opening stock	20	
Purchases	210	
Carried forward	230	350

	£'000	£'000
Brought forward	230	350
Closing stock	15	215
Gross profit		135
Administration expenses	38	
Selling and distribution expenses	10	
Financial charges	6	
Depreciation on fixed assets	15	69
Net profit		66
Share of profit: Axon	33	
Barrow	33	66

Balance sheet as at 30 April 19-9

	£'000	£'000		£'000	£'000
Fixed assets at cost	300		Capital accounts		
Less aggregate			Axon	150	
depreciation	50	250	Barrow	50	200
Current assets			Current accounts		
Stock	15		Axon	31	
Trade debtors	35		Barrow	19	50
Balance at bank	40	90			250
			Long term bank loan		
			at 10% per annum		60
			Current liabilities		
			Trade creditors	20	
			Accrued expenses	10	30
		340			340

The partnership accountant suggested that since the business had grown significantly, the partners would be wise to prepare annual forecast budget accounts.

The first year's budget forecast was to be based on the following information:

(1) The partnership agreement was to be modified as follows:

   (i)   Interest on fixed capitals at 9% per annum is to be allowed. Previously this did not form part of the agreement.

   (ii) Barrow is to be paid a salary at 3% of the projected annual turnover.

   (iii) There are no other changes in the partnership agreement.

(2) Total annual sales are forecast to increase to £550,000, with a gross profit margin of 40%.

(3) It is anticipated that the closing stock at 30 April 19-0 will be £45,000.

(4) It is expected that increased efficiency will allow administrative expenses to be held at the 19-8/-9 level.

(5) Selling and distribution expenses are expected to be 5% of turnover.

(6) The existing freehold premises (cost £100,000) are to be re-furbished and extended. The capital cost will be £60,000. No depreciation is provided on the premises.

No new other fixed assets will be purchased, and the present depreciation charge of 10% per annum on cost will continue.

(7) In order to finance the expansion of the business the following loans were negotiated:

   (i)   On 1 August 19-9 the long term loan is to be increased to £90,000 with a reduction in the interest charge to 8% per annum.

(ii)   The partnership's bank have agreed to an overdraft limit of £50,000, and the projected overdrawn balance as at 30 April 19-0 will be £45,000. Overdraft interest charges are expected to be £5,000 for the year.

(8)   At 30 April 19-0 it is forecast that £39,000 will be held in short term investments pending further capital expenditure.

(9)   Anticipated drawings for the year:

Axon £45,000   Barrow £48,500

(10)   Other forecast figures as at 30 April 19-0.

	£'000
Trade debtors	60
Trade creditors	15
Accrued expenses (other than interest charges)	1
Expenses in advance	3
Cash in hand	5

(11)   All bank interest charges will be paid on 1 May 19-0.

REQUIRED

(a)   Forecast trading, profit and loss, and appropriation accounts for the year ending 30 April 19-0.

(9 marks)

(b)   A forecast balance sheet as at 30 April 19-0.

(10 marks)

(c)   List six advantages that can arise from the introduction of a system of budgeting.

(6 marks)

(Total 25 marks)

19 STANDARD COST AND VARIANCE ANALYSIS

Questions on standard costs and variance analysis cover:-
- explanation of the concept of standard costing
- advantages of standard costing
- flexing budgets
- calculating sales, direct labour, direct materials and overhead variances
- explanations for variances and possible relationships between different kinds of variances

---

STANDARD COSTS

Definitions

Standard Costs

Predetermined calculations of the components which contribute to the costs of a business under given conditions.

Standard Costing

The use of standard costs, principally in the preparation of budgets for the purpose of controlling operations and functions of a business through variance analysis. Standard costs are also used in the production of estimates, quotations, etc.

Standard Time

The time, in minutes or hours, in which a given quantity of work should be completed. In addition to the basic time required for completing the work, allowance is included in the standard for contingencies and permitted relaxation. Standard time is, paradoxically, a measure of work, not of time. Standard hours produced = SHP

Overhead Absorption Rate (OAR)

Overheads are 'absorbed' into total costs by the application of an Overhead Absorption Rate. The rate is calculated by dividing period budgeted overheads by the Standard Hours (or by some other measurement of activity such as units or weights produced) for the period.

Variance

The difference between actual revenue or costs and budgeted (or planned or standard) revenue or costs.

Variance Analysis

The examination of variances using calculations to discover the factors which have contributed to the variances, and the magnitude and nature of those contributions. Variances are described as 'favourable' (F) if they contribute to the profitability of a business. If they diminish the profitability, they are described as 'adverse' (A). These are the usual descriptions, but others may be used in practice.

Flexible Budget

An indispensible tool for variance analysis; flexible budgets recognise the different behaviours of fixed and variable costs at varying levels of activity.

Setting standards.

1. Standards must be reasonable; possible of attainment under conditions of an acceptable degree of efficiency.
2. Standards based upon ideal conditions will be regarded as normally unattainable, and disregarded by those who are meant to be achieving them.
3. If standards are set too low, they conceal inefficient performance and offer no challenge to staff to give of their best efforts.

19.1 FLEXING THE BUDGET

Comparison of actual performance with budget requires comparison of 'like with like'. If actual activity differs from budgeted activity, the budget must be 'flexed' to produce one for the actual level of activity.

19.1.1 EXAMPLE 1 (Flexing a simple budget)

A budget has been prepared for the production of 1,000 units of X in March. The actual output for March was 1,100 units.

Using the budget given below for the production of 1,000 units you are required to flex the budget for 1,100 units of X.

		Budget for 1,000 units	Budget for 1,100 units.
		£	£
Direct materials		6,000	6,600
Direct labour		15,000	16,500
Production overheads	– variable	9,000	9,900
	– fixed	22,000	22,000
Selling and distribution expenses	– variable	10,000	11,000
	– fixed	20,000	20,000
Administration costs			
	– fixed	8,000	8,000
		90,000	94,000

EXAMPLE 2 (A slightly more difficult example)

A budget was prepared for the production of Bantam Bits at output levels of 1,000 and 2,000 Bits respectively, as shown below. Actual production was 1,800 Bits.

You are required to prepare a budget for the production of 1,800 Bantam Bits.

ANSWER	Budget (1,000)	Budget (2,000)	Budget (1,800)
	£	£	£
Direct materials	21,000	42,000	37,800
Direct labour	35,000	70,000	63,000
Production overheads	60,000	80,000	76,000
Selling and distribution	45,000	60,000	57,000
Administration	29,000	29,000	29,000
	190,000	281,000	262,800

Tutorial note: Production overheads and selling and distribution expenses do not vary proportionately to production. The increases in these costs for an additional 1,000 units are: Production costs £20,000; selling and distribution £15,000. These are the variable elements in these costs per 1,000 units. The balances of £40,000 of Production overheads and £30,000 of selling and distribution expenses are fixed costs.

Therefore:

Production costs for 1,800 Bantam Bits = £40,000 + (1.8 × £20,000) = £76,000

Selling and distribution = £30,000 + (1.8 × £15,000) = £57,000

19.1.2 EXERCISE 1 (Flexing a budget)

The budget for the production of 200,000 packets of 'Brekkinuts' was as follows:

	£'000
Direct materials	10
Direct labour	12
Production overheads – variable	5
– fixed	6
Carried forward	33

	£'000
Brought forward	33
Selling and distribution	11
Administration	8
	52

10% of the Selling and distribution expenses are variable; all Administration costs are fixed.

The actual production of 'Brekkinuts' was 190,000 packets.

You are required to prepare a budget for the production of 190,000 packets of 'Brekkinuts'.

19.2   SALES VARIANCES

The variances are-

Volume variance: Master budget sales – Flexible budget sale (MBS – FBS)

Price variance: Flexible budget sales – actual sales (FBS – AS)

19.2.1 EXAMPLE A budget for the sales of Product 'Q' was as follows:

1,000 units of Product 'Q' at £12 per unit: £12,000

1,300 units were sold for total revenue of £15,200.

Find the volume and price variances for the actual sales.

ANSWER

Flexed budget: 1,300 units at £12 each = £15,600

Volume variance

	£	
MBS	12,000	
FBS	15,600	
	3,600	(F)

Price variance

	£	
FBS	15,600	
AS	15,200	
	400	(A)

Summary:	£	
Volume variance	3,600	(F)
Price variance	400	(A)
Total variance (MBS - AS)	3,200	(F)

19.2.2 EXERCISE 1. (Calculation of sales variances.)

Reflections Ltd. produce 'Car Shine' polish. The budgeted sales for 19-2 were 150,000 tins at £3 a tin.

Actual sales of 'Car Shine' polish for 19-2 were 148,600 tins which produced total revenue of £448,950.

REQUIRED

Calculations of the sales variances for the sales of 'Car Shine' polish for the year 19-2.

19.3   TOTAL VARIANCES – COSTS

TOTAL COST VARIANCE: Total costs per Master Budget (MBTC)
                                            less Actual total costs (ATC)

The total cost variance will be explained in broad terms by the following variances, which will in turn be explained by sub-variances.

QUANTITY VARIANCE: Total costs per master budget (MBTC)
                                            less Total costs per flexible budget (FBTC)

Once the total cost and quantity variances have been calculated, all the other variances will be calculated using the flexed budget. There will be no further use for the master budget as far as the calculations are concerned.

In all the calculations of variances that follow, deduct 'actual' from 'budget'; a positive remainder will indicate a favourable variance, and a negative remainder will indicate an adverse balance.

TOTAL DIRECT LABOUR VARIANCE:
Direct labour per flexed budget (FBDL)
less Actual direct labour (ADL)

TOTAL DIRECT MATERIALS VARIANCE:
Direct materials per flexed budget (FBDM)
less Actual direct materials (ADM)

* TOTAL OVERHEAD VARIANCE:
Total overheads per flexed budget (FBTO)
less Actual total overheads (ATO)

* This variance may be split between fixed overhead variance (FBTFO–ATFO) and variable overhead variance (FBTVO - ATVO)

TOTAL COST VARIANCE =
Quantity variance (F) or (A)
plus or minus Total Labour variance (F) or (A)
plus or minus Total Direct Materials variance (F) or (A)
plus or minus Total Overhead variance(s) (F) or (A)

19.3.1 EXAMPLE

Meniss Ltd. manufactures skateboards. The budget for March19-3 for the production of 4,000 skateboards was as follows:

	£
Direct materials	5,000
Direct labour	12,000
Overheads - variable	6,000
fixed	8,000
	31,000

4,400 skateboards were produced in March 19-3 and the actual expenditure was as follows:

	£
Direct materials	5,600
Direct labour	13,100
Overheads - variable	6,800
fixed	7,750
	33,250

You are required to calculate the main variances for March 19-3.

ANSWER

Flexed budget for 4,400 skateboards:	£
Direct materials	5,500
Direct labour	13,200
Overheads – variable	6,600
fixed	8,000
	33,300

Total cost variance (MBTC – ATC) = £(31,000 – 33,250) =	£2,250	(A)
Quantity variance (MBTC – FBTC) = £(31,000 – 33,300) =	£2,300	(A)
Total direct materials variance = (FBDM – ADM) = £(5,500 – 5,600) =	£100	(A)

Total direct labour variance = (FBDL – ADL) = £(13,200 – 13,100) =	£100	(F)
Total variable overheads variance = (FBTVO – ATVO) = £(6,600 – 6,800) =	£200	(A)
Total fixed overheads variance = (FBTFO – ATFO) = £(8,000 – 7,750) =	£250	(F)
	£2,250	(A)

19.3.2 EXERCISE (Calculation of total variances)

Laser, Digit and Co. produce compact disc players. Their budget for April 19-4 and the actual outturn were as follows:

	Budgeted production 1,500 players	Actual 1,800 players
	£	£
Direct materials	90,000	110,000
Direct labour	45,000	52,500
Overheads – variable	42,000	55,000
fixed	72,000	70,000
	249,000	287,500

REQUIRED

An analysis of the total cost variance for the production of CD players in April 19-4.

19.4 SUB-VARIANCES

Sub-variances are used to analyse total variances to provide further information to management.

As with total variances, deduct 'actuals' from budget in every case; then positive remainders = favourable variances, negative remainders = adverse variances.

DIRECT LABOUR SUB-VARIANCES

Standard rate = SR; Actual rate = AR; Standard hours = SH; Actual hours = AH.

DIRECT LABOUR EFFICIENCY VARIANCE: (SH – AH) × SR

DIRECT LABOUR RATE VARIANCE: (SR – AR) × AH

EXAMPLE

Direct labour budget for 100 units = 4 hours per unit at £6 an hour. Actual time taken to produce 100 units was 385 hours; actual rate paid = £6.15 an hour.

Budgeted direct labour cost = 100 × £24 =	£2,400	
Actual direct labour cost = 385 × £6.15 =	£2,367.75	
Total direct labour variance =	£32.25	(F)
Direct labour efficiency variance = (400 – 385) × £6 =	£90	(F)
Direct labour rate variance = £(6 - 6.15) × 385 =	£57.75	(A)
as above	£32.25	(F)

DIRECT MATERIAL SUB-VARIANCES

Standard price = SP; Actual price = AP; Standard usage = SU; Actual usage = AU

DIRECT MATERIAL USAGE VARIANCE: (SU – AU) × SP

DIRECT MATERIAL PRICE VARIANCE: (SP – AP) × AU

EXAMPLE

The direct materials budget for 100 units of production requires 10 kilos of 'X' per unit produced. 'X' costs £20 per kilo. Actual production was 105 units and 1,058 kilos of 'X' was used at a cost of £19.80 per kilo.

Budgeted direct material cost = 100 × 10 × £20 =	£20,000	
'Flexed' budget: 105 × 10 × £20 =	£21,000	
Actual direct material cost = 1058 × £19.80 =	£20,948.40	
Total direct material variance =	£51.60	(F)
Direct material usage variance = (1,050 – 1,058) × £20 =	£160	(A)
Direct material price variance = £(20 – 19.80) × 1,058 =	£211.60	(F)

OVERHEAD SUB VARIANCES

(SHP= standard hours produced; OAR = Overhead absorption rate)

When fixed and variable overheads are treated together:

Total overhead variance =   Overhead expenditure variance

       + Overhead efficiency variance

       + Overhead volume variance

Overhead expenditure variance =   Actual total overheads

       – (Flexed) Budgeted total overheads

Overhead volume variance =   (Flexed) Budgeted total overheads

       – Actual hours worked × OAR

Overhead efficiency variance =   Actual hours worked × OAR

       – SHP × OAR

19.4.1 EXAMPLE 1 (Calculation of total and sub variances for materials and labour)

Ebor plc manufactures 'After-U' chocolates. The budget for production costs for 25,000 boxes of chocolates for June 19-5 was as follows:

	£
Direct materials (10,000 kilos at £2.50 per kilo)	25,000
Direct labour (1,000 hours at £5 an hour)	5,000
	30,000

Actual results were as follows:

No. of boxes of chocolates produced:	27,500
	£
Direct materials (11,300 kilos at £2.48)	28,024
Direct labour (980 hours at £5.20 an hour)	5,096
	33,120

REQUIRED

The following variances: Total cost, quantity, total materials, total labour, materials usage, materials price, labour efficiency and labour rate.

ANSWER

Flexed budget for 27,500 boxes.	£	
Direct materials (11,000 kilos at £2.50 per kilo)	27,500	
Direct labour (1,100 hours at £5 an hour)	5,500	
	33,000	
Total budget variance £(30,000 – 33,120) =	£3,120	(A)
Quantity variance £(30,000 – 33,000) =	£3,000	(A)
Total materials variance £(27,500 – 28,024)	£524	(A)
Total labour variance £(5,500 – 5,096)	£404	(F)
as above	£3,120	(A)
Materials variances		
Materials usage variance (11,000 – 11,300) × £2.50	£750	(A)
Materials price variance £(2.50 – 2.48) × 11,300	£226	(F)
Total materials variance as above	£524	(A)
Labour variances		
Labour efficiency variance (1,100 – 980) × £5	£600	(F)
Labour rate variance £(5.00 – 5.20) × 980	£196	(A)
Total labour variance as above	£404	(F)

EXAMPLE 2 (Calculation of overhead variances)

The Top Hat Company prepared the following overheads budget for March 19-1:

Variable overheads	£12,750
Fixed overheads	£16,000
Hours to be worked	5,000
Standard hours of production	5,000

At the end of March 19-1 the following were the actual results for the month

Variable overheads	£13,220
Fixed overheads	£16,280
Actual hours worked	4,850
Standard hours produced	4,900

REQUIRED

The overhead expenditure, volume and efficiency variances and the total overhead variance.

ANSWER

$$\text{Overhead absorption rate (OAR)} = \text{Total overheads/SHP} = \frac{28,750}{5,000} = £5.75$$

$$\text{Flexed overhead budget: Variable overhead absorption rate (VOAR)} = \frac{£12,750}{5,000} = £2.55$$

overheads = £[16,000 + (4850 × 2.55)] = £28,367.50

Expenditure variance £(29,500 – 28,367.50) =	£1,132.50	(A)
Volume variance £[28,367.50 – (4,850 × 5.75)]		
= £(28,367.50 – 27,887.50) =	£480	(A)
Efficiency variance £[27,887.50 – (4,900 × 5.75)]		
= £(27,887.50 – 28,175) =	£287.50	(F)
Total overhead variance	£1,325	(A)

19.4.2 EXERCISE 1. (For practice in calculating variances)

P.A.M. Sportsgear Ltd. manufactures 'Pulchra' Keep Fit machines.
The standard cost for one machine is:

	£
Direct materials (14 kilos at £6 per kilo)	84
Direct labour (6 hours at £10 per hour)	60
Production overheads	36
	180

25% of the production overheads are variable and the standard costs are based on budgeted production of 600 machines per month.

In October, 650 machines were made and the actual costs for the month were:

	£
Direct materials (8950 kilos at £7.15 per kilo)	63,992.50
Direct labour (3,850 hours at £10.15 per hour)	39,077.50
Production overheads (Fixed: £16,000)	22,000.00
	£125,070.00

REQUIRED

Produce a table showing all the main and sub-variances, and reconcile them.

EXERCISE 2. (Calculation of overhead variances)

The following budget was produced for November 19-3:

Variable overheads	£24,640
Fixed overheads	£38,080
Hours to be worked	6,400
Standard hours of production	6,400

The actual results for November 19-3 were

Variable overheads	£25,200
Fixed overheads	£39,250
Hours actually worked	6,600
Standard hours produced	6,800

You are required to calculate the expenditure, volume, efficiency and total overhead variances for November 19-3.

19.5   EXPLANATIONS FOR VARIANCES

When required to suggest causes of variances in examination questions, make sure your suggestions are reasonable and avoid making assertions which cannot be substantiated from information supplied in the questions. Variance analysis, particularly at the stage required at this level of study, only indicates areas where management should direct their further attention in order to decide what corrective action needs to be taken.

It is important to realise the possible inter-relationships between different variances.

A common cause of variances unfortunately lies in the fact that all too often there are inherent errors in the budget preparation.A favourable labour rate variance may arise because of the employment of a lower grade of labour than that embodied in the budget; but that may be more than offset by adverse labour efficiency and materials usage variances.

A favourable materials price variance may indicate that materials have been purchased 'on the cheap'; the materials in question may prove to be sub-standard as a result, which may reflect in a substantial adverse materials usage variance and an adverse labour efficiency variance.

An adverse labour rate variance may be the result of a wage award which was not foreseen when the budget was prepared. This is most unlikely to be reflected in the workers' performance and would be unlikely, in itself, to reflect in other variances. But if the adverse variance is caused by the employment of more highly skilled workers than those envisaged in the budget, their improved performance may be expected to show in other favourable variances (e.g. usage, efficiency).

A little imagination is helpful when commenting on variances, but the comments must stand up to reason, in the context of the facts, or absence of facts, in the question.

It is important that management be informed about variances as soon as possible after the event in order that they can take necessary remedial action without delay.

'Management by crisis' applies to managers who spend their time 'fighting fires' instead of 'preventing fires'. They are unaware of approaching difficulties until they are hit by crises, and then have to spend all their time and energy getting out of the difficulties; by which time the business has suffered.

Management by exception. Too much detailed information given to managers may be counter productive. They need not know specially about items that are favourable compared with budget; but they do need to know about those that are adversely deviating from budget so that they can concentrate on the important matters that require their particular expertise. It may be desirable, in fact, not to report any variance which is not really significant.

Permanent, significant changes in factors upon which a budget is based may require that the budget be revised; an out-of-date budget is of no use to management.

19.6   KEY POINTS TO REMEMBER

1.   Standard costs are predetermined costs which are possible of attainment under conditions of an acceptable degree of efficiency.

2. Standard costs are used in the preparation of budgets and in preparing quotations for contracts.

3. Flexible budgets recognise the different behaviours of fixed and variable costs as activity levels vary, and in that way, allow actual performance to be compared with budget at various levels of activity and meaningful variances to be calculated.

4. It may be necessary to flex the budget in examination questions.

5. Memorise all the variances covered in this chapter and the method of calculating each one.

6. Be prepared, not only to suggest reasons for variances, but also to say how they may relate to each other.

7. Variances indicate to management areas where further enquiry may be necessary before any decision can be made about remedial action to be taken.

COMMON ERRORS
- failure to flex budgets
- inability to calculate variances
- inadequate, poorly expressed explanations as to possible causes of variances and lack of appreciation of the relationships between variances.

19.7 EXAMINATION QUESTIONS

QUESTION 1 (London June 1987)

(a) Examine three different levels of activity which may be used when setting activity levels for standard costing. Identify the strengths and weaknesses of each. *(7 marks)*

(b) Calculate material and labour variances from the following:

	Standard	Actual
Price of material (£ tonne)	6.40	6.30
Usage of material (tonnes)	570	610
Wage rate (£ per hour)	3.42	3.22
Direct labour hours	120	140

(4 marks)

(c) State with reasons those variances in (b) above which the production manager may be able to control. *(4 marks)*

(Total 15 marks)

QUESTION 2 (London January 1989)

(a) Brunswick Products uses a system of standard costing. The following details relate to Dec. 19-8:

	Department	
	Blasting	Painting
Direct labour hours worked	3,400	9,200
Direct wages earned	£12,648	£38,272
Units produced	900	2,400
Standard hours per unit	4	3
Standard hourly wage rate	£3.70	£4.00

For each department, you are required to calculate:
- (i) the standard direct labour cost per unit;
- (ii) the direct wages (direct labour) variance;
- (iii) the direct wages *rate* variance;
- (iv) the direct wages *efficiency* variance. *(8 marks)*

(b) What do the answers to (a) above indicate to the production manager of Brunswick Products about the performance of the two departments and why? *(7 marks)*

(Total 15 marks)

QUESTION 3 (JMB June 1987)

The Delta Company makes one product and the following relates to production during April.

	Actual Cost	Finished goods During April at Standard Cost	Work in Progress at the end of April at Standard Cost
	£	£	£
Direct Materials used	204,000	200,000	2,500
Direct Labour	52,000	50,000	625
Fixed Overheads	52,000	50,000	250
Variable Overheads	102,500	100,000	1,250
	410,500	400,000	4,625

There was no opening stock of work in progress at the beginning of April. The standard cost per unit is:

	£	
Direct Material	10.00	(Standard Cost £2 per lb.)
Direct Labour	2.50	(Standard Cost £1.25 per hour)
Fixed Overheads	2.50	(£1 per £ of direct labour))
Variable Overheads	5.00	(£2 per £ of direct labour)
	20.00	

During April 104,000 lbs. of material were used and 41,000 direct labour hours were worked.

You are required to calculate:

(a) the material price variance and usage variance;   *(6 marks)*
(b) the labour rate variance and efficiency variance   *(6 marks)*
(c) the total fixed overhead variance   *(4 marks)*
(d) the total overhead variance   *(4 marks)*

(Total 20 marks)

QUESTION 4 (JMB June 1988)

Alpha Company Limited operates a standard costing system. One of the recently recruited production staff does not understand how a standard costing system operates.

You have been given the following information with regard to the 'deluxe model' of the company's product range.

Standards per deluxe product
Direct Materials   4 kilos at £1.50 per kilo
Direct Labour   2 hours at £3.20 per hour

Information relating to the previous month
Number of products produced   38,000 (units)
Direct Materials: purchased 180,000 kilos for use in production
            150,000 kilos   £252,000
Direct Labour: 78,000 hours worked for   £273,000

There was no work in progress at the beginning or end of the month.

You are required to:

(a) calculate:

   (i)   the material price variance,
   (ii)   the material usage variance,
   (iii) the labour rate variance,
   (iv)   the labour efficiency variance;   *(10 marks)*

(b) explain the meaning, potential significance and limitations of the variances, as calculated in your answer to part (a) above, to the recently recruited member of the production staff.   *(10 marks)*

(Total 20 marks)

QUESTION 5 (WJEC June 1987)

Describe the cost control features that standard costing and budgetary control have in common and the ways in which standard costing and budgetary control differ from each other. *(18 marks)*

QUESTION 6 (AEB November 1987)

RGK Ltd. commenced business as a manufacturer of a single product on 1 July 198-6. At the request of the managing director the firm's cost clerk operated a system of standard costs for the control of the direct material and direct labour costs.

The following information was available on 30 June 19-7 the end of the first year of its manufacturing operations:

(1) **Standard Unit Costs**

Direct material	2 kg at £3 per kg.
Direct labour	30 mins. per unit at £6 per hour

Actual Unit Costs

Direct material	1.8 kg at £3.10 per kg.
Direct labour	35 mins. per unit at £6.50 per hour

(2) **Balances as at 30 June 19-7**

	£
Direct expenses	80,000
Maintenance expenses	40,000
Depreciation: plant and machinery	30,000
Factory rent paid	15,000
Wages: maintenance labour	16,000
Other fixed factory overhead	20,500
Selling and distribution expenses	31,000
Administration expenses	45,000

(3) The firm achieved its production budget target of 50,000 units. Of this output 40,000 units were sold at £20 per unit.

There were no closing stocks of raw materials or work-in-progress.

(4) The following expense adjustments were necessary:

   (i)   the factory rent had been paid for a period of fifteen months commencing on 1 July 19-6.

   (ii) wages were owing for maintenance labour £3,700.

   (iii) administration expenses owing were £2,100.

(5) The firm valued its stock of finished units at prime cost.

REQUIRED

(a) A manufacturing, trading and profit and loss account for RGK Ltd. for the year ended 30 June 19-7.
(12 marks)

(b) Calculate the total direct material and total direct labour variances. Analyse these variances to provide the managing director of the company with management information on the use of the direct materials and direct labour.
(6 marks)

(c) If the managing director's primary objective is the maximisation of profit, explain why a policy of calculating the variances on an annual basis is inadequate.
(7 marks)

(Total 25 marks)

QUESTION 7 (AEB November 1988)

Scotia Ltd. manufactures a toy which is produced by cutting shapes from plastic sheeting. A system of budgetary control and standard costing is in operation and the following information is available for period 6, 19-8:

(1) Standard unit product cost

	£
Direct material	1.00
Direct wages	0.68
Carried forward	1.68

	£
Brought forward	1.68
Production overhead	1.60
Total standard cost of production	3.28

The budgeted production for period 6 was 17,500 units.

(2)   Standard unit cost specification

Direct material: 0.25 sq.metres at £4.00 per square metre

Direct labour: 0.20 hours at £3.40 per direct labour hour.

(3)   Production overhead details

All production overhead is fixed and the following variances have been established for period 6:

	£	**Comments**
Efficiency variance	1,200	favourable
Activity/volume variance	4,000	adverse
Capacity variance	5,200	adverse
Expenditure variance	1,480	adverse

(4)   Actual production data for period 6

Production, in units	15,000
Production overhead incurred	£29,480
Direct wages paid	2850 hours at £3.80 per hour
Direct material used	3,900 square metres at £3.60 per square metre.

REQUIRED

(a)   Outline the benefits to Scotia Ltd. of a system of budgetary control and standard costing.   *(5 marks)*

(b)   A computation of the overall direct labour total variance for period 6 analysed into:

(i)   efficiency variance

(ii)   rate variance   *(4 marks)*

(c)   A computation of the direct material total variance for period 6 analysed into:

(i)   usage variance

(ii)   price variance   *(4 marks)*

(d)   Outline possible reasons for each of the variances calculated in (b) and (c).   *(4 marks)*

(e)   Discuss possible inter-relationships between the material, labour and fixed overhead variances.

(6 marks)

(Total 25 marks)

QUESTION 8   (AEB November 1989)

Dour Ltd. manufactures moulded furniture including chairs for general purpose use. These chairs are manufactured from a chemical mixture purchased in a prepared state. Details of the contribution made by these chairs to the overall company results for the year ended 31 October 19-9 were:

**Contribution statement for chairs for
the year ended 31 October 19-9**

	£	£
Sales		112,500
less variable costs		
Raw materials	55,000	
Direct labour	26,000	81,000
Contribution		£31,500

Additional information.

(1)   There were no opening or closing stocks of chairs.

(2)   The budget and standard cost details prepared prior to 1 November 19-8 revealed:

(i)   budgeted sales of chairs 18,000 at £8.00 each:

(ii)   each chair should take 3 kg of chemical mixture at £1.00 per kg.

(iii)   each chair should take 20 minutes of direct labour time;

(iv)   the direct labour rate per hour was £6.00.

(3) In investigating the actual results for the year ended 31 October 19-9 the following information came to light:

    (i)   15,000 chairs were sold;

    (ii)   44,000 kg of raw material was used;

    (iii) 4,000 hours of direct labour time was clocked.

REQUIRED

(a) Calculate the overall sales variance for the year ended 31 October 19-9.   *(2 marks)*

(b) Calculate the overall labour variance for the year ended 31 October 19-9 analysing it into:

    (i)   rate variance

    (ii)   efficiency variance   *(6 marks)*

(c) Calculate the overall material variance for the year ended 31 October 19-9 analysing it into:

    (i)   price variance;

    (ii)   usage variance   *(6 marks)*

(d) Prepare a statement that shows the budgeted contribution for the year ended 31 October 19-9.

(4 marks)

(e) Examine the variances calculated in (a), (b) and (c) above and give possible reasons for each.

(7 marks)

(Total 25 marks)

QUESTION 9   (London June 1987)

(a) What is meant by (i) management by exception and (ii) management by crisis?   *(8 marks)*

(b) Discuss how far standard costing might be viewed as (i) management by exception and (ii) management by crisis.   *(12 marks)*

(Total 20 marks)

20 CAPITAL EXPENDITURE APPRAISAL

Questions on this topic require:-

- an appreciation of the particular nature of capital expenditure and the importance of basing capital expenditure decisions on as much information as possible
- an understanding of profitability, risk and the time-value of money in relation to capital expenditure
- ability to calculate accounting rate of return(ARR), payback period, net present value(NPV) and Internal Rate of Return (IRR)
- critical analysis of the various appraisal methods used – recognition of the non-financial factors which may affect capital expenditure decisions

20.1   CAPITAL EXPENDITURE

(i)   Capital expenditure is expenditure on fixed assets (including additions to fixed assets) which is intended to benefit future periods.

(ii)   It usually involves very large sums of money.

(iii)   In the case of the construction of very large assets such as factories, ships, bridges, oil rigs, etc., the expenditure may be committed for 20, 50 or more years ahead.

(iv)   Capital expenditure may well decide the 'shape' (i.e. the location, size, pattern of operations, efficiency, ability to compete in the market, etc.) of a business for a very long time.

(v)   Errors of judgement made in capital expenditure decisions cannot easily be reversed, and may indeed be irreversible. The expenditure may be irretrievably lost.

(vi)   It is therefore particularly important that as much information as possible should be available to management to enable it to make prudent capital expenditure decisions.

(vii)   Some pieces of information provided for management may contradict other information because the different methods used to provide the information assess the proposed expenditure from different viewpoints. It is then that management judgement is required to decide how much weight should be given to each piece of information.

(viii) Management often have to take non-financial information into account. Capital expenditure may be necessary even if it will not in itself be profitable; this will be true when the expenditure is required simply to preserve the business. For instance, a factory which is polluting the atmosphere with obnoxious fumes, or a river with effluent, risks being closed down by environmental authorities unless it spends money on abating the nuisance. Health and Safety at Work legislation may force a firm to spend money on making its premises and machinery safe if it is not to be threatened with closure by Government Inspectors. Profitability is not a prime consideration in these cases.

20.2   ACCOUNTING RATE OF RETURN (ARR) (Also known as Return on Capital Employed (ROCE))

Profitability is measured by calculating expected profit from a project as a percentage of the capital expenditure involved.

It must be emphasised that profit for this purpose is the <u>additional</u> profit that will be earned by the business, and the capital expenditure is the <u>additional</u> capital required for the project.

The return on capital from the project will be compared with the return being earned on the capital already invested in the business. For example, if a business is earning a profit of 20% on its capital, it will not be particularly interested in a new product which will earn a profit of only 15% on the capital required to produce the new product, because the new product will dilute present profitability.

20.2.1 EXAMPLE (A calculation of the accounting rate of return)Venture Ltd. presently earns a return on its capital of 18%.

It proposes to manufacture and market a new product, Truveen.

The manufacture of Truveen will require the purchase of a new machine at a cost of £100,000 and additional working capital of £40,000.

Sales of Truveen are expected to be £66,000 per annum. The cost of manufacture will be £25,000 per annum. Selling and distribution costs will amount to £3,000 per annum. There will be no additional administration expenses.

Venture Ltd. depreciates its machinery at the rate of 10 % on cost each year.

REQUIRED

(a) Calculate the accounting rate of return expected from Truveen.

(b) State, with your reasons, whether or not Venture Ltd. should proceed to make and market Truveen.

(c) Your views on the advantages and disadvantages of using the accounting rate of return to assess capital expenditure.

ANSWER

(a)

Venture Ltd.
Statement of profitability of Truveen (annual)

	£	£
Sales		66,000
less Cost of manufacture	25,000	
Selling and distribution	3,000	
Depreciation	10,000	38,000
Net profit		28,000
Additional capital employed:	£	
Machinery	100,000	
Additional working capital	40,000	
	140,000	

Accounting rate of return: $\dfrac{28,000}{140,000} \times 100 = 20\%$

(b) Venture Ltd. may proceed to produce and market Truveen as the accounting rate of return at 20% is greater than its present rate of return on capital employed of 18%. This is subject to any other factors which are not discoverable from the question.

(c)

Advantages:

1. Management can compare the expected profitability of a project with the present profitability of the business.

2. ARR is easy to calculate

Disadvantages:

1. ARR is based on 'average annual profit' which may not be typical of any year.

2. The timing of cash inflows and outflows is ignored. (Obviously, the earlier cash comes in, and the later cash goes out, the better.)

3. ARR does not show whether, or how soon, the net receipts will cover the initial outlay; it ignores the risk factor.

4. ARR ignores the time-value of money.

5. 'Profit' cannot be defined objectively. Depreciation, provisions for bad debts etc. are subjective judgements. Profit may be before or after tax. The timing of cash flows is more objective.

6. There is no commonly accepted method of calculating capital employed. It may or may not include additional working capital. It may be based upon the initial expenditure on the project, or it may be the average capital employed.

7. ARR takes no account of the duration of the project.

20.2.2 EXERCISE (Use of ARR to compare projects)

A company is considering whether to invest in project A, project B, or project C. It will be unable to invest in more than one of those projects. (i.e. the projects are mutually exclusive). Each project will entail an initial outlay of £150,000.

Forecast profits:		Project A	Project B	Project C
		£	£	£
Year	1	15,000	8,000	8,000
	2	15,000	12,000	12,000
	3	15,000	20,000	15,000
	4	15,000	30,000	20,000

The company is presently earning a return of 10% on capital 60,000   70,000   55,000.

REQUIRED

Calculate the Accounting Rate of Return for each project and comment on which project you consider the company should adopt.

20.3   PAYBACK PERIOD

Risk is an important factor to be considered in capital expenditure decisions. The sooner the outlay on a project is covered by the inflow of cash, the better; this is the payback period. A long payback period increases the risk that the outlay will not be recouped.

The payback period is measured in years. Only cash paid or received enters into the calculations; non-cash items such as depreciation and accruals and prepayments are ignored.

20.3.1 EXAMPLE (Comparison of the payback periods of two projects.)

P446

	Project 1 Cash inflow/ (outflow)	Balance	Project 2 Cash inflow/ (outflow)	Balance
Years	£	£	£	£
0	(100,000)	(100,000)	(100,000)	(100,000)
1	20,000	(80,000)	15,000	(85,000)
2	40,000	(40,000)	20,000	(65,000)
3	40,000	–	25,000	(40,000)
4			30,000	(10,000)
5			30,000	20,000

REQUIRED

(a) Calculate the payback periods for projects 1 and 2 and state which project would be the better one to choose.

(b) Comment on the advantages and disadvantages of the payback period as an aid to making investment decisions.

Tutorial note: By convention, initial investment is shown as taking place on the last day of year 0, the first year's receipts occur on the last day of year 1, and so on.

ANSWER

(a) Payback periods:

Project 1, the original outlay of £100,000 is paid back after 3 years.

Project 2. At the end of year 4, £10,000 still remains to be paid back. Assume that net receipts accrue evenly throughout the year; the initial outlay will be recouped $1/3$ of the way into the fifth year. Payback period = 4 years 4 months.

Project 1 would appear to be the better of the two projects as the period of risk is less than that of Project 2. However, much more information would be necessary in order to make a balanced decision between the two options, such as the life expectancies and comparative profitability of the two projects.

Non financial factors, if any, must be considered.

(b) Advantages:

1. Payback periods are relatively simple to calculate.
2. Calculation of net cash flows is more objective than calculation of profitability.
3. Payback indicates the project which is at risk for the least time before the initial outlay has been recouped.
4. Short payback periods benefit a firm's liquidity and facilitate faster growth.

Disadvantages:

1. Payback ignores the life expectancy of a project. In the example above, Project 1 may produce no further cash receipts after year 3, whereas Project 2 may continue to generate cash for 10 years.
2. Two projects may have the same payback period although they have different patterns of cash inflows; one may make a more immediate improvement in the firm's liquidity position than the other.
3. Payback takes no account of the time-value of money.

20.3.2 EXERCISE (Calculation and interpretation of payback periods.)

Flexi-Budgets Ltd. plans to market packaged systems for companies to use when evaluating capital expenditure proposals.

The choice is between three packages: Uniflex, Duoflex and Triflex. Each system will involve an initial outlay of £10,000.

The net receipts for each package are as follows:

	Uniflex £	Duoflex £	Triflex £
Year 1	2,000	4,000	2,000
Year 2	3,000	4,000	2,000
Year 3	5,000	2,000	2,000
Year 4	4,000	3,000	3,000
Year 5	4,000	3,000	3,000
Year 6	4,000	3,000	4,000

REQUIRED

Calculate the payback period for each package and state which package you consider Flexi-Budgets Ltd. should market. Give your reasons.

20.4 NET PRESENT VALUE (NPV) AND DISCOUNTED CASH FLOW (DCF)

Accounting Rate of Return and Payback period have been criticised for not taking account of the time value of money.

The time value of money recognises that £1 received now is worth more than £1 received in one year's time. For example, £1 received now, if invested at 10% per annum at compound interest will amount to £1.10 in one year's time and to £1.21 in two years time and so on. If £0.909 were invested now at 10% compound interest, it would amount to £1 in one year's time. If £0.826 were invested now at 10% per annum compound interest, it would amount to £1 in two year's time. Therefore using a discounting rate of 10%, £1 received in one year's time is equivalent to having 90.9p now, and £1 received in two year's time is equivalent to having 82.6p now.

If meaningful comparisons are to be made, they must be made 'like with like'. If future receipts are to be compared with present outlay, they should be discounted to present day values. The Net Present Value of a project is calculated by discounting the cash flows (DCF).

A positive net present value suggests that the project concerned is worthy of further consideration; the larger the amount of the NPV the better. A negative NPV indicates that the project should not be considered.

The discounting factors required for DCF may be calculated, but are available from tables (Present value of £1) (see 20.7 pages 301 and 302).

When the net receipts for a project are a constant amount for several years, save time in discounting them by using the appropriate factor from Present Value Annuity tables if one is available. Otherwise total the factors for those years from the Present Value of £1 tables; this usually achieves almost the same result. (There may be a small difference due to roundings.)

e.g. Net receipts for each of years 1,2 and 3 are £20,000.

Discounting rate being used: 10%

Year 1	£20,000 × 0.909	=	£18,180
Year 2	£20,000 × 0.826	=	£16,520
Year 3	£20,000 × 0.751	=	£15,020
	2.486		£49,720

Using a Present Value Annuity table:

Year 3	£20,000 × 2.487	=	£49,740

The discounting rate used is normally that of the cost of the capital required for the project. If the project is being financed by an issue of 12% debentures, the cost of capital, will be taken as 12%; if the finance is provided by shares on which a dividend of 10p per £1 share is paid, the cost of capital is 10%, and so on.

20.4.1 EXAMPLE (Selection of an option by finding the net present value of each available option.)

Discount (Factors) Ltd. are considering marketing a new product, but they have to choose between two possibilities: Product M and Product Q.

Either product will require the purchase of a new machine costing £110,000.

The estimated receipts for the two products are as follows:

	Product M	Product Q
	£	£
Year 1	40,000	20,000
Year 2	35,000	25,000
Year 3	30,000	30,000
Year 4	25,000	35,000
Year 5	20,000	40,000

Discount (Factors) Ltd. cost of capital is 12%

REQUIRED

(a) Calculations to show which of the two products Discount (Factors) Ltd. should market, with reasons.

(b) The advantages and disadvantages of using the Discounted Cash Flow technique for making decisions about capital expenditure.

ANSWER

Year	Product Discounting Factor at 12%	M £	NPV £	Q £	NPV £
0	1	(110,000)	(110,000)	(110,000)	(110,000)
1	0.893	40,000	35,720	20,000	17,860
2	0.797	35,000	27,895	25,000	19,925
3	0.712	30,000	21,360	30,000	21,360
4	0.636	25,000	15,900	35,000	22,260
5	0.567	20,000	11,340	40,000	22,680
Net Present Values			2,215		(5,915)

(a) Discount (Factors) Ltd. should market Product M as it has a positive Net Present Value of £2,215 showing that future net receipts at present day value exceed the initial cost of the outlay.

Product Q should not be considered as it has a negative NPV, indicating that Discount (Factors) Ltd. might do better to invest £110,000 at 12% compound interest rather than use the capital for this product.Note: Both products will produce (undiscounted) net receipts of £150,000, but they arise earlier in Product M than in Product Q.

(b) Advantage: The method recognises the time-value of money and produces more meaningful results than the simple Payback method. DCF can be applied to the Payback method, however.

Disadvantage: It is more complicated than ARR and Payback and in practice can require a large volume of complicated calculations to be made. This does not have to be a problem if a computer with a suitable program is available.

20.4.2 EXERCISE (The comparison of two projects using DCF)

Wyezed Ltd. is contemplating the purchase of a new machine and must choose between two models: 'Goliath', which costs £80,000 and is capable of producing 12,000 units per year, and 'Cyclops' which costs £100,000 and is capable of producing 14,000 units per year.

The costs of production are: 'Goliath' £6 per unit; 'Cyclops' £5 per unit.

All units produced by either machine can be sold at £8 each.

All purchases and sales are on a cash basis.

Both machines have an estimated useful life of 5 years and will be depreciated at the rate of 20% per annum on cost.

REQUIRED

Calulate the net present values for the two machines, using a rate of 15%, and state which of the two machines Wyezed Ltd. should consider purchasing and why.

20.5   INTERNAL RATE OF RETURN (IRR)

The Internal Rate of Return is the rate of discount which equates the net receipts from a project to the cost, i.e. the rate which produces a nil NPV. IRR is an alternative to NPV for deciding whether or not a project is acceptable. The IRR should be compared with the cost of capital.

IRR may be found by

(i)   discounting the cash flows using two different rates sufficiently wide apart to give a positive NPV in one case, and a negative NPV in the other.

(ii)   interpolating the two NPVs to arrive at the IRR.

20.5.1 EXAMPLE (Finding the internal rate of return for a project.)

A project involves an initial cost of £100,000. The annual net receipts for a period of 5 years are estimated to be £28,000.

NPV at a discount rate of 10% = £6,148

NPV at a discount rate of 14% = (£3,876)

$$IRR = 10\% + (14 - 10) \times \frac{£6,148}{£(6,148 + 3,876)}$$

$$= 10\% + 4\% \times \frac{£6,148}{10,024} = 12.45\%$$

NPV and IRR compared

(i)   NPV is easier to calculate than IRR.

(ii)   NPV is a better method for ranking projects in order of priority.

(iii)   Normally NPV and IRR agree on the acceptability or non-acceptability of a project.

(iv)   IRR is frequently used in business in spite of its limitations.

20.5.2 EXERCISE (Calculation of IRR)

Abednego can borrow £20,000 at 12% per annum. He is considering a particular venture which involves an initial outlay of £20,000.

The venture will produce net receipts of £6,000 per annum for five years.

REQUIRED

Calculate the Internal Rate of Return for the venture and advise Abednego whether or not he should go ahead with it.

20.6   KEY POINTS TO REMEMBER

1. Capital expenditure decisions are especially important because of the large amounts of money often involved and the long term effects on the business. Bad decisions are usually not easily reversed.

2. Management needs as much information as possible to enable it to make capital expenditure decisions. Some of the information may be of a non-financial nature. See 20.1 above and Chapter 24.

3. Each method of appraisal has advantages and disadvantages. Be prepared to discuss these in an examination.

4. Whichever method of appraisal is used, the results depend upon the accuracy of the profit forecasts and estimates of future receipts and payments.

5. The longer the period covered by a forecast, the less accurate it is likely to be.

6. Risk and the time-value of money are two important factors in capital appraisal.

7. Payback period, DCF and IRR are concerned only with cash inflows and outflows; depreciation is not relevant in these calculations, but it must be included for ARR purposes.

8. Questions which incorporate extracts of Net Present Value tables require DCF calculations to be made (a fact not readily recognised by some examinees!)

9. **A SUNK COST** is expenditure which has already been incurred; it is represented by assets which may continue to be used to serve their present purpose but have little or no resale value for any other purpose. Sunk costs should be ignored in capital expenditure appraisal calculations.

10. Ignore book values of assets in capital expenditure calculations.

11. **OPPORTUNITY COST** is the value of a benefit foregone, or the value of the next best alternative course of action which is eliminated by the chosen project.

COMMON ERRORS

- inclusion of depreciation in Payback period, DCF and IRR calculations.
- discounting annual revenue and expenditure separately instead of calculating net receipts before discounting.
- omitting to include the proceeds of sale or scrap of an asset as a receipt in the DCF calculation in the final year.

20.7   EXAMINATION QUESTIONS

PRESENT VALUE OF £1

Years	10%	11%	12%	13%	14%	15%
1	0.909	0.901	0.893	0.885	0.877	0.870
2	0.826	0.812	0.797	0.783	0.769	0.756
3	0.751	0.731	0.712	0.693	0.675	0.658
4	0.683	0.659	0.636	0.613	0.592	0.572
5	0.621	0.593	0.567	0.543	0.519	0.497
6	0.564	0.535	0.507	0.480	0.456	0.432
7	0.513	0.482	0.452	0.425	0.400	0.376
8	0.467	0.434	0.404	0.376	0.351	0.327
9	0.424	0.391	0.361	0.333	0.308	0.284
10	0.386	0.352	0.322	0.295	0.270	0.247

Years	16%	17%	18%	19%	20%
1	0.862	0.855	0.847	0.840	0.833
2	0.743	0.731	0.718	0.706	0.694
3	0.641	0.624	0.609	0.593	0.579
4	0.552	0.534	0.516	0.499	0.482
5	0.476	0.456	0.437	0.419	0.402
6	0.410	0.390	0.370	0.352	0.335
7	0.354	0.333	0.314	0.296	0.279
8	0.305	0.285	0.266	0.249	0.233
9	0.263	0.243	0.225	0.209	0.194
10	0.227	0.208	0.191	0.176	0.162

QUESTION 1 (Cambridge June 1988)

Elder Plc is currently considering a single capital investment project. The Company has sufficient financial resources to undertake the project which will not affect any other part of Elder's business.

The project will involve initial capital outlay of £3,700,000 which will be spent at the beginning of year 1.

Cash flow returns on the project are expected to be:

End of years	Cash Flow
	£
1 – 3	1,200,000
4 – 6	800,000

The project will have a six-year life at the end of which it will be closed down and sold realising scrap proceeds of £250,000.

Elder's directors ask you to advise them regarding investment appraisal techniques. They have heard of the 'pay-back' and 'discounted cash flow' methods but are unsure how to apply them. However they set out the following criteria.

1. Any project to be undertaken must yield a positive net present value when discounted of 15%.
2. Any project must be excluded if it yields less than 17% when measured by the internal rate of return method.

REQUIRED

(a) Calculate for the project
   (i) the payback period
   (ii) the net present value
   (iii) the internal rate of return. *(13 marks)*

(b) Advise the directors as to whether or not the project should be undertaken on the basis of the criteria they have laid down. *(3 marks)*

(c) Briefly discuss the advantages and limitations of the three methods of project appraisal applied in part (a) above. *(9 marks)*

(Total 25 marks)

QUESTION 2 (London June 1988)

Street-Wise Boutiques are considering re-equiping one of their city-centre stores at a cost of £35,000. It is estimated that the new fittings and equipment will have a life of five years, after which they may be sold for £2,000.

The company estimates that the new appearance of Street-Wise will increase net cash inflows by £10,500 per annum.

(a) Calculate the Net Present Value (NPV) of the investment if the company expects a 20 per cent rate of return on their investment. Assume that the capital expenditure occurs at the beginning of Year 1, and that all cash inflows occur at the end of the respective years. *(4 marks)*

(b) Show the maximum interest that Street-Wise should pay if it needs to borrow money to finance the project. *(4 marks)*

(c) Calculate the Payback period. *(2 marks)*

(d) Using your answers, advise Street-Wise upon their planned investment. *(5 marks)*

QUESTION 3 (JMB June 1987)

Speedy Limited, a sports equipment manufacturer, has been offered a five year contract to manufacture a special exercise machine for a retailer. The machines would be sold to the retailer for £60 each, and the retailer guarantees to take 1,000 machines per annum.

The company's accountant has calculated the annual costs of fulfilling the contract as follows.

	£
Materials	9,000
Labour	17,500
Machinery Lease	15,000
Machinery Depreciation	12,000
General Overheads (100% of Labour)	17,500
Cost Per Annum	71,000

His advice is not to accept the contract.

You are given the following additional information:

(i)   the machinery only has to be leased if the contract is accepted;

(ii)   the machinery depreciation relates to existing machinery that the company already owns and that will last for at least five years.

(iii)   the general overheads would directly increase as a result of taking the contract by only £3,000 per annum.

(iv)   if the contract is not accepted then the existing machinery and facilities could be utilised on another contract to produce £8,000 per annum over the next two years and £15,000 per annum over the following three years.

(v)   the company has a cost of capital of 15% per annum.

You are required to write a report to the management of Speedy Limited presenting the information relevant to the evaluation of the two alternatives and explaining, given the above information, which is financially the more attractive.

(Total 25 marks)

QUESTION 4 (JMB June 1988)

The management of Theta Company are considering the capital budget for 19-9. They are considering whether or not to replace some existing machinery with some new machinery which uses more modern technology and, as a result, can reduce labour costs and material costs. The situation at 1 January 19-9 is estimated to be as follows:

	Existing machinery £	New Machinery £
Original Cost	30,000	240,000
Net Book Value	18,000	–
Net Realisable Value	10,000	–
Depreciation per annum	2,000	24,000
Labour Costs per annum	40,000	12,000
Material Costs per annum	500,000	485,000
Power per annum	10,000	12,000
Maintenance per annum	4,000	5,000
Estimated physical life remaining	10 years	10 years
Estimated scrap value in 10 years	0	0

Both machines have the same capacity. The company's cost of capital is 12%

You are required to calculate the financial implications of the alternative choices as at 1 January 19-9, and suggest what action the company should take, given the above information.

(25 marks)

QUESTION 5 (AEB June 1987)

Hirwaun Pig Iron Co. operate a single blast furnace producing pig iron. The present blast furnace is obsolete and the company is considering its replacement.

The alternatives the company is considering are:

(i)   Blast furnace type; Exco. Cost £2 million.

This furnace is of a standard size capable of a monthly output of 10,000 tons. The company expects to sell 80% of its output annually at £150 per ton on a fixed price contract.

The remaining output will be sold on the open market at the following expected prices:

	19-8	19-9	19-0	19-1
Price per ton	£150	£140	£140	£160

(ii)   Blast furnace type; Ohio. Cost £3.5 million.

This large furnace is capable of a monthly output of 20,000 tons. A single buyer has agreed to buy all the monthly output at a fixed price which is applicable from 1 January each year.

The prices fixed for the next four years are as follows:

	19-8	19-9	19-0	19-1
Price per ton	£130	£130	£140	£170

Additional information.

(1)   Blast furnaces operate continuously and the operating labour is regarded as a fixed cost. During the next four years the operating labour costs will be as follows:

    Exco £1.2 million per annum

    Ohio £2.5 million per annum

(2)   Other forecast operating payments (excluding labour)

Payments per ton of output

	19-8	19-9	19-0	19-1
Exco	£130	£130	£135	£135
Ohio	£120	£120	£125	£125

(3)   It can be assumed that both blast furnaces will have a life of 10 years.

(4)   The company's cost of capital is 12% per annum.

(5)   It should be assumed that all costs are paid and revenues received at the end of each year.

REQUIRED

(a)   The forecast budgets for each of the years 19-8 - 19-1 and for each of the blast furnaces being considered. Show the expected yearly net cash flows.   *(7 marks)*

(b)   Appropriate computations using the net present value method for each of the blast furnaces, Exco and Ohio for the first four years.   *(8 marks)*

(c)   A report providing a recommendation to the management of Hirwaun Pig Iron Co. as to which blast furnace should be purchased. Your report should include a critical evaluation of the method used to assess the capital project.   *(10 marks)*

(Total 25 marks)

QUESTION 6 (AEB June 1988)

Concentric Ltd., a manufacturing company, has recently appointed a new managing director.

After completing a review of the company's machinery he reported to the Board of Directors that the present machinery was out-of-date and incapable of sustaining high production levels without frequent breakdowns, and that the quality of the present production was poor.

The managing director proposed that the company should change to robotic machines.

The following information was available on the robots being considered for purchase.

(1)

	Robot A	Robot B	Robot C
	£M	£M	£M
Purchase cost of machines	10.0	9.0	15.5
Estimated net cash inflows			
Year 1	3	3	3
Year 2	3.5	3	5
Year 3	4	3.5	6
Year 4	4	4	6

(2)   The company's cost of capital is 12%.

(3)   Owing to their productive efficiency the robots would make the following number of manufacturing workers redundant:

At end of	Robot A Number of workers	Robot B Number of workers	Robot C Number of workers
Year 1	50	50	50
Year 2	60	60	80

(4)   The manufacturing workers' unions were opposed to the implementation of robotics, but in negotiations they had indicated that they would agree to the following:

Redundant workers should each receive

  (i)   an amount equal to half a year's wages at the end of the year in which they were made redundant, and

  (ii)   an additional flat rate terminal payment of £2,000 per worker.

Note: The average annual wage is £6,000.

(5)   All estimated net cash inflows arise at the end of the relevant year. The net cash inflows in (1) above do not take account of the redundancy payments.

REQUIRED

(a)   (i)   Appropriate computations using the net present value method for each of the robots being considered.   *(12 marks)*

  (ii)   A report to the Board of Directors of Concentric Ltd advising them as to which robot should be purchased, based on your results in (i) above.   *(4 marks)*

(b)   (i)   Give **five** factors which the directors should consider before reaching their final decision.

                                                                                          (5 marks)

  (ii)   Briefly outline the aspects of social accounting that the company needs to consider before making a final decision.   *(4 marks)*

                                                                                    (Total 25 marks)

QUESTION 7 (AEB November 1988)

Esana Plc were considering diversifying their business activities. A director had suggested that the leisure industry was an expanding market and as a result the company was examining the purchase of one of two blocks of apartments in Buenoland, a popular holiday destination.

The buildings under consideration were:

Apartments	Cost	
	£M	
Oriente	20	Consists of 150 high quality apartments.
Benimas	5	Consists of 50 apartments, but with basic facilities only.

The company accountant prepared the following forecast operating budgets for each of the buildings:

BUILDING	ORIENTE		BENIMAS	
YEAR	ESTIMATED REVENUE RECEIPTS	ESTIMATED OPERATING PAYMENTS	ESTIMATED REVENUE RECEIPTS	ESTIMATED OPERATING PAYMENTS
	£M	£M	£M	£M
19-9	4.0	2.0	2.0	1.5
19-0	7.6	3.0	2.6	1.8
19-1	12.0	5.2	4.5	2.0
19-2	14.0	6.0	5.2	2.2
19-3	15.5	6.5	6.1	2.6

Further market analysis provided the following information:

(1) Initial budget predictions were made on the assumption that 65% occupancy of the apartments could be achieved. The latest information shows that if £100,000 a year advertising payments were made, the occupancy rate of each building could be increased to 70% and that revenue receipts would increase by an additional 5% in each of the budget years forecasted, without any increase in the operating costs.

(2) Fifty per cent of all operating payments (except advertising) were paid in Buenolands currency, zen. The budgets assume an exchange rate of 200 zen=£1 sterling.

A recent economic forecast predicted that the £1 sterling would gradually weaken against the zen. For the purpose of making projections, it is to be assumed that the rate remains at 200 zen up to the end of 19-1, but falls to 150 zen from 1 January 19-2.

Additional information.

(3) The company's cost of capital is 12% per annum.

(4) It should be assumed that all costs are paid and revenues received at the end of each year.

REQUIRED

(a) Revised operating budgets for 19-9 - 19-3 inclusive, for each of the buildings being considered.

(9 marks)

(b) Net present value computations for each of the buildings for the period 19-9 - 19-3.   *(8 marks)*

(c) Prepare a brief report advising Esana Plc which apartment block they should purchase. State any reservations that you may have.   *(8 marks)*

(Total 25 marks)

INTERPRETATION OF ACCOUNTS

Questions on accounting ratios require:-
- an understanding of the use of ratios
- calculation of specified ratios
- selection of appropriate ratios to demonstrate aspects of a business
- trend analysis and inter-firm comparison
- an appreciation of possible relationships between ratios
- comments on ratios, the information they convey about a business and suggested factors which may underlie the ratios.
- an understanding of, and ability to comment critically upon, the gearing of a company
- limitations of ratios

21.1   RATIOS

The purpose of accounting is to convey information, but 'absolute' numbers in isolation are generally meaningless. A profit of £10,000 could be very satisfactory or most unsatisfactory. It may be very good for a small business with a capital of £25,000 for it would represent a return of 40% on capital. The same profit in a larger business with a capital of £1,000,000 would represent of return of 1% which would be a poor result indeed. It is only possible make a judgement about profit if it can be related to some other figure such as the amount of money invested in the business. It would be difficult to find an alternative investment which would give a return of more than 40%, but an investor in a company which yields a return of only 1% should have little difficulty in finding a more profitable investment.The small business above appears to be managed more efficiently than the larger one. However, further enquiry might reveal the following:

	Small business		Larger business	
	£		£	
Year before last	50,000	(profit)	(20,000)	(loss)
Last year (as above)	10,000	(profit)	10,000	(profit)
Next year (forecast)	(20,000)	(loss)	100,000	(profit)

Clearly, the small business appears to be in decline whilst the larger one is becoming more successful. One year's results do not reveal these trends, but the results of several years have given a new and important perspective to the relative results.

From the above, the following basic points emerge which must be continually borne in mind when appraising any business by its accounts:

1. Figures in isolation are meaningless; they need to be related to other figures (ratios) to put them in perspective.

2. Trends in the same business over a number of years will show whether it is progressing or deteriorating.

3. Results in one business may be compared with the results of other businesses (inter-firm comparison) to see if it is performing as well as it should, provided:

    (i)   they are in the same line of business (it would not be sensible to compare the accounts of a fish shop with the accounts of an iron foundry.) and

    (ii) the structures of the businesses are similar (it would not be realistic to compare a sole trader with a large company because they are two different kinds of entity.)

4. The ratio of profit to capital has not explained why the businesses have been performing differently, or why one is in decline and the other growing. There are other ratios which will further analyse the operations of a business and show how they have contributed to a particular rate of return on capital. They will not explain the operations; but they will assist management by

indicating areas where the operations of the business need to be investigated and corrective action taken. It is very important to bear this last point in mind when commenting upon a business. Examination questions generally do not give sufficient information to allow for identification of precise causes for the results or state of a business.

21.2   A PYRAMID OF RATIOS

The ratios covered in this chapter are represented in the following 'pyramid', which shows their inter-relationship.

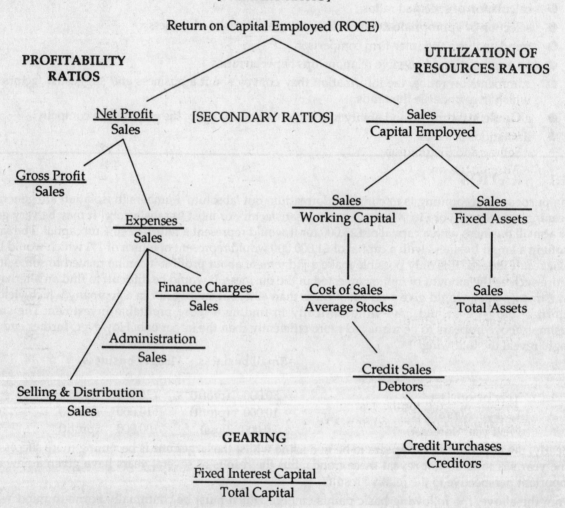

Ratios are calculated to be used; to be useful they must be meaningful. To be meaningful, there must be a direct relationship between the constituent parts of each ratio.

21.3   USERS OF RATIOS

1.   Management,
     (a) to analyse past results
     (b) to plan for the future (e.g preparation of budgets)
     (c) to control their business.
2.   Investors, to compare their investments with alternative forms of investment.
3.   Bankers and Finance Houses, to assess the credit worthiness of businesses.
4.   Financial analysts working for the financial press, trade associations, trade unions etc.
5.   Government statisticians, to compile tables of national statistics.

21.4 RATIO ANALYSIS

THE HORATIO COMPANY PLC
Trading and Profit and Loss Account
for the years ended 31 December

	19-1		19-2	
	£'000	£'000	£'000	£'000
Sales (all on credit)		1,000		1,220
less Cost of Sales:				
Opening stock	60		68	
Purchases (all on credit)	710		812	
	770		880	
less closing stock	68		72	
		702		808
Gross Profit		298		412
less				
Selling and distribution	60		78	
Administration	105		134	
		165		212
Operating profit		133 *150*		200 *260*
Interest payable		5 *10*		15 *20*
Profit before tax		128 *140*		185 *240*
Taxation		47 *50*		57 *70*
Profit after tax		81 *90*		128 *170*
Preference dividend	4 *5*		4 *5*	
Ordinary dividend	25 *30*	29	50 *60*	54 *65*
		52		74
Transfer to General Reserve		30		50
Balance of profit for the year		22		24
Balance brought forward from 19-0		4		26
Retained profit carried forward		26		50

Balance Sheet as at 31 December

	19-1		19-2	
	£'000	£'000	£'000	£'000
Fixed Assets (net book value)		316		520
Current assets				
Stock	68		72	
Trade Debtors	83		112	
Balance at Bank	85		77	
	236		261	
less Current Liabilities				
Trade Creditors	80		120	
Taxation	47		57	
Preference and ordinary dividends	29	156	54	231
Net working capital		80		30
Carried forward		396		550

	£'000	£'000	£'000
Brought forward	396		550
less 12^1/$_2$% Debentures	40		120
	356		430
Share capital and reserves			
Ordinary shares of £1	250		250
8% Preference shares	50		50
General reserve	30		80
Retained profit	26		50
	356		430

The ratios that follow are grouped according to their characteristics, i.e. profitability ratios, liquidity ratios, utilisation of resources etc. For each ratio the model is given, followed by the calculation of the ratio, using The Horatio Company plc., and appropriate comments. Each of these is important in examination answers on ratio analysis.

PROFITABILITY RATIOS

RETURN ON CAPITAL EMPLOYED (R.O.C.E.), This is sometimes called return on net assets although the calculation may also be made using gross assets.

R.O.C.E. is the PRIMARY RATIO as it is considered to be the most important of the ratios and the one that forms the starting point in ratio analysis. It is expressed as a percentage.

Model:

$$\frac{\text{Profit before interest}}{\text{capital employed}} \times 100$$

19-1

19-2

$$\frac{133}{396} \times 100 = 33.59\% \qquad \frac{200}{550} \times 100 = 36.36\%$$

ROCE relates profit to the resources employed in earning the profit. It shows how much profit has been earned per £100 of long term capital. In the case of this company, £33.59p profit was earned for every £100 of the long term capital in 19-1. In 19-2, the profit increased to £36.36p for every £100 of capital employed showing that there had been an improvement in profitability.

This ratio is important because:

1. A low percentage is indicative of a profit which could quickly be turned into a loss with a reversal of the company's fortunes.

2. Additional borrowings will have an adverse effect upon profitability if the cost of borrowing is higher than the percentage return on capital.

3. It serves as a 'benchmark' against which to measure the accounting rate of return when assessing a new project, the purchase of a new business etc.

4. If the ratio is available for separate parts or activities etc. of a business, any part or activity with a percentage return below the average for the business as a whole may be considered for disposal, closure or cessation.

5. Investors use this ratio when considering alternative forms of investment.

When comparing ROCE for different firms it is important to ensure that they are all in the same line of business and their operations are similar. A firm which produces bicycles, making all the parts itself, will be more capital intensive than another firm which merely assembles bought-in parts.

For examinations, unless required to do otherwise by the question, use profit before interest. In practice, accountants may use different profit figures for this ratio, e.g. profit after tax. The use of profit before tax recognises that tax liabilities largely depend upon the annual budgets of the Chancellor of the Exchequer and regard taxation as a factor over which directors have little control. The use of profit after tax affixes the directors with the responsibility for managing company affairs in such a way as to reduce the tax liability. Capital employed should be taken to mean:

Issued share capital + reserves + long term loan capital
(unless otherwise stated in the question.)

Alternative definitions of capital employed for this ratio give:

Return on equity: i.e. ordinary share capital + reserves.

(in this case 'return' would be profit before tax less any preference dividend.)

Return on total funds employed: i.e. all issued share capital + reserves + long term liabilities + current liabilities.

Note: The reserves should always be included as part of the 'equity'.

Net Profit Percentage

This is known as one of the secondary ratios as, with the other secondary ratio, $\dfrac{\text{Sales}}{\text{Capital employed}}$, (see below), it helps to explain ROCE. The net profit percentage expresses the net profit as a percentage of sales or turnover. (Turnover= net sales or sales less sales returns.)

Model:

$$\frac{\text{Profit before interest and tax}}{\text{sales}} \times 100.$$

HORATIO:

	19-1		19-2
$\dfrac{133}{1,000} \times 100 =$	13.3%	$\dfrac{200}{1220} \times 100 =$	16.39%

This shows that in 19-1, out of every £100 of sales, £13.30 was left as profit after deducting the cost of sales and all operating expenses. This had improved to £16.39 per £100 of sales in 19-2. This could have happened if Horatio had increased its selling prices without increasing its costs proportionately; or it could have reduced its costs; or there could have been a combination of both factors.

When comparing the net profit percentage of different firms, it is important to ensure that they are in the same line of business. A retail grocery chain needs to sell its stock quickly while it is fresh and to ensure this, will operate on a narrower profit margin than firms which sell electrical equipment. Profit margins, which will be studied below, together with the overheads of the business, will decide the net profit percentage. The next five ratios will help to explain the net profit percentage.

Gross Profit Percentage

The gross profit percentage shows the margin which is being earned on sales.

Model:

$$\frac{\text{Gross profit}}{\text{sales}} \times 100$$

HORATIO:

	19-1		19-2
$\dfrac{298}{1,000} \times 100 =$	29.8%	$\dfrac{412}{1220} \times 100 =$	33.77%

This shows that the margin (gross profit) on every £100 of sales made by Horatio in 19-1 was £29.80p; in 19-2, the margin had improved to £33.77p.

The gross profit percentage will vary with the type of business; a business which needs to turn its stock over quickly (e.g. fish shop) will work on a low gross profit percentage to encourage sales. A shop which sells television sets will have a lower rate of stock turnover and will expect a higher profit percentage.

The gross profit achieved on sales can be compared with the expected gross profit, using the mark-up/margin relationship where necessary. (See Chapter 4.3). A lower than expected gross profit percentage may be explained by:

1. An increase in the cost of goods sold has not been passed on to customers.

2. In order to dispose of old or slow moving stocks, the selling price has been reduced e.g. 'winter sales'.

3. The business has adopted a policy of giving bulk discounts to major customers.

4. A 'price-cutting' policy has been adopted in the face of local competition.

5. 'Shop soiled' or damaged stock has been sold below the normal price.

6. Stock which has been stolen but not identified as such has been included in cost of sales. (Where stock losses have been identified, the value of the goods should be taken out of the cost of sales by crediting purchases and debiting profit and loss account so as not to distort the gross profit percentage.)

Operating Expenses/Sales

Total operating expenses are related to the sales.
Model

$$\frac{\text{Total operating expenses}}{\text{sales}} \times 100$$

HORATIO

	19-1		19-2

$$\frac{165}{1000} \times 100 = 16.5\% \qquad \frac{212}{1220} \times 100 = 17.38\%$$

In 19-1 Horatio spent £16.50 on overheads for every £100 of sales; this had increased to £17.38 in 19-2. There may be good reasons for this, but the next two ratios will help the management understand why the increase has taken place.

Selling and Distribution Expenses/Sales

Selling and distribution expenses are related to sales. These expenses are expected to vary with sales, not necessarily proportionately, but it is important to compare the rate of change with the rate of change in turnover.
Model

$$\frac{\text{Selling and distribution expenses}}{\text{sales}} \times 100$$

HORATIO

	19-1		19-2

$$\frac{60}{1000} \times 100 = 6\% \qquad \frac{78}{1220} \times 100 = 6.39\%$$

Horatio's selling and distribution costs show an increase of 0.39% in 19-2 which suggests slightly less efficiency in this aspect of the business. It may be explained by the increase in turnover being attributable to sales to a number of small customers resulting in higher distribution costs per sale.

Administration/Sales

Administration overheads are related to sales.
Model

$$\frac{\text{Administration expenses}}{\text{sales}} \times 100$$

HORATIO

	19-1		19-2

$$\frac{105}{1000} \times 100 = 10.5\% \qquad \frac{134}{1220} \times 100 = 10.98\%$$

Whereas in 19-1 Horatio spent £10.50 on administration overheads for every £100 received from sales, this expenditure had risen to £10.98 percent in 19-2. Administration overheads may normally be expected to consist mainly of fixed costs and should not increase in line with turnover. The expenditure for 19-2 could have been expected to be nearer the 19-1 expenditure of £105,000 after making allowance for inflation, etc. How much of the increase, if any, can be justified will only be ascertained by an examination of Horatio's expenditure on administration.

UTILISATION OF RESOURCES RATIOS

These ratios are used to measure the efficiency with which the resources (fixed assets etc.) have been used. The method is to calculate the amount of sales that have been generated per £100 of resources.

Utilisation of Capital Employed

This ratio is used to show how effectively the capital employed has been used to generate sales. It is one of the secondary ratios.

Model

$$\frac{\text{Sales}}{\text{capital employed}}$$

HORATIO

19-1		19-2	
$\frac{1,000}{396} =$	2.53 times	$\frac{1220}{550} =$	2.22 times

The capital employed in 19-1 produced 2.53 times the amount in sales, i.e. each £100 of capital produced £253 sales. In 19-2 the ratio had fallen to 2.22. The higher the ratio, the more effectively the capital is being employed. The capital employed in Horatio has increased by £154,000 [£(550,000 - 396,000)]. £80,000 of the increase is accounted for by the issue of £80,000 debentures which were evidently required to help finance the purchase of additional fixed assets (£204,000). The interest debited in the profit and loss account (£15,000) in 19-2 indicates that the debentures were issued at the beginning of that year, but the assets acquired may not have started to earn revenue until later in the year. There would not in that case be a full year's incremental revenue as a return on the additional capital employed.

Strictly, the capital employed should be the average capital employed during the year and this would take account of the time for which additional share capital, debentures and other long term loans had been enjoyed by the business; it would also include a proportion of the profit earned in that year.

Relationship between the Primary and Secondary Ratios

The product of the secondary ratios = the primary ratio i.e. Net profit percentage × utilisation of capital = ROCE

HORATIO

19-1:	$13.3\% \times 2.5252512 =$	33.585852%
19-2:	$16.39344\% \times 2.2181818 =$	36.363636%

(More exact figures than those previously calculated have been used to demonstrate conclusively the relationship between the secondary and primary ratios)

A business dealing in goods with a low profit margin must turn its stock over more quickly than a business earning a high profit margin in order to achieve the same net profit percentage.

The utilisation of capital employed can be further analysed in the following ways:

$\frac{\text{Sales}}{\text{fixed assets}}$	Horatio: 19-1;	$\frac{1000}{316}$	=	3.16 times
	19-2;	$\frac{1220}{520}$	=	2.35 times
$\frac{\text{Sales}}{\text{total assets}}$	Horatio: 19-1;	$\frac{1000}{552}$	=	1.81 times
	19-2;	$\frac{1220}{781}$	=	1.56 times
$\frac{\text{Sales}}{\text{current assets}}$	Horatio: 19-1;	$\frac{1000}{236}$	=	4.24 times
	19-2;	$\frac{1220}{261}$	=	4.67 times

WORKING CAPITAL RATIOS

Working capital is the amount by which total current assets exceed total current liabilities. The ratios test the ability of a business to pay those creditors who are due to be paid within twelve months (usually within two or three months).

Current Ratio (Sometimes called the working capital ratio)

This ratio shows how many times current liabilities are covered by current assets; it is usually expressed as a true ratio. The right hand term of ratios (in this case, current liabilities) should always be expressed as unity.

Model

> Current assets: current liabilities
> HORATIO

	19-1		19-2
236:156 =	1.51:1	261:231 =	1.13:1

A ratio of between 1.5:1 and 2:1 may generally be considered reasonable. Therefore Horatio's working capital seems barely satisfactory in 19-1 and has fallen to a very low level in 19-2. A current ratio in excess of 2:1 may indicate poor management of resources with capital tied up in stocks, debtors or lying idle in the bank instead of being put to work to earn profit.

Various factors must be considered when commenting on this ratio:

1. The nature of the business. The business may require large stocks to be carried; or one in which sales are mainly on credit can be expected to have substantial debtors. These two factors will increase the current ratio.

2. The working capital of a seasonal business will fluctuate more than a non-seasonal business which has a steady working capital.

3. The component parts of working capital need to be examined in order to see how sound the working capital is. Slow moving stocks and slow paying debtors may give a favourable appearance to the current ratio but will be little help in paying creditors already due for payment.

Liquid Ratio (Also known as the 'Quick' ratio or the 'acid test')

Liquid assets are those which are in the form of cash and those which can readily be converted into cash. The least liquid form of current asset is stock whether of materials, work in progress or finished goods. The liquid ratio tests the ability of the current assets other than stock to meet the current liabilities.

Model

> Current assets less stock: current liabilities
> HORATIO

	19-1		19-2
168:156 =	1.08:1	189:231 =	0.82:1

A liquid ratio of 1:1 is generally considered satisfactory but it may be allowed to fall to 0.9:1 if the debtors pay promptly and there is a regular inflow of cash from them. A business which sells almost wholly for cash but enjoys normal credit terms for its purchases may well have a liquid ratio of 0.5:1 or even less. A supermarket would be a good example of this.Horatio's liquid ratio was satisfactory in 19-1 but has fallen to a level at 31 December 19-2 which would be dangerously low for many businesses, but without knowing more about this particular company, no definite judgement can be made.

Three ratios are commonly used to test the various components of working capital:

Stockturn

Model

$$\frac{\text{Cost of sales}}{\text{average stocks}}$$

Stock turn indicates how many times during a year stock is turned over. (For examination purposes,

$$\text{average stock} = \frac{\text{opening stock + closing stock}}{2}.)$$

> HORATIO

Average stocks: 19-1: $\dfrac{60{,}000 + 68{,}000}{2} = 64{,}000$

19-2: $\dfrac{68{,}000 + 72{,}000}{2} = 70{,}000$

$$\begin{array}{ll} \text{19-1} & \text{19-2} \\ \dfrac{702}{64} = \quad 10.97 \text{ times} & \dfrac{808}{70} = \quad 11.54 \text{ times} \end{array}$$

The rate of stock turnover has improved slightly in 19-2.

The more quickly stock is turned over, the sooner the profits are earned on it and the more times the profit can be earned.

A shop selling fresh food will have a much quicker stockturn than one selling high class jewellery; but the jeweller will make a much larger profit margin on his sales.

Debtors' Ratio

This may be expressed as sales/debtors but is more usually expressed as the average period of credit taken by customers.

Model

$$\frac{\text{Debtors}}{\text{credit sales}} \times 365 = \text{average days credit}$$

HORATIO

$$\begin{array}{ll} \text{19-1} & \text{19-2} \\ \dfrac{83}{1000} \times 365 = \quad 30.3 \text{ days} & \dfrac{112}{1220} \times 365 = \quad 33.5 \text{ days} \end{array}$$

It would appear that on average, the debtors were taking 3 days longer to pay their invoices in 19-2 than in 19-1.

The period of credit being taken must be compared with the period normally allowed by Horatio.

A period of credit may appear to be unduly long simply because a large volume of credit sales has taken place in the last week of the year and the debtors were given four weeks credit.

One factor that must be borne in mind is that the older a debt is allowed to become before it is collected, the greater the risk that it will not be collected at all. There is then a potential risk that the working capital is less than it appears on the balance sheet.

Creditors Ratio

This may be expressed as credit purchases/trade creditors, but is more usually used to calculate the period of credit being taken from suppliers.

Model

$$\frac{\text{Trade creditors}}{\text{credit purchases}} \times 365 = \text{days credit taken}$$

HORATIO

$$\begin{array}{ll} \text{19-1} & \text{19-2} \\ \dfrac{80}{710} \times 365 = 41.1 \text{ days} & \dfrac{120}{812} \times 365 = 53.9 \text{ days} \end{array}$$

Horatio has taken 13 days longer in 19-2 to pay creditors than in 19-1. Whether this is good or bad depends upon the time allowed for payment by suppliers. Extended credit benefits Horatio's cash flow but it may be at the expense of the goodwill of the suppliers.

INVESTMENT RATIOS

Gearing

The gearing of a company may be calculated in one of the following ways:

Model 1

$$\frac{\text{Fixed interest capital}}{\text{total capital}} \times 100$$

(Fixed interest capital = long term loans + preference shares, if any; total capital = fixed interest capital + equity. Equity = issued ordinary share capital + reserves.)

HORATIO

	19-1		19-2

$$\frac{40 + 50}{306 + 40 + 50} \times 100$$ 　　　　　　　　　　$$\frac{120 + 50}{380 + 120 + 50} \times 100$$

$$= \frac{90}{396} \times 100 = \quad\quad 22.7\% \quad\quad\quad = \frac{170}{550} \times 100 = \quad\quad 30.9\%$$

Model 2 Debt/equity ratio

$$\frac{\text{Fixed interest capital}}{\text{equity}} \times 100$$

HORATIO

	19-1		19-2

$$\frac{40 + 50}{306} \times 100 = \quad\quad 29.4\% \quad\quad\quad \frac{120 + 50}{380} \times 100 = \quad\quad 44.7\%$$

The gearing of a company's capital is assessed as follows:

	Debt/total capital	Debt/equity
High gearing	more than 50%	more than 100%
Neutral gearing	50%	100%
Low gearing	less than 50%	less than 100%

The effect of gearing on the holders of a company's equity:

	Company A (Low gearing)	Company B (High gearing)
	£'000	£'000
Ordinary shares	80	20
10% debentures	20	80
	100	100
If profits before interest are	10	10
deduct debenture interest	2	8
profits available for ordinary shareholders	8	2
representing return on equity of	10%	10%
If profits double:	20	20
deduct debenture interest	2	8
profits available for ordinary shareholders	18	12
representing return on equity of	22.5%	60%
or, an increase in return of	225%	600%

From this it will be seen that in a situation when profits are increasing, the rate of increase in the profits available for the equity shareholders in a highly geared company is greater than in a low geared company. It follows that a drop in profits in a high geared company affects the ordinary shareholders more severely than in a low geared company.

Earnings per Share (EPS)

Earnings are profits after tax and preference dividends.

Model

$$\frac{\text{Earnings (in pence)}}{\text{no. of ordinary shares}}$$

HORATIO

	19-1	19-2

$$\frac{81,000,000 - 4,000,000}{25,000,000} = \qquad 30.8p$$

$$\frac{128,000,000 - 4,000,000}{25,000,000} = 4 \qquad\qquad 49.6p$$

The earnings per share have increased by 18.8p in 19-2.

Investors regard Earnings per Share as a convenient measure of the success of a company.

Price Earnings Ratio (PER)

The P/E ratio relates the market price of a share to the earnings per share.

Model

$$\frac{\text{Market price of share}}{\text{earnings per share.}}$$

HORATIO

(Assume that the market price of The Horatio Company's shares was as follows: at 31 December 19-1 was £2.50 and at 31 December 19-2 was £4.50)

	19-1		19-2	

$$\frac{250}{30.8} = \qquad 8.1 \qquad \frac{450}{49.6} = \qquad 9.1$$

The Price Earnings Ratio may be regarded as the number of years' earnings that investors are prepared to pay for in the purchase price of the company's shares. The higher the PER, the greater the confidence of investors in the future of the company.

21.5   SUMMARY OF MOST USEFUL RATIOS

Return on capital employed

$$\frac{\text{Profit before interest and tax}}{\text{capital employed}} \times 100$$

Net Profit percentage

$$\frac{\text{Profit before interest and tax}}{\text{sales}} \times 100$$

Gross Profit percentage

$$\frac{\text{Gross profit}}{\text{sales}} \times 100$$

Utilisation of capital

$$\frac{\text{Sales}}{\text{capital employed}}$$

Utilisation of fixed assets

$$\frac{\text{Sales}}{\text{fixed assets}}$$

Utilisation of total assets

$$\frac{\text{Sales}}{\text{fixed assets + current assets}}$$

Stockturn

$$\frac{\text{Cost of sales}}{\text{average stock}}$$

Debtors ratio

$$\frac{\text{Trade debtors}}{\text{credit sales}} \times 365$$

Creditors ratio

$$\frac{\text{Trade creditors}}{\text{credit purchases}} \times 365$$

21.6 LIMITATIONS OF RATIOS

1. Ratios only show the results of carrying on business; they do not indicate the causes of poor ratios. Further investigation is required.

2. The accuracy of ratios depends upon the quality of the information from which they are calculated; the required information is not always disclosed in accounting statements and account headings may be misleading.

3. Ratios can only be used to compare 'like-with-like'.

4. Ratios tend to ignore the time factor in seasonal businesses e.g. widely fluctuating stock levels and debtor levels.

21.7 RATIOS IN EXAMINATIONS

1. Calculations of ratios. Name the ratio, show the model and all workings.

2. Selection of ratios. Choose ratios that are relevant to the question whether it be about profitability, liquidity or some other aspect of a business.

3. Comments. These should be concise and relevant. Avoid making assumptions which are not in the question unless your answer makes it clear that it is based on assumptions.

4. Comparison of the financial statements of two different businesses, or of the same business for different years, may require adjustments to be made to one or both sets of statements to place them on the same basis. The usual adjustments are for a management salary in the profit and loss account of a sole trader when comparing it with that of a limited company; or the inclusion of a 'notional' rent in a business which owns its own premises when the comparison is with another business which rents its premises.

21.7.1 EXAMPLE 1.(Calculation of profitability and liquidity ratios)

The trading and profit and loss accounts and balance sheets of Laurel, a sole trader, and Hardy Ltd. at 30 June 19-1 were as follows:

Trading and profit and loss accounts

	Laurel		Hardy Ltd.	
	£	£	£	£
Sales		100,000		200,000
less Cost of sales				
Opening stock	6,000		29,000	
Purchases	44,000		94,000	
	50,000		123,000	
Closing stock	5,000		31,000	
		45,000		92,000
Gross profit		55,000		108,000
Operating expenses		25,000		58,000
Net profit		30,000		50,000

Balance sheets

	Laurel		Hardy Ltd.	
	£	£	£	£
Fixed assets		80,000		145,000
Current assets				
Stock	5,000		31,000	
Debtors	4,000		25,000	
Bank balance	6,000		18,000	
	15,000		74,000	
less				
Current liabilities				
Creditors	9,000		51,000	
		6,000		23,000
		86,000		168,000
Capital		86,000		
		86,000		
Ordinary shares of £1				125,000
Retained profit				43,000
				168,000

Both Laurel and Hardy Ltd. are in the same line of business. All purchases and sales of both businesses are on credit.

Laurel has been offered a position with another company at a salary of £15,000 per annum. He manages his own business and if he were to employ somebody to manage it for him, he estimates he would have to pay the manager £10,000 per annum. If Laurel sold his business he could reinvest his capital at 15 percent per annum.

REQUIRED

(a) Three ratios to compare the profitability of the two businesses.

(b) Three ratios to compare the liquidity of the two businesses.

(c) Comment on the businesses, using the ratios prepared for(a) and (b) above.

(d) Advise Laurel on the best way of maximising his income in the future.

ANSWER

Adjustment of Laurel's net profit:

	£
Profit per profit and loss account	30,000
less: Notional management salary	10,000
Adjusted profit	20,000

(a)

	Laurel	Hardy Ltd
Return on capital employed		
$\dfrac{\text{Net profit}}{\text{capital employed}} \times 100$		
$\dfrac{20,000}{86,000} \times 100$	26.26%	
$\dfrac{50,000}{168,000} \times 100$		29.76%
Net profit percentage		

	Laurel	Hardy Ltd

$\dfrac{\text{Net profit}}{\text{sales}} \times 100$

$\dfrac{20,000}{100,000} \times 100$ — 20%

$\dfrac{50,000}{200,000} \times 100$ — 25%

Gross profit percentage

$\dfrac{55,000}{100,000} \times 100$ — 55%

$\dfrac{108,000}{200,000} \times 100$ — 54%

(b)

Current ratio

Current assets:current liabilities

15,000:9,000 — 1.67:1

74,000:51,000 — 1.45:1

Liquid ratio

Current assets - stock:current liabilities

10,000:9,000 — 1.11:1

43,000:51,000 — 0.84:1

Debtors ratio

$\dfrac{\text{Debtors}}{\text{sales}} \times 365$

$\dfrac{4,000}{100,000} \times 365$ — 14.6 days

$\dfrac{25,000}{200,000} \times 365$ — 45.6 days

(c)   After adjusting Laurel's profit for a notional management salary of £10,000 his net profit has been reduced by 33^1/$_2$%. The remaining profit of £20,000 more truly represents the return he is getting on his capital.

Laurel's return on capital is 26.26% compared with a better return of 29.76% for Hardy Ltd. This is explained partly by the fact that Laurel's net profit percentage, allowing for his notional management salary, is only 20% against that of 25% for Hardy Ltd. A comparison of the gross profit percentage, however, shows that Laurel's is a little better at 55% as against 54%. This indicates that Laurel appears to be managing the overheads of his business less efficiently than Hardy Ltd.

His overheads (including management salary) are 35% of turnover as compared with 29% in Hardy Ltd's.

Laurel's utilisation of capital ratio is $\dfrac{100,000}{86,000}$ or 1.16 compared with 1.19 ($\dfrac{200,000}{168,000}$) for Hardy; there is little difference between them.

The current ratio for Laurel's business (1.67:1) is slightly better than Hardy Ltd's (1.45:1). Without any information about the nature of the business being carried on by the two concerns, the adequacy of these ratios is difficult to judge: normally a current ratio between 1.5:1 and 2:1 is considered to be satisfactory. The liquid ratio of Laurel's business is 1.11:1 which may be considered satisfactory, but Hardy Ltd.'s liquid ratio is 0.84:1 which seems very low. A noticeable feature of the two businesses is the disparity between their respective stock turnovers: Laurel: 45,000/5,500 = 8.2 times; Hardy Ltd: $\dfrac{92,000}{30,000}$

= 3.1 times. The information in the question does not reveal the likely cause of this difference but the substantial difference between Hardy Ltd's current and liquid ratios, combined with its stockturn suggests very strongly that Hardy Ltd. may be carrying unduly high stocks.

Another noticeable disparity between the two businesses is the surprising difference between their debtors' ratios. The average period of credit taken by Laurel's customers is only 14.6 days, while that taken by Hardy Ltd. is 45.6 days. The difference between the two credit periods is one month, and that is itself a normal time allowed for credit. It would appear that Laurel may be too strict in his allowance of credit to customers whilst Hardy Ltd. suggests a lax control over credit.

It is not surprising, given the above information, that Hardy Ltd is taking extended credit from its suppliers; the surprise is the extent of the creditors ratio, which is $\frac{94,000}{51,000} \times 365 = 184$ days which must surely mean impending trouble for Hardy Ltd. from its creditors.

Hardy Ltd. is clearly suffering from the effects of overtrading i.e. expanding its business with inadequate working capital to support the expansion. This seems to be borne out by stockpiling, substantial debtors, and creditors nearly three times the amount of the liquid funds available.

(d) Laurel has three options:

1. To employ a manager for his business at a salary of £10,000 per year, reducing his annual profit to £20,000 per annum. He could then accept the offer of employment with another company at a salary of £15,000 per annum, giving a total income of £35,000 per annum.

2. To accept employment with another company at a salary of £15,000, sell his own business for £86,000 and invest the capital at 15 percent per annum giving him further income of £12,900, making a total income of £27,900.

3. To continue to run and manage his own business on his existing income of £30,000 per annum.

Option 1. would give Laurel the largest income, but he should seek a suitable contract of employment from his prospective employer before committing himself. He may possibly prefer the freedom of self-employment to an additional income of £5,000 per annum.

EXAMPLE 2 (Reconstruction of trading and profit and loss accounts and balance sheet from given accounting ratios.)

Redvers was in business and at 31 December 19-4 his capital was £40,000. All his sales and purchases were on credit.

The following information is available for the year to 31 December 19-5:

At 31 December 19-5 stock was valued at £19,000, which was £5,000 less than at the end of the previous year.

    Rate of stockturn: 6 times.
    Mark up 25%.
    Selling and distribution expenses: 8% of sales.
    Other overheads ?
    Net profit percentage 10%.
    Sales/fixed assets: 5 times.
    Sales/current assets: 4 times.
    Average period of credit taken by debtors: 30 days.
    The only current assets are stock, debtors and balance at bank.
    Average time taken to pay creditors 60 days.

REQUIRED

Prepare the trading and profit and loss account for the year to 31 December 19-5 and a balance sheet as at that date.(Make all calculations to the nearest £)

ANSWER

Workings:

    Opening stock £(19,000 + 5,000) = £24,000
    Average stock £24,000 + 19,000/2 = £21,500
    Cost of sales: £21,500 × 6 = £129,000
    Sales: £129,000 × $\frac{125}{100}$ = £161,250

Purchases: (Cost of sales + closing stock - opening stock)

$$= £(129{,}000 + 19{,}000 - 24{,}000) = £124{,}000$$

Selling and distribution: 8% of £161,250 = £12,900

Net profit: 10% of £161,250 = £16,125

Fixed assets: $\dfrac{£161{,}250}{5} = £32{,}250$

Debtors: $\dfrac{£161{,}250}{365} \times 30 = £13{,}253$

Total current assets $\dfrac{£161{,}250}{4} = £40{,}313$

Creditors: $\dfrac{£124{,}000}{365} \times 60 = £20{,}384$

Redvers
Trading and profit and loss account
for the year to 31 December 19-5

	£	£
Sales		161,250
Less Cost of sales		
Opening stock	24,000	
Purchases	124,000	
	148,000	
less closing stock	19,000	129,000
Gross profit (20% of £161,250)		32,250
Selling and distribution	12,900	
Other expenses (balancing figure)	3,225	16,125
Net profit (10% of sales)		16,125

Balance sheet as at 31 December 19-5

	£	£
Fixed assets		32,250
Current assets		
Stock	19,000	
Debtors	13,253	
Bank (balancing figure)	8,060	
	40,313	
less Current liabilities - Creditors	20,384	19,929
		52,179
Capital at 1 January 19-4		40,000
Net profit for the year		16,125
		56,125
Drawings (balancing figure)		3,946
		52,179

21.7.2 EXERCISE 1 (Calculation of accounting ratios)

Anita and Leila are partners in business. Their Trading and profit and loss accounts for the years ended 31 December 19-2 and 19-3, and the balance sheets of their business at 31 December 19-2 and 19-3 respectively are as follows:

Trading and profit and loss accounts
for the years ended 31 December

	19-2		19-3	
	£	£	£	£
Sales		125,000		150,000
Less Cost of sales				
Opening stock	8,500		11,500	
Purchases	88,000		95,125	
	96,500		106,625	
less Closing stock	11,500	85,000	12,125	94,500
Gross profit		40,000		55,500
Wages	17,125		21,400	
Rent and rates	5,600		5,600	
Sundry expenses	4,025		4,500	
Depreciation	2,000		3,000	
		28,750		34,500
Net profit		11,250		21,000

Balance sheets as at 31 December

	19-2			19-3	
	£	£	£	£	£
Fixed assets (NBV)					
Premises		–		25,000	
Equipment	24,000			20,000	
Motor vehicles	12,000			15,000	
Office furniture	2,250			3,270	
		38,250			63,270
Current assets					
Stock	11,500			12,125	
Debtors	9,590			14,380	
Bank balance	2,010			–	
	23,100			26,505	
less					
Current liabilities					
Creditors	10,800		10,425		
Bank overdraft	–		4,600		
		12,300	15,025		11,480
		50,550			74,750
Capital accounts					
Anita	25,000			35,000	
Leila	25,000	50,000		35,000	70,000
Current accounts					
Anita	1,000			2,000	
Leila	(450)	550		2,750	4,750
		50,550			74,750

REQUIRED

(a) Calculate the following ratios for Anita and Leila:

    (i)   Return on capital employed;

    (ii)   Gross profit percentage;

    (iii)   Net profit percentage;

    (iv)   Current ratio;

    (v)   Liquid ratio;

    (vi)   Stockturn;

    (vii)   Debtors ratio;

    (viii) Creditors ratio.

EXERCISE 2 (Preparation of Trading and profit and loss account and balance sheet using given ratios.)

John Kelworthy is considering purchasing the business of Ken Porter and is looking into the financial aspects of the business. Kelworthy is waiting for a copy of the accounts for the past year, to 30 June 19-3, from Porter but in the meantime he is trying to reconstruct the accounts from statistical information which Porter has already given him.

The information is as follows:

All sales and purchases are on credit.

Net book value of fixed assets at 30 June 19-3 (i.e. after depreciation has been provided for the year): £42,000

Porter has charged depreciation on his fixed assets on the reducing balance method using a rate of 20% per annum. There were no purchases or sales of fixed assets during the year to 30 June 19-3.

Other information for the year to 30 June 19-3:

Sales:fixed assets ratio 5.5:1.

Mark-up 33$^1/_3$%

Stock turn 15 times. The average stock maintained by Porter during the year to 30 June 19-3 was £7,700. At the end of the financial year, the closing stock was 50 per cent higher than the stock at the beginning of the year.)

Net profit percentage: 12$^1/_2$%

Average period of credit taken by debtors: 28 days.

Average time taken to pay creditors: 35 days.

Current ratio at 30 June 19-3: 2:1.

The only current assets are stock and debtors. The bank account is overdrawn.

Porter has drawn £100 per week for living expenses.

REQUIRED

Prepare a Trading and profit and loss account for Ken Porter for the year to 30 June 19-3 and a balance sheet as at that date. (Calculations should be to the nearest £).

21.8   KEY POINTS TO REMEMBER

> 1. Answers involving the calculation of ratios should always give the names of the ratios, the model in each case and show the workings. (If the calculation is arithmetically incorrect, the model may still earn a mark.)
>
> 2. Make sure the ratios are always relevant to the question.
>
> 3. Learn the form in which each ratio is normally shown e.g. percentage, no. of times, days, or as true ratios.
>
> 4. When required to select ratios, choose the more common or obvious ones for the purpose; avoid the temptation to select unusual ratios just for the sake of being seen to be clever or different from other students.

5. Take care to calculate ratios accurately. It is not necessary to take answers to too many places of decimals; use discretion. It would be quite unnecessary to express the debtors' average period of credit as 28.645 days; 28.6 will do.

6. When commenting on ratios, express the answer clearly, noting any relationships between the ratios concerned. Avoid being 'dogmatic' about causes of adverse ratios as the question will almost certainly not give sufficient information for a definitive answer.

COMMON ERRORS

- selecting wrong amounts from accounts; eg. taking the figure of net current assets when gross current assets are required for the current ratio.
- failure to reduce the right hand term of a ratio to 1 e.g. 3.5:2 instead of 1.75:1.
- 'inventing' ratios by selecting items between which there is no real relationship.

21.9   EXAMINATION QUESTIONS

QUESTION 1   (Cambridge November 1989)

The summarised final accounts of two companies are set out below. Both companies have many features such as products, geographical areas and selling organisations in common. It would appear therefore that a comparison of the two companies by using selected ratios of their financial performance would be beneficial.

Trading results
Financial years ending in 19-9

	R.CIRCLE PTE.LTD.COMPANY £M		S.ROOT PTE.LTD.COMPANY £M	
Sales		700		1,050
Less Cost of Sales				
Opening Stock	240		300	
Purchases	560		780	
	800		1,080	
Closing Stock	300	500	330	750
		200		300
Interest	–		15	
Expenses	85	85	95	110
		£115		£190

Balance sheets as at date in 19-9

	R.Circle £M	S.Root £M		R.Circle £M	S.Root £M
Ord.Sh.Cap.			Fixed assets	210	340
£1 ord.Sh	300	300	Stock	300	330
General Reserve	200	150	Trade Debtors	140	180
P&L Balance	60	50	Cash	50	–
Loan(repayable 19-2)	–	150			
Trade creditors	140	120			
Bank Overdraft	–	80			
	£700	£850		£700	£850

You should note that all sales and purchases are conducted on a credit basis. Further the directors of both companies believe that these figures reflect the relatively stable business environment and are not affected by any significant distortions.

REQUIRED

(a) Calculate for each company the following ratios:

Net Profit to Sales	Stock Turnover
Quick/Liquid ratio	Return on Equity
Return on NET total assets employed	Earnings per share

FOR EACH RATIO YOU SHOULD SHOW THE BASES (FIGURES) USED IN YOUR CALCULATIONS.

(12 Marks)

(b) Compare the performances of the two companies using three criteria:

(1) Profitability,

(2) Utilisation of resources,

(3) Return to ordinary shareholders.

You should use selected ratios from your answers to part (a). *(9 marks)*

(c) Although the use of ratios is widespread in business these techniques do have limitations. Identify three possible limitations. *(4 marks)*

(Total 25 marks)

QUESTION 2   (London June 1988)

An individual with £10,000 to invest in ordinary shares is considering the respective merits of two companies, Ainsdale Limited and Formby Limited. Both companies were formed on 1 June 19-7.

Their balance sheets at 31 May 19-8 were as follows:

	Ainsdale	Formby
	£	£
Fixed Assets (net book value)	159,000	173,000
Current assets:		
Stock	32,000	27,000
Debtors	41,000	22,000
Bank	–	13,000
Total Assets	232,000	235,000
Less Creditors; amount falling due within one year	62,000	65,000
	170,000	170,000
Share Capital:		
Ordinary Shares of 25p each	50,400	162,000
Profit and Loss account	(400)	8,000
Creditors: amounts falling due after more than one year:		
7% Debentures	120,000	–
	170,000	170,000

Note: Profits (before interest deductions in the case of Ainsdale Limited) of both companies were expected to increase from the 19-8 level of £8,000 to £22,000 in 19-9 and £24,000 per annum thereafter.

You are required to:

(a) Advise the investor as to which, if any, of the two companies is the better investment. State reasons for your choice. *(7 marks)*

(b) State two items of further information which might be needed before making a final decision.

(8 marks)

(Total 15 marks)

QUESTION 3 (Oxford June 1987)

The following figures relate to Rowring plc, a small retailing company:

1 January 19-6	Reserves £40,000
	Book value of fixed assets £359,900
31 December 19-6	Creditors £18,420 (the only current liability)
	Capital employed £360,000 (includes Debentures)
	Cost of Sales £437,850
	Reserves £40,000 (excluding Profit and Loss A/C balance.)
	Debentures £100,000

Some of the relevant ratios for the year ended 31 December 19-6 were:

Current ratio	2:1
Acid Test ratio	3:2
Stock Turn	29.19 times
Gross Profit Margin (on sales)	30%
Dividend cover	3 times
Coverage of fixed charges	4.75 times
Collection period for debtors	12 days (assume 300 days per year)
Net profit to Ordinary shares	15%

Ordinary dividend paid at 5p per share

All sales are on credit.

The capital consists of Ordinary shares only.

The nominal value of shares is £1 and the market price at 31 December 19-6 is £1.50.

Debentures in issue are at 8%

You are required to:

(a) prepare the trading and profit and loss account of the company for the year ended 31 December 19-6 and the balance sheet at that date, using any format that you prefer. Your answer should show at least opening and closing stocks, expenses and as much balance sheet detail as is possible.

(34 marks)

(b) Calculate:
   (i)   The yield on Ordinary shares
   (ii) Earnings per share
   (iii) Price/earnings ratio

(6 marks)

ALL WORKINGS MUST BE SHOWN

NOTE: IGNORE TAXATION

(Total 40 marks)

QUESTION 4 (Oxford June 1987)

When comparing the accounts of two companies to assess their performance and efficiency what factors would you have to take into account concerning the companies? Give an example of two ratios that could be affected by these factors and explain why. *(8 marks)*

QUESTION 5 (Author's question, after JMB)

Colin Henry has received the published accounts of Juniper PLC. He is puzzled by some of the items in the accounts and has written to the managing director requesting explanations of those items, which are included in the following extracts from the Directors' report and accounts:

Juniper PLC Extracts from the Directors' report and accounts:

	Years to 30 June		
	19-5	19-6	Item
	£m	£m	
Turnover			
UK sales	90.7	93.5	
Overseas sales	2.6	4.0	
Total	93.3	97.5	

327

	Years to 30 June		
	19-5	19-6	Item
	£m	£m	
Profit before taxation	6.7	7.2	
Taxation on profit for the year	3.3	2.8	
Earnings attributable to ordinary shareholders	3.4	4.4	1
Dividends	1.1	1.1	
Retained profit for the year	2.3	3.3	2
Total capital employed	26.4	28.9	
Net asset value	25.0	27.8	3
Ratios	%	%	
Profit /turnover	7.2	7.4	4
Asset turnover	3.3	3.4	5
Profit/total capital employed	25.4	24.9	6
Profit/net asset value	26.8	25.9	7

	Pence per Share	Pence per Share	
Earnings	34.0	44.0	8
Dividends	11.1	11.1	9
Net asset value	250.0	278.0	10

You are required to draft a letter for the managing director to send to Colin Henry, explaining

(a) The meanings and significance of the items numbered 1 to 10 above; *(20 marks)*

(b) Why the net asset value of each share is only 278p although they are quoted on the Stock Exchange at 345p *(10 marks)*

(c) The relationships between items 4 to 7. *(10 marks)*

(Total 40 marks)

QUESTION 6 (Author's question, after JMB)

Woodman is considering investing in Sycamore PLC and has sent you relevant data he has received from that company for your opinion. In order to help you form an opinion, you have also obtained similar data for other comparable companies.

	Sycamore PLC			Comparable Companies
	19-1	19-2	19-3	19-3
Return on long-term capital employed	13%	14%	16%	17.5%
Gross profit as a percentage of sales	20%	23%	25%	25%
Net profit as a percentage of sales	8%	10%	13%	14%
Stock turnover (times)	7	8	10	12
Debtors collection period (in weeks)	6	5	4	5
Current ratio	1.3:1	1.5:1	1.8:1	1.75:1
Liquid ratio	0.7:1	1:1	1.2:1	0.9:1

You are required to draft a letter to Woodman

(a) Analysing and commenting on Sycamore PLC's profitability and asset utilisation *(6 marks)*

(b) Analysing and commenting on Sycamore PLC's liquidity *(6 marks)*

(c) Outlining the dangers of using inter-firm comparison *(8 marks)*

(Total 20 marks)

QUESTION 7 (AEB June 1989)

The following summarised financial information is available on two companies for the year ended 31 December 19-8.

	Amigo plc £million	Barres plc £million
Sales	50	10
Administration charges	1.5	0.4
Selling and distribution charges	2.5	0.8
Gross profit percentage	25%	50%
Other balances at 31 December 19-8	**£million**	**£million**
Fixed assets at cost less aggregate depreciation	21	2.9
Net current assets	16	3.23
Balances as at 1 January 19-8		
Issued capital £1 ordinary shares fully paid	15	2
Share premium	5	Nil
Retained earnings	8	3
10% Debentures	5	Nil

The balances at 1 January 19-8 had remained unchanged throughout the year.

Additional information.

(1)   Both companies had declared and paid a final dividend as follows: Amigo plc 10% Barres plc 50%.

(2)   The directors of Amigo plc were considering buying shares in Barres plc as an investment. On 31 December 19-8 Barres plc ordinary shares were quoted on the Stock Exchange at £4 per share.

REQUIRED

(a)   For the year ended 31 December 19-8:

(i)   summarised revenue statements

(ii)   profit and loss appropriation accounts for each of the companies.   *(8 marks)*

(b)   Calculate **three** suitable ratios to illustrate the profitability of each of the companies. Comment on the profitability of each company.   *(7 marks)*

(c)   What is the minimum amount that Amigo plc must invest in the equity of Barres plc in order to achieve a controlling interest?   *(3 marks)*

(**Note:** use the share price quoted on 31 December 1988.)

(d)   Write a brief report giving reasons why Amigo plc may see Barres plc as a suitable investment.

(5 marks)

(e)   Prepare a balance sheet extract to show how Amigo plc would record its investment in Barres plc on the assumption that 1.1 million shares were purchased on 1 January 19-9.   *(2 marks)*

(Total 25 marks)

QUESTION 8 (AEB November 1989)

The following financial information is available on two companies Telven plc and Sendra plc as at 31 March 19-9.

	Telven plc £'000	Sendra plc £'000
Authorised share capital		
£1 Ordinary shares	500	1,500
10% £1 Preference shares	500	–
Issued share capital		
£1 Ordinary shares fully paid	500	1,200
10% £1 Preference shares fully paid	400	–

	£'000	£'000
Reserves		
Share premium	250	400
Retained earnings	350	550
Loan capital		
11% Secured debentures - 2005	500	–
10% Debentures 19-5 - 2000	–	200

Unwin, a shareholder who owns ordinary shares in both companies, had recently been reading the annual reports, in which Sendra plc anticipated little growth over the next financial year, whereas the chairman of Telven plc was very optimistic and indicated in the report that further long term fixed interest borrowings had been arranged to finance an acceleration in development.

Unwin extracted the following additional information from the annual reports.

(1)

	Telven plc £'000	Sendra plc £'000
19-8/-9 Net trading profit before interest charges	300	380
19-9/-0 Forecast net trading profit before interest charges	600	400

(2) Both companies would make transfers to general reserve in 19-9/-0 of £200,000 and both forecast the declaration of a 20% ordinary share dividend. The preference share dividend would also be paid.

(3) Telven plc issued £300,000 of 8% debentures 2010 at par on 1 April 19-9. Unwin decided to consult his financial adviser since he could not understand why Telven plc, a company with substantial fixed interest borrowings, was going to get itself further into debt. He was afraid that his future Telven dividends would be reduced owing to heavy interest payments.

REQUIRED

As the financial adviser to Unwin:

(a) Explain the term 'gearing' and distinguish between high and low gearing ratios. *(5 marks)*

(b) Calculate a gearing ratio for each company as at 1 April 19-9. *(6 marks)*

(c) Prepare forecast profit and loss appropriation accounts for each company for 19-9/-0.

(8 marks)

(d) Prepare a brief report to Unwin indicating why the gearing ratio in a company is important to an ordinary shareholder. Your report should also consider the points about which Unwin expressed concern. *(6 marks)*

(Total 25 marks)

22 THE MANAGEMENT OF WORKING CAPITAL AND SHORT-TERM FINANCE: LONG-TERM FINANCE

Questions concerned with these topics require:-
- an appreciation of the importance of working capital and its vital role in business
- an understanding of the circulating nature of current assets
- recognition of the necessity for adequate liquidity
- ability to explain ways in which working capital may be controlled so as to maintain liquidity
- discussion of sources of short-term and long term finance

This chapter should be studied with Chapters 12 (Statements of Source and Application of Funds) and 21 (Interpretation of accounts and accounting ratios) in mind.

22.1   WORKING CAPITAL

Exhibit 1 is a diagrammatic representation of the flow of funds into a business and the way they circulate internally.

Some of the funds are used to purchase fixed assets which are required for retention in the business for the purpose of providing goods or services; fixed assets are not acquired with the intention of reselling them in the normal course of trading.

When fixed assets are of no further use to the business, they are disposed of, and any proceeds provide another source of funds for the business.

The operation of fixed assets needs to be supported with an adequate supply of WORKING CAPITAL. For example, manufacturing machinery requires:

> raw materials,
>
> labour to operate and maintain the machines,
>
> overhead expenditure, such as rent of the factory,
>
> power to drive the machinery etc.

Raw materials, while being worked on become work in progress; work in progress becomes finished goods. The finished goods may be sold for cash which becomes another source of funds for the business. If the goods are sold on credit the asset of finished goods is replaced by another asset: debtors. When the debtors pay for the goods they provide more funds for the business.

Meanwhile cash has had to be paid to the suppliers of the raw materials (creditors), the workforce and for the business overheads; more raw materials have had to be purchased for future production.

The way in which cash circulates around the working capital system of a business in various guises as stocks of raw materials, work in progress, finished goods, debtors, and returns as cash again may clearly be seen in Exhibit 1.

It is easy to appreciate why current assets are known as the CIRCULATING CAPITAL of a business.

As with any circulatory system, whether it be in the human body or in a machine, the health or efficiency of the whole entity depends upon the efficiency of the circulatory system. For this very reason, the analysis of business performance uses ratios to test the state of working capital and its constituent parts.It should also be remembered that a business is expected to generate funds internally by its operations and not to depend on external sources except when a major expansion is being considered. No doubt the study of Statements of Source and Application of Funds will have made this point apparent already.

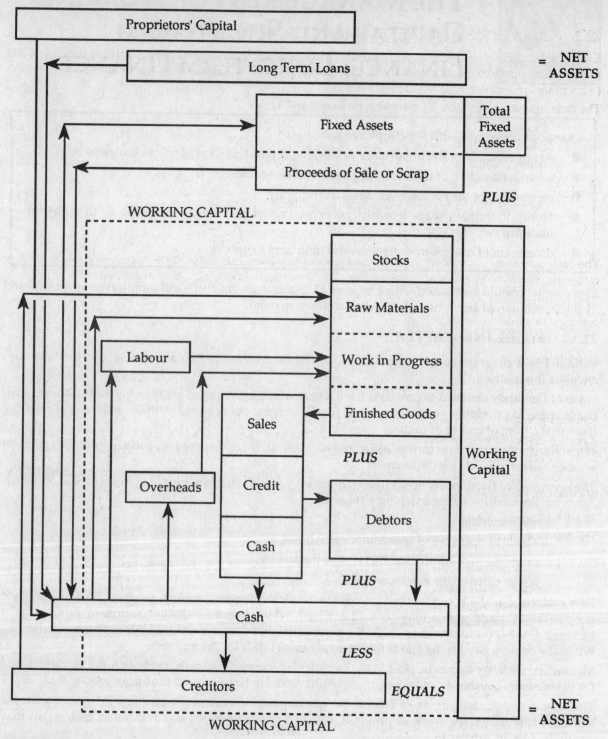

EXHIBIT 1

Examination questions are usually based upon:

(a) The distinction between profitability and liquidity

(b) The role of profitability in the generation of funds

(c) The effect of the generation of funds on the working capital

(d) Analysis and assessment of working capital

(e) Management of working capital

(f) Methods of raising additional short-term and long-term funds.

Items (a) - (c) have already been dealt with in Chapters 12 and 21; this chapter will now deal with (d),(e) and (f).

22.2 ANALYSIS AND ASSESSMENT OF WORKING CAPITAL

Every business needs to recover, with as little delay as possible, cash from sales to replace the cash it has to pay to its suppliers for its stock. The CASH OPERATING CYCLE measures the time it takes for 'cash' to circulate around the working capital system.

The cash operating cycle for a trader will be found as follows:

	Days
Stock turnover	X
plus Average period of credit taken by customers	X
	X
Average period of credit taken from suppliers	(X)
Cash operating cycle	X

The cash operating cycle for a manufacturing company takes into account the turnover periods for raw materials, work in progress, and finished stocks. These periods are calculated as follows:

Raw materials:

$$\frac{\text{Average stock of raw materials}}{\text{Cost of raw materials used}} \times 365 = x \text{ days}$$

Work in progress:

$$\frac{\text{Average stock of work in progress}}{\text{Cost of goods manufactured}} \times 365 = x \text{ days}$$

Finished goods:

$$\frac{\text{Average stock of finished goods}}{\text{Cost of goods sold}} \times 365 = x \text{ days}$$

If the cash operating cycle is too long, the cause should be apparent from the ratios used in the calculation; further investigation of the causes will lead to the taking of corrective action.

22.2.1 EXAMPLE (Calculation of cash operating cycle for a sole trader)

The following is the trading account for B. Ingo Ltd. for the year to 31 December 19-5:

	£	£
Sales (all on credit)		45,000
Less: Cost of sales		
Opening stock	3,100	
Purchases (all on credit)	28,000	
	31,100	
Closing stock	3,310	27,790
Gross profit		17,210

Other information:

	At 31 December 19-5
Debtors	£5,918
Creditors	£4,600

REQUIRED

A calculation of the cash operating cycle for B.Ingo Ltd.

ANSWER

Stock turnover:

$$\text{Average stock} = \frac{3,100 + 3,310}{2} = 3,205$$

		Days
No. of days $= \dfrac{3,205}{26,000} \times 365 =$		45
Debtors period of credit $\dfrac{5,918}{45,000} \times 365 =$		$\underline{48}$
		93
Time taken to pay creditors		
$\dfrac{4,600}{28,000} \times 365 =$		$\underline{(60)}$
Cash operating cycle		33

22.2.2 EXERCISE (Calculation of cash operating cycle for a manufacturing company)

The following information is available for The Batwing Manufacturing Company for the year to 31 December 19-3:

Direct materials used:	£99,985
Cost of goods produced:	£151,072
Cost of sales:	£181,100
Sales (all on credit)	£211,970
Purchases of raw materials (all on credit)	£95,900
Raw materials:	
Stock at 1 January 19-3	£6,500
Stock at 31 December 19-3	£8,840
Work in progress:	
Stock at 1 January 19-3	£7,800
Stock at 31 December 19-3	£7,100
Finished goods:	
Stock at 1 January 19-3	£15,000
Stock at 31 December 19-3	£16,754
Debtors at 31 December 19-3	£18,000
Creditors at 31 December 19-3	£15,764

REQUIRED

Calculate the cash operating cycle for The Batwing Manufacturing Company.

22.3 MANAGEMENT OF WORKING CAPITAL AND SHORT-TERM FINANCE

A satisfactory cash operating cycle requires good management of working capital. The cycle will be lengthened by excessive stock levels, inadequate control over the period of credit taken by customers or by failure to take full advantage of the period of credit allowed by suppliers.

Management of Stock

Stockturn should be compared with the rate which might be expected in an efficiently run business in the same trade. Too high stock levels are costly:

1. Capital 'locked up' in the stocks is idle money which is not earning profits.
2. Storage of stock is costly and should be kept to a minimum consistent with efficient storage. The costs include rent, heating and lighting and maintenance of stores or warehouse, wages of staff, handling costs etc.
3. Stock may be lost through deterioration, evaporation etc.
4. Stock may become obsolete.

On the other hand, stock levels which are too low may lead to:

1. 'Stockouts' which may interrupt production or result in a failure to meet orders.
2. Excessive purchasing department costs resulting from the large volume of small orders.
3. Loss of quantity discounts obtainable for bulk orders.

Maximum and minimum levels should be fixed for each item of stock and re-order levels should take account of the minimum permitted stock level, the rate of usage and the lead-time required for the receipt of stock after placing the order.

Excessive stock levels may be reduced by:

1. Delaying re-ordering until the stock has been reduced to the desired level. This will gradually decrease the stock level and increase the liquidity of the business. The current ratio should not be affected (in theory), but the liquidity ratio should gradually improve. The cash operating cycle will be shortened.

2. Disposal of surplus stock by sale; the current ratio should not, in theory, be affected but there should be an immediate improvement in the liquidity ratio and in the cash operating cycle.

Management of Debtors

Capital is sometimes referred to as being 'locked up' in debtors. In reality, such cash is financing other peoples' businesses instead of the one for which it was intended.

Granting credit to customers is an essential part of business, especially if trade is to be encouraged. However it requires, on the part of the creditor, credit control and credit management.

Credit Control

It is implicit in credit transactions that the customer agrees to pay on or before an agreed date. Failure on the part of the customer to pay as agreed constitutes the breaking of the agreement by the customer. The creditor should take such action as is possible to obtain payment without further delay. Further credit allowed to defaulting debtors before they have paid overdue debts will only worsen the working capital position of the creditor. Debts become more difficult to collect the older they are allowed to become and the rate at which they become bad debts increases rapidly once they pass the due date. No further credit should be extended to such debtors until they have paid the overdue debts; until then further dealings should require 'cash with order'.

Credit Management

An efficient system of credit management will minimise credit control problems. Credit management involves enquiring into prospective customers' credit-worthiness and their past payments records with other suppliers before allowing them credit terms. Special agencies exist to supply such information to businesses.

Discounts for Prompt Payment

Debtors may be encouraged to pay promptly by the offer of cash discounts if they pay within a stipulated time. On no account should they be permitted to take the discount if they do not pay within the time allowed.

Debt Factoring

This is the sale of book debts to a Factoring Company which exists to buy other peoples' book debts at a discount. The selling company receives the money for the debts, less the discount, at once. The Factoring Company collects the debts; its profit comes from the discount. If the factoring is 'without recourse', the Factoring Company has to bear the loss if any of the debts prove to be bad. If the factoring is 'with recourse', the selling company must compensate the Factoring Company for bad debts.

A company which factors its debts may improve its cash operating cycle quite considerably but its current and liquid ratios remain virtually unchanged, being only slightly worsened by the discount allowed to the factor.

Management of Cash

This is done by the preparation of cash budgets. Annual cash budgets must be broken down into monthly cash budgets and prior to the commencement of each month the monthly budget should be further broken down into weekly budgets. If the cash situation is critical, the weekly budget will be further broken down into daily forecasts. It should be remembered that cash budgets show the expected cash position on the last day of the budget period but the incidence of cash inflows and outflows may produce quite unexpected and critical positions within the period.

Where the cash situation is seen to become critical it may be necessary to take steps to expedite the collection of debts or to delay some payments. Capital expenditure may be deferred, or alternative ways of acquiring the assets considered, such as:

1. Purchase on credit terms. Payment of the capital outlay is delayed for a limited period. This has the effect of worsening the working capital ratios because creditors will be increased by the amount of the outlay. However, the liquidity of the company will not be depleted until the debt becomes due.

2. Hire purchase. Payment is made by instalments over a period of time. Each instalment consists of part of the cash price of the assets and an element of interest. The asset will be shown at its full cash price in the fixed assets on the balance sheet with a corresponding amount as a creditor in the current liabilities. This will result in a worsening of the working capital ratios but cash will be reduced only by the amounts of the instalments instead of by the full cash price.

3. Leasing. The assets are leased or hired. Working capital is reduced only by the periodic leasing payments.

4. Sell/lease back. Assets are sold to a finance company which then leases them back to the user. This is similar to leasing (above) except that the assets have already been purchased by the user. The sale of the assets to a finance company produces cash for the business without the loss of the use of the assets.

The importance of making arrangements in good time for anticipated requirements for bank overdrafts or loans by an early approach to the bank manager with a competently prepared budget cannot be emphasised too strongly.

Off Balance Sheet Financing

This term describes sources of finance which do not appear on the face of the balance sheet such as factoring trade debts and leasing fixed assets.

Management of Surplus Funds

Too much liquidity in a business can be harmful inasmuch as money is lying idle in a bank account instead of being used to earn revenue. If it is surplus to immediate requirements it should be invested. The following are some of the opportunities available:

1. Loans to other companies in the group, if any.

2. Bank deposit account.

3. Purchase of Treasury Bills.

4. Loans to Finance Houses, Merchant Banks overnight or for longer periods.

5. Loans to Local Authorities for 7 days or longer periods.

(Options 4 and 5 are only possible where substantial sums of money are surplus to requirements, usually in excess of £10,000 in the case of 4. and £50,000 in the case of 5.)

Any of the above investments would appear as working capital in the balance sheet.

Management of Creditors

It is important to recognise the risks of delaying payment of creditors when trying to overcome liquidity problems:

1. Loss of discounts.

2. Loss of credit facilities.

3. Risk of losing suppliers

4. Risk of legal action

5. Reputation of poor credit rating in the trade.

22.4 OVERTRADING

Overtrading occurs when a business expands too quickly without adequate working capital to support the expansion.

In order to meet the expansion, stocks are built up; as sales increase so do the book debts. Because of the increase in stock, creditors also increase. The liquidity of the business is inadequate to meet the situation. The cash operating cycle is too extended and there is insufficient cash in the system. When the creditors press for payment the business defaults on payment and collapses.

22.5. LONG TERM SOURCES OF FINANCE

1. ADDITIONAL SHARES ISSUED FOR CASH

Advantages

(i)   If existing shares in issue are popular with investors, there may be little difficulty in raising additional capital by increasing the shares in issue.

(ii) If existing shares are exchanging hands above their par value, the additional shares may be issued at a premium, increasing the inflow of cash to the company.

(iii) The shares may be issued as redeemable shares to avoid permanent dilution of the share capital.

(iv) Unless the shares are redeemable, there is no requirement to repay the capital at some future date when it may be inconvenient.

(v)   Unlike loans, on which interest has to be paid whether profits are being made or not, dividends are only paid on shares if profits are available.

Disadvantages

(i)   The high cost of making a new issue of shares.

(ii) Unless there is an immediate increase in profit, the dividend cover, and therefore dividends, may be diluted.

(iii) The voting rights of existing shareholders may be affected unless the shares form a rights issue.

2. LONG TERM LOANS: DEBENTURES

Advantages

(i)   Debentures can be redeemed at a future date.

(ii) Debenture holders are not normally entitled to voting rights.

(iii) Debentures do not interfere with the benefits accruing to equity shareholders in periods of increasing profitability.

Disadvantages

(i)   Debenture interest must be paid whether or not the company has made a profit.

(ii) The debentures will have to be redeemed at some future date which may cause liquidity problems.

(iii) Possible adverse effect on 'gearing'.

(iv) Debenture holders are entitled to repayment of their loan in priority to the repayment of capital to shareholders in a winding up.

22.6 OTHER SOURCES OF FINANCE

GOVERNMENT GRANTS aimed at attracting industry to development areas. The grants may be towards operating costs (e.g. labour costs) or capital expenditure (e.g. towards cost of construction of a factory.)

22.7 CAPITAL STRUCTURE GENERALLY

Any consideration of the capital structure of a business takes into account the proportion of the total assets which should be financed by long term capital and how much by short term sources of finance (i.e. current liabilities). Furthermore, the proportion of long term borrowing to proprietors' capital (i.e.gearing or leverage) needs to be considered.

Obviously, it is impossible to make hard and fast rules to decide the proper capital structure for any business. However, the following are some of the matters relevant to this topic.

Long term investment (i.e.fixed assets) should be financed by long term capital. If it were financed by short term sources of finance the assets may have to be sold in order to repay the short term indebtedness; that could eventually lead to there being no business left to continue.

If it is accepted that a particular current ratio is appropriate for any business in question, that will suggest the proportion of current assets which may be financed by short term creditors. For instance, a current ratio of 1.5:1 indicates that about $66^2/3\%$ of the current assets may be financed by the creditors and the remainder by long term capital.

From the above, it may be argued that long term capital should therefore equal the total of the fixed assets plus at least one third of the current assets. It must again be emphasised that no hard and fast rule can be laid down.

The next consideration is how much of the long term capital should be subscribed by the proprietors (equity shareholders) and how much by fixed interest capital (debentures, preference shares). This will be decided by the required gearing, neutral gearing being equal contributions to the long term capital by the ordinary shareholders on the one hand and the debenture/preference share holders on the other.

22.7.1 EXAMPLE (The diagrammatic representation of the capital structure of a company)

The following is the abbreviated balance sheet of Snodix Ltd. at 31 December 19-2:

	£'000	£'000
Fixed assets		850
Current assets	300	
less Current liabilities	150	150
		1,000
less Long term liabilities:		
Debentures		100
		900
Ordinary share capital and reserves		900

REQUIRED

(a) Prepare a suitable diagram, using the information in the balance sheet, to show as at 31 December 19-2,

    (i)   the various sources of finance

    (ii) the spread of the total funds over the various categories of assets.

(b) Comment briefly on the capital structure and the working capital of Snodix Ltd. as at 31 December 19-2.

ANSWER

(a) See diagram on following page.

(b) The current ratio of Snodix Ltd. at 31 December 19-2 was $\dfrac{300}{150} = 2{:}1$ which may be considered to be satisfactory for most businesses.

As 50% of the current assets are financed by the current liabilities, the remaining 50% (£150,000) plus the fixed assets are financed by the long term capital.

Snodix Ltd. is a low geared company as only 10% of the long term finance is supplied by the debentures.

$$\left(\frac{100,000}{900,000 + 100,000} \times 100\right).$$

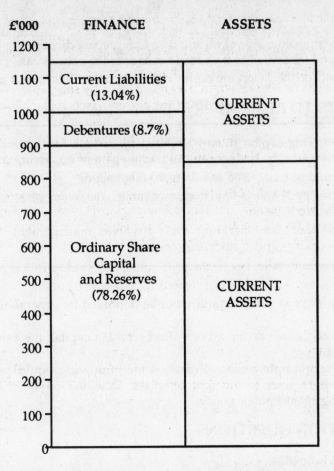

£'000   FINANCE   ASSETS

Diagram to show the sources of finance and spread of total funds

Tutorial note. The finance and asset columns should be equal in height and width, giving them equal areas. Show the scale in £'000s and calculate the percentages of the components of finance.

22.7.2 EXERCISE (To compare the capital structure of two companies)

Apex Ltd. and Base Ltd. both have financial years ending on 31 March. Their balance sheets as at 31 March 19-1 were as follows:

	Apex Ltd.		Base Ltd.	
		£'000		£'000
Fixed assets		1,200		1,400
Current assets	800		700	
less				
Current liabilities	500	300	420	280
		1,500		1,680
less 10% Debentures		300		–
		1,200		1,680
Share capital and reserves:				
Ordinary shares of £1		800		800
8% Preference shares of £1		–		500
Profit and loss account		400		380
		1,200		1,680

Both companies made a profit of £60,000 before interest in the year to 31 March 19-1

REQUIRED

(a) For each of the two companies Apex Ltd. and Base Ltd. prepare diagrams to represent their various sources of finance and the spread of their total funds over the various categories of their assets.

(b) Make brief comments on their working capital ratios, capital structure, and earnings. (Ignore tax.)

22.8 KEY POINTS TO REMEMBER

1. Adequacy of working capital must be related to various factors such as the industry concerned, the nature of the business and its trading pattern e.g. giving credit etc.

2. Overtrading should be recognised as a dangerous situation.

3. The cash operating cycle shows how long, on average, the outlay on stocks of goods or raw materials is recovered in sales.

4. Management of the cash operating cycle involves management of the individual components of working capital; stock, debtors etc.

COMMON ERRORS

- failure to identify ways in which liquidity can be improved by generating cash from stock and debtors.

- failure to understand how various actions affect working capital, the bank balance or the cash operating cycle.

- failure to make appropriate recommendations for improving liquidity e.g. delaying capital expenditure or alternatives to outright purchase. Delaying payment of tax is not a good suggestion, it being against public policy.

22.9 EXAMINATION QUESTIONS

QUESTION 1 (Oxford June 1987)

Explain why profit earned in a business is not automatically followed by a similar increase in cash resources.

(8 marks)

QUESTION 2 (JMB June 1987)

Below are some of the financial statistics for The Playfull Toy Company PLC.

£'000

	19-3	19-4	19-5	19-6
Sales	33,400	38,800	43,200	42,000
Net Profit (Loss) Before Taxation	4,050	2,700	1,520	(2,100)
Stocks	12,300	14,800	16,400	19,200
Debtors	8,900	8,400	10,500	11,100
Bank Overdraft	2,400	6,700	10,600	23,100
Creditors	8,200	8,100	9,300	11,100

The company did not have any cash balances during this period.

You are required to:

(a) calculate the following ratios for each year:

   (i)   the net margin;

   (ii) the current ratio;

   (iii) the acid-test ratio;

   (iv) the debtors days ratio;

(10 marks)

(b) comment on the financial state of the company given the above information and the ratios you have calculated;

(10 marks)

(c) explain in principle, based upon the ratios that you have calculated, what courses of action you would advise management of Playfull Toys to take.

(10 marks)

(Total 30 marks)

QUESTION 3   (JMB June 1988)

Businessman:'The successful management of a business is concerned with increasing its profitability'.

Businesswoman:'Not really, businesses do not cease trading due to a lack of profitability, but due to a lack of liquidity. Therefore, liquidity of the business is primary'.

Accountant:'You both have a point, but you have ignored the importance of the financial structure of the business'

Taking account of the above conversation, you are required to:

(a) explain the meaning of the following terms:
     (i)   profitability
     (ii)   liquidity
     (iii) financial structure;   *(12 marks)*

(b) critically evaluate the arguments in the above quotations, and devise a response to the three people.   *(18 marks)*

                                                                            (Total 30 marks)

QUESTION 4   (WJEC June 1986)

'Liquidity', that is the provision of liquid assets, can lead to considerable difficulties if not adequately maintained.

(a) Explain why liquidity is important in a business and the difficulties that may arise from neglect of attention to the maintenance of adequate liquidity.   *(6 marks)*

(b) Explain why the maintenance of liquidity may pose problems in a rapidly expanding business in particular.   *(5 marks)*

(c) Explain the main techniques that may be used to ensure that adequate liquidity is maintained and give an illustration of **one** of the techniques.   *(7 marks)*

                                                                            (Total 18 marks)

QUESTION 5   (AEB November 1989)

Extracts for the last two available balance sheets of Dee Ltd., whose financial year ends on 30 September.

	19-8	19-8	19-9	19-9
	£'000	£'000	£'000	£'000
Current assets				
Stocks	24,000		35,000	
Trade debtors	16,000		18,000	
Prepayments	2,000		1,500	
Balance at bank	4,000	46,000	–	54,500
Creditors due in less than one year				
Trade creditors	20,950		39,000	
Dividends proposed	3,500		4,700	
Corporation Tax	4,300		5,100	
Balance at bank	–	(28,750)	19,325	(68,125)
Net current assets (liabilities)		17,250		(13,625)
Creditors, due in more than one year				
12% Debentures, 1991	36,600		31,700	

REQUIRED

(a) Define and calculate two ratios relating to the liquidity of Dee Ltd. for **each** of the two years.

                                                                            (4 marks)

(b) From the information given explain the possible causes of the change in the liquid position of Dee Ltd. over the two years.   *(6 marks)*

(c) Advise the management of Dee Ltd. how the liquid position of the company could be improved.

                                                                            (4 marks)

                                                                            (Total 14 marks)

23 COMPUTERS IN ACCOUNTING

Questions on computers in accounting require:-

- an acquaintance with some basic computing terms
- some knowledge of computer hardware
- a general understanding of computer software - ability to explain how computers can be used in accounting
- discussion of the advantages of computer systems and some of the problems associated with them

---

23.1   SOME COMPUTER TERMINOLOGY

Hardware

The computer itself and its associated peripheral equipment. The computer, or Central Processing Unit, consists of:

> Internal storage facility for data being processed,
>
> An arithmetic and logic unit to operate on data
>
> A control unit to manage the processing of data.

The associated peripheral equipment consists of:

> A data inputting device (e.g. keyboard, optical character recognition scanners etc.)
>
> External backing storage to hold data until it is required for processing (e.g. hard or floppy disks.)
>
> Output devices (e.g. laser printers, print wheel printers.)

Software

The name given to the programs or packages that control computer functions. Examples of programs are those written to maintain sales ledger or purchases ledger accounts; general ledger accounts; preparing payrolls, stock records,or final accounts from the financial records. The appropriate program must be loaded into the Central Processing Unit before data processing can begin.

File

This may be likened to the files in any office filing system; a computer system file is a collection of related records (e.g. clock cards for a payroll) kept on disk. The file, and any record in it can be 'accessed' through the appropriate 'key' data field.

Batch Processing

Refers to the method of processing batches of similar data in the same run; e.g. all sales invoices for a week may be processed together in a single weekly run in much the same way as an accounts clerk might set time aside each week to post the invoices to the sales ledger.

On-Line Processing

The input of data takes place at the point of origin. e.g. where the Central Processing Unit is situated at Head Office, data may be input from remote terminals at branches.

Time Sharing

An arrangement that allows on-line users to access different files and programs simultaneously.

Real-Time

A further development of 'on-line' processing. Data originating at a branch office may be input to the Head Office computer, processed, and the results transmitted back to the branch immediately. Examples of this may be seen in travel offices where they are used for booking air tickets etc.

23.2   EXAMPLES OF COMPUTER APPLICATIONS IN ACCOUNTING

Financial accounting:

(i)   Sales ledger

(ii)   Purchases ledger

(iii)   General ledger

(iv)   Payroll records

(v)   Stock records

(vi)   Trading and profit and loss accounts

(vii)   Balance sheets.

Management and cost accounting:

(i)   Costing calculations and costing records.

ii)   Forecasting/budgeting

(iii)   Estimating job costs

(iv)   Project appraisal

(v)   Credit control

23.3   DATABASE SYSTEMS

Data stored in these systems has to be input only once; it is then accessible for any process for which it is required. For example, data concerning the sale of an item of stock, once input to the database, will be used to create an invoice, make appropriate entries in the Sales ledger and General ledger accounts, update the stock record and be used for management accounts, costing purposes and statistical returns.

Each of the applications in the paragraph above would require data to be recopied each time with the risk of errors if done manually. Provided data is input correctly to the database in the first instance, it will be copied accurately to every other record in which it is required. On the other hand, if data is input to the system incorrectly, the error will be perpetuated in all the accounting and statistical operations carried out by the computer.

It should be apparent that database systems are of immense use in accounting and statistical work.

23.4   SPREADSHEETS

A spreadsheet is a computer program which provides the user with a template of rows and columns via the screen. By using the rows and columns of the template, the user can build financial and statistical models. Where the entries in some of the positions in the template derive from arithmetical operations performed on data entered elsewhere in the template, the program can be designed to calculate and make the entries automatically with a speed and accuracy greatly in excess of that to be expected from the user.

There are many spreadsheet applications; the following are but a few:

(a)   Operational or functional budgets

(b)   Master budgets (forecast profit and loss accounts and balance sheets)

(c)   Cash flow charts

(d)   Capital expenditure appraisals (NPV and IRR)

(e)   Estimates for jobs and contracts

(f)   Stock records

(g)   Financial and statistical projections of sales

(h)   Profit projections (e.g. marginal costing applications)

Some of the more important facilities offered by spreadsheet software are:

1.   The ability to manipulate data in the spreadsheet to discover the effect upon the model. This is very useful for what are known as 'what if' calculations. For example, in budgeting, it is important to know the effect a reduction of, say, 5% on sales would make to the final result. As the level of sales is varied on the spreadsheet, the program will recalculate other items in the spreadsheet to show, apart from other things, the effect on gross and net profit etc.

2.   The ability to print spreadsheets or any part(s) of them. The print facility includes the ability to print 'graphics' (diagrams, charts etc.)

23.5 WORD PROCESSING

The combined use of word processing with computers enables the production of financial reports for management, sales catalogue information for mailing to customers etc.

Credit control is a particularly important application of word processing as individual letters can be produced for debtors whose accounts are overdue, incorporating the balance on their accounts extracted from the database.

23.6 ADVANTAGES OF COMPUTERS IN ACCOUNTING

1. They process data at phenomenally faster speeds than is possible by manual methods.
2. They are capable of handling vast quantities of data which could only be processed by a large number of clerks if done manually.
3. They are extremely accurate. Nearly every reported 'computer error' is, in fact, a user error.
4. They make the provision of financial and statistical information available which would otherwise be too difficult or expensive to produce within the required time-scale.
5. They enable 'exception reports ' to be produced easily. These are reports of any item which does not conform to specified limits of acceptability. These reports facilitate 'management by exception'.

23.7. DISADVANTAGES OF COMPUTERS

1. Installation costs are high. This is often compensated for later by a reduction in staff costs.
2. Operating and user staff need special training.
3. 'Garbage in, garbage out' means that if data input to a computer is faulty, the computer will produce faulty results. Computers cannot think for themselves; they will only do what they are programmed to do with the input data..
4. Once a computer system has been designed and installed, it may be very difficult and expensive to change if modification is required. It may take some time to modify it. This contrasts with manual systems in which clerks can change the system instantly once they have received the necessary instruction to do so.

23.8 EXERCISES

(You will need to visit dealers and exhibitions to answer the following exercises.)

1. How many makes and models of microcomputers can you find which would be suitable to perform the accounting function in a small business?
2. How much does the most expensive microcomputer in your list for Exercise 1 cost? How much does the cheapest one cost.

   What additional capabilities does the most expensive microcomputer have over the cheapest?
3. What peripheral equipment is available for each of the computers you have listed in Exercise 1? To what extent are the computers compatible with each other? (i.e. can they be linked in any way? Can they use common software? Can they use peripheral equipment produced by another manufacturer?)

23.9 KEY POINTS TO REMEMBER

1. Advanced level accounting papers do not require an in-depth knowledge of computer systems; that is reserved for advanced level computer studies papers. However, a good understanding of the uses of computers in accounting is expected and students should take every opportunity to obtain some 'hands on' experience and to visit computer exhibitions.

2. Show some practical knowledge of the subject in your answers if you can, and be prepared to discuss the disadvantages as well as the advantages of computers.

23.10 EXAMINATION QUESTIONS

QUESTION 1 (Oxford June 1986)

What is a posting run in a computer accounting system? Give **two** examples of such runs and explain what information is being posted. *(8 marks)*

QUESTION 2 (Oxford June 1987)

Name and explain **four** types of accounting information that you would expect to obtain from a computer by using **either** a sales ledger or a stock control package. *(8 marks)*

QUESTION 3 (WJEC June 1986)

Since the Second World War, technological changes and similar factors have brought about many changes in the environment in which accounting systems operate.

Explain what you consider to be the most important of these changes and factors, and explain their effects upon the development and use of accounting systems. *(18 marks)*

QUESTION 4 (Oxford June 1986)

Explain 'Management by exception' and state what accounting systems are available to enable managers to apply this principle in their work. *(8 marks)*

SOCIAL ACCOUNTING

Questions on social accounting require:-

● an understanding of the limitations of financial statements as bases for management decision making

● a recognition of factors, other than financial ones, which must be taken into account in the management of a business

24.1 THE LIMITATIONS OF FINANCIAL STATEMENTS AS BASES FOR MANAGEMENT DECISIONS

The concept of money measurement results in the limitation of entries in financial records to those transactions which can be expressed in money terms. As a result there are many factors affecting business which must be omitted from financial statements. Examples are:

(i) Staff morale

(ii) The quality of staff (its degree of skill, training etc.)

(iii) The quality of the management of the business

(iv) The attitude of the public towards the business

(v) The effect of the business upon the local community

(vi) The contribution, for good or·ill, of the business to the environment (e.g 'green' issues.)

(vii) Where the business stands on political issues e.g. trading with countries with which there are trading sanctions; trading in arms etc.

At this point it should be mentioned that attempts have been made to place values on many 'social' factors, but these are economists' values rather than accountants' values and, whatever their validity as economic concepts, are not generally recognised by accountants as complying with the accounting concept of money measurement.

There are situations in which profitability alone should not be the sole or main determinant of policy.

For ease of memory, and as a guide to the approach to social accounting aspects in examination questions, the non financial factors to be considered are summarised under the broad headings of THE FOUR P's:

> PEOPLE
>
> PLACES
>
> PRODUCTS
>
> POLITICS.

It will often be found that there is a close relationship between these four factors. For example, people are involved because of a threat to the environment (place) or because some political issue is at stake.

24.2 PEOPLE

People may be affected by the conduct of a business in varying degrees of involvement. One way of ranking peoples' involvement could be: first in order, the employees and the proprietors; next the customers; people living in the immediate locality and the local authority; more remotely, the general public and government. The degree of involvement will obviously depend upon the situation in question and it is easy to think of a situation in which government is more concerned about the conduct of a business than are people living in the vicinity.

Employees

These may be affected by:
- redundancy, particularly in rural areas, inner cities or other regions where unemployment may be high.
- introduction of advanced technology.
- the use of dangerous materials
- inadequate Health and Safety at Work protection.
- psychological factors relating to premature retirement.
- lack of consultation or information about changes which affect them
- being expected to contribute to economies of cost in a business while management make no contribution at all. (e.g. wages being cut at the same time as the managing director gets a big pay-rise.)

Some points to bear in mind:
(a) Is a trade union involved?
(b) If a grievance is not removed, what consequences may result? Disaffection of the employees? Industrial action? What will be the effect upon the business and its profitability, goodwill, even its continued existence?
(c) Costs of redundancy.
(d) Is there any alternative to making workers redundant? Can they be retrained for other jobs or re-located elsewhere within the organisation?
(e) Is any action contemplated or possible to soften the blow to workers being made redundant
(f) It may be easy to recruit unskilled labour, but if skilled labour is made redundant, will it be as easy to re-employ or replace them later if the need arises?

The Local Population

Consider the effect on the local population if a business:
- has a poor reputation as an employer
- causes a nuisance because of noise, fumes, use of large or heavy lorries to transport materials, goods etc.

Some points to bear in mind:
(a) effect on trade of business.
(b) the business's dependence upon the local population for staff recruitment.

The Local Authority

The local authority will be concerned with local amenities, environmental issues, Health and Safety at Work conditions, trading standards etc. It may become involved because of complaints received from local residents.

It has powers to enforce abatement of nuisances, enactment of statutory requirements regarding working conditions, trading standards etc. It may take legal action which could have unfortunate consequences e.g. heavy fines etc.

The General Public

A business which infringes the law, causes a nuisance or conducts its business in an ecologically unacceptable manner risks unwelcome publicity in the Press, on Radio or Television.
This could adversely affect its trade.

Government

Government is concerned with political implications such as illegal trading in arms, drugs etc., trading with countries subject to embargoes.Government is also concerned with the collection of taxes and duties. Taxpayers are entitled to conduct their affairs with a view to minimising their liability to tax (tax avoidance); it is illegal for them to evade payment of their proper tax liability e.g. by supplying the Inland Revenue with false information. (tax evasion).

24.3 PLACES

Ecology, or the care of the environment, is a popular issue today and is a favourite topic with examiners. It features prominently daily in the media.

'Places' should be interpreted widely to include, as appropriate, the rain forests, the ozone layer etc.

Typically, questions are based on businesses which seem unable to afford necessary modifications to their buildings or plant to make them ecologically acceptable. A careful examination of the facts in the question may show that there is a financial aspect as well as a social one:

A division of a large manufacturing concern has a factory in a rural area. The factory is annoying the local community by emitting obnoxious fumes into the atmosphere and the local inhabitants are complaining that the fumes are affecting their health.

The latest accounts for the factory show the following results for the past year:

	£m
Gross receipts	100
Operating expenses	(65)
Fixed overheads	(45)
Loss for year	(10)

Fixed overheads include an annual charge of £25m from the Head Office of the undertaking.

The capital cost of modifying the production process so as to abate the nuisance caused by the fumes would be £5m and the directors have stated that the company cannot afford the cost of modification.

In this example, the factory is making a profit of £15m before taking Head Office fixed costs into account. If the Local Authority were to use its powers to close the factory because it failed to abate the nuisance, Head Office would lose that contribution to its fixed costs which would have to be shared by the remaining part of the organisation. The directors' contention that the factory cannot afford the additional expenditure can not be supported.

The social aspects to be mentioned are the effect of the nuisance on the local population; the factory's reputation; the risk of compulsory closure of the factory if the nuisance is not abated, probably with heavy fines imposed as well; unwelcome bad publicity in the national Press, etc.

24.4 PRODUCTS

Consideration of these must include:

- their compliance with trading standards
- the use of rare or scarce materials
- the use of dangerous materials (link with people, place) - ethical or social acceptability (tobacco, publication of a book which might be offensive racially or religiously etc.)
- unethical advertising

24.5 POLITICS

This heading should be interpreted widely to include any matter which appertains to government, but not party politics in the narrower sense.

Government is concerned with trading:

- in illegal commodities (e.g.drugs, arms, etc.)
- in markets on which there is a trade embargo.

Government is also concerned with fiscal policies and taxation; and with legislation affecting the whole of the industrial, commercial and service industry environment.

Businesses should be conducted in such a manner as to comply with all legal requirements at all times.

24.6   KEY POINTS TO REMEMBER

1. Financial considerations are important, but by no means the only matters to be taken into account in the management of a business.

2. Financial statements are limited in the amount of information they convey; they cannot convey information about anything which cannot be quantified in money terms.

3. Businesses should be managed in a socially responsible manner as well as a financially prudent manner.

4. Any statement of business objectives which fails to take account of social implications may be setting the wrong objectives. For instance, an objective to maximise profit may be counterproductive if it fails to recognise the need to appear to be socially responsible. The attempt to achieve a big profit (at all costs!!) may alienate its market.

5. It is worthwhile to keep abreast of social issues as they affect business by reading a good newspaper regularly.

6. The purpose of this chapter has been to stimulate thought. Many students do not know how to approach social aspects of accounting in examinations or what is expected by the examiner.

7. Do not, on any account, express your own political views or views on social matters, in the examination. The examiner may not agree with your views and is entitled to have his own thoughts on these matters. An examination is not the occasion to win support for your views. The examiner is only interested to find out if you can recognise social accounting topics and offer some objective comments on them. Social accounting usually forms part only of a question and may only have 4 or 5 marks allocated to it. It is not, for that reason, to be left unattempted. 5 marks can make a difference of two grades to the examination result in some circumstances. On the other hand, 5 marks does not warrant a thesis for a degree! The maximum amount of time that should be spent on a 5 mark question is nine minutes, which is time enough to show recognition of the aspects of social accounting involved and give a sufficient reason for their importance.

24.7   EXAMINATION QUESTIONS

QUESTION 1   (AEB November 1988)

The following profit statement relates to a division of Citizen plc:

Profit statement for the year ended 31 October 19-8

	£	£
Sales		300,000
Less Expenses		
Direct production expenses		
Material	110,000	
Labour	75,000	
Overhead	30,000	
Indirect production expenses		
Depreciation of machinery	30,000	
Fixed	15,000	
Administration and selling expenses		
Variable	6,000	
Fixed	18,000	284,000
Profit		16,000

Additional Information.

(1) The division's machinery had a net book value at 31 October 19-7 of £90,000 and is being depreciated at £30,000 per annum.

(2) Citizen plc is actively considering a proposal to close the division at the end of a financial year on or before 31 October 19-1.

The Management has estimated the resale values of the machinery as follows:

	£
at 31 October 19-8	70,000
31 October 19-9	50,000
31 October 19-0	36,000
31 October 19-1	Nil

(3) Certain costs have been estimated to increase in *each* of the following three years as follows:

	£
Direct labour	5,000
Direct material	9,000
Indirect fixed production expenses	2,000
Fixed selling expenses	2,000

(4)   (i)   Sales – sales volume will not change but selling prices will increase by 10% on 1 November 19-8 and not increase thereafter.

    (ii)   Direct production overheads - are expected to remain at the same percentage of direct labour as in the year ended 31 October 19-8.

    (iii)   Variable selling expenses - as a percentage of sales value are expected to remain constant.

REQUIRED

(a)   (i)   Forecast profit statements, in columnar format, for **each** of the three years to 31 October 19-1 assuming that the division continues until that date. *(9 marks)*

    (ii)   An accounting statement showing the financially optimum date for the closure of the division. *(4 marks)*

(b)   A brief outline of the non-financial relevant factors to be borne in mind when considering the future of the division. *(5 marks)*

(Total 18 marks)

QUESTION 2   (AEB November 1988)

The following financial information was available on Yeso Ltd. as at 31 March 19-8.

	£		£
Current assets	70,000	Retained earnings at 31 March 19-7	32,000
Fixed assets (at net book value)	126,000	General reserve	15,000
Current liabilities	45,000	Share premium	18,000
Net profit for the year		Ordinary share capital	
ended 31 March 19-8	6,000	£1 shares fully paid	80,000

Additional information.

(1) No interim dividend had been paid, but the directors decided to recommend a final dividend of 10% and to transfer £10,000 to general reserve.

(2) The recently appointed managing director wishes to improve the profitability of the business and he issued a policy statement that all new capital investment must show a minimum return on capital employed of 15% per annum.

(3) Adam, a sole proprietor about to retire, offered to sell his business to Yeso Ltd.

    (i)   The recent financial history of the business is as follows:

	19-4	19-5	19-6	19-7
	£	£	£	£
Net assets employed	35,000	40,000	39,000	46,000
Net profit for year	7,000	7,700	8,100	8,600

350

The price Adam has set for his business is the 19-7 net assets valuation plus £5,000 for goodwill.

    (ii)   An examination of Adam's books, by the managing director of Yeso Ltd. revealed that the net assets included an unused derelict building with book value of £5,000. The market valuation of the site was £20,000.

REQUIRED

(a) The profit and loss appropriation account of Yeso Ltd. for the year ended 31 March 19-8.   *(5 marks)*

(b) Calculate the return on capital employed for Yeso Ltd. for the year ended 31 March 19-8 using two definitions of capital employed.   *(4 marks)*

(c) Prepare a brief report advising whether Yeso Ltd. should purchase Adam's business. Your report should include appropriate calculations to support your argument.   *(6 marks)*

(d) Identify ways, through appropriate action, in which the company may be able to raise the return on capital employed of Yeso Ltd.   *(5 marks)*

(e) If a company continues to earn a persistently low return on capital employed, what are the implications for:

    (i)   the financial position of the company

    (ii) the social accounting aspects relating to the employees?   *(5 marks)*

(Total 25 marks)

APPENDIX 1
PRACTICE EXAMINATION PAPER 1
(AEB TYPE)

THREE hours allowed

In Section A answer all questions.

In Section B answer either Question 4 or Question 5
In Section C answer either Question 6 or Question 7

You must show all workings.

SECTION A

Answer all questions in this section.

QUESTION 1 (23 marks)

Alan Saltmarsh has produced draft accounts for his business for the year to 31 December 19-0, and the draft balance sheet as at that date was as follows:

	£	£	£
Fixed Assets			
Premises at cost		48,000	
less Provision for depreciation		9,600	38,400
Plant and equipment at cost		23,000	
less Provision for depreciation		11,500	11,500
Motor vehicles at cost		13,800	
less Provision for depreciation		5,170	8,630
			58,530
Current Assets			
Stock		7,200	
Debtors		4,170	
Balance at bank		6,733	
		18,103	
less Current Liabilities			
Creditors	5,523		
Other credit balances (see note below)	4,225	9,748	8,355
			66,885
Financed by			
Capital: balance at 1 January 19-0			59,000
profit for the year			20,215
			79,215
deduct: drawings for the year			12,330
			66,885

	£
Note: Other credit balances comprise:	
Proceeds of disposal of machine	3,000
Suspense account	1,225
	4,225

Since preparing the draft accounts, Alan Saltmarsh has made the following discoveries:

1. Goods which had been sold on credit for £1,450 but not despatched to the customer before the year end had been included in stock. The customer had been invoiced before the year end and the invoice had been entered into the books. The customer had not paid the invoice by 31 December 19-0.

2. Goods had been sent on 'sale or return' to a customer. The customer had been invoiced for these goods in the sum of £1,200, but had not indicated by 31 December that he intended to accept the goods.

3. During the year to 31 December 19-0 Alan Saltmarsh had paid builders and decorators the sum of £10,000 to carry out work on the premises. The whole of this work had been debited to Repairs and Redecoration of Premises account. He has now been advised that only 40% of this work should be treated as revenue expenditure.

4. A machine which had cost £8,000 and had been purchased on 1 January two years earlier had been sold for £3,000 The proceeds of sale had been recorded in the books but no other entries had been made.

5. A credit balance of £195 on a supplier's account in the Purchases Ledger had been omitted from the list of balances extracted from the ledger on 31 December 19-0.

6. The remaining balance on the Suspense account was caused by the total of one page in the Sales Day Book being posted, in error, to the debit of the Purchases account.

Additional information

(i) Alan Saltmarsh sells his goods at a mark-up of 25% on cost.

(ii) Purchases Ledger and Sales Ledger control accounts are not maintained.

(iii) Alan Saltmarsh provides for depreciation on the fixed assets appearing in his books at 31 December at the following rates:

Premises:	2% of cost
Plant and machinery:	20% of cost
Motor vehicles:	25% of cost.

REQUIRED

(a) Prepare journal entries to correct the above errors and omissions. (Narratives are required.)

(12 marks)

(b) Prepare a statement of corrected net profit for the year ended 31 December 19-0. *(4 marks)*

(c) Prepare a balance sheet as at 31 December 19-0 after the corrections have been made. *(7 marks)*

QUESTION 2 (16 marks)

Denis Muir's balance sheet at 31 March 19-1 was as follows:

	£	£
Fixed Assets		
Motor vehicles at cost	8,000	
less Provision for depreciation	5,600	2,400
Fixtures and fittings	7,200	
less Provision for depreciation	3,500	3,700
Carried forward		6,100

	£	£	£
Brought forward			6,100
Current Assets			
Stock		6,150	
Trade debtors		6,210	
Rent prepaid		1,375	
Bank		6,445	
		20,180	
Less			
Current Liabilities			
Loan interest	75		
Trade creditors	5,400	5,475	
			14,705
			20,805
Less			
Loan from brother (interest at 10% per annum			
payable 30 June and 31 December)			3,000
			17,805
Financed by			
Capital at 1 April 19-0			19,000
Add profit for the year			8,405
			27,405
Deduct drawings			9,600
			17,805

Further information

1. Forecast sales for the year to 31 March 19-2:

		£
19-1		
April	– June	21,000
July	– September	25,500
October	– December	28,500
19-2		
January	– March	24,000

All sales are on credit, the terms being payment at the end of the month following the month of sale. 5% of debts prove to be bad; Denis Muir allows a cash discount of 4% for prompt payment.

2. Purchases for the year to 31 March 19-2 will be as follows:

		£
19-1		
April	– June	15,000
July	– September	18,000
October	– December	18,000
19-2		
January	– March	21,000

All purchases are on credit; Denis Muir receives two months credit from his suppliers.

3. Wages are paid currently at the rate of £1,000 per month. An 8% wage award is expected to be given on 1 July 19-1.

4. Rent of premises is £6,000 per annum payable on March 25, June 21, September 29 and December 25.

5. In April 19-1, Denis Muir will sell some fixtures which cost £3,000 three years ago, at a loss of £650. Fixtures in the books at 31 March each year are depreciated at 15% per annum. on cost.

6. Muir plans to purchase an additional vehicle for £6,000 in October 19-1. Vehicles in the books at 31 March each year are depreciated at the rate of 20% per annum.

7. Muir will draw £1,000 per month for living expenses.

8. Closing stock at 31 March 19-2 will be £8,000

REQUIRED

(a) A cash forecast for Denis Muir for the year to 31 March 19-2.   *(10 marks)*

(b) A trading and profit and loss account for the year to 31 March 19-2 and a balance sheet as at that date.   *(6 marks)*

QUESTION 3 (17 marks)

The following is an extract from the balance sheet of R.T.Fax plc. at 30 June 19-5.

		£
Share capital and reserves.		
Authorised: 1,000,000 ordinary shares of £1	1,000,000	
300,000 10% preference shares of £1	300,000	
	1,300,000	
Issued:	600,000 ordinary shares of £1 fully paid	600,000
	Share premium account	120,000
	Revaluation reserve	250,000
	General reserve	300,000
	Retained profit	220,000
		1,490,000

The directors of R.T.Fax plc are investigating ways of raising an additional £2.5m. to finance a programme of expansion of the company and have decided to proceed as follows:

1. To increase the ordinary share capital of the company by an issue of bonus shares to the existing shareholders on the basis of two bonus shares for every three already held. The reserves of the company are to be preserved in the most flexible form possible.

2. To make a rights issue of ordinary shares on a one for one basis, taking the bonus issue into account, at £1.50 per share.

3. To issue 300,000 10% preference shares of £1 each at par.

4. To issue as much $12^1/_2$% debenture stock as necessary to raise the additional finance required.

Note: The necessary steps will be taken to increase the authorised share capital of the company.

REQUIRED

(a) An extract of the balance sheet of R.T.Fax plc assuming that effect is given to the above programme and all shares and debenture stock are taken up.   *(8 marks)*

(b) Calculations of the value of 100 ordinary shares

   (i) before the issue of the bonus shares and

   (ii) immediately after the issue of the bonus shares.

   (Calculations are to be based on balance sheet values.)   *(4 marks)*

(c)   Calculation of the value of the holding of someone who originally held 1,000 ordinary shares assuming he took up all the shares to which he was entitled under the above plan.   *(2 marks)*

(d)   A brief explanation of what you understand by gearing, including a calculation of the gearing of R.T.Fax plc using your answer to Part(a) as the basis for your calculation.   *(3 marks)*

SECTION B

Answer either Question 4 or Question 5.

QUESTION 4 (22 marks)

The Wee Makeit Manufacturing Company produces a new, improved model of compact disc player, for which the following information is available.

	Year ended 30 June 19-1	Year ended 30 June 19-2
Sales in units	1,200	2,400
	£	£
Selling price per unit	330	300
Direct materials per unit	60	70
Direct wages per unit	40	50
Variable overhead expenses per unit	60	75
Fixed expenses	200,000	250,000

The cost of developing the player was £270,000 and was wholly incurred before 1 July 19-0. The development costs are being written off in equal instalments over the first three years of the product's life and are included in the fixed expenses.

The Production Director believes that the pattern of costs for the year ended 30 June 19-2 will remain the same for subsequent years but that if the price is further reduced to £280, the volume of sales will increase by a further 25%.

REQUIRED

(a)   A calculation of the break-even point of the product for each of the years ended 30 June 19-1 and 30 June 19-2.   *(6 marks)*

(b)   A calculation of the profit or loss on the players for each of the years ended 30 June 19-1 and 19-2.

   (6 marks)

(c)   Your advice to the directors as to whether or not the company should continue the production of the players in the years ended 30 June 19-3 and subsequently.   *(10 marks)*

QUESTION 5 (22 marks)

On 1 April 19-3 Cognito Ltd. started to manufacture an electronic control known as 'Pacemaker'. Each Pacemaker requires one unit of direct material, of which Cognito Ltd. receives 1,000 units per month. The cost of the raw material was £8 per unit until 1 September 19-3 when Cognito found a new source of supply from which the material could be obtained at £5 per unit. Cognito receives the raw material on the first day of each month.

In addition to the cost of the direct material, the other costs of production are (per unit): Direct labour £10; variable factory overheads £5.

The following further information is also available for the six months to 30 September 19-3:

Number of Pacemakers produced per month: 800 units

Total number of Pacemakers sold: 4,200 units

Selling price per Pacemaker: £50

Fixed factory costs for the period: £36,000

Administration costs for the period: £50,000

Depreciation of factory plant and equipment (6 months) £15,000

All sales are made through agents who are entitled to a commission of 5% on the sales.

REQUIRED

(a) Prepare a manufacturing, trading and profit and loss account for the six months to 30 September 19-3 showing each of the alternative profit/loss figures if the closing stock of finished goods is valued at:

    (i) prime cost or

    (ii) total factory cost.   *(16 marks)*

Note: Cognito values its stocks of raw materials using the FIFO method.

(b) Explain what is meant by the FIFO and LIFO methods of valuing stock issues and the effect of each on the profit of a firm at a time of changing price levels.   *(6 marks)*

SECTION C

Answer either Question 6 or Question 7.

QUESTION 6 (23 marks)

Omnipres plc is a holding company with interests in many parts of the world. It has a number of problem areas and decisions have to be made as to the proper course of action to be taken in each case.

(1) The company has been producing a material, Plastinium, which has been used extensively in industry for advanced technology. The material costs £15 (total or absorption cost) per kilo to produce and there are 3,000 kilos of the material in stock at the factory. Recently, a rival manufacturer has started to market another material, Duroplas, which sells for £12 per kilo, and is a suitable substitute for Plastinium. The sales of Plastinium have started to suffer considerably as a result of the introduction of Duroplas.

(2) A factory in the U.K. produces a fertiliser under the brand name of 'Supagro'. The product, when mixed with certain other chemicals, produces a powerful explosive. It is the only product of the factory, which employs 150 people in an area of high unemployment. The factory is unsuitable to be used for any other purpose unless a considerable sum of money is spent on modifications to it. The factory will only 'break even' if it sells 15,000 tons of 'Supagro' per annum.

Barrenland is a third world country which suffers from the terrible ravages of famine and, in order to improve the agriculture of that country, has entered into a contract for the supply of 7,000 tons of 'Supagro' per annum.

Bulliboyne is a country which is adjacent to Barrenland and a state of war exists between the two countries, frequent incursions being made into Barrenland by Bulliboyne.

Bulliboyne has offered to buy 12,000 tons of 'Supagro' at an advantageous price to the U.K. factory providing supplies of the fertiliser to Barrenland cease.

The only other customers of the factory altogether account for the purchase of 4,000 tons of 'Supagro'.

(3) A factory producing parts for washing machines has been poorly managed and has been making unacceptably high losses for the past three years. The losses have averaged £120,000 per annum (including share of Head Office fixed costs of £185,000) The factory is in an inner city area and employs 400 workers. The managing director has been reasonably popular with the workforce whose morale is nevertheless not very high; he is paid £20,000 per annum.

The Board of Omnipres plc have concluded that the only chance of making the factory competitive and profitable is to replace the present managing director with a very capable chartered accountant at a salary of £75,000 per annum. His remit will be to increase productivity by 15% and to reduce wage rates by 5% in order to achieve profitability. Failure to achieve profitability will result in closure of the factory. The average redundancy payment would be £1,500 per worker.

REQUIRED

Prepare a report advising the company as follows:

(a) Whether Omnipres plc should continue to produce 'Plastinium'.

(7 marks)

(b) Whether Omnipres plc should accept the offer from Bulliboyne for the purchase of 'Supagro'.

(8 marks)

(c) Problems which may beset Omnipres plc's plans for making the washing machine parts factory profitable and whether there is any possible alternative to make the factory competitive and profitable.

(8 marks)

State any assumptions that you make. Your report should consider both financial and non-financial factors.

QUESTION 7 (23 marks)

Cedric has been appointed as accountant to Titan Ltd., a company which has been in existence for some years. Titan Ltd. has developed a new product which it proposes to add to its range. The new product will require additional machinery for its manufacture and the machinery will cost £1.5m. and have a life expectation of 10 years.

Cedric has been given the job of evaluating four alternative methods of financing the acquisition of the new machinery which are as follows:

(1) To lease the machinery from Hiraplant Ltd. on terms by which Titan Ltd. will pay £300,000 per annum, for the period of ten years.

(2) To purchase the machinery on credit under terms which will provide for five annual payments of £490,000, the first payment to be made on the last day of the first year. The annual payments have been calculated on the basis that the interest accrues evenly over the period of the loan.

(3) To issue 400,000 £1 ordinary shares at £3.75 per share. The annual dividend paid to ordinary shareholders in recent years has been 15% and the directors expect that rate to be maintained in the foreseeable future.

(4) To locate the production of the new product in a region 180 miles from Titan Ltd.'s factory. The region being considered is one of high unemployment where the government has introduced a scheme to encourage job creation within the region. Under the scheme, Titan Ltd. would be eligible for interest free finance of £1,500,000 which would have to be repaid over a five year period in equal annual instalments. The additional production costs incurred as a result of locating the manufacture of the new product in this region would be £50,000 per annum. Production of existing products will remain unaffected by the selection of this option.

REQUIRED

(a) The entries which would appear in the revenue accounts of Titan Ltd. in the first year of production of the new product in respect of each of the above options.

(8 marks)

(b) A statement of the implications for Titan Ltd. of each of the four proposals which Cedric should include in his report to the directors.

(15 marks)

APPENDIX 1
PRACTICE EXAMINATION PAPER 2
(AEB TYPE)

THREE hours allowed

In section A answer both questions
In Section B answer either Question 3 or Question 4
In Section C answer either Question 5 or Question 6

You must show all workings.

SECTION A

Answer both questions in this section.

QUESTION 1 (25 marks)

The balance sheets of Stradma Ltd. at 31 December 19-1 and 31 December 19-2 were as follows:

	19-1			19-2		
	£'000	£'000	£'000	£'000	£'000	£'000
Tangible Fixed Assets (Note 2)						
Freehold property			300			470
Plant and machinery			185			215
			485			685
Investments at cost			100			50
Current Assets						
Stocks		140			170	
Trade Debtors		162			153	
Balance at bank		–			65	
Cash		20			27	
		322			415	
Less Current Liabilities						
Trade Creditors	64			54		
Proposed dividend	25			30		
Bank overdraft	42	131	191	–	84	331
			776			1,066
Less: Long term liability						
12% Debentures			100			60
			676			1,006
Financed by:						
Share Capital						
£1 Ordinary shares fully paid			300			800
Share premium			185			25
Retained earnings			191			181
			676			1,006

Additional information

(1) Profit and loss appropriation for the year ended 31 December 19-2.

		£'000
Net profit		35
Less: Interim dividend paid	15	
Final dividend proposed	30	45
Transfer to retained earnings		(10)

(2) Fixed Assets:

	Freehold Property £'000	Plant & Machinery £'000
At cost		
Balance at 1.1. 19-2	380	280
Revaluation at 1.1.19-2	100	
Disposals		(110)
Additions		160
	480	330
Depreciation		
Balance at 1.1.19-2	(80)	(95)
On revaluation	80	–
On disposals	–	30
Charge for the year	(10)	(50)
	(10)	(115)
Net book values	470	215

(3) During the year to 31 December 19-2, machinery which had cost £110,000, was sold for £40,000.

(4) Investments which had cost £50,000 prior to 1 January 19-2 were sold on 1 July 19-2 for £65,000.

(5) On 1 July 19-2, a Rights Issue of ordinary shares was made on the basis of one new share for every three shares already held. The shares were issued at a price of £1.60 each.

(6) On 1 December 19-2, the issued capital of the company was further increased by a bonus issue of ordinary shares on the basis of one new share for each share already held, using first the balance on the Freehold Property Revaluation Reserve, then the Share Premium account.

(7) During the year to 31 December 19-2, 12% debentures were redeemed at par.

REQUIRED

(a) A statement of source and application of funds for Stradma Ltd. for the year to 31 December 19-2.

(15 marks)

(b) An explanation of the purpose of statements of source and application of funds. *(3 marks)*

(c) An explanation of the causes of the changes in the working capital of Stradma Ltd. between 31 December 19-1 and 31 December 19-2. *(5 marks)*

(d) Stradma Ltd. has a budget target for return on equity capital employed for the year ending 31 December 19-3 of 18%; what net profit must the company earn in order to meet its target?

(2 marks)

QUESTION 2 (25 marks)

The directors of Broadline (US) Limited were considering purchasing an additional lorry; their choice of vehicle lay between three different makes of lorry: 'Butchboy', 'Barberdon', and 'Rowbo-Loney'. The lorries had specifications which were technically similar in most respects and each had an expected working life of 5 years.

The following information was available on the lorries being considered:

(1)

	LORRIES		
	'Butchboy'	'Barberdon'	'Rowbo-Loney'
Purchase price	£60,000	£70,000	£80,000
Estimated scrap value after 5 years	£12,000	14,000	£16,000
Fixed costs other than depreciation	£	£	£
Year 1	3,000	2,500	1,800
Year 2	3,000	2,500	1,800
Year 3	3,300	2,500	1,600
Year 4	3,600	2,800	1,600
Year 5	3,600	3,000	1,600
Variable costs per road mile	8p	10p	12p

(2) Broadline (US) Limited charges 40p per mile for all journeys irrespective of the length of journey and the expected annual mileages over the 5 year period are:

	Miles
Year 1	50,000
Year 2	60,000
Year 3	70,000
Year 4	80,000
Year 5	90,000

(3) The company's cost of capital is 10% per annum.

(4) It should be assumed that all operating costs are paid and revenues received at the end of the year.

(5) Present value of £1 at interest rate of 10% per annum:

Year 1	0.909
Year 2	0.826
Year 3	0.751
Year 4	0.683
Year 5	0.621

REQUIRED

(a) (i) Appropriate computations using the net present value method for each of the lorries under consideration. *(14 marks)*

    (ii) A report to the directors of Broadline (US) Limited advising them as to which lorry they should purchase. *(6 marks)*

(b) A brief outline of the problems encountered in evaluating capital projects. *(5 marks)*

SECTION B

Answer either Question 3 or Question 4.

QUESTION 3 (25 marks)

Parsloe Ltd. make and sell a single product known as A1-XL and the following information has been extracted from the records of the company for the financial years ending 31 May:

	Actual results	Forecast results	
	19-2	19-3	19-4
Costs per unit produced	£	£	£
Direct materials	30	31.2	31.8
Direct labour	12	13.2	13.2
Variable production overheads	9.6	9.6	10.2
Variable sales overheads	7.2	7.2	7.8

Additional information

(1) The company's sales are:

	Price per unit	Unit volume
	£	000s
Actual sales 19-2	72	36
Forecast sales 19-3	69	60
Forecast sales 19-4	68	96

(2) The fixed costs in 19-2 were £120,000; they are expected to remain constant in 19-3 and 19-4.

(3) All expense and revenue relationships are expected to remain unchanged except where identified.

REQUIRED

(a) Calculate the number of sales units necessary to break even for each of the years 19-2 - 19-4.

(6 marks)

(b) Prepare a single graph showing break-even points for 19-2, 19-3 and 19-4 and clearly indicating the break-even points.

(6 marks)

(c) For each of the years 19-2, 19-3 and 19-4, calculate the margin of safety.

(2 marks)

(d) Explain why in spite of

(i) rising variable costs

(ii) rising break-even points

the total annual profits are expected to be higher in 19-3 and 19-4 than in 19-2.

(4 marks)

(e) If the company decided to revise its 19-4 forecast unit sales, what sales unit price would have to be charged in order to break-even at 30,000 units?

(3 marks)

(f) State **three** limitations of break-even analysis.

(4 marks)

QUESTION 4 (25 marks)

Eden Decor Ltd. manufactures garden furniture. One of the lines it produces is a bird table and the contribution made by the bird tables to the overall company results for the year ended 30 June 19-5 was as follows:

Contribution statement for bird tables for the year to 30 June 19-5.

	£	£
Sales		162,000
less variable costs		
Raw materials	53,280	
Direct labour	47,680	100,960
		61,040

Additional information.

(1) The budget for the production and sales of bird tables for the year to 30 June 19-5 was prepared on the following bases:

   (i) budgeted sales of bird tables: 15,000 at £10 each.

   (ii) each bird table requires 4 kg of materials at a cost of 80p. per kg.

   (iii) three bird tables should be made per hour of direct labour.

   (iv) the direct labour rate is £7.20 per hour.

(2) The actual results for the year to 30 June 19-5 revealed the following:

   (i) 18,000 bird tables were sold.

   (ii) 74,000 kg of raw materials were used.

   (iii) direct labour amounted to 6,400 hours.

(3) There were no stocks of bird tables at 1 July 19-4 or at 30 June 19-5.

REQUIRED

(a) Calculate the overall sales variance for the year ended 30 June 19-5. *(2 marks)*

(b) Calculate the overall labour variance for the year ended 30 June 19-5 analysing it into:

   (i) rate variance;

   (ii) efficiency variance *(6 marks)*

(c) Calculate the overall material variance for the year ended 30 June 19-5 analysing it into:

   (i) price variance;

   (ii) usage variance *(6 marks)*

(d) Prepare a statement that shows the budgeted contribution for the year ended 30 June 19-5.

   (4 marks)

(e) Examine the variances calculated in (a), (b) and (c) above and give possible reasons for each.

   (7 marks)

SECTION C

Answer either Question 5 or Question 6.

QUESTION 5 (25 marks)

Codd, Liversidge and Doyle are in partnership in a retail trade. Their shop in Citiville also serves as Head Office and provides administrative support for the other two branch shops which are situated in Nereham and Hilton. The Citiville shop purchases, stores and distributes goods to the branch shops for resale as well as selling goods itself. Draft trading and profit and loss accounts for the Head Office shop and branches have been prepared as follows for the year ended 31 December 19-4.

	Citiville (Head office)		Nereham		Hilton	
	£'000	£'000	£'000	£'000	£'000	£'000
Sales		400		210		120
Cost of sales						
Opening stock	52		20		22	
Goods from head office	–		150		60	
Goods from Nereham					20	
Purchases	550		40*			
Goods to branches	(264)					
Closing stock	(49)		(32)		(14)	
		289		178		88
Gross profit		111		32		32
Less expenses						
General expenses	30		11		12	
Fixed administrative expenses	13**		5		8	
Variable costs	42		12		15	
		85		28		35
Profit(Loss)		26		4		(3)

* Included in this figure is £23,000 representing goods sent to Hilton.
** £26,000 less amounts charged to branches.

Additional information

(1) On 31 December 19-4 Citiville had sent goods, at cost, to the branches as follows:

	£'000
Nereham	34
Hilton	20

These goods were received by the branches on 3 January 19-5.

(2) Some goods were purchased locally by Nereham and some of these were transferred at cost to the Hilton branch. On 30 December 19-4, Nereham sent goods costing £3,000 to Hilton, and these goods were not received by Hilton until 4 January 19-5.

(3) After the draft profit and loss accounts had been prepared, the following stock losses, which had occurred before 31 December 19-4, were discovered.

	£
Citiville	460 loss
Nereham	900 loss
Hilton	350 gain

(4) The partnership agreement provides for

(i) partners' salaries of

	£
Codd	8,000
Liversidge	10,000
Doyle	5,000

(ii) Interest at 8% per annum on the partners' capital account balances which were as follows throughout the year to 31 December 19-4:

	£
Codd	40,000
Liversidge	32,500
Doyle	50,000

(iii) Partners share the balances of profits and losses equally.

(5) Codd, Liversidge and Doyle wish to improve the profitability of the partnership and consequently are considering how to improve the profitability of the Hilton branch. They are looking at two options:

Option A Increase the sales of the Hilton branch by more effective advertising and changing the type of goods sold there. It is considered that the gross profit of the branch would be increased by 50%; the additional advertising would increase general expenses by £8,000 and variable expenses would increase by £2,000.

Option B Close the Hilton branch and transfer the business to Nereham. As a result, Nereham branch's gross profit would be increased by £14,000 but its fixed administrative expenses would increase by £2,000 and its variable costs by £4,000. Overall fixed administrative expenses would be reduced by £3,000. Redundancy costs, not included above, would amount to £7,000.

REQUIRED

(a) Prepare a trading and profit and loss account for the partnership for the year ended 31 December 19-4 that EXCLUDES the options outlined in (5) above. (Separate accounts for the branches are NOT required.) *(10 marks)*

(b) Prepare a statement of the appropriation of net profit as calculated in (a) between the partners. *(8 marks)*

(c) Prepare a statement which shows the financial impact of each of the options in (5) above and critically evaluate the options. *(7 marks)*

QUESTION 6 (25 marks)

Greta Gabor owns 10,000 £1 ordinary shares in Arliss plc. She has received the annual report and accounts of the company for the year ended 30 September 19-2. In summarised form, the financial information is as follows:

Profit and loss account for the year ended 30 September 19-2.

	£'000	£'000
Turnover		1,000
less Cost of Sales		450
Gross profit		550
less Establishment expenses	155	
Depreciation	65	220
Net profit		330
Retained earnings at 1 October 19-1		70
		400
Ordinary dividends proposed		200
Retained earnings at 30 September 19-2		200

Balance sheet as at 30 September 19-2

Fixed assets	At cost	Aggregate Depreciation	Net
	£'000	£'000	£'000
	700	–	700
Other fixed assets	740	320	420
Carried forward	1,440	320	1,120

		£'000	£'000	£'000
Brought forward		1,440	320	1,120
Current assets	Stock		385	
	Trade debtors		189	
	Balance at bank		16	
			590	
less	Current liabilities			
	Trade creditors	110		
	Proposed dividend	200	310	280
				1,400

Capital and reserves	
Authorised and Issued Capital £1 ordinary shares fully paid	800
Share premium	400
Retained earnings	200
	1,400

The dividend was paid on 2 December 19-2.

Greta Gabor purchased all her shares in Arliss plc during the year to 30 September 19-2 at £2.80 per share in the expectation that the dividend would be much larger. On receiving the above information she has written to the chairman of the company expressing her disappointment, especially after she has compared the financial statements of Arliss plc with those of other businesses. Greta Gabor has suggested the following ways in which further funds could be made available to pay a higher dividend:

(1) The share premium account and the retained profits are reserves which belong to the ordinary shareholders and should be distributed as dividends.

(2) The freehold property was purchased many years ago and has appreciated in value since then. She has been advised that the property now has an open market value of £1,100,000. The property should therefore be revalued in the books at its full market value and the profit used to pay a dividend.

(3) Instead of making such large 'appropriations' of profit for depreciation, the maintenance of the 'other fixed assets' should be upgraded so as to keep them in 'as good as new' condition. If this is done in the year to 30 September 19-3, it will not be necessary to provide for depreciation and the cash may be used instead to pay a larger dividend.

(4) The stocks are maintained at too high a level and immediate steps should be taken to sell the excess stocks. This would produce additional profits which could be used to pay dividends.

REQUIRED

(a) Use appropriate ratios to determine
   (i) the profitability of the company
   (ii) the liquidity of the company
   (iii) Greta Gabor's rate of return on her investment.
   (10 marks)

(b) What further information is required in order to assess the company's profitability and liquidity more reliably.
   (4 marks)

(c) What are the main limitations of using ratios for comparison of the results of different businesses.
   (3 marks)

(d) Draft a reply for the chairman of Arliss plc to send to Greta Gabor, dealing with the suggestions she has made for improving the dividends. Include in your reply an assessment of each of the proposals, based on normally accepted accounting principles.
   (8 marks)

APPENDIX 1
PRACTICE EXAMINATION PAPER 3
(AEB TYPE)

THREE hours allowed

In Section A answer all questions
In Section B answer either Question 4 or Question 5
In Section C answer either Question 6 or Question 7

You must show all workings.

SECTION A

Answer all questions in this section.

QUESTION 1 (21 marks)

Brando plc manufactures and sells three products: Product X, Product Y and Product Z. The following profit/volume graph has been compiled for the three products for the year ended 31 December 19-2.

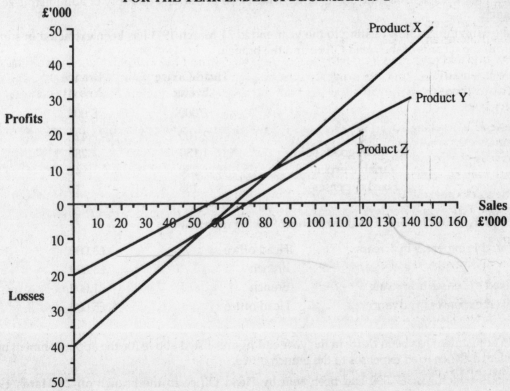

BRANDO plc
PROFIT/VOLUME GRAPH FOR PRODUCTS X,Y AND Z
FOR THE YEAR ENDED 31 DECEMBER 19-2

The average selling prices of each of the three products, X,Y and Z are as follows:

Product	Selling price (per unit)
	£
X	10
Y	12.5
Z	8

The directors wish to introduce a new product, Product W, as from 1 January 19-3. They are assuming that the data for the three existing products X,Y and Z, as shown in the profit/volume graph above, will remain unchanged in 19-3, but that the introduction of the new product, W, will increase the total fixed costs of Brando plc to £100,000 per annum. If the unit price of Product W is fixed so as to give a contribution/sales ratio for that product of 40%, 12,000 units of W will be sold, bringing the total sales revenue of Brando plc to £560,000 for the year to 31 December 19-3.

REQUIRED

(a) Prepare a profit/volume graph for Product W. (There is no need to show Products X,Y and Z on the graph.)
(6 marks)

(b) Prepare a forecast total profit statement for Brando plc for the year to 31 December 19-3. Assume that Product W is introduced.
(5 marks)

(c) Calculate the break-even point for each of the products, W,X,Y and Z.
(4 marks)

(d) Prepare a break-even graph for Brando plc, using the total figures you have prepared in (b) above.
(4 marks)

(e) Using the break-even graph you have prepared in (d) above, state the level of sales at which the department will break-even.
(2 marks)

QUESTION 2 (21 marks)

Branston and Pickles are in partnership in a retail business. Branston, the senior partner, manages the main outlet in Exeter, whilst Pickles, the junior partner, manages a branch outlet in Yeovil. Goods are purchased for the branch by the Exeter office which also performs a quantity of administrative work for the branch.

The following information relating to the year ended 31 March 19-3 has been extracted in summarised form from the records of the Head Office and the branch:

	Head Office Exeter	Branch Yeovil
	£'000	£'000
Sales	2,100	420
Cost of goods sold	1,150	285
Variable expenses	250	42
Fixed expenses	185	10

The above figures do not take account of the following information:

(1) Variable expenses in arrears: Head office   £8,000
                                    Branch   £3,000
     Fixed expenses in arrears: Branch   £1,000
     Fixed expenses in advance   Head office   £5,000

(2) No adjustment has been made in the year end figures listed above for the apportionment of £70,000 of Head Office fixed expenses to the branch office.

(3) Goods which cost £7,000 had been sent by Head Office to the branch on 29 March 19-3; they arrived at the branch on 4 April 19-3. The goods in question had not been included in the closing stocks of Head Office or the branch. Head office had not yet made the necessary entries in its books recording the despatch of the goods to the branch.

Goods are transferred to the branch at cost price.

(4) The stocks of goods held at 31 March 19-3 had been valued at cost as follows:

£

Head Office 45,000
Branch   12,000

These figures do not include goods in transit at 31 March 19-3.

Of the goods held at the branch, goods which had cost £4,000 had become damaged by water and had a resale value now of only £1,000.

(5) The partnership agreement provides for each partner to be credited with a commission based upon the gross profit of the Head Office or branch managed by him. The commission is to be based on 10% of the gross profit after charging the commission.

Branston and Pickles have become concerned about the poor trading performance of the branch. Branston has suggested that the branch should be closed and Pickles has responded by saying that he would be prepared to take it over from the partnership and carry on the business in Yeovil as a sole trader.

REQUIRED

(a) For the year ended 31 March 19-3, separate trading and profit and loss accounts for the branch and Head Office in columnar form.   *(10 marks)*

(b) (i) Calculate the contribution made by the branch to the profits of the business as a whole.

    (ii) Comment upon the partners' suggestions for the future of the branch.   *(9 marks)*

(c) Determine the value of the closing stock of the business as a whole as at 31 March 19-3.

    (2 marks)

QUESTION 3 (13 marks)

Gerald has prepared draft accounts for his business for the year to 30 June 19-1 and the net profit for the year appears to be £21,420. However, he has now discovered that no entries have been made for the following items:

(1) During the year he had accepted a painting from John Quirk who owed the business £5,000 and was unable to pay the debt. Gerald had accepted the painting, which was valued at £2,000, in full settlement of the debt.

(2) One of Gerald's employees had stolen goods worth £2,200 and cash totalling £900 during the year. The employee had been prosecuted and had been ordered by the court to repay £800. Gerald had made a claim on his insurance company for the balance of the loss but the insurance company was denying liability. Gerald does not consider the matter to be finally settled yet.

(3) During the year, Gerald had some work done to the business premises as well as to his own private residence. Some of the materials used had been included in the purchases account and had cost £5,000 less 5% trade discount. He had also used his firm's labour for the work at a cost of £4,000. 20% of the work done had been on his own residence. Of the remainder, 50% was estimated to be improvement to the premises and the balance reckoned to be premises maintenance.

(4) Gerald had overlooked the charge for depreciation of the firm's motor van for the year. The van was purchased two years ago when it was priced at £6,000: Gerald had traded in the firm's old motor van and paid £4,800 in cash for the present van. Gerald depreciates the motor van by the reducing balance method using the rate of 25%.

REQUIRED

(a) Prepare journal entries to correct the above mentioned matters.   *(6 marks)*

(b) Prepare a statement showing how the revised net profit is calculated after the foregoing corrections have been made.   *(7 marks)*

SECTION B

Answer either Question 4 or Question 5.

QUESTION 4 (25 marks)

The following is the balance sheet of Camelot plc as at 30 June 19-4:

	£'000	£'000	£'000
Fixed assets			
Freehold premises at cost			1,100
Fixtures and fittings at net book value			580
			1,680
Current assets			
Stocks		220	
Debtors		415	
		635	
less			
Current liabilities			
Creditors	460		
Bank overdraft	75	535	100
			1,780
less			
Long term liabilities: 10% Debentures			250
			1,530
Share capital and reserves			
Authorised and issued			
4,000,000 Ordinary shares of 25p each fully paid			1,000
Share premium			160
General reserve			200
Profit and loss			170
			1,530

The directors of Camelot are seeking to rationalise the company and their plans include the discontinuance of part of the operations of the company. The relevant division is represented in the balance sheet by the following valuations:

	£'000
Freehold premises	200
Fixtures and fittings	65
Stock	80
Debtors	135
Creditors	110

The directors are considering two schemes:

SCHEME 1.

The division can be closed down completely, the assets sold, the debtors collected and the liabilities settled. The assets can be expected to realise the following amounts:

	£'000
Freehold premises	250
Fixtures and fittings	40
Stock	55

Debtors would be collected subject to discounts of £5,000.

Creditors would be settled subject to discounts of £2,000.

Closure would involve redundancy payments to 30 workers totalling £90,000.

SCHEME 2.

The directors have received an offer from the local management to buy the division and to continue to operate it as a going concern. A new company would be formed for the purpose and would purchase the division on the following terms:

Camelot plc would receive:

200,000 Fully paid Ordinary £1 shares in the new company at par.

40,000 12$\frac{1}{2}$% debentures 2000 at par.

£100,000 in cash.

REQUIRED

Prepare a report for the directors, showing clearly:

(a) detailed calculations for each of the two options; *(5 marks)*

(b) the option recommended and the reasons (include non-financial factors); *(15 marks)*

(c) the balance sheet of Camelot plc assuming that Scheme 2 was adopted. *(5 marks)*

QUESTION 5 (25 marks)

The balance sheet of Buckley Ltd. as at 31 May 19-2 was as follows:

	£	£	£
Fixed assets			
Freehold premises at cost		250,000	
Fixtures and fittings at net book value		64,000	314,000
Current assets			
Stocks		71,500	
Debtors		22,300	
		93,800	
Less			
Current liabilities			
Creditors	43,200		
Bank overdraft	5,600	48,800	45,000
			359,000
Long term liabilities: 10% Debentures 1999			25,000
			334,000

	£	£	£
Capital and reserves			
250,000 Ordinary shares of £1 fully paid			250,000
Profit and loss			84,000
			334,000

Additional information

(1) The authorised share capital of Buckley Ltd. is 500,000 Ordinary shares of £1 each.

(2) Thomas Hardy has approached the directors of Buckley Ltd. with a view to selling his business to the company and has produced his latest balance sheet which is as follows:

	£		£	£
Capital	65,000	Freehold premises		25,000
Long term liability	10,000	Fixtures and fittings		40,000
Creditors	15,000			65,000
		Stock	24,000	
		Balance at bank	1,000	25,000
	90,000			90,000

(3) The directors of Buckley Ltd have made the following offer to Hardy:

(i) Buckley Ltd. will acquire the business of Thomas Hardy and take over the following assets at the values stated:

	£
Freehold premises	40,000
Fixtures and fittings	35,000
Stock	23,000

(ii) Buckley Ltd. will be responsible for the payment of Hardy's creditors.

(iii) Hardy will retain the cash at bank and discharge the long term liability.

(iv) Buckley Ltd. will settle the purchase consideration as follows:

By the issue to Hardy of

(a) 25,000 Ordinary shares of £1 each in Buckley Ltd. at a valuation of £3 per share.

(b) £10,000 in $12^1/2$% Debentures 1999 at par.

and payment to him of £5,000 in cash.

(4) Buckley Ltd will finance the acquisition and provide much needed cash for future expansion with a rights issue of 2 ordinary shares for every 5 shares held, at a price of £2.50 per share. The issue will be fully underwritten and the issue expenses will be £5,000.

REQUIRED

(a) Prepare a statement showing the value of the consideration offered to Thomas Hardy.   (2 *marks*)

(b) Prepare a statement showing a calculation of the difference between the consideration offered by Buckley Ltd. and the net assets acquired by the company.   (2 *marks*)

(c) Explain the reason for the difference calculated in (b) and also how it could be dealt with in the accounts of Buckley Ltd.   (4 *marks*)

(d) Prepare the balance sheet of Buckley Ltd. as it will appear if the take-over and the rights issue take place.   (14 *marks*)

(e) Explain what is meant by a rights issue and how such an issue differs from a bonus issue. (3 *marks*)

SECTION C

Answer either Question 6 or Question 7.

QUESTION 6 (20 marks)

Gray and Sons Department Stores has three departments:

> Furniture and furnishings
> Clothing
> Restaurant

The following balances have been extracted from the books at 31 December 19-2:

		£	£
Salaries and wages			180,000
Rent and rates			48,000
Heating and lighting			15,000
Insurance			9,000
Discounts received			3,600
Commissions			8,800
Purchases	– Furniture and furnishings	120,000	
	– Clothing	60,000	
	– Restaurant	10,000	190,000
Opening stocks	– Furniture and furnishings	40,000	
	– Clothing	12,000	
	– Restaurant	1,200	53,200
Sales	– Furniture and furnishings	280,000	
	– Clothing	160,000	
	– Restaurant	28,000	468,000
Closing stocks	– Furniture and furnishings	44,000	
	– Clothing	14,000	
	– Restaurant	800	58,800

Expenses are to be apportioned as follows:

	Furniture & Furnishings		Clothing		Restaurant
Salaries and wages; insurance:	7	:	4	:	1
Rent and rates Heating and lighting }	4	:	3	:	1
Discounts received	2% of purchases		2% of purchases		nil
Commissions payable	2% of sales		2% of sales		nil

The management of Gray and Sons Departmental Stores is considering whether or not the Restaurant should be closed.

REQUIRED

(a) Prepare departmental trading and profit and loss accounts in columnar form for Gray and Sons Ltd. for the year to 31 December 19-2. *(16 marks)*

(b) Briefly state, with reasons, whether or not you think the restaurant should be closed. *(4 marks)*

QUESTION 7 (20 marks)

Bertram Bartok has received a legacy from his aunt and he wishes to invest it wisely. He believes that two factors which should be considered when investing in shares are the profitability and financial stability of the company concerned.

Two companies in which Bartok is interested are Stockhausen (UK) plc and Webern plc. He has obtained the following information about the companies:

	Stockhausen (UK) plc £'000	Webern plc £'000
For the year to 31 March 19-3		
Turnover	900	436
Cost of sales	612	283.4
Net profit (before interest)	117	47.96
As at 31 March 19-3		
Gross capital employed	1,000	410
Total fixed assets	600	120
* Closing stock	90	190
Liabilities due for settlement within one year	300	115
Long term loans	250	

* Both companies maintain their stock at constant levels throughout the year.

REQUIRED

Using appropriate ratios, draft a memorandum to Bertram Bartok advising him on the relative profitability and financial stability of the two companies. Include any other observations which you think may help Bartok to make up his mind. *(20 marks)*

APPENDIX 1
PRACTICE EXAMINATION PAPER 4
(AEB TYPE)

THREE hours allowed

In Section A answer both questions
In Section B answer either Question 3 or Question 4
In section C answer either Question 5 or Question 6

You must show all workings.

SECTION A Answer both questions in this section.

QUESTION 1 (25 marks)

Fred Moxon, a sole trader, has been in business for some years but has not maintained proper books of account. He has paid income tax in the past, based on estimated assessments and now feels he has paid too much tax. The Inspector of Taxes has told Moxon that no repayment of tax is possible until he can produce evidence of his profits for the two years to 5 April 19-1 and 19-2.

Moxon has produced the following information:

	5 April 19-0	5 April 19-1	5 April 19-2
	£	£	£
Freehold premises at cost	37,000	37,000	62,000
Fixtures and fittings	8,000	9,000	14,000
Motor vans	10,000	8,000	6,000
Stock (valued at cost at these dates)	35,000	32,000	40,000
Trade debtors	21,400	19,800	20,900
Trade creditors	900	1,300	1,150
Accrued expenses	1,000	720	800
Prepaid expenses	100	80	100
Balance at bank	-	5,000	18,000
Bank overdraft	9,000	-	-
Cash	1,000	700	400

Further information.

(1) Fred Moxon has not introduced any additional capital into the business between 5 April 19-0 and 5 April 19-2.

(2) Moxon had improvements made to the premises in November/December 19-1. The total cost of the work was £45,000, of which Moxon had paid £25,000 at 5 April 19-2. The balance of the money owing is not included in the creditors at that date.

(3) On 28 March 19-1, fire destroyed stock which had cost £8,400. The claim against The Frugal Insurance Company plc was not agreed until 5 February 19-2, when it was agreed that the claim would be settled in the sum of £3,200. Moxon had not received the compensation at 5 April 19-2. This matter is not reflected in the figures of debtors shown above.

(4) Since producing the above figures, Moxon has learned that two of his debtors have become bankrupt and there is unlikely to be any money available for their creditors. Details are as follows:

Date of debt	Amount
	£
4 January 19-1	2,000
3 December 19-1	3,300

375

(5)   There were no motor vans in the business until 6 April 19-9, when Moxon purchased two vans:

Van no.	Cost
	£
EYO 999 W	6,000
XZX 001 P	11,000

EYO 999 W was sold on 6 July 19-1 for £3,000 and was replaced by QQY 747 Z at a cost of £9,000. The values shown above for the motor vans are Moxon's estimates. He has now been advised that more realistic figures would have been calculated if the vehicles had been depreciated at 20 per cent per annum on cost.

(6)   Moxon's drawings and private expenditure paid out of the business bank account were as follows:

	Years to 5 April	
	19-1	19-2
	£	£
Drawings	7,200	10,800
Payment to gardener for work at private residence	2,000	2,000
Family holidays	3,000	2,800
School fees	5,000	5,800

REQUIRED

(a)   A statement showing the detailed calculation of the profit earned by Fred Moxon for each of the years ended 5 April 19-1 and 19-2.   (12 marks)

(b)   A balance sheet for the business as at 5 April 19-2.   (7 marks)

(c)   Write a brief memorandum to Fred Moxon giving **six** possible advantages that he would gain by maintaining accounting records on double entry bookkeeping principles in future.   (6 marks)

QUESTION 2 (25 marks)

The directors of Allegro plc are considering buying shares in Scherzo plc. The shares in Scherzo plc are currently quoted on the Stock Exchange at £3.50 per share.

The following information is available for the two companies for the year ended 31 December 19-3.

	Allegro plc	Scherzo plc
	£m	£m
Sales	88	?
Cost of sales	?	20
Selling and distribution costs	3.5	0.85
Administration expenses	2.5	0.75
Gross profit percentage mark-up on cost	$33^1/_3$%	
Gross profit percentage margin on sales		$33^1/_3$%

Other balances at 31 December 19-3

	£m	£m
Fixed assets at cost less aggregate depreciation	60	18
Net current assets	30.75	2.6

Balances as at 1 January 19-3	£m	£m
Issued capital		
£1 ordinary shares fully paid	50	12
Share premium	10	Nil
Retained earnings	12	5
12½% Debentures	10	Nil

The balances at 1 January 19-3 did not change during the year.

Both companies had declared and paid a final dividend as follows:

Allegro plc 12%   Scherzo plc 40%

REQUIRED

(a) For the year ended 31 December 19-3:

    (i)   summarised revenue statements

    (ii) profit and loss appropriation accounts for each of the companies. *(8 marks)*

(b) Calculate three suitable ratios to illustrate the profitability of each of the companies. Comment on the profitability of each company. *(7 marks)*

(c) What is the minimum amount that Allegro plc must invest in the equity of Scherzo plc in order to gain a controlling interest? (Use the share price quoted on 31 December 19-3.) *(3 marks)*

(d) Prepare a balance sheet extract to show how Allegro plc would record its investment in Scherzo plc, on the assumption that 1.2 million shares were purchased on 1 January 19-3. *(2 marks)*

SECTION B

Answer either Question 3 or Question 4 in this section.

QUESTION 3 (25 marks)

Botulnex Ltd. manufactures three chemical products: Botinex, Lunex and Nextubol.

The budgeted output for twelve months is as follows:

Botinex	12,000 kilograms.
Lunex	15,000 kilograms
Nextubol	8,000 kilograms

Three machines are used for the manufacture of the products and the machine time required for the production processes are (per kilogram):

	Botinex	Lunex	Nextubol
Machine No.1	4 minutes	2 minutes	–
Machine No.2	2 minutes	–	6 minutes
Machine No.3	–	4 minutes	3 minutes

Each machine is budgeted to be manned for 1300 hours during the twelve month period.

Lunex is the only one of the three products for which there is an alternative process. This involves using Machine No.1 and Machine No. 2. If Machine No. 2 is used, 15 minutes of that machine's time will be required for the production of 1 kilogram of Lunex, but the resulting product will be a concentrated chemical mixture of double the normal strength. The concentrated mixture can be diluted in another department of Botulnex Ltd. to normal strength.

Further information.

Per kilogram	Botinex	Lunex	Nextubol
	£	£	£
Selling price	6.60	6.00	7.80
Direct materials	2.40	1.90	2.40
Direct labour	1.90	1.80	2.00
Variable overheads	1.25	1.40	1.30

The fixed costs of Botulnex Ltd. for the same twelve month aperiod will amount to £37,000.

377

REQUIRED

(a) Prepare a statement that shows whether or not the production forecast for the twelve month period can be achieved. Support your answer with detailed workings. *(10 marks)*

(b) Prepare a statement which shows:

(i) the total budgeted contribution of the three products.

(ii) the maximum contribution achievable, using the information contained in your answer to Part (a).

(iii) the difference between the budgeted net profit and the maximum achievable net profit.

(5 marks)

(c) Discuss the problems that arise when:

(i) production falls short of budgeted sales.

(ii) production exceeds budgeted sales. *(6 marks)*

(d) What information is of use when there is a factor which limits output below demand. *(4 marks)*

QUESTION 4 (25 marks)

Constance Fabrications Ltd. 'buys in' component parts and assembles them before painting the assembled products and transferring them to the warehouse as finished goods.

The company operates a system of standard costing and budgetary control. The budget statement for October 19-4 contains the following information:

	Assembly Dept.	Painting Dept.
Standard cost per unit		
Direct material	£8	–
Direct labour	£21	£7.20
Budgeted output in units	15,000	15,000
Budgeted direct labour hours	45,000	22,500

Note: The output of the Assembly department becomes the input to the Painting department. There were no opening or closing stocks of work in progress.

Further information

(1) Actual production details for October 19-4 were as follows:

(i) Output passing through both processes was 13,000 units. There were no stocks of opening or closing work in progress

(ii) Direct material used at standard prices: £106,800

(iii) Direct material used at actual prices: £105,465

(iv) Direct wages paid and direct labour hours worked for the Assembly department were as follows:

Wages paid £282,000

Hours actually worked 40,000

(2) There was no labour rate variance in the Painting department but the Painting department's labour efficiency variance was £3,000 (adverse).

REQUIRED

(a) Calculate the total direct material variance and analyse it into:

(i) direct material usage variance

(ii) direct material price variance *(6 marks)*

(b) Calculate the overall direct labour variance for the Assembly department and analyse it into:
   (i) direct labour efficiency variance
   (ii) direct labour rate variance   (*6 marks*)

(c) Identify the possible reasons for each of the variances calculated for the Assembly department in (a) and (b) above and for the variance given for the Painting department.   (*8 marks*)

(d) Discuss possible inter-relationships between these variances.   (*5 marks*)

SECTION C
Answer either Question 5 or Question 6 in this section.

QUESTION 5
The Vortex Manufacturing Co. plc owns a factory in Newborough, where it is the town's largest employer. It is the company's policy to encourage sport in the town, which has a high level of unemployment. The company has its own Soccer Club and gives it practical support in many ways, including financial help. The club's pavilion and pitches are situated on freehold land owned by The Vortex Manufacturing Co. plc adjacent to its factory and the company makes no charge to the club for the use of the land. However, the club's premises are in a dilapidated state and now need replacing at an estimated cost of £30,000.

For some years, the club has organised an annual 'Charity Day', an event to raise funds for local charities.

Bilditkwik and Scarper are property developers who have made a very generous offer to The Vortex Manufacturing Company plc for the land occupied by the Soccer Club.

The accounts of the club are maintained by the company's accountant, but are kept separate from the company's accounts.

The trial balance of the club at 31 December 19-3 was as follows:

	Dr £	Cr £
Clubhouse at cost	6,750	
Fixtures at cost	13,500	
Provision for depreciation of fixtures at 31.12.19-2		9,450
Equipment for maintenance of sports ground at cost	10,800	
Provision for depreciation of equipment for maintenance of sportsground at 31.12.19-2		4,860
Sports equipment	1,890	
Subscriptions		17,550
Donations		2,600
Bar sales		67,500
Bar stocks	5,400	
Bar purchases	45,900	
Discounts received on bar purchases		675
Creditors for bar purchases		4,050
Surplus on 'Charity Day'		9,855
Wages	15,525	
General expenses	12,285	
Repairs to clubhouse	2,295	
Cash at bank	7,280	
Cash in hand	90	
Accumulated fund		4,995
Sales of house journal		1,440
Cost of house journal	1,260	
	£122,975	£122,975

Further information

(1) The bar stocks at 31 December 19-3 were valued at £4,320 (cost).

(2) Included in subscriptions were prepayments of £350.

(3) General expenses amounting to £324 were accrued at 31 December 19-3.

(4) The surplus on the 'Charity Day' is distributed to local charities in early April.

(5) The club depreciates fixtures by 10% per annum on the straight line basis and sportsground maintenance equipment by 15% per annum on the straight line basis.

(6) It is the club's policy to write off sports equipment to revenue in the year of purchase.

(7) The donations have been received as a result of an appeal for the creation of a fund to be used for training promising young footballers.

(8) The Vortex Manufacturing Co. Ltd. produces a house journal which is distributed through the Soccer Club. The journal has a selling price of 10p, but The Vortex Manufacturing Company Ltd. sells it to the club at £8.75 per 100 copies, allowing the club make a profit on sales.

(9) In order to encourage support for the soccer club, The Vortex Manufacturing Co. Ltd. has agreed that as from 1 January 19-3, it will supplement the club funds by a subsidy of 20p for every £1 of annual subscriptions received in each financial year. The subsidy is payable in the April following the end of each year. No provision has been made for the subsidy in the above trial balance.

REQUIRED

(a) An income and expenditure account for the year ended 31 December 19-3 of The Vortex Manufacturing Co. Ltd.'s Soccer Club. *(11 marks)*

(b) A balance sheet as at 31 December 19-3 for The Vortex Manufacturing Company Ltd.'s Soccer Club. *(6 marks)*

(c) A report advising the directors of The Vortex Manufacturing Company Ltd. on the future of the Soccer Club including an evaluation of the present financial state of the club. *(8 marks)*

QUESTION 6 (25 marks)

Orbital Holidays Ltd. is a travel agency which has carried on business for many years. It sells holidays offered by holiday tour operators, for which it receives commissions equal to 10 per cent of the value of the holidays sold. The following information has been extracted from the books of Orbital Holidays Ltd. at the end of its financial year on 31 January 19-3.

	Dr £	Cr £
Commission received		360,000
Wages (including commission)	72,000	
Rent and rates	25,000	
Advertising	40,000	
General expenses	28,000	
Debenture interest	1,000	
Depreciation : fixtures & fittings		18,000
motor vehicles		8,000
Fixtures and fittings		
at cost	42,000	
Motor vehicles at cost	14,000	
10% Debenture (issued 1 Feb 19-1)		20,000

Further information

(1) At 31 January 19-3 rent of £5,000 was owing and £6,000 for advertising had been paid in advance.

(2) Orbital Holidays Ltd. pays 10% of the commission it receives to the staff as a bonus.

(3) All costs are fixed with the exception of the commission paid to staff.

(4) It is the policy of the company to depreciate its motor vehicles by 25% per annum on cost, and its fixtures and fittings by 10% per annum on cost.

The tour manager is interested in a new type of foreign holiday which he wishes to offer to customers next year. The company accountant has produced the following estimated costs of selling 400 holidays as follows:

	£
Hotel costs (£200 per holiday)	80,000
Travel costs (£100 per holiday)	40,000
Advertising costs	25,000
General administration costs	45,000
	190,000

Average cost per holiday: £475

The managing director has expressed concern because whilst the holiday can be sold at £600 in the peak holiday season, it would be unlikely to sell at more than £400 outside the peak holiday season.

REQUIRED

(a) An operating statement for the year ended 31 January 19-3.   *(6 marks)*

(b) Calculate the value of holidays the company had to sell to break even during the year ended 31 January 19-3.   *(11 marks)*

(c) Comment on the company accountant's approach to the calculation of the cost of the proposed new holiday.   *(8 marks)*

APPENDIX 1
PRACTICE EXAMINATION PAPER 5
(LONDON TYPE)

THREE hours allowed

Answer FIVE questions, choosing TWO from section A, TWO from Section B and ONE from Section C
All calculations must be shown.

You are reminded of the necessity for good English and orderly presentation in your answers.

Section A

Answer TWO questions from this Section. (Each question carries 25 marks).

QUESTION 1

Adam, Eve and Pinchmee are in partnership, sharing profits and losses in the ratio 3:2:1. At 31 December 19-1 their balance sheet was as follows:

	£	£
Fixed Assets		106,644
Current Assets		
Stock	71,116	
Debtors	42,655	
Bank	24,863	
	138,634	
Less Current Liabilities		
Trade creditors	35,278	103,356
		210,000
Capital accounts		
Adam	100,000	
Eve	50,000	
Pinchmee	25,000	175,000
Current accounts		
Adam	24,000	
Eve	10,000	
Pinchmee	1,000	35,000
		210,000

Adam decided to retire from the partnership on 1 January 19-2.

Accordingly, it was agreed between the partners that:

(1) The balances on their current accounts would be transferred to their respective capital accounts.

(2) Goodwill would be valued at £24,000, but no goodwill would be recorded in the firm's ledgers.

(3) Fixed assets would be revalued at £100,000, stock at £60,000 and a debtor for £240 would be written off as bad.

(4) Of the amount due to Adam, £100,000 would be transferred to a Loan account and the balance settled in cash immediately. A bank overdraft facility would be available for this purpose,if necessary. The loan would be repayable to Adam in four equal annual instalments, the first being due on 31 December 19-2.

Eve and Pinchmee decided to form a limited company, Evenmee Ltd., to acquire the partnership business on 2 January 19-2. The company had an authorised share capital of 100,000 ordinary shares of £1 each and acquired the partnership assets and liabilities, including the loan from Adam, at their revised book values. Shares were issued to Eve and Pinchmee at par value in the ratio 3:2. An appropriate cash payment was made by one of these partners to the other to adjust their rights, and the partner receiving the payment immediately used the cash to subscribe for further shares in Evenmee Ltd. at par.

REQUIRED

(a) The capital accounts of Adam, Eve and Pinchmee showing the entries in respect of Adam's retirement and the acquisition of the business by Evenmee Ltd. *(18 marks)*

(b) The opening balance sheet of Evenmee Ltd. as at 2 January 19-2. *(7 marks)*

QUESTION 2

The chief accountant of The Geekay Manufacturing Company plc prepared forecast draft accounts for the company for the year ended 31 December 19-0. The following were included in the schedule of balances at that date:

	Dr. £	Cr. £
Ordinary shares of 10p each, fully paid		500,000
8% Redeemable Preference Shares, of £1 each, fully paid		100,000
Share Premium Account		50,000
Asset Replacement Reserve		80,000
Provision for unrealised profit on stock of finished goods		12,500
Interim Ordinary Dividend	25,000	
Preference dividend	4,000	
Net Profit for the year		314,000
Retained profit brought forward 1 January 19-0		232,000
Trade debtors and other debit balances	70,000	
Trade creditors and other credit balances		38,000
Cash at bank	65,000	
Stocks at 31 December 19-0:		
Raw materials	82,000	
Work in progress	64,000	
Finished goods	76,500	

Note: The authorised share capital is 6 million ordinary shares of 10p each and 100,000 8% Redeemable Preference Shares of £1 each.

The company chief executive has informed the chief accountant that the directors have made the following decisions:

(1) The preference shares are to be redeemed at par on 31 December 19-0 but no new shares will be issued to finance the redemption.

(2) £40,000 is to be transferred to the Asset Replacement Reserve.

(3) The chief executive is preparing a schedule of his expenses for the year amounting to £11,000. The chief accountant had not previously been aware of these expenses.

(4) Apart from the preference dividend to be paid, the directors will recommend a final ordinary dividend of 2.5p per share. These dividends will be paid in March 19-1.

The chief accountant estimates that taxation on the profit for the year will amount to £52,000.

You are required:

(a) (i) to prepare the profit and loss appropriation account for the year ending 31 December 19-0.

(8 marks)

(ii) a balance sheet at 31 December 19-0 for The Geekay Manufacturing Company plc showing clearly the total of fixed assets, the current assets, current liabilities, net working capital, net worth, share capital and reserves in as much detail as is possible from the information given above.

(14 marks)

(b) Explain why a company is required to maintain the total of its share capital and reserves at their pre-redemption level after redeeming redeemable shares. *(3 marks)*

QUESTION 3

The following information is available from the accounts of Enigma Variations plc for the year ended 31 March 19-2.

1. Exceptional items

   A major customer owing Enigma Variations plc £110,000 has gone into Creditors' Voluntary Liquidation. No dividend is expected for the unsecured creditors.

2. Extraordinary items

   During the year to 31 March 19-2, Enigma Variations plc sold a factory for £5.5m. The factory had a book value of £1.5m (cost) when sold.

3. Taxation

	£m
Corporation tax on the profits of the year	40.5
Corporation tax on the gain on the sale of factory	1.2
Overprovision for corporation tax on profits of previous year	(3.8)

4. Dividends

	£m
Paid	0.8
Proposed	2.0

5. Reserves

19-1		19-2
£m		£m
–	Asset Revaluation reserve	25
–	Capital redemption Reserve	50
18.6	General Reserve	38.6
84.2	Profit and Loss account	137.5
102.8		251.1

6. Post balance sheet events

   A contract worth £120m was signed with an overseas customer on 10 April 19-2.

384

You are required:

(a) to prepare, as far as the information permits, the profit and loss account of Enigma Variations plc in vertical form for the year ended 31 March 19-2.   *(16 marks)*

(b) to explain the meaning of the terms

   (i)   post balance sheet events

   (ii) extraordinary items

   (iii) exceptional items.   *(9 marks)*

Section B

Answer TWO questions from this section. (Each question carries 15 marks.)

QUESTION 4.

Flybird plc has prepared the following draft statement of accounting policies as a note to its published accounts for the year ended 31 May 19-4.

1. **Accounting Convention**

    Three of the company's main competitors have gone into voluntary liquidation during the past year. Accordingly, the fixed assets of Flybird plc have been valued on a conservative basis at estimated realisable values.

2. **Turnover**

    Value Added Tax has been included in the Turnover shown in the profit and loss account.

3. **Stock**

    Manufactured stock has been valued at prime cost of production.

4. **Research and Development**

    Research expenditure which is not expected to lead to a viable product is written off in the accounts. Expenditure on research which is expected to lead to viable products, together with all development expenditure has been capitalised.

5. **Fixed Assets**

    Plant and machinery to the value of £1.8m (normal cash price) has been obtained during the year on Hire Purchase. As this plant and machinery will not legally become the property of Flybird plc until 30 April 19-9 when the final H.P. instalment has been paid, it is not included in the fixed tangible assets shown in the balance sheet.

Comment on the acceptability of each of the five accounting policies listed. You should refer, where appropriate, to recognised accounting concepts, conventions and Statements of Standard Accounting Practice.   *(15 marks)*

QUESTION 5

Audico Ltd. was formed for the purpose of manufacturing 'Walkman' type personal stereo units. It commenced operations on 1 June 19-3.

Initially it was planned to make and sell 35,000 units at £56 per unit in the first year. The variable costs of production per unit would be:

	£
Direct materials	14
Direct wages	10
Other direct expenses	7

Audico Ltd.'s fixed overhead budget was £420,000 per annum. of which 60 per cent would be incurred in the factory, 25 per cent in the office and 15 per cent by the selling and distribution department.

After four months of production, a more realistic appraisal of the market indicated that a maximum of 30,000 units would be sold in the year to 31 May 19-4. The directors accordingly decided to maintain production at the originally budgeted level and to keep the unsold units in stock in readiness for a new market to be opened overseas in Deffenland in the following year; the directors believed that the units would sell well in Deffenland providing the price there was cut to £48.

Stocks of raw materials sufficient for current production needs only are ordered so that there were no stocks of raw materials on hand at 31 May 19-4; neither was there any work-in-progress at that date.

You are required:

(a) to prepare an estimated manufacturing, trading and profit and loss account for Audico Ltd. for the year to 31 May 19-4, based on the revised sales total. *(11 marks)*

(b) to calculate the sales value at which Audico Ltd. will 'break-even' in the year to 31 May 19-4.

(4 marks)

QUESTION 6

Robin Adair, an inexperienced accounts clerk, extracted a trial balance from his firm's books. When the trial balance failed to agree, Adair opened a suspense account for the difference and proceeded to prepare a trading and profit and loss account and balance sheet. The profit and loss account showed a net profit for the year of £14,236.

Control accounts are not kept.

The following items were discovered subsequently:

1. A sales invoice for £150 had not been entered into the Sales Day Book.

2. The discount allowed column in the cash book totalled £549 in February; this amount had been posted to the credit of Discounts Received account.

3. During the year, a motor van had been sold for cash to Jon Pettigrew. The van had cost £6,000 when new and at the date of sale, the accumulated depreciation on the van amounted to £3,800. The sale proceeds of £1,500 had been entered in the cash book and credited to Jenny Potter's account in the Sales Ledger. No other entries had been made in the books for this transaction.

4. A debit balance of £246 on the account of Fairfax Supplies Ltd. in the Purchases ledger had been wrongly extracted from the ledger as a credit balance.

5. Discounts received account had been entered on the wrong side of the Profit and Loss account as an expense. The balance on the account was £3,200.

After these errors had been corrected, there was a 'nil' balance on the suspense account.

You are required:

(a) to prepare journal entries, where appropriate, to correct the above errors. (Narratives are NOT required.) *(9 marks)*

(b) to show the suspense account as it will appear in the ledger after the correcting entries have been made. *(2 marks)*

(c) to prepare a statement of the revised profit for the year. *(4 marks)*

Section C

Answer ONE question from this section. (Each question carries 20 marks.)

QUESTION 7

(a) Prior to the introduction of Statement of Standard Accounting Practice No.12, many companies did not provide for depreciation of freehold property because the value of such property usually appreciated over a period of time.

You are required to state the requirement of SSAP 12 as regards depreciation of freehold property and explain how that requirement is justified. *(8 marks)*

(b) INTERNAL MEMORANDUM

To Accountant

From Managing Director.

Replacement of machinery.

You will be aware of the fact that at the last Board meeting, I persuaded my fellow directors to agree to the replacement of a considerable amount of our machinery which has become very old and inefficient.

Year after year I have had to agree to considerable sums of money being put aside for depreciation of the machinery, and dividends have had to be reduced as a result.

I am now informed that the company bank balance is quite inadequate for the purchase of the new machinery which is urgently required.

Kindly let me have, without delay, your explanation of the reason for the money which you were putting aside for depreciation not being available now that it is required.

Unless the explanation you give is satisfactory, I shall request our auditor, Mr. Checkitt, of Messrs. Checkitt, Tickitt and Wink, chartered accountants, to carry out a thorough examination of the company's books.

(Signed)
Kurt Kummuppance
Managing Director

You are required to draft a reply from the accountant to the chairman explaining why the bank balance is low although yearly provision has been made for the depreciation of the machinery.

Your answer should include a recommendation to the chairman of a way of ensuring that funds are available for renewal of fixed assets in future. (Make any assumptions you wish to make in drafting your answer) *(12 marks)*

QUESTION 8

The Companies Act 1985 contains provisions relating to Group Accounts.

(a) Explain what is meant by:
  (i) holding company
  (ii) subsidiary company *(4 marks)*

(b) Explain the purpose of consolidated accounts. *(4 marks)*

(c) How do consolidated accounts help to show the strengths or reveal the weaknesses of individual companies within the group? How may these matters be obscured by the consolidation of the accounts? *(12 marks)*

APPENDIX 1
PRACTICE EXAMINATION PAPER 6
(LONDON TYPE)

THREE hours allowed

Answer FIVE questions, choosing TWO from Section A, TWO from Section B and ONE from Section C. All calculations must be shown.

Your are reminded of the necessity for good English and orderly presentation in your answers.

Section A

Answer TWO questions from this section. (Each question carries 25 marks.)

QUESTION 1

(i) What is the difference between

(a) allocation of overheads and (b) apportionment of overheads?

Give an example of each.   *(6 marks)*

(ii) Explain what is meant by overhead absorption rate and mention three bases on which the rate may be calculated.   *(5 marks)*

(iii) Diversity Ltd. has three production departments: Machining dept., Assembly dept., and Painting dept. There are also two service departments, Dept. A and Dept. B.

Dept. B services all the other four departments, whilst Dept. A services only the production departments.

The following are the overhead costs of the departments for the four weeks to 28 March 19-1:

Department	Machining £	Assembly £	Painting £	Dept A £	Dept B £
Indirect labour	25,000	20,000	10,000	6,000	8,000
Other overheads	10,000	8,000	6,000	3,000	2,000

The service departments' overheads are charged to the other departments as follows:

	Machining	Assembly	Painting	Dept A
Dept. A	50%	25%	25%	–
Dept. B	40%	30%	20%	10%

The Machining dept. recovers overheads on the basis of machine hours whilst the Assembly and Painting departments recover overheads on the basis of labour hours worked.

The following information is available for the production departments:

Machining department: machine hours worked, 400 per week.

Assembly department: hourly rate of pay £5.

Painting department: hourly rate of pay £4.

Calculate the overhead recovery rates for each of the production departments.   *(14 marks)*

QUESTION 2

(i) The following information is available for PAM Industries Ltd.:

	Budgeted	Actual
Total fixed expenses	£336,000	£312,000
Total variable expenses	£240,000	£260,000
Volume of production (standard machine hours)	4,800	5,120
Units produced	120	152

You are required to calculate the following variances for PAM Industries Ltd.:

   (a) Fixed overheads: the expenditure and volume variances;

   (b) Variable overheads: the expenditure and efficiency variances.   *(12 marks)*

(ii) The managing director of PAM Industries Ltd. is uncertain as to the meaning and significance of the four variances you have calculated in (i) above. Draft a memorandum to the managing director to help him understand the meaning and significance of the variances.   *(13 marks)*

QUESTION 3

(a) Differential Products Ltd. commenced manufacturing on 1 January 19-2. The directors have been studying the company's results for the years ended 31 December,19-2 and 19-3. The company has hitherto calculated profits using marginal costing principles. The directors have now been advised by their accountant that they should have based their profit calculations on absorption costing methods and they wish to know what effect absorption costing would have had on the company's profits.

The following information is available for the two years:

	19-2	**19-3**
Sales (in units)	2,000	2,300
Price per unit	£45	£50
No. of units produced	2,500	2,700
Direct materials per unit	£9	£11
Direct labour per unit	£12	£14
Direct expenses per unit	£4	£5
Fixed overheads (factory)	£49,000	£49,000

Stocks of finished goods are valued on the FIFO basis.

You are required to calculate the profits of Differential Products Ltd. for the years ended 31 December 19-2 and 19-3 using (a) marginal costing and (b) absorption costing.   *(16 marks)*

(b) Explain why the profits calculated using absorption costing differ from those calculated under marginal costing.   *(4 marks)*

(c) Prepare a statement which shows clearly how the different profits for 19-2 and 19-3 have arisen.

    (5 marks)

Section B

Answer TWO questions from this section. (Each question carries 15 marks.)

QUESTION 4

(i) The employees of Kwidzin Ltd. are holding a meeting to discuss proposals which have been made by management for revising the method of remunerating the staff. Their Trade Union representative has been referring to 'piece rates', 'time rates' and 'standard hours'. Some of the employees are not sure what he means by these terms.

Explain briefly what is meant by:

   (a) piece rates

   (b) time rates

   (c) standard hours.   *(4 marks)*

(ii) Indentures Ltd. employs a number of trainee workers and has devised a scheme for their remuneration as follows:

$$\text{Earnings} = \text{hourly rate} \times \sqrt{\text{Standard hours} \times \text{Clock hours}}$$

If the hourly rate of pay is £6 and 4 standard hours are allowed for a job, calculate the earnings if nine clock hours are recorded.   *(2 marks)*

(iii) Simon has very recently become employed by Crockett Ltd. and was pleased when he was told that the company operates a bonus scheme for its employees.

The scheme rewards its employees by paying them a bonus of 50% of the time saved on the completion of jobs.

Simon now feels that the scheme works to his disadvantage because he has been studying the following situations:

	If no time saved	**If time saved**
Time allowed	10 hours	10 hours
Time taken	10 hours	6 hours
Rate per hour	£8	£8
Basic pay	£80	£48
Bonus	-	£16
Total pay	£80	£64

You are required to prepare a brief, simple explanation for Simon to show how he can benefit from the bonus scheme.

(4 marks)

(iv) Briefly explain the essential difference between the Halsey and the Rowan bonus systems.

(5 marks)

QUESTION 5

(a) Explain what is meant by a 'flexible budget'.

(3 marks)

(b) From the following information produce a flexed budget for direct materials and direct labour:

	Master budget	**Actual**
Units of production	1,000	1,500
Direct materials usage (total)	2,000 kgms	3,150 kgms
Direct materials cost (total)	£4,500	£6,772.5
Direct labour hours (total)	4,500	7,125
Direct labour cost (total)	£40,500	£64,481.25

(5 marks)

(c) Using the information contained in (b) above, calculate the following:

    (i)   Quantity variance

    (ii)   Direct materials (total) variance

    (iii)   Direct materials usage variance

    (iv)   Direct materials price variance

    (v)   Direct labour (total) variance

    (vi)   Direct labour efficiency variance

    (vii) Direct labour rate variance

(7 marks)

QUESTION 6

(a) Identify and explain three disadvantages to a business of holding excessive stocks of raw materials or finished goods.

(6 marks)

(b) Gamma Ltd. uses a chemical mixture in the production of moulded products. The mixture is liable to deteriorate if it is kept in stock for too long and instructions have been given to the storekeeper to keep a strict control on the re-ordering of the mixture so as to avoid the risk of deterioration on the one hand, and 'stock-out' on the other.

The following information is relevant to the chemical mixture:

Minimum stock level	4,000 tonnes
Monthly usage	1,800 tonnes
Estimated delivery time	1.5 months
Estimated cost of placing an order	£36
Holding costs per tonne	£4 per month

You are required to calculate:
- (i) the re-order level
- (ii) the economic order quantity *(6 marks)*
- (c) What is meant by the 'imprest' system of store keeping? *(3 marks)*

Section C

Answer ONE question from this section. (Each question carries 20 marks.)

QUESTION 7

Distinguish between the terms in each of the following pairs:

(a) break-even point, and margin of safety

(b) mark-up, and C/S (or P/V) ratio

(c) management by exception, and management by crisis

(d) accounting rate of return, and internal rate of return. *(20 marks)*

QUESTION 8

A firm employs the following accountants:

(i) management accountant

(ii) financial accountant

(iii) cost accountant.

Write a brief job description for each, indicating the data each is likely to use in the job, the kind of information each may be expected to produce and the relationships which should exist between them.

(20 marks)

APPENDIX 2 ANSWERS

CHAPTER 1

1.6.2

Colombo
Trial balance as at 31 December 19-9

	Dr £	Cr £
Premises	80,000	
Plant and machinery	65,000	
Office furniture	15,000	
Provision for depreciation: plant and machinery		35,000
Provision for depreciation: office furniture		10,000
Stock at 1.1.-9	6,000	
Debtors	5,500	
Creditors		2,700
Purchases	47,000	
Carriage inwards	1,200	
Carriage outwards	2,100	
Sales		90,000
Returns inwards	2,600	
Returns outwards		1,400
Provision for doubtful debts		500
Selling and distribution expenses	20,800	
Administration expenses	15,400	
Discounts receivable		2,000
Discounts allowed	1,800	
Drawings	12,600	
Capital		133,400
	275,000	275,000

Note: Closing stock does not appear in the books at all until the trading account is prepared.

CHAPTER 2

2.1.2

Total Controls Ltd.
Sales ledger control account for the month of September 19-0

19-0		£	19-0		£
Sept 1	Balance b/f	5,000	Sept 1	Balance b/f	76
30	Sales for the month	21,790	30	Sales returns	1,760
	Bad debt recovered	70		Discounts allowed	580
	Cash book-dishonoured cheques	826		Cash book - cash received from debtors	20,450
	Interest debited to accounts	36		Cash book- bad debt recovered	70
	Balance c/d	150		Bad debts w/o	424
				Contras-Purchases ledger	1,200
				Balance c/d	3,312
		27,872			27,872

Oct 1	Balance b/d	3,312	Oct 1	Balance b/d	150

Purchases ledger control account
for the month of September 19-0

19-0		£	19-0		£
Sept 1	Balance b/d	124	Sept 1	Balance b/d	3,600
30	Purchases returns	440	30	Purchases for the month	14,500
	Discounts received	276		Balance c/d	80
	Cash paid	11,120			
	Contras - sales ledger	1,200			
	Balance c/d	5,020			
		18,180			18,180
Oct 1	Balance b/d	80	Oct 1	Balance b/d	5,020

Tutorial notes:

1. Cash sales and cash purchases are irrelevant as far as control accounts are concerned and so are ignored in this exercise.

2. The provision for doubtful debts is irrelevant and is also ignored.

2.2.2

Dodgson
Purchases ledger total account for the three months ended
30 June 19-3

19-3		£	19-3		£
Apr 1	Balance b/d	625	Apr 1	Balance b/d	32,000
30	Purchases returns	3,200	30	Purchases	120,000
	Bank	100,200		Balance c/d	410
	Discounts	2,500			
	Balance c/d	45,885			
		152,410			152,410
May 1	Balance b/d	410	May 1	Balance b/d	45,885
31	Purchases returns	4,800	31	Purchases	160,000
	Bank	148,000		Balance c/d	570
	Discounts	3,800			
	Balance c/d	49,445			
		206,455			206,455
Jun 1	Balance b/d	570	Jun 1	Balance b/d	49,445
30	Purchases returns	4,000	30	Purchases	144,000
	Bank	130,000		Balance c/d	220
	Discounts	2,700			
	Balance c/d	56,395			
		193,665			193,665
Jul 1	Balance b/d	220	Jul 1	Balance b/d	56,395

2.3.2 (a)

Datchett
Purchases Ledger Control Account (corrected)
for the month of January 19-9

19-9		£	19-9		£
Jan 31	Balance b/d	540	Jan 31	Balance b/d	
	Discounts received	1,026		(balancing figure)	10,915
	Balance c/d (see (b) below)	13,960		Correction of casting error in P.D.B.	1,250
				Correction of cash posting for month	1,800
				Cancellation of discounts allowed posted in error	1,321
				Balance c/d (see (b) below)	240
		15,526			15,526
Feb 1	Balance b/d	240	Feb 1	Balance b/d	13,960

(b) **Calculation of the corrected totals of the debit and credit**
balances in the Purchases ledger as at 31 January 19-9

	Dr £	Cr £
Purchases ledger balances as included in the trial balance	540	15,240
Correction of posting error to Sawyer's account		(600)
Cancellation of credit note erroneously posted to W. Lynne's account	(300)	100
Credit note now posted to L.Wynne's account		(400)
Transfer to James' account from sales ledger		(380)
	240	13,960

CHAPTER 3

3.2.2

(a)

G.Sobers
Suspense account

19-3		£	19-3		£
	Sales	180	Jun 30	* Difference on trial balance	35
				Lloyd	45
				Bad debt w/o	100
		180			180

* In this type of question, when the difference on the trial balance is not given, the difference is found by calculating the amount required to make the suspense account balance.

(b) **Journal**

			Dr £	Cr £
2.	Machinery at cost		750	
		Machinery repairs		750
	Profit and loss		75	
		*Provision for depreciation of machinery		75
4.	Purchases		300	
		F Engineer		300

* Additional depreciation must be calculated and provided on machinery as the calculation of depreciation in the draft accounts would not have taken account of the improvement.

(c)   **Statement of corrected profit for the year to 30 June 19-3**

	Decrease	Increase	
	£	£	£
Profit per draft accounts			7,550
Reduction in machinery repairs		750	
Increase in provision for depreciation of machinery	75		
Increase in sales		180	
Increase in purchases	300		
Increase in bad debts w/o	100		
	475	930	
		475	
Net increase in profit			455
Revised net profit			8,005

3.2.3

P.Hendrie

(a)   **Journal**

		Dr	Cr
		£	£
1.	Repairs to motor cars	2,780	
	Suspense	90	
	Motor cars at cost		2,870

(Cancellation of amount debited in error to Motor cars at cost and posting of cost of repair work to Repairs to motor cars; consequent reduction to 'difference on trial balance' in Suspense account.)

2.	Suspense	500	
	Sales		500

(Sales understated by £500 because of omission of Boon's invoice from Sales Day Book. Consequent reduction to 'difference on trial balance' in Suspense a/c.)

3.	Suspense	3,600	–

(Opening stock figure overstated by £3,600 in trial balance, causing a trial balance difference, but double entry not affected.)

4.	Stock	1,300	
	Cost of sales		1,300

(Closing stock understated by omission of stock sheet)

5.	Suspense	320	–

(Credit balance of £160 in sales ledger extracted as debit balance causing a trial balance difference of double that amount but not affecting the double entry)

(b)   **Suspense account**

19-2		£	19-2		£
Mar 31	Motor car at cost	90	Mar 31	Difference on trial balance	4,510
	Sales	500			
	Adjustment of stock at 1 Apr 19-1	3,600			
	Adjustment of trade debtors	320			
		4,510			4,510

(c)

Calculation of adjusted net profit for the year ended
31 March 19-2

	Decrease £	Increase £	£
Net loss per draft profit and loss account			(2,300)
Increase in motor repairs	2,780		
Increase in sales		500	
Reduction in cost of sales (decrease in opening stock)		3,600	
Reduction in cost of sales (increase in closing stock)		1,300	
	2,780	5,400	
		2,780	
Net reduction in loss			2,620
Adjusted net profit			320

4.1.2

Mr. Blower

Statement of Affairs as at

	1 July 19-2 £		30 June 19-3 £
Fixed assets:			
Premises at valuation	8,000		8,000
Motor van	4,000		3,200
Motor car	–		5,500
Plant and equipment	900		1,000
	12,900		17,700
Current assets:			
Stock of materials	100	175	
Debtors for work done	1,250	640	
Balance at bank	2,400	120	
	3,750	935	
less Current liabilities:			
Owing to suppliers	(975)	(1,800)	
Rates owing	–	(400)	
Telephone owing	(15)	(40)	
	2,760	(1,305)	
	15,660		16,395
Less long term liability:			
Loan from father	–		(2,000)
Capital	15,660		14,395
less capital at 1 July 19-2			(15,660)
			(1,265)
Add Drawings during year (52 × £80)			4,160
			2,895
Deduct capital introduced during year (motor car)			5,500
Net loss for the year to 30 June 19-3			(2,605)

4.2.2

A Smith Purchases total account

19-4		£	19-3		£
March 31	Cheques	168,000	April 30	Creditors b/f	14,640
	Discounts	6,400	19-4		
	Creditors c/f	16,100	March 31	Purchases (bal.fig.)	175,860
		190,500			190,500

Sales total account

19-3		£	19-4		£
April 30	Debtors b/f	19,730	March 31	Cash	199,700
	Sales (bal.fig.)	205,940		Discounts	4,820
				Debtors c/f	21,150
		225,670			225,670

4.3.2

Mr. Peters
Trading account for the year to 30 September 19-5

	£	£
Sales		260,000
less Cost of sales Stock at 1 Oct 19-4	11,000	
Purchases	211,000	
	222,000	
Stock at 30 September 19-5	14,000	208,000
Gross profit (20% of sales)		52,000

4.5.2

J.T.Forster
Profit and loss account for the year to 31 December 19-3

	£	£
Work done (40,764 - 3,000 + 6,000)		43,764
less cost of materials (9,000 + 2,000		
2,600 + 4,250 - 2,700 - 3,500)		11,650
		32,114
Wages (6,000 + 1,800)	7,800	
Rates (1,000 + 400 - 500)	900	
Electricity (800 - 200 + 280)	880	
Advertising (700 + 120 - 340)	480	
Motor expenses (2,100 - 900)	1,200	
Loss on sale of motor lorry	2,200	
Depreciation of motor lorries	1,800	
Depreciation of plant and equipment	1,400	16,660
Net profit		15,454

Balance sheet as at 31 December 19-3

		£
Fixed assets:	Premises	45,000
	Motor lorry (10,000 - 1,000)	9,000
	Plant and equipment	11,000
	Carried forward	65,000

			£	£	£
	Brought forward				65,000
Current assets:	Stock			3,500	
	Debtors			6,000	
	Prepayments:	rates		500	
		advertising		340	
	Cash at bank			3,540	
	in hand			450	
				14,330	
less Current liabilities:					
	Creditors		4,250		
	Accrual – electricity		280		
	Mrs. Forster		2,500	7,030	7,300
					72,300

	£
Represented by	
Capital at 1 Jan 19-3	66,896
Net profit	15,454
	82,350
Drawings (10,000 + 50*)	10,050
	72,300

* cash shortage.

Depreciation of motor lorries: 20% of £8,000 for six months

20% of £10,000 for six months)

Loss on sale of motor lorry:

	£
CWT100R at 1 Jan 19-3	£8,000
less depreciation as above	800
	7,200
less sale proceeds	5,000
	2,200

4.6.2.

Conn, Flagge, Ray & Son
Calculation of claim for stock lost in fire on 5 November 19-1

Proforma trading account for the period 1 Jul 19-1 to 5 November 19-1:

		£
		£
Sales (17,220 + 61,000 + 18,780 - 16,000)		81,000
Less		
Stock at 1 July 19-1	23,750	
Purchases (59,630 + 14,210 - 11,520)	62,320	
	86,070	
Stock at 5 November destroyed	26,070*	
salvaged	6,000	32,070 → 54,000
Gross profit (33⅓% of £81,000)		27,000

*   Stock destroyed: £26,070 (balancing figure)

CHAPTER 5

5.2.2   **Diplock, Pibworth and Parkland Sports and Social Club**

Bar Trading Account for the year ended 31 December 19-1

	£	£
Bar takings		4,100
Bar stocks at 1 Jan	800	
Purchases (2,050 + 430 - 350)	2,130	
	2,930	
Bar stocks at 31 Dec	600	2,330
		1,770
Barman's wages		750
Bar profit carried to Income and Expenditure Account		1,020

Income and Expenditure Account for the year to 31 December 19-1

Income	£	£	£
Members' subscriptions			
(2,100 - 60 + 180+ 130 - 110)			2,240
Profit on bar			1,020
Annual dinner/dance: Sale of tickets		2,400	
less expenses:			
catering	1,440		
dance band	300	1,740	660
Sale of raffle tickets		180	
less cost of prizes		60	120
			4,040
Expenditure			
Subscriptions written off		140	
Hire of hall (1,500 + 100 - 150)		1,450	
Printing and postage		200	
Lighting and heating (581 - 105 + 140)		616	
Hon. Secretary's expenses		122	
Affiliation fees		100	
Repairs to equipment		300	
Depreciation of equipment (2,500 + 800 - 2,800)		500	3,428
Excess of income over expenditure			612

Balance sheet as at 31 December 19-1

		£
Fixed assets:	Equipment. Balance at 1.1. -	2,500
	Additions during year	800
		3,300
	less depreciation	500
		2,800

		£	
Current assets:	Bar stocks	600	
	Subscriptions in arrear	180	
	Balance at bank	1,300	
Carried forward		2,080	2,800

		£	£	£
Carried forward			2,080	2,800
less				
Current liabilities:	Subscriptions in advance	110		
	Creditors for bar stocks	430		
	Accrued expenses (140 + 100)	240	780	1,300
				4,100
Accumulated fund: Balance at 1 1.-1				3,488
Excess of income over expenditure				612
				4,100

CHAPTER 6
6.2.2 Exercise 1

Gray and Green
Profit and loss appropriation account
for the year ended 31 March 19-0

		£	£
Net profit b/d (8,000 - 500*)			7,500
Partners' current accounts:	Gray	3,750	
	Green	3,750	7,500

Note: In the absence of a partnership agreement, Gray is entitled to interest at 5% on his loan, such interest being debited in the profit and loss account, and the partners are entitled to equal shares of the profit.

Balance sheet extract as at 31 March 19-0

		£	£
Capitals: Gray		20,000	
Green		14,000	34,000

Current accounts:	Gray	Green	
	£	£	
Balances b/f	7,000	2,000	
Interest on loan	500	–	
Share of profit	3,750	3,750	
	11,250	5,750	
Drawings	(4,000)	(3,000)	
	7,250	2,750	10,000
			44,000
Long term liability: Gray - Loan			10,000
			54,000

Exercise 2
(a)

Palmer and Green
Profit and loss account for the year ended 31 December 19-0

	£	£
Gross profit b/d		80,000
Selling and distribution (23,500 + 1,500)	25,000	
Administration (16,400 - 800)	15,600	
Interest on loan – Palmer	800	
Depreciation: Premises	4,000	
Motor cars	3,200	48,600
Net profit (carried forward)		31,400

		£	£
Net profit (brought forward)			31,400
Interest on drawings:	Palmer	700	
	Green	800	1,500
			32,900
Interest on capitals:	Palmer	3,500	
	Green	2,000	5,500
			27,400
Salary: Green			8,000
			19,400
Share of profits: Palmer (³/₅)		11,640	
Green (²/₅)		7,760	19,400

Partners' Current accounts for the year ended 31 December 19-0

		Palmer £	Green £			Palmer £	Green £
19-0				19-0			
Jan 1	Balance b/d		3,000	Jan 1	Balance b/d	4,000	
Dec 31	Interest onDrawings	700	800	Dec 31	Interest on loan	800	
	Drawings	7,000	8,000		Int. on Caps.	3,500	2,000
	Balances c/d	12,240	5,960		Salary		8,000
					Profit	11,640	7,760
		19,940	17,760			19,940	17,760
				19-1			
				Jan 1	Balance b/d	12,240	5,960

Balance sheet as at 31 December 19-0

		Cost £	Depn £	Net £
Fixed assets				
	Premises	100,000	29,000	71,000
	Motor cars	16,000	11,200	4,800
		116,000	40,200	75,800
Current assets				
	Stock		12,000	
	Debtors		36,000	
	Prepayment		800	
			48,800	
less				
Current liabilities				
	Creditors	8,300		
	Bank overdraft	3,600		
	Accrued expense	1,500	13,400	35,400
				111,200
Deduct long term liabilities: Bank loan			30,000	
	Palmer		8,000	38,000
				73,200

Represented by

	Capitals	Current accounts	Total
	£	£	£
Palmer	35,000	12,240	47,240
Green	20,000	5,960	25,960
	55,000	18,200	73,200

Exercise 3

Doyle, Lee and Carter
Appropriation account for the year ended 31 December 19-3

		£	£
Net profit b/d			7,000
less Interest on Capitals	Doyle	2,500	
	Lee	1,700	
	Carter	600	4,800
			2,200
less Guaranteed share of profit: Carter			5,000
			(2,800)
Share of loss:	Doyle ($^5/_8$)	(1,750)	
	Lee ($^3/_8$)	(1,050)	(2,800)

Exercise 4

(a)

Bath and Wells
Forecast trading and profit and loss account for the year to 31 December 19-1

	£	£
Sales (70,000 + 10,000 + 120,000)		200,000
less Cost of sales (balancing figure)		132,000
Gross profit (40% of £80,000) + (30% of £120,000)		68,000
less		
Salaries and wages (10,000 + 4,000)	14,000	
Rent and rates	3,600	
Insurance	800	
Entertainment	1,000	
Car expenses (2,600 × 2)	5,200	
Advertising	3,300	
Sundry expenses	1,000	
Depreciation: Motor cars (25% of (3,000 + 5,000)	2,000	
Fixtures and fittings	600	31,500
Net profit		36,500
Interest on capital: Bath	680	
Wells	1,000	
	1,680	
Salary: Wells	8,000	9,680
		26,820
Share of profit: Bath ($^3/_5$)	16,092	
Wells ($^2/_5$)	10,728	26,820

Forecast balance sheet as at 31 December 19-1

			£	£
Fixed assets				
Motor cars (3,000 + 5,000)			8,000	
less depreciation			2,000	6,000
Fixtures and fittings			3,000	
less depreciation			600	2,400
				8,400
Current assets				
Stock (2,200 + 8,000)			10,200	
Debtors			9,000	
Bank (balancing figure)			29,500	
			48,700	
Less Current liabilities				
Creditors			3,800	44,900
				53,300
Represented by				
Capitals	Bath		6,800	
	Wells		10,000	16,800
Current accounts		Bath	Wells	
Interest on capital		680	1,000	
Salary			8,000	
Share of profit		16,092	10,728	
		16,772	19,728	36,500
				53,300

(b) Bath should consider taking wells into partnership for the following reasons:

(i) His share of the profit will give him a greater income than he can expect as a sole trader as the question states that his profit in recent years has remained static at around £6,800 p.a.

(ii) The liquidity of the business, which is beginning to cause Bath concern, will greatly improve if Wells is admitted as a partner. The bank overdraft of £2,500 will be repaid and replaced by a satisfactory balance at the bank.

CHAPTER 7

7.1.2 Exercise 1

Toll, Puddle and Martyn
Trading and profit and loss account
for the year to 31 December 19-2

	£	£
Sales		74,000
less Cost of sales		38,000
		36,000
less		
Wages	8,000	
General expenses	3,000	
Depreciation	1,000	12,000
Net profit c/d		24,000

	1 Jan-30 Jun £	1 Jul-31 Dec £	Total £
Net profit b/d	12,000	12,000	24,000
Salary – Toll (6/12× 3,000)		(1,500)	(1,500)
	12,000	10,500	22,500
Share of profit			
Toll (³/₆)	6,000	(¹/₃) 3,500	9,500
Puddle (²/₆)	4,000	(¹/₃) 3,500	7,500
Martyn (¹/₃)	2,000	(¹/₃) 3,500	5,500
	12,000	10,500	22,500

Exercise 2

Crook, Shank and Spindle
Trading and profit and loss account
for the year to 31 March 19-2

		£
Sales		190,000
less Cost of sales		100,000
Gross profit c/d		90,000

	1 Apr-30 Sep £		1 Oct-31 Mar £		Total £
Gross profit b/d		30,000		60,000	90,000
less					
Wages & salaries	10,500		10,500		21,000
Rent and rates	3,000		3,000		6,000
Lighting and heating	2,000		2,000		4,000
General expenses	1,100		1,300		2,400
Loan interest					
Crook			600		600
Depreciation:					
Motor cars	2,000		2,800		4,800
Provision for					
doubtful debts	(20)	18,580	80	20,280	60 38,860
Net profit		11,420		39,720	51,140
Interest on capitals					
Crook			2,000		
Shank			1,500		
Spindle			1,000		
			4,500		
Salary - Spindle			2,000	6,500	6,500
		11,420		33,220	44,640
Shares of profit					
Crook	6,852		13,288		20,140
Shank	4,568		13,288		17,856
Spindle	–	11,420	6,644	33,220	6,644 44,640

7.2.2

(a)

Legge and Spinner
Journal

		Dr.	Cr.
		£	£
Premises		30,000	
	Revaluation a/c		30,000
Revaluation a/c		5,000	
	Plant and machinery		5,000
Revaluation a/c		8,000	
	Motor van		8,000
Revaluation a/c		6,000	
	Stock		6,000
[i.e.£(7,000 - 3,000) + 2,000]			
Revaluation a/c		400	
	Provision for doubtful debts		400

(b)

Revaluation account

19-2		£		19-2		£
Dec 31	Plant & machinery	5,000		Dec 31	Premises	30,000
	Motor van	8,000				
	Stock	6,000				
	Sundry debtors	2,000				
	Provision for doubtful debts	400				
	Capital:Legge 4,300					
	Spinner 4,300	8,600				
		30,000				30,000

(c)

Legge and Spinner; Capital accounts

		Legge	Spinner				Legge	Spinner
		£	£				£	£
19-2					19-2			
Dec 31	Bal. c/d	44,300	44,300		Dec 31	Bal b/f	40,000	40,000
						Profit on Reval.	4,300	4,300
		44,300	44,300				44,300	44,300
					19-3			
					Jan 1	Bal b/f	44,300	44,300

7.3.2 (a)

Carey and Street
Journal

	Dr	Cr
	£	£
Revaluation a/c	1,000	
Provision for depreciation of plant		
and equipment	9,000	
Plant and equipment		10,000

405

	£	£
Revaluation a/c	700	
Provision for depreciation of motor vans	8,300	
Motor vans		9,000
Provision for depreciation of office machinery	2,800	
Office machinery		1,000
Revaluation a/c		1,800
Revaluation a/c	940	
Sundry debtors		800
Provision for doubtful debts		
[(5% of £5,200) - 120]		140

(b)

Carey and Street
Revaluation account

19-2		£	19-2		£
June 30	Plant and equipment	1,000	June 30	Office machinery	1,800
	Motor vans	700			
	Sundry debtors	940		Capitals	
				Carey	504
				Street	336
		2,640			2,640

Plant and Equipment

19-2		£	19-2		£
Jun 30	Balance b/f	14,000	Jun 30	Revaluation	10,000
				Balance c/d	4,000
		14,000			14,000
Jul 1	Balance b/d	4,000			

Provision for depreciation of plant and equipment

19-2		£	19-2		£
Jun 30	Revaluation	9,000	Jun 30	Balance b/d	9,000

Motor Van

19-2		£	19-2		£
Jun 30	Balance b/d	11,000		Revaluation	9,000
				Balance c/d	2,000
		11,000			11,000
Jul 1	Balance b/d	2,000			

Provision for depreciation of motor van

19-2		£	19-2		£
Jun 30	Revaluation	8,300	Jun 30	Balance b/d	8,300

Office Machinery

19-2		£	19-2		£
Jun 30	Balance b/d	5,000	Jun 30	Revaluation	1,000
				Balance c/d	4,000
		5,000			5,000
Jul 1	Balance b/d	4,000			

Provision for depreciation of Office Machinery

19-2		£	19-2		£
Jun 30	Revaluation	2,800	Jun 30	Balance b/d	2,800

Sundry debtors

19-2		£	19-2		£
Jun 30	Balance b/d	6,000	Jun 30	Revaluation	800
				Balance c/d	5,200
		6,000			6,000
Jul 1	Balance b/d	5,200			

Provision for doubtful debts

19-2		£	19-2		£
Jun 30	Balance c/d	260	Jun 30	Balance b/d	120
				Revaluation	140
		260			260
			Jul 1	Balance b/d	260

7.5.2
(a)

Parchment, Deedes and Tape
Journal

	Dr.	Cr.
	£	£
Freehold premises	30,000	
Revaluation		30,000
Revaluation	5,000	
Motor cars		5,000
Revaluation	5,000	
Office furniture and equipment		5,000
Revaluation	2,400	
Provision for unpaid costs		2,400

(b)

Partners' Capital accounts

		Parchment	Deedes	Tape
19-3		£	£	£
Dec 31	Balances b/f	100,000	100,000	
	Revaluation (loss)	8,800	8,800	
		108,800	108,800	
19-4				
Jan 1	Bank			50,000
	Motor car			12,000
	Goodwill	5,000	5,000	(10,000)
		113,800	113,800	52,000

Note: Goodwill

	Old firm	New firm	Adjustment to Capital accounts	
	£	£	£	
Parchment	25,000	20,000	5,000	Cr
Deedes	25,000	20,000	5,000	Cr
Tape		10,000	10,000	Dr
	50,000	50,000		

(c)

Parchment, Deedes and Tape Balance Sheet as at 1 January 19-4

	£	£
Fixed assets:		
Freehold premises		130,000
Motor cars (35,000 + 12,000)		47,000
Office furniture and equipment		1,000
		178,000
Current assets		
Stock	20,000	
Debtors (48,000 - 2,400)	45,600	
Bank (12,000 + 50,000)	62,000	
	127,600	
less		
Current liabilities - creditors	8,000	119,600
		297,600

Represented by

	Capitals	Current Accounts	
	£	£	£
Parchment	113,800	12,000	125,800
Deedes	113,800	6,000	119,800
Tape	52,000		52,000
	279,600	18,000	297,600

7.6.2

(a) and (b)

Johanne, Sebastian and Bach
Trading and profit and loss accounts for
(a) six months to 31 December 19-2 and
(b) six months to 30 June 19-3

	£	£
Sales		96,000
less cost of sales		
Stock at 1 Jul 19-2	8,000	
Purchases	29,000	
	37,000	
Stock at 30 Jun 19-3	4,000	33,000
Gross profit c/d		63,000

	1 Jul – 31 Dec 19-2		1 Jan – 30 Jun 19-3		Total	
	£	£	£	£	£	£
Gross profit b/d		31,500		31,500		63,000
Selling expenses	3,600		3,600		7,200	
Distribution expenses	2,400		2,400		4,800	
Wages and salaries	10,000		10,000		20,000	
General expenses	1,600		1,600		3,200	
Depreciation:						
Freehold premises	500		750		1,250	
Motor cars	2,000		600		2,600	
Office machinery	2,250		500		2,750	
Interest on loan			1,500		1,500	
		22,350		20,950		43,300
Net profit		9,150		10,550		19,700
Interest on drawings						
Johanne	200					
Sebastian	300					
Bach	250	750				750
		9,900		10,550		20,450
Salary Johanne	5,000				5,000	
Sebastian			3,500		3,500	
Bach			1,500		1,500	
Interest on capitals						
Johanne	1,500				1,500	
Sebastian	750				750	
Bach	750				750	
		8,000		5,000		13,000
		1,900		5,550		7,450
Share of profit						
Johanne (¹/₂)	950				950	
Sebastian (¹/₄)	475		(¹/₂) 2,775		3,250	
Bach (¹/₄)	475	1,900	(¹/₂) 2,775	5,550	3,250	7,450

(c)

Sebastian and Bach
Balance Sheet as at 30 June 19-3

Fixed assets	At valuation	Depn.	Net
	£	£	£
Freehold premises	60,000	750	59,250
Motor cars	6,000	600	5,400
Office machinery	4,000	500	3,500
	70,000	1,850	68,150
Current assets			
Stock		4,000	
Debtors		5,000	
Bank		15,100	
Carried forward		24,100	68,150

	£	£	£
Brought forward		24,100	68,150
Less Current liabilities			
Creditors	7,000		
Accrued expenses	2,200		
Interest on loan	1,500	10,700	13,400
			81,550
Less long term liability: Loan from Johanne			30,000
			51,550

Represented by	Capital	Current a/c	Total
	£	£	£
Sebastian	25,000	2,275	27,275
Bach	25,000	(725)	24,275
	50,000	1,550	51,550

(d)

Partners' Capital accounts for the year to 30 June 19-3

		Johanne	Sebastian	Bach
		£	£	£
19-2				
Jul 1	Balances b/f	30,000	15,000	15,000
Dec 31	Current accounts	8,250	(2,075)	(10,025)
	Goodwill	10,000	(5,000)	(5,000)
	Revaluation	16,175	8,088	8,087
	Motor car	(4,000)		
	Loss on disposal of motor car	(800)	(400)	(400)
	Transfer to Loan account	(30,000)		
	Bank	(29,625)	9,387	17,338
19-3				
Jun 30	Balance	–	25,000	25,000

Partners' Current accounts for the year to 30 June 19-3

		Johanne	Sebastian	Bach
		£	£	£
19-2				
Jul 1	Balances b/f	5,000	3,000	(6,000)
Dec 31	Salary	5,000		
	Interest on capitals	1,500	750	750
	Share of profit	950	475	475
	Interest on drawings	(200)	(300)	(250)
	Drawings	(4,000)	(6,000)	(5,000)
	Balance to capital accounts	8,250	(2,075)	(10,025)
19-3				
Jun 30	Salaries		3,500	1,500
	Share of profit		2,775	2,775
			6,275	4,275
	Drawings		(4,000)	(5,000)
Balances c/f			2,275	(725)

CHAPTER 8

8.1.2.

(a)

Fortnum, Marks & Co.
Revaluation accounts

	Fortnum & Mason £	Marks & Spencer £
Fixtures	400	
Freehold property	4,000	
Creditors	320	280
Stock	(400)	(1,000)
Vehicles	(400)	(400)
Debtors	(800)	(1,000)
Profit/(loss) on revaluation	3,120	(2,120)
Capital accounts: Fortnum	(1,664)	
Mason	(1,456)	
Marks		1,272
Spencer		848

(b)

Partners' Capital Accounts – old firms

	Fortnum £	Mason £	Marks £	Spencer £
Balances b/f	24,000	21,000	22,000	15,600
Current accounts	2,000	1,200		
Goodwill	8,000	7,000	6,000	4,000
Profit on revaluation	1,664	1,456		
Profit on realisation			4,320	2,880
	35,664	30,656	32,320	22,480
Investments	(2,400)			
Loss on revaluation			(1,272)	(848)
Loss on realisation	(320)	(280)		
Balances c/f	32,944	30,376	31,048	21,632

(c)

Partners' Capital Accounts – new firm

	Fortnum £	Mason £	Marks £	Spencer £
Balances b/f	32,944	30,376	31,048	21,632
Cash	4,556	874	202	3,368
	37,500	31,250	31,250	25,000
Goodwill	(7,500)	(6,250)	(6,250)	(5,000)
Balances c/f	30,000	25,000	25,000	20,000

(d)

Fortnum Marks & Co. Cash account

	£	£		£
Balance b/f				
Fortnum & Mason	8,400		Balance c/f	43,600
Marks & Spencer	26,200	34,600		
Carried forward		34,600		43,600

411

	£	£
Brought forward	34,600	43,600
Partners' capital a/cs		
Fortnum	4,556	
Mason	874	
Marks	202	
Spencer	3,368	
	43,600	43,600
Balance b/f	43,600	

(e)

Fortnum Marks & Co.
Balance Sheet as at 1 September 19-1

	£	£
Fixed assets		
Freehold property		19,000
Fixtures		4,000
Vehicles		7,600
		30,600
Current assets		
Stock	23,800	
Debtors	25,400	
Bank balance	43,600	
	92,800	
less Creditors	23,400	69,400
		100,000
Capital accounts		
Fortnum		30,000
Mason		25,000
Marks		25,000
Spencer		20,000
		100,000

Workings:

Disposal Accounts

	Fortnum & Mason	Marks & Spencer
	£	£
Cash book – proceeds		20,000
Capital account – Fortnum	2,400	
Freehold property		(10,000)
Fixtures		(2,800)
Investments	(3,000)	
Profit/(loss) on disposals	(600)	7,200
Capital accounts: Fortnum	320	
Mason	280	
Marks		(4,320)
Spencer		(2,880)

412

8.2.2

(a)

Penn, Punch and Staple
Realisation account

19-0		£	19-0			£
Jun 30	Leasehold premises	5,000	Jun 30	Penn – Capital		2,500
	Delivery vans	2,000		Staple – Capital		6,000
	Fixtures and Fittings	2,000		Bank		11,500
	Stocks	12,000		Capitals –		
	Debtors – diff.	175		Penn	470	
				Punch	470	
				Staple	235	1,175
		21,175				21,175

(b)

Bank

19-0		£	19-0		£
Jun 30	Realisation	11,500	Jun 30	Balance b/f	900
	Sundry debtors	3,225		Sundry creditors	3,900
	Staple – capital	2,535		Loan – Quire	3,000
				Penn – capital	5,430
				Punch – capital	4,030
		17,260			17,260

(c)

Partners' capital accounts

		Penn	Punch	Staple
		£	£	£
19-0				
Jun 30	Balances b/f	5,000	2,000	2,000
	Current accounts	3,400	2,500	1,700
	Realisation a/c – van	(2,500)		
	Realisation a/c – stock			(6,000)
	Realisation a/c – loss on realisation	(470)	(470)	(235)
		5,430	4,030	(2,535)
	Bank	(5,430)	(4,030)	2,535

8.3.2 (a)

Bent, Bold and Broke
Realisation account

19-2		£	19-2		£
Jan 1	Fixed assets	22,000	Jan 1	Bank	20,000
	Stock	18,000		Capitals (loss)	
	Debtors – diff.	1,000		Bent ($^3/_6$)	10,500
				Bold ($^2/_6$)	7,000
				Broke ($^1/_6$)	3,500
		41,000			41,000

(b)

Bank

19-2		£	19-2		£
Jan 1	Balance b/f	3,000	Jan 1	Sundry creditors	6,000
	Realisation	20,000		Capitals –	
	Debtors	4,000		Bent	10,750
				Bold	10,250
		27,000			27,000

(c)

Partners' capital accounts

		Bent	Bold	Broke
19-2		£	£	£
Jan 1	Balances brought forward	20,000	20,000	5,000
	Current accounts	2,000	(2,000)	(3,000)
	Loss on realisation	(10,500)	(7,000)	(3,500)
		11,500	11,000	(1,500)
Debit balance on Broke's capital account (20:20)		(750)	(750)	1,500
		10,750	10,250	–
Bank		(10,750)	(10,250)	–

8.4.2

(a)

Dee, Emma and Fay
Realisation account

19-5		£	19-5		£
Mar 31	Sundry fixed and current assets	75,000	Mar 31	Enterprise Ltd.	90,000
	Capitals – Dee	5,000			
	Emma	5,000			
	Fay	5,000			
		90,000			90,000

(b)

Enterprise Ltd.

19-5		£	19-5		£
Mar 31	Realisation a/c	90,000	Mar 31	8% Debenture stock	5,000
				Ordinary shares – Enterprise Ltd	60,000
				Bank	25,000
		90,000			90,000

8% Debentures in Enterprise Ltd.

19-5		£	19-5		£
Mar 31	Enterprise Ltd.	5,000	Mar 31	Dee - loan	5,000

Ordinary shares in Enterprise Ltd.

19-5		£	19-5		£
Mar 31	Enterprise Ltd	60,000	Mar 31	Capitals – Dee	20,000
				Emma	20,000
				Fay	20,000
		60,000			60,000

Bank

19-5		£	19-5		£
Mar 31	Enterprise Ltd.	25,000	Mar 31	Capitals – Dee	15,000
				– Emma	10,000
		25,000			25,000

Dee – Loan

19-5		£	19-5		£
Mar 31	8% Debentures	5,000	Mar 31	Balance b/f	5,000

(c)   **Partners' Capital accounts**

		Dee	Emma	Fay
19-5		£	£	£
Mar 31	Balances b/f	30,000	25,000	15,000
	Realisation account	5,000	5,000	5,000
		35,000	30,000	20,000
Ordinary shares in Enterprise Ltd.		(20,000)	(20,000)	(20,000)
Bank		(15,000)	(10,000)	–

Note: Allocation of shares:

Capital/profit sharing ratio	Dee	Emma	Fay
Capitals	£30,000	£25,000	£15,000
Profit sharing ratio	1	1	1

Fay has lowest capital/psr; her capital account will be satisfied in full by allocation of shares, which will then be divided between the partners in profit sharing ratio.

CHAPTER 9

9.4.2   **Chance Ltd.**

(i)   If 10% preference shares are non-cumulative

	19-1	19-2	19-3	19-4	19-5
	£	£	£	£	£
Profit	22,000	6,000	11,000	7,000	10,000
10% Pref. share dividend	8,000	6,000	8,000	7,000	8,000
Profit available for ordinary dividend	14,000	–	3,000	–	2,000
Pref. div. %	10	7.5	10	8.75	10
Ord. div.%	11.7		2.5	–	1.7

(ii)   If 10% preference shares are cumulative

	19-1	19-2	19-3	19-4	19-5
	£	£	£	£	£
Profit	22,000	6,000	11,000	7,000	10,000
10% Pref. share dividend	8,000	6,000	8,000	7,000	8,000
			+2,000		+1,000
Profit available for ordinary dividend	14,000	–	1,000	–	1,000
Pref. div %	10	7.5	(10+2.5)	8.75	(10+1.25)
Ord. div.	11.7	–	0.8	–	0.8

9.5.2

The Goodbuy Co. plc
Application & allotment

	£		£
Bank (monies returned)	11,750	Bank (on application)	186,750
Ordinary share capital	225,000	Bank (on allotment)	125,000
Share premium	75,000		
	311,750		311,750

Bank

	£		£
Application and allotment	186,750	Application and allotment	11,750
do.	125,000		
Call	75,000	Balance c/d	375,000
	386,750		386,750
Balance b/d	375,000		

Ordinary share capital

	£		£
Balance c/d	300,000	Application and allotment	225,000
		Call	75,000
	300,000		300,000
		Balance b/d	300,000

Share premium

	£		£
		Application and allotment	75,000

Call

	£		£
Ordinary share capital	75,000	Bank	75,000

9.6.2

Jollysticks Ltd.
Application and allotment

	£		£
Bank (returned money)	3,300	Bank	21,300
Ordinary share capital	30,000	Bank	15,903
Share premium	4,200	Forfeited shares	297
	37,500		37,500

Bank

	£		£
Application & allotment	21,300	Application & allotment	3,300
Application & allotment	15,903	Balance c/d	34,343
Forfeited shares	440		
	37,643		37,643
Balance b/d	34,343		

Ordinary share capital

	£		£
Forfeited shares	550	Application & allotment	30,000
Balance c/d	30,000	Forfeited shares reissued	550
	30,550		30,550
		Balance b/d	30,000

Share premium

	£		£
Forfeited shares	77	Application & allotment	4,200
Balance c/d	4,343	Forfeited shares	220
	4,420		4,420
		Balance b/d	4,343

Forfeited shares

	£		£
Application & allotment	297	Ordinary share capital	550
Forfeited shares reissued	110	Share premium	77
Share premium	220		
	627		627

Forfeited shares reissued

	£		£
Ordinary share capital	550	Bank	440
		Forfeited shares	110
	550		550

9.8.2

Jill Ltd.

		£
(i)	Valuation of an ordinary share:	
	based on balance sheet values:	
	Total of net assets	147,000
	Deduct Preference share capital	25,000
	Ordinary share capital and reserves	122,000

Value of one ordinary share: $\dfrac{£122,000}{75,000} = \underline{£1.63}$

		£
(ii)	Valuation based on realisable values of net assets:	
	Fixed assets at realisable values	86,000
	Current assets at realisable values	48,000
		134,000
	less creditors	9,000
	Net asset value	125,000
	Value of one ordinary share:	
	Net asset value	125,000
	less Preference share capital	25,000
		100,000

$\dfrac{£100,000}{75,000} = \underline{£1.33}$

Splendiferous plc

	£	£
The retained profit		10,000
less:		
Debenture interest	600	
Preference share dividend	160	760
Profit available for ordinary dividend		9,240

	£
But:	
Balance at bank	8,000
less debenture interest and preference dividend as above	760
Maximum cash available for ordinary dividend	7,240

Note: The cash position may be different when the dividend becomes payable. Also the General reserve may be available to increase the profit available for dividend if, in the opinion of the directors, that reserve is in excess of the company's requirement.

CHAPTER 10

10.4.2

The Wooden Box Co. Ltd

Note to the accounts - Tangible fixed assets.

	Freehold Land & Buildings	Leasehold property	Plant & Machinery	Motor Vehicles	Total
	£	£	£	£	£
Balance at 1.1. 19-2	400,000	–	396,000	130,000	926,000
Increase on revaluation	600,000				600,000
Disposals			(106,000)	(20,000)	(126,000)
Additions		100,000	110,000	32,000	242,000
	1,000,000	100,000	400,000	142,000	1,642,000

DEPRECIATION Provisions at					
1.1. 19-2	–	–	(127,200)	(42,500)	(169,700)
Provisions on disposals			52,100	11,250	63,350
Charge for year	(40,000)	(5,000)	(69,000)	(33,500)	(147,500)
	(40,000)	(5,000)	(144,100)	(64,750)	(253,850)
Balance sheet	960,000	95,000	255,900	77,250	1.388,150

TANGIBLE FIXED ASSETS

Freehold land and buildings have been revalued by Messrs. Coffyn, Paul, Bayer and Stone, Chartered Surveyors on 1 July 19-2 at £1m., of which £200,000 relates to the value of the land.

Depreciation is calculated to write off the cost of the fixed assets on a straight line basis over the expected useful lives of the assets concerned.

The annual rates used for this year are:

Freehold buildings	5%
Leasehold property	5%
Plant and machinery	20%
Motor vehicles	25%

The rates shown above are consistent with those used in the previous year. Freehold buildings are being depreciated for the first time this year at 5%, based upon the revalued amount and the expected remaining useful economic life of 20 years. The additional annual charge resulting from the revaluation amounts to £40,000. Freehold land is not depreciated.

The leasehold property is being amortised over the period of the lease, which is 20 years. The additional annual charge resulting from this is £5,000.

CHAPTER 12

12.3.2

Mary
Statement of source and application of funds
for the year to 31 March 19-4

	£	£
Profit for the year		18,940
Add amortisation of lease	2,000	
depreciation: equipment	1,400	
motor van	1,600	
office equipment	400	5,400
		24,340
Other sources of funds		
Proceeds of sale of word processor		200
		24,540
Applications of funds		
Purchase of equipment	(9,000)	
Drawings	(14,440)	(23,440)
		1,100
Increase/(decrease) in working capital		
Increase in stock	3,000	
Increase in debtors	1,000	
Increase in creditors	(2,580)	
	1,420	
Movement in net liquid funds – Bank	(320)	1,100

12.4.2

Andrew and Demetriou plc
Calculation of net profit before tax.

	£'000
Retained profit for the year (85 - 110)	(25)
Increase in General Reserve (230 - 200)	30
Increase in asset replacement reserve (185 - 160)	25
Provision for proposed dividends	600
Provision for taxation	540
Net profit for the year before tax	1,170

12.5.2

Pondayne plc

Workings

Freehold premises at valuation

19-4		£'000	19-4		£'000
Jan 1	Balance b/f	900	Dec 31	Balance c/f	1,200
Dec 31	Property revaluation reserve	300			
		1,200			1,200

Plant and machinery at cost

19-4		£'000	19-4		£'000
Jan 1	Balance b/f	450	Dec 31	Disposal	80
Dec 31	Purchases (bal.fig)	320		Balance c/f	690
		770			770

Provision for depreciation of plant and machinery

19-4		£'000	19-4		£'000
Dec 31	Disposals	64	Jan	Balance b/f	376
	Balance c/f	520	Dec	P & L (bal. fig.)	208
		584			584

Disposal of plant and machinery

19-4		£'000	19-4		£'000
Dec 31	Plant & machinery	80	Dec 31	Prov. for depn.	64
				Cash	8
				P & L (bal. fig.)	8
		80			80

Fixtures and Fittings at cost

19-4		£'000	19-4		£'000
Jan 1	Balance b/f	60	Dec 31	Disposals	40
Dec 31	Purchased (bal. fig.)	20		Balance c/f	40
		80			80

Provision for depreciation of fixtures and fittings

19-4		£'000	19-4		£'000
Dec 31	Disposals	38	Jan 1	Balance b/f	54
	Balance c/f	30	Dec 31	P & L (bal.fig.)	14
		68			68

Disposal of fixtures and fittings

19-4		£'000	19-4		£'000
Dec 31	Fixtures & fittings	40	Dec 31	Prov.for depn.	38
	P&L (bal.fig.)	3		Cash	5
		43			43

(a)   Non-cash items:

Revaluation of premises	£300,000	(not shown in statement of source and application of funds)
Depreciation for year:		
Plant and machinery	£208,000	
Fixtures & fittings	£14,000	
Loss on disposal of		
Plant and machinery	£8,000	
Profit on disposal of		
Fixtures and fittings	£3,000	

(b)   Utilisation of funds for purchase of tangible fixed assets:
          Plant and machinery   £320,000
          Fixtures and fittings   £20,000

12.8.2   **The Vortex Puzzle Co. Ltd.**
                                    Taxation

19-6		£'000	19-5		£'000
Jun 30	Provision (19-6)		Jul 1	Provision (19-5)	
	c/f	201	19-6	b/f	157
	Paid (bal.fig)	166	Jun 30	P&L	210
		367			367

12.9.2   **Portable Grummitts plc**
                                   Dividends

19-4		£'000	19-3		£'000
May 31	Paid in year		Jun 1	Proposed div. b/f	300
	(bal fig)	330	19-4		
	Proposed div.c/f	250	May 31	P&L	280
		580			580

Extract from Portable Grummitt plc statement of source and application of funds:
Application of funds
Payment of final and interim dividends £330

12.10.2   **The Ovid Egg Products Ltd.**
             Statement of Source and Application of Funds
                    for the year to 31 December 19-1

	£'000	£'000
Profit before tax		97
Add: Depreciation	63	
Loss on disposals of fixed assets	9	72
Funds generated by operations		169
Other sources of funds		
Issue of shares for cash	50	
Premium on shares	10	
Issue of debentures	30	
Proceeds of sales of fixed assets	45	135
		304
Application of funds		
Purchase of fixed assets	118	
Taxation paid	49	
Dividends paid	45	212
		92
Increase/(decrease) in working capital		
Increase in stock	40	
Increase in debtors	26	
Decrease in creditors	13	
	79	
Movement in net liquid funds		
Increase in bank	13	92

(b) Answer, which should be in letter form, should make reference to:

1. Funds generated by operations amounted to £169,000.
2. New issue of shares for cash produced £60,000.
3. Increase in company's debentures produced £30,000.
4. Disposal of fixed assets produced £45,000.
5. Purchases of fixed assets accounted for £118,00.
6. Taxation and payment of dividends accounted for another £94,000.

   The sources of funds (1 to 4 above) exceeded the applications (5 and 6) by £92,000 which equals the increase in working capital.

(c) Statements of Source and Application of Funds show what funds have been received by a business during a year and how they have been used. They show what factors have affected the working capital during the year. Working capital is the life blood of any business.

The statements also serve as a link between the balance sheets of two consecutive years of a business. That link is difficult to establish without such a statement. Balance sheets show the position of a business at particular moments in time and exhibit the assets and liabilities of the business without showing the results of carrying on business in the intervening period. Profit and loss accounts, on the other hand, take no account of capital expenditure, and account for revenue and expenses on an accruals basis so that cash flow is obscured.

SSAP 10 is designed to establish statements of source and application of funds as a link between balance sheets.

CHAPTER 13

13.1.2

Pinewood plc

Working

	Balance sheet 31.1.-3	Bonus issue	Rights issue	Revised balance sheet
	£	£	£	£
Ord. share cap.	200,000	700,000	300,000	1,200,000
Share premium	53,000	(53,000)	30,000	30,000
General reserve	600,000	(600,000)		
Profit & loss	85,000	(47,000)		138,000
				1,368,000

Answer:

Revised balance sheet as at 1 February 19-3

	£'000	£'000
Fixed assets		852
Current assets (377,000 + 330,000)	707	
less Current liabilities	191	516
		1,368
Financed by		
Share capital and reserves		
1,200,000 ordinary shares of £1 fully paid		1,200
Share premium		30
Profit and loss account		138
		1,368

13.2.2
(a)

Pinewood Ltd.
Capital Reduction account

	£		£
Profit and loss	44,000	Ordinary share cap.	50,000
Provision for depn. of fixed assets	5,000		
Provision for bad debts	1,000		
	50,000		50,000

(b)

Re-drafted balance sheet

	£	£	£
Fixed assets (45,000 - 5,000)			40,000
Current assets (28,000 - 1,000)		27,000	
less Current liabilities Creditors	12,000		
Bank overdraft	5,000	17,000	10,000
			50,000
100,000 Ordinary shares of 50p fully paid			50,000

13.3.2 Exercise 1
Working

Penguin Beakers Ltd.

	Before redemption	New issue	Redemption of pref. shares	New bal. sheet
	£'000	£'000	£'000	£'000
Net assets	101	12.5	(12)	101.5
Ord. shares	75	10		85
Red. pref. shares	10		(10)	–
Share premium	6	2.5	(2)	6.5
Retained profits	10			10
	101			101.5

Answer

Revised balance sheet

	£'000
Net assets	101.5
Capital and reserves	
85,000 ordinary shares of £1 fully paid	85.0
Share premium	6.5
Retained profit	10.0
	101.5

Exercise 2
Working

Flamingo plc

	Before redemption	Create CRR	Redeem Pref. shares	New bal. sheet
	£'000	£'000	£'000	£'000
Net assets	1,250		(110)	1,140
Ord. shares	750			750
Pref. shares	100		(100)	–
Cap. Red. Res.		100		100
Share premium	40			40
Revenue reserves	360	(100)	(10)	250
	1,250			1,140

Answer   **Balance sheet after redemption of preference shares**

		£'000
Net assets		1,140

Capital and reserves

	£'000
750,000 ordinary shares of £1 fully paid	750
Capital redemption reserve	100
Share premium	40
Revenue reserves	250
	1,140

Exercise 3   **Ostrich Ltd.**

Balance sheet as at 30 September 19-2

	£
Net assets (13,000 - 4,000)	9,000

Capital and reserves

	£
6,000 ordinary shares of £1	6,000
Capital redemption reserve	3,000
	9,000

Note: The Companies' Act 1985 permits a private limited company to use capital reserves to create a capital redemption reserve if the revenue reserves are insufficient for the purpose provided the revenue reserves are exhausted for this purpose first. It further allows such a company to create a capital redemption reserve less than the amount of the shares being redeemed if all the reserves, revenue and capital, are insufficient.

CHAPTER 14

14.1.2   **Merger (19-1) Ltd.**

Working: Calculation of goodwill.

	Gerald Menswear	Mercer Fashions	Combined
	£'000	£'000	£'000
Freehold premises	75	25	100
Delivery vans	8	5	13
Fixtures & fittings	4	11	15
Office equipment	3	1	4
Stock	38	55	93
Debtors	4	60	64
	132	157	289
less creditors	(48)	(98)	
Net assets	84	59	
Purchase consideration	100	60	
Goodwill	16	1 Total	17

Calculation of share premium.	£
Total consideration	160,000
Cash payments	40,000
Consideration payable in shares	120,000
Number of shares to be allotted	100,000

Each share is therefore valued at £1.20 i.e. at a premium of 20p

Answer
Merger (19-1) Ltd.
Balance sheet as at 1 July 19-1

	£'000	£'000
Fixed assets		
Intangible: Goodwill		17
Tangible		
Freehold premises	100	
Delivery vans	13	
Fixtures and fittings	15	
Office equipment	4	132
		149
Current assets		
Stock	93	
Debtors	64	
Bank (100 - 16 - 22 - 40)	22	
	179	
Current liabilities: Creditors(32+76)	108	71
		220
Capital and reserves		
200,000 Ordinary shares of £1		200
Share premium		20
		220

14.3.2

Exercise 1
Doulla Ltd. and subsidiaries
Consolidated balance sheet as at 31 December 19-1

		£'000	£'000
Fixed assets			
Intangible:	Goodwill (see below)		11
Tangible:	Freehold land and buildings	100	
	Plant and equipment	185	
	Motor vehicles	105	
	Office machinery	65	455
			466
Current assets			
	Stock	164	
	Debtors	113	
	Bank	117	
		394	
Amounts due for settlement within one year:			
	Creditors	120	274
			740
Share capital and reserves			
Ordinary shares of £1			600
Reserves			140
			740

Goodwill			£'000
Rosalia Ltd.	Purchase consideration		200
	Net asset value acquired		182
	Goodwill		18
Tracey Ltd.	Purchase consideration		150
	Net asset value acquired		157
	Negative goodwill		(7)
Goodwill (18 - 7)			11

14.3.2

Exercise 2

Hon Wai Ltd. and subsidiaries

Consolidated balance sheet as at 30 April 19-4

	£'000	£'000
Intangible Fixed Assets		
Goodwill (see below)		13
Tangible Fixed Assets		
Freehold property	180	
Plant and machinery	219	
Motor vehicles	103	502
		515
Current assets		
Stock (153 - 8)	145	
Debtors (99 - 5)	94	
Bank	48	
	287	
Less amounts due to be paid within one year		
Creditors (76 - 5)	71	216
		731
Share capital and reserves		
Ordinary shares of £1		700
Reserves		31
		731

Goodwill	Mei Yiu Ltd	Sing Yiu Ltd
	£'000	£'000
Cost of acquisition	195	150
Value of ordinary shares and reserves	177	155
	18	(5) Net 13

Exercise 3

Buckle Ltd. and subsidiaries

Consolidated Balance Sheet as at 1 January 19-0

	£'000	£'000
Intangible Fixed Assets		
Goodwill (see below)		10
Carried forward		10

	£'000	£'000
Brought forward		10
Tangible Fixed Assets		
Freehold premises	40	
Motor vehicles	135	
Equipment	75	250
		260
Current assets		
Stock	106	
Debtors	92	
Bank	24	
	222	
Amounts due to be paid within one year		
Creditors	60	162
		422
Capital and reserves		
Ordinary shares of £1		300
Retained profit		46
		346
Minority interests (see below)		76
		422

Goodwill		**Lace Ltd.**		**Pin Ltd.**
		£'000		£'000
Cost of acquisition		100		70
Value of shares & reserves				
acquired	(80% of 110)	88	(75% of 96)	72
Goodwill		12		(2)
Net goodwill 10				
Minority interests	(20% of 110)	22	(25% of 96)	24
Add Preference shareholders		30		
		52		24
Total 76				

Exercise 4   **Wader Ltd. and subsidiaries**

Consolidated Balance Sheet as at 1 May 19-5

	£'000	£'000
Intangible Fixed Assets		
Goodwill (see below)		31
Tangible Fixed Assets		
Freehold property	384	
Plant and machinery	277	
Motor vehicles	88	749
Carried forward		780

	£'000	£'000
Brought forward		780
Current Assets		
Stock (140 - 6)	134	
Debtors (134 - 7)	127	
Bank	85	
	346	
Amounts due for payment within one year		
Creditors (111 - 7)	104	242
		1,022
Amounts due for settlement after more than one year		
Debentures (60 - 20)		40
		982
Share capital and reserves		
Ordinary shares of £1		800
Retained profits		101
		901
Minority Interests (see below)		81
		982

Goodwill	Swan Ltd.		Heron Ltd.	
	£'000		£'000	
Cost of acquisition		180		75
Share capital and reserves	205		120	
less preference shares	25			
	180			
less minority interest (20%)	36	144	(⅓) 40	80
Goodwill		36		(5) = 31

Minority Interests	£'000
Ordinary shares in Swan Ltd. (as above)	36
Ordinary shares in Heron Ltd.(as above)	40
Preference shares in Swan Ltd. (20%)	5
	81

14.4.2

Exercise 1

Box Ltd. and its subsidiary
Consolidated Profit and Loss Account
for the year to 31 March 19-1

	£'000	£'000	Note
Turnover		162	1
Cost of sales		95	2
Gross profit		67	
Distribution costs	13		
Administration expenses	35	48	
Profit on ordinary activities before taxation (carried forward)		19	

	£'000	£'000
Profit on ordinary activities before taxation (brought forward)		19
Taxation on profit on ordinary activities		7
Profit on ordinary activities after taxation		12
Extraordinary profits net of tax		7
Profit for the financial year		19
Retained profit brought forward		20
		39
Proposed dividend	8	
Transfer to reserve	18	26
Retained profit carried forward		13

Note 1. Combined turnover less inter-company sales of £18,000

Note 2. Combined cost of sales less inter-company sale as above and deletion of unrealised profit £3,000 on unsold stock.

Exercise 2

Bat Ltd. and its subsidiary
Consolidated Profit and Loss Account
for the year ended 30 September 19-3

	£'000	£'000	Note
Turnover		1,726	1
Cost of sales		1,193	2
Gross profit		533	
Distribution costs	54		
Administrative expenses	120	174	
Profit on ordinary activities before taxation		359	
Taxation on profit on ordinary activities		117	
		242	
Minority interests		64	3
		178	
Extraordinary profit net of taxation		39	4
Profit for the financial year		217	
Retained profit from the previous year		176	5
		393	
Proposed dividends	120		
Transfer to reserves	104	224	6
Retained profit carried forward		169	

Note 1. Turnover 1,000 + 750 - 24
  2. Cost of sales 684 + 525 -24 + 8 (unrealised profit)
  3. Minority interests: Pref. div. $^1/_3 \times 42 = $ 14
     Ord.shareholders
     $^1/_4 \times 242 - 42$ (pref.div.)
     $= ^1/_4 \times 200$ 50   64
  4. Extraordinary profit 24 + $^3/_4 \times 20 = 39$
  5. Retained profit from previous year 116 + $^3/_4 \times 80 = 176$
  6. Transfer to reserves 80 + $^3/_4 \times 32 = 104$

CHAPTER 15

15.1.2

1.
The Jobbitt Co. Ltd.
Manufacturing, trading, profit and loss account for the year ended 30 September 19-8

	£	£
Raw materials	115,000	
less stock at 30 Sep 19-8	13,000	102,000
Direct labour		200,000
PRIME COST		302,000
Add factory overheads		
Indirect materials	10,000	
Indirect labour	25,000	
Rent and rates	35,000	
Electricity	8,000	
Salaries	20,000	
Depreciation: machinery	12,000	110,000
		412,000
Less Work in progress at 30 Sep 19-8		9,500
COST OF GOODS PRODUCED		402,500
Sales		700,000
Less cost of goods sold		
Cost of goods produced	402,500	
less stock of finished goods		
at 30 Sep 19-8	2,800	399,700
GROSS PROFIT		300,300
Less Salaries	40,000	
Rent and rates	15,000	
Electricity	2,000	
Sundry expenses	2,000	
Depreciation: office equipment	1,000	60,000
NET PROFIT		240,300

Balance sheet extract:

		£	£
Current assets:	Raw materials	13,000	
	Work in progress	9,500	
	Finished goods	2,800	25,300

2.
Collette Fabrications Ltd.
Manufacturing, trading, profit and loss account for the year ended 30 April 19-9

		£	£
Raw materials:	Stock at 1 May 19-8		15,000
	Purchases	176,000	
	Carriage inwards	15,340	
			191,340
	Carried forward		206,340

	£	£
Brought forward	206,340	
Stock at 30 April 19-9	17,500	188,840
Direct wages		195,000
PRIME COST		383,840
Factory overheads		
Indirect wages	26,000	
Rent and rates (75% of 51,000)	38,250	
Heating and lighting ($^2/_3$ of 60,000)	40,000	
Insurance ($^9/_{10}$ of 3,000)	2,700	
Motor van expenses (50% of 8,000)	4,000	
Depreciation: Loose tools (5,000+9,000-4,000)	10,000	
Factory building	4,000	
Machinery	14,000	
Motor vans (50%)	5,000	143,950
		527,790
Work in progress at 1 May 19-8	24,000	
30 April 19-9	(21,000)	3,000
Cost of goods produced		530,790
Sales		800,000
Cost of sales Stock at 1 May 19-8	36,000	
Cost of goods produced	530,790	
	566,790	
Stock at 30 April 19-9	32,000	534,790
Gross profit		265,210
Discounts receivable		4,125
		269,335
Office salaries	68,600	
Rent and rates (25% of 51,000)	12,750	
Heating and lighting ($^1/_3$ of 60,000)	20,000	
Insurance ($^1/_{10}$ of 3,000)	300	
Carriage outwards	3,360	
Motor van expenses (50% of 8,000)	4,000	
Depreciation: Motor vans	5,000	
office machinery and equipment	5,000	119,010
Net profit		150,325

15.2.2

Exercise 1

Bonnie and Clyde
Manufacturing, trading, profit and loss account
for the year ended 31 March 19-7

	£'000	£'000
Raw materials Stock at 1 April 19-6	7	
Purchases	96	
	103	
Stock at 31 March 19-7	13	
Carried forward		90

	£'000	£'000
Brought forward		90
Direct labour		124
Prime cost		214
Factory overheads	85	
Depreciation: Factory	8	93
		307
Work in progress at 1 April 19-6	8	
31 March 19-7	(15)	(7)
Cost of production		300
Factory profit		50
Transfer to trading account		350
Sales		400
Cost of sales Stock of finished goods 1 April 19-6	14	
Goods transferred from factory	350	
	364	
Stock of finished goods 31 March 19-7	24	340
Gross profit		60
Rent receivable		20
		80
Office overheads	64	
Depreciation: Offices	2	66
		14
Factory profit		50
Net profit		64

Exercise 2

Kontakki Ltd.
Manufacturing, trading, profit and loss account
for the year ended 30 June 19-8

	£'000	£'000
Raw materials Stock at 1 July 19-7	40	
Purchases	110	
	150	
Stock at 30 June 19-8	55	95
Direct wages		85
Prime cost		180
Rent and rates (75% of 40,000)	30	
Heating and lighting (75% of 16,000)	12	
Repairs to factory	20	
Depreciation: machinery	30	92
		272
Work in progress at 1 July 19-7	16	
30 June 19-8	(14)	2
Factory cost of goods produced (carried forward)		274

		£'000	£'000
Factory cost of goods produced (brought forward)			274
Factory loss			(24)
Goods transferred to trading account			250
Sales			300
Cost of sales	Stock of finished goods at 1 July 19-7	32	
	Cost of goods manufactured	250	
	Purchases of finished goods	60	
		342	
	Stock of finished goods at 30 June 19-8	30	312
Gross loss			(12)
Office salaries		28	
Rent and rates (25% of 40,000)		10	
Heating and lighting (25% of 16,000)		4	
Redecoration of offices		15	
Depreciation: Salesmens' cars		15	(72)
			(84)
Add factory loss			(24)
Net loss			(108)

15.3.2
Exercise 1

Dorritt and Dombie Ltd.
Manufacturing, trading, profit and loss account
for the year to 31 March 19-2

		£'000	£'000
Raw materials	Stock at 1 April 19-1	28	
	Purchases	300	
		328	
	Stock at 31 March 19-1	32	296
Direct wages			360
Licence fees			104
Prime cost			760
Indirect wages		88	
Property expenses ($4/5 \times 90$)		72	
Canteen expenses ($4/5 \times 40$)		32	
Depreciation: machinery		36	
canteen equipment ($4/5 \times 10$)		8	236
			996
Work in progress	1 April 19-1	58	
	31 March 19-2	(54)	4
Factory cost of goods produced			1,000
Factory profit (10% of £1,000,000)			100
Transfer to trading account			1,100

		£'000	£'000
Sales			1,800
Cost of sales	Stock at 1 April 19-1	33	
	Transferred from factory	1,100	
	Purchases	58	
		1,191	
	Stock at 31 March 19-2	66	1,125
Gross profit			675
Office salaries		50	
Property expenses ($^1/_5 \times 90$)		18	
Canteen expenses ($^1/_5 \times 40$)		8	
Selling and distribution		40	
Other administration		45	
Depreciation: office machinery		5	
canteen equipment		2	
Increase in provision for unrealised profit		3	171
			504
Add factory profit			100
Net profit			604

(b) Balance sheet extract at 31 March 19-2:

		£'000	£'000
Current assets			
Stocks	Raw materials		32
	Work in progress		54
	Finished goods	66	
	less provision for unrealised profit	6	60
			146

(c) Calculation of absorption cost of each unit completed in the year to 31 March 19-2:

	units
Sales	4,500
Increase in stock	132
less 'bought in'	(232)
Manufactured	4,400

Absorption cost per unit: $\dfrac{£1,000,000}{4,400} = £227.27$

Exercise 2

The Premier Manufacturing Co. Ltd.
Manufacturing, trading, profit and loss account
for the year to 31 December 19-8

		£	£	£
Raw materials	Stock at 1 Jan 19-8		18,000	
	Purchases	245,500		
	Carriage inwards	1,350	246,850	
			264,850	
	Stock at 31 Dec 19-8		22,000	
	Carried forward			242,850

	£	£
Brought forward		242,850
Direct wages		351,000
Prime cost		593,850
Factory overheads		
Indirect wages	22,900	
Rent and rates	58,000	
Electricity	27,000	
Repairs and maintenance	10,000	
Insurance	10,200	
Motor vehicle expenses (50%)	8,800	
Cost of loose tools (15,000+13,650-13,400)	15,250	
Depreciation: Freehold premises	7,200	
Plant and machinery	43,000	
Motor vehicles	10,500	212,850
		806,700
Work in progress at 1 Jan 19-8	27,800	
31 Dec 19-8	(24,500)	3,300
		810,000
Factory profit on completed goods		90,000
Finished goods transferred to trading account		900,000
Sales		1,200,000
Cost of sales Stock at 1 Jan 19-8	42,500	
Goods transferred from factory	900,000	
	942,500	
Stock at 31 Dec 19-8	67,500	875,000
Gross profit		325,000
Discounts received		1,760
		326,760
Administration	74,000	
Selling and distribution	55,190	
Rent and rates	30,000	
Electricity	13,500	
Repairs and maintenance to offices	8,200	
Insurance	3,400	
Motor vehicle expenses (50%)	8,800	
Discounts allowed	2,140	
Debenture interest (800 + 800)	1,600	
Depreciation: Freehold premises	2,400	
Motor vehicles	10,500	
Office machinery	5,200	
Provision for unrealised profit	2,750	217,680
		109,080
Factory profit		90,000
Net profit		199,080

Balance sheet as at 31 December 19-8

	Cost £	Depn £	Net £
Fixed assets			
Freehold property	240,000	105,600	134,400
Plant and machinery	215,000	168,000	47,000
Motor vehicles	84,000	63,000	21,000
Office machinery and equipment	26,000	23,200	2,800
	565,000	359,800	205,200
Current assets			
Stocks Raw materials		22,000	
Work in progress		24,500	
Finished goods	67,500		
less provision for unrealised profit	6,750	60,750	
Loose tools		13,400	
		120,650	
Debtors		114,640	
Bank		54,260	
Prepayments (1,800 + 600 + 1,000 + 800)		4,200	
		293,750	
Amounts due to be settled within one year			
Creditors	23,540		
Accrued expenses (6,000+1,900+ 5,000+2,800+3,000+800)	19,500	43,040	250,710
			455,910
Amounts due to be settled after more than one year			
8% Debentures			20,000
			435,910
Share capital and reserves			
150,000 ordinary shares of £1			150,000
Retained profits (86,830 + 199,080)			285,910
			435,910

(b) Answer should include reference to:

(i) Accruals or matching concept: expenditure has been matched to revenue included in the accounts, and to period of time covered by the manufacturing, trading, profit and loss account. e.g. rent, wages, selling and distribution expenses have been adjusted for accrued expenditure; rates and insurance have been adjusted on a time basis for amounts prepaid.

(ii) Cost concept: All expenses and fixed assets have been recorded in the books at their cost to the company rather than at some other value. The net book value of the fixed assets represents the amount of the original cost of those assets being carried forward to be set against the revenue which those assets will earn in future periods. (Another example of the matching concept)

(iii) Going concern concept: The business has been regarded as likely to continue its operations in their present form for the foreseeable future. If there had been any likelihood of the present operations being discontinued or curtailed in the foreseeable future, fixed assets should have been shown in the balance sheet at their likely realisable values. Stocks of raw materials, work in progress and finished goods should have been valued on the basis of worth in an enforced sale instead of at cost.

Note: The question specifically requires you to comment on the concepts in relation to your answer to Part (a). A general discussion of the concepts unrelated to Part (a), no matter how good, would not be regarded as an answer to the question as set.

CHAPTER 16

16.1.2 **Archer, Bowman and Chieftan**

Standard time for 115 units = 35 hrs. i.e 18.26 minutes per item.
If number of units completed is 138, that is equivalent to 42 standard hours.
Therefore time saved = 7 hours

(i)		£
Archer:	Basic wage	84
	Bonus: hourly rate = £2.40	
	£2.4 × 50% of 7 hours	8.40
		92.40
	Equivalent to an hourly rate of £2.64	
Bowman	Basic wage	84
	Bonus: hourly rate = £2.40	
	£84 × $^{7}/_{35}$	16.80
		100.80
	Equivalent to an hourly rate of £2.88	
Chieftain	Basic wage	84
	Hourly rate = £2.40	
	Pay = £2.40 × $\sqrt{42 \times 35}$ = £2.40 × 38.34 =	£92.02
	Equivalent to an hourly rate of £2.63	

(ii) If number of units completed is 184, that is equivalent to 56 standard hours
Therefore time saved = 21 hours.

		£
Archer:	Basic wage	84
	Bonus: hourly rate = £2.40	
	£2.40 × 50% of 21 hours =	25.20
		109.20
	Equivalent to an hourly rate of £3.12	
Bowman	Basic wage	84
	Bonus: hourly rate = £2.40	
	£84 × $^{21}/_{35}$	50.40
		134.40
	Equivalent to an hourly rate of £3.84	
Chieftain	£2.40 × $\sqrt{56 \times 35}$ = £2.40 × 44.27 =	£106.25
	Equivalent to an hourly rate of £3.035	

16.2.2 **The Beta Manufacturing Co. Ltd.**

Manufacturing accounts for the three months to 31 May 19-2

	FIFO	LIFO	AVCO
	£	£	£
Direct materials Purchases	10,150	10,150	10,150
less closing stock	(2,210)	(2,070)	(2,163)
Carried forward	7,940	8,080	7,987

	£	£	£
Brought forward	7,940	8,080	7,987
Direct wages	16,500	16,500	16,500
Prime cost	24,440	24,580	24,487
Variable overheads	4,000	4,000	4,000
Fixed overheads	11,200	11,200	11.200
Depreciation	3,180	3,180	3,180
Factory cost	42,820	42,960	42,867

CHAPTER 17

17.2.2
Bigthings Ltd.
Absorption cost statement for the month of March 19-2

Number of units: 2,000

	Unit cost	£
	£	
Direct materials	15	30,000
Direct labour	26	52,000
Prime cost	41	82,000
Factory overheads	($^1/_{12}$)	42,500
Depreciation: factory		1,500
plant and machinery		20,000
Factory cost		146,000
Salaries: sales staff		4,167
Wages: delivery van drivers		2,833
Motor van running costs		4,000
Depreciation of motor vans		1,250
Office rent		2,750
Other administration costs		21,000
Total cost		182,000

(a) If selling price is £100 per Whopper
sales will be £200,000;
Net profit will be £18,000

(b) Total profit of 40% of total cost = £72,800
Selling price = £254,800 ÷ 2,000 = £127.40

17.4.2
D.Brown Ltd.

Marginal cost of 5,000 bicycles:

		£
Direct expenses:	Materials	300,000
	Labour	400,000
	Royalties	50,000
Other variable costs:		
	Selling and distribution	20,000
	Administration	10,000
		780,000

Marginal cost per bicycle £156
Selling price per bicycle £260
Contribution per bicycle £104

		£
Total fixed costs:		
Selling and distribution		200,000
Administration		220,960
		420,960

(i)   Break even point: 420,960/104 = 4,047.69
        or 4,048 bicycles
        or sales total of £1,052,399.40

(ii)   Margin of safety: (5,000 - 4,048) = 952 or 19.04%

Exercise 2   **Mei Ling Ltd.**

Marginal cost of each lantern:

	£	£	
Direct material	8		
Direct labour	12	20	
Unit selling price	£25	£23	£22
Unit contribution	£5	£3	£2
No. sold	400	600	1,100
Sales	£10,000	£13,800	£24,200
C/s ratio	20%	13.04%	9.09%
Total contribution	£2,000	£1,799	£2,199.78
Fixed costs per week	£700	£700	£805
Profit	£1,300	£1,099	£1,394.78

Provided there is a demand for 1,100 lanterns per week, Mei Ling Ltd. should reduce the unit price of lanterns to £22.

Exercise 3   **T.Lambrou Ltd.**

The answer, which should be in good report form, should contain the following information.

Calculation of contribution per unit of accessory

	£
Components	25
Labour (4 × £9)	36
Other variable costs	6
Marginal cost	67
Contribution	13
List selling price	80

Proposal 1.
Selling price will be reduced by 10% to £72. This is £5 in excess of the marginal cost and will produce a unit contribution. The proposal may therefore be acceptable. Profit would be increased by 1,000 × £5 (£5,000)

Proposal 2.
Selling price will be reduced by 20% to £64. This is £3 below marginal cost and is therefore unacceptable. Acceptance of the proposal would affect profit adversely by 2,000 × £3 (£6,000)

Exercise 4   Ninasim & Son Ltd.

The 'bought in' price of each product should be compared with the marginal cost of its production. Ignore variable selling and distribution costs as these will be incurred whether the products are manufactured by Ninasim or Husseyin & Husseyin.

Marginal cost per unit of production:

	Ninabits	Simlabits	Sonybits
	£	£	£
Direct materials	18	7	9
Direct labour	25	21	26
Marginal cost	43	28	35
'Bought in' price	50	30	33

Ninasim & Son Ltd. should continue to manufacture Ninabits and Simlabits as they can do so more cheaply than they can buy the items from outside.

It would appear that Sonybits should be bought from Husseyin & Husseyin and Co. Ltd. but this might be subject to other considerations such as the cost of discontinuing production, costs of making workers redundant, the possibility of using the freed resources profitably for other purposes etc. etc.

Exercise 5   C.Yiannakou

This is a question concerning limiting factors and is solved by finding the contribution per unit of limiting factor for each product.

	Boxydon	Doxydon	Moxydon
	£	£	£
Unit cost			
Material	6	12	8
Labour	32	40	40
Marginal cost	38	52	48
Selling price	50	64	60
Contribution	12	12	12
Contribution per sq. metre of Boxium	4	2	3
Rank as follows:	1	3	2

Revised production schedule:

Item	Production in units	Usage Sq. metres	Balance Sq. metres	Contribution £
Boxydons	10,000	30,000	62,000	120,000
Moxydons	11,000	44,000	18,000	132,000
Doxydons	3,000	18,000	–	36,000
				288,000

CHAPTER 18

18.1.2

M.Cohen
Sales Budget for the year to 31 December 19-4

19-4	Volume	Product A Price	Amount	Volume	Product B Price	Amount	Total
		£	£		£	£	£
Jan	1,000	100	100,000	500	120	60,000	160,000
Feb	1,000	100	100,000	530	120	63,600	163,600
Mar	1,050	110	115,500	530	120	63,600	179,100
Apr	1,050	110	115,500	530	120	63,600	179,100
May	1,050	110	115,500	530	126	66,780	182,280
Jun	1,050	110	115,500	583	126	73,458	188,958
Jul	1,050	110	115,500	583	126	73,458	188,958
Aug	1,134	110	124,740	600	126	75,600	200,340
Sep	1,134	115.5	130,977	600	126	75,600	206,577
Oct	1,134	115.5	130,977	624	168	104,832	235,809
Nov	1,134	115.5	130,977	624	168	104,832	235,809
Dec	1,134	115.5	130,977	624	168	104,832	235,809
	12,920		1,426,148	6,858		930,192	2,356,340

18.3.2

Exercise 1

Murude plc
Production Budget for the year to 31 December 19-2

Quarter to	Mar 31	Jun 30	Sep 30	Dec 31
Balance b/f	16,000	19,000	12,000	2,000
Production	45,000	45,000	45,000	45,000
	61,000	64,000	57,000	47,000
Sales	42,000	52,000	55,000	32,000
Balance c/f	19,000	12,000	2,000	15,000

Exercise 2

Shwish Ltd.
Production Budget for the year to 31 December 19-3

Quarter to	Mar 31	Jun 30	Sep 30	Dec 31
Balance b/f	600,000	650,000	600,000	400,000
Production	300,000	300,000	300,000	300,000
	900,000	950,000	900,000	700,000
Sales	250,000	350,000	500,000	400,000
Balance c/f	650,000	600,000	400,000	300,000

Exercise 3

The Aaisha Company
Production Budget for the year to 31 December 19-5

Month	January	February	March	April
Balance b/f	1,000	2,000	4,000	5,000
Production	7,000	10,000	8,000	7,000
	8,000	12,000	12,000	12,000
Sales	6,000	8,000	7,000	8,000
Balance c/f	2,000	4,000	5,000	4,000

18.4.2

Pi Manufacturers Ltd.

Purchasing budget for four months to 30 June 19-1

	March	April	May	June
Kilos purchased	2,400	3,000	2,700	1,800
Price per kilo	£1.50	£1.50	£1.50	£2
Cost of purchases	£3,600	£4,500	£4,050	£3,600

Note: Purchases in March will be in respect of the material forming the product to be sold in May (3 kilos per unit sold), and so on.

18.5.2

Kadriye

Cash budget for the year to 31 December 19-2

Quarter to	March 31 £	June 30 £	Sept. 30 £	Dec. 31 £
Receipts				
Cash received from debtors	10,000	21,000	28,000	34,000
Sale of car		3,500		
Loan			6,000	
	10,000	24,500	34,000	34,000
Payments				
Creditors	28,000	16,000	20,000	17,000
Purchase of motor van	5,000			
Wages	6,000	6,000	6,000	6,000
Rent	1,200	1,200	1,200	1,200
Drawings	1,500	1,500	1,500	1,500
Bank interest		795		580
	41,700	25,495	28,700	26,280
Net receipts/(payments)	(31,700)	(995)	5,300	7,720
Balance b/f	15,800	(15,900)	(16,895)	(11,595)
Balance c/f	(15,900)	(16,895)	(11,595)	(3,875)

18.6.2

(a)

Courante Ltd.

Cash budget for four months to 30 April 19-2

	January £	February £	March £	April £
Receipts				
Sales - cash	10,000	11,200	12,000	13,200
Debtors	17,000	15,000	16,800	18,000
	27,000	26,200	28,800	31,200
Payments				
Creditors	9,000	10,000	8,000	12,000
Selling and distribution	1,200	2,500	2,800	3,000
Administration	8,000	8,000	8,000	8,000
Interim dividend				2,500
Plant & machinery			24,000	
	18,200	20,500	42,800	25,500
Net receipts/(payments)	8,800	5,700	(14,000)	5,700
Balance b/f	9,500	18,300	24,000	10,000
Balance c/f	18,300	24,000	10,000	15,700

(b)

Forecast profit and loss account for the four months to 30 April 19-2

	£	£
Sales		116,000
Cost of sales:		
Stock at 1 Jan 19-2	12,000	
Purchases	45,000	
	57,000	
Stock at 30 Apr 19-2	9,000	48,000
Gross profit		68,000
Selling and distribution	12,600	
Administration	34,100	46,700
		21,300
Interest on debentures		400
		20,900
Interim dividend		2,500
		18,400
Transfer to general reserve		10,000
Retained profit for the year		8,400
Retained profit brought forward		2,700
Retained profit carried forward		11,100

Forecast balance sheet as at 30 April 19-2

	Cost	Depn	Net
	£	£	£
Fixed assets			
Freehold premises	20,000	4,200	15,800
Plant and machinery	39,000	10,800	28,200
	59,000	15,000	44,000
Current assets			
Stock		9,000	
Trade debtors		19,800	
Prepaid expenses		1,300	
Bank		15,700	
		45,800	
Amounts due to be paid within one year			
Trade creditors	15,000		
Selling and distribution	3,300		
Debenture interest	400	18,700	27,100
			71,100
12% Debentures			10,000
			61,100
Share capital and reserves			
Ordinary shares of £1			25,000
General reserve			25,000
Retained profit			11,100
			61,100

443

(c)

Forecast statement of source and application of funds
for four months ending 30 April 19-2

	£	£
Net profit		20,900
Add depreciation		2,000
Funds generated by operations		22,900
Applications of funds		
Purchase of machinery	24,000	
Payment of interim dividend	2,500	26,500
		(3,600)
Increase/(decrease in working capital		
Decrease in stock	(3,000)	
Increase in debtors	2,800	
Decrease in prepayments	(1,100)	
Increase in trade creditors	(6,000)	
Increase in accrued expenses	(2,500)	
	(9,800)	
Movement in net liquid funds		
Increase in bank balance	6,200	(3,600)

CHAPTER 19

19.1.2

Brekkinuts
Flexed budget for 190,000 packets.

	£	£
Direct materials		9,500
Direct labour		11,400
Variable overheads		
Production		4,750
Selling & distribution		1,045
		26,695
Fixed overheads		
Production	6,000	
Selling & distribution	9,900	
Administration	8,000	23,900
		50,595

19.2.2

Reflections Ltd

Total sales variance £(450,000 - 448,950) = £1,050 (A)

	£	
Master budget sales: 150,000 tins @ £3 =	450,000	
Flexed budget sales: 148,600 tins @ £3 =	445,800	
Volume variance	4,200	(A)

	£
Flexed budget sales	445,800
Actual sales	448,950
Price variance	3,150 (F)

19.2.3   Laser, Digit and Co.

Total cost variance (MBTC - ATC)= £(249,000 - 287,500) = £38,500 (A)
Quantity variance (MBTC - FBTC) = £(249,000 - 284,400) = £35,400 (A)

	Flexed budget 1,800 players	Actual	Total variances
	£	£	£
Direct materials	108,000	110,000	2,000 (A)
Direct labour	54,000	52,500	1,500 (F)
Variable overheads	50,400	55,000	4,600 (A)
Fixed overheads	72,000	70,000	2,000 (F)
	284,400	287,500	3,100 (A)

19.4.2
Exercise 1   P.A.M. Sportsgear Ltd.

		Master budget	Flexed budget	Actual
		£	£	£
Direct materials		50,400	54,600	63,992.50
Direct labour		36,000	39,000	39,077.50
Production overheads-				
	variable	5,400	5,850	6,000.00
	fixed	16,200	16,200	16,000.00
		108,000	115,650	125,070.00

Total variances

	£	
Total budget variance	17,070	(A)
Quantity variance	7,850	(A)
Total materials variance	9,392.50	(A)
Total labour variance	77.50	(A)
Total overhead variance	250	(F)

Sub-variances

	£	
Materials usage variance (9,100 - 8,950)kilos × £6	900.00	(F)
Materials price variance £(6 - 7.15) × 8950	10,292.50	(A)
	9,392.50	(A)
Labour efficiency variance (3,900 - 3,850)hrs × £10	500.00	(F)
Labour rate variance £(10 - 10.15) × 3,850	577.50	(A)
	77.50	(A)

Overhead variances - Variable	50	(F)
Fixed	200	(F)
	250	(F)

Exercise 2

	£	
Actual overheads £(25,200 + 39,250) =	64,450	
Total budgeted overheads £(24,640 + 38,080) =	62,720	
Overhead expenditure variance	1,730	(A)
Total budgeted overheads	62,720	
Actual hours × OAR (6,600 × 9.8)	64,680	
Overhead volume variance	960	(F)
Actual hours × OAR	64,680	
Standard hours produced × OAR (6,800 × 9,80)	66,640	
Overhead efficiency variance	1,960	(F)

CHAPTER 20

20.2.2

	Project A £	Project B £	Project C £
Total profits (4 years)	60,000	70,000	55,000
Average profits p.a.	15,000	17,500	13,750
ARR (on £150,000)	10%	11.67%	9.16%

Whilst B would seem to be the more attractive project, the ARR on B is only slightly better than the ARR on A. If, for this purpose, the funds generated by the operations can be roughly equated with cash inflows, A has the better profile in the earlier years.

There is insufficient information to make a proper judgement between the three projects as the question gives no indication of the their life expectancies. Furthermore, ARR does not take account of the time-value of money.

The judgement is being made on estimated figures of profit which may, with time, prove to be materially inaccurate.

20.3.2   Flexi-Budgets Ltd.

Uniflex and Duoflex both have pay-back periods of 3 years. Duoflex would appear to entail less risk than Uniflex because the cash inflow is greater in years 1 and 2. It would therefore be preferred to Uniflex although the cash inflow of Uniflex is expected to be better in the later years than would be the case with Duoflex.

Triflex would not be considered as the payback period is over 4 years.

20.4.2

Wyezed Ltd.

Year	Discounting factor 15%	Goliath Net receipts £	NPV £	Cyclops Net receipts £	NPV £
0	1	(80,000)	(80,000)	(120,000)	(120,000)
1	0.870	24,000	20,880	42,000	36,540
2	0.756	24,000	18,144	42,000	31,752
3	0.658	24,000	15,792	42,000	27.636
4	0.572	24,000	13,728	42,000	24,024
5	0.497	24,000	11,928	42,000	20,874
			472		20,826

Both machines have positive net present values when the net receipts are discounted at 15% although the NPV for Goliath is very small and could become negative given the uncertainties connected with forecasting.

As Cyclops has the much larger NPV, Wyezed Ltd. should consider purchasing that machine.

20.5.2   **Abednego**

Net receipts of £6,000 for 5 years discounted at 14% produce NPV of £20,592; less initial outlay of £20,000 = £592

Discounted at 16%, NPV = (£356)

Therefore IRR = $14\% + (2\% \times \frac{592}{592 + 356}) = 15.25\%$

CHAPTER 21

21.7.2

Exercise 1   **19-2**   **19-3**

(i) R.O.C.E
net profit/capital employed

$\frac{11,250}{50,550}$ 22.26%

$\frac{21,000}{74,750}$ 28.09%

(ii) Gross profit percentage
gross profit/turnover

$\frac{40,000}{125,000}$ 32%

$\frac{55,500}{150,000}$ 37%

(iii) Net profit percentage
net profit/turnover

$\frac{11,250}{125,000}$ 9%

$\frac{21,000}{150,000}$ 14%

(iv) Current ratio
Current assets:current liabilities
23,100:10,800   2.14:1
26,505:15,025   1.76:1

(v)   Liquid ratio
Current assets less stock:current liabilities

11,600:10,800	1.07:1
14,380:15,025	0.96:1

(vi)   Stockturn
cost of sales/average stock

$$\frac{85,000}{10,000.0}$$ 8.5 times

$$\frac{94,500}{11,812.5}$$ 8 times

(vii)   Debtors' ratio
debtors/turnover × 365

$$\frac{9,590}{125,000} \times 365$$ 28 days

$$\frac{14,380}{150,000} \times 365$$ 35 days

(viii)   Creditors' ratio
creditors/purchases × 365

$$\frac{10,800}{88,000} \times 365$$ 44.8 days

$$\frac{10,425}{95,125} \times 365$$ 40 days

Exercise 2

John Kelworthy
Ken Porter
Trading, profit and loss account for the year to 30 June 19-3

	£	£
Sales		231,000
Cost of sales		
Opening stock	6,160	
Purchases	118,580	
	124,740	
Closing stock	9,240	115,500
Gross profit		115,500
Expenses other than depreciation	76,125	
Depreciation	10,500	86,625
Net profit		28,875

Balance sheet as at 30 June 19-3

	£	£
Fixed assets		42,000
Current assets		
Stock	9,240	
Debtors	17,721	
Carried forward	26,961	42,000

		£	£
Brought forward		26,961	42,000
Current liabilities			
Creditors	11,371		
Bank overdraft	2,110	13,481	13,480
			55,480
Capital at 1 July 19-2 (balancing figure)			31,805
Net profit			28,875
			60,680
Less drawings			5,200
			55,480

CHAPTER 22

22.2.2

The Batwing Manufacturing Company
Cash operating cycle

	Days
Raw materials turnover	
Average stock = $\frac{1}{2}(6,500 + 8,840) = 7,670$	
$\frac{7,670}{99,985} \times 365$	28
Work in progress turnover	
Average work in progress = $\frac{1}{2}(7,800 + 7,100) = 7,450$	
$\frac{7,450}{151,072} \times 365$	18
Finished goods turnover	
Average stock of finished goods	
$\frac{1}{2}(15,000 + 16,754) = 15,877$	
$\frac{15,877}{181,100} \times 365$	32
Debtors ratio	
$\frac{18,000}{211,970} \times 365$	31
	109
Creditors ratio	
$\frac{15,764}{95,900} \times 365$	60
Cash operating cycle	49

22.7.2   **Apex Ltd. and Base Ltd.**

(a)

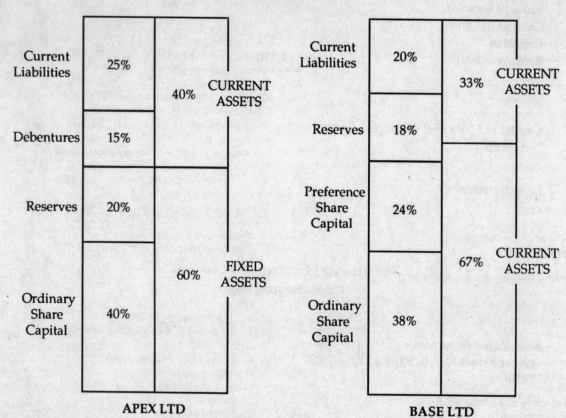

Diagrammatic representation of the sources of finance and utilisation of funds by Apex Ltd. and Base Ltd as at 31 March 19-1.

(b)   Answer should include reference to:

	Apex Ltd.	Base Ltd.
Current ratios	1.6:1	1.67:1
Capital structure: gearing	none	29.76%
Earnings (after interest/preference dividend)	£30,000	£20,000
Earnings per share	3.75p	2.5p

INDEX

Costing
3rd edition
T LUCEY

620pp 1989
(Also available as ELBS edition in member countries at
local currency equivalent price of £3.00)

This book provides a thorough coverage of cost accountancy. It is widely used as a course text on both accountancy and other courses. The text includes many self-testing exercises, examination questions and case studies.

Courses on which this book is known to be used

ACCA; CIMA; AAT, BSc Combined Studies; BA (Hons) Accounting; BA (Hons) Business Studies; BA (Hons) Business Administration; BTEC HND Business and Finance; RSA Costing; SCOTVEC HND Accounting; Institute of Purchasing and Supply.
On reading lists of ACCA, AAT and SCCA

CONTENTS

THE FRAMEWORK OF COST ACCOUNTING
CLASSIFICATION AND CODING

MATERIALS
PURCHASING, RECEPTION AND STORAGE
STOCK RECORDING AND INVENTORY
  CONTROL
PRICING ISSUES AND STOCKS

LABOUR
REMUNERATION METHODS
RECORDING, COSTING AND ALLIED
  PROCEDURES
OVERHEADS
COST ACCOUNTS

COSTING METHODS
INTRODUCTION
JOB AND BATCH COSTING
PROCESS COSTING JOINT PRODUCT AND BY-
  PRODUCT COSTING

PLANNING, CONTROL AND DECISION
  MAKING
COST BEHAVIOUR
MARGINAL COSTING AND ABSORPTION
  COSTING
MARGINAL COSTING AND DECISION
  MAKING
BREAK EVEN ANALYSIS
CAPITAL INVESTMENT APPRAISAL
BUDGETS

STANDARD COSTING
INTRODUCTION
VARIANCE ANALYSIS (MATERIAL, LABOUR
  AND OVERHEADS)
VARIANCE ANALYSIS (SALES AND
  STANDARD MARGINAL COSTS)
UNIFORM COSTING
COSTING AND COMPUTERS
CASE EXERCISES

LECTURERS' COMMENTS

'*Lucey has bravely attempted to bring the subject into the 1990s ... There is a useful new chapter on Costing and Computers ... The price is right, and the technical quality is there. What more could a student ask?*'
ACCA Students Newsletter December 1989

'*Brilliant!*'
Lecturer

Free Lecturers' Supplement

Intermediate Accounting
J R Dyson

650pp 1989

This book provides coverage of the Basic and Intermediate accounting examinations set by AAT, RSA and LCCI. In doing so, it covers the ground of many BTEC National and HNC/D courses and Certificate, Diploma or Degree courses. Main points are covered in a summary form with comprehensive examples and exercises with solutions. Case studies are included for assignment work.

CONTENTS

BASIC ACCOUNTING
The Background to Accounting
Debit and Credit Transactions
Double-entry Bookkeeping
Discounts
Value Added Tax
The Cash Book and Other Ledgers
Bank Reconciliation Statements
The Petty Cash Book
Day Books
The Journal
Bills of Exchange
Control and Total Accounts
Stock
Accruals and Prepayments
Bad and Doubtful Debts
Depreciation
Final Accounts
Error Correction
Incomplete Records

SPECIAL TYPES OF ACCOUNT
Departmental Accounts
Manufacturing Accounts
Container Accounts
Contract Accounts
Investment Accounts
Consignment Accounts
Royalty Accounts
Club and Society Accounts
Partnership Accounts
Company Accounts
Branch Accounts
Hire Purchase Accounts
APPRAISAL OF ACCOUNTS
Cash Flow Statements
Source and Application of Funds'
    Statements
Value Added Statements
Accounting for Changing Prices
Interpretation of Accounts
CASE STUDIES

LECTURERS' COMMENTS
'Dyson gets to the heart of the subject without confusion and highlights possible errors.' 'I particularly like the list of common errors at the end of each chapter.' '..covers our HNC Business Studies requirements ideally.' 'Good layout, well written.'

Free Lecturers' Supplement

Foundation Accounting
2nd edition
A H MILLICHAMP

512pp 1989

This book provides a thorough coverage of the theory and practice of accounting at Foundation level. Carefully graded exercises and examination questions (with and without answers) provide plenty of practice and self review.

Courses on which this book is known to be used

Foundation Accountancy courses; ACCA; CIMA; AAT; ICSA; BA (Hons) Accounting and Business Studies; BTEC HNC/D Business and Finance.
On reading lists of ACCA and SCCA

CONTENTS

LECTURERS' COMMENTS

'Basic accounting textbooks need not only to cover the techniques, underlying theory and interpretation of accounts, they need to reach the right balance between the three elements. This book achieves that right balance.'
Accountants Record

'I have used the book with my Foundation Accountancy courses for years now – it's ideal for them.'
Lecturer

Free Lecturers' Supplement

A First Course in Cost and Management Accounting
T Lucey

256pp 1990

This book provides a broad introduction to cost and management accounting for those who have not studied the subject before. It is written in a clear, straight forward fashion without technical jargon or unnecessary detail. The text includes many practical examples, diagrams, exercises and examination questions. Features include several objective tests for self-assessment and assignments for activity-based learning.

Courses on which this book is known to be used

BTEC National Business and Finance; RSA; LCCI; AAT; Management and Supervisory Studies; Business Studies and Marketing courses; Access courses; Purchasing and Supply and any course requiring a broad, non-specialist treatment of cost and management accounting.

CONTENTS

COST ANALYSIS AND COST ASCERTAINMENT
What is Product Costing and Cost Accounting?
Elements of Cost
Labour, Materials and Overheads
Calculating Product Costs
Job, Batch and Contract Costing
Service, Process and Joint Product Costing
INFORMATION FOR PLANNING AND CONTROL
What is Planning and Control
Cost Behaviour
Budgetary Planning
Budgetary Control
Cash Budgeting
Standard Costing
Variance Analysis
INFORMATION FOR DECISION MAKING AND PERFORMANCE APPRAISAL
What is Decision making?
Marginal Costing
Break-even Analysis
Pricing Decisions
Investment Appraisal
Performance Appraisal of Departments and Divisions

Free Lecturers' Supplement